THE
FASTEST
MEN
ON
EARTH

Published in 2021 by Welbeck

An Imprint of Welbeck Non-Fiction Limited, part of Welbeck Publishing Group.

20 Mortimer Street London W1T 3JW

A CIP catalogue record for this book is available from the British Library

ISBN 9781787396661

Typeset by Design To Print Solutions Ltd.
Printed in the United Kingdom

10 9 8 7 6 5 4 3 2 1

THE FASTEST MEN ON EARTH

**THE INSIDE STORIES OF
THE OLYMPIC MEN'S
100 METRES CHAMPIONS**

NEIL DUNCANSON

WELBECK

Neil Duncanson runs North One Television, one of Britain's most creative and successful independent production companies, and has won three BAFTAs for sports coverage. He began as a news reporter in east London before moving into the world of television, first with Thames News and then Thames Sport and LWT. At the age of 30 he started Chrysalis Sport, which produced Channel 4's *Football Italia*, the BBC's *Rugby Special*, the famous Graham Taylor documentary *An Impossible Job* and ITV's *Formula One*. In 2003 the company was bought and re-named North One and now boasts a vast output, including *MotoGP*, *Formula E*, *Extreme E*, *Travel Man*, *The Gadget Show* and all Guy Martin's television programmes. Neil remains CEO of the company he started 30 years ago, now one of the most respected in television. As an author, his book credits include *Tales of Gold*, *Crown of Thorns* (on heavyweight boxing champions) and two children's books. He is a member of the International Society of Olympic Historians and lives in Essex.

Contents

Foreword

By Usain Bolt

'The World's Fastest Man' … these are words that I never get tired of hearing. I am honoured to be in an exclusive group of humans who have a talent for running fast.

The 100 metres is the blue-ribbon event of the Olympic Games. It is the event that the world stops to watch to see who is going to win the title of world's fastest man. I won my first Olympic Games gold in Beijing in 2008. After that, I spent the next four years training to be the first person to successfully defend my titles. When I managed to achieve this in London in 2012, I tried to do what some people thought was impossible – win it all again in Rio 2016, and become a legend in sport. I retired from running in 2017, with eight Olympic Games gold medals, eleven World Championships gold medals and world records in the 100 metres (9.58 seconds), 200m (19.19 seconds) and 4 x 100m (36.84 seconds).

I admit that I am not someone who studies the history of the sport. Growing up I was very familiar with the Jamaican heroes – the likes of Donald Quarrie, Herb McKenley and Arthur Wint. My first memory of watching the Olympics was the 1996 Games in Atlanta, when I was ten years old, where Donovan Bailey won the 100 metres and Michael Johnson was the star in the 200 metres and 400 metres.

This book shows the kind of effort required to be an Olympic 100-metre champion and how winning a gold medal and being the fastest man on earth has sometimes been as much of a curse as it has been a blessing.

Some of my predecessors didn't do so well when their speed faded, but I am fortunate to have been born in an era in which I could be well rewarded for my speed. I hope I did my bit too. I competed clean. I brought attention to the sport by entertaining the crowd, making them smile and putting on a show. I opened doors for the next generation of athletes to benefit in many ways.

I do miss the thrill of competition, the atmosphere of the big stadiums. I don't miss the training though…! I plan to enjoy the next period of my life watching the new athletes fight to become champions, win medals and set records. I hope my success can encourage and motivate the next generation to continue to push the limits of human performance and, just as I was inspired by Michael Johnson and Donald Quarrie, I hope my legacy will inspire the athletes of the future. As I always say, 'Don't Think Limits, Anything is Possible'.

Introduction & The Early Years

Tom Burke & Frank Jarvis

Eight men will line up on the start line of the Olympic 100-metres final at Tokyo's lavishly re-built National Stadium, just before ten o'clock on the night of Sunday, August 1, 2021 – a little over a year later than planned – all believing they can join the greatest club in athletics history.

Inside ten seconds, seven of them will be forgotten.

The 'Fastest Men On Earth' is a truly elite club: membership is limited and demanding, requiring an Olympic gold medal or a world record in the 100 metres – ideally both. Very few athletes make the grade.

The men who meet the club's requirements are the modern-day equivalent of gunfighters, whose quick-fire reactions to a pistol shot and breathtaking speed separate them as winners from the losers. A modern example of 'the quick or the dead'.

The 100 metres remains the glamour event of the Olympic Games and its stars are still the most lauded and rewarded of all athletes. They range from celebrity, multi-million-dollar heroes to lonely victims of tragic suicide; from enduring legends to forgotten heroes; prison in-mates to government ministers; pharmaceutically enhanced cheats to innocent nineteenth-century college boys.

But they all have one thing in common. On one day of their lives they laid a genuine claim to the title of fastest man on earth. They all pushed the boundaries of human speed and endurance.

The supposedly immutable laws of physics, biomechanics – even physiology – are pushed and pulled on a daily basis in the world of sport, where defying them, even for a fleeting moment, creates the indelible memories of sporting history and magic we all love to talk about.

In the sport of sprinting, we measure these limits in the tiniest of fractions and over the years success has been observed in almost imperceptible increments. A hundredth of a second here, a thousandth there. Hardly the stuff of dreams. Until now: until Usain Bolt. Bolt didn't so much *challenge* the accepted laws of physics, biomechanics and physiology … as blow them completely apart.

In the history of record books, nobody has re-written them by such jaw-dropping margins or with such effortless speed and swagger as the big Jamaican sprinter. He won three gold medals in Beijing. Three more in London. Three more again in Rio de Janeiro.

Usain Bolt's world records in the 100 metres and 200 metres could last for decades. He is unarguably the greatest sprinter there has ever been. A year after Rio he retired from the track – a wealthy, contented global superstar – and joined the ranks of the sporting immortals.

Bolt was simply a phenomenon. He single-handedly re-invented the sport of sprinting, dragging it kicking and screaming from the depths of drug-fuelled despair to the heights of Hollywood fantasy. Before he arrived on the scene the world of sprinting was sinking, due to the widespread use of performance-enhancing drugs by some athletes. A sceptical public viewed sprinting in much the same way as cycling, bodybuilding and weightlifting. Drugs had killed their belief – athletics fans were leaving in droves.

Then a 21-year-old Jamaican strode purposefully onto centre stage, mugging to the cameras, playing to the crowd and running like a god. No one had ever seen his like and even seasoned veterans of the sport stood in awe and marvelled as titles were claimed and records destroyed.

History was re-cast and a new hero was born. But talk to the man and he will tell you that he never saw himself as a saviour. All he really wanted was to be a legend. The fastest man on earth – ever. And to be remembered for it – forever.

So what now for Usain Bolt's sport? What now for those who have to pick up the baton and follow him? He has set the bar stratospherically high, but if the history of the event has taught us anything it is that records will *always* be broken. New heroes will come. Though we may have to wait some time for one like Usain Bolt.

So it might come as something of a surprise, not least to Bolt himself, that there have in fact been faster men. Not recently, of course, but back in the depths of time when men were real men and there were no television pictures, multi-billion global audiences, digital timing, high-tech spiked shoes, synthetic running tracks or scientifically designed diets. Only cave drawings and a race for the next meal.

A few years ago, on the edge of a lake in New South Wales, Australia, anthropologists discovered 20,000-year-old fossilized footprints sealed in the mud that showed that our cave-dwelling ancestors were running at around 37 kilometres per hour. Given that Usain Bolt's top speed in winning gold at the Beijing Olympics was 42kph, this is quite incredible. Our Pleistocene Age men were running barefoot, on undulating terrain and armed with heavy spears. No high-tech assistance was available. The scientists believe that these aboriginal ancestors would have been capable of speeds of more than 45kph if they'd had the same modern advantages of Usain Bolt.

Of course, these Stone Age fast men were also well motivated, either chasing dinner or being chased as dinner. There's clearly no better way of improving your speed than being pursued by something unpleasant with sharp claws and pointed teeth.

It is a widely held anthropological view that 21st-century man is the worst example of physical manhood in history and that the comforts of modern life and a bewildering array of distractions have left him soft, slow and vulnerable. All the evidence points to the fact that Stone Age men would have beaten today's Olympic athletes out of sight – at everything.

But while such anthropology may give us pause for thought, it also gives us a clue as to why we have always been fascinated about speed – and why we care passionately about who is the fastest human on the planet. It is clearly an innate fascination that goes all the way back to those sabre-toothed days, whether it is running as children or watching others run faster than ourselves. This leads to questioning just how fast we can run – and whether it's faster than a wild animal, a chasing mob of ruffians or, in more modern times, a bike or a car.

It could also be connected to how precisely we can measure the world's fastest man. He's the one with the Olympic gold medal and/or the world record. In almost every other sporting discipline this individual sporting and physical excellence is impossible to measure. Who's the toughest man on the planet? It used to be the world heavyweight boxing champion, but today there are so many different belts in that sport that the title has been completely devalued. Who's the cleverest man? Da Vinci, Newton, Einstein? It's all so subjective. On the contrary, the fastest man on earth is an easy icon to identify.

But just how far can we go? Scientists will tell you we're reaching our physical capacity for speed, but they've been saying that for years and every time a record is set it seems there is always someone out there who will one day break it. Hard though it is to imagine, at some point in the future someone will break the records of Usain Bolt.

And the identity of the world's fastest man is just as important as the records he sets, especially when his speed seems as effortlessly God-given and thrilling as it is in the case of Bolt. Such speed, power and athletic grace offer a visceral experience that has the capacity to catch the breath and raise the neck hairs of even the most ambivalent sports fan.

So who were these fastest men on earth? And why were they fast? How did they rise to the top and, perhaps even more intriguingly, what happened to them when they weren't fast any more?

Clearly there were no organized games or records in Stone Age times, so we have to fast forward to the ancient world to find the identity of the first acclaimed fastest man on earth. Sporting games and challenges can be traced to 5,000BC in Ancient Egypt, but historians suggest they were largely horse sports and fighting. It was a trend continued by the Romans, who eschewed the idea of simple foot races for the better-paying gladiatorial events so well documented by history. In the meantime it was left to the Ancient Greeks to set the athletic bar and then wait nearly three thousand years for the rest of the world to follow.

The original Olympic Games, which can be traced back to 776BC, lasted five days, of which the first was reserved for traditional ceremonies, the second for boys, the third for men, the fourth for horses and chariot racing and the fifth for prize giving. There were a number of foot races, and the ancient equivalent of today's sprints was called the Stade – simply a race from one end of the famed Olympia stadium and back again, a distance estimated at 200 yards. There was also a semi-endurance race called the Diaulos and an endurance race called the Dolichos, which was 24 turns of the stadium while armed with a warrior's shield. A race not for the faint-hearted.

In the first six hundred years of the ancient Olympics, two men stood out in the

Stade race – each winning three titles in three separate Games. The first real ancient fast man was Chionis of Sparta, who won in 664, 660 and 656BC; then there was Astylos of Croton who won in 488, 484 and 480BC and, for the controversy he aroused, could be called the Ben Johnson of his day. After winning his third title, he took money to run for a rival Greek state and was thrown out of his town, shunned by his family and had his house pulled down and turned into a prison.

But the greatest ancient hero of all arrived in 164BC – at the 154th Olympiad – and he was a young man called Leonidas, a teenager from the island of Rhodes, not to be confused with Leonidas, the King of Sparta. Said to have the speed of a god, the young Leonidas was the Games' first real superman, and by all accounts he might have given Usain Bolt a run for his money too.

At his first games he won all three running events – Stade, Diaulos and Dolichos – and then went on to repeat this extraordinary feat three more times in consecutive Games. He finished his athletic career as the only man in a thousand years of Olympic competition to win all 12 titles over four Games.

The ancient Olympics were certainly the world's premier physical games, but they were also regarded as important political events, chronicled in detail by the serious writers of the times. So surviving texts and records show that while prize money was not allowed and only laurel wreaths were presented to the winners, the prestige of winning an Olympic title was immense, and towns and cities lavished gifts and favours on their successful athletes. Most never had to work again. Leonidas of Rhodes certainly didn't, and he spent the rest of his life regarded by his contemporaries as a minor deity, helping would-be athletes, living quietly on his home island in a house paid for by the state, with a comfortable monthly income.

An ancient historian called Eusebios Pamphilos described Leonidas as simply 'the fastest man in the known world, who will be embraced by history and his statue in Altis will vouch for his unsurpassed feat for the coming centuries'. Not a phrase you are likely to find in the back copies of *Track and Field News*.

Modern Olympic Games founder Baron Pierre de Coubertin would be more than a little surprised to see how, in contrast to the ethos he promoted, money and not the Corinthian spirit dominates the Games today, but times have changed dramatically and even he would have to concede that the origins of the Games were always rooted in tangible reward as well as glory.

The works of Homer often included tales of sprint races. In some areas of Ancient Greece, queens even selected their kings by means of a sprint, and the sport became embedded in Greek philosophy as a means of combining mind, body and spirit.

The Greeks constructed some magnificent stadiums and even introduced some early technology in response to teething problems – most notably the starts, where cheating was commonplace. At first they tackled this by placing a judge on the start line armed with a menacing trident. Athletes who jumped the start – and remember they all ran naked – could be given a sharp reminder of their transgression. After a few Olympiads, starting sills were adopted, which were simply grooved slots in which the runners had to stand. Then there were starting stones, and there is even evidence in old drawings of a rudimentary starting gate system, called a husplex, that is reminiscent of the stalls used in modern-day horse racing.

In the late 4th century AD, after a thousand years of competition, some historians suggest that a spoilsport by the name of Theodosius I, who as Roman emperor ruled Greece, misguidedly put an end to the Olympics as part of a campaign to quash paganism and impose Christianity as a state religion. Apparently, organized Games had no part in his vision of the future. However, more recent studies have revealed that the Olympic Games continued well into the 5th century AD, before gradually fading from view due to the crippling costs of staging them.

It is there that our history of fast men goes dark, save for fleeting descriptions of foot racing at medieval fairs, religious ceremonies and rites of passage across the world.

Organized athletic meetings with money prizes have been recorded throughout Europe, in the Middle East and in North America, where the Native Americans were renowned exponents of sprinting. But it was in Britain, toward the end of the eighteenth century, that professional running began to increase in popularity.

One of the early heroes was the Reverend Lord Frederick Beauclerk, who was reputed to be the great-grandson of King Charles II and Nell Gwynne. While he raced all over London, the real hotbed of foot racing was Kent, and the men of the county were said to be the swiftest in England.

Throughout the nineteenth century the sport continued to grow, especially in London and the thriving industrial cities in the North. Among the early professional racing personalities was Jem Wantling, who was discovered in a Derby pottery factory and was so dominant that by 1822 he had virtually run out of opponents to race. Wantling was a powerful man and ran in constant fear of pulling muscles, so he always turned out for races with his legs strapped in leather thongs. He was reputed to have run 100-yard races in nine seconds – on gravel roads.

He was followed by Connecticut-born George Seward, the 'American Wonder', who arrived in England in 1843, having exhausted competition in the United States. The following year, just a few days before his 27th birthday and in front of more than 3,000 people, Seward ran 100 yards in 9 and a quarter seconds on a turnpike road in Hammersmith, though it later transpired that the course was downhill and he had been allowed a ten-yard flying start.

Seward was a big crowd-puller, especially in London, and in 1847, on a newly built running ground in Barnet, north of the city, he was timed at 19 and a half seconds for the 200 yards, a record that remained intact until the end of the century. It took him less than five years to run out of opponents in England, so he would tour the country offering to run against six different men over 100 yards, racing them individually at five-minute intervals. Still he always won. A muscular 5ft 8in tall, the articulate and intellectual Seward was one of the first athletes to rely on an almost vegetarian diet. He spent a lot of time in England and died in Birkenhead in 1883, aged 66.

The old turnpike roads were a favourite location for professional sprinting in the early days, but later grass cricket fields were used, and finally, when sprinting became really popular, purpose-built cinder tracks or 'running paths' were constructed around the country.

However, despite its popularity, the professional racing circuit was always shrouded in disrepute because of its domination by a collection of greedy and selfish promoters, rather than one overall controlling body. As a result, spectators could never be certain whether the races they were watching were genuine or 'fixed', which largely depended on the wagers involved. There were no cohesive rules to govern procedure, and it was common for spectators to try to interfere with the runners or even for rival sprinters to clash during a race.

When contracts were drawn up for races, which were between two men only, the small print included details on how the race should be started. In the early days this usually took the form of 'starting by consent', whereby one runner would just take off when he felt so inclined, but if the other runner did not wish to start at the same time, the first competitor would have to return to the start.

This sometimes lasted for hours and, in one infamous case, four hours and 200 false starts. Eventually, common sense prevailed and a rule was made stipulating that the athletes had to begin racing within 15 minutes or a pistol would be used to start the race. It was only a matter of time before everyone realized the pistol was, in fact, a far better way of starting and, from 1857 onwards, starting sprint races by pistol became the standard practice.

At about the same time, the first 'spikes' came into use, and athletes who had been running in moccasins or boots, or else barefoot, began to wear custom-made cricket shoes with spiked soles, which enabled them to run quickly on cinders. The first mention of these shoes in race reports appeared in 1844; George Seward was an early adopter. On a tour of America in the early spring of 1847, he wore bespoke spikes which had been made in Bishop Auckland from expensive cordovan – a soft, pliable horse-hide leather. Apart from the top professional runners, however, it was not until the 1860s that spikes were widely used by athletes.

Race timing was also a hit and miss affair. Even when races were timed, the authenticity of the figures recorded and the standard of the watches themselves were often open to question. The goal for amateurs back in the mid-nineteenth century was to beat 'even time' – which was ten seconds for the 100 yards.

The first athlete credited with such a time was Thomas Bury, who was timed in ten seconds flat at Cambridge University. After that there were Americans Rene La Montagne, William Wilmer and John Owen; Scot Milroy Cowie and Ghanaian Arthur Wharton, who ran ten flat twice inside an hour at the 1886 AAA Championships, at London's Stamford Bridge.

The extraordinary Wharton would twice win the Amateur Athletic Association (AAA) 100-yard title and become the world's first black professional footballer, keeping goal for Preston North End, Sheffield United and Rotherham United. Struggling with a drink problem, he retired from football in 1902 and worked at the Yorkshire Main Colliery, in

Edlington. He died in 1930 and was buried in a pauper's grave, though a headstone was added in 1997. Despite the proliferation of races and runners in the nineteenth century, one man stood out head and shoulders above the other pros, and that was Londoner Harry Hutchens.

Born in Putney, just south of the River Thames, in 1856, Hutchens would become the greatest sprinter of his day, and his record suggests that he was one of the fastest men ever, although it is difficult to determine exactly how good he was as timing was haphazard at best and, more often than not in those days, downright dishonest. However, Olympic sprint champions right up to the First World War held him in very high regard, and even in the 1930s a magazine article written by 1924 Olympic 100 metres champion Harold Abrahams compared him seriously with Jesse Owens.

Hutchens first realized his fleetness of foot while working as a delivery boy for the newsagents W.H. Smith, and while still a teenager he found a sponsor and took up a career in sprinting. He won his first race in Wimbledon, winning an electro-plated silver tea service, but after that the real money began to pour in.

The purses on offer for the big sprint races were large enough to attract would-be fast men from all over the world, and the boom period for the sport began around 1870, when two prestigious, purpose-built stadiums were erected, Powderhall, in Edinburgh, and Lillie Bridge, in West London. With only a few exceptions all the top races of the age were held at these venues.

From the mid-1870s, Hutchens established himself as the fastest man in Britain, if not the world, with a series of handicap wins around the country. He was big crowd-puller for the promoters but, with long shorts and a big droopy moustache, he was hardly the quintessential athlete, standing at 5ft 10in, with a wiry frame that belied his natural speed. However, what made him particularly viable as a business proposition was a certain moral flexibility in accepting 'race orders' from the promoters.

So he ran to form whenever the bookies backed him to win, but lost a few races he ought to have won easily, when his backers wanted to make a quick killing. Of course, he received a share of the proceeds, but the management and the promoters made their money too. However, when Hutchens ran seriously there was no one who could stay with him at any distance from 100 to 300 yards.

In 1878 Hutchens, christened 'Greased Lightning' by the British press, won the first Sheffield Handicap – given a five and quarter yard start by champion George Wallace, who started from scratch, Hutchens won by a foot – and the following year he threw down the gauntlet in the press for someone to challenge him over 130 yards for £500. On that occasion there were no takers, but when he later ran at Powderhall his fans from all over the country packed into special trains to make the journey. A crowd of more than 10,000 paid to see him run, but he failed to get out of first gear and lost his one and only handicap competition.

But it was on the same track in the winter of 1884, at the famous New Year Sprint, which became something of a tradition in Scotland and continued there until well into the 1960s, that he set the pro racing world alight. After running a 300-yard heat on a freezing cold morning he sat down to a big traditional lunch of roast beef and potatoes and then went out less than an hour later to run the distance in exactly 30 seconds, a record that stood until well after the Second World War.

In 1887 he went to Australia for the winter, where he made a great deal of money winning – and losing – a series of sprint races against some of the top local runners. On returning home, however, he discovered to his horror that he had been replaced as Britain's premier sprinter and that a new man was calling himself Britain's number one.

Harry Gent, a 26-year-old Geordie, had won some important handicap races in Hutchens's absence and fancied his chances against the older man. The promoters could see a very big pay day and arranged for the two men to meet over 120 yards at Lillie Bridge for the official championship of the world, with prize money of £200.

The big race, which attracted a tremendous amount of publicity, took place in September 1887, and the promoters must have been rubbing their hands with glee when they saw the thousands of fans streaming into the ground to watch what the newspapers had described as 'The Race of the Century'. An extraordinary crowd of more than fifteen thousand had paid a shilling each to get in, and queues formed immediately around the stalls of the various bookmakers on duty inside.

However, the promoters' master plan had one fatal flaw, and it would not only cost them a small fortune but would ultimately sound the death knell for the entire professional running culture in England.

While Hutchens and Gent went out and thrilled the crowd with a short warm-up routine on the track, back in the dressing-room a fearful row broke out between the rival backers as to who should be declared the winner of the race. It was generally agreed between them that the result should be 'fixed', so that they could place some heavy bets. However, the pride of both runners, or the lack of suitably persuasive compensation, prevented either from giving way and agreeing to lose. The argument culminated in Hutchens's backers whisking their man out of the dressing-room, into a waiting carriage and away from the ground, hastily followed by Gent and his entourage.

Meanwhile, outside in the stadium the big crowd was rapidly running out of patience. When it finally became clear that the race was not going to happen and that both the runners they had waited so long to see had long since decamped, their shock quickly turned to anger and then to violence. In scenes never witnessed before in Victorian England, the beautiful ground was smashed to pieces, with a huge mob of hooligans, hell-bent on revenge, tearing down the wooden stadium buildings, uprooting the perimeter railings and then setting fire to everything that remained. While the majority of the crowd tried desperately to get away, the small police presence was powerless to stop the rampage, which ended with what one local newsman described as 'groups of men dancing like savages around the embers of the ruined stadium'.

Such was the scale of the violence that terrified spectators climbed over the fence between the stadium and the local railway and ran along the tracks to get to the nearest station. The ageing stationmaster tried vainly to stop the first bunch, but when he saw the huge mob behind them he suffered a massive heart attack and dropped dead on the spot.

This black day destroyed Britain's premier athletics stadium and it was never rebuilt. For many years it was an overflow car park for the Earl's Court exhibition centre, but today it is home to the Lillie Square housing scheme. Far more importantly, the riot killed off the popularity of professional sprinting in England, though it continued on a much smaller scale in the North and was always popular in Scotland.

As for Hutchens and Gent, they finally got together in a park in Gateshead, in the North East, about a month later, where some nine thousand fans turned out to see Gent beat the favourite, this time with an apparently suitable agreement on the finances.

In the following year at Powderhall, after a decade as the top sprinter, Hutchens had to give way to Gent in the New Year competition, but he continued to run and the records show that he won his fourth Sheffield Handicap in 1891, at the age of 35, and even finished fourth in the same race in 1898 at the amazing age of 42. Hutchens maintained a keen interest in the sport, coaching promising youngsters on the professional circuit during the early 1900s. He died in relative obscurity in 1939, at the advanced age of 81, at his home in Catford, South London. Incredibly, even his own local newspaper did not seem to realize his reputation and gave his death scant coverage, whereas *The New York Times* gave him a substantial obituary, with reverential tributes from some of the top US sprinters.

Timekeeping being what it was and race-fixing being the order of the day in his time, it is difficult to determine how good Hutchens really was, although if even some of his recorded times were genuine he has to be bracketed in the top class. At the turn of the century he still had no fewer than nine world records to his name between 50 and 350 yards, including 9 and three-quarter seconds for the 100 yards and 21 and four fifths of a second for the 200 yards.

After the Lillie Bridge scandal many sprint racing fans turned to other sports, most notably football, and their growing disillusionment with professional sprinting, together with the lack of a proper governing body and the mercenary attitude of the promoters, meant that fans of the track in general also began to look elsewhere. Inadvertently, the popularity of the professionals had encouraged the development of amateur athletics in Britain, which had been growing steadily from about the 1860s but had hitherto been confined mainly to the Armed Services, a few upmarket clubs and the universities. Now the amateurs began to take over the athletics scene, and the approach of the new century heralded the arrival of a new breed of sprinters, including Englishman Charlie Bradley and the Jamaican-born Scot Alf Downer.

Yorkshireman Bradley, who was a member of the Huddersfield Cycling & Athletics Club, did not start running until he was 20 and would go on to win four AAA 100 yards titles in a row between 1892 and 1895, including one at Northampton's County Cricket Ground, in which he was told by the officials that there was no chance of him claiming a record because the track was slightly downhill and there was a following wind. Bradley promptly told them he would run the race in the opposite direction and did so in ten flat, uphill and into the wind! Many years later he recalled: 'There was a gradual rise of two feet and it was undoubtedly my best performance.'

But Bradley's luck didn't hold when he travelled to America in search of new opponents. In September 1895 he narrowly lost to the rising young American star Bernie Wefers, who had just won the AAU sprint double a few weeks earlier, when they raced in Manhattan in a London AC vs New York AC meet. The US team won all eleven events and local reports suggest more than 12,000 fans were in attendance.

Shortly after that Bradley was banned for life by the AAA – along with five other athletes – for taking under-the-counter payments or 'excessive expenses' to run. A talented all-round sportsman, Bradley continued to play local cricket and for many years ran the Shakespeare Hotel, a popular Huddersfield public house. He died aged 71 in a Blackpool nursing home in July 1940, and the legendary distance runner Walter George sent a flower from his garden to be dropped into his grave.

Alf Downer was Bradley's chief rival in the 1890s and for three consecutive years won the 100, 220 and 440 yard Scottish titles – all run on the same afternoon. However, he was also thrown out of the sport in sensational fashion after he dared to disclose some of the shady 'shamateur' dealings that went on even in those seemingly innocent days. He revealed that he was regularly paid under-the-table money for running, usually about ten pounds a time, by clubs up and down the country who saw his value as a big crowd-puller.

Downer's revelations hit the sport hard, and the Amateur Athletic Association reacted by embarking on a witch-hunt, throwing out selected athletes for receiving illegal payments. Downer always spoke disparagingly about their selective action, claiming that 99 per cent of British athletes were not real amateurs, and observing that the AAA had not penalized the clubs that had made the payments. At the famous hearing in London, in 1896, Downer and the five other athletes were suspended for life from amateur competition, an ordeal he later described as akin to being tried for manslaughter.

So Downer and the AAA went their separate ways. He thrived for a time on the professional circuit and made some decent money in some of the famous handicap races, but when his speed began to fade he found it difficult to cope. After several mental breakdowns and a lengthy illness, he died in Edinburgh aged just 39 – with local newspapers reporting: 'Sad to relate, he became afflicted with religious mania and latterly had to be kept in restraint.'

Meanwhile, in the amateur world, the race to break 'even time' for the 100 yards had continued apace. At the first New Zealand national championships – held in Dunedin, in 1889 – local reports suggested Kiwi sprinter Jack Hempton had clocked an incredible 9.6 for 100 yards, though it was never officially recognized. In 1892 he twice ran official times of 9.8. Hempton was killed in one of New Zealand's first automobile accidents, in 1914.

However, the title of fastest amateur of the nineteenth century goes to a shy, young American named John Owen, who was the first sprinter to run an officially recognized 9.8 seconds for the 100 yards, at the AAU championships of 1890 in Washington DC.

Owen was born in Detroit in 1861, the son of a wealthy banker, iron manufacturer and shipyard owner, who joined his father's business instead of going to college. Around the same time, he joined the newly-formed Detroit Athletic Club and in his first ever race – an indoor 40-yard dash – surprised his friends, rivals and even himself by winning with consummate ease. Renowned trainer Mike Murphy was persuaded to take Owen under his wing and, in September 1889, less than a year after that first race, he won the American national 100- and 220-yard sprint double title in New York.

More than a thousand people were at Detroit's railway station to greet Owen and he was carried shoulder-high in a torchlight procession all the way to a celebration dinner at the athletic club. The following year he won the 100 yards title again and set the new world record, but soon afterwards, not long after the death of his father, he decided to retire from the track and take over the family business. Armed with a fortune estimated at more than a million dollars and a sizeable inheritance from his mother, as well as a sound entrepreneurial instinct, Owen developed a huge part of the east side of Detroit – known as Indian Village – into one of the most affluent parts of the city, making himself a multi-millionaire in the process.

John Owen died in 1924 at his summer home in Mackinac Island, some 250 miles north of Detroit, after succumbing to injuries received after being thrown from his horse. The Detroit Free Press remembered him as being 'closely identified with the growth of the city from the small community it was at the close of the Civil War to its present position as the fourth largest city in the United States'.

There was no doubt that the amateur movement around the world was going from strength to strength, but it was a young French aristocrat named Baron Pierre de Coubertin who really put the sport on the international map. He had visited Britain in 1890 and toured the top public schools, including Eton, Harrow and Rugby, where he was particularly impressed by the strong sporting traditions that accompanied the academic schooling. He also visited a tiny market town in Shropshire by the name of Much Wenlock. From 1850 this sleepy hamlet had staged the Wenlock Olympian Games, an annual festival created by a local doctor named William Penny Brookes, which was open to local inhabitants, rich or poor, young or old. It included standard athletic events, but also arts, crafts and games – even a popular event called tilting, which was a modern version of medieval jousting. Brookes had campaigned vociferously to restore the ancient Olympics and fought successfully for the inclusion of physical education on the national schools curriculum. The young Frenchman shared the same Olympian ideals as Brookes, and De Coubertin left England convinced that the entire edifice of the British Empire was founded on the sporting orientation of these schools, building such qualities as leadership, loyalty, national pride, character and morale – a kind of muscular Christianity that he had read about in books such as Tom Brown's Schooldays and had now seen for himself. De Coubertin had a vision of uniting the nations of the world in sporting competition, and from that dream would soon come the modern Olympic movement, although it owed more to Tom Brown, a tiny Shropshire town and the British Empire than the ancient games of the same name.

Central to de Coubertin's thinking was the Victorian notion of the amateur; of gentlemen running together in friendly competition without the taint of money prizes.

With this philosophy, he captured the mood of the times and, by 1894, he had won international approval to stage the very first modern Olympic Games.

So it was that in Athens, on Monday, April 6, 1896, in the flower-covered royal box of a magnificent new stadium, which a rich Greek merchant had paid for, King George I of Greece declared the Games open and resurrected the Olympics after a lapse of more than 15 centuries.

Although the organization was good, it was an unusual competition, which included such diverse events as mountain climbing, bell ringing and choral singing, as well as the more traditional athletic endeavours. The white marble stadium, erected on the ruins of an ancient sports complex, was an impressive sight and every day during the Games it was filled to capacity with forty thousand spectators. However, the construction was too narrow, and the pillared corners of the track were so tight that the athletes kept slowing down, often running into each other and falling over while trying to negotiate them. For some unknown reason the races were also run in the opposite direction to that of today.

Thirteen nations entered the competition, although they could hardly be described as truly national teams, because most of the athletes entered as groups of individuals who happened to be in Greece or somewhere nearby at the time. The US team comprised such a party, mainly from the East Coast clubs and most notably from the famous Boston Athletics Association. However, it was this last group of athletes who almost missed the Games completely as they had not been notified that designated dates were set using the Greek calendar. They had set sail from New York on March 20 on the 8,000-ton German steamer *Barbarossa* with four weeks to cruise to the Games – or so they thought. About ten days after leaving port they arrived in Gibraltar, and sprinter and quarter-miler Tom Burke sent a letter to the *Boston Post*, which they received and published about a fortnight later. In it he explained in some detail the rather laid-back nature of an average day in the first US team's preparations for the Olympic Games. 'We usually arise at 7.30am and an ice-cold salt water bath awaits us. We breakfast at 8 and the rest of the morning is spent on deck or writing in the saloon. On deck we amuse ourselves with the usual ocean games of ring toss and shuffleboard.

'We have lunch at 12.30 and after lunch we lounge about the deck or read until 3.30 when the exercise begins. We have our exercise on the lower deck and crowds of passengers are attracted. The exercise is heavy and lasts about an hour. The deck aft is crowded with passengers and all seem to take great interest in watching the men work. Manager Graham has laid out a 24-lap track and the sprinters have a thirty-yard straight. We also skip the rope and have a regular course in arm drill.

'As for myself, I am not feeling as well as I would like, as it is too early in the year for me to be right. I have been working hard, however, and Graham says that I don't need to train and will win anyway.

'We dine at 6 and the steamer orchestra renders selections from operas during this meal, which is anxiously awaited because of the peaches and ice cream we have for dessert. The evening is spent listening to music and we retire to our outside staterooms at 10.'

Sadly this apparently serene progress would soon be disrupted. The boat left Gibraltar for Naples, after which they caught a train to Brindisi, a steamer to Corfu, another to the port of Patras and then began a 10-hour train journey to Athens. When, after their tortuous journey the exhausted Boston contingent finally reached Athens, they believed they had a relaxed 17 days ahead of them for training and preparation. Unbeknownst to them, the opening ceremony was due to commence in just 10 minutes.

Triple jump champion James B. Connolly, one of the East Coast contingent, recalled many years later: 'A committee in frock coats and tall hats received us at the station in Athens and put us into open carriages and hurried us to the Chamber of Deputies, where the athletes of a dozen nations were already seated. Speeches were made, wine passed around and healths drunk. We stayed clear of the wine until the German crowd stood up, held their glasses high, looked to us and gave us three loud "Hochs!" and "Americanische" and emptied their glasses.

'Burke, Blake, Barry, Hoyt and me were sitting together. We were all teetotallers, or practically so, but the honour of our country demanded that something be done now; so we filled glasses, gave the Germans nine "Rahs!" and an "Allemande" and emptied our glasses.'

But still they weren't aware the competition was upon them, even when woken by a blast of martial music outside the window of the Hotel d'Angleterre, where they were staying, at four o'clock in the morning. It wasn't until breakfast later that morning, when athletes Connolly, Burke and Barry were handed a copy of the programme, that they realized the competition started that same day.

Among the latecomers was the only reigning American champion to make the trip. Tom Burke was rated as probably the best quarter-miler in the world, having won the AAU 440-yard title in 1895, and he was a red-hot favourite for the 400 metres. However, he knew that some of the world's top sprinters had not made the journey to Athens, notably the reigning American sprint champion Bernie Wefers, a Georgetown medical student who had claimed a share in the 100-yard world record of 9.8 seconds less than a year earlier. The New Jersey flyer was 4,000 miles away competing in the Boston College Indoor Games. He would claim three AAU sprint doubles and was regarded as the fastest man in the world in the mid-1890s. It was reported that he had once run a 9.4-second 100 yards, but despite the three watches corroborating the time, the chief timekeeper, none other than the AAU boss Bill Curtis, refused to believe it, stating 'no man can run that fast'. The lanky Wefers, who put his success down to clean living and never taking a drink in his life, became a hugely successful coach at New York AC and Rutgers University, coaching 42 national and Olympic champions. He died after a long illness in 1957, aged 84, at a hospital in the Bronx.

The 100 metres world record at the time stood at 10.8 seconds and there was a long line of athletes laying claim to it – though the disparity in the quality of the events in which they were set, and the timing methods employed made it nigh on impossible to accurately put a name to the first man to break 11 seconds.

This confusion of contenders included New Yorker Luther Cary, one of the greatest sprinters of the late nineteenth century, who had retired in 1893 shortly after allegations were made suggesting that he had secretly run as a professional. This was vehemently denied by the Princeton athlete, who had won the AAU sprint double in 1891, then came to England and won the AAA 100 yards title. He was famously described by the New York Times as 'a powerful, ugly, natural flyer' and on his European summer tour with the Manhattan AC Club, Cary told the publication Umpire about his training and nutrition regimen. 'Eat well and heartily', he advised. 'Two hours before a contest take a good solid meal of half a chicken (roast); then rest for an hour. A drink of cold water won't do you any harm if you feel thirsty, but cold tea is better.' He also recommended retiring to bed at 9.30pm and rising at 6.30am every day of the year. Cary clearly ran some stunning times, but few of them were ever confirmed as official records and he often despaired as another set of record claims were turned down by the AAU, often for jump starting, including a well-publicized 9-and-three-quarter seconds for 100 yards, at Princeton. His 100 metres record, set in Paris, at the Bois de Boulogne, on Independence Day 1891, appears similarly suspect. One timer had him at 10 and three quarter seconds, but a white handkerchief had been used to start the race, which gave rise to serious doubt over the quality of the officialdom on the day. His time was eventually rounded back to 11 seconds.

A year later, at the Belgian championships, the Australian-born British teenager Cecil Lee, a student at South Eastern College, in Ramsgate, laid claim to being the first man to break 11 seconds, but once again it was never officially ratified. There were three timekeepers and they had stopped their watches at 11.0, 10.8 and 10.6 respectively. The following summer, at the same championships in Brussels, local boy Etienne de Ré thought he had cracked the 11-second mark, only to find similar time discrepancies.

It was not until 1895 that a genuine 10.8-second mark could be reasonably believed – and then it happened twice. First, in April, it was the 24-year-old British Army officer Llewellyn Atcherley who ran the time in a first-round heat at the so-called 'Frankfurt Olympics', a multi-sport tournament between the local club, Suddeutsche Athleten & Fussballspieler, and Blackheath Rugby Football Club, at the city's Palmengarten cycle track. Contemporary reports in German newspapers suggest, however, that there was only one timekeeper. Atcherley would go on to become Major General Sir Llewellyn and a Chief Constable in both Shropshire and Yorkshire.

Four months after Atcherley's run, it was the turn of Harry Beatton, a Suffolk football star and the son of a Saxmundham publican, who clocked 10.8 seconds at the Dutch championships in Rotterdam, just a week after his 21st birthday.

Whatever the veracity of their world record claims, the fact remains that none of the world's genuine fast men of the day were taking part in Athens. So, perhaps not unreasonably, Tom Burke decided to take advantage of this dearth of talent and have a go at the 100 metres himself. After all, he had not travelled such a long way to compete in just one event. Burke was born in the West End area of Boston in 1876, the son of an undertaker. Described as a tall, skinny kid, he attended the English High School, the first public high school opened in the United States, but he suffered badly from rheumatism and at one point it was feared he would have to spend his life on crutches.

Happily he outgrew his health problems, taking the New England 220-yard and quarter-mile championships as an 18-year-old, and in 1895 was selected to race for New York AC in the famous 11-0 rout of London AC, at Manhattan Fields.In Athens, when the heats of the 100 metres began, 'Long Tom' and his compatriots Tom Curtis and Frank Lane adopted their usual crouch start, much to the amazement of the crowd and the European athletes who had never seen anything like it before. It had been introduced in America in the 1880s by coaching legend Mike Murphy and was first demonstrated by Yale sprinter Charles Sherrill, a future US General and politician, who used it to win the US 100-yard title in 1887.

Resolutely sticking to their standing start, the other athletes in Athens watched the three Americans win their heats easily, albeit against very mediocre opposition, and qualify for the final.Curtis, an electrical engineer from MIT (Massachusetts Institute of Technology), recalled his heat in an American magazine article more than thirty years later: 'Entered in the heat with me were a German, a Frenchman, an Englishman and two Greeks. As we stood on our marks, I was next to the Frenchman, a short, stocky man. He, at that moment, was busily pulling on a pair of white kid gloves and having some difficulty in doing so before the starting pistol. Excited as I was, I had to ask him why he wanted the gloves. "Ah-ha" he answered, "zat is because I run before ze Keeng!". Later after the heat was run [Curtis won it at a canter] I asked him in what other events he was entered. He was in only two, the 100 metres and the Marathon, to me a curious combination. He went on to explain his method of training. "One day I run a leetle way, vairy quick. Ze next day, I run a long way, vairy slow."'

Such was the tone of the first Olympic Games. Despite qualifying for the first Olympic 100 metres final, Curtis then decided to drop out to conserve his energy for his favourite event, the 110 metres hurdles, which was the next final on the programme. He duly won it.

So it was five men – the two remaining Americans, a German, a Hungarian and a Greek – who eventually lined up on the rough, deep cinder track for the start of the first Olympic 100 metres final, surrounded by spectators who had crowded on to the track itself for a better view.

The sun was shining brightly, the stadium was packed, and according to contemporary newspapers the hills above were bristling with another 60,000 spectators. As the pistol cracked, a great roar went up from the crowds both inside and outside the stadium as the six-foot-tall Tom Burke powered away from the rest of the field, his long legs easing him across the line in a sedate 12 seconds flat, a poor time and one-fifth of a second slower than he'd run in the heats, but sufficiently fast to beat off the challenge of second-placed German Fritz Hoffman, better known for rope-climbing, and the Hungarian Alajos Szokolyi who came in third. Hoffman, who was the captain of the German team, went onto the compete in the 1900 and 1906 Games. He died in Berlin in 1927. The hugely popular Szokolyi returned to his family estate in Hungary and ran a military hospital through the First World War; while Frank Lane became one of America's leading eye specialists. He died at just 52, in Rockford, Illinois, in 1927.

Back in Athens, a few days after the 100 metres, Burke went out for the final of the

400 metres and again won easily – a feat that he would most probably have repeated even if all the world's top athletes had been on show, although his time of 54.2 seconds was six seconds slower than his best time for the distance. Burke collected his two medals – both silver, as there were no gold medals at the first Games in Athens – and returned home a hero.

The Greeks regarded Burke as the biggest star of the Games and one Athenian reporter managed to find an interpreter and asked him what he trained on. 'Beans' answered Tom. At the entrance to the stadium there was a flagpole on which the colours of the winning nation were hoisted after each event. After winning the 100, Burke told his manager: 'By the Lord, we'll keep that old fabric of glory up there all day.' And so it remained.

The Americans won nine of the 12 track and field events, and when the all-conquering Boston athletes finally returned home, the city went wild and turned out in force to show its appreciation, parading its heroes through the streets and staging banquets for them.

At one of these banquets – at the Boston Athletic Association clubhouse, an uproarious night by all accounts – Burke rose to speak and all hell broke loose. Known for his keen sense of humour, he told the black tie gathering. 'I'll try and make this speech as short as my 100-yard dash. It's been said that we were all amateurs. But I have to confess to having received a dozen silk neck-ties from an Athenian dry goods dealer!'

In a lengthy, but possibly tongue-in-cheek report in the *Boston Globe*, published about a week after the race, the Boston team manager John Graham described how Burke had been escorted to the Temple of Zeus after his victory 'by a procession of great magnificence' and adorned with an olive wreath by the King of Greece. He ended his report, filed by long-distance phone call, explaining: 'Tom Burke has just gone to bed with his crown on.'

Burke continued to run with some considerable success, winning the AAU 440 yards title in 1896 and 1897 and the 880 yards in 1898. He also took a college title in 880 yards while a graduate student at Harvard.

The Olympic experience was clearly an inspiration to Burke and he became one of the initiators of the Boston Marathon, which was launched in 1897, the same year he ran 57 and four fifths seconds for the unusual 500 yards, clipping a fifth of a second off Lon Myer's world record, at a track meeting in Newton, near Boston.

After retiring from the track, Burke practised law in his native Boston and coached briefly at Mercersburg Academy, but his real passion was for writing. During the Olympics he had sent back regular dispatches about his experiences to the *Boston Post*, and he eventually gave up the law and in the years that followed worked regularly as a columnist for the *Post* and the *Boston Journal*.

In May 1905, a burglar broke into Burke's home, in the Roxbury district of the city, and stole $200 in cash and all his athletic trophies, medals and watches, including his Olympic medals, despite being attacked by Burke's Boston terrier. They were never recovered.

While working on the *Boston Journal* he met and married Ruth Bodwell, who wrote under the pen name of Peggy Quincy, and in 1912 they welcomed a daughter, Alice. When the First World War broke out he enlisted in the Army, one of the oldest men in the US

Signal Corps, and won his aviator's wings. As a commissioned lieutenant, he worked as a physical training instructor at aviation fields around the country until 1919.

Burke's interest in athletics continued right up to his death in 1929, at the age of 54. The *Boston Globe* reported that he suffered a heart attack and collapsed on the Narrow Gage Ferry, on a cold February morning, while on his way to work in the city. He died a week later in the Haymarket Relief Hospital. In an obituary in his old paper, the *Boston Post*, his great running rival Bernie Wefers was quoted saying that few could equal Burke's great running achievements, and the newspaper mourned the passing of 'one of the greatest athletes of all time'.

The author of the article was journalist Arthur Duffey, who had gone to the 1900 Olympic Games in Paris as the out-and-out favourite to succeed Burke as the 100 metres champion. The diminutive Duffy, who had just turned 21, had beaten everyone out of sight during the run up to the Games and while in Europe, just before leaving for Paris, he beat his two closest rivals, the Americans Frank Jarvis and Walter Tewkesbury, at the AAA Championships, held at Stamford Bridge, in west London.However, once in the French capital all kinds of things started to go wrong. Instead of one US team, there were 55 American competitors who had been sent from a variety of colleges. They had all been told that they were competing in an international exhibition meeting, which was to run alongside the Paris Exposition. They subsequently insisted they never even knew they were competing in an Olympic Games until they received their medals some months later. Indeed, the newspaper reports of the day did not mention the word 'Olympics' at all.

The Games were poorly organized from the start, mainly due to the fact that de Coubertin had lost his grip on them. Although he had successfully fought off an attempt by the Greeks to keep the Games permanently in Athens, he had little influence and plenty of enemies in France, and thus the Olympics were wrenched from his control and run by a group of French officials, merely as an unimportant sporting sideshow to the trade exposition.

The athletics events were held at the Racing Club, in the Bois de Boulogne, but there was not even a proper cinder track, so the officials marked out a course on a grass arena, with a 100-metre stretch which rose and fell like a rollercoaster and was full of bumps and holes.

The French decided to open the Games on Sunday, July 15, but the USA protested that this was an 'unGodly act' and demanded they should start on Saturday. The French countered that this was Bastille Day and opening the competition then would be impossible. After a long and bitter battle it was decided that the Games would open on Saturday and, with some athletes allowed to miss Sunday, would start in earnest again on Monday. Most school sports days were better organized.

The reporter attending from the *Boston Globe* remarked: 'The natty college costumes of the Americans were a decided contrast to the home-made attire of some of the best European athletes, who, instead of donning a sweater or bathrobe after the trials, walked about in straw hats and light overcoats.'

The heats and the final of the 100 metres competition were staged on that disputed opening Saturday, and consequently less than a thousand of people turned out to watch. As one newspaper remarked, there were more people on the track than in the two small stands, and most of those were American tourists. It was closer to a US college sports event than an Olympic Games.

The locals who did turn up failed to appreciate the proliferation of Stars and Stripes or the raucous American cheering. One US newspaper observed: 'The Frenchmen could not become reconciled to this form of cheering and they were heard to frequently exclaim, "What a bunch of savages."'

Arthur Duffey, the pride of Georgetown University, was still the clear favourite to win, despite the 21-year-old Jarvis and Tewkesbury equalling the world record of 10.8 seconds in the heats. However, there was some evidence to suggest that the French timekeeping was a little on the generous side to say the least.

In glorious sunshine, the final field of just four men shot out of their marks at the sound of the gun and, as expected, Duffey charged into an early lead. The race looked done and dusted. Then disaster struck. At 50 metres the favourite leaped into the air and crashed spectacularly to the ground, while the Princeton University senior Jarvis hurtled past him and crossed the line in first place with watches stopping at 11 seconds dead.

Tewkesbury, a dental graduate, was just a few feet behind in second place, but went on to win two gold medals in the 200 metres and 400 metres hurdles, for which he had practised by leaping over the gravestones in a cemetery near his home in Pennsylvania. Australia's Stan Rowley took third.

Duffy told waiting pressmen: 'I don't know why my leg gave way. I felt a peculiar twitching after 20 yards. Then I seemed to lose control of my leg and suddenly it gave out, throwing me on my face. But that is one of the fortunes of sport and I cannot complain. But I don't think I can compete here again.'

He later confirmed that he had pulled a tendon and subsequently tripped over one of the low ropes that separated the lanes. Nearly all the press reports majored on Duffy's catastrophe and hardly a mention was made of the actual winner of the event, Frank Jarvis.

There were no winners' medals in Paris, but *objets d'art*, valued at $80, $50 and $10, were presented to the first-, second- and third- placed athletes. Bronze competitor medals were issued some months later. Second-placed Tewkesbury recalled a bizarre conclusion to the event when, at ninety years old, he was a special guest at the 1968 Penn Relays. 'I was at a banquet at the end of the Games and a member of the British royal family suggested I deserved better. I don't know why. He asked if there was anything I wanted and I said I'd like one of those new French motorcycles. He said he'd see that I got one. I got more enjoyment out of that motorcycle than anything else.' Jarvis went on to take part in the triple jump and the rather more curious standing triple jump, but without winning another medal, and as the Games lurched on, watched by dwindling crowds, they proved to be the dismal failure everyone expected.

Afterwards Duffy found fame as a top sports writer in Boston, while Jarvis returned home to the quiet life and, soon after the Games, graduated from Princeton, then the law school at the University of Pittsburgh, before being admitted to the Bar in 1903.

He married in 1906 and both his children shared his passion for sport. Son Frank junior captained his school football and baseball teams, while daughter Dorothy won a Pennsylvania state tennis championship.

Jarvis practised as an attorney in Pittsburgh until his death in 1933 from a heart ailment at the age of 55, and such was his prominence in the city, both within his own practice and the wider legal community, that on the day of his funeral all the federal, state and county courts were adjourned as a mark of respect.

St Louis 1904

Archie Hahn

Two years after his disastrous final in Paris, Arthur Duffey created something of a sporting sensation by smashing the world 100 yards record. The old record of 9.8 seconds, set way back in 1882, had been matched by more than 20 athletes around the world and it was a widely held view of the time that this was a barrier that was unlikely to be broken.

When Duffey ran an electrifying 9.6 seconds for Georgetown University at the 1902 intercollegiate championships – the IC4A in New York – the reaction in the athletic world was one of incredulity. It was like a sub four-minute mile moment for sprinting.

In a sports magazine article he wrote shortly afterwards, Duffey memorably explained: 'I went to the mark all in a tremble. When we drew for positions I got a bad lane. The man who had used it in the semi-final had dug holes like graves. I filled them, but that made loose cinders under my feet and was worse than ever. I do not remember much about the start; I never do. I get set and think of nothing but the pistol. I suppose I must be in some sort of hypnotic state. The next thing I remember is that we were going down the track, probably twenty yards from the start, and Bill Schick was leading. I have known Schick for a long time. We ran against each other in high school and I had always beaten him. Now I saw that he had beaten me. I thought I must have got a bad start, and it came over me that if he beat me at the start he might win at the finish, too.

'Every runner has a different way of covering the course. Schick seems to go like a steam engine from the start to finish. I go in two bursts or beats. When I felt that my first burst was over, I could still hear Schick at my side. I thought at the time he must be about a foot ahead and I was never scared so badly before. I let out harder and worked as I had never done in any other race. It seemed as though something was pulling my head back and my arms up. But I knew I must hold myself and not let that happen. So I gripped my palms, shoved my head forward and tried to run harder than ever. Then I pulled away.'

Three of the four official timers stopped their watches at 9.6 seconds, but the other one had Duffey at 9.4. It was one of the most extraordinary sprint runs in history and the record would not be broken for 27 years.

As the fastest man on earth, Duffey looked the red-hot favourite to erase the disappointment of Paris and take the sprint crown at the 1904 Olympic Games, which were to be held on American soil for the first time. However, injury dogged him once again and he was forced to withdraw from the June AAU Championships, which were effectively the Olympic trials.

A few months later, instead of competing in the Olympics, Duffey sailed to Britain to try and add to his four consecutive AAA 100 yards titles – unsuccessfully as it turned out – and spent several months touring the tracks of England, Scotland and Ireland. When he finally returned, long after the St Louis Games were over, he decided to hang up his spikes for good.

'All lovers of the cinder sport will grieve over the passing of Duffey,' bemoaned the *Boston Globe*. 'He was a fine figure from his first race and a cleaner, more likeable athlete has never competed here or abroad.'

A year later Duffey's story took another surprising turn, one that would permanently end his running career. In an article in *Physical Culture Magazine* he admitted receiving generous expenses from race promoters since the turn of the century and suggested most other leading athletes had done the same. The secretary of the American Athletic Union (AAU) James E. Sullivan was incandescent and threatened to prosecute him as a criminal. Informed that this was legally shaky, he instead banned the 26-year-old Duffey from amateur athletics for life and wiped all his records from the sport's famed *Spalding Official Athletic Almanac* – a publication edited by Sullivan.

So with no Duffey and reigning champion Frank Jarvis now retired, there seemed precious little excitement in the sprinting world to whet the appetites of the public or the sportswriters as the Olympic Games approached, to be held in the American midwest city of St Louis. As an international competition the 1904 Olympics were laughable, with hardly anyone, bar the United States, sending a truly representative team. Britain and France didn't bother at all, and even the countries that did, of which there were only 11, sent merely the barest collection of athletes, such were the financial realities of taking a team halfway across the world.

Just as in Paris four years earlier, the St Louis Games were held as a sporting adjunct to a trade fair, in this case the World's Fair, and were in effect just an overblown American club meeting. But with major clubs such as New York AC and Chicago AC battling it out to determine bragging rights for which was the best club in the country, the performances remained very much in the major league.

While newspapers around the world devoted their attention to the Russo-Japanese war, President Theodore Roosevelt opened both the Fair and the Games in late August, but whereas tens of thousands flocked to the Fair, only a few thousand watched the third modern Olympics.

The United States won every track and field event except one, where a Montreal policeman named Etienne Desmonteau triumphed in throwing the 56-pound weight. In the sprints the fastest man of the day was reckoned to be Chicago AC's Bill Hogenson, the captain of the USA team and a celebrated college football star, but the events in St Louis were dominated by the diminutive figure of fast-starting Archie Hahn, christened the 'Milwaukee Meteor' by the sportswriters at the Games.

Hahn was the eldest child of a German immigrant father who arrived in the United States in the 1860s, opened a tobacconist store in rural Wisconsin and married a local girl. Archie arrived in September 1880 and he, his brother and three sisters grew up in Dodgeville, a small farming town, but he never set foot on a track until he was 19 years old. His high school didn't have a track team – or a track – and despite his height of just 5ft 5in and weight of just 135 pounds, his extraordinary speed made him a regular on the Portage High School football team.

He ran his very first race in 1899 at a county fair and finished third in the 100-yard dash, but he returned the following year and won the same event at a canter. His time of 10.1 seconds impressed the crowd, especially the observers from the University of Michigan, who invited him to study law and turn out for their track team.

Hahn wanted to play football at college, but the coach of the day, Fielding Yost, dismissed the idea on the grounds that he was too small. So Hahn turned all his sporting energies to running, particularly the sprints.

In the four years he spent at Michigan, Hahn was the sprint champion of the 'Big Ten' colleges every season and served notice of his Olympic intent when he won both the US and Canadian sprint titles in 1903. In order to qualify to run at the Olympics in those days, however, you had to be a member of an athletic club, not simply a college, so Hahn signed up with Milwaukee AC and joined them for the trip to St Louis.

There were three sprint events at the 1904 Games, at 60, 100 and 200 metres, and Hahn outpaced his rivals in the shorter dash in just seven seconds. With that edge he entered the 200 metres, which was a straight course rather than the familiar curve of today, and of the four starters, all of them American, three jumped the gun in successive attempts to get the race away and were penalized with two-metre deficits.

So all Hahn's rivals started behind him and they never caught up. He crossed the line a comfortable three metres ahead of them, with the powerful Louisville sprinter Nat Cartmell second and Bill Hogenson third. Hahn's time of 21.6 remained the Olympic record until the Games returned to the States in 1932.

All he needed for a clean sweep was victory in the classic 100 metres, in which again all six finalists were American. At the gun, the field got away together and charged into a strong headwind, but by the 20-metre mark Hahn was already edging ahead of his two nearest rivals, Cartmell and Hogenson, and he hit the tape a good two metres clear to claim his third gold medal of the Games, one of four athletes to achieve the feat in St Louis.

Cartmell, who took the silver, went on to break the world 50 yards record in 1905. Following the London Olympics in 1908, he turned professional and won the world sprint championship. After retiring in 1912 he enjoyed a hugely successful coaching career at the universities of North Carolina, West Virginia, Penn State, Manhattan College and the US Military Academy at West Point. He died in New York in 1967 aged 85.

Hogenson, who took another bronze, was the son of Danish and German immigrants and went on to a stellar career in the ceramic industry. He founded the Porcelain Enamel Institute and was a fellow of the American Ceramic Society. He died in 1964.

Shortly after returning home from St Louis, Hahn graduated from Michigan with a law degree, but he never practised his profession, deciding instead to devote his life to sport, particularly the track. At about this time it was decided that Athens would stage an 'Interim Games' in 1906 to try and bring back the international flavour to the Olympics, something that had been lost by the lack of foreign participants in St Louis and a complete lack of organization in Paris. So Hahn decided to go back into training to compete for the USA in the sprints and took a job as a teacher in a Michigan high school while he prepared for the competition.

For the first time in American track history, a genuine US team was selected from the clubs and colleges, ruled over by the newly formed American Olympic Committee, headed by Theodore 'Teddy' Roosevelt, and Hahn was selected for the 100 metres.

With his toughest rivals, Cartmell and Hogenson, not taking part, Hahn won it easily. However, it was rumoured that he took advantage of a lenient starter by tearing out of his marks when the Greek command *Etami* or 'Get set' was made. He apparently left his rivals on the start line and actually eased up as he won the race, but the starter did not recall the runners and the result stood.

Hahn's American teammate, Kansas City AC's Fay Moulton, who was fourth in St Louis, took the silver and Australia's Nigel Barker the bronze.

For more than a hundred years Archie Hahn remained the only sprinter to retain an Olympic 100 metres title on the track, although the Athens competition, which became known as the 'intercalated' or 'renegade' Games, was only two years after St Louis and could not really be described as a genuine Olympic Games. Hahn himself was happy with his success, and the following year he decided to retire from the amateur track world, turn professional and earn some money from his talents. In a short report on his retirement a *Washington Post* correspondent described him as 'probably the greatest sprinter the world has ever seen'. More personally, it continued: 'Hahn has never refused to meet a rival athlete or to give him a chance to redeem himself. His courtesy, courage and splendid sportsmanship have made him one of the best-liked men in American athletics.'

Hahn ran in pro races all over the USA and performed stunts at fairs, including a famous occasion in Wisconsin when he outran a racehorse over 50 yards. He was still winning races until 1918, when he finally gave up competing at the advanced age of 38.

In a rare public appearance in Washington, in 1913, Hahn named two sprinters who had never won medals at the Olympics as his toughest opponents, Harvard's Bill Schick, who equalled the 100 yards world record in 1905, and Boston AC's fast-starting Billy Eaton.

It was about that time that he began to coach at colleges up and down the country, including Brown University, Princeton and his alma mater Michigan. Later he was appointed to replace the legendary 'Pop' Lannigan as head coach at the University of Virginia, where he moulded some of the Cavaliers' best track and football teams, claiming 17 state championships. During these years, Hahn majored in track and football, but he also dabbled in just about every other sport, including a stint as a boxing coach during the Second World War.

Earlier in his career he put together a landmark book on training for the track called

How to Sprint, published in 1929, which was the first major work of its kind and remains a classic text on the sport. Illustrated by dozens of photographs and drawings, it describes in forensic detail every facet of sprinting, from the basic techniques to fast starting and finishing, and includes important tips on how to dig correctly shaped holes in the cinder tracks, choosing the best shoes and the correct diet.

The book even included copious notes on how sprinters should conduct themselves before a race. 'Many athletes make a great mistake by walking about the field before competition and generally exhaust their physical and nervous energy before the event,' he wrote. 'A certain amount of nervous excitement will aid a sprinter, if controlled. Talking with well-wishers and amateur advisers tends to confuse, and certainly exhausts, the competitor. The sprinter – or any athlete – should make a point of keeping to himself before he actually takes to his marks.'

Always seemingly ahead of his time, Hahn also took the advertiser's dollar, appearing in newspaper ads plugging the dubious energy-giving value of a vitamin-enriched chocolate drink called Cocomolt.

After a lifetime in coaching, during which he became something of a legendary figure on the college circuit, Hahn finally decided to hang up his coach's cap and retire in 1951, at the grand old age of 70. He later suffered a lengthy illness and in January 1955, after a heart attack, he died at his home in Charlottesville, Virginia, leaving wife Sarah, son Archie Junior, two daughters and six grandchildren.

Archie Hahn's name lives on and he is widely regarded as the most outstanding sprinter of the early Olympic era. That was certainly the view of his country's modern-day athletic powers, who elected him to the National Track and Field Hall of Fame, in Indianapolis, where the giant trophy he won during the 'renegade' Games of 1906 is on permanent display.

London 1908 & Stockholm 1912

Reg Walker and Ralph Craig

The American dominance of the sprints was expected to continue when the Games came to Edwardian London and the newly created 'technical marvel' of the White City Stadium in 1908. The Games had originally been assigned to Rome, but after the eruption of the volcano Vesuvius in April 1906, the Italian Government decided to redirect huge funds to reconstruct the devastated city of Naples. They informed the International Olympic Committee (IOC) that they could no longer afford to stage the event, and a late switch was made to London.

Sadly, the Olympics were beset with problems from start to finish, including widespread international bickering and bad feeling, especially between the hosts and the Americans, which earned the 1908 Games the unfortunate title of 'The Battle of Shepherd's Bush'.

In the sprinting world, it was 24-year-old James Rector, an American law student from the University of Virginia, who was the favourite to take the 100-metre laurels back to the United States.

Rector was a fascinating figure. The first athlete from the state of Arkansas to compete in the Olympics, he was known by friends and family simply as 'Indian' (surprisingly even recorded as his name in a 1901 state census), because from a very young age he was so naturally fleet of foot, it was said, that he ran like a native American.

Rector came from a rich and powerful political family and both his grandfathers were state governors – one in Arkansas and the other in Mississippi.

He was sent to the best schools and excelled academically and athletically, starring on the football, baseball and track teams at his prep school in New Jersey before arriving at college.

Once settled at the University of Virginia, he set countless indoor and outdoor records at distances from 50 to 220 yards. In Olympic year he equalled the American 100 metres record of 10.8 seconds and matched the world 100 yards record of 9.6. The odds on another American Olympic champion were shortening by the day.

But just across the border in Canada there was another contender for the big sprinting prize – Irish-born Bobby Kerr. The 26-year-old had emigrated with his parents from Enniskillen, in Ireland's County Fermanagh, when he was just five. He only took up sprinting seriously as a way of keeping fit when he joined the fire brigade of an agricultural machinery factory in his hometown of Hamilton, Ontario. After winning a few local races he was encouraged to enter the 1904 Olympics and saved $75 to make the trip. He slept on the floor of a friend's apartment before going out in the semi-finals of the 100 metres competition.

Four years later Kerr had grown stronger and faster, winning almost every Canadian sprint title with ease. He also won the English AAA 100 yard title in the build-up to the 1908 Games, and in the absence of a competitive British sprinter he soon became a crowd favourite.

However, they had not taken into consideration one of the most unlikely heroes yet discovered by the Olympics, a waif-like 19-year-old clerk from South Africa by the name of Reg Walker. An unlikely-looking athlete, Walker stood just 5ft 7in tall and tipped the scales at barely nine stone, giving the impression that a light breeze would blow him over, yet when he ran, he was a quite different human being. As a teenager, his only sporting experience had been in lacrosse, a sport that regularly drew big crowds in South Africa, where he was a fleet-footed winger on his local team in Durban. It was the team's managers who persuaded him to take up sprinting and he joined the city's Albion Harriers Club.

It was in 1907 that Walker first came to the attention of the sporting world in general, when he turned out for the South African Championships wearing plimsolls. The meet officials sent him back to get some proper spiked shoes, which he had to borrow, and he then went out and beat the favourite, Transvaal's Eddie Duffy. The IOC had given permission for the four British colonies in Southern Africa – the Cape of Good Hope, Natal, the Orange River Colony and the Transvaal – to participate in the 1908 Olympics under the umbrella name of South Africa. In the January of Olympic year a national Olympic Committee was formed under the leadership of mining magnate and former athlete Henry Nourse.

There was little time and funds were scarce, but they scraped together enough money to send a team of 15, including seven track and field athletes. It would be the first time South Africa had competed and the first time they would wear their now familiar green outfits with the yellow springbok on the chest.

One of the great myths that sprung up over Walker was that he had been left out of the team because of his youth and inexperience, and was only able to make the Games because Natal raised enough money to send him independently. Documents from the archives of the South African Olympic Association, including hand-written minutes from the Executive Committee, describing the selection process, prove this was not the case and that Walker was selected as the number two sprinter behind South African champion Eddie Duffy. However, it is true that a significant public fundraising effort was made in Natal to ensure Walker's travelling expenses were covered, along with entry fees for some of the warm-up events that were to be held in London.

Walker arrived in London in mid-June, about a month before the opening of the Games, in order to get acclimatized to the European conditions and test himself against some of the likely opposition in a few races in the intervening weeks. Just a week after arriving in Britain, Walker lined up in the AAA Championships in London, and lost by a decisive margin to the Canadian Kerr.However, watching from trackside was the man who would enable Walker to make the jump from also-ran to Olympic champion. Sam Wisdom was a former pro sprinter and an old-fashioned coach from the halcyon days of professional sprinting and had been the motivating force behind the great Harry Hutchens. He was impressed with Walker's natural sprinting talent and also realized that the main reason for his inability to win at the highest level was his below-average starting prowess.Wisdom, who was nearly 60 at the time, was a London plumber by trade. However, he had not only trained Hutchens in his prime, but even paced him to his English 50 yards sprint record. Wisdom also introduced Walker to the top pro of the day, the Australian Arthur Postle, and they practised together in the build-up to the Olympics.

It also came to light that Walker's great rival James Rector lent a helping hand when Wisdom asked him to help the young South African adapt to the low crouch starts favoured by the Americans. In those more innocent days, the US star was happy to assist. It seems inconceivable today, but on the eve of the Olympic final Rector spent most of the day perfecting the starting technique of one of his greatest rivals. Would his noble sportsmanship prove his undoing?

Wisdom also ensured that the youngster maintained an almost regimental training schedule in the manner of the old pros and ate what in those days passed for a healthy diet.

The regime had an electric effect on the quiet and modest Walker and he took the 100 metres by storm. The heats began shortly after King Edward VII opened the Games, on July 13, an appearance that heralded almost continuous rain for the remainder of the competition.

What made the sprints even more exciting than usual was the 'sudden death' nature of the heats, as only the winner of each race was guaranteed to go through. As predicted, James Rector looked the most impressive runner on view; he tied the Olympic record in the heats with a run of 10.8, and equalled the performance in the semi-finals. Not to be outdone, the fast-improving Walker also tied the record in his semi-final.

A few years later Walker wrote: 'I was practising my starts with unfailing regularity, but in the second round of the competition when Rector showed faster than I did, I realized even then I was not fast enough and during the morning of the final I went down to Stamford Bridge and did some more practising. The result was that when the final was decided in the afternoon, I was quicker away than the other competitors.'

Walker felt that the chief requisite for a top sprinter was an abundance of what he referred to as nervous energy and the ability to channel that energy into running. He also kept to a strict diet, which included boiled lamb chops, rusks and weak tea for breakfast; roast beef and vegetables, stale bread and milk puddings for lunch; and fish, toast and stewed fruit for late tea!

So, with his starting technique now near perfect and his diet in trim, Walker lined up in the final, alongside Rector, Kerr and the 1904 silver medallist Nat Cartmell, on Wednesday, July 22. Because there were no Englishmen in the final, the home crowd were all rooting for Walker and a colonial victory to wrest the title from the Americans.

But all the experts, including the morning's papers, were still predicting a win for the speedy Rector, despite the American's strange windmill arm action, which seemed to propel him along the track. In the corner of the stand was an American 'compound' packed with noisy fans from the United States, yelling and chanting for Rector, waving huge banners and flags and playing fanfares on their bugles.

As the four men crouched into their starting holes a hush fell over the stadium, followed by a huge roar as the pistol cracked and the sprinters sped away. Walker, vivid in his dark green, showed first and then Rector passed him at 30 metres. Walker drew level at about halfway and they ran neck and neck until about 20 metres from the finishing line, when the young South African seemed to find another gear and flew past the American, hitting the tape a good half metre in front, with Rector snatching second place from the fast-finishing Kerr.

Walker had again equalled the Olympic record of 10.8 – indeed, two of the five stopwatches had stopped at a new world record of 10.7 seconds. As he crossed the line, the whole stadium erupted and the fifty thousand-strong crowd went wild, hurling their hats and programmes into the air, jumping on their seats and flooding on to the track. To his obvious embarrassment, Walker was swept up by the crowd and carried shoulder high around the track, and with a giant South African flag waving at his side he was paraded all the way to the dressing-room, even receiving a huge ovation from the American 'compound' as he passed. After changing and catching his breath, he was presented to the royal box for special congratulations. Walker's victory was one of the outstanding performances of the Games and was heralded by the British press as a huge colonial success in the absence of serious competition from their own runners. In the ugly 'Anglo-American cold war' of the 1908 Games, Walker was also celebrated for defeating the US athletes.

While the newspaper column inches on his victory rivalled those of the little Italian Dorando Pietri, who was picked up by officials as he staggered towards the finish of the marathon and manhandled across the line, it still could not camouflage the bitter squabbling between the hosts and the Americans. The following morning his unexpected success knocked even the Suffragettes off the front pages of the British newspapers, and when the news finally reached South Africa, its press reacted with wild enthusiasm about the nation's first ever gold medal winner. The USA had lost the Olympic 100 metre final for the first time and their mood darkened further when Bobby Kerr beat the two American favourites to take the gold medal in the 200 metres.

Before returning home, Walker took part in a small British tour, equalling the British 100 yards record of 9.8 seconds, despite a strong head wind, in a bank holiday athletics festival at Ibrox Park, in Glasgow. He then beat that time with a 9.6-second run in a meeting in Halifax, only to see it chalked off due to a following wind. He rounded off the tour in Abergavenny, Wales, where he was timed at 9.4 in the 100 yards – but the AAA refused to ratify it as a world record because the track was slightly downhill.

There were calls for Walker to be given a top job for life when he finally arrived home, in December, and Natal's prime minister sent a telegram of congratulation, while in his native Durban an unofficial Reg Walker Day was declared, with schools and offices closing early and celebrations held in the streets.

Walker may have been treated like royalty and acclaimed as one of the nation's greatest heroes, even by the government, but when all the fanfare, parties, parades and hero worship eventually faded away there was, of course, no job for life. In fact, there was no job at all, and Walker could not make any money running as an amateur.

However, he managed to survive for the next couple of years, living on handouts and backing from various athletic associations, and winning titles both in South Africa and Britain, including the AAA 100 yards championship in 1909. His old coach Sam Wisdom watched happily from the stands, but his health was deteriorating and he retired shortly afterwards and died, following a heart attack, at his home at a west London hotel in 1912.

For a year after the Olympics, Walker had turned down lucrative offers to race the world's top professional sprinters. By the end of 1910, however, he was still unemployed and virtually penniless, so he decided he was going to make his fortune as a professional, despite protests from South Africa, who wanted him to run in the 1912 Olympics. Reg's stepson, Bill Walker, who also lived in Durban, related a story of how South African millionaire R. Edgar Walker offered him the staggering sum of £250,000 to stay as an amateur, run in the 1912 Olympics and never turn pro, but Walker could be stubborn and headstrong and wouldn't change his mind once he'd made a decision. Walker junior believed that his stepfather probably made about £1,000 out of pro racing, despite the big purses – the majority of the money going to managers, coaches, promoters and hangers-on – whereas when the old millionaire died he left his £6 million estate to various charities for cats and dogs.

For five years Walker certainly made a decent living as a pro, racing against the top sprinters on the circuit, including his old friend Postle and Jack Donaldson, both from Australia, where pro sprinting was big business and purses for each race could be as much as £500. However, his career was cut short by the First World War and after first serving in German West Africa – now Namibia – he returned to England in 1917, enlisted with the Expeditionary Forces, and fought as an infantryman on the Western front.

A bout of malaria and a gunshot wound to the head took a heavy toll on Walker's health, and for years after the war he suffered bouts of trench foot from standing knee-deep in water-filled trenches. The terse wording on his military discharge card, issued in January 1919, simply stated that he was 'surplus to requirements having suffered impairments'.

After the war, Walker attempted to re-ignite his track career and even won a couple of races at meetings in England, but time and the war had taken their toll and he returned to his previous work as a clerk, this time for a rug, mat and canvas company in Manchester. During Walker's time in England his Olympic gold medal and Springbok blazer were stolen and never seen again, although some years later a bizarre advertisement appeared in a British newspaper suggesting that the medal might be returned if he went home to South Africa. Eventually he did go home, where he dabbled in a little coaching, including training his nephew Reg Kitchin, a good hurdler, who still credits his uncle for giving him an extra six yards. But the gold medal never reappeared.

He had married 23-year-old Londoner Maisie Hill in 1917 but divorced soon after. He then married a Manchester war widow, Sarah Lynch, just before Christmas 1926. However, after she died in 1941 aged just 46, Walker became lonely and there were reports that he began to drink heavily. It appeared he had been disinherited by his wider family because of his passion for running and his wealthy great aunts left their entire fortunes to the Silver Leaf Cat's Home, in London. His final residence was listed as a small room in the Hotel Riviera, on Durban's waterfront. Walker died in 1952 from tuberculosis, aged 62, in Durban's King George V Hospital, and left barely enough money to cover his funeral.

Today he is still revered as one of his country's finest sportsmen and remains one of the star names in the country's sports hall of fame in Pretoria, where some of his track kit is displayed.

Walker's fellow medallists, Rector and Kerr, both went onto enjoy impressive careers in their chosen professions. The year after London, Rector graduated with his law degree, retired from the track and joined one of the premier legal firms in St Louis. He toyed with a comeback at the 1912 Olympics, but after a few races in 1910 decided against it. During World War 1 he served in the US secret service and was about to be deployed to Europe when the conflict ended. He retired from his law practice in 1943 to look after the family's estate trust and died, aged 65, in March 1950.

Kerr continued running until 1919, but also decided against an Olympic return, figuring he was past his best. He saw active service in Europe during the Great War, first with the 205th (Tiger) Battalion, then the 164th and finally the pioneering 1st Tank Battalion. After the war he started an impressive coaching career, in both track and football, and was Canadian team captain at the 1928 Olympics and team manager at the 1932 Games. Kerr also helped organize the first British Empire Games, held in Hamilton, Ontario in 1930. He died in his native city in 1963, aged 80. A park named after him remains an enduring memorial to one of Canada's first sporting heroes.

With Reg Walker plying his trade on the world's professional sprinting circuit, the way looked clear for the Americans to move in and reclaim their lost sprint title when the Olympics reconvened in Stockholm, Sweden, in 1912. The United States team looked an awesome athletic force and included three exceptional sprinters, Ralph Craig, Howard Drew and Don Lippincott, any one of whom was capable of winning the gold medal.

The favourite had been Detroit's Ralph Craig, a tall 23-year-old from Michigan University who had to be cajoled into making the trip to Sweden at all. He had twice equalled Bernie Wefers's 1896 world record of 21.2 seconds for the 220 yards, and in 1910 had added the national collegiate 100 yards to his collection of trophies. But Howard Drew, the first top-class black sprinter to run in the Olympics, had beaten him in the 100 metres during the US trials, so the forecasters were struggling to predict a winner.

Craig was born and raised in Detroit, and attended Central High School, where he was spotted and coached as a hurdler by ex-boxer Jack Collins. At Michigan, he was trained by Archie Hahn's old mentor Keene Fitzpatrick, who recalled: 'Craig was as great an all-round sprinter as I ever knew. He was a bit slow off the marks but had tremendous drive. He was a good quarter-miler and, I believe, could have broken the world record at 300 yards if he had tried it. The funny thing about Craig was that he was a hurdler when he came to Michigan, but we quickly converted him.'

However, when Craig graduated in 1911 he was genuinely anxious about competing in the Olympics and was close to giving up the sport. He had just got engaged and started a new job – as an industrial chemist at Frederick Stearns & Co, a big pharmaceutical outfit in Detroit – so he felt he couldn't take the time off he needed to devote to training. He was only persuaded to carry on running when an old school friend intervened. When they were kids, Charley Burton and Craig used to race each other down the city's back alleys, around Charlotte and Second streets, and Burton convinced him that he could make the necessary arrangements. He even won over Craig's new employer, Fred Stearn himself, who gave him the time off, with full pay, so that he could concentrate on his training, go to Sweden and bring back gold medals and glory for the United States.

Craig was finally persuaded to go, and he joined the Detroit YMCA's track club and began serious training to get back into running shape.

Little was then known about a chunky 18-year-old called Don Lippincott, but he'd been spotted by the American Olympic authorities running for Penn State as a freshman and offered a place on the team – if he could fund his own travel. That seemed simple enough as he came from one of the most affluent banking families in Philadelphia, but with the recent *Titanic* disaster still fresh in the memory, his mother was terrified his ship to Europe would sink and persuaded his father not to fund the trip.

Stubbornly, Lippincott managed to raise enough money from friends and alumni at Penn State to make the journey. It gave the young economics student the opportunity to take a unique place in sprinting history.

Of course there were other sprinters capable of snatching a medal as well as the Americans, including the talented German Richard Rau, who claimed the unofficial world record of 10.5 seconds, and Britain's Willie Applegarth, a top performer at both sprint distances.

Stockholm, bathed in July sunshine, was a breath of fresh air for the Olympic movement after the feuding and fighting of London. During the intervening years there had even been calls for the Olympics to be abandoned, as they were thought by some to be damaging international harmony rather than promoting it. De Coubertin needed Stockholm to succeed or the entire movement would be in serious danger of collapse. Fortunately, the 1912 Games proved to be a genuine hit and Stockholm is still regarded as one of the greatest of all time.

Stockholm had no Olympic village, so the teams were scattered around the city in various hotels, while the Americans preferred to stay on board their luxury steamer in the harbour. This time 28 countries took part, with nearly four thousand athletes competing in a purpose-built stadium, where an early form of electronic timing was being tested at the Olympics for the first time. The Games were formally opened on Saturday, July 6, by King Gustav V before a crowd of almost 100,000 people, and most of them stayed to watch the first heats in the 100 metres competition.

In the 16th heat, Don Lippincott created a lasting piece of Olympic and sporting history. As usual the young sprinter went to his marks squeezing a cork to help relieve nerves, but he tore down the cinder track and hit the tape just a few feet ahead of Britain's Willie Applegarth. The three straw-hatted timers studied their watches. All had stopped at 10.6 seconds.

Lippincott had smashed the old 10.8 mark and with electronic timing being experimented with at the games for the first time, it would be the first official IAAF world record for the 100 metres. It stood for nearly nine years. Lippincott's picture appeared on the front page of his hometown *Philadelphia Inquirer* alongside banner headlines. But medals weren't being handed out for the heats. There was still a semi and a final to negotiate.

As expected, all the top American sprinters made it comfortably through their respective preliminaries to qualify for the semi-finals, which like the final would be held on the following day. Lippincott served warning to his rivals that, although young, he could not be taken lightly, when he ran another superb race to win his semi. Craig looked comfortable in his semi, but unknown to the big crowd, Drew had pulled a muscle winning his and now faced a race against time to be fit for the final.

With five US athletes in the final alongside the only non-American, South African George Patching, the press were speculating on a clean American sweep of the medals. Craig had an unusual practice he followed when he raced, though it's not known if he employed it in Stockholm. He placed a tiny pebble in his mouth, under the tongue, which he insisted kept his mouth moist while running. How he kept from swallowing it we will never know.

As the time of the final approached, the runners began to go through their usual warm-up routine, but a buzz started to run through the crowd when the pre-event favourite Howard Drew limped off the track, his face contorted in pain. The muscle tear he suffered in his semi had not responded to vigorous treatment, but he had decided to go on to the track and try to warm up in the vain hope that the adrenaline might push him through the pain barrier. However, the warm-up simply made the injury worse and he had to be helped off the track and back to the dressing-room.

With Drew out of the equation, Craig and Lippincott were now clear favourites to take medals for the United States, but the final was marred by no fewer than seven false starts, including one in which Craig and Lippincott, so intent on beating each other, sprinted the entire distance on their own without realizing there had been a recall.

Eventually, at the eighth attempt, the anxious starter managed to get the field away, and it was the speedy South African Patching who made the early break and led the race to half distance, before the slower-starting Americans Craig, Lippincott and New Yorker Alvah Meyer got into their stride and drew level. As the tape neared, Craig edged ahead, but then the whole field seemed to cross the line en masse – in fact the crowd could not tell who had won or who had come second or third.

But it didn't take the judges long to award the gold medal to Ralph Craig, whose strength over the final 20 metres had brought him home first by less than two feet in a time of 10.8 seconds, with the unfancied Meyer second and Lippincott third. The Americans revelled in the sight of three United States flags rising up on the stadium's flagpoles, only the second time it had happened in Olympic history.

A few days later Craig and Lippincott lined up for the final of the 200 metres, this time with the German Rau and Britain's Applegarth alongside them. But the elegant Craig proved his superiority a second time as he powered his way past the field, after another slow start, to win in 21.7, with Lippincott second and Applegarth just holding off Rau for third.

So Craig finished the competition with two gold medals and naturally became the toast of the American team, although the real hero of the Games was the brilliant all-round athlete Jim Thorpe, a Native American who took gold in both the pentathlon and the decathlon. Even though he was cruelly stripped of both titles in January the following year, because he had once been paid $60 for playing baseball, Thorpe remains one of the greatest stars ever seen at the Olympics.

When Ralph Craig returned home to Detroit he was acclaimed as the hero of the city, and for the rest of his life he wore a diamond ring presented to him by the Mayor in honour of his success in Sweden. In the two years that followed the Games, before the outbreak of the First World War, both Drew and Lippincott equalled the world 100 yards record of 9.6, while Applegarth tied the world 100 metres mark of 10.6. A few months after the Games all three of them equalled Craig's world 220 yards record of 21.2.

Lippincott went back to life as an economics student at Penn State, graduating in 1915, and served as a lieutenant in the US Navy during the war, before returning home to start an impressive career in banking, stocks and securities. He died in 1963.

Drew's story was even more remarkable. Though 21 when he competed in Sweden, he was still in high school, having skipped school as a teenager to look after his family and work as a bellhop. During the First World War, he served as a supply sergeant in the 809th Pioneer Infantry, and shortly after returning home he graduated from Drake University School of Law. He began his law practice in Hartford, becoming one of only four black attorneys in Connecticut and retired as its first black judge. He died in 1957 and was widely revered for his work in fostering better racial understanding across the state. Despite their achievements, both Lippincott and Drew have sadly been reduced to footnotes in sporting history, but the name of Ralph Craig would never be forgotten, thanks to his performances in those two Stockholm finals. He returned home and promptly quit the track, enjoying his new job and family life, with his two gold medals safely tucked away. In the 1920s he left his native Detroit and moved to New York, where he worked as an administrator in the State unemployment insurance office, a job he held until his retirement in the early fifties. At the same time, Craig worked tirelessly in the Olympic Council, furthering the movement in the United States and promoting athletics and water sports, the latter having been something of a passion for him since childhood.

He had sailed and rowed for the Detroit Boat Club as a young man, and as he got older his interest and expertise grew until he was generally recognized as one of the most proficient yachtsmen in the country. He wrote papers for the North American Yacht Racing Union and also compiled *The History of Yachting in the Olympic Games*, which remained one of his proudest achievements. His work over three decades in the Olympic Council and his eminence in the yachting world earned him selection as a reserve skipper for the US yachting team, in the American Dragon Class, at the 1948 Olympics in London. But an even greater honour was kept a closely guarded secret until a few hours before the US team's ship docked in England. This was his selection as the man to carry the US flag in the opening ceremony parade, an honour announced in front of the whole team by American Olympic Committee chief Avery Brundage, who had been a team-mate of Craig's at the 1912 Games.

The New York Times reporter at the scene described the 59-year-old Craig as 'a tall, distinguished-looking gentleman, with a full head of grey hair and close-cropped moustache'.

Understandably, the thrill of carrying the Stars and Stripes around Wembley Stadium, filled with more than 100,000 people, remained one of his greatest moments and more than made up for the disappointment of not being needed to actually participate in the yachting competition.

Craig married his wife Elizabeth back in 1913 and they had two children, a daughter Elisabeth and a son Bruce. During the 1950s, especially after his official retirement, Craig spent a great deal of time writing for the *Detroit News*, where he specialized in Olympic matters, but he also became something of an expert on the breeding and keeping of spaniels, writing a number of articles and a book on the subject. He died in July 1972, at the grand old age of 83, at his home on Lake George, at Ticonderoga, New York, but his exploits are kept alive at the National Track and Field Hall of Fame, where he is remembered not only as one of the finest sprinters of his era, but also as the only gold medallist ever to return to the Olympic Games in a completely different sport, an achievement that is unlikely to be matched.

Antwerp 1920

Charley Paddock

By the time the 1920 Olympics arrived in the war-torn city of Antwerp, the world had been starved of international athletic competition for eight years. The planned 1916 Games in Berlin had been cancelled as the Great War raged, so the only major meeting held between Stockholm and Antwerp was the Inter Allied Games, staged in 1919, in Paris, where servicemen from all the Allied Forces gathered to compete in what contemporary reporters described as the 'Military Olympics'.

One of the big stars of these Games and the man everyone would fear on the track a year later in Belgium was the brash, confident American speedster Charley Paddock, a striking, muscular athlete from California, who would not only become a dominant force in the sprints for the next decade but also the world's first real track superstar – a genuine showman who delighted in entertaining the crowds with a trail-blazing series of stunts and gimmicks.

As Hollywood boomed, Paddock not only hung out with the biggest screen stars of the day, he actually starred in movies himself and was seldom out of the newspapers. When he was on the track he made sure that every pair of eyes was trained on him and him alone, and his life, both on and off the track, was always controversial, highly colourful, guaranteed to entertain, but tragically very short.

He was born in August 1900 in Gainesville, Texas, but when doctors said they were worried about young Charley's lack of weight – at seven months he weighed just seven pounds – and suggested that the hot, humid Texan climate was to blame, the family moved to the healthier climate of California.

The move was clearly beneficial and Paddock soon developed into a fit, powerful, barrel-chested young man. Although his parents tried to encourage him to play sports as a child, the only pastime that seemed to interest him was throwing rocks at the older boys and then running away to see if they could catch him. Fortunately for him, he was always too fast for them, or a glittering career on the track might have been halted there and then.

As a teenager, he began to take an interest in athletics and was encouraged in this both by his father, who was a keen miler in his day, and by local track star Forrest Stanton, who trained on the beach close to the affluent Paddock family's summer home at Hermosa.

Young Paddock used to sit and watch him work out, and as a result Stanton took him under his wing, even inviting him to his house and letting him take home some of his medals. Paddock vowed that one day he would win medals of his own. His first competitive races were over cross-country courses, and then he took up miling before eventually converting to the sprints, in which he immediately began to win school titles at all ages, including the California high school title while still only 15.

However, he abandoned his senior year at high school, just a few months short of graduation, and enlisted in the US Army, joining a field artillery camp in Kentucky. By the time he was 18 he had reached the rank of 2nd lieutenant.

Army life clearly did not have an adverse effect on his running, and early in 1919 he ran an impressive 9.8 for the 100 yards, a time that earned him an invitation to compete for a place in the American forces team which was shortly to leave for the Inter Allied Games. Again he ran impressively and was picked for both sprints and the relay in Paris where, despite the chaos that ruled throughout Europe, many of the world's top athletes were on show.

These Games provided Paddock with his first major competitive test – one that he passed with flying colours by winning both the 100 and 200 metres, plus a further gold in the relay. Among the spectators was Nicholas 1, the King of Montenegro, who was becoming increasingly alarmed at the miserable way in which the small band of athletes representing his tiny Balkan state was performing and decided to 'adopt' some of the stars of the Games by knighting them in the stadium. So it was that Paddock became Sir Charley of Montenegro, although it was a title he seldom used in later life.

When Paddock returned to the United States, news of his success in Europe had gone before him and he was already becoming something of a celebrity. He loved to entertain and the fans enjoyed his stagey appearances, which often included multi-coloured tracksuits and exotic silk running shorts. In addition to this sartorial showmanship, he had a number of other gimmicks with which the crowds could readily identify, including a superstitious routine before each race, during which he would walk around the track looking for a piece of 'friendly' wood, more often than not a hurdle, knock on it three times, cross his hands and return to his marks. Apart from being a crowd-pleasing act, this also served as perhaps the first overt piece of psychological one-upmanship seen on the track.

His capacity for drawing crowds and for almost limitless self-promotion was something he carried off from head to toe, quite literally, as his son Charley junior recalled: 'He certainly was a showman and he really enjoyed running. Apart from his garish track outfits he insisted on having specially made running shoes, in deer or elk skin, so that when they got wet they would shrink and conform to exactly the shape of his feet, like they were glued to them.'

But Paddock reserved his theatrical *pièce de résistance* for the end of the race, when he performed his famous jump finish, taking off from the track some 10 or 12 feet from the tape and hurling himself through it in mid-air.

Track purists were horrified by the stunt and always felt it was the reason why he lost so many races that he really ought to have won, but Paddock always maintained that this finish gave him about an extra fifth of a second over his rivals at the tape. He also realized that it would catch the eyes of the judges, who would see nothing at the end of a closely contested race but the flying figure of Charley Paddock.

Athletics historian Tom McNab rates Paddock as one of the track's first great personalities. 'He was certainly the first star of amateur sprinting and undoubtedly one of the first great "shamateurs". He wandered all over America setting all sorts of weird and wonderful records in the type of races no one but he would tackle. But he saw the value in doing it and similarly he saw the value in the jump finish, which from a coaching point of view was a complete waste of time, but it was a great grandstand ploy and people flocked from all the States to see Charley Paddock run.'

But before those barnstorming racing days began, there was the challenge of the 1920 Olympic Games, and Paddock, who had won a scholarship to the University of Southern California, where he came under the influence of the famous US coach Dean Cromwell, had already begun to hone his skills in readiness for Antwerp.

Paddock was hardly the ideal shape for a sprinter, in fact he looked more like a shot putter, standing about 5ft 8 in tall, weighing about 170 pounds, stockily built and muscular, with short, powerful legs. Cromwell began correcting a poor start, a short stride and Charley's habit of using just his shoulders and arms to run, although he remained essentially a power runner, with one of the highest knee lifts of any athlete on the track.

After winning the Far West sprint title, Paddock qualified automatically for the US Olympic team, joining an impressive sprinting line-up, which included two Texans, Loren Murchison and Morris Kirksey, alongside the 'New York Thunderbolt' Jackson Scholz, who had just graduated with a journalism degree from the University of Missouri after spending two years in the US Navy Flying Corps. They were all aboard the steamship USS *Princess Matoika* when it eventually set sail from New York. This vessel would become infamous in newspapers around the world by the time it reached Europe, as the US team carried out a 'mutiny' on board, with some of the athletes threatening not to compete in the Games when they arrived.

The 'Mutiny on the *Matoika*' is now long forgotten, and the American track authorities certainly prefer it to be so. However, the original protest petition containing the names of the mutineering athletes still survives, a document organized and delivered by a seven-man committee that included Charley Paddock. It was the first, but by no means the last, time that he would run foul of the US track powers. It was probably the most publicized of all the events in which he was involved, and so it was no small wonder that under such pressure he went on to achieve what he did at the Games after creating such a furore.

The story surrounding the mutiny began when the US Olympic Committee realized that they had had run out of time to secure adequate passage for the team on conventional trans-Atlantic liners. The effects of the war and the impact of the global flu pandemic were still causing chaos to shipping and all the luxury steamers were booked solid for months ahead, so they went cap in hand to the US Government, which decided that the Army could lend a hand by providing a ship to transport the team to Europe at no cost, a scheme that pleased the cash-conscious USOC immensely as it saved them the $70,000 needed for conventional passage.

The ship selected for the journey was the modern transport steamer *Northern Pacific*, which was as fast as the top commercial liners of the time and could make the crossing in seven or eight days. Arrangements were made for the ship to leave New York just after the final Olympic trials in Boston, in order to arrive in Antwerp about a fortnight before the competition began. Then disaster struck. The *Northern Pacific* loosened a huge plate on her hull, below the waterline, and had to be hauled into dry dock for repair, leaving the Army and the USOC in something of a quandary and the entire US team stranded in New York, temporarily barracked in a basic army camp just outside the city.

After lengthy negotiations, another vessel was found, but there was now little choice and the one finally handed over, the 20-year-old transport ship *USS Princess Matoika*, was certainly not in the same class as the *Northern Pacific*; it was old, slow and had hardly any of the comforts to which the team were accustomed. The few cabins and staterooms that did exist were quickly snapped up by the officials and their wives, while the team had to make do with what were essentially troopship quarters. The US athletes immediately christened it a 'rusty old troop ship' and as simmering resentment and discontent on board began to spread, a wire from Europe was intercepted on the ship by a member of the team indicating that their situation on the *Matoika* was a garden party compared to what awaited them when they arrived in Antwerp.

This unwelcome news triggered a team meeting, hastily convened deep in the bowels of the ship. A huge petition was drawn up and signed demanding that the USOC take some action. The signatures of all the athletes were written in a large circle just as on the old-style mutiny papers of the past, so that the authorities could not identify the ringleaders. It listed all their grievances, which ranged from general complaints about the awful conditions to specific examples of appalling food, over-crowding, poor sanitation and the fact that many athletes were sleeping in a stinking hold which was over-run with rats. They wanted action and a promise that such a situation would never be allowed to happen again – or they would not compete in the Olympics.

Fortunately for the bewildered officials, common sense prevailed and the USOC pacified and eventually persuaded the athletes that the return journey would be much better and that the emergency measures they were enduring would never be repeated.

But when the team finally arrived in Belgium, the 'Mutiny on the *Matoika*' very nearly became the 'Revolt of Antwerp' when the team discovered it was to be barracked in the cramped classrooms of an old school, with hardly any food during a Belgian public holiday, with insufficient beds or proper facilities and no one available to solve its problems until after the holiday was over.

Paddock and his close friend Loren Murchison had suffered enough and decided to 'jump ship' and take an apartment a short distance away where they could eat properly and avoid the mayhem caused by the USOC's patent lack of planning. Having been delayed in New York and taken twice as long to cross the Atlantic as originally planned, instead of the expected two weeks' preparation, they now had just a few days to acclimatize in Antwerp before the Games opened.

The 100 metres competition began the day after the opening ceremony, so the four American sprinters were ordered not to march behind the US flag, but to watch from the stands to conserve their energy.

Some thirty thousand people packed into the impressive white-walled stadium, which had been built in just under a year by the Belgians despite the difficult circumstances created by the war. Apart from the four US stars, there was tough competition in the sprints from Harry Edward, the first black athlete to represent Britain at an Olympic Games, and the French–Algerian Emile Ali Khan, who had won the French sprint title and equalled the 60 metres world record in 6.8 seconds. It was no surprise when all six breezed into the semi-finals.On a sunny August Monday morning, the semis saw all six favourites make it through to what looked like an incredibly tight final, which was to take place later in the afternoon. The hours of waiting in the stadium must have felt like an eternity to the athletes. Murchison spent the entire time wandering around in a daydream, muttering to himself that he was going to win and trying to summon up his nervous energy, while the rest of the finalists sat around and pretended to ignore him.

Finally, when it was time to go out on to the track and warm up, Lawson Robertson, the American team's Scottish-born sprint coach, came up with a novel distraction. The wily old coach, who had taken part in the 1904 and 1906 Olympic 100 metres finals, told the four American runners: 'What you fellas need to warm you up is a glass of sherry and a raw egg.' The athletes looked at him in total disbelief, but Morris Kirksey leaped at the idea, seeing a possible psychological advantage if the others didn't follow suit.

'It would make me sick,' moaned Murchison. 'I could never drink and raw eggs turn my stomach inside out.'

Jackson Scholz looked similarly unimpressed with the plan. Robertson turned to Paddock and asked him if he wanted a glass. 'What's Kirksey going to do?' he asked. 'He's on his way to the sherry and egg,' said Robertson.

That did it. Paddock saw what Kirksey was trying to do and decided to do likewise. In his book *The Fastest Human*, published toward the end of his career, he recalled: 'Though I was considerably upset as to what a stimulant might do to me, I realized the tremendous moral advantage Kirksey would have on the rest of the field if he were the only one to follow Robbie's advice. I am not sure Kirksey was keen on the idea himself, but he probably thought the rest of us would not follow suit and he was always willing to gamble on anything. When he drank his sherry and egg he had three companions and it did warm us up and bring back the punch and pep we sorely needed.'

When the finalists were called forward, Paddock began to go into his good luck routine at the start and found himself a piece of 'friendly' wood, crossed his hands and prepared for the gun. He also had a habit, when called to his mark, of putting his hands way over the start line and then drawing them back slowly as the second command of 'Get set' was given. He was in the process of doing just that when the starter, unaware of this ritual, told him in French to pull his hands back. He then called *Prêt*, the French for 'Ready, Get set' and off went the gun.

However, both Murchison and Edward misinterpreted what had happened and thought they were being ordered to stand up, so both had relaxed when the gun went off and were left trailing yards behind. Kirksey went off like a bullet and took an early lead, but by the halfway mark it was Scholz with a two-foot advantage, with the fast-finishing Edward, who was making up for his bad start, closing quickly. Kirksey began to overtake the field, but Paddock was right on his shoulder, straining every sinew to ease past his team-mate on the boggy cinder track. The race was almost over.

'Then I saw the thin white string stretched to breaking point in front of me,' wrote Paddock, 'and I drove my spikes into the soft cinders and felt my foot give way as I sprang forward in a final jump for the tape, and just as my feet left the ground Kirksey turned his head towards me and for a single instant lost his forward drive.'

Paddock's description of the closing split second of the race is shown perfectly in the photograph taken at the finish, one of the most famous in Olympic history, with Paddock, arms spread wide, crashing, airborne, through the tape, while Kirksey had turned his head to the right in an apparent anguished realization of defeat. That fatal mistake cost Kirksey the race and made Charley Paddock the Olympic champion.

'Nothing else mattered,' wrote Paddock, 'my dream had come true and I thrilled to the greatest moment I felt I should ever know. The hands so eager to shake mine now might be doubled against me tomorrow and the autographs burned or forgotten. The real pleasure had been in the anticipation and in that single moment of glorious realization.'

Britain's Harry Edward was awarded third place – although the photographs taken from the stand side of the track clearly show Scholz was ahead of him. Some 40 years later, written in an unpublished memoir, Edward remembered the controversial start and the race with extraordinary clarity: 'I had drawn the outside lane near the grandstand. I loosened up, especially my shoulder and arm actions, and dribbled a short distance. Some of my opponents had a few bursts out of the starting holes dug into the cinder track, others bent and stretched, loosening up in their own fashion. The band stopped playing and a hush settled over the stadium. Then came the starter's voice: "*A vos marques!*" And we responded by digging the balls of our feet into the pre-dug holes, placing our fingers behind the white starting line.

"*Preparez-vouz!*" shouted the starter and we got set, awaiting the crack of the pistol and the release of concentrated tension of mind and muscles. While in the momentary, nervous suspense the starter's aide and linesman at my right said in English: "Paddock, take your hands back behind the line!" This broke my tension just as a false start would have done. Then the pistol went off. I jumped out of the holes more vertically than in the proper forward direction. I put tremendous effort into my strides, found myself about four feet behind the leaders at half distance, regained an improved forward-leaning position and ended with a tremendous burst, passing everybody at the end.

'Alas, I passed them about three feet behind the finishing line. The judges gave me third place behind Paddock and Kirksey of the United States. There was a great delay before the results were announced. Every participant sensed or knew that the start had been a doubtful one. Scholz said to me at the end of the race that it had been a false start.'

Edward even filled out a protest form in the hope of getting the final re-run and Ali Khan persuaded the French team to push for an annulment. The British team made discreet enquiries and were told it was unlikely the starter would reverse his decision so, keen not to start a fight they couldn't win, Edward's protest was quietly dropped. The French team went ahead with their protest, which was considered by the IOC committee the following day and rejected by 4 to 0.

Edward's extraordinary life story is worthy of brief summary. He was actually born in Berlin, in 1898; his father was a waiter and circus performer from Dominica, in the British West Indies; while his mother was a Prussian piano teacher. Fascinated by the Olympic Games at an early age, Edward was starting to make a name for himself as a young sprinter when war was declared. He actually ran his first races in the newly built Berlin Olympic Stadium, winning at 200 metres and placing second in the 100, on the very day that Archduke Ferdinand was assassinated.

In 1915 he was interned, as a de facto British subject, in the grim Ruhleben civilian detention camp, just to the west of Berlin. Conditions were awful and he spent almost four years enduring meagre rations and witnessing daily violence, sickness and death before he was liberated to Scotland when the war ended. But in the camp he also won the running races that were organized by the internees and believes 'the exceedingly rough conditions' toughened him up.

Edward found his way to London, took work as a French and German teacher and signed up with the Polytechnic Harriers in Chiswick, where he became an almost instant star by winning the English AAA 100 and 220 yards titles in the summer of 1920. This famous double won him selection to the British Olympic team in Belgium, so he took a fortnight's holiday from his job to make the trip.

After the controversial start in the 100, he was not unreasonably disappointed to win only bronze and his despair only deepened when a tendon injury restricted his running in the 200 metres final – where he won another bronze medal.

Charley Paddock was also disappointed – losing almost on the line to fellow American Allen Woodring, a shy young man from Syracuse University, who only made the race as a late replacement for the exhausted Jackson Scholz.

Paddock was also very tired, but he dearly wanted to complete the sprint double, something he looked odds-on to do as he charged into the lead in the final and came out of the turn almost five metres clear of the field. But he'd gone off too quickly and there was little gas left in the tank, and as the finish neared Woodring closed on Paddock's shoulder and the two seemed to hit the tape together. The judges rightly awarded the gold to the boy from Syracuse, who had just sneaked past Paddock on the line as he made his customary leap for victory.

The long-legged Woodring, who had borrowed a pair of spikes before the race because his own had split, had to be convinced by Paddock that the 100 metres champion hadn't sportingly allowed him to win by slowing up in the last 25 metres. The damaged shoes must have struck a chord with Woodring, as he went on to be a salesman for the Spalding athletic equipment company.

In his memoir, called *When I Passed The Statue Of Liberty, I Became Black – The Autobiography of an Ex-European,* which is housed in the Amistad Research Center in New Orleans, along with all his papers and photographs, Harry Edward recalled Woodring telling him 'that was your race, Edward'. A pulled tendon in the semi-finals meant he ran the final in a 'grimace of suppressed and conquered pain and strode as far as the pain would permit me'. He never got over his double Olympic disappointment, despite winning more English titles, including an extraordinary performance at the 1922 AAA championships where he won the 100, 220 and 440 yards titles, all in under an hour, after which he was personally congratulated by King George V.

In 1923 he emigrated to America, where racial prejudice initially confined him to menial jobs such as a dishwasher, longshoreman and labourer, but as the years rolled by he found his calling as an aid worker and civil rights activist and used his language skills working for humanitarian causes at the United Nations. He died in Augsburg, on a visit back to Germany in 1973, and his passing didn't merit a single line in the British newspapers. Back in Antwerp, Paddock wasn't finished with the competition and after leading off the impressive US sprint relay team to another gold medal and a world record of 42.2 seconds, along with Scholz, Murchison and anchorman Kirksey, Paddock returned home to a hero's welcome with three medals and a solid reputation on which to build and promote his future both on and off the track.

Bizarrely, 24-year-old Morris Kirksey won a second gold medal in the rugby tournament, when the US team, heavily populated by students from Stanford University, shocked pre-event favourites France 8–0. Kirksey would later graduate from Stanford, then St Louis Medical College, and enjoy an eminent career as a psychiatrist in the US prison system, working at San Quentin and Folsom.Paddock had never shunned publicity, in fact he openly courted and encouraged it, finding journalists and the media fascinating and generally easy to manipulate and exploit. He had enjoyed writing since his play-producing days at school, adapting the classic works in the eighth grade, and he'd been working for a newspaper in Pasadena since he was14 years old, so it came as little surprise to anyone who knew him that writing would play a major part in his future career.

He contributed articles to newspapers and magazines, commented on people and events, wrote speeches for his motivational lecture tours and would later travel the world covering athletic meetings. However, all this literary activity took a back seat in the spring of 1921, when he embarked on a wholesale assault on the world's sprint records as well as inventing a few new ones of his own.

Paddock was driven compulsively to win and break records, and by the end of his career he had established no fewer than 17 different world marks, ranging from the more traditional sprint distances to the typically Paddock-esque runs of 90 yards, 110 yards, 135 yards, 250 metres, 300 metres and so on. In April 1921, running for USC in front of 3,000 fans at a southern Pacific AAU meeting in Redlands, California, he broke four world records and tied another in the space of a few hours. And he only ran in two races! In the first he tied Arthur Duffey's 100 yard record of 9.6, but he also beat Don Lippincott's 10.6 100-metre mark with a jaw-dropping new world record of 10.4 seconds. He had tapes set up at both distances.

After a short rest he ran a second race – with tapes set at 220 yards, 200 metres, 300 yards and 300 metres on a straight track. He was outside the 220 yards record, but set a new world record in the 200 metres of 21.2, then set new world marks of 30.3 in the 300 yards and 33.8 in the 300 metres.

'Trojan Speed Artist Shows Dazzling Form', screamed the *Los Angeles Times*. 'Greatest Of All Time' boomed the *Brooklyn Standard Union*. 'Wonder Runner', shouted the *Detroit Free Press*.

Paddock lapped it all up and a few months later, in Pasadena, he broke three more world records and tied another in one race – with the clocks stopping at 8.8 for a new record in the 90 yards, once again equalling the 9.6-second 100 yards record and then setting a new record for the 110 yards of 10.2. This was also a new world record for the 100 metres, but it was never officially ratified because the AAU refused to put the time forward, explaining that the course was actually *longer* than 100 metres! Paddock had run 100.584 metres in 10.2 seconds.

As the next Olympic Games – this time in Paris – loomed on the horizon, Paddock was out on his own as the world's premier sprinter and was already dubbed the 'world's fastest human', a title invented by a west coast sports writer and adopted enthusiastically by Paddock. However in some ways the title could also be a millstone around his neck, and early in 1923 he seriously considered retirement, feeling he had little to gain and a lot to lose from appearing on the track, with every sprinter gunning for him. It was left to one of Paddock's close friends, the great movie star Douglas Fairbanks, to persuade him to continue competing until at least after the next Olympics, although Paddock's insouciant contempt for the US track powers almost cost him a place on the team.

It was during 1923 that he received and accepted an invitation to run in a student games competition in Paris, despite threats from the AAU that he might lose his amateur status if he took part, as the Americans had decided not to permit any athlete to compete abroad in the year preceding the Olympics. However, they did allow a Harvard and Yale team to race against Oxford and Cambridge, in England. True to form, Paddock treated the AAU with his customary disregard and told the authorities, via one of his newspaper columns, that he would go where he pleased because he was 'over the age of 21, free and white'. He travelled to Paris, won all three sprint events in the competition, including a world record-equalling run of 10.4 in the 100 metres, and promptly returned home to face the music. The furious AAU wanted to suspend him and ban him from the forthcoming Olympics, but Paddock found an ally in the other major US athletic force, the National Collegiate Athletic Association (NCAA), and a huge power battle ensued, fought for the most part in the pages of American newspapers. Paddock was finally reinstated, but not before he dropped a bombshell on the AAU by suggesting that they were aware of professionalism creeping into the sport and that some athletes were being paid secretly. Whether his revelations disturbed their cosy world is unclear, but it was not long after his disclosures were made that the Paris affair was quickly settled. In the years that followed, the AAU never missed an opportunity to snipe at Paddock. And he never missed an opportunity to snipe right back.

If his troubles with the AAU weren't enough, Paddock almost eliminated himself from the Olympics when he broke his ankle playing basketball during a lecture tour in Iowa, just before the Christmas of 1923. He kept it secret, but it was months before he was strong enough to run properly and, though running seriously under par, he did just enough at the Olympic Trials in Boston to stake his claim for a place in both the 100 and 200 metres.

So Paddock and the rest of the US sprint team – Scholz, Murchison, George Hill, Bayes Norton and newcomer Chester Bowman – travelled to Europe for the 1924 Games.

Never before had there been such a red-hot favourite for a sprint gold medal as Charley Paddock. However, when he arrived in Paris self-doubt began to creep in, especially when he began running poorly in the heats, while the rising British star Harold Abrahams ran exceptionally well. Nor did it help when Bellin de Coteau, an eminent French physician who had examined Paddock before the Games, proclaimed: 'Paddock's a freak. He's fat, has curvature of the spine and shoulder blades that stick out, his nasal respiration needs attention and when he runs he looks like a calf with two heads!'

Paddock had travelled to Paris with 14-year-old Douglas Fairbanks Junior and his mother Anna Beth, who was an old friend. This was a trip that young Douglas would never forget. 'I remember Charley as a jolly, chunky fellow, though it was always a mystery to me how he could be such a speed demon on the track built like he was,' he recalled a few years before his death in 2000.

'He was a great one with the girls and I remember being terribly envious. We were on our way to Paris on the same ship as the team, which included Charley, the other great sprinter Loren Murchison and the swimmer Johnny Weissmuller. I remember working out with them on the ship and I hero-worshipped them. When we landed on the other side they let me train with them. Charley trained every day and he would give me a 60 yard start in a 100 yard race and still beat me.'

Sadly for Paddock, the races in the Paris Olympics were not quite as easy, and the best he could do in the 100 metres final was a poor fifth place. 'It's no use, I just haven't got it any more,' he told Fairbanks Senior. 'My legs tie up, my speed is gone. I'm an old man sure enough this time.'

Fairbanks tried to cheer him up and he was wined and dined by his movie star clan, including new wife Mary Pickford and the French star Maurice Chevalier, who livened up proceedings by doing outrageous impressions of the Games' two big stars, Paavo Nurmi and Harold Abrahams.

The break from the competition clearly did Paddock some good and he went back into the fray in much better shape, managing another silver medal in the 200 metres, just an agonizing few inches behind Jackson Scholz. But he damaged a thigh muscle leaping for the tape and had to sit out the relay as the American squad romped to another gold medal.

After a short but successful post-Olympic tour of Europe, which redeemed some of Paddock's lost prestige, he returned home to the United States. While in Europe, he met the founder of the Olympic movement Baron Pierre de Coubertin, who saw Paddock's value as a persuasive promoter and publicist and suggested a plan for both Paddock and Murchison to embark on a massive world tour, which the Baron described enthusiastically as 'Sprinters Around the World', in order to spread the gospel of track, sportsmanship and the Olympic ideal. The idea appealed to Paddock, and early in 1925 he and Murchison left on an epic four-month tour that took them to the athletic outposts of Japan, China, the Middle East and back to Europe. In every country they visited, the two sprinters raced, spoke at meetings and banquets, met civic leaders and were generally hailed as great sporting ambassadors.

Tragically, a few months after returning home from the tour, Murchison was struck down with spinal meningitis and spent the rest of his life paralysed and wheelchair-bound. He died in a nursing home in New Jersey in 1979.

As for Paddock, nothing, it seemed, could ever go completely smoothly, and when he returned to the United States he discovered that allegations of expense fiddling had been levelled against him and Murchison. They had allegedly been pocketing large amounts of money from the countries they had visited, far in excess of their genuine expenses. Both athletes were flabbergasted and vehemently denied the charges, but only after a lengthy and much publicized investigation by Paddock's old friends, the AAU, were they finally cleared.

Towards the end of 1925, Paddock was again considering retiring from the track and focusing more on his writing career, but an inner voice kept nagging him to break a few more records, and he wanted to try and make up for the disappointment of Paris by making the US Olympic team for a third time, in Amsterdam in 1928.

He even turned down a monumental offer from the top sports promoter C.C. Pyle to turn pro and run a series of races for a minimum fee of $30,000, a sizeable sum in those days. But he had other irons in the fire, and after emerging unscathed from another row with the AAU over his bucking of amateur rules by appearing in a gasoline advertisement, he decided to take up Douglas Fairbanks's suggestion and try his luck in the fastest growing and most lucrative business in California – the movies. They had been doing their growing in a small Los Angeles outpost just a stone's throw from Paddock's Pasadena home, in a place called Hollywood.

Apart from the premier silent movie stars and heavyweight boxer Jack Dempsey, Paddock was just about the most famous face on the West Coast, and Paramount Pictures decided to invest in that fame by casting him alongside one of their top stars, Bebe Daniels, in one of the first co-ed college life comedies, in which he played himself as a coach at the college. The five-reel silent *Campus Flirt* was moderately successful at the box office, but all the headlines were reserved for the off-screen relationship between the two stars. Rumours circulated about a possible real-life romance during the shooting of the movie, which was released in the late summer of 1926, and the Hollywood gossip columnists, including the legendary Louella Parsons, had a field day speculating on a possible wedding, even though Daniels had previously been linked with many of the rich and famous and had apparently broken off an earlier engagement with fighter Dempsey.

'Bebe Daniels To Wed Sprinter King', 'Charley Paddock Captures Film Star's Heart In Five Weeks' and *'Yes Sir She's My Bebe'*, crowed the LA papers, and the couple were seen around the best Hollywood nightspots and parties for about 18 months, although there is no evidence to suggest they were ever engaged, and the romance, if it ever existed beyond the film company press departments, appeared to die a natural death.

But Paddock's movie career continued and he starred, often as himself, in a number of sports-based films and a few B westerns, in which he got a reputation as something of a daredevil stuntman. He also produced a few minor pictures of his own and finally starred in a movie loosely based on his own life called *The All American*, in which he played a sprinter called Charley Patterson.

His attempts to promote it during the Olympic year of 1928 landed him in even more hot water with the AAU and there were inevitable calls, from other countries too this time, for him to be barred from the Games. But once again he managed to ride out the storm.

In May 1926, he decided to run one more race – against the up-and-coming West Coast sprinter Charlie Borah over 100 yards at the Los Angeles Coliseum. Before the confrontation, he billed the meeting as his farewell performance, but after he beat the young pretender and smashed the world record in 9.5 seconds, he reversed his decision yet again and returned to serious training in readiness for the 1928 Olympics. Sadly, the record was never ratified officially, as in those days a record had to be broken by two-tenths of a second for a new one to qualify.

But as the Games approached Paddock's form began to fall away and another youngster from California, Frank Wykoff, who was soon to be the first man to register a 9.4 for 100 yards, beat him in two races over both sprint distances. Despite doubts over his form, Paddock was still chosen for the US Olympic team, albeit only for the 200 metres, but he was beaten in the semi-finals.

'After 1928 he saw people coming along that he no longer had the stamina to race against,' said stepson Prisk Paddock. 'He had been in the sport a long time and he wrote about the track scene and went to a lot of meetings, so he saw what people were doing and how they were coming along, so he decided it was time to retire.'

This time there would be no comebacks, so with his track career over and work in the movie business at an end, he wrote a book about his running career and settled down to pursue his newspaper career. In December 1930 he met and married divorcee Neva Prisk Malaby, the 26-year-old daughter of the publisher of the *Pasadena Star-News* Charles Henry Prisk, and took over the job of business manager of the *Press-Telegram* newspaper, in Long Beach, California, and then also the *Star-News*, in Pasadena, both family concerns.

He became an increasingly successful and influential figure on the West Coast, managing the two newspapers as well as writing features, articles and editorials. Gradually he became more interested in politics, and by the time the Second World War began his editorial messages had become more political and more widely read.

It was because of his growing influence on the political scene, his family believed, that a local political rival, who sat on the draft board, tried to get Paddock called up to the services, despite the fact that at 42 he was bumping the upper age limit.

Paddock saw what was happening and decided to beat his rival to the punch by joining the Marines, where his prior service and long association with the reserves enabled him to enter as a captain. He was assigned as an aide to Major-General William Upshur, first as a public relations man and then as a morale officer, based at the Pacific HQ, in San Francisco. It was on the final leg of a tour of the Pacific war front, in July 1943, that Paddock was killed in a plane crash, over Alaska, along with Upshur and four others.

He was not brought back to Pasadena, but buried at Sitka, Alaska, in accordance with family wishes, and a few months after his death a commercial freighter was named after him, along with a sports field in Pasadena. The news of his untimely death made front-page news in *The New York Times* and most of the other American newspapers. Had he not been killed it is likely that Paddock would have returned home to become an even more successful publisher and probably a successful politician.

Charles W. Paddock, the 'California Comet', was the first track superstar and not only goes down in athletic history as one of the greatest sprinters of all time, but also as a flamboyant personality who did an immense amount to raise the level of awareness and popularity of sprinting all over the world. He may have been guilty of blithely ignoring the authorities on occasions, but that was because he was highly individualistic and held strong opinions on how the sport ought to be run. Meanwhile he was a huge crowd-puller and certainly gave the sport a much higher profile than it might otherwise have enjoyed. For these reasons alone, Paddock must rank as a giant amongst the sprinters of the last hundred years.

The last word ought to go to Rube Samuelson, the sports editor of Paddock's main newspaper rivals the *Pasadena Post*, whose heartfelt personal tribute bettered anything else written at the time: 'Upon entering, the editorial room of *The Post* was strangely hushed yesterday afternoon. Everyone was working with unusual diligence and concentration, each at his own desk. There was no greeting, no banter, no conversation. What was wrong? Then came the sudden realization, almost without being told. Charley Paddock was gone.

'Words come awfully hard as this is written. That rollicking laugh, that spirit of fierce, determined competition, be it in athletics or business or Marine life, that tremendous vitality, that positive individualism that Pasadena knew so well – all that and more has been stilled.

'No track man captured the imagination more than Charley. He gave life to track and field meets – life that they had never before known. What colour! What a come through performer! What an individual!

'You might not have agreed with him at times, but what forceful personality can always be agreed with? Or should be? Or wants to be? Charley Paddock provoked thought. He had to. He was that kind of vital human being. Only big men in spirit and action fall into that category, while others forever debate their conclusions. Charley Paddock didn't borrow someone else's thoughts to present as his own. He lived in his own right, gave his own opinions fearlessly, awoke many from their lethargy and fought the good fight.'

Paris 1924

Harold Abrahams

When the 1920 Olympic Games ended, the elder statesmen of British athletics returned home vowing never to send another team. Even after the dust had settled, there was serious discussion about abandoning the Games and not sending a team to Paris in 1924. While they probably felt humiliated at collecting only four athletic gold medals, despite an excellent performance by the track team, the few British Olympic records that survive indicate that there were several other reasons for their sudden disenchantment with the Games.

Both the British Olympic Association and the AAA felt that everything had gone wrong in Antwerp. The general public, they said, were totally apathetic about the competition; the Games had become alien to British ideals; professionalism was creeping in; the organization of the Olympics needed a complete overhaul; and, moreover, the athletic bodies still had to plead with potential sponsors just to raise the few thousand pounds needed to finance an Olympic trip.

All these problems were aired regularly during countless committee meetings in the years that followed Antwerp, but after much wrangling common sense finally prevailed and, with assurances on at least some of their gripes, the 'old guard' decided to bite the bullet and go to Paris. Had they decided otherwise, one of Britain's most successful track teams might never have set foot in the Olympic Stadium and one of the country's most enduring athletic legends might never have snatched his moment of glory.

That man was Harold Abrahams, now immortalized in the hugely successful, Oscar-winning, though factually hazy 1981 film *Chariots of Fire*. For most people, the film version of Abrahams's story is the real one, but his family all agree that, for the most part, it is a fairy tale. As Harold's nephew Anthony Abrahams succinctly put it: 'They got three things right. Harold was Jewish, he went to Cambridge and he won the 100 metres. The rest you can just "enjoy". It was a good film in the *Boys' Own* paper style.'

Abrahams's Olympic ambitions were fired just before the outbreak of the First World War, when his two eldest brothers, Adolphe and Sidney, both top athletes, took him along to Stamford Bridge, London's premier athletics stadium at the time, to watch the 1914 AAA championships. Harold never forgot the experience and the huge impression made on him by the running of the then British sprint king Willie Applegarth, who had been a double medal winner in the 1912 Olympics.

Born in December 1899, Abrahams came from a privileged background. His father was a wealthy City financier, a heavy-drinking Lithuanian Jewish immigrant, a man prone to violent tempers and who could not even write his own name in English. Despite this disadvantage, he achieved great wealth and power in his adopted country.

Harold was born prematurely, weighing barely 2lb, and was not expected to survive. Consequently, he was spoiled by all the family. He was the youngest, by some years, of six children, four boys and two girls, and grew up in Bedford. He was acutely aware of the sporting achievements of brothers Adolphe, a good half-miler, and Sidney, who represented Britain in the long jump at the 1906 and 1912 Olympics, finishing a respectable fifth and twelfth. They were always pushing and bullying young Harold, and the need to be better than them was a constant spur to him.

'Harold told me,' recalls Anthony, 'that when he first started showing signs of being a good athlete, they would make him run everywhere. Their favourite game was to make him run around the houses in Bedford. They'd give him a time to beat and if he didn't make it they used to hit him over the head with rolled newspapers.' With such family support, it came as no surprise to the family when Harold made a successful racing debut at Stamford Bridge – at the age of 10.

By the outbreak of the First World War, most of the family had grown up and left home, but Abrahams was just entering his teens, and when his parents split up, it was decided that he should be sent away to be a boarder at Repton, a long-established and expensive public school. In the film *Chariots of Fire*, Abrahams's prime motivation for running is his fight against anti-Semitism which, claims the film, dogged him throughout his early life. However, there is little evidence for this view and if it did exist at any time in his life, then it was probably at Repton, where he spent some lonely years. Indeed, he does not appear to have been a dedicated Jew, as all the athletics meetings in those days were held on Saturdays – the Sabbath. 'What drove Harold,' says Anthony, 'was firstly the need to be better than his brothers; secondly, that throughout his life he was a perfectionist and wanted to succeed. He knew he had great athletic and intellectual powers. The family expected him to do well and that made him even more determined.'

By the end of the war he was already making a name for himself as a sprinter and long jumper, winning titles in the 1918 public schools championships and in the following year beating his former idol Willie Applegarth in an exhibition race, accepting a two-yard start, but winning by six. Two months later, he followed the tradition of his brothers and sisters and went up to Cambridge, where he studied law at Caius College and quickly earned his athletic blue, although he never ran around the university quadrangle as depicted in *Chariots of Fire*; that was Lord Burghley some years later.

Less than a year after settling into college life, while still a freshman, he was selected for Britain's track squad for the 1920 Olympics. However, at this early stage of his athletics career Abrahams was not in the same class as the cream of the world's sprinters – the likes of the Americans Paddock and Scholz, or even Britain's Harry Edward – and although he won his first heat, he went out in the next round. But he was philosophical about the trip. 'I had a long-distance view of Charley Paddock's large back,' he once said, 'and although my competing at Antwerp was far from distinguished, I benefited enormously from the experience and I'm sure it played a large part in my good fortune at Paris four years later.'

In those intervening years he enjoyed mixed fortunes on the track, including a world record in the rarely run 75 yards at Stamford Bridge, only for it to be disallowed when it was discovered that the track was eight inches too short. It was not until 1923 that things began to move forward quickly for Abrahams – a year that saw him leave Cambridge and join forces with the now legendary coach Sam Mussabini. Mussabini, half-Arab, half-French, a cycling and billiards expert, had coached sprinters Willie Applegarth and Harry Edward, as well as the double gold medal-winning middle distance runner Albert Hill, in addition to helping out on the professional circuit, which had not endeared him to the athletics establishment.

Nevertheless, Abrahams sought him out and trained with him relentlessly for almost a year before the 1924 Games. His single-minded desire for success in Paris set him apart from every other athlete in the country. New Zealander Arthur Porritt was running at Oxford during this time and recalled the effect that Abrahams had on his contemporaries. 'His training methods were today's training methods. I was always very impressed with his effort. His methods were absolutely unknown at that time and I couldn't help admiring the way he trained, practised, dieted, did this, didn't do that, just to keep fit. This was entirely out of keeping with the spirit of the time. Harold was almost professional, though obviously not to the extent of getting any remuneration. For the rest of us, our training, by today's standards, would do nothing but make people laugh. A few hours on a Sunday morning, perhaps a few starts, a couple of hundred yards and some chatting. Whereas Harold was training long hours and three or four times a week.'

A highlight of the 1923 season and a measure of how far Harold needed to progress was to have been the AAA championships, in which he was destined to take on the rising Scottish star Eric Liddell in the 100 metres. Liddell had played rugby for Scotland and was a strangely unorthodox runner, with a windmilling arm action and his head pulled back as if he was gasping for air. But he was quick. Their first meeting on the track turned out to be the semi-final of the 220 yards, at the 1923 AAAs, where the Scot blitzed Harold and the rest of the field in a record 21.6 seconds. Abrahams was taken aback by the power and speed of his rival and, as fastest loser, was offered a run-off to qualify for the final. Stunned by the margin of defeat he instead withdrew from the competition.

The 100 yards was the following day and a 20,000-strong crowd packed into Stamford Bridge expecting to witness the big showdown between Liddell and Abrahams for the title of Britain's fastest man. But it never happened. In an interview some years later, Harold blamed a throat infection for pulling out of the 100 yards, though he was well enough to win the long jump title on the same day. A case, perhaps, of Liddell-itis, rather than laryngitis.

In blazing sunshine, Abrahams watched from trackside as Liddell ran away with the 100 yards in a new British record of 9.7 seconds. Throughout his life Harold poured cold water on the Scot's record, questioning the veracity of the time to cloud the victory. Most felt it was sour grapes on his part, as the three timekeepers all clocked Liddell at under 9.7 and a fourth unofficial timekeeper stopped his watch at 9.62 – a hair's breadth from the world record.

For added drama, the producers of *Chariots of Fire* did put Liddell and Abrahams together in the 100 yards final, with Liddell winning convincingly and Harold turning to Mussabini for help. But they never met on the track over the 100. Perhaps mercifully for Harold, Liddell was never due to compete in the 100 metres at the Paris Olympics because the heats were to be staged on a Sunday and he was a devout Christian, though he triumphed in the 400 metres and took a bronze in the 200. After Paris he returned to his missionary work in China, where he died, in a Japanese internment camp, in 1946.

After the 1923 AAAs, Mussabini took Abrahams's running apart, and together the coach and athlete worked at rebuilding every facet of his sprinting, aimed at just one goal – a gold medal in the Olympic 100 metres in Paris.

Athletics historian Tom McNab, the historical consultant on *Chariots of Fire*, believes that Mussabini's influence cannot be overestimated. 'Abrahams was the first British athlete to be thoroughly trained in a very professional manner. The anti-Semitism in the film was there for added drama, when in fact it didn't really exist, except possibly for a general level of anti-Jewish feeling which pervaded the twenties. But it may have been the grit in the oyster that produced the pearl of the 1924 Olympic winner, though he never made any point about it. Mussabini was far more important; he came from the traditions of professional running, the lore and mystique of the old "pro" racers of the nineteenth century. He knew the likes of Harry Hutchens and much of what he had learned came from that era.'

Abrahams himself wrote: 'Sam was "dead nuts" on the arm action, with the arms kept low, bent at the elbows. He maintained that the action of the arms controlled the poise of the body and the action of the legs. So my training sessions consisted largely of perfecting the start and practising the arm action over and over again.

'There were no starting blocks in those days, so we took meticulous care with the placing and digging of the starting holes and the accurate control of the first few strides. I always carried a piece of string the length of my first stride and marked the spot on the track, at which I would gaze intently on the word "set".'

Mussabini was a stickler for stride length and Abrahams always believed that not over-striding gave him an extra yard and a half. To ensure he was running properly, Mussabini would place pieces of paper at measured points along the track and Abrahams would have to run and pick them up on his spikes. After perfecting the stride length, Mussabini then taught Harold to adopt what became his famous 'drop' finish, in which he leant into the tape to drop his chest on to it. So by the spring of 1924, Abrahams emerged as a completely different athlete from the one who had failed at the Olympics four years earlier. As if to prove his new standing, he ran a wind-assisted 9.6, which would have equalled the world record had it been officially ratified, and then raised his national long jump record to 24ft 2½in (7.38m), a mark that remained unbeaten for 32 years. The Olympic Games were beckoning.

To his amazement, Abrahams was selected to run at the Games in the 100 metres, the 200 metres, the sprint relay and the long jump. An angry letter, published in the *Daily Express* a few days later, suggested that this was too much for one man and that he should be omitted from the long jump. It was signed by 'A Famous International Athlete'. Incredibly, the selectors took heed and he was duly dropped from the long jump. The author of the letter was, of course, Abrahams himself.

Although there was nothing like today's media interest in the Olympics, the British press latched on to Abrahams and reported his every movement and opinion, including his view that there was little chance of him winning the 100 metres. 'This wasn't mock modesty,' he wrote some years later, 'for I always (according to my friends) had far too high an opinion of my ability. But the Americans appeared to me to be in a different class from myself.'

Arthur Porritt was selected to run for New Zealand in the sprints. 'By and large we expected the Americans to more or less clean up the show, except for Harold. He was, if you like, the Great White Hope,' he said.

A glance at the quality of the opposition bore out Abrahams's pessimism, especially with the Americans in fighting mood after a poor performance, by their standards, in Antwerp. No expense had been spared to ensure that the United States team would return triumphant from these Games, and after the American trials, chief coach Lawson Robertson pronounced the team to be the greatest athletic force ever to leave the country. A huge amount of money had been raised to ensure that the team arrived in Europe at the peak of fitness, especially after the Antwerp debacle, and the giant *SS America* was chartered specially to transport the team in the lap of luxury. The promenade deck was even fitted out with a 220-yard cork track so that the athletes could train during the week-long trip. When they arrived in Paris they were greeted by thousands of cheering fans and boarded a convoy of 70 cars taking them to their own US Olympic village, an estate in the countryside outside the capital that was once the stately home of one of Napoleon's marshals.

What a contrast to the preparation of the British team. 'We went from Newhaven to Dieppe, then to Paris, because it was the cheapest as well as the longest route,' Abrahams once said, 'and we all stayed in a rather miserable little hotel.'

The Games opened on Saturday, 5 July, and the first heats of the 100 metres began on the following day, with no fewer than 75 athletes taking part. The first round soon sorted out the men from the boys and Abrahams cruised comfortably to victory in a sedate 11 seconds, although he needed to run faster in a much more competitive second round, where he won his heat in 10.6, equalling the Olympic record. After a tense 24-hour wait, the semi-finals took place the following afternoon and Abrahams later admitted that he nearly failed to qualify for the final. Drawn in his heat were the Australian champion Edwin 'Slip' Carr and the Americans Paddock and Chester 'Chet' Bowman, a 22-year-old from Syracuse University who had just won the junior AAU 60 yard title. 'I did a very stupid thing that nearly cost me the race. Out of the corner of my eye I saw Carr move. Bang! The gun went and I was certain there would be a recall, but I was wrong and immediately running nearly two yards behind the others. A small voice inside me said, "Keep your form, don't panic," and gradually the gap closed and I dropped down for the tape and thought I broke it. I walked disconsolately back to the start. Had I won?

Had I even qualified? To feel the tape break is no criterion. An agonizing few minutes, which seemed like hours, followed, and then at last the loud speaker gave my number and time. I had qualified and equalled the Olympic record for the second time. The relief was tremendous and from that moment I felt certain that I would win the final.'

The final, the ultimate goal in the Abrahams master plan, was to be run nearly four hours later, and he admitted afterwards that he felt like a condemned man just before going to the scaffold. But he still found time to come to the aid of his fellow Empire athlete, Arthur Porritt, who against all the odds had battled his way through to the final as well. Porritt still remembers it clearly. 'Because Harold had been working for this one race for a solid year, he and Mussabini had arranged to have a special hut just outside the stadium. After the semi-final Harold came to me and said that as I was the only other Briton left against the four Americans, would I like to share his hut with him in those awful hours before the final. I thought this was a superb gesture, because here was a man who had devoted his whole life for a year to winning this race and it had now reached its most crucial stage, yet he was willing to take in somebody he only knew vaguely to let him share the peace and quiet of his hut at this very last stage.'

'We mostly just lay on our backs, chatted a little, listened to Mussabini and had a rub down. It was very quiet and restful. I don't know what the Americans were doing, but Harold and I were now in a totally different state of mind. Just before the race we were taken to a holding room, prior to going on to the track, and while we were there the Prince of Wales, the future King Edward VIII, came down to see the two British athletes and wish us well. It was quite a kick.'

The six finalists – Abrahams, Porritt, Paddock, Jackson Scholz, Bowman and Loren Murchison – began to assemble on the track just before seven o'clock. Harold had read a note from Mussabini saying that he would win, and old Sam's parting words were ringing in his ears: 'Only think of two things, the report of the pistol and the tape. When you hear the one, run like hell till you break the other.'

An eerie hush came over the packed grandstand at the Stade Colombes as the athletes took their marks, but a huge roar went up as the starter got the field away, and by the halfway point Harold, 'scudding along like some great bird,' as one reporter lyrically put it, was leading, slightly up on Scholz and Bowman, with the favourite and world record holder Paddock nowhere near them. In the final 50 metres Harold managed to stretch his lead to about a yard and he hit the tape, with the newly adopted drop finish, in 10.6, ahead of Scholz in 10.7 and, incredibly, the fast-finishing Porritt in 10.8, beating the other three Americans out of a medal. The noise from the crowd was deafening.

'My victory was a great piece of luck,' Abrahams wrote later. 'I won't say it was only luck, for I trained solidly for over nine months. But it is luck just to find your very best form at the right moment. The start was a perfect one. I soon felt myself going a tiny bit faster than the others and in just over ten seconds I had achieved the ambition of a lifetime. One chance every four years and I was never to compete in the Games again. Ten seconds out of a lifetime.

'The smallest error, less than one per cent, and all would be lost. What is the good of being second in an Olympic final? Forever one's name appears on the roll of Olympic champions, while the second man is soon forgotten. The winner gets all the flowers; it may not be justice, but it is life.' Shortly before he died aged 89, at his home in Delray Beach, Florida, in 1986, Jackson Scholz was asked what he remembered of Abrahams. 'I remember his ass,' he said, with a wry smile. A couple of years earlier, Scholz, who spent a lifetime writing sports-based fiction, made an amusing TV commercial for American Express with actor Ben Cross, who played Harold Abrahams in the film *Chariots of Fire*.

White-haired and sharply dressed, seated in a restaurant, Scholz looks straight to camera and announces: 'You know me.'

Cross interrupts: 'I beat him in the movie *Chariots of Fire*.'

Scholz retorts: '*You* didn't beat *me*!'

'Well, I beat the chap who played you!' said Cross.

It was well received and proved a great success for the credit card company. It was ironic that Scholz would associate him himself with the movie, as he had become extremely fed up with constant requests from the public to reveal the content of the religious note his movie character had pressed into the hand of Ian Charleson, who played Eric Liddell, just before the 400 metres final. In real life, he'd done no such thing. 'I don't remember ever speaking to Liddell, much less writing him a note,' he recalled.

Scholz initially refused to watch the movie simply because they had mispronounced his name – it was *shoals*, not *shol-ze* – but in the end he relented. He said: 'One day I'll go and see it, but for now I'd rather have my own memories of how things were.' And there were plenty of memories in a stellar running career. 'I'd like for people to remember me as a winner, a successful runner a decent writer and a gentleman,' he said. 'And one other thing ... I was fast.'

Scholz was a decent writer, penning 31 bestselling books of sports fiction over 31 years, with titles such as *Dugout Tycoon, Backfield Buckaroo* and *Split Seconds*, before he retired in the early seventies. It was said he kept a detailed diary of his running career and sold a hugely witty autobiography about his life. Its whereabouts are still unknown.

He went downhill quickly after the death of Phyllis, his wife of 50 years. They had no children. He requested not to have a funeral and for his ashes to be scattered at sea.

Arthur Porritt, later Lord Porritt, also enjoyed an extraordinary life after athletics, with a distinguished career as surgeon to the Royal Household, including Her Majesty the Queen, and later as Governor-General of New Zealand, and he remained a lifelong friend of Abrahams; they even met for dinner, with their wives, every year at the precise time of the 1924 final, a race he too regarded as the run of his life. Recalling the final a few years before his death in 1994, Porritt said: 'I got a good enough start, but a slow one, and halfway through the race I was exactly where I expected to be, running nicely last. Then something, which I've never understood to this day, bit me and I just started getting into high gear and I could feel myself going through the whole crowd, passing one after the other. Had there been another five yards I'd have been second, I was catching up so fast. But I'd never have caught Harold, he was a clear yard ahead.

'My reaction was complete disbelief; I'd won a medal in the final. Harold was obviously delighted, you could feel it. But being Harold it didn't show, not on the outside. There was no arm waving or great joy, he just smiled. On the other hand I could sense that all his tension had gone. He'd achieved what he'd set out to do. Harold did a lot after that race, but I think it was an apex in his life. The whole of his subsequent life depended on the fact that he'd won the Olympic 100 metres.'

Abrahams had become the first European to win an Olympic sprint title, the perfect example of an athlete who peaked at precisely the right moment. However, there was an interesting addition to the story many years later, when he revealed that he had been using a special tonic, called Easton Syrup. This tonic contained a small amount of strychnine, a stimulant that can be found on the current IAAF list of banned drugs. Had there been dope testing at the 1924 Olympics, Abrahams would probably have been disqualified.

The effort he put into winning the gold medal had clearly taken its toll, and in the 200 metres that followed he managed to make the final but ran in a very tired-looking last. He always maintained that he ran the first half of the race too slowly. Scholz took the gold from Charley Paddock, with Eric Liddell taking the bronze. It was the second and final time he and Abrahams would meet on the track, both ending in defeat for the Englishman, but Abrahams did win a silver medal in the sprint relay, behind the United States, alongside Walter Rangeley, Lancelot Royle and Wilfred Nichol. Running the first leg, he was two yards down on the American lead-off runner Francis Hussey, a high school kid, at the changeover.

There were no medal ceremonies at the Games, and the French authorities sent his gold and silver medals through the post. They arrived about a month after the Games and, because the French had put insufficient stamps on the package, Abrahams had to pay the excess postage. Sadly, some fifty years later, the gold medal, which he had framed along with the autographs of the 1924 finalists, was stolen from his home, although a replica was organised for him by the British Olympic Committee.

With the Paris Olympics over, Abrahams set his sights on the next Games, in Amsterdam, where he decided to ignore the track and concentrate on the long jump. However, it was during a minor long jump competition, in May 1925, that his athletic career came to an abrupt and painful end. He was competing for Bedfordshire against his old London Athletic Club, at Stamford Bridge, when he missed the board on his second jump, twisted his foot as he jumped and landed on it awkwardly, falling sideways. Cambridge athlete Rex Alston, who would team up with Abrahams in later life as a BBC radio commentator, was in the stadium that day.

'I had already run that afternoon and was getting changed in the dressing-room when there was a great shout outside. A few minutes later the door opened and Harold was carried in by three ambulancemen.

'He looked absolutely ghastly, as white as a sheet and only barely conscious from the pain. I have never seen a man look so ill or in such terrible pain. As he fell into the pit the momentum of his body tore all the muscles and nerves of his leg and he said himself that he heard them ripping and rending like a piece of sailcloth. For a while it was feared he would never walk again and he never put his foot on the ground for six months. Of course, that was the end of his athletics career and for the rest of his life he walked with a limp.'

Abrahams was his usual philosophical self, saying: 'I wonder, if, in a sense, that it was not another piece of good-bad luck. How many people find it almost impossible to retire at the right time? Would I have gone downhill and tried to go on? That was the decision I never had to make. It was made for me. Rather painfully, but it was made.'

The accident formed another watershed in his life and to son Alan marked the division between two distinct phases in his life: the first, as a highly ambitious young man, driving to succeed, very aggressive, totally competitive and single-minded; the second, with the pressure removed, as a much more relaxed, easy-going man.

His sudden departure from competitive athletics – although he did act as the non-competing captain of the British athletics team at the 1928 Olympics – prompted him to venture into other spheres of his beloved sport, notably journalism, broadcasting and administration. His standing in the sport earned him the post of athletics correspondent of the *Sunday Times*, a job he held from 1915 until he retired in 1967. When the BBC began to broadcast athletics it was to Abrahams, with his polished approach and in-depth knowledge, that they turned to get their early programmes off the ground, and he became a cornerstone in the BBC sports department for more than forty years.

Despite serious reservations about the Nazi regime, he attended the Berlin Olympics as British team official, *Daily Sketch* journalist and part-time BBC commentator, and his frantic, partisan radio commentary on the 1500 metres victory of his New Zealand friend Jack Lovelock remains a piece of cheerleading brilliance even today.

Abrahams described his experiences in Berlin to his family, explaining that while he loved the Games he felt nothing but contempt for the atmosphere of oppression and hatred. He famously told his son Alan that he was once close enough to Hitler to have shot him if he'd had a gun in his pocket – and wished that he had.

He also wrote a popular athletics book, with brother Adolphe, which dealt primarily with training but also advocated the radical idea, certainly by 1928 standards, of broken-time payments for athletes. In *Training for Health and Athletics*, they suggested: 'It is, of course, an easy task to ridicule the whole of the amateur-professional position, and we have often wondered whether much harm would result to sport if the distinctions were abolished in their entirety. Eventually, we think, they will be.'

From 1926 he became interested in the administration of athletics and joined the AAA's general committee. Until his death more than 50 years later, he held a variety of posts, his reputation as a great athlete guaranteeing him the respect necessary to climb the ladder to the front benches of the controlling bodies, while his legal brain and keen intellect enabled him to manage the sport efficiently. He was a pivotal figure in the organization of the 1948 London Olympics and even acted as one of the timekeepers when his great friend Roger Bannister broke the four-minute mile in Oxford in 1954, later presenting him with the stopwatch he had used.

As his career in administration burgeoned, alongside his work in journalism and broadcasting, his life at the Bar, at which he had built quite a reasonable practice by the outbreak of the Second World War, took something of a back seat. However, he did find time to meet and marry divorcee Sybil Evers, a light opera singer he met in 1935 – and certainly not, as depicted in *Chariots of Fire*, before the 1924 Olympics, though it was at a Gilbert & Sullivan production. It was a happy marriage and they adopted two children, Alan and Sue. As Alan recalled: 'He'd always go along to her productions, and at home they'd listen to the gramophone, the old wind-up things with 78s. I think our entire record collection was Gilbert & Sullivan, I don't think we had anything else.'

Abrahams was devastated when Sybil died suddenly in 1963, after being struck down with blood poisoning. The doctors suggested it was a rare virus she had picked up from gardening and there was nothing they could have done to save her. In his excellent 2011 biography on Abrahams, *Running With Fire*, author Mark Ryan described the devastating impact of her death on Harold. 'Sybil's death had indeed marooned Harold,' he wrote, 'and in some ways he never recovered. All his life he feared putting "all his eggs in one basket" in case he lost the thing he loved most.' After the war, during which he served in the Ministry of Economic Warfare as head of the statistics section, he joined the Ministry of Town and Country Planning and in 1950 became Secretary of the National Parks Commission, a post he held for 13 years and which earned him the CBE. However, his passion for athletics continued and as he got older his control over the sport in Britain grew. Together he and his colleague Jack Crump ruled athletics, and his powerful position drew him into two clear areas of controversy.

Tom McNab, a national coach from 1963, thinks that Abrahams was more interested in controlling the sport on his own terms and that he was deeply suspicious about the growing role of coaches. 'Abrahams was a poacher turned gamekeeper. In his athletic days he had a professional coach and often went against the mainstream of athletics thinking. But when he became part of the establishment he became a reactionary.'

This manifested itself when Britain's first national coach, Geoff Dyson, was appointed and began trying to modernize the sport and update the coaching methods. His theories were adopted by Eastern Bloc countries and are still valid today. But to Abrahams, Dyson constituted a threat.

'He was one of the main antagonists and was undermining everything Dyson was trying to do,' says McNab. 'He got on very well with many athletes, but he had a very imperious view of his own position. He felt he and his class ran the sport and that everything else had to relate to them. But times were changing and the balance of power had to change. People like Abrahams could not develop from the public school–Oxbridge ethos. He was not well liked by the coaching fraternity and he had little time for professional coaches, which was a little ironic. I always considered him to have a first-class intelligence, but he carried with him the shadows and attitudes of the twenties. He looked upon coaches like Sam Mussabini as social inferiors, people who should speak when they were spoken to, instead of people who were going to help the sport develop to meet modern demands.'

There were others too who thought that Abrahams and his colleagues at the British Board were actually holding back athletics, preventing athletes from competing abroad and halting the development of the sport in a truly international sense. Among those who experienced the rough side of Abrahams's policy was the top sprinter Peter Radford, who would win a 100 metres bronze medal in the 1960 Rome Olympics and had broken the world 200 metres record in 20.5, but had never competed against anyone who had run under 21 seconds. Before the Games he wrote to the Board asking if he could go to the US Olympic trials to see how he would fare against the top Americans. 'But that wasn't met at all favourably,' recalls Radford, 'and the answer I got was a firm no. They said my duty was to run in the Midland County Championships, which were on the same day, as I'd climbed the sport's ladder through the county, area and eventually the AAA championships. So I dutifully went to the Midland County Championships, on a soggy track, with no competition, won as I pleased and came away having learned absolutely nothing.'

Radford went to Rome knowing nothing about world-class 200 metres running and, despite his vast natural talent and his world record, failed to reach the final.

Abrahams's son Alan, however, feels that his father has been much maligned and disagrees with suggestions that he was suffering from a degree of athletics megalomania. 'He appeared to me to be a born compromiser,' he says, 'and seemed to spend an enormous amount of time running around acting as a kind of "sweeper" to all the others, who seemed to be scoring own goals. He would try and take the heat out of situations and try and stop squabbling parties from getting their hands around each other's throats.'

However, Abrahams also antagonized the press. He was instrumental in drawing up many of the rules that governed the sport, including one forbidding athletes to write or broadcast about athletics without the permission of the Board, a body run by himself and Crump. Permission was rarely given, and the two of them monopolized the media market: Harold worked for BBC Radio, Times Newspapers, Thomson Newspapers and *World Sports* magazine; while Crump plied his trade with BBC TV, the *Daily Telegraph* and *L'Equipe*. Apart from annoying some of the athletes, who saw their 'elders' doing exactly what they were forbidden to do, the position of these two men gave them a unique insight into the sport and much privileged information, which caused understandable friction between them and other journalists on the 'outside'.

Among them was the late John Rodda, athletics correspondent of the *Guardian* from 1948 to 1995. 'Overall, during his time he did much good, or what he thought was good. But my feeling, one that is shared by others, was that his position was an iniquitous one. Here was one of the senior officials in the BAAB, where he held posts as treasurer and chairman, a man with great influence in the sport. Should he have been working for all these media organizations?

'It's obvious to me now that he was holding things back, though perhaps not deliberately. I suppose some would say it's sour grapes, but in some cases it could be quite damaging. I remember when Harold attended the selection meeting for Britain's Olympic team for 1952. We were all to be told on Monday, the day after the meeting, so our stories would appear on Tuesday. Harold sat down after the meeting, wrote his story for Thomson Newspapers, popped it into their offices on Sunday night and it promptly appeared in all their provincial papers the next morning. He'd forgotten to put an embargo on. Even the Press Association complained.'

Although Abrahams, who compounded his situation by refusing to join the National Union of Journalists, did not seem perturbed by the dissent, all these things failed to endear him to many people in and around the sport. Nor was he an easy person to get along with; even his friends and family admit that he could be difficult. He could be condescending and arrogant, and he sometimes spoke his mind when it simply inflamed a situation, a characteristic recognized by Lord Porritt.

'There's no doubt he could be a prickly character. He said what he thought, he said it quite openly and he said it pretty hard. Perhaps he wasn't feeling enough, but I think that after going through all the pain and agony in those early days to win that medal, he felt he was boss.'

Abrahams's friends always talk of his intense loyalty, his modesty, his keen sense of humour, his skills as a great entertainer, and of an extremely kind-hearted and generous man. He was certainly a complex personality.

Throughout his life he always remained a somewhat eccentric character, and one of his legendary quirks was his fascination with time. Naturally he took a keen interest in times on the track and spent hours documenting athletics statistics, but he took this passion a stage further. Time governed his life. He always got up at six, went to bed at ten and wore three stopwatches.

'He was always timing things,' says his son Alan. 'He did small things like timing an egg, catching a bus or even going to the toilet, but he also timed things like flying from London to Australia – not just the flight, but all the various stages, like how long it took to get to the airport, time in the air, time to land. He just had this mania to time things.'

As he got older and the sport began to change, Abrahams believed that professionalism in athletics would become inevitable, although he never came to terms with athletes receiving money for races, and he loathed political interference. He was a strong believer in the theory that athletes should run as individuals, without flags or countries. As a member of the sport's hierarchy he did much to rationalize the laws as athletics grew more complicated, and he served for many years on the IAAF, especially on the technical committee.

A close colleague for many years and someone who knew what Abrahams had achieved was Sir Arthur Gold, the last real patriarch of British athletics, who died in 2002. He recalled: 'Harold was the voice of British athletics for more than 40 years, especially in the days before television. He was the John Arlott of his sport. Some of the comments about him are fair, he certainly wasn't blameless, but some are completely unfair. Harold was a lawyer and had all the skills of a cross-examining counsel, but he often didn't remember when he was speaking to people that he wasn't cross-examining them in the witness box. It was unintentional, but it was unfortunate. He did not suffer fools gladly and many people found him intimidating.

'There was clearly a personality clash between Harold and Geoff Dyson and they argued over who had responsibility. But that argument continues today. Harold would get Dyson to justify everything he said and there were problems between them.

'It was obvious there was a criticism of Harold because of his position as an administrator and a journalist. When I took over from Jack Crump I took this criticism to heart and I never wrote another sentence. I don't think Harold abused the situation . but I always felt it was unwise. He was a great loss to athletics because it was impossible to replace a man who had such a depth of knowledge about the sport. Remember, he attended every Olympics, with the exception of 1932, from 1920 until he died. He also contributed greatly to framing various rules in the sport and his clear legal mind helped minimize the ambiguities in the sports rules and regulations.'

In the winter of 1977, less than two months before his death, Harold had been buoyed by the news that there was to be a film made about his exploits in 1924 and, despite reports to the contrary, was apparently quite positive about it when he met screenwriter Colin Welland to discuss early plans for what would be *Chariots of Fire*. He also felt compelled to write to Robert Marchant, the grandson of his old coach Sam Mussabini. Sam had collapsed and died more than 50 years earlier while travelling home to London from the South of France on the 'Blue Train'. The letter explained that Harold still had appreciation for old Sam's help even 53 years later, and he enclosed a copy of the letter Mussabini had sent to his hotel just before the 100 metres race in 1924. It read:

'Dear Mr Abrahams

You must please pardon my not coming to see you, much as I would have liked to. However, I believe and hope you will win the 100 metres. Go out determined to do your best and don't forget to go down on the first stride. A sponge and some cold or preferably iced water used around the nape of the neck, under the ears and at the wrists and elbows, will brace you up. Get nicely warmed up and react to the gun. I should use the springy old 6-spiked shoes. All the best of luck from

Yours truly

S.A. Mussabini'

The essence of the note was used to great effect in the final version of *Chariots of Fire*, which not only immortalized Abrahams and his teammate Eric Liddell, but went on to win four Oscars, including best picture and best original screenplay.

Abrahams remains one of the greatest figures in British athletics, both on and off the track. When his death was caused by a stroke, in January 1978, hundreds turned up for his memorial service and his friend, writer and statistician Norris McWhirter, began the eulogy thus: 'To deliver a remotely adequate address on the life and achievement of Harold Abrahams would require an inordinate amount of time. In his life Harold timed everything and everybody. He quite unfortunately specialized on sermons and on addresses at memorial services.' It was somehow strange that Abrahams never received any public recognition for his work in athletics, something that clearly disappointed him, especially as his elder brothers were both knighted.

However, he dominated athletics in its three main areas: first as a competitor, where winning the gold medal changed his life dramatically and gave him the platform from which, at a very early age, he broke into the two other areas of the sport, administration and the media. For Abrahams, winning the gold medal was critical, and he would have been the first to admit that he effectively lived off those 10 seconds of glory for the rest of his life. What a contrast there would be in the man who succeeded him as the 100 metres champion and holder of the 'Fastest Man on Earth' title in 1928.

Amsterdam 1928

Percy Williams

Percy Williams was always an unlikely, as well as an unwilling, sporting hero. The son of a tram conductor, he was born in May 1908 and grew up in Vancouver. His parents separated when he was quite young and he was brought up by his mother.

Although they did not live in abject poverty, money was certainly scarce. Young Percy was never especially interested in sport as a child, although his first recollections were of winning a junior cycle race, and there are records of him winning a school sports 100-yard race, at just 13 years old. Two years later, however, he suffered a bout of rheumatic fever that damaged his heart so badly the doctors told his mother he should never again be allowed to over-exert himself.

This ban on active sports did not bother him unduly – his general indifference was supported by a poor physique, which was hardly in the sportsman mould. He was thin and frail with a delicate constitution, but his interest in sport was re-awakened at high school, where after two years of inactivity he ignored doctors' orders and began winning prizes in shooting and tennis.

The sports-minded principal of the school encouraged him and his classmates to compete in all kinds of sports, including running, and it was he who convinced Williams that he should enter a sprint race against Vancouver champion Wally Scott in 1926. 'You kinda got pushed into these things,' Williams said many years later. 'You were a bum if you didn't try out.'

The race brought Williams into contact with a man who would have a lasting effect on his life – track coach Bob Granger. Granger was coaching Scott and watched in complete disbelief as this skinny, almost wraith-like 18-year-old ran his man to a dead heat. He later recalled: 'I think he violated every known principle in the running game during that race. He ran with his arms glued to his sides. It actually made me tired to watch him.' But Granger recognized the young man's promise and immediately took him under his wing.

It is clear now that without the fanatical support of Bob Granger, Williams would never have competed in the Olympic Games, or any other Games, a fact that he himself confirmed many years later. He bullied, cajoled and persuaded Williams to achieve success after success, in a sport to which he clearly was not much attracted. His enthusiasm waned even further, if that were possible, when he learned that Granger had banned his real sporting love – swimming.

The coach, by today's standards, had some bizarre ideas about training and technique. Granger maintained that Williams possessed 'precious energy' which should be preserved at all costs. If possible he would always avoid letting the frail Williams burn himself out in training. He mapped out special training sessions and designed racing tactics geared to conserving the athlete's valuable energy reserves.

On cold days Granger would rub him down with cocoa butter and keep him covered with layers of clothing, even blankets, to keep in his body heat and stop his muscles from getting cold. At one meeting, much to the amusement of the crowd, Williams emerged from the dressing-room wearing four tracksuits and three sweaters, looking like a visitor from another planet. Such was Granger's fascination with preserving Williams's 'precious energy' that he even organized groups of boys to demonstrate starts and arm actions so that he could watch, save his strength and practise later in front of a mirror.

Gradually his style and technique began to improve and Granger started entering him in local meets, where he set records that would survive in Canada for more than a quarter of a century. At a rain-sodden high school meet he set records for the 100 and 220 yards on a boggy grass track, where the first 50 yards were run uphill and the last 10 yards were virtually under water.

It was during the 1927 season that Williams had his first unhappy brush with officialdom, the first of many as it turned out, and the root of his bitterness toward athletics in his declining years. He won the British Columbia sprint title and this qualified him to run in the Canadian championships in Hamilton.

In a rare interview, not long before his death, with Vancouver sports columnist Jim Kearney, Williams recalled: 'The official here, who was supposed to look after my travel, had already gone east. He'd decided before I even ran that I wasn't good enough to go, so he went instead. Bob Brown, the baseball man, bought my ticket and sent me. But Bob Granger had to work his way there washing dishes on the railway diner.'

By the back door route both men duly arrived in Hamilton for the championships, but it was time for the Canadian officials to upset the young runner again. 'Tracks in those days had only six lanes, not eight,' said Williams, 'or at least they were supposed to have six. After the heats, six of us qualified for the final of the 100. Then one of the officials suddenly discovered – I think he may have taken off one of his shoes and counted his toes to make sure – that the track had only five lanes, not six. But they had the solution. There were two runners from western Canada, Buster Brown, from Edmonton, and myself. So they tossed a coin to see which one of us would drop out. I lost and didn't get to run.'

The following year, a little older and wiser, Williams again won the state sprint title and headed east across Canada for the national championships, which this time would be the Olympic trials. This time the officials paid his fare, but the Trans Canada Railway again had the pleasure of Coach Granger's company as a dishwasher and pantry boy. Some of Canada's top sprinters were on show, many of whom had been training at US colleges, and Williams, still a relative unknown even in his own country, caused something of a stir by taking both the 100 metres in 10.6 seconds and the 200 metres in 22 flat, booking his ticket for the Olympics in convincing style.

The Canadian assault on the 1928 Games was launched on a shoestring budget, and once again there was no ticket for poor Granger – and this time no trains across the Atlantic or dishes to pay the way.

Seeing how this might affect Williams's performance, his mother Dot, who worked as a theatre cashier and was a woman totally devoted to her only child, toured Vancouver raising money to send Granger with her son. She managed to raise $350 from 19 Vancouver businessmen, enough to keep him in the same hotel as the Canadian team, but Granger still had to find passage on a boat from Quebec City. Once again the coach's ingenuity came to the rescue.

'The team sailed for Europe on a liner,' Williams remembered, 'but Granger had to work his way over on a cattle boat. It was headed for Amsterdam, he knew that, but he didn't know how many stops it would make before it got there, or even if he'd arrive on time. As it happened he got there only three days after we did and took over my training.'

But Granger didn't let the small inconvenience of different ships slow down his training plans. By befriending his ship's wireless operator, he managed to send messages to Williams's ship during the night reminding him to do his stretching exercises and not let anyone massage him too roughly.

In Amsterdam, Williams's room in the Canadian team's third-rate hotel, on the edge of the city's seedy red-light district, became his training headquarters. A mattress was pushed against a wall to use as a buffer for starting practice – much to the consternation of the management and the guests next door. Granger, who refused to leave his protégé in the hands of team coach Cap Cornelius, always maintained that these bedroom practice sessions gave Williams the rocket starts that marked his racing in Amsterdam.

The personal care that Granger gave Williams was certainly unique, and another member of the sprint team, Harry Warren, who would go on to enjoy a fine academic career as professor of geology at the University of British Columbia, has every reason to remember his own role in Granger's unusual training methods.

'Percy was a delicate boy,' he recalled, 'and Granger wouldn't let him out of his sight for a minute if he could help it. Percy had this habit at night of pulling the sheet over his head when he went to sleep and Granger was afraid he might suffocate.

'I was sleeping in the same room as Percy and I'd usually go over and check and pull the sheet down. But Granger was sleeping on a chair outside the door in the corridor and there would always be a note stuffed under the door asking if he was all right. I'd push a note back under the door saying yes he was.'

The Games opened on Saturday, 28 June, without the presence of their creator Baron de Coubertin, who was lying seriously ill in France. He sent a poignant message to the athletes saying: 'I should be wise to take this present opportunity of bidding you farewell.' Although it was another nine years before he died, he never saw another Olympics.

The day after the opening ceremony, on the Sunday afternoon, Percy Williams and 86 other hopefuls began the 100 metres heats. He cantered easily through the first round, equalled the Olympic record of 10.6 in the second round and started to win the attention of the 40,000 spectators, who were clearly warming to this slightly built 'unknown' from Canada. In the semis, held on the following day, Williams started badly and could only finish second to the American Bob McAllister, who was a New York cop. However, it was enough to carry him safely into the final several hours later.

By now the Americans were worried and began to make excuses about how and why Williams was winning. The track had only been finished the day before the competition started and was very soft, so the US coaches and pressmen claimed that their runners were all 'pounders' and could not run in such conditions, whereas Williams was a floater and made light of the boggy surface. When he went on to trounce the same US sprinters on the indoor circuit, one wry Canadian pressman observed that all the sprints must have been run on soft wood tracks!

Two hours before the final was due to start, Granger took Williams to the dressing-room and gave him a book to read, supervised a short warm-up and rubbed him down with cocoa butter, a large consignment of which had survived its trip on the cattle boat. The line-up for the final was impressive: towering over the diminutive Williams, as they dug their starting holes and warmed up, were the giant 6ft 2in British sprint star Jack London; New Yorker McAllister, who had beaten Percy in the semis; the Californian pre-race favourite Frank Wykoff; the German Georg Lammers, and the white South African Wilfred Legg.

Williams was still the real underdog, but after two false starts – by Legg and Wykoff – he tore out of his holes and led the field all the way to the tape, holding off late challenges from the fast-finishing London, Lammers and Wykoff, to win by a yard in 10.8. The crowd went wild with delight. They were surprised, Williams was surprised and so too were the Olympic officials – they could not find a Canadian flag or a record of the Canadian national anthem, and so the medal ceremony had to be delayed while they searched frantically for both. Winning the title was the climax of nearly two years' hard work for Williams, but it also had its dark side. He wrote in his diary that night: 'So I'm supposed to be the world's 100 metres champion. Crushed apples. No more fun in running now.'

However, the victory also had its lighter side and many years later Williams remembered: 'People don't believe me when I tell them, but I didn't know any of those people I ran against. I didn't even know what they looked like until I saw them on the track. And certainly very few people over there could recognize me. In the age of television people think this is impossible. But let me give you an example. A few hours after I won the 100, Doral Pilling, a Canadian javelin thrower, and I saw this big crowd outside our hotel. So we came out to see what it was all about. We joined the mob, looking over their shoulders. I asked a person in front of me why they were there and he said, "We're waiting for the Canadian runner Williams to come out of the hotel." I didn't tell him who I was. I stood around waiting for him too and talking to some of the people. It was much more fun.'

A little like his predecessor Harry Edward back in 1920, Britain's silver medallist Jack London had been airbrushed from the nation's sporting memory. That is until his medals turned up in 2019 on a popular BBC television programme called *Antiques Roadshow*.

His great niece had taken his collection of medals, trophies and memorabilia to the show to get them valued and ended up selling them at auction for £8,000 and prompting fresh interest in his incredible story – culminating in him featuring prominently in the BBC's *Black History* month.

London was born in British Guyana in 1905 and moved to London as a baby. His father was a teacher and church minister and came to England to train as a doctor. Young Jack excelled as an athlete and joined the Polytechnic Harriers, where he came under the coaching eye of Sam Mussabini. Fast and powerful, he began to dominate the sprint scene in England and easily won a place on the Amsterdam Olympic team. He won the AAA 100 yards title in 1929, but his career was cut short by injury in 1930 and he hardly ran again. But that's when his story took some unusual turns. As a talented pianist, he was part of the original cast of Noel Coward's musical *Cavalcade* in London's West End; then appeared alongside comic Will Hay in the film *Old Bones of the River*; before writing a coaching manual and ending his working life as a hospital porter in St Pancras. He was just 61 when he died in London after a stroke in 1966.

In his 1948 coaching book, *The Way To Win*, Jack wrote some prescient words to encourage up-and-coming young sprinters. 'Please don't think that what I have said about the size of sprinters is a hard and fast ruling. Two of the record holders, for instance, are quite unlike each other in build. Owens is 5ft 10in and built like a boxer; Wykoff, on the other hand, is tall and slender. I too am an exceptional height for a sprinter, being 6ft 2in, but heavily muscled above the waist. In spite of these differences in build, there is always that one common factor where sprinters are concerned – they are all nervous, highly strung types of humanity.'

Back in Amsterdam, there was little time for Williams to relax and savour his 100 metres success, as the heats of the 200 metres were already upon them and, despite his gold in the 100 metres, Williams was again given little chance, especially against a field of fresh runners that included the American gold and silver medallists from the event four years earlier, Jackson Scholz and Charley Paddock. But again he proved the doubters wrong, easing into the final, whereas both Paddock and his highly fancied US team-mate Charlie Borah were edged out.

Coach Granger, still obsessed with Percy's well-being, was now beside himself, spending hours roaming the streets outside the hotel trying to quieten the rowdy taverns and clubs so that his charge could get some sleep. On the day, Granger once again marked Williams's card and perceived the German Helmut König as the danger man. He told Percy to stick with König coming out of the bend and to pull him in down the home straight. Sure enough, Williams was sitting a yard or so behind the German as they came out of the curve and, as they entered the straight, he seemed to find another gear and came home a yard clear, with Britain's Walter Rangeley overhauling König for the silver. The German dead-heated with the fast-finishing Scholz for third and the following day the judges offered them a re-run. But Scholz had, in his own words 'tied one on the night before', so he magnanimously declined and gave the bronze to König. The stadium rose to cheer the first double sprint champion since 1912, and the first man to reach him was the 1908 Canadian 200-metre champion Bobby Kerr, who heard the unassuming Williams say simply: 'Won't Granger be pleased?' Even the great Charley Paddock was in awe of the new champion, telling reporters and anyone else who would listen: 'That boy doesn't run – he flies. He's a real thoroughbred. He starts a race as a pull runner, with his leg action in front of him and his knees high. But in the closing metres of a race he's not a pull runner, but a driver. In all my years of running and watching runners, I've never seen a sprinter who could employ two methods in one race.'

Williams failed to win a third gold medal, as the Canadian sprint relay team was disqualified for running out of lane and the US team took first place and equalled the world record. However, there was one last award for the Canadian before he left Amsterdam – and a rather surprising one. A massive medical survey had been conducted throughout the Games by a team of Dutch doctors and scientists to try and pinpoint the perfect Olympic athlete. Every one of the three thousand athletes at the Games had to fill in forms and undergo medical tests, which included details about their height and weight measurements, and tests on breathing, weight-lifting and chest expansion. At the end of this exhaustive study the researchers announced, to the amazement of everyone, including the athlete in question, that the skinny looking 5ft 7in, 125lb Percy Williams was the most perfect athlete at the Olympics.

With the main show over, Williams and some of the Canadian team were dispatched on a European tour by their official overlords, to earn back some of the money spent on transporting them to the Games. They insisted, however, that Percy ran only relays so as to preserve his unbeaten record before returning to Canada. For this journey the officials delved deep into their pockets and came up with a ticket to get Granger home alongside Percy and the team, rather than with the cattle.

Almost overnight, Williams was transformed from a nobody in his own city into an international celebrity, and the trip back across Canada to Vancouver was just one long string of civic receptions, parties and celebrations. No other Canadian has taken the country by storm as Williams did during those few weeks. At each major city he was hauled off the train and taken to special welcoming receptions. At Winnipeg he was given a golden retriever, which sparked his lifelong interest in hunting dogs; and in Regina, his old friend Harold Wright, the sprinter, who just missed the 1928 team but ran in 1932, dragged him off to the city theatre for a huge party. Wright, who became Canadian Olympic Association President, remained one of Williams's few close friends.

But the biggest welcome of all was reserved for his triumphant homecoming in Vancouver. 'City Goes Wild as Percy Comes Home' screamed the front page of the Vancouver Sun on the day that he finally arrived in mid-September. The city's schools were closed, the state Premier Simon Fraser Tolmie and the city mayor sat with Williams in an open-topped car as a vast motorcade snaked through the streets, while some thirty thousand cheering people lined the route to show their appreciation of what he had achieved in Europe. He even got an escort from the Mounties. After all the speeches, congratulations, dinners and parties, Williams, now hailed as Vancouver's Charles Lindbergh, was presented with a new Graham-Paige sports car, $500 in gold and, later, a $15,000 trust fund.

'If we received anything over $25 we were supposed to be professional,' recalled Williams. 'But the officials had an out. If they said it was OK, then it could be done.' By now several universities in the United States were vying with each other to enrol him, but he eventually accepted an offer of a place at the local University of British Columbia. Such were the demands on his time and his lack of enthusiasm for studying that he caused a furore by leaving college and running off to compete in the US indoor season. There were calls in the Canadian press for his trust fund to be withdrawn, but he managed to ride the storm. Throughout 1929 and 1930, Williams was simply the best sprinter in the world and ran his way across the United States, a month-long extravaganza dubbed 'The Iron Guts Tour', winning an astonishing 21 out of 22 races. His feat prompted US Olympic team manager General Douglas MacArthur to pronounce him 'The greatest sprinter the world has ever seen.' Track fan and comic Will Rogers joined the complimentary bandwagon when he told a radio audience: 'The United States must annex Canada to acquire Williams.'

During this indoor extravaganza he posted a new 45-yard world record of 4.9 seconds, equalled three other world records and beat the rising US star Eddie Tolan, whose day would come during the 1932 Olympics. Years later, Williams maintained that his indoor tour of the USA was the highpoint of his career, and not the 1928 Olympics. 'I think I came up with my best performances in the winter of 1929. I had never run indoors before, but I ran 22 races in 21 days and I came second in one and won all the others. Everyone remembers Amsterdam, but nobody remembers that.

'Louis D. Taylor, who was the Mayor of Vancouver, sent me a wire urging me to come home before I burned myself out. But I was enjoying myself. I was running so often I didn't have to train. I liked the indoor circuit better than outdoors. It had a real circus atmosphere. It was more fun.'

When the fun was finally over, he returned, early in 1930, to a Depression-hit Vancouver to look for a job. But memories were short, and all the back-slapping businessmen of two years earlier could only apologize and tell him that times were hard and there just were not any suitable openings. So he continued to run and in August, at the Canadian national championships, set a new world record of 10.3 for the 100 metres – a mark that stood unbeaten for six years. 'I'm glad I don't have to run like that every day,' he told pressmen. Sadly his running days would come to an end sooner than he thought.

About 40 miles from Toronto, where he set his world record, preparations were well underway in Hamilton for the staging of the first British Empire Games – now the Commonwealth Games. The day of the 100 yards final – the Empire had not yet gone metric – was freezing cold and the rain was sheeting across the stadium, so Bob Granger cocooned Percy in blankets until the very last moment and gave him his usual cocoa butter rub-down. He was perfectly warmed up as the runners went down on the starting line and waited for the gun. Then, just as the starter raised his pistol, a national anthem suddenly came blaring through the PA system. Some athletes from a previous event were receiving their medals on the podium and the organizers decided to delay the start of the race until it was over. By the time the race was ready to start, the finalists, including Williams, were all shivering and soaking wet.

Williams took up the story: 'Forty yards from the tape I felt the muscle go. Two things can happen. The leg collapses and you fall down. Or it keeps flipping and you manage to finish the race. Mine kept flipping and I managed to win.' Old newsreel film of the race shows Williams's hand reacting at the precise moment of the tear and clutching at his left thigh. It was a miracle that he kept going at all, let alone won the race, and he almost fell through the tape.

'The Canadian team didn't have a doctor there,' recalled Williams, 'and nobody seemed concerned except Bobby Robinson, who was promoting the Games, and his only concern was that he would be out of the $700 he'd been promised if he could deliver me to a meet in Chicago the following week.' The damage was a severe muscle tear high up on the thigh, in the groin area, and although he managed to resume training, the injury never healed properly and Williams never again scaled the heights of his early racing career.

But so outstanding was he that, despite this injury, he still managed to qualify for Canada's sprint quartet at the Los Angeles Games in 1932, captaining the team. 'Before I went to LA, I had a physical and the doctor told me that an operation right after the injury in Hamilton would have repaired the damage completely. But it was too late at this point.'

He recalled bitterly how they were treated this time around by Canadian officialdom. 'After the team was named, a man from the Canadian National Railways arrived on my doorstep. He'd been authorized by the AAU in the east to offer me a one-way ticket to LA and $10 in expense money. I thanked him and told him I'd make other arrangements.' Some of us ended up driving down with George Irvine, who owned a Seven-Up plant here in Vancouver. We kept track of all our expenses, divided them up among us and handed them in. A team official said we'd be reimbursed but couldn't say when, so we told him if it wasn't by opening day we wouldn't be running.

'We were angry. The team officials had come in by train from eastern Canada, travelling first class. One of the hurdlers told us the athletes from the east had been offered a choice. If they rode the day coach they could eat in the diner. But if they wanted a berth to sleep in they'd have to grab their food at the station sandwich counters whenever the train stopped.'

The LA experience was just another that soured Williams's memories of athletics. In addition to the problems with the officials, his injury meant elimination in the semis of the 100 metres and anchoring the Canadian relay team to fourth spot, just outside a medal place. It was the last track and field meeting in which he raced and the last he ever attended. After returning to Vancouver he made an abortive attempt to set up an indoor track meeting, which was thwarted by his old friends at the Canadian AAU, and then abandoned the sport forever and, in his own words, 'grabbed a pencil and started writing insurance'.

He was a keen aviator and acquired a commercial pilot's licence, which he put to good use during the Second World War by training navigators. After the war he returned to insurance and set up his own company, which he ran until a few years before his death. Throughout his life he enjoyed shooting, golf, dogs and horses, but never athletics.

When Vancouver opened its new athletics stadium in 1954, for that year's Empire Games, there was a suggestion that it should be named after Williams, as a few years earlier he had been voted the nation's outstanding track and field performer of the century. It was greeted unenthusiastically by officialdom, who felt that he had done little to encourage sport in the city since retiring from the track. But Williams was always candid about the motives behind his track career. Interviewed in the early 1950s he admitted: 'I never did like running. Anything I accomplished I did because of the determination of Bob Granger. I always thought it was a lot of hogwash to say that you ran for your flag and country. I was out there to beat the guy beside me.' But the Games organizers did manage to persuade him to 'turn the first sod' of the new stadium.

In 1970 he attended the funeral of his old mentor Bob Granger. They had hardly spoken since 1932 and for years Granger had been living a sad, reclusive life on Vancouver Island, existing solely on a meagre state pension. But when Williams was asked by reporters to rate his old coach's impact on his career, he replied: 'Offhand, I'd say a hundred per cent.'

In 1972, he was voted Canada's all-time greatest Olympic athlete and should have played a role in the massive publicity drive aimed at successfully launching the Montreal Olympics of 1976. This was orchestrated by the COA President Harold Wright, his great old friend, but Williams refused to take part. 'I was one of his few good friends and I'd known him for years,' says Wright, 'but he wouldn't even do it for me. He wouldn't do anything that would put him in the limelight.'

In 1978, on the fiftieth anniversary of his Olympic feat, he was given the Vancouver Civic Recognition Award, and two years later he received the Order of Canada, one of the nation's highest awards. However, he refused to travel to Ottawa to receive it, so Governor General Edward Shreyer came to Vancouver to perform the ceremony.

In January of the same year his gold medals were stolen from the British Columbia Sports Hall of Fame (they were never recovered) and two weeks later his beloved mother Dot, his lifelong companion, died aged 92.

Wright agrees that especially towards the end of Williams's life he became a sad figure. 'He was a real reluctant hero. I suppose he was just a terribly shy, introverted and lonesome guy. The only way he would come out was if my wife would call and tell him we were picking him up at a certain time. Even then he'd be waiting in the street outside his front door. We'd never go in. He felt people had taken advantage of him during his athletic career and I suppose that was true. But he was a true friend and he didn't have many close friends because of his shyness. But he really was a nice person.'

Columnist Jim Kearney, probably the last journalist to conduct an in-depth interview with Williams, agrees that he was a deeply embittered man. 'He felt very bitter about the treatment of the athletes in his time, especially compared to the ritzy lifestyles of some of the officials. He lived with his mother until she died and from then on lived alone. I think he had a bit of a drink problem and he avoided all publicity. I know he suffered terribly from arthritis and swallowed a dozen aspirins a day to ease the pain in his knees and ankles.'

After his heart condition worsened and he had suffered two strokes, Williams sought a quick end to his relentless pain, and in November 1982 he took a twelve-gauge shotgun out of its rack at his West End apartment, climbed into the bath, put the gun under his chin and pulled the trigger.

Over two hundred people attended his memorial service more than fifty years after his double Olympic triumph. The Reverend Dr Gerard Hobbs told the gathering: 'Percy Williams proved a difficult hero. Shy by disposition, he found himself uncomfortable in the spotlight, reluctant to exploit the opportunities for glory that fame threw his way. When injury brought an end to his brief running career, he withdrew to a quiet life of friends, of work, of the sport he could still enjoy without fanfare, hesitatingly accepting the honours that continued to come his way.'

For the few who managed to get close to him, Williams was a kind and honest friend, but to those who did not, and there were many, he could be a difficult, introverted and bitter man, who put nothing back into the sport that had made him famous. But Williams's dilemma was that he had never wanted to be famous. It seemed everyone knew Percy Williams the legend, but very few knew the man.

Los Angeles 1932

Eddie Tolan

As the 1930s began, a new crop of sprinters arrived on the scene ready to replace the recently injured Olympic champion Percy Williams and prepare for the next Games in Los Angeles in 1932. For the first time, an increasing number of black American athletes were emerging, especially among the new wave of sprinting talent, alongside some of the more established white track stars. A few black Olympic athletes, rare though they were, had been selected for USA teams since the early Games, but the American college system, particularly in the east, was now waking up to the fact that black students and black athletes were just as talented as their white counterparts. Progress was beginning to be made towards offering them more in terms of sports scholarships and educational opportunities, but these were still the early days and opportunities were still extremely limited. Two men who managed to take advantage of this small step forward were the black sprinters Ralph Metcalfe and Eddie Tolan, a pair who would go on to dominate the sprint events at the Olympics.

Metcalfe, a tall, powerful athlete, famed for his slow start and astonishing finish, ran for Marquette University in Milwaukee, whereas Tolan, a tiny, bespectacled figure, hailed from America's traditional 'school of sprint champions', the University of Michigan, where Olympic sprint champions Archie Hahn and Ralph Craig were produced. They were challenged in the United States by the improving Frank Wykoff, who had made the 1928 Olympic final at just 18, and the Ohio State star George Simpson, who had claimed a new world record of 9.4 seconds in the 100 yards in 1929, only to see it rejected by the IAAF because he had used an illegal piece of equipment to help give him a better start – namely, starting blocks.

The only competition for the superior US sprinting force came from the tough German Arthur Jonath, South African Daniel Joubert and the 24-year-old Australian Jimmy Carlton, who ran an incredible 20.6 for the 220 yards in Sydney during January of the Olympic year only to see it ignored by the authorities because the judges ruled that there was a following wind, although eyewitness reports maintained that there was no wind at all and that Carlton had won by about 15 yards. So incensed was Carlton about the decision that he promptly quit athletics, refused to go to Los Angeles, became an ordained priest and entered a monastery in New South Wales.

Despite Carlton's disappearance, the scene was set for a high standard of sprint competition in Los Angeles, and although Metcalfe was almost everyone's clear favourite, it was generally agreed that the race would be close. However, no one could have foreseen just how close it would actually be, nor predict that the result of both sprint finals would still be the subject of doubt, controversy and debate even in today's athletic circles.

To the day he died, as a respected Chicago Congressman in the late 1970s, Metcalfe insisted that he did not lose the 100 metres final, a view that seems to be reinforced by the official black and white film of the event, although the camera itself was not directly in line with the tape.

The athlete actually declared the winner of the contest was Detroit's Eddie Tolan who, at just 5ft 4½in, remains the smallest ever Olympic sprint champion. With his horn-rimmed glasses taped to his head, size six-and-a-half feet and a bandage around his left knee to protect an old football injury, a more unlikely-looking champion would be difficult to find. But if the tale of Percy Williams was a sad one, then Tolan's life story was one of similar misfortune and, despite triumphing against all the odds to take his place in Olympic history, his life was dogged by bad luck, misery, setbacks and ultimately, life-shortening illness. Tolan was born in Denver, Colorado, in September 1908, and grew up with his brother and two sisters in Salt Lake City, realizing at an early age that he was faster than most of his friends when outrunning the angry neighbouring farmers from whom he stole watermelons. His parents came from Texas; father Tom was a hotel cook and his mother Alice a washerwoman, whose father had been born into slavery, and in 1924 they moved the family east to Detroit to look for work. A year later, young Eddie started at the local Cass Tech High School, just as his father started work as a paint sprayer at one of the big automobile plants. Despite his obvious talent for running, Eddie's first love was football, and he always maintained that his older brother Hart was the real athlete of the family. Eddie looked up to Hart, and when his big brother's sporting prowess saw him become the first athlete to win six 'school letters' (represent his school in six different sports) in the state of Utah – in their Salt Lake City days – he knew that sport was where his own future lay. When the two boys enrolled at Cass Tech, Eddie started his football career as a reserve for his brother on the school team, but when the track coach saw his speed he convinced him to try out for the track.

Eddie was a worker and trained hard, and while Hart did not have the necessary application to make it to the top, Eddie always delighted in relating a story about how a short time after graduating from college he was due to run in a big track meeting in Detroit but fell ill. Hart, who had been out of competition for about five years, put on a pair of spikes and went out and won the 100 yards to keep up the family name. During his three years at Cass Tech, Eddie Tolan won 17 out of the 18 state indoor and outdoor competitions he entered, and his bedroom was bedecked with the countless medals and ribbons that he had won, including those he was given for winning the national interscholastic meeting in both the sprint distances.

In 1928 he chose to attend the University of Michigan, despite great interest from six other top colleges, hoping to play football for the great coach Fielding Yost. He managed to pick up a scholarship for the college, but it did not cover all his fees, and so his mother had to work around the clock, doing mostly menial jobs, to pay his way. But Tolan was not destined to become the great football player he had always dreamed of being, although he always considered his six touchdowns as a quarterback for Cass in a 48–6 win over great rivals Western High his greatest sporting thrill, rather than his Olympic success in 1932. It was football that almost cost him his future in sport when he ripped the ligaments in his left knee during a junior game and was told that he might never run again. Of course he did, but it was always with that famous elasticated bandage protecting the damaged knee, and he walked with a limp from that day. 'It was a surgical miracle,' he once told a Detroit sportswriter, 'I didn't think I'd be able to walk properly again, much less run.' It was for precisely that reason that when he joined Michigan, head track coach Steve Farrell managed to persuade the college powers to have him barred from football so that he could concentrate his efforts on running – a decision that deeply upset the young athlete. But Farrell managed to convince Tolan that he was doing the right thing, and many years later Eddie admitted: 'The track team did a lot more travelling then, so I saw the opportunity to travel on a Pullman and see the country. People would say on the streets of Chicago when they saw me, "That's Eddie Tolan of Michigan."

'That was something, because I wouldn't have been allowed in a lot of hotels and places if I hadn't been with the Michigan team.' Had he continued to play football in addition to his track running, he would never have made the 1932 Olympic team, let alone the winner's rostrum.

As a freshman at Michigan the press dubbed him the 'Midnight Express', for obvious reasons, a nickname that stuck with him throughout his running career, although some of his college friends liked to call him 'Twinkle Toes' because of his amazing leg speed. Tolan did have a try at making the 1928 Olympic team, but he wasn't quite ready for the major league. His opportunity came the following summer after an indifferent start to his intercollegiate racing, when he took his first top-class title by winning the 100 yards at the Big Ten Championship, at the Dyche Stadium at Evanston, Illinois, sprinting to a new world record of 9.5 *and* beating the highly rated George Simpson. The trip also revealed the realities of how different it was being a black athlete on the road, even if it was with a top college.

'It was my first Big Ten meet and there was one other coloured fellow in the team, a weight man called Booker Brooks,' Tolan revealed during a rare newspaper interview in the 1950s. 'We went to three hotels before one would take us. Then they told us we would have to eat in the kitchen. I wanted to go back home to my college in Ann Arbor and I told Farrell I was quitting. I remember what he told me. "You are the only coloured boys on any Michigan team. If you quit you will hurt your people." I called friends in Detroit and they told me to stay, so during the meet we ate our three meals each day at the YMCA, a coloured YMCA.'

He also got a reputation for his gum-chewing, which started out as a simple way of relieving stress before a race, but he accidentally ran a 100 metres while still chewing and realized he was actually chewing in sync – his mouth moving faster when he needed to accelerate.

Later that year he won both sprints at the national 1929 AAU meeting, a success that earned him a place on a small US track team to tour Europe, where he twice equalled the world 100 metres record of 10.4 and earned rave reviews from sportswriters throughout the continent. Even though he worked hard, Tolan did not enjoy training, and if he could win a race without turning on the gas then he would do it. A track official who held watches on races in Michigan for 40 years, Phil Diamond, remembered: 'If someone else could run 100 yards in 9.6 seconds, Eddie would beat him by a foot. If the competition could do only 10.1, Eddie would still only win by a foot.' Diamond remembered some of the stunts that Coach Farrell used to get Tolan to train harder. 'Farrell knew all the gadgets and stunts used in the professional races in England. One morning he offered theatre tickets as prizes for the winners at different distances, but Tolan wasn't interested.

'He knew he could beat all the other sprinters so why bother? Finally, Farrell called over Roddy Cox, a big hammer thrower and football player. He put another man on Cox's back and then bet Tolan he couldn't run 100 yards faster than Cox could run and carry his rider 50 yards. Tolan bit at that. The suggestion that he couldn't beat a slow man with a heavy load, even with a 50-yard head start, was too much. But Farrell knew what he was doing. Tolan couldn't win no matter how much he tried. Farrell knew from experience that one man would carry another 50 yards in 9.1 or 9.2 seconds. Tolan was the fastest sprinter in the world, but even if he equalled his own world record of 9.5 he was still going to lose.'

When the 1930 track season began, Tolan was already established as one of the world's top sprinters, if not *the* top sprinter. But by his standards it was a poor season, with only one major title, the AAU 100 yards, plus a win at a bizarre meet in Canada to show for his efforts. His trip to Vancouver was for the Dominion Day competition, and on a warm July afternoon he amazed the crowd and the judges by clocking an astonishing 10.2 for the 100 metres, on a track that was proven to be slightly uphill. He then followed that performance by taking second place behind Simpson, by a whisker, in the 200 metres, where both athletes clocked a world record equalling 20.6. For some reason the wind conditions were not known and the records were never officially ratified by the IAAF. A month later Percy Williams set a new world mark of 10.3, and an official 10.2 would not be set for another six years.

After that disappointment, Tolan continued to enjoy mixed fortunes on the track, losing some races, winning others, and in 1931, the year in which he graduated from Michigan, he was rated the best in the world over 220 yards, with both the NCAA and IC4A titles, but he had little success in the shorter sprint.

Although he had graduated and set his sights on becoming a doctor and studying at medical school, he put the plans on ice so that he could concentrate on making the 1932 Olympic team and took a job as a teacher, working at the West Virginia Institute, near Charleston. The job did not pay much, but what little he earned was sent back home, where his entire family were out of work and suffering like so many others in the Depression. When he eventually returned to Detroit in the spring of 1932, ready to start training for the Games, he did not have enough money to make the daily trips out to Ann

Arbor to run on the University of Michigan track, which was a necessity because Detroit didn't have a track and his coach Steve Farrell was based there.

At first he had to be content with barricading some of the streets around the Tolans' west side home so he could practise on the road, but later an old Cass Tech friend, then a chauffeur, drove him back and forth to the track so he could qualify for the Mid West trials. He attended the Chicago trials thanks to a donation from a member of the Michigan Olympic Committee, but his benefactor was unable to help when it came to travelling to the final Olympic trials out in Palo Alto, California. Tolan had decided the only way to reach the trials was to hitch-hike the 1,800 or so miles, when another benefactor, former Governor Alex Gorsebeck, rallied to his aid, signing a cheque for his fare and living expenses in California.

In the trials, however, he was dominated by the rising star from Marquette University, Ralph Metcalfe, who eclipsed him in both the 100 and 200 metres, with Tolan coming second and George Simpson assuring himself of a place in both sprints by nipping third. Whereas Eddie had been the number one US sprinter in the pre-Olympic year, Metcalfe had breezed through the 1932 season undefeated, and his awesome form made him the out-and-out favourite to beat the apparently fading Tolan in Los Angeles.

Whoever was going to win, the US press seized on the angle that for the first time it would be a black sprinter. The sports columnist Braven Dyer wrote in the *Los Angeles Times*: 'Metcalfe and Tolan make the ace of spades look positively pale by comparison, but boy can these boys run. And they figure to do even better here than they did in Palo Alto because it's warmer now and they enjoy the heat.'

Naturally the Americans were heralding the Games as the greatest leap forward in Olympic history and despite concerns that they would fail because of the global depression, they were carried off in some style by the organizers, with more than 1,500 athletes, from 34 nations, arriving to compete and in excess of 1,250,000 spectators paying to sit and watch the Games unfold. Although just half the number of athletes who competed in 1928 would take part in Los Angeles, they turned out to be among the most successful in Olympic history, the first to boast a healthy cash surplus at the end, which ran to almost $1 million, and in the course of the Games 16 new world records were set, two were equalled and 33 new Olympic marks were made.

On Saturday, July 30, with a mammoth crowd of nearly 105,000 packed into the city's Memorial Coliseum Stadium, Vice President Charles Curtis declared the Games open in the absence of President Herbert Hoover, who was too busy campaigning in the forthcoming presidential elections, which he then lost, to spare time for the Olympics.

The 100 metres competition, which began soon after the opening, was a record-breaking affair from start to finish, with German Arthur Jonath shaving a tenth of a second off the Olympic record in running 10.5 in the first round of heats, only to see Eddie Tolan lower the record to 10.4 in the second round. In the first semi-final, Tolan was awarded first place in 10.7 ahead of the South African Joubert, while the Japanese star Takayoshi Yoshioka edged out the reigning champion Percy Williams for a place in the final. However, as if to presage the chaos of the final, photographic evidence suggested Joubert, who had travelled for 38 days to get to the Games, had actually won ahead of Yoshioka, with Tolan only third, two feet ahead of Williams.

In the second semi, Metcalfe was still steamrollering the opposition and cantered to victory in 10.6, with team-mate Simpson second and Jonath in third. These six sprinters made up the field for probably the most talked-about Olympic sprint final in history, a final that was held under clear blue skies and high temperatures on Monday, August 1. The American fans were keen to re-establish their supremacy in an event that they had not won for 12 years, and a hush fell across the crowd as the lane announcements were made, putting Tolan out in lane six, by the stands, with Jonath inside him, while Metcalfe drew lane three. All attention was on the six runners as they stripped off their tracksuits and limbered up, dug their starting holes and got to their marks.

At the gun, the visibly nervous Joubert got a flyer and the athletes were called back for another start, but this time they were away cleanly and it was the Japanese star Yoshioka who shot out of his holes the fastest and held the lead for the first 40 metres. But then Tolan began to assert himself, and at about 50 metres he had a definite lead. As the rest of the field drew level with the fading Japanese sprinter, it was Ralph Metcalfe who began to put on his famed finishing burst and from 80 metres onwards there was almost nothing to separate the two runners; Tolan's piston-like leg speed keeping him level with the fluent power of Metcalfe until they both seemed to hit the tape together in a dead heat. Tolan pulled up just past the tape,

while Metcalfe eased off the power and cantered around the bottom turn before he finally turned and casually walked back to the finish line. Although it was uncertain who had won the race, it was totally clear that Jonath had pipped Simpson for the bronze. He would be the first athlete to gain a medal running in Adidas shoes.

Metcalfe went straight over to Tolan and shook his hand, then arm-in-arm they walked back to the start, photographers clustered around them, talking animatedly. It was some time before the announcement came booming over the public address system that Tolan had been declared the winner, just two inches in front of Metcalfe, in a new Olympic record of 10.3, which also equalled Williams's world record. Metcalfe was given the same time, but a silver medal, a fact that haunted him for the rest of his life. Shortly before he died he said: 'I have never been convinced I was defeated. It should have been a tie. The seven judges took a lot longer than they normally did and they awarded me the same time as Eddie Tolan.'

He took it sportingly at the time, but a close look at the photographs and the film of the event adds credence to Metcalfe's claim for a dead heat. But the result wasn't actually officially ratified until the following morning, after the Olympic officials had, for the first time, been able to study film footage as well as a variety of still photographs of the finish.

Had the race been run a year later Metcalfe would probably have won, because the rules were changed as a result of the controversy over the finish, so that crossing the line determined the winner of the race, not just breasting the tape, which is how Tolan just edged out Metcalfe. At their next annual meeting the AAU convention voted retroactively and awarded the 100 metres title to both Tolan and Metcalfe, but not the gold medal – the

Olympic organizers never accepted their vote as binding, and Tolan's name stands alone in the record books.Bronze medallist Arthur Jonath, who had only taken up sprinting after a hand injury ended his boxing career, returned to a hero's welcome in Germany, but not before Hollywood stars Greta Garbo and Marlene Dietrich personally begged him to stay in America. He was offered US citizenship and a college scholarship, but his family persuaded him to return home. During World War Two he fought in the German Army on the Russian front, was captured and survived a Soviet POW camp before being returned to Germany. Post-war, he ran a petrol station in Frankfurt and coached at the local athletic and football club until his death in 1963, at the age of just 53.

Ralph Metcalfe, meanwhile, had his best event at Los Angeles to come, where his speed and power in the 200 metres would surely count, and again he was everyone's favourite to win. The final was held on Wednesday, August 3, after some fierce heats where yet more records had fallen, with the old Olympic mark of 21.6 broken no fewer than four times, first by Metcalfe and Tolan who brought it down to 21.5, and then by Jonath and the Argentinian Carlos Bianchi Luti, who lowered it to 21.4. In the first semi, Metcalfe won easily, but in the second Eddie Tolan only narrowly managed to hold off the fast-finishing Canadian Harold Wright to take third place and qualify for the final.

In the final, Luti had the faster start, but as the runners came out of the turn and into the home straight Simpson was about a yard in front, with Tolan closing fast. The gum-chewing Detroiter caught and passed Simpson with 50 metres to go and won by a clear margin of about six feet. Tolan's time was clocked at 21.2 by electronic timing – an official world record for the distance and a new Olympic record. The crowd cheered another American victory, but were puzzled about what had happened to pre-race favourite Metcalfe. His bad luck story had continued, and even today some doubt remains over his part in the race because officials spotted from the film of the start that he had started three or four feet behind where his mark should have been.

He was offered a re-run by the officials, but rejected it because he did not want to jeopardize the clean sweep of the event by the Americans, with Simpson taking the silver and Metcalfe performing miracles to finish third. There is a counter-theory to this suggesting that the film is an optical illusion created by the fact that Metcalfe dug his starting holes on the inside of his lane, whereas Simpson, in the next lane out, dug his on the outside, giving the impression that they were too far apart. However, the faulty lane measurement theory was the more likely explanation and just one more reason why Metcalfe felt so frustrated after the Games.

Metcalfe would go on to live an extraordinary life, starring in the Berlin Olympics of 1936, lecturing in political science, serving as a 1st lieutenant in the US Army transportation department during the Second World War and becoming a successful Chicago businessman, entering politics in the 1940s and eventually becoming a democratic Congressman. He died in 1978 a revered and respected figure across the United States.

Just after the sprint events had concluded, in a newspaper interview conducted with Tolan and Metcalfe in the room they shared in the Olympic village, Metcalfe teased Tolan for being lucky. Tolan replied: 'Yeah, I had it all right, but it's about time, Ralph.

First little old luck I had in eight years.' Some years later, in an article he penned for the *Detroit Free Press*, he described the long wait for the final result of the 100 metres, rather than actually winning it, as his biggest thrill.

'This may sound a little strange,' he wrote, 'but I've never experienced a real thrill in running. I beat Ralph in one of the most controversial finishes in Olympic history and headed for the cottages provided for the US team. Just as I reached my room, the radio announced that the winner of the 100 metres race would not be known until the judges reviewed pictures the following morning.

'I felt certain that I had won the race, but I didn't get much sleep that night – just wondering. The following morning we saw the movies of the race and the judges awarded me first place. That's when I began two days of planning, working out a certain way to prove my superiority over Metcalfe. I analyzed every race I had ever run. I recalled a previous meeting between Metcalfe and myself in Nebraska when I came up in the final yards to beat him.

'Never in my racing career had I been more keyed up. I had every step of that 200 metres planned. As fate would have it, Metcalfe, Simpson and I qualified for the final. We went to the starting line. There was a false start, someone jumped the gun. That seemed to take the pressure off me. Call it sixth sense, or what you will, but I felt certain that this race was in the bag. The anticipated stretch drive didn't materialize. Metcalfe faltered and I won, with Simpson finishing second.

'There wasn't any thrill in winning the race. the anticipation of the victory, those hours of anxiety, the careful planning and the hope provided an even greater emotional kick than the triumph.'

Eddie Tolan was now the athletic toast of America, the only man to win two gold medals on the track at the Games, and his homecoming to Detroit was eagerly awaited. But while their hero returned to the city's main station with two gold medals in his pocket, he was soon forced to face the realities of the Depression – he was black, unemployed and penniless.

He was looking forward to seeing his mother at the station, as they were very close and wrote regularly to each other during the Games. Beforehand, he had asked her permission to forget the family's plight during these few days so that he could concentrate on racing and wrote: 'I want so much to send the American flag to the top of the winner's staff. I want to see our name head the list when the result is announced, for I know if I can win the two dash events our worries will be lessened and some brightness will return to our lives.' Mrs Tolan told a reporter from the *Detroit Free Press*: 'I've worked hard, but it's worth it. If my menfolk could only find jobs I could ease up a bit and a mighty big worry would be off Eddie's mind. Just before he left for California he visited me, told me, "Mom, don't you worry".

'I don't know how he got to California. Folks, I suppose. Folks are always being kind to us. When he won his first race I sent him a telegram. I couldn't afford it but I had to tell him not to worry his head about my troubles.'

But on his return to Detroit, Eddie found that nothing had changed. There may have been thousands of people cheering him at the station and a seemingly endless supply of glib, smiling politicians eager to shake his hand and pose with him for photographs, but he did not have a job, his father had not worked for two years and his two brothers and two sisters were also out of work. Only his mother was working and keeping the family from starving. Just before Tolan arrived home his mother received a phone call from the Governor of Michigan who made an elegant speech about her son's achievement. She thanked him politely but told him about the family's real problems, and he vowed to do something to get them all work. So it was that on the very day that Tolan returned home, his brother Fred was working outside the railway station picking up the waste paper dropped by the crowd who had come to pay tribute to his brother. The rest of the family were still out of work.

In December of 1932, the Mayor of Detroit presented him with the official thanks of the city, in the form of a beautifully crafted leather-bound resolution, after which Tolan made a short speech intimating that something a little more tangible would have been preferred. More promises were made by the councillors, who all agreed that the Tolan family could not eat a resolution. One of the many offers, most of them bogus, that were made to Tolan on his return home was from dancer Bill 'Bojangles' Robinson, who invited him to tour with him on the vaudeville circuit, relating stories about his running career and his success at the Olympics. Tolan saw this as a way of providing much-needed money for his family and helping him pay his way through medical school, so he jumped at the chance. He was booked for a 103-show tour at $1500 dollars a week and it seemed that all their problems were over. However, the Depression forced the cancellation of the show after just one week and Tolan returned home broke and conscious that his dream of becoming a doctor was gone forever. Early in 1933, he finally got the job the city had been promising him – as a filing clerk in the city's Registry of Deeds. He stayed there for nine years, with only a short break during 1935 when he travelled to Australia to take part in the professional sprint circuit.

There he took part in a four-race tournament against some of the top pro sprinters of the day, including the Australians, Austin Robertson and Tom Roberts, and Scotsman Willie MacFarlane. Eddie won three of the four races and took the world pro title, running on grass, at night, under floodlights. And although it was all a million miles from the Olympics, he managed to return home with a suitcase full of trophies and medals and a wallet full of foreign currency, which went straight into the family's still empty coffers.

During the Second World War he worked as a stock control officer in the giant Packard car plant, and later he ran a petrol station for eight years before giving up and selling burial insurance. Eventually he returned to teaching and became a substitute physical education teacher at Irving Elementary, on Detroit's west side, working for the city right up to his death in 1967, at the age of 57. Two years earlier he had suffered kidney failure, which needed daily dialysis, and this finally prompted the heart attack from which he died.

Tolan's Olympic feats are remembered in several track and field halls of fame, and shortly after his death a playing field in Detroit was named after him close to the Detroit

Medical Centre. He once said: 'Most people think a tall man has a better chance of winning because his feet are in the air over a longer stretch. But height is not a factor. A small man's ability to get speed can be compared to the pistons of an automobile. His pistons generate a lot of power if he has the legs and the heart.'

Eddie Tolan, a lifelong bachelor, certainly had plenty of heart, and throughout his life, despite all the setbacks that he suffered, he remained a kind-hearted and affable man, shrugging his shoulders at his misfortunes. His epitaph should read: Eddie Tolan tried hard and deserved better.

Berlin 1936

Jesse Owens

After the deep disappointment of his defeats in the 1932 Olympics, and with Eddie Tolan now retired, Ralph Metcalfe emerged as the world's premier sprinter, taking both sprint titles in the US championships in 1933 and 1934. But his lack of good fortune dogged him yet again, because in 1935, just a year before the next Olympic Games in Berlin, his complete dominance was challenged by two newcomers to the sprinting scene. The first was Eulace Peacock, the Philadelphia flyer from Temple University, who took Metcalfe's national 100-metre title in 1935, beating him into second place. The other was the athlete who finished third in that particular race, but would go on to become one of the greatest names in athletics history – Jesse Owens. More than 80 years after his Olympic achievements the name of Jesse Owens is still known throughout the world, while his influence on the track scene, particularly on the sprints and the athletes who followed him, is incalculable. But like most legends his is founded in part-fact and part-fiction, and as the years of his rollercoaster life went by it became increasingly difficult to separate the two. Stripped of all publicity hype, gloss and modern re-touching, the real story of his life does not always correspond to its familiar public image.

Owens first burst on to the track scene as an 18-year-old trying out for a place in the 1932 Olympics, when despite a brave showing he was knocked out in the preliminary heats. However, he was still hailed as a future track star in Cleveland, Ohio, the city to which he and his family had moved just after the First World War to escape the grinding poverty and violent racism that abounded in rural Alabama, in the Deep South.

Owens was born in 1913, the youngest of ten children, and as a child he suffered a serious bronchial illness which threatened his life on several occasions. But he recovered and on arriving in Cleveland was packed off to the local elementary school where he earned his famous name. He had been christened James Cleveland, and when his new teacher asked his name he drawled, in southern fashion, 'J.C. Owens, ma'am.' The teacher, misunderstanding him, wrote down Jesse Owens, and the eager-to-please newcomer did not have the heart to correct her. From that day onwards, he adopted his new name.

His athletic talents were spotted at junior high school by the part-time Irish coach Charles Riley, a wily old mathematics professor, who recognized Owens's natural ability but had difficulty in convincing him to take track and field seriously. Eventually he persuaded Owens to train with him for an hour before school every morning, and during this time Riley bred excellent habits, making him watch how effortlessly horses ran and coaching him to run as if he were treading on hot coals, which produced the aesthetic running style that is marvelled at even today.

Owens began to win a handful of junior high competitions, but his eyes were not set on the Olympic Games until a visit to his school by the 1920 sprint king Charley Paddock, during one of his famed lecture tours in 1928. Paddock's persuasive speaking convinced Owens that he wanted to follow in his footsteps, and from that day Paddock became his idol and the Olympics his ultimate goal.

In September 1930, Owens joined East Tech High School, but asked Riley to continue coaching him, which he did gladly, working for the next two years to make Owens the brightest track prospect in Ohio. After failing to qualify for the 1932 Games, Jesse became even more determined and, the following year, won three titles in the national interscholastic meeting in Chicago, taking the long jump and the 220 yards, and equalling the world record in the 100 yards in 9.4 seconds.

His performance enabled East Tech to win the event and, for the first time, Owens became something of a hero in Cleveland, with the mayor even organizing a parade to City Hall in his honour.

His fame spread, and when the time came for him to leave East Tech and select a college, there were countless offers to sign him up, and his decision and the reasons for it became the subject of hot local debate. After much haggling over the incentives that each college was prepared to offer, including a stipulation that his unemployed father was offered a job, Owens chose Ohio State University, despite the fact that racism was quite prevalent on the campus and he was barred from using the men's dormitories because of his colour.

He was not even allowed to live on the campus. Instead he shared a boarding house with the small number of other black students at Ohio State, about a quarter of a mile away.

At this time, the percentage of black students in American colleges was small, and sports scholarships, as we know them today, were extremely rare, especially in track, so Owens only received a partial scholarship and had to make up the rest of the money by working before and after school. One of the most celebrated of these part-time jobs was operating a lift in the State office building in Columbus – a simple enough job that paid a reasonable wage, but further illustrated the deep divide between black and white students even in 'modern' Ohio. Whereas the white students manned the main lifts for the employees and visitors, Owens was not permitted to be seen at the front of the building and had to operate the freight lift at the back.

Although he was a great athlete, Owens was not the greatest scholar, and after his freshman year at Ohio State he was placed on academic probation because of his poor grades. Though a bright, articulate and street-smart man, he would never acquit himself well in the classroom. His main ability, off the track, was his passion for public speaking and he could hold an audience spellbound with a well-rehearsed speech, something at which he was already earning money even in these early pre-Olympic days, touring schools and clubs for $50 a time. He also spent some of his time helping out needy organizations for no reward, and he soon realized that the speaking circuit was something that he could work on in the future.

In the spring of 1934, he reached another landmark in his track career when his coach, Riley, handed over his 'rough diamond' to the young, ambitious new track coach at Ohio State, Larry Snyder, whose job it would be to hone Owens's natural talent and polish his technique. Snyder entered him in countless meetings when his college track career began in 1935, and such was his popularity that twelve thousand people turned out to watch him compete in a dual meet between Ohio State and Notre Dame, in which Owens won all three of his events.

This local popularity turned to international fame at the Big Ten Championship at Ann Arbor, on 25 May, when to the astonishment of the crowd and everyone connected with track and field, Jesse broke three world records and equalled a fourth in less than one hour, a feat that is still unparalleled in track and field history and regarded by many people as greater than his performances in the Olympics a little over a year later.

'The Day of Days', as it became known, was held on a warm, clear afternoon, but there was one athlete who was not looking forward to the event at all. Owens felt awful because he was still aching from falling down a flight of stairs while horsing around with a college friend five days earlier and he had not been able to train all week. As he made his way to the stadium he was so sore that Snyder and several athletes had to help him into the rumble seat of a car, help him out and almost carry him to the locker-room, where he sat for half an hour in a steaming hot bath.

Owens remembered some years later: 'Some of my team-mates had to help me get on my running gear. Our trainer put a big swab of hot liniment on my back and they had to help me get on my sweat suit to keep me warm. I got out to the track and hoped I would feel better after I did my usual warm-up of jogging a 440 and then stretching, but I couldn't even jog, let alone stretch.'

Owens propped himself up against a flagpole at one end of the stadium and watched the other athletes darting up and down the cinder track as Coach Snyder tried to persuade him to pull out of the competition. But Owens decided to have a go at the first race – the 100 yards – and slowly pulled himself to his feet and walked gingerly to the start. Little did he know that he was about to step into the history books.

At 3.15pm, the starter called the field to their marks and suddenly the pain in Owens's back, which had even hindered him digging his starting holes, disappeared. 'It was completely gone. I couldn't feel anything. I didn't know why then and I don't to this day,' he once said. At the gun he sprang out of the holes and burst smoothly down the track to equal the world record of 9.4, a clear tenth of a second ahead of the second-placed man. Ten minutes later he moved across to the long jump pit, which had been dug recently in front of the stands, and a white handkerchief was placed on the 26ft 2¼in (7.98m) world mark of Japan's Chuhei Nambu, set in 1931. As a hush fell over the crowd, Owens took off down the runway and got tremendous lift off the board, landing six inches beyond the handkerchief and smashing the record. His mark of 26ft 8¼in (8.13m) would not be beaten for more than 25 years. It was the only jump that Owens made that day and he enjoyed the thundering applause of the crowd, the officials and the other athletes in the stadium for a full five minutes.

At 3.45pm, he stepped up for the 220 yards and was well clear of the field after just 10 yards, cruising down the straight and breaking the tape in a remarkable 20.3, knocking three tenths of a second off Ralph Metcalfe's record. At 4pm he tackled the 220 yards low hurdles, and though he was not a technically good hurdler he tore the opposition apart, winning by a clear second from the next placed man and breaking the world record by four tenths of a second in 22.6, even though two of the three timers clocked him in 22.4. In the two-furlong races, Owens had also set metric world marks, and thus in effect he had broken five world records and tied a sixth in less than 60 minutes, despite his back injury. Afterwards he had to be helped into the shower and then into a car to get home.

It was a subject that Owens loved to talk about and he later revealed: 'Actually all I thought about was the next event. I never thought about records, I just wanted to get through what was next and do my best. I wanted to do well in my first Big Ten meet but I never expected anything like close to what happened. Afterwards, the only real pressure I felt was that I was a target for other people, the guy to knock off. The records were a launching pad for Olympics, the Big Ten was the starting point where I first knew I could compete against top-class athletes and achieve things. But the Games were the ultimate, the biggest competition against the very best.'

After touring the country, performing in various meetings, he returned home in July 1935 and married his childhood sweetheart, Ruth Solomons, whom he had met at junior high. They already had a daughter, Gloria, who was born back in 1932, but the marriage seemed to have an adverse effect on his track performances, and these coincided with the rise to prominence of Eulace Peacock, a tall, powerful athlete in the mould of Metcalfe, and on the ten occasions that they met in the sprints or in the long jump during 1935, Peacock beat Owens seven times – so much so that Charley Paddock publicly put his money on Peacock to beat Owens in Berlin.

The likeable and quietly-spoken Peacock, who died in New York in 1996, aged 82, was always modest about his achievements and what could have been, even though Owens himself admitted that he was the only man he ever feared on the track. Peacock recalled: 'I remember Jesse once said to me, "You know, I never could beat you, I didn't know how to handle you." I was like Metcalfe, but Jesse was so smooth he could run all by himself in world record time. But Metcalfe and I knew if we came out even with him, or just a yard behind, we could overtake him, because in the last 20 or 30 metres we'd close right down on him.'

Peacock's victory over both Metcalfe and Owens in the 1935 AAU championships in Lincoln, Nebraska, made him the favourite for the Olympic team, but then tragedy struck and during an anchor leg in the Penn Relays he pulled a hamstring so badly that it put him out of the reckoning. 'I went to the final trials and gave it a go but it pulled again,' he says, 'and that was that. But I never got down in the dumps about it; I never worried about what might have happened. There would have been some interesting races in Berlin with Owens, Metcalfe and myself, because with the three of us it was a case of who felt right on the day.'

There are those who suggest that, had Peacock travelled to Berlin in full health, he would have taken at least two of the four gold medals that Owens eventually went on to win. No one will ever know, but with Peacock out of the way, Owens knew that his only real competition in the sprints came from his team-mate Metcalfe. Meanwhile the big man's form had dipped slightly since his almost invincible years of 1933 and 1934.

However, like all black athletes of the day, Owens had to face other pressures as well as athletic competition: overt racism, which so often made life on and off the track a misery. It ranged from a poisonous off-hand remark to being refused entry to restaurants and hotels and being forced to ride at the back of a bus. Peacock suffered just like Jesse and remembered: 'It was pretty rough at times, but you tried to adjust yourself to it. It was part of America then and you had to take those knocks. Jesse, Metcalfe and me all had these problems and we had to handle it, though there was never a question of fighting. We would go into restaurants to eat and get thrown out, hotels would refuse to let in the black members of our team and we'd eat in kitchens.

'I remember one time on our way to the AAUs in 1935 when the train we were on was re-routed because of a storm. It stopped and a conductor got on and said to the guy on our train, "I understand you've got some niggers on the train, what are you going to do about it?" We were in bed, but we were all awake and heard the guy on our train say we were fellas from the top colleges in the east and we weren't causing a problem. He told the conductor, "If you want to throw them off the train, you do it," but no one bothered us. You can imagine how we felt. Here we were on our way to the national championships and this happens, but we played it cool and kept quiet.

'We always felt we could do more by actions on the track rather than fighting and knocking somebody down. Our attitude towards these people was if that's the type of person he is, then fine, just walk away.' It was an attitude shared by Owens and many of his generation, and one that would get him involved in trouble later in his life, because for all the changes that followed he remained very much a man of the thirties.

It was not until early in 1936 that Owens began to return to his Big Ten form, running a new world record of 10.2 seconds for the 100 metres in Chicago in June, a record that would last for twenty years. By the time the *SS Manhattan* sailed for Europe he was already being touted as a favourite for three gold medals, in the 100 and 200 metres and the long jump. Just before the team left for Europe, America's other big black sports hero, heavyweight boxer Joe Louis, was beaten in humiliating fashion by Adolf Hitler's favourite, Max Schmeling, and although Louis would be back it was left to his great friend Jesse Owens to shoulder the nation's sporting hopes in Germany.

The awarding of the Games to Berlin had been made prior to the rise of the Nazis, and as the Olympic year grew closer there were calls to boycott them because of the human rights violations in Germany, protests that grew more vociferous when Jews were banned from German sports clubs. By then Hitler had grasped the propaganda value of staging the Olympics and performed an amazing bluff on the Olympic committees from around the world by convincing them that the stories that visitors had heard about persecution and violence were pure invention. In fact, those who attended the Games returned home enormously impressed with their organization and with Germany itself, thanks to a massive cover-up operation mounted by the Nazis.

The 1936 Olympic Games would be the first, but not the last, to be exploited for political gain, and more than 80 years later it is difficult to understand how the rest of the world fell for Hitler's deception. The leading advocate of US participation was AOC President Avery Brundage, a hard-line right-winger who persuaded the committee to vote for participation after a spurious fact-finding mission to Berlin as the guest of the Nazis. Despite protests about the treatment of Jews and blacks in Germany, the AOC finally voted to compete, as did Britain, which was even slower to mobilize opposition than the USA. Their decisions were backed by the IOC, which argued blindly that politics had no part to play in sport. For Hitler, the Games were a political and moral fillip because the world had come to Berlin and, with very few exceptions, had left the city liking what they had seen. Had the Games not been held, maybe the world would have been prompted to examine what was really happening in Germany and what Hitler's true motives were.

Berlin was completely transformed for the Games, decorated from top to bottom, with all racist graffiti and offensive newspapers removed and giant swastika posters and flags draped from every building. Some four thousand athletes and officials were billeted in the Olympic village, along with nearly three thousand pressmen.

On board the *SS Manhattan*, Ralph Metcalfe, now one of the older athletes, spoke to his black colleagues urging them to resist emotional involvement in the political atmosphere, a move that seemed to calm some of the athletes' anxieties about what they might expect in Berlin. Shortly after Metcalfe's death, Owens recalled: 'When we got to Germany there was this ... political aroma. As we sat around the cottages at night he counselled us. He was the guy who set us straight. He told us the deeds we were supposed to do. He said we were not there to get involved in the political situation. He said we were there for one purpose – to represent our country. That led to our success. He was the guy who did it for us.'

The Games opened, under cloudy skies, on Saturday, August 1, in the spectacular new Olympic stadium, before 100,000 clamorous spectators, and as the US team swept into view they whipped off their straw boaters and clasped them to their chests. In the team was the young Jewish sprinter Marty Glickman, who went on to be one of the elder statesmen of American broadcasting. 'We kind of shuffled into the stadium, the US team never really marched, and it was the first time we were going to see Adolf Hitler and company. We were among the last to enter the stadium and as we walked down the track in front of Hitler's box, flanked by all the Nazi bigwigs, Goering, Goebels, Hess and all that gang, he looked sternly down at us and we looked up at him and you could hear the comment go through our ranks, in fact I said it as well – he looks just like Charlie Chaplin – and that's the way we felt about him. He was like some two-bit South American dictator who might last a few months; he was not to be taken seriously. Little did we know what was about to take place.'

Despite the political differences, the German people made everyone extremely welcome, particularly the American team, and Jesse Owens became their hero, although there were racial overtones from some sections of the Nazi media which accused the United States of relying on 'black auxiliaries' to win their medals, a race that the Nazis regarded as sub-human.

Owens himself once recalled: 'We all knew about the racial thing but we couldn't read German so we couldn't read what was being written about us, being animals and all that. But the German people were tremendous. Every day we got a standing ovation from the multitude of people. They were looking at you, not as a black man, but in terms of the ability you displayed. This was the Olympics and there was spill over into your own country. You made headlines here and people saw them and they had second thoughts about you and about blacks, instead of making just a categorization.'

There was no doubt that Owens was the focus of the public's attention in Berlin, and everywhere he went in the city he was pursued by fans clutching autograph books; they even pushed photos and autograph books through his bedroom window at night while he tried to sleep. Glickman recalled: 'His popularity was such that in order to get him safely in and out of the stadium each day he had to use a secret tunnel entrance and exit, otherwise he would have been mobbed by the adulating crowd.'

This adulation grew still further when the competition began, and from the first day he appeared on the track a deafening chant of 'Oh-vens, Oh-vens, Oh-vens' would go up every time the crowd spotted him. The competition itself was not a great challenge for him, and when his first event – the 100 metres – began, the day after the opening ceremony, he had little trouble in living up to German expectations. In the first round he tied the Olympic record of 10.3; in the second round he ran a wind-aided 10.2, and then he eased off to win his semi-final in a sedate 10.4, while Metcalfe strolled the other in 10.5.

In the final, it was a one-horse race from the start, with Owens leading from the gun to build a two-yard lead by the halfway mark which was enough for him to thwart Metcalfe's strong finish and still win the race by a yard at the tape, with Holland's Martinus Osendarp third, Frank Wykoff fourth, and Hitler's favourite, Erich Borchmeyer, back in fifth. Round one of the Jesse Owens Olympic show was complete.

Of course, one of the most famous stories surrounding Jesse Owens was his supposed snub by Hitler, who refused to shake his hand after his 100 metres victory, or so the story goes. It was pure invention by the American press and if there was any snub at all, which is doubtful, then it certainly did not involve Owens.

On the first afternoon of competition, when Jesse was running just heats, Hitler sat in his box and watched with glee as two German athletes won gold medals, summoning them immediately to his box for personal congratulations. Later the same afternoon, he did likewise for a Finnish athlete, but when Owens's friend, the black high-jumper Cornelius Johnson, won the gold medal, Hitler decided that it was getting late and left the stadium before Johnson was awarded his medal. He was not invited to the box because

Hitler was not there. The official explanation was that the Führer had left at a prearranged time and that no snub was intended, but before the Games reconvened the following day – when Owens would run in the 100 metres final – the IOC officials informed Hitler that he would have to congratulate every winner in his box or none at all. Hitler agreed and thereafter he received no other athlete for the duration of the Olympics.

So when Owens won his gold medal there was no invitation to Hitler's box, nor should there have been, but the American press decided to build themselves a story, running headlines all over the country like 'Hitler Snubs Jesse'. When he returned home, at first Jesse tried to put the record straight, but he later found that continually denying the tale was increasingly tedious, so he began agreeing with it and later even embellishing it.

He had little time to savour his win in the 100 metres, in which he equalled the Olympic record of 10.3, despite a heavy track soaked by a sudden downpour just before the race. The following day, he was plunged straight into the 200-metre heats and the long jump competition, the latter being where his stiffest competition lay, in the blonde, blue-eyed German Luz Long, a model of Hitler's supposed Aryan supremacy. For the first time in the Games, Owens felt a little nervous and, still in his tracksuit, took a practice run down the runway and into the pit. To his surprise, the German officials counted it as his first jump, and he was so rattled by this that he fouled his second and had only one jump remaining to make the final or face elimination from the competition.

At this point, Owens was approached by Long, who introduced himself in perfect English.

'Glad to meet you,' said Owens. 'How are you?'

'I'm fine,' replied Long. 'The question is how are you?'

'What do you mean?' said Owens.

'Something must be eating you,' said Long, demonstrating his knowledge of American slang. 'You should be able to qualify with your eyes closed.'

With more than 100,000 pairs of eyes, including those of Hitler and the other top Nazis, gazing down on them, Owens and Long chatted in the middle of the stadium. Long joked about how much he looked like the typical Aryan model, a theory in which he did not believe, and then suggested that Owens should aim to jump from just behind the board to ensure that he did not foul. Owens made the qualifying distance by just one sixteenth of an inch on his final jump.

In the final, held the same afternoon, Owens started the competition with a new Olympic record of 25ft 5½in and then followed up with 25ft 9¾in. However, in the fifth of the six rounds Luz Long brought the huge crowd to their feet by matching Owens's leap exactly. Inspired by Long's challenge, Owens then jumped 26ft ¾in and went on to better that with his last jump of 26ft 5½in to clinch the gold. The first person to offer his congratulations was Long, and Owens wrote later: 'You can melt down all the medals and cups I have and they would be a plating on the 24-carat friendship I felt for Luz Long at that moment.'

Sadly, Long was killed while fighting in the German Army at the Battle of St Pierre in 1943, but Owens continued to correspond with his family for many years, and in 1951 he honoured a promise he'd made to Long by tracking down his son Kai in Germany. 'I've seen Luz again,' Owens said, 'in the face of his son.'

On day three of the competition, having qualified easily for the 200 metres final, Jesse eased his way around the damp, red clay track to his third gold medal in a new Olympic record of 20.7, beating Mack Robinson, the older brother of Brooklyn Dodgers star Jackie, by an incredible four yards, with Osendarp taking another bronze. Despite the light rain that fell all day, making the track even heavier, Owens looked absolutely effortless, while the athletes behind him strained and grimaced their way to the tape. He had become the first athlete to win three track and field golds since the Games of 1900. 'He was markedly better than anyone,' recalled Marty Glickman. 'He was also the smoothest runner I have ever seen and the most physically co-ordinated. When he ran it was like watching water flowing downhill.

'The sprint team used to practise on the cinder track and we would all dig up the cinders where we ran – except Jesse. When we looked at his lane all you would see were six spike marks for each step where his spikes had gone into the cinders and come out clean. It was as if he was running six inches off the ground.'

After Owens received his third gold medal, his Olympics ought to have ended, and at this point 18-year-old Marty Glickman's should have begun. American track tradition dictated that such was the depth and strength of its sprinters that the first seven past the post in the US Trials 100 metres then made up the sprint team in Berlin – and all seven competed. The first three, Owens, Metcalfe and Wykoff, would run in the individual race, and the next four home in the trials, Foy Draper, Marty Glickman, Sam Stoller and Mack Robinson, would then make up the 4 x 100m relay team.

But it was here that a really sinister story unfolded at the Berlin Olympics, certainly as far as the Americans were concerned. The first change to the team, an understandable one, came when Robinson qualified for the 200 metres final and decided not to run in the relay. He was replaced by Wykoff, who had something of a relay pedigree, having been in the last two US Olympic teams, both of which had won gold.

The track team was run by two men, Lawson Robertson and Dean Cromwell, and shortly after the 200 metres Robertson was quoted as saying: 'Owens has had enough glory and collected enough gold medals to last him a while. We want to give the other boys a chance. Marty Glickman, Sam Stoller and Frank Wykoff are assured places on the relay team. The fourth choice rests between Foy Draper and Ralph Metcalfe.' Two days later, however, the situation had changed and, despite a time trial held in Berlin, where Stoller won, Glickman came second and Draper third, it seemed that the two Jewish boys were going to be kicked off the team. Newspapers were full of the coach's indecisiveness and the whole affair smacked of backroom politics. The athletes involved are now all deceased, but much of what they had to say at the time and since is still on record.

Glickman explained: 'The relay team was composed of Wykoff and Draper, both of the University of Southern California, Sam Stoller, the only other Jew on the US track team, and me. We'd practised passing the baton the several weeks we were in Berlin. The morning of the day we were supposed to run we were called into a meeting by Lawson

Robertson, the head track coach, and Dean Cromwell, the assistant head, and we were told that because of a rumour that the Germans had been hiding their best sprinters and saving them to upset the American team in the relay, that Sam and I would be replaced by Jesse and Ralph Metcalfe. Now there's no question that Owens and Metcalfe were faster than Sam and I, a yard faster at least, but we'd been practising. In fact, years later Wykoff said we probably would have run faster because of our superior baton passing.

'I was a brash kid and I said, "But coach, that's silly, you can't develop world-class sprinters unless you run in world-class competition."'

Metcalfe and Wykoff reportedly blamed Owens for selfishly campaigning to be permitted a crack at a fourth gold medal, but Glickman's account differs greatly and he stresses that Metcalfe uttered not one word of protest. 'I said we'll win by 15 yards no matter who runs, but they said, "You'll do as you're told and that's the way the team's going to be."'

Owens, to his everlasting credit, and to Glickman's undying gratitude, said, 'Coach, let Marty and Sam run. I've already won my three gold medals. I'm tired, I've had it, let them run, they deserve it.'

Glickman continued: 'At that, Cromwell pointed his finger at him and said, "You'll do as you're told," and in those days black athletes did as they were told. So Sam and I watched the race from the stands. In the entire history of the Games, as far as I know, no American athlete, physically able, has ever been there and has not competed except for Sam and myself.

'Mere coincidence, was it, that we were both Jewish, or out-and-out anti-Semitism? As it turned out later, Avery Brundage, head of the AOC, and Cromwell, turned out to be America Firsters, which was the group that was sympathetic to the Nazi cause. Brundage was one of the founders so there was no question about his sympathies.'

The suggestion was that Brundage and Cromwell had pulled out the Jewish pair to spare any embarrassment on Hitler's part at seeing them on the victory rostrum. Naturally, the relay was won by the US squad in world record time, with Owens leading off and handing to Metcalfe, by which time they were so far ahead that the two white members of the team, Draper and Wykoff, could have run in backwards and still won. The German team, which featured no new names, finished third.

Clearly, there were several motives behind the relay debacle and probably some of them will never be known, although anti-Semitic feelings loomed large. However, it was unforgivable for the US organizers to have brought two young athletes halfway across the world, only to dash their hopes at the last moment. Besides, had they been serious about improving the quality of the US relay teams they would have been better served working on the 4 x 400 squad, where medal winners Archie Williams, Jimmy LuValle and Glenn Hardin were all left out and the original quartet promptly lost to the British foursome by more than 12 yards.

There was one touching moment in the miserable affair, and that came when the relay team received its medals and Owens insisted that Ralph Metcalfe, an Olympic bridesmaid, should stand at the top of the rostrum.

In 1998 the US Olympic Committee chairman Bill Hybl awarded special medals to Glickman and, posthumously, to Stoller. Hybl stopped short of a full apology, but said: 'We regret this injustice and we feel it was an injustice. We're not only atoning for this but recognizing two great individuals.'

Within a few years of receiving the award, Glickman died after a major heart operation; Stoller had died in 1985 after trying his luck in the movie business; Robinson returned to California, working in a variety of jobs for the City of Pasadena, and died in 2000; while Draper was killed during the Second World War when the bomber he was piloting crashed during an offensive in North Africa. Dutch policeman Martinus Osendarp, bronze medallist in both the 100 and 200 metres, dropped the baton in the relay final, but still clearly enjoyed the Nazi Olympic experience. Often billed as the world's fastest white man, he took both European sprint titles in 1938 and was something of a Dutch sporting hero; however, when Germany occupied Holland during the war, he joined the German SS. He was held responsible for the arrests and deaths of scores of Dutch Jews and resistance fighters and in 1948 was jailed for 12 years for his collaboration. He was released early in 1953 and for a while was forced to work in the mines, but he eventually went into coaching. He died in Heerlen, near the German border, in 2002 at the age of 86.

As for Jesse Owens, he won his four gold medals and the achievement made him a household name all over the world – even the Southern newspapers in the USA carried reports and pictures about him – so when, after the Games, the AAU began a barnstorming tour of Europe with some of their star athletes, to try and make up their expenses on the Olympic trip, he was the man everyone wanted to see. But he was exhausted and just wanted to go home and, as he dragged himself from meeting to meeting around Eastern Europe and finally to London, his performances deteriorated and his desire to return to the States grew stronger. Both he and his coach, Larry Snyder, were made aware of a number of lucrative offers from show business which had arrived by telegram from the States, and that made matters worse, as he was not being paid for running. The last straw came when he learned that the tour was to go to Sweden, Norway and Finland before heading home.

Owens decided that he had had enough, and wanted to go home to seek his fortune and earn the dollars that were being waved in his direction. He ran the third leg of a relay at a packed White City Stadium in London – and then jumped on a ship bound for New York. It was to be his last ever serious race.

Brundage and the AAU were furious when they realized that their star attraction had gone home, especially as they were guaranteed 15 per cent of the gate money with Jesse appearing in the team and only 10 per cent without him. In typically cavalier fashion, Brundage and his colleagues suspended Owens for life for refusing to compete, even though he was an amateur and had never signed a contract to run in Scandinavia. As Owens said at the time: 'The suspension is very unfair to me. There's nothing I can gain out of this trip. All we athletes get out of this Olympic business is a view out of the plane or train window. It gets tiresome, it really does.'

So just two weeks after he had taken the athletics world by storm and won four gold medals for the United States, his country's athletics chiefs effectively kicked him out of the sport. He returned home to a hero's welcome in the streets of New York, and later in Cleveland and Columbus too, but most of the attractive offers made in the immediate aftermath of the Games quickly turned to dust. A $40,000 offer to appear on the Eddie Cantor radio show proved to be false, as did most of the show business offers, and the only concrete ones he received were to appear on stage with Bill 'Bojangles' Robinson, who had hired Eddie Tolan, or to coach track at Ohio's premier black college, Wilberforce.

Owens chose the dancing, but before he signed a contract he had a change of heart and asked to be reinstated as an amateur. The AAU refused, and to most people it seemed that he had thrown away his athletics career for a pile of empty promises.

Two weeks after returning home as a hero, he was still looking for the job that would set him up for life, but it never came. 'One day he was riding at the head of the parade,' recalled Marty Glickman, 'and the next he was just another black man in America, once again riding in the back of the bus, and he had a very difficult time for several years after the Games.'

Owens himself, talking some years later about his dilemma, said: 'I was taught at a very early age by my coaches that even though ours was a social structure which prohibited people from mingling and eating and living and riding together, that eventually things would change through deeds. I thought then about those things, because when I came back after all the stories about Hitler and his snub, I came back to my native country and I couldn't ride in the front of the bus, I had to go to the back door, I couldn't live where I wanted. Now what's the difference? I wasn't invited to shake hands with Hitler, but I wasn't invited to the White House to shake hands with the President either.' It was true that nothing had changed for the better; and President Roosevelt never even sent a message of congratulations.

However, Professor William Baker, who spent five years researching Jesse's life story for the biography *Jesse Owens: An American Life*, maintains that much of the hardship was a myth. 'The suggestion is that when Owens came back he couldn't get a job and he couldn't make any money, so he had to race against horses, motor cycles and automobiles and that sort of degrading activity. The truth is that he came home from Berlin and did find some of the offers he received were bogus, but in fact he made a lot of money. He gave his support to the Democratic presidential candidate, Alf Landon, and made $10,000 for that, he made a lot of public appearances and late in the year he did race a horse, in Cuba, but was paid $2,000 for that, which was a lot of money for 1936.

'The fact is between '36 and '39 he held more than a dozen jobs, made a lot of money and didn't spend it wisely. He had a dry-cleaning business go bankrupt, he lost money on a touring basketball team and a softball team, but every year he bought a brand new Buick and kept a fabulous wardrobe for himself and his wife. He made a lot of money and he spent a lot.'

Only a year after the Berlin Games, however, Jesse Owens's fame was waning, and until after the Second World War he became something of a forgotten man, working during the war as the personnel director of black workers at the Ford Motor Company. He then resigned and went back on the road, touring as a special attraction alongside the Harlem

Globetrotters and working in dead-end jobs, never seeming to be able to break out of the racial stranglehold under which the majority of blacks suffered in America at the time. Athletically, Owens was still a force, and in 1948 he produced an exhibition long jump of 25ft 11in and was reputed to have run 100 yards in 9.8 seconds as late as 1955. The turnaround for Jesse, one that saw a renaissance of interest in him and his name, came in the early 1950s, and from then on he never looked back.

In 1950, Associated Press voted him the greatest athlete of the half-century and he began to get involved in youth work. In 1953 he was appointed secretary of the Illinois State Athletic Commission and started working in radio and television.

Professor Baker has an interesting theory to account for his sudden re-emergence into the public consciousness. 'I am convinced that were it not for the Cold War Jesse Owens would have been forgotten. America desperately needed to have some black, visible hero who had made it in American society, because the race question was the Achilles heel of US propaganda. The only other candidates were Paul Robeson, a communist living in Paris, Jackie Robinson, who was too outspoken, and Joe Louis, whose career was on the down.

'Jesse Owens was a wonderful spokesman for Americanism. He had made it, he was enthusiastic, he had a work ethic about him and he was very patriotic.'

Owens became something of a roving ambassador for President Eisenhower, visiting Third World countries in Ike's 'People to People' programme and attending Olympic Games, starting in 1956, as the official presidential representative. Appearing alongside other celebrities such as Bob Hope, Jesse Owens had finally made the big league in the fame stakes and he never let it slip away again. Despite his overt patriotism, he still managed to fall under the scrutiny of the FBI during the fanatical 'reds under the beds' purges led by J. Edgar Hoover. A file existed on him, following a three-year investigation, which was headed 'Foreign Inspired Agitation Among the American Negroes', prompted by his once having sent a greeting to the National Negro Congress. Eventually he was exonerated, and it was probably the only time in his life that Jesse Owens was ever described as a radical.

At about the same time he became something of a corporate figure, endorsing multi-national companies and working as a 'front man' for them, making speeches to employees, attending meetings, making commercials and generally representing their interests. These included Ford, ARCO, Greyhound, Paramount and Lincoln Mercury, plus a selection of smaller concerns. Owens was an inspirational speaker and throughout his career used just six basic speeches, each one lasting about half an hour and intended to be motivational, thoughtful and entertaining, which they all were. He told one interviewer: 'I'm not in the entertainment field; my business is primarily to be able and willing to talk to people from a motivating and inspirational standpoint. I talk about people who have succeeded with a great deal of handicaps.'

On top of his corporate commitments, Jesse had more than a hundred requests each year to make speeches to various groups, of which about thirty were accepted, at around $2,000 a time, although he also worked on charitable and civic groups for nothing, as well as for hospitals, boys clubs and the Salvation Army.

As the sixties arrived, he was caught up in the racial tension that swept America, and some critics maintain that he should have presented a much higher profile in the civil rights movement. He was condemned by some radicals for staying on the side of the establishment, but they forgot that Owens was still a man of the thirties, and although they considered him a poor role model, to others he was someone with whom they could readily identify as an athlete and as a man who had made it against all the odds.

After avoiding a four-year prison term for non-payment of taxes in 1965, he was caught in the middle of the Black Power rows during the 1968 Games in Mexico, and he alienated himself still further from the angry young black athletes when he tried to intervene on behalf of the US Olympic Committee after the famous Black Power salutes of John Carlos and Tommie Smith. He was attacked as an 'Uncle Tom' figure and a tool of the white establishment. 'I just tried to get them to realize nobody owes you anything in this country,' he once said. 'Whatever you want is there for the taking, if you have the ability and desire to take it.'

The New York Times athletics correspondent Frank Litsky remembers: 'The US Olympic Committee was aghast at what was happening and they looked for help, for someone to reason with the black athletes. They asked Jesse and he tried to intervene, but I don't think he really understood the thinking of the modern black athlete and he was not treated with huge respect by these people, they weren't listening to him and I think he was hurt very much by it.'

'To these angry young blacks, Jesse Owens was frankly something of a fossil,' says Professor Baker. 'He was a man of the thirties and had been taught to smile and turn the other cheek and to say "yessir". Blacks in the sixties were no longer willing to do that, so to them Owens seemed utterly outdated. There was even conflict at home with his three daughters who were into the civil rights movement.'

Sprinter Mel Pender, who had returned from fierce fighting in the Vietnamese jungle to run in the Games, recalled in his 2017 book *Expressions of Hope*: 'Owens should have been on our side. He should have supported the cause since he himself was so poorly treated. To us, he was a spy for the white establishment and therefore had no place with us. We saw him as someone who had been sitting on the 50-yard line with all the VIPs and he had really forgotten that he had been a struggling athlete. He spoke to us as if he were Avery Brundage.'

Owens returned home from Mexico and penned the book *Blackthink*, in which he attacked the black power movement as pro-negro bigots. It included the line: 'The black fist is a meaningless symbol. When you open it you have nothing but fingers – weak, empty fingers. The only time the black fist has significance is when there's money inside. There's where the power lies.'

It was powerful material and got a mixed reaction in the black press, so much so that two years later he published another book called *I Have Changed*, in which he watered down some of his previous statements and philosophy. In it he explained: 'I realize now that militancy in the best sense of the word was the only answer where the black man was concerned, that any black man who wasn't militant in 1970 was either blind or a coward.' Throughout the seventies, Jesse acted as an Olympic elder statesman, raising funds, attending banquets, making speeches and becoming what one writer described as a 'professional good example, a combination of nineteenth-century spellbinder and twentieth-century PR man'. He received dozens of awards, including America's highest civilian decoration – the Medal of Freedom Award. In 1971, he suffered a severe attack of pneumonia, which almost killed him, and he was forced to give up his daily packet of cigarettes, something he had enjoyed since his teens, for a fittingly dignified pipe. In 1978, he had a jolt when his old rival Ralph Metcalfe died from a heart attack, and less than a year later Jesse himself fell ill while filming an American Express commercial and was rushed to hospital, where doctors diagnosed lung cancer, almost certainly caused by cigarette smoking. The condition was inoperable and so he returned to his home in Phoenix, Arizona, where he died in hospital in March 1980, aged 66, still vehemently opposing President Carter's planned boycott of the Moscow Olympics in protest at the Russian invasion of Afghanistan.Amid heavy snowfalls, more than two thousand people turned out for his funeral at the Rockefeller Chapel at the University of Chicago.

Despite their political differences on the 1980 Olympic boycott, President Carter said: 'Perhaps no athlete better symbolized the human struggle against tyranny, poverty and racial bigotry. His personal triumphs as a world-class athlete and record holder were the prelude to a career devoted to helping others. His work with young athletes, as an unofficial ambassador overseas and a spokesman for freedom are a rich legacy to his fellow Americans.'

But the most poignant line came from another speaker, who said: 'No doubt the first man to meet him at the pearly gates will be Ralph Metcalfe saying, "I beat you this time."'

There are dozens of monuments to, and memories of, Jesse Owens scattered around the world – even the street leading to the Berlin Olympic Stadium was renamed after him. There are many different points of view about him, some complimentary and others not, but ask anyone who knew him well and they find it difficult to say anything unflattering about him without a smile.

As Frank Litsky says: 'Jesse was a nice human being. He was warm, he'd put his arm around you, he'd tell you a story, he was full of stories and they were nice stories, they were inspiring. When you left him you had a feeling that something good had happened and you smiled. Your day had been made and he did that for a lot of people.'

Those who knew him less well, or not at all, found it easier to be uncharitable. Professor Baker feels that he was a plastic man who sold his name and fame, whereas many others regard him as a man with a turn of speed and a commanding presence who lived a lifetime spinning the legend he created in those few far-off days in Berlin.

Owens was not an intellectual and he never did get his degree from Ohio State – although he was awarded an honorary doctorate in 1972 – but he survived on his wits and his charm. 'He was articulate, he was well mannered, he was very handsome, he was the life of the party,' says Marty Glickman, who remained a friend until Owens's death. 'He was a terrific guy. But he was no Albert Einstein. He lived out his life as the figure he was in 1936. He was always Jesse Owens, 1936 quadruple Olympic champion.'

But for all his frailties, Jesse Owens was a good man, an athlete of unrivalled talents who saw an opportunity to make a better life for himself and his family and took it. In today's athletics market he would be a multi-millionaire, but back in the 1930s and 1940s he did what was necessary to survive, and after some difficult years it paid off. His name will live forever in Olympic history and will always be synonymous with speed, while his influence on thousands of young athletes is impossible to measure – almost all subsequent Olympic sprint champions admit that they owe him a debt.

'You learn to play the game of life according to the society in which we live,' he once said. 'If you remember these things and try to live them day by day, then I think there are people you talk to day after day who won't forget the things you did. Therefore, you walk the streets of your home ten feet tall because you never know how many kids wish to emulate what you have done.'

Owens's legacy is well cared for. Shortly after his death, friends and family established the Jesse Owens Foundation, a non-profit organization still overseen by his three daughters, Gloria, Marlene and Beverly, which provides financial assistance and support to help under-privileged kids through college. In 1990, President George W. Bush posthumously awarded him the Congressional Gold Medal.

And the legend shows no sign of fading. In recent years a US postage stamp featuring Owens was issued; Ohio State's new 10,000-seater stadium was named in his honour; shoe giants Adidas produced a retro training shoe – in red, white and blue – to mark his Olympic achievements; a major highway in Cleveland was re-named Jesse Owens Way; and Ohio's newest state park was named after him.

In February 2016 *Race*, a feature film about his life, was released starring Stephan James as Owens, Jason Sudekis as Larry Snyder and Jeremy Irons as Avery Brundage. The racing sequences were filmed at the old Olympic Stadium in Berlin. It received mixed reviews, with *Rolling Stone* opining that 'without diminishing the accomplishments of Owens, the film reminds us of our blinkered history with race and the hurdles still ahead,' while *Time* magazine suggested that '*Race*, whose title has obvious multiple meanings, lets us down on too many fronts. It's a dropped baton of a movie.'

While the critics were lukewarm, Owens's story was still regarded as valid enough to warrant the full Hollywood treatment 80 years after his extraordinary Olympic exploits.

The name of Jesse Owens will never die, but for a man with apparently effortless, God-given talent, perhaps the most insightful description of him came from the man himself: 'We all have dreams. In order to make dreams come into reality, it takes an awful lot of determination, dedication, self-discipline and effort.'

London 1948

Harrison Dillard

Among the thousands who packed the streets of Cleveland to see Jesse Owens's triumphant return home from the Berlin Olympics was a young 13-year-old from the lower east side of the city called Harrison Dillard.

He and some of his friends had persuaded their parents to let them go and watch the parade, and ran over a mile from their homes to the centre of the city's black district where Owens was due to pass.

They forced their way through the crowd and were standing on the edge of the kerb as Owens, dressed immaculately in suit and tie and sitting in the back of a huge convertible car, glided slowly by. Owens spotted them looking up at him, gave a big smile and a wink and shouted out, 'Hi kids, how are ya?'

Naturally they all thought that this was the greatest thing that had ever happened – their hero had actually spoken to them – and young Harrison ran all the way home, burst into the kitchen, almost pulling the door off its hinges, and breathlessly told his mother, 'I've just seen Jesse Owens and I'm going to be just like him.'

She just smiled, as mothers do, and said, 'Yes, son, I'm sure you will be.' She may have had her own private doubts, but for Harrison his Olympic dream began that very afternoon.

Mrs Dillard, however, had other more pressing things on her mind, like feeding the family; times were tough during the Depression, and Cleveland had been hard hit. Harrison's father, who sold ice and coal from door to door from a horse-drawn wagon, suffered like everyone else and for some years the family led a hand-to-mouth existence in suffocating poverty. Despite the hardship of his childhood years, young Dillard's love of running began on the back streets of the city and at a very early age he realized that he had a talent for running fast, something he especially enjoyed when it meant beating the older children.

He also watched the young Jesse Owens running and jumping at the local high school, only a mile from the Dillard home, but his first memory of Owens was as a high-jumper. His other heroes were the fighters Joe Louis and Henry Armstrong, but whenever he boxed he always seemed to end up with a bloody nose, so he chose to follow in the footsteps of his track idol.

What was particularly interesting about his early development as an athlete was his passion for hurdling, an event to which he had a very bizarre introduction, thanks to a friend who ran on a local high school track team. 'His name was Jimmy White, I'll always remember him,' recalled Dillard. 'He was the only kid in the neighbourhood who had a pair of running spikes and we thought they were marvellous.

'There was an alley behind our street and Jimmy would set up obstacles for us. We took the seats out of old cars, set them on fire to burn off the fabric, so there was just the springs remaining, then used them as hurdles. They were light so you didn't hurt yourself if you hit one and they were low enough for us to jump over.'

So from the tender age of eight, using burned-out car seats as hurdles, Dillard began to acquire a technique for hurdling that would one day make him not only the greatest of his time, but also one of the best in history. With that early training and the guiding light of Mr Owens to motivate him, it was not long before he was making a name for himself in athletic circles, although mostly it was not his real name.

When Harrison was just six years old he acquired the nickname 'Boney Babe' because he was so thin, a name that was then shortened to just 'Boney' and later to 'Bones'. The latter stuck and even close friends who knew him for forty or fifty years always called him 'Bones'. In 1941, it was Owens who took a special interest in the 18-year-old Dillard's exploits at East Tech High School, although the famous story about how he got a pair of the great man's track shoes is not absolutely true. 'It's a little apocryphal,' admitted Dillard. 'We were at school and he went into the locker room and brought out a brand new pair of shoes, suggesting I give them a try. Though they were his shoes he hadn't actually worn them himself, but he'd given them to me so of course I wore them till they just disintegrated!'

After high school, Dillard enrolled at Baldwin-Wallace College, in the Cleveland suburbs. His training was more sophisticated than leaping car seats in alleys, but only just. 'We had a small gym that enabled me to set up one hurdle and run the 15 yards to it, get over it, hit the ground and have just enough room to stop by going through a door on the opposite side of the building. That's how small it was.'

To perfect his timing outdoors, he placed matchboxes on top of the hurdles and attempted to knock them off cleanly with his spikes to ensure that he was clearing them by the barest margin.

In the summer of 1942, Dillard took part in his first national championships, albeit in the junior section, finishing a creditable second in the low hurdles and fourth in the high hurdles. However, it was not long before the war took an active role in his life and in the following spring, during his second year as a business student at Baldwin-Wallace College, he was drafted into the US Army.

He saw plenty of combat and matured physically, serving in the 92nd Infantry Division, the 'Buffalo Soldiers', a famous segregated division, dating back to the days after the Civil War. The all-black 'Buffalo Soldiers' fought the German Army in the mountains of Italy. Dillard, a private first class, won master sharpshooter badges both with the M1 rifle and .45 calibre pistol. 'I never fired guns before or after the war. It was just something I was good at,' he said.

He spent 32 months in Italy, eight months of them in active combat. In the final months of the European war, the 'Buffalo Soldiers' entered an Italian town whose name he has now forgotten. The Germans had just fled. 'Normally, we felt like liberators,' he said. 'But every door was closed and every blind was drawn. We found out that other American troops had told the Italians that our division would rape all the women,' Dillard said. Later, the townspeople held a banquet for them. They had come to realize the 'Buffalo Soldiers' lived by the division's motto, 'Deeds, not words'.

It was not until May 1945, when the war was drawing to a close, that he was able to start running again and he competed in a number of army meetings in some of the Italian cities close to where he was stationed.

Then he travelled to Frankfurt, Germany, for his first taste of real international competition, the 'GI Olympics', where Allied troops from all over Europe and the Mediterranean theatre of war competed. Dillard took them by storm, emerging with no fewer than four gold medals for sprinting and hurdling. There was a special spectator among the crowd that day, General George S. Patton, and the American reporters asked him what he thought of this young private winning all the medals. Pausing for a moment, Patton finally declared in his inimitable style, 'He's the best goddam athlete I've seen in my life,' which Dillard considered a great compliment.

In the winter of 1945, Harrison returned home to Baldwin-Wallace to start training with coach Eddie Finnigan, but already his sights were set firmly on the forthcoming 1948 Olympic Games in London. His confidence was strengthened further in the summer of 1946, when he won two major US hurdle titles and broke Jesse Owens's record for the 220 yards low hurdles with a run of 22.5.

In 1946 one of his potential Olympic rivals was removed from the equation. Harold 'Hal' Davis, the California Comet, was the pre-eminent sprinter of the war years and tied both Jesse Owens's 100 metres world record of 10.2 in 1941 and, a year later, Frank Wykoff's 100 yards record of 9.4 seconds. He won countless US and NCAA titles and, incredibly, lost only three 100 races in his life.

Had the Olympics happened in 1940 or 1944, he would have been odds-on to have taken gold at both, but instead he left college and joined the Marines. He saw active service in the Pacific and was among the first US soldiers into Hiroshima and Nagasaki after the atom bombs had been dropped. When he finally returned to California he was still only 25 years old, but a serious hamstring injury in 1946 finished his career and his Olympic dreams. He died in his native Morgan Hill, near San Jose, in 2007, aged 86, and was one of the first inductees to the National Track & Field Hall of Fame, along with Jesse Owens and Harrison Dillard.

Dillard's path to Olympic glory began seriously in 1947, when he tore into an awesome series of 82 straight wins in sprints and hurdles, indoors and outdoors, at home and abroad, that would take him to the very brink of the Olympic Games. It included two more world records, the first in June 1947, during the NCAA championships in Salt Lake City, where he lowered his own 220 yards low hurdles mark to 22.3, a record that would stand for nine years. Then, in the following spring, at the Kansas Relays, he clipped a tenth of a second off the 120 yards high hurdles record with an electrifying run of 13.6 seconds – but it could so easily have been faster.

Ted Theodore, a close friend and later team-mate of Dillard and latterly Alumni Director at Baldwin-Wallace, explained: 'He'd run a tremendous race in the preliminaries and looked so free and easy. In the final I was at the finish line and saw him run one of the most amazing races I have ever witnessed. I was really excited because Bill Porter, who was second, was just coming off the last hurdle when Harrison was crossing the finish line. The three starters were looking in amazement at their watches and as I peered over their shoulders I saw two watches at 13.5 clean and the other one at 13.6. I said hurray he's got a 13.5, but no, lo and behold they were reluctant to award such a fine time and gave him a 13.6. He was cheated out of a tenth of a second.'

This incredible winning streak established him as the world's premier hurdler, but it was finally broken when he lost four races in quick succession during the run-up to the Olympics. It started with defeat over 100 metres at the AAU Championships at the hands of Barney Ewell, who, along with Hal Davies, would probably have challenged for the 1944 Olympic sprint title had it been held. Less than an hour later, he lost the 110 metres hurdles to fellow American Bill Porter and suddenly the man who everyone thought was invincible, and the favourite for a gold medal in London, was looking decidedly shaky.

Incredibly, the next two races he lost were in the final US Olympic trials themselves. First, he was beaten into third place in the 100 metres, a race won in a world record-equalling 10.2 seconds by the in-form Ewell. Mel Patton, who had smashed the world 100 yards record with a run of 9.3 seconds a few months earlier, took second place. But a third spot at least meant a guaranteed place in the US 100 metres team for London and a run in the sprint relay.

In the 110 metres hurdles trial, Harrison, despite the recent setbacks, remained odds-on favourite – he was still faster than anyone in the world and no one could match his incredible speed between the hurdles or his silky technique over them. It would take a disaster to rob him of a gold medal, said the press – and a disaster they got.

'All I had to do was finish third and I was in the team,' says Dillard, 'but on that particular day, as history shows, I finished dead last. I hit the first hurdle, got over the second and then hit every other hurdle in succession, stopping completely at the eighth. I had totally lost the rhythm of the race and my timing was so completely destroyed I just stopped and didn't even finish. Here I was, the world record holder and American champion, and it all went for nought because under the American system you qualify on that day or you don't make it at all.'

The 25,000 crowd at the stadium in Evanston, Illinois, were stunned by his spectacular failure and the race made headlines all over the country, but thanks to his scraping a place in the sprint Dillard avoided missing the Games altogether, so he was not totally crushed by the hurdles catastrophe.

There was the inevitable inquest between the athlete and his coach Eddie Finnigan into what went wrong, and Dillard said: 'We came to the conclusion I simply wasn't getting my lead leg up, because I was running so fast my timing was just a fraction off, but it was enough to make my lead heel catch the hurdles.'

So he had to be satisfied with a crack at the sprints, joining Barney Ewell and Mel Patton on the sprint team, and in July the US squad set sail for austerity London, a city in turmoil after the horrors of German bombing during the war and still living with strict food and clothes rationing. Despite the fact that great areas of the city still lay in rubble, the awarding of the Games to London was acclaimed universally and 59 countries, with more than 4,500 athletes, flooded into Britain. 'There's no atmosphere like the Olympic Games,' recalled Dillard, 'nothing like it anywhere in sport in the world. In America, we have the World Series, the Super Bowl and the Kentucky Derby, but they're nothing like the Olympics.'

The site for the athletics was Wembley Stadium, the traditional home of British football, while the athletes themselves were barracked in school buildings and service camps at RAF Uxbridge and Richmond Park. The public responded in magnificent style, packing the stadium throughout the competition, and for once even the unpredictable British weather managed to smile on the proceedings.

'We certainly had everything we wanted at Uxbridge,' Dillard remembered, 'including good training facilities, a laundry, a bank, even a motion picture theatre. But our food was flown in from the States, even the meat, vegetables and milk, because of the rationing in Britain and because we all liked to eat the type of food we were accustomed to, so we also brought our own cooks to prepare the food once it arrived. The British people were very friendly, I think they were glad to have something to celebrate after the years of bombing, so we had an excellent time sightseeing or renewing old acquaintances.'

As was common practice, the 100 metres competition was among the first track events to be held, so Dillard was confined to the barracks during the opening ceremony and listened to it on the radio. When the sprint heats got underway, all eyes were on the American pair Patton and Ewell, plus the Panamanian student Lloyd La Beach, who had also equalled the world record of 10.2 a few months before the Games. The American track coach Dean Cromwell had been widely quoted in the press, saying that he felt Patton would win both sprint events, but there seemed nothing to choose between the three favourites. One name was not mentioned at all during the pre-race hype, and that was Harrison Dillard, but he was not worried about all the publicity surrounding the big names because he knew that he was going to win.

He looked impressive in the heats and in the semi-final beat his friend and rival Barney Ewell, but even that victory could not persuade the experts that he had a medal chance in the final.

The six men who lined up for the final, held in blazing sunshine, on Saturday, July 31, were Dillard, the British duo of McDonald Bailey and Alistair McCorquodale, La Beach, Ewell and Patton; all took special care with their starting blocks, which were being used for the first time in an Olympic Games.

'I just knew I was going to win,' said Dillard. 'The only unknown quantity in the race was McCorquodale, because none of us knew anything about him. But a few days before the final I had what amounted to a vision and I saw myself crossing the line first. Barney Ewell and I were sharing a room and we were sitting on his bunk when I turned to him and said, "Barney, I'm gonna beat you, I just know I'm gonna win on Saturday." He just smiled and laughed it off, saying, "Yeah, big deal," probably thinking I was trying to psyche him out, but I really could see myself winning that race.'

On the eve of the final, few of the masses of international pressmen would rate Dillard in the company of the real sprinting 'heavyweights', and opinion seemed to be divided between Patton and Ewell. 'I was so relaxed between the semi and the final, I managed to get a nap for 20 minutes on the dressing-room table, but Barney was so highly strung before a race you daren't talk to him or he'd snap your head off, while Mel got so nervous he'd throw up before most competitions.'

Dillard had been drawn in the outside lane, with the 31-year-old Ewell in lane two and Patton on the inside. After a Bailey false start, the pistol cracked and Dillard flew off his blocks like a bolt of lightning. By the second stride he was already ahead and he led all the way and seemed to hit the tape first, with Ewell a fraction behind him, but it was a real photo finish. Naturally Ewell could not see Dillard in the outside lane and thought that he had won and began to dance and jump around the track with his hands in the air. Even Mel Patton, who finished a disappointing fifth after a poor start, came over to Ewell to offer his congratulations as the crowd of 83,000 cheered wildly. But when the judges studied the photo finish picture, it was clear that Harrison had won by a couple of feet in 10.3, equalling the Olympic record, with Ewell second in 10.4 and La Beach third.

When the result was finally announced after a few minutes' wait, Ewell sportingly accepted it immediately and impressed the crowd by going straight over to Dillard to offer his congratulations. 'By the time I got to the finish "Bones" was halfway to Cleveland,' Ewell would always say with a smile, when asked about the race.'I knew that winning hinged on the start I got,' said Dillard, 'and I spent the entire time between the US trials and the Games working on nothing but starts. For a hurdler I was a pretty good starter, but that still wasn't good enough for the sprints, so I worked on them for three weeks and I lost about five pounds in weight – and there wasn't much to lose – just practising.

'I remember the race vividly. I was right up against the stands, which was the worst possible lane in normal circumstances, but this year they were using the electric photo, so it wasn't so bad. I remember hitting the middle of the race and I was definitely in front, no question about it, so the problem was to keep running fast without tying up. But I was able to stay relaxed and keep driving and praying for the tape to just hurry up and get there.

'I remember lunging for the tape and out of the corner of my eye I saw another white American jersey, which was Barney Ewell, and he thought he'd won and started that victory dance. But I remember Lloyd La Beach, who finished third in the lane next to Barney, saying to him, "Man, you no win, 'Bones' win." That reassured me because I thought I'd won too.'

The gold medal more than compensated for the disappointment of not making the team in the hurdles, and his performance earned rave reviews in the press, particularly the American newspapers, where it was headline news. Coach Finnigan was the proudest man in the stadium and raced from his seat in the stands and tried to leap the rail and get on to the track. It was not the first time that he had done so – he'd done it back in 1942 when Harrison was placed fifth in his first senior AAU championship in New York. On that occasion, Finnigan raced down the stands and as he attempted to jump on to the track he was stopped by a big Irish New York policeman.

'Where d'you think you're going?' he demanded.

'That's my youngster out there, I wanna go out and congratulate him,' replied Finnigan in his strong Irish accent.

The policeman asked, 'What would your name be?'

'Finnigan,' replied the coach.

'Go right ahead, my boy,' said the policeman.

Now, at Wembley, the same thing happened again and this time he was stopped by a British bobby and they went through the same routine. Finally the policeman asked his name.

'Finnigan,' he replied.

'Get back in the stands, you bloody Irishman!' came the answer.

Dillard loved to tell the story, although Finnigan was a resourceful man and did find his way on to the track eventually, lifting his charge off his feet, tears streaming down his face. Overcome with emotion, he returned to his hotel room and left a note for Dillard's close friend Jack Clowser of the *Cleveland Press*, which said: 'This is the day we waited for so long. To think it came not in the hurdles but in the event we all thought Dillard couldn't win. Fate is strange and wonderful. I'm going out to find a church somewhere. My heart is bursting.'

The unhappiest man in the stadium must have been Mel Patton. Many reasons were given for his disappointing performance. He blamed the lack of training and top-class races, whereas Coach Cromwell attributed his failure to the humidity and the chewed-up inside lane of the track. It has also been suggested that he was too nervous before the race, got off to a bad start and seized up trying to catch a fast field. The real answer is probably a combination of all these factors. In later years Patton explained: 'It was hot and humid in London that summer. It had an effect on me. The most I ever weighed at the time was 151 pounds and I was down to 143 then. I was pretty disturbed before the 100. I wasn't running on all eight cylinders. I wasn't physically strong. I was unbelievably disappointed, but it wasn't the end of the world. I still had the 200.' He certainly returned with a vengeance in the 200 metres and won the gold by a clear yard from Ewell and La Beach. Harrison did not run in the 200 metres, and he watched the 110 metres hurdles with mixed feelings as Bill Porter won the gold and the United States went 1-2-3 in an event that he could have won easily. But he was selected for the sprint relay, a competition that proved to be one of the most controversial in the Games, with the US team boasting the gold and silver medallists in the 100 metres and the winner of the 200 metres, Dillard,

Ewell and Patton, and the talented long-jumper Lorenzo Wright. They made the final comfortably. There was little competition and, as expected, the US squad took first place with relative ease, Ewell leading off, handing to Wright and then Harrison blazing around the bend, leaving Patton to canter down the home straight practically unopposed to win by about six yards. However, then the alarm bells rang as one of the judges claimed that Ewell had run beyond his restraining line as he passed the baton to Wright, and the US team was disqualified, much to their amazement.

Barney Ewell was so upset about the decision, insisting that he had not run out of the zone, that he asked the coaches to make an official complaint. The strength of Ewell's protest convinced the US team managers to lodge the complaint, but it could not prevent the medal ceremony from taking place, with the British team receiving the gold medal while the Americans looked on in disbelief.

Three days later at a jury of appeal the film of the race was studied and it became clear that the judge was wrong. 'The moving pictures showed Barney had another four or five feet before he crossed the line,' said Dillard. 'We discovered that the judge who made the decision was a Scottish Presbyterian minister, so nobody could question his honesty, it was just a simple mistake. Coming into that first turn there was a proliferation of lines and he just got confused and watched the wrong line.'

So Harrison received his second gold medal and became one of the heroes of the Games, no mean achievement when you consider that these were the Olympics of Emil Zatopek, Fanny Blankers-Koen and the 17-year-old decathlete Bob Mathias. Dillard was in great demand when the US team embarked on its usual European tour, and it was some weeks after the closing ceremony when he finally arrived home in Cleveland to the sort of welcome he had seen Jesse Owens receive all those years before. It really was the stuff that dreams were made of. As for his team-mates, due to the war, the unlucky Barney Ewell had almost certainly missed his best opportunity of Olympic glory, being perhaps past his best at the age of 30. Post-London, he turned professional for a few years, running in Australia, New Zealand and Scotland, before retiring from the track in 1952. He returned home to Lancaster, Pennsylvania, and spent a lifetime coaching and encouraging kids at his old high school. They even named a sports complex after him.

Ill health dogged Ewell in later life, but despite the amputation of both legs he remained his up-beat, affable self to the very end. He died in April 1996, aged 78.

Californian Mel Patton fared better, and after winning the 200 metres in 1948 he coached track in several US colleges before directing the national sports programme in Saudi Arabia and managing an electronics company. He died, aged 89, at his home in Fallbrook, California, in 2014. Panama's Lloyd LaBeach returned home a national hero. It would be sixty years before the nation tasted another track and field medal. He retired from running in 1957 and moved his family to Nigeria, where he ran a successful agricultural import/export business. He died in 1999 at the age of 76.

For Dillard, when the dust had finally settled on London, there was still the matter of winning the gold medal he had always wanted, the 110 metres hurdles. He was still the world record holder and had spent most of his time training for the event. He felt that he could not retire without having one more crack at it, even though it would mean another four years in competition before he could make the team for the 1952 Olympics in Helsinki.

He took a job as a public relations officer for the Cleveland Indians baseball team, where the general manager Hank Greenberg, a baseball Hall of Famer, gave him plenty of time to train. He did a lot of running indoors, and in the run-up to the 1952 Games he was allowed to disappear to the warm climate of California for special training, and the Indians even sent his pay cheques out to him. He decided not to defend his 100 metres title, feeling that at 29, and with many up-and-coming younger track stars, it would simply be too tough.

In the summer of 1952, Dillard made no mistakes in the national championships or the Olympic trials, winning the hurdles in both, but although he was the favourite to win the gold medal in Finland there was no room for complacency, as fellow American Jack Davis was beginning to run him very close. Once in Helsinki, Dillard began to look and feel sharp, equalling the Olympic record of 13.9 in the semi-finals while easing up, so he went into the final itself in very good shape.

From the start, it was a two-horse race, with big Jack Davis, who dwarfed him at 6ft 3in and 190lb, on the inside, but it was Dillard who got away quicker and led to about the sixth hurdle. 'Then I saw a big foot on my left, then a head and then the whole of Jack's body,' he recalled. 'I knew I just had to clear the last few hurdles and if I could hit the ground off the last one just ahead or even with Jack I knew I would win because I could run faster than him. Jack knew he had to be in front, so he was trying hard to get even and in doing so clipped one of the hurdles, and I hit the ground running after the last hurdle well in front and I guess I won the race by a couple of feet.' The time was a new Olympic record of 13.7.

Dillard had finally achieved his ultimate goal of winning the gold medal that he had worked so hard for all his life. Jack Davis, at 21, would live to race another day and would go on to win another silver medal in the 1956 high hurdles. Dillard's joy was completed in Helsinki with another gold medal, the fourth of his collection, in the sprint relay – this time on the second leg around the first turn. Although he continued to run and even made an unsuccessful attempt to make the US Olympic team for Melbourne in 1956, his performances in Helsinki were the peak of his athletics career and thereafter it was all downhill. When he finished sixth in the trials in 1956, just a week before his thirty-third birthday, he decided to quit and he never raced competitively again.

Jesse Owens's old coach, Larry Snyder, once said of Dillard that if he had abandoned the hurdles and concentrated on the sprints he could have been one of the all-time greats, and it is a theory that he did not dismiss. 'There's no question that I could have been a better sprinter. The fact that I won the Olympics without concentrating on it throughout my career would certainly indicate that, but I enjoyed running the hurdles, they were a distinct challenge, and when people asked me about the two events I would tell them that sprinters were a dime a dozen! I've always maintained that hurdling is one of the high arts in track and field. When you run outdoor hurdles you have ten obstacles to negotiate cleanly and clearly – that's ten opportunities you have to fail.

He was still working with the Indians after the 1956 trials, but a few years later the ownership of the club had changed hands and, struggling with financial problems, it had to make economies and Dillard was among the first people to be laid off. He moved from job to job, working full-time in radio and television and then, after a spell of selling life insurance, went back into radio work before finally, in the mid-1960s, joining the Cleveland Board of Education, in what was called a Manpower Training Programme, which helped people who had dropped out of high school and were lacking basic skills. Dillard recalled: 'I had a friend who had been looking for a job, and one day he told me he'd applied for this job but said he couldn't get it because he didn't have a college degree. He said I should apply, so almost as a lark I did. I was hired a couple of days later and stayed for good.' He stayed on that programme for five years before being promoted downtown to executive level in the city's business department within the Board. Meanwhile, he was continuing his media career with a regular chat show on Cleveland's WABQ Radio and a weekly column in the *Cleveland Press*.

The Board of Education was his career for nearly thirty years, and after successive promotions he retired in the early nineties as the Business Chief of the department, where he was responsible for the maintenance of all the city's schools and the acquisition of books and supplies, a demanding post that he took over amid apparent political controversy and one that regularly hit the headlines.

Dillard remained a popular figure in Cleveland and was often seen at track meets encouraging young athletes. Baldwin-Wallace's Ted Theodore says: 'I've seen Harrison around athletes, men and women, and he never turned his back on them. He was always ready to give them advice, to give them encouragement, to suggest ways they could improve. We're really proud of the fact that he cared about his own roots and helping others, hopefully, to aspire to the same kind of greatness.'

Although he admitted that track and field and the Olympic Games has changed, Harrison still enjoyed the sport and always said he would love to be out there running today. 'I was just born 40 years too early,' he smiled. 'Look at the money some of these guys are earning.'

Ask anyone involved in track in the USA about Dillard and the answer will always be prefaced by a smile of affection or a kindly remark or anecdote. He is held in high regard for his ability, modesty and humour by everyone who met him. Sadly he lost his wife of more than 50 years in 2009. He was introduced to Joy at an athletes' reception by track star Herb McKenley, in Jamaica, where she was a left fielder on the national softball team. He was in the middle of a 93-day State Department goodwill trip and was having a well-earned day off. She moved to the States to marry him in 1955. At the time of her death they had only just moved to the Richmond Heights area of Cleveland to share a house with their daughter Terri and three grandchildren.

He would always get a little starry-eyed when there was talk of Jesse Owens and rated him as probably the greatest sprinter of all time, although he admired Bob Hayes and admitted that he might have struggled to beat the current Olympic champion. 'I question that I could beat a Usain Bolt. The extent to which these guys train now, I really question if I could beat them. On second thought, maybe if Jesse and I trained we'd be able to take them.'

Winning the gold medals during his track career certainly had a positive effect on his life. 'There's every chance I would not be in the position I am today had I not been a gold medal winner,' he admitted candidly. 'It opened a lot of doors, but once you go in those doors you have to produce the goods. In life in general there are places I can go where I am still recognized and it's still a good feeling. But just competing in sport gave me a great deal of self-confidence and enabled me to travel and meet people and made me an all-round, better individual.'

Harrison Dillard, quietly spoken and mild-mannered, remains one of the great post-war athletes and the only man ever to win an Olympic gold in both the sprint and the high hurdles, a record that is unlikely to be matched. At one period he held no fewer than 11 records, world, Olympic or American, and his run of 82 straight wins stood for 35 years. His list of titles could fill several pages, but the most impressive include eight AAU indoor hurdles titles, seven of them in succession, and victory in nine successive years in the Millrose Games hurdles. He has been enshrined in no fewer than four national track and field halls of fame, and his achievements form the bulk of a museum at his alma mater Baldwin-Wallace College, where an impressive indoor track was recently opened and named after him.

'I think it's great just to see the photographs and the history,' said Dillard, when the museum opened. 'It makes me feel good that I'm part of it. Occasionally I'll run into somebody who will say I saw you at Baldwin-Wallace and they didn't know who I was, so that's nice.' In 2012 Dillard published a belated memoir about his life, simply entitled *Bones*. The foreword was written, without the benefit of hindsight, by his long-time friend, the television and movie star Bill Cosby. Today Cosby's name may be disgraced, after he was convicted for a number of sex offences in 2018, but some of his words about Dillard are worth a second look. 'This man, this Harrison Dillard, is an amazing man. He is an admirable character not only for his athletic accomplishments, but also for his character, showing a unique awareness of how the choices we make define ourselves. He has faced crucial and challenging decisions and issues throughout his life and never turned away, not one time.'

Identifying Dillard at Baldwin-Wallace may be a little easier today. In April 2015, a life-sized bronze statue of the Olympian, in full flight, was unveiled near the entrance to the college stadium. 'This is indeed a wonderful, wonderful day,' he told the 300-plus gathering. 'I don't know how many of you wake up sometimes and dream that you're going to be perpetuated in the form of a statue. First you have to do something, right?'

The statue was the dream of Dillard's long-time friend Ted Theodore, who said simply: 'Harrison would have been a champion even if he'd never put on a pair of track shoes. He's a champion's champion, he's proven himself both as an athlete and as a human being. He is one of the most humble, gentle human beings you can find. He's a wonderful family man, a person who dedicated himself to serving the city in which he grew up. He never made millions like today's track men, but he is a man of character and humility.'

By then, time was beginning to lean more heavily on Dillard. At 96-years-old his once fluid mobility had disappeared and old age, frailty and ill-health had taken their place. After being diagnosed with stomach cancer he died in hospital in Cleveland, Ohio, in November 2019.

The New York Times concluded its obituary report with an apposite quote from Dillard about the importance of being a role model: 'I have always felt that you present yourself in public as one to be respected and remembered, someone people can say, here is a human being and a great guy.'

Helsinki 1952

Lindy Remigino

Every Olympic Games throws up a romantic story of triumph against all the odds, but few could match the tale of a young American sprinter who came from nowhere to win the Olympic title at Helsinki in 1952.

Little Lindy Remigino was not regarded as a world-class sprinter; he was not even considered as national class; in fact, he was only rated as the third-best sprinter on his college team. However, fate decided to smile on the young New Yorker, and while one by one the strongly fancied athletes fell by the wayside, Remigino just kept on running – right into the pages of Olympic history.

The story of 'Cinderella' Lindy, had it been written as a movie script, would have been rejected as unbelievable. But being an Olympic sprint champion is much more than being the best in the world; it is also an exercise in supreme timing – first it's about qualifying, then arriving at the Games in peak fitness, and then getting it absolutely right on the only day that matters: the day of the final. This particular 100 metres final, in Helsinki, proved to be one of the closest in the Games' history and, just like the final 20 years earlier, it still remains a topic of hot debate among track fans and historians, with the silver medallist insisting to the day he died that he was not beaten. But it all could have been so different for Remigino had he not been accidentally chosen for his high school sprint team when its first-choice sprinter fell sick. Born in Queens, New York, in 1931, Remigino and his family moved a hundred miles north to Hartford, the state capital of Connecticut, when he was just six years old. His father was clearly a fan of the famous and christened his eldest son Rudolf, after Valentino, and the youngest Lindbergh, after the aviator, although both boys shortened their names – to Rudi and Lindy. Even before high school Remigino was a keen runner, chasing cars and running to school, but he was not bitten by the competitive bug until he was about 14 years old, when he entered a race at his local YMCA.

Remigino recalled: 'My brother and I went down to see what was going on and there were all kinds of events, so I entered a 40-yard dash. We had to run up and touch the far wall of the hall, turn around and come back. I won it and the guy handed me a little blue ribbon. I thought, "Hey, that's a lot of fun, I think I'll keep this up when I get to high school," and that was my introduction to track and field, and I still have that blue ribbon.'

However, when he eventually got to Hartford Public High School the coaches immediately pigeon-holed him as a quarter-miler rather than a sprinter. His first competitive run was inauspicious. He shot off his marks like a bullet and with the tape just in sight and the rest of the field some 30 metres behind, his legs turned to rubber, he fell flat on his face and vomited in front of the stands.

'That's when I found out I was a sprinter,' laughed Remigino, 'and not a quarter-miler. I was humiliated. My brother was in the stands and at first he was ready to pass out cigars, but after that he was hiding. He was so disappointed and I decided not to run any more quarters.'

A little while later, he got the opportunity to run a shorter distance when the school's senior sprinter reported sick just before a meeting and Remigino was drafted in as a late replacement. Determined never to run any longer races again, he charged down the track in the 100 yards, winning the race in 10.3, and never looked back. He went on to excel as a high school sprinter, winning the state championship in both the 100 and 220 yards in 1948 and 1949, and claiming the New England 100 yards title in the same years.

But despite a prediction in the 1949 Hartford High School yearbook that Remigino would win in the 1952 Olympics, in reality the Games seemed an impossible goal, and he was considering giving up the track altogether when, during a New England meeting, he was approached by a man who said: 'I like the way you run, we'd like you to come to Manhattan.' That man was coach George Eastment and thanks to him Remigino was able to improve his sprinting and set his sights on reaching those Games.

Although he became a member of Manhattan College's successful track team, he still did not reach the standard required for Olympic team selection, and during 1950 and the following year he did little on the track that merited newspaper ink. It was not until the beginning of the 1952 indoor season that he started to train hard, but even then his form was inconsistent and there were times when he genuinely felt like quitting.

'I was certainly my own worst enemy,' admitted Remigino, 'because whenever I got beat I took it real hard, but when I won I felt great.'

His first big win early in 1952 came at the Millrose Games, in New York's Madison Square Garden, where he won a 60-yard dash. During that indoor season he had to race with his two Manhattan team-mates John O'Connell and Joe Schatzle almost every time, and he only managed three victories, finishing up with another 60-yard win at the Knights of Columbus Games, also at Madison Square Garden. Despite Millrose Games tournament director Fred Schmertz publicly announcing to the press that he felt Remigino was going to win at the Olympics, few people felt that he was going to be a serious contender. The US press had already singled out the likely trio for Helsinki. It included Chicago's Jim Golliday, a hugely powerful 21-year-old from Northwestern University, who was the world number one in 1951 and won the Big Ten and, just a fortnight before the 1952 Olympic trials, claimed the NCAA 100- and 220-yard titles. Alongside him was the long-striding 'Handy' Andy Stanfield, from Jersey City, who was more of a 200 metre specialist and fancied his chances at the shorter distance. And there was Morgan State's Art Bragg, from

Baltimore, who had won the 1951 NCAA 100 yards title as a sophomore. And that was just the main competition in his own country. Remigino wasn't close to this impressive trio, but his coach George Eastment felt that there was more to come from his protégé and tried to boost his ego with the help of a friend on the *New York Herald Tribune*, the great track and boxing writer Jesse Abramson.

'Do you think Remigino is a great sprinter?' asked Eastment.

Abramson agreed that he was.

'Then will you please write a piece saying so? I can't make him believe it.'

The article did not immediately galvanize Remigino into action, and with only four major meetings left before the boat sailed for Helsinki, his form remained painfully erratic. At the IC4As in New York he could place only third in the 100 metres, but won the 200 metres. However, his chances improved soon afterwards when Andy Stanfield announced that because of his susceptibility to muscle pulls he was going to run only in the 200 metres in Finland.

Remigino's luck turned still further when he won a tight four-man battle for fifth spot in the NCAA final at Berkeley, which guaranteed him a place in the Olympic trials. However, a week later more disappointment followed when he performed poorly at the AAU Championships in Long Beach, California, failing to make the final of the 100 metres. The race was won by 20-year-old Texan Dean Smith, but ominously, the favourite Jim Golliday pulled up halfway through the final with a muscle problem and had just a week to get himself right for the trials.

So, in the late June heat at the Los Angeles Coliseum, it was anybody's guess who would pull out a performance and book a place on the 100 metres team. In the very first heat of the trials, Golliday catapulted off the start, then immediately jerked upright and slowly hobbled the rest of the distance. A pulled thigh muscle had ruined his Olympic dream. 'I knew I was through as soon as I left the holes,' he told reporters. 'The pain was there and I had to quit. Not a very good time to get hurt, is it?'

The final was close, with fast-starting Bill Mathis flying into an early lead and finishing within a yard of the winner. But he could still only place fifth. Art Bragg won the race, in 10.5 seconds, a clear foot in front of Remigino with AAU champion Dean Smith tied for third with the US Air Force flyer Jim Gathers. Smith would eventually get the nod for the 100 team, while Gathers would run in the 200.

Remigino had made it, but the US press remained steadfastly underwhelmed by the performances and suggested their chances of retaining the prized 'Fastest Man on Earth' title were remote. One writer even criticized Remigino's running style, commenting that he looked like a dairy farmer when he ran, with shoulders hunched together as though he was carrying two milk churns across a barnyard!

'Of course, Jimmy Golliday was the favourite in the trials. I think he was the fastest of all of us,' recalled Remigino. 'But he got injured. When I ran against him I'd be hitting the ground like a machine gun but I wasn't going anywhere. He just held on to his lead.' Golliday, according to track experts, might well have won the Olympic final by a couple of yards, but he will always be remembered as the man who might have been. Sadly, the same catastrophe befell him just before the 1956 Games, and not long afterwards he quit the track and went into the insurance business. But he always struggled with his health and in 1971 he died from pneumonia after a long illness at the age of just 39. With his berth on the boat assured, it began to dawn on Remigino that he had a real chance of winning. Golliday was out, Stanfield was only running the 200 (he broke the world record with a 20.6 in the trials) and Bragg was now only just beating him. He was not particularly afraid of the international competition, namely Jamaica's classy Herb McKenley, the 400 metres silver medallist in 1948 who was destined to repeat the feat at Helsinki but was dropping down to the 100 metres for some speed-work, and Britain's McDonald Bailey, who finished last in the 1948 final after coming back from injury, but was now the joint world record holder.

Mac Bailey had become something of a fan favourite in Britain, despite being born in the then colonial outpost of Trinidad. He grew up as the son of a strict schoolmaster in the fantastically named village of Hard Bargain, near San Fernando, and his natural speed was first spotted at school where he routinely won races against much older boys. Inspired by the feats of his hero Jesse Owens, Bailey attended the athletics-obsessed Queen's Royal College, in the capital Port of Spain, and quickly began to win sprinting titles. He spent hours poring over British and American coaching manuals in the local library, but his track career was nearly derailed when the family doctor diagnosed him with a weak heart and advised him to give up active sports. Mercifully, a second opinion proffered a different view and after a series of rigorous medical tests he was declared fit to continue.

It was toward the end of the second world war that he finally found himself in England, when he decided to sign up for the RAF and, in his own words 'do a little bit for the war effort'.

Within a few months the war was over and Bailey stayed in England to push his athletic career, with half an eye on the upcoming London Olympics. He could have run for Trinidad, but they didn't decide until late about sending a team to the Games and by then he had elected to run for his adopted home. Marred by injury, the Games were a disappointment for him, but he would go on to rack up no fewer than seven AAA 100 and 200 metre titles. In the summer of 1951, running for Great Britain against Yugoslavia, he matched Jesse Owens' world 100 metre record of 10.2 seconds at a match in Belgrade. By the time he reached Helsinki, the smooth-running Bailey was approaching 32 years of age and time was running out for him to win a major international championship. Meanwhile, Remigino was improving all the time and his confidence rocketed during a pre-Olympic training camp at Princeton, where the US coaches got him into excellent shape. 'I felt really good. After all, the Americans had dominated the event for so long and we felt confident one of us was going to win,' he said.

Remigino's belief was strengthened still further when the training workouts began in Finland and he won every starting practice, thanks to his indoor running earlier in the year. He was still out in front at 60 metres, something that delighted the crowd at the practice sessions, especially a large Italian contingent which shouted continually, 'Bravo, Remigino.' The atmosphere in Helsinki was also a huge boost to his confidence, with 21 hours of sunshine every day, enabling the athletes to have two or even three workouts if they wished.

Helsinki was a particularly friendly Games, even though the Russians had their own Olympic village away from the capitalist influences of the Western athletes. Remigino remembered: 'We had the western camp, and the Russians, the East Germans and the rest of the Eastern Bloc nations had the eastern camp. They were completely separated from us and I remember them coming into the stadium, all dressed in white, and nobody knew who they were, because we didn't know what CCCP meant, so there was a great mystique about them.

'But our shot putters Jim Fuchs and Parry O'Brien decided to pay them a visit and they went over to the eastern training camp. They weren't supposed to go, the place was covered with barbed wire and there were secret police walking around everywhere, but it didn't bother them. After all, who's going to argue with two guys who weigh 280 pounds and stand about six four? But they didn't show for a couple of hours and we started to get worried about them, when finally they came back carrying piles of souvenirs from the Soviet Union.'

Again, as happened in 1948, with the 100 metres competition due to start the following day the American sprinters were not permitted to march in the opening parade, and Remigino and his team-mate Dean Smith watched from the stands as the rain poured down on the athletes who filed into the stadium, with tears pouring down their faces.

When the parade finished, doves were released, a cannon boomed a 21-gun salute and then out of the tunnel ran a small, balding man carrying the Olympic flame. It was the legendary Finnish runner Paavo Nurmi, a nine-time gold medallist in the 1920s and holder of no fewer than 29 world records who, despite rumours that he was suffering from rheumatism, bounded youthfully into the stadium. He then passed the flame to fellow countryman, 61-year-old Hannes Kolehmainen, the winner of three gold medals in the 1912 Olympics, and he jogged to the cauldron at the top of the opposite stand and lit it. The seventy thousand-strong crowd, undaunted by the appalling conditions, cheered wildly as the spectacle unfolded. The first day of the Games was reserved for the qualifying rounds of the 100 metres, and with 72 entrants the competition took its time. 'It seemed like an endless number of heats were being run,' said Remigino. 'While waiting for your turn you're pacing up and down under the stadium because you're not allowed to go on the track. I must have run the 100 metres about fifty times, up and down, up and down that stadium – and then you're on. So I got up on the track and what a feeling that is, especially at your first Olympics, with all the people watching. We had to learn the Finnish commands, then the gun goes off like a cannon and you're flying, running much faster than you have ever run in your whole life.'

Remigino cruised through the first heat, easing up in 10.4, then took his quarter-final in the same time, still looking relaxed and comfortable, just like his closest rivals Bragg, Smith, McKenley and Bailey, who all ran well. The next day saw the semis and the final, and Remigino was hoping that he would draw Bailey in his semi because he'd beaten him in practice. But, as luck would have it, he drew the fast-finishing McKenley, and as if to preview what was to come in the final, they seemed to hit the tape together in a photo finish, with the Jamaican getting the vote over Remigino by the merest whisker.

However, the Olympic sprint still had another twist before the final. This time it was appalling luck for the American number one Art Bragg, who crashed out of the competition when he suddenly pulled up in his semi and jogged in a dejected last. Bragg had pulled a hamstring just before the Games and had hoped it would heal quickly enough to compete, but despite heavy strapping it gave way at the worst possible moment. 'I have no alibi,' he told the American reporters. It was a sad conclusion to Bragg's Olympic dreams and he retired from the sport in 1954. 'Whenever I watch the Olympic 100 metres on television I just break down in tears,' he told an interviewer many years later.

Bragg became a probation officer in Los Angeles and died in 2018, aged 87. Asked about the 1952 Games, his widow Maria told a *Baltimore Sun* reporter: 'It always brought sadness to his mind knowing he'd come so close to his chance to excel before that terrible injury. It was something he was never quite able to rise above.'

One by one the potential winners were whittled away, until there were only a quartet of athletes – Smith, Bailey, McKenley and Remigino – with a genuine shot at the gold.

'Now I knew that any of the four of us could win,' recalled Remigino, 'and it was all going to boil down to just 10 seconds in the final.' There were a few hours' break between the end of the semi-final and the start of the final, and all the athletes were asked to leave the track and return to their dressing-rooms.

'The main dressing-room was under the stadium and there were tables there, but I didn't want to get a rub-down, I just wanted to have my legs relaxed, so I laid on one of the tables and covered myself with a large white towel. So I'm laying there and trying to get my thoughts together on how to tackle the race when in pops McKenley for heaven sakes and he's got a big smile on his face.

'He says to me, "Lindy, McDonald Bailey is ready to be had, he's so doggone nervous. I just left him and he's so nervous you can forget him." So that kind of perked me up.'

The tall, smooth-running McKenley didn't remember the incident, although he agrees that Bailey did have the jitters. 'I really didn't expect to get to the final,' he said. 'I just went into the competition for the speed and I just kept going all the way to the final.'

Finally the athletes were called, returned to the track and began to warm up in preparation for the big race. Mac Bailey, the 31-year-old whom even the American press had voted the favourite, looked the most ill at ease of the whole bunch. 'When I was named favourite I became very tense and nervous,' recalled Bailey. 'Remigino, by contrast, was probably the most relaxed person there, because no one was looking for him, in the same way no one was looking for Dillard in 1948. What unnerved me was the track. The conditions were awful, it was a very heavy, sodden surface and my lane was the worst of the lot. Water was pouring off the stand roof and right onto my lane. I looked down at my running shoes and I couldn't see the spikes because of the huge cake of mud and cinders on them. The track was so bad they even poured kerosene over it and set light to it to try and dry it off.'

As the six finalists lined up at the start – the Russian Vladimir Sukharyev, McKenley, Remigino, Smith, Bailey and the Australian John Treloar – only one thought flashed through Remigino's mind and that was to get out of the blocks like a bolt of lightning. Meanwhile McKenley, the world 400 metres record holder, had been trying to convince himself throughout the competition to stay down at the start and not pop up too early.

As the gun fired, it was Lindy who sprang into the lead and just when it mattered McKenley got off to a bad start, standing straight up after just a few strides, so that by about 50 metres Remigino was way out in front. However, with about 20 metres to go, the rest of the field began to bear down on him, particularly the powerful McKenley and Mac Bailey. 'It was then I did something tactically wrong,' admitted Remigino. 'When I saw the tape coming up real fast at me I thought, "I'm gonna win this damn thing," and I stuck my chest out, but I wasn't anywhere near the tape. I'm leaning and I didn't realize how far away I really was. So instead of hitting the tape and leaning, I started slowing up because my stride is getting shorter, then everyone is coming at me and as we hit the tape I thought McKenley had got me, and I was angry because I thought I'd blown it.'

The last 10 metres of that final were among the most dramatic in Olympic sprint history, and even today there is disagreement over exactly what happened. It is true that Remigino had leaned far too early, and as he reached the tape his right shoulder and arm flicked towards the line, just as McKenley came flying past him like an express train. The photo showed that he had just beaten 'Hustling Herb' on the line by getting his shoulder there first, but the judges had to study it closely and even had a set square brought in to ensure that they made the correct decision. Some journalists felt that McKenley had won it, some thought it had been a dead heat, whereas others agreed with the judges, but even with the aid of the old black and white moving pictures it is still difficult to tell. The BBC announced stiffly that McKenley had won the race, while in Jamaica, a little less stiffly, an emotional local commentator screamed that Herb had taken the gold. In the end, the final verdict was Remigino by one inch, in 10.4, with McKenley second in the same time, Bailey third in the same time and Smith fourth, also in the same time. The distance between first and fourth was just 14 inches.

Remigino said: 'I thought Herb had won, as other people were congratulating him, so I shook his hand and said, "I think you won it." He said he thought it was close, and then I saw the photo. My name went up and I just jumped for joy. That moment has stayed with me for the rest of my life.'

The Jamaican team manager, Herb McDonald, conferred with the Olympic jury, asked to see the photo and then said that he felt it should have been a dead heat, but added that he had no intention of lodging a formal protest. The New York Times considered that McKenley had done no better than barely draw even with Lindy, whereas Peter Wilson, the doyen of British track writers, was never convinced that the gold medal had gone to the right man and always maintained that McKenley had won it by a whisker. One of the abiding memories of the Games, Wilson recalled, was of McKenley sitting in an empty stadium still studying the photograph and insisting that he had won.

'If the tables were turned, I'm sure I'd feel the same way,' said Remigino. 'But I think I won and Herb and I remained friends for years.' McKenley went on to coach the Jamaican national team, serve as president of the Jamaican AAA and create the programmes that made the country the athletic force it is today. A revered sporting figure in Jamaica, with a road named after him in Kingston, McKenley died in the capital in 2007 following heart by-pass surgery.

Mac Bailey knew it was his last shot at Olympic glory but reacted in his standard calm and low-key manner. 'Almost apologetically Remigino said to me after the dramatic photo finish, "You know, Bailey, you should have been running more often in the States, where you learn to stick your chest out in our close indoor finishes." Perhaps he was right.'

One of the first people to rush to congratulate Remigino was the giant shot putter Parry O'Brien, who had just won a gold himself, and he bounded across the infield after the result of the 100 metres was announced and grabbed him in a bear hug, lifting him off his feet. 'He took all the wind out of me and said, "Lindy, you've just won a gold medal, you don't realize what you've done, it's going to change your whole life." Lo and behold he was right because once you're a gold medallist, you're a gold medallist for ever.'

After the medal ceremony the organizers whisked him into a giant press conference, where he was positioned behind a large desk on which were placed dozens of microphones. When the conference began, Britain's Harold Abrahams stood up and began to ask a question, but he was interrupted by Red Smith of the *Herald Tribune*, who said: 'Wait a minute now, this guy's a New Yorker, I get first shot.' Remigino answered in Italian and English as all sorts of questions were thrown at him, especially about the American sprinters who did not make the final. 'Are you kiddin'?' he told one interviewer, who asked about being the world's best. 'If those guys were in I wouldn't be here.'

Eventually he managed to escape the media madhouse and returned to his room in the village to think about what he had achieved. But there was little time for relaxation – he was in the relay team, alongside his own teenage hero Harrison Dillard, Dean Smith and Andy Stanfield, so there was still practising to be done, even though it nearly ended in disaster on the day.

Dillard, who had been wishing that he had entered the 100 metres, never practised the relay at full speed – in fact, the US team rarely got together at all, such was the strength of the sprinting.

Remigino explained: 'During one practice we would all be tearing about, but Harrison would just jog up and give me the stick and I would give it to Andy. So in the final we're in with the Soviets, who didn't have any outstanding individuals, but were a pretty good team. Smith starts off and he hands to Harrison, who comes barrelling down the straight and almost whizzes straight past me. Because we haven't been practising at full speed I have no timing and he was going so fast I almost missed him. But I got the stick and got round the bend and handed to Andy Stanfield, who drew away to win by two metres. Later he tells me I wouldn't let the stick go and he had to pull it out of my hand!'

Stanfield, who led an American 1-2-3 in the 200 metres, would run again successfully in the Melbourne Olympics four years later, before joining the federal government and leading teams to combat the United States' spiralling drugs problem. He died in 1985 aged 57, after a lengthy illness at his home in Orange, New Jersey.

Lead-off relay man Dean Smith had an even more colourful post-Olympic career. After graduating from the University of Texas he played professional football for the Los Angeles Rams and the Pittsburgh Steelers before heading to Hollywood and a stellar career as a stuntman. He was a talented horseman and rodeo performer and appeared in scores of daredevil western action sequences in such movies as *Rio Bravo, The Alamo, True Grit* and countless TV shows. He also performed some of the big stunts in *The Birds, The Sting, The Towering Inferno* and *Westworld*. He remains the only Olympic gold medal winner to be enshrined in the Hollywood Stuntman's Hall of Fame and in 2013 wrote a hugely entertaining book about his extraordinary life entitled *Cowboy Stuntman – From Olympic Gold To The Silver Screen*. In it he explained how in 1959 his Olympic teammate, decathlete Bob Mathias, introduced him to John Wayne, which led to him appearing in almost every subsequent film he made. Wayne asked if Smith was up to the job and his legendary stuntman Cliff Lyons told him: 'He's faster than a turpentined cat and he can ride a horse too.'

A spry 89 years old, Smith still lives in his native Texas.

As for Britain's Mac Bailey, Helsinki was pretty much the end of the line. The following year the AAA banned him for breaching his amateur status and allowing his name to be used to sell starting blocks at the Lilywhites department store. He won the appeal and a few months later in 1953, in what turned out to be his farewell track performance, he won a final AAA sprint double at London's White City. After publishing an autobiographical coaching guide, called *If It's Speed You're After*, he again landed in trouble with the sport's governing body, so he announced his retirement and quit as a champion.

After a fine amateur career which delivered little financial reward – save for a few under-the-table payments from promoters, a room full of trophies and, on one occasion, even a toaster – he decided to cash in on his fame and speed, sensationally signing for £1,000 to play rugby league for Leigh. However, in more than six months, injuries and lack of rugby experience restricted him to just one friendly game, against rivals Wigan – although 15,000 fans turned up to see him finish the game and score a try. He worked for several years for a food wholesaler in Guyana, dabbled in journalism and television, then coached the Trinidad & Tobago team at the 1964 Olympics before opening a restaurant in Port of Spain with his wife Doris. In the late 1990s, after suffering for many years with glaucoma, he lost his eyesight, but remained bright and active until his death at home in the capital in 2013, aged 92.

As for Remigino, the Helsinki relay victory meant he could return to the States with two gold medals in his pocket. Before heading home for Hartford he ran a series of races all over Europe, and during that post-Olympic period he remained almost unbeaten, running against Smith, Bragg and Thane Baker, who was a silver medallist behind Stanfield in the 200 metres. He won every 100 metres, but McKenley got his revenge by beating him in the 200 metres. In Oslo Remigino even managed to tie the world record of 10.2, but the mark was said to have been wind-aided and was never officially ratified by the IAAF.

He finally returned to Connecticut and a huge welcome party was held in his home town, with parades, banquets, speeches and awards. He was really looking forward to seeing his fiancée, June, after his long absence, and they were married in 1953 – the same year he graduated from Manhattan. He continued his coaching career, something he had set his sights on before going to Helsinki, and joined Hartford Public High School, where he became one of the most successful track coaches in the country.

Between 1952 and the next Olympic year, he continued to run competitively and set his sights on the 200 metres in Melbourne, feeling that he would be outgunned in the 100 metres by the newcomers to the sprint scene. Shortly before the Olympic trials, he beat the reigning champion, Andy Stanfield, only to be struck down with a throat infection, so while Stanfield went off to Los Angeles to train in the warm climate before the trials began, Remigino was languishing in bed. He stayed there until just a few days before the trials, and although he felt very weak he then flew to California, where he was promptly wiped out of the competition. It was the greatest disappointment of his track career and at the age of 25 he retired from athletics.

'So I went back to my coaching career. I knew I could coach, I knew I could help youngsters and I started going to clinics to become a better coach, then before long I was giving the clinics and writing papers. I really enjoyed it.' When he retired as a coach in 1984, Lindy had stacked up no fewer than 31 state championships, coaching 10 all-Americans and presiding over 11 undefeated seasons on the track. He won the National High School Coach of the Year Award three times, and one of his closest coaching rivals, Irv Black, of the New Britain High School, said: 'We had some great rivalries, but our athletes were always friends. He had the credentials to be an Olympic coach. He had good technique for training sprinters, but a lot of Olympic champions wore it on their sleeves. Of all the guys I knew, Lindy used it less than anybody.'

Remigino retired from teaching in 1991 and the sports store he opened in the eighties – called, naturally enough, Remigino's 1st Place – closed a few years later. He continued to be involved in many of the US Olympic initiatives, attending Games and even working on New York's abortive 2012 bid. In 2002 he carried the flag for the American delegation at the fiftieth anniversary of the 1952 Olympics, in Helsinki. 'The Olympic 100 metres is a marquee event,' he said on his 80th birthday, 'and I'm very proud of what I was able to achieve and to say that my story is part of its wonderful history.'

In 2010, Hartford Public High School changed the names of its annual indoor and outdoor track meets to the Lindy Remigino Invitational, in recognition of the long-standing contribution he had made as a coach. In the same year, he met Usain Bolt at an event in Connecticut. 'He was a very nice, impressive guy. A good foot taller than me too. He could give Carl Lewis in his prime a head start and still beat him. Just amazing.'

Winning the gold medal certainly opened a lot of doors for Remigino and he admitted that getting his first teaching job might not have been so easy had it not been for his Olympic success. He took full advantage of the opportunity and paid the investment back in full. Many people dismissed him as a lucky winner, but that is far too much of a simplification. It takes more than luck to win an Olympic title, and although some of the big names were missing, that was hardly his fault. It is all part of the Olympics – getting there is the first part of the race, while winning a gold medal comes later.

Frank Litsky, of *The New York Times*, probably put it best when he said: 'It's true that Lindy was the third-best sprinter on the Manhattan College team. In his defence it was a very good team, but he wasn't the greatest sprinter. It was a time when many sprinters were eliminated for one reason or another and he survived. People say he wasn't the greatest, maybe not, but he's an Olympic champion and there's no asterisk in the record book that says, "Not as good as he should be." He was there when he had to be there and while he never really won anything huge again, he won the gold medal at the Olympics.'

The city of Hartford mourned when Remigino died in July 2018, aged 87, after a long fight with pancreatic cancer. Tributes from coaches all over the state poured in. 'In the 1980s I took my teams to his Hartford Invitationals. He was always very gracious. A great guy,' said one. 'All the things he did as a coach and in the Olympics, he left a tremendous legacy,' said another. 'He could reach kids and when he saw someone had great natural talent he could produce it. He was Mr Track. He really was.' While another added: 'He was the standard. Everyone was hoping they could do what he was doing. His teams were always that good. He was a gentleman, a class act. He set the example for everyone. What being an athlete, a person, a coach, was all about.'

A smart, proud family man with a great sense of humour, Remigino left behind June, his beloved wife of 65 years, five children – a son and four daughters – ten grandchildren and five great grandchildren. Yet despite the Olympic memories, it's probably his outstanding coaching career and the hundreds of young athletes he inspired that may prove the more lasting legacy.

Melbourne 1956

Bobby Morrow

Lindy Remigino's scepticism about successfully defending his title at the 1956 Olympics was well founded. In the years that followed Helsinki, three new young stars exploded on to the American track scene all hoping to write their own names into the history books – they were Chicago's diminutive but fast-starting Ira Murchison, Duke University's giant teenager Dave Sime and the smooth-running Texan Bobby Morrow.

But America's embarrassment of sprinting riches didn't end there. In addition to this talented trio there was the promising Leamon King, who twice equalled the world 100 metres record a month before the Games, plus the 1952 Olympic 200 metres champion Andy Stanfield and runner-up Thane Baker returning to do battle again. So even making the US Olympic team for Melbourne in 1956 was going to be an uphill struggle for all the top sprinters.

But one man did rise above the pack and go on to dominate the Games in Australia and that was the tall, handsome figure of Bobby Morrow, the quintessential all-American boy, who was rated by many as the most relaxed sprinter of all time, possibly even more so than his hero Jesse Owens.

But Morrow would go on to discover that winning a haul of Olympic gold medals had a downside as well as an upside, and he was never sure whether they were a blessing or a curse.

It is possible that his sheltered upbringing was inextricably linked to what happened to him after his Olympic success, closeted, as he was, in a strict and devoutly Christian family, growing up on a remote cotton farm in San Benito, way down in the lower Rio Grande Valley.

For Morrow the home atmosphere was one of discipline and regular trips to church, three times a week and twice on Sundays, and he never tasted a beer until after he left high school. Such a puritanical upbringing hardly equipped him to deal with the enormous pressures that would be placed on him in the wake of his Olympic triumph, and Morrow, the man some writers liked to call America's 'Mr Clean', would have his name dragged through the mud by unscrupulous people who sought to exploit his success on the track.

But, as he often pointed out, were it not for his God-given speed he probably would never have attended college and would have remained in San Benito working quietly on the farm.

Bobby Joe Morrow, as he was christened, was born in Harlingen, Texas, in October 1935, but he did not realize his natural ability for sprinting until junior high, when he was already 16. The coach at San Benito High School, Jake Watson, spotted his potential and set to work to fulfil it. Watson was an uncommon talent, a high school coach who actually knew something about track, and Morrow was always keen to acknowledge the debt he owed him. Watson set him on the road toward the Olympic Games, though they were far from his thoughts at the time, and began to teach him the rudiments of relaxation as a key to top-class sprinting – something that he would later perfect at college.

Morrow had not considered going to college – his plan on leaving high school was to marry his childhood sweetheart, Jo-Ann, and return to the farm, but Watson convinced him that he could be a great sprinter and persuaded him to sign up for summer school to build up enough credits to get to college. By this stage, he had already excelled on the track as a high school athlete, with a schoolboy record of 9.6 in the 100 yards, so there was no shortage of offers when the time came to leave San Benito High.

One came from Lamar Hunt, the owner of the Dallas Texans football club, who had seen Morrow excel as a tailback for his school team and wanted him to try out as a pro. However, in those days the money in football was nothing compared to the sums that players can earn today and Morrow decided against it, preferring to travel around the country on the free trips he was being offered by some of the top colleges who were keen to sign him up.

In the end, he opted for Abilene Christian College, a Church of Christ school, the conservative organization to which he and his family belonged, and the school his older brother attended. But there were other reasons for choosing Abilene. Morrow liked the smallness of the school – with only two thousand students, compared to forty thousand at the big colleges – and as a shy, farm boy he felt happier in the more modest surroundings at Abilene.

Most important of all, he knew the pedigree the school had in track, where despite its size it had won a pile of national titles and boasted one of the best sprint relay teams in the country.

Now married to Jo-Ann, Morrow settled straight into the Abilene track team. In his first outings for the college, as a freshman in 1955, he began to run some impressive times, culminating in June with an astonishing run in Abilene, at a cold and rainy NAIA meet, where he tore down the track to register a 9.1 for 100 yards, which was two-tenths of a second better than Mel Patton's world record. Unfortunately for Morrow, the win was wind-assisted so the record did not stand, but the run convinced him that he could make it to the very top – the Olympic Games.

The man responsible for his improvement was the Abilene coach Oliver Jackson, who honed Morrow's natural speed, polished his technique and taught him how to relax and run. Relaxation was the key to his form, and the fluidity that Jackson managed to build into his running was something to behold. One writer described Morrow's style quite succinctly: 'He doesn't appear especially to pull, push or drive as he runs. He's never struggling. He just runs. He's like a wheel rolling down the track.'

A test used by Morrow to ensure that he was running properly was to waggle his jaw muscles as he ran, especially coming off the curve in a 200-metre race, where lots of athletes tended to tighten. Films of his races show this technique, with an action that looks as if he is running in his sleep.

Early in 1956, Abilene had the best sprint quartet in the United States, with Morrow, Bill Woodhouse, James Segrest and Waymond Griggs, and in the two years that followed they would break or equal world records a staggering 11 times. Training was quite advanced for its time, with Jackson supervising weight-training, almost unheard of in those days, and insisting that Morrow ran throughout the year, although it was mostly cross-country during the off-season and then running bare-foot on grass before moving on to the track. Of course he was barred from playing football at college because Jackson feared that he might get injured, and the coach also stopped him long jumping, an event in which Morrow had shown great promise at high school.

'Most of my work was done barefoot on the grass,' recalled Morrow. 'In fact, I hardly got on the track before the season began and then only to get conditioning for the 200 metres. We always concentrated on relaxation. We trained so your cheeks would bounce up and down when you ran, making sure your arms were relaxed and we worked on that every day of the week. I worked on starting a lot because I never tried to roll with the gun, like a lot of other sprinters, so consequently I was usually behind at the start and had to make up a lot of ground. I was never a great starter.'

One of Jackson's chief ploys to ensure that Morrow would never tighten up, even if he was a long way behind the rest of the field, was to have a training colleague start about 10 yards in front of him in a 220-yard run, and tell Morrow to catch up without tensing while keeping his jaw muscles bouncing. All this training paid off when the Olympic year finally arrived, and after a short tour of Australia, which proved invaluable experience, he tore into the opposition around the United States.

At the same time, newcomer Dave Sime was hitting the headlines with a series of spectacular indoor wins, and the two finally met at the Drake Relays in Iowa, in April, where during a torrential downpour the 19-year-old leaped out of the blocks to beat Morrow by a yard. It was his first defeat over 100 yards for three years and it would be his last defeat of the season in major competition. There are those who maintain that Sime would have presented Morrow with a tougher challenge at the Olympics than the athletes who eventually competed in the final, but Dave Sime never made it to Melbourne. Shortly after his victory over Morrow he was thrown by a horse and injured his groin muscle. The following week he ran in California and smashed the world 220 yards record in 20.0, but in doing so aggravated the injury, leading to complications that dogged him throughout the season. When he and Morrow met again at the NCAA championships in Berkeley, California, in June, Sime could only manage a third place, blaming the injury, while Morrow cantered home by two yards.

Despite these victories, many sportswriters still did not rate his chances of making the team, especially with the line-up of sprinting talent in the US all vying for places, but Morrow shocked them all by winning the AAU 100 metres and followed that with a sprint double in the Olympic trials, at the Los Angeles Coliseum.

The trials, held in late June, saw Morrow, US Air Force Lieutenant Thane Baker and the pint-sized US Army Private Murchison – nicknamed 'The Human Sputnik' – selected in the 100 metres, and Morrow, Stanfield and Baker in the 200 metres, with the University of California's Leamon King as the odd man out who travelled as part of the relay team.

The unlucky Dave Sime lasted four strides into his first 100 metres heat before collapsing onto the track and crawling onto the in-field with a recurrence of his old muscle injury. He would miss the Olympics.

The Games were not held until November of 1956, the end of Australian springtime, so there were another four months in which to both prepare and stay healthy. During that time the Americans led a wholesale assault on the sprint records, with the once more fit Dave Sime twice equalling the 100–yard mark and Leamon King matching it once. In the 100 metres, Morrow three times equalled the world record of 10.2 seconds and his teammate Murchison equalled it twice.

Then there was Private Willie Williams, a slightly-built GI stationed with a US Army tank division at Fort Knox. He had missed the Olympic team in 1952, finishing sixth in the trials, but in the following years he became the man to beat. He topped the 100 metre world rankings in 1953, won two consecutive NCAA championships and nine Big Ten sprint titles, and in 1956 he was running into some fine form. However, in the Olympic trials disaster struck. He had cruised through the semi-final heat – albeit trailing Morrow's world-record equalling 10.2 seconds – but in the final, in front of 42,000 fans, he suffered cramp and crashed over the finish line dead last, his Olympic dream over.

Nonetheless, he would still take his place in the history books.

Five weeks later, in the heats of the International Military Sport Council Championships in Berlin, the 24-year-old Williams became the first man to run the 100 metres in 10.1 seconds. In the process, he broke his hero Jesse Owens' twenty-year-old world record, which had been set in the very same Olympic stadium. In fact, Williams achieved this feat on the exact same cinder track and in the very same lane that Owens had run in 20 years earlier. The following day his Army buddy Ira Murchison equalled the mark in the semi-finals and the day after that, below an overcast sky and with a light, but legal, wind at his back, the fast-starting Williams beat Murchison by barely a foot in the final, with another 10.1. After the race Williams told reporters he'd been suffering from stomach problems, hadn't trained and nearly withdrew from the event. After an Army hospital check-up in Nurnberg he felt better and explained: 'It's unbelievable. I am really surprised, but I always had it in the back of my mind to break the world record. Today I felt relaxed all the way. I started fast and then I just kept picking up speed. But I don't think there is any chance of me becoming a member of the Olympic team. Such matters are decided at the trials. I missed the boat and this was my Olympics.'

In his 2013 book *Sprinting Through Life*, Williams recalled being captivated by Owens speaking at his high school in 1948. As he walked into the stadium eight years later an official pointed out a plaque to the great man. 'It was then that an indescribable feeling overcame me that brought tears to my eyes,' he wrote. 'It was a combination of my awareness of how Hitler had reacted to Jesse Owens winning four gold medals in this stadium and a deep internal feeling that shouted: "I am here at this moment in time to do something outstanding".'

Williams was a hugely popular athlete and as the first man to hit 10.1 seconds his name would forever be in the roll call of 100 metres record holders – but he still wouldn't be going to Melbourne. Strangely, his book doesn't make any mention of what must have been a crushing disappointment.

A year after his world record, Williams left the Army and began a hugely successful coaching career – at both high school and college level – retiring as associate head coach at his alma mater, the University of Illinois, in 2000. He died in his native Gary, Indiana, in 2019, aged 87.

Back in the run-up to Melbourne, records continued to tumble. During October Leamon King hit form and twice equalled the new 10.1-second record in California – on both occasions beating Morrow and Murchison. Meanwhile, in the 200 metres, Morrow had equalled the 20.6 world record twice, so it was still anybody's guess which of the American stars would hit form on the day and take the top prize.

Morrow's surprising defeats had come during a specially selected series of pre-Olympic tests, but it was reported widely that he was suffering from a debilitating virus infection, which caused weight loss and a general loss of sparkle. But by the time he left for Australia, he was well on the road to recovery.

The journey, undertaken a fortnight before the Games were due to start, was a tortuous one. 'Back in '56 we had no jets,' recalled Morrow, 'so we travelled by a prop-driven Pan-Am Clipper. The team was broken up and I was travelling with the lady swimmers, which was a great experience for me, but it was a long trip, about 48 hours' flying time, and it was horrendous sitting there all that time with no sleep. We all tried to find somewhere to lie down and my feet swelled up and I couldn't get my shoes on. We made three stops, at Honolulu, Fiji and Canton, but we were glad to get off when we finally arrived.'

Despite the political turmoil around the world, Melbourne was a happy place for the Olympics. There was still fighting between Hungary and the Soviet Union, while the Suez crisis continued to bubble, so it was no surprise that there were suggestions that the Games should be scrapped and a number of countries chose to boycott them in the belief that turbulent world events prevented them being staged in the right spirit. But the charm and efficiency of the Australian organizers and the amazing enthusiasm of the fans meant that the Olympics not only went ahead but proved a tremendous success, with 120,000 enthusiasts packing the main stadium, the Melbourne Cricket Ground, during every day of competition.

Morrow realized immediately that Melbourne was a sports-minded city when he saw the kids heading for the tennis courts instead of church on a Sunday morning. 'I loved Australia,' he said. 'I loved the people there, they packed the stadium and there were thousands of people outside who couldn't get in. It was a warm experience, especially visiting the various athletes from all over the world and to be able to talk to them and learn their training methods. Of course we were particularly interested in talking to the Russian athletes and they were keen to talk to us, so we'd sit down and find out about each other's training, eating and preparation.'

For the first time at the Olympics, the Soviet Union team took its place in the main village, at Heidelberg, where the Australian Government had built houses, each accommodating four athletes during the Games. The US team had all their supplies flown in, even their water, and the village cafeteria was open 24 hours a day and became a popular meeting-place for the athletes.

Morrow said: 'I was just in a fantasy land being one of the youngest members of the Olympic team – just 21 – and being able to meet and talk to all the athletes from around the world. Sport was the international language and everyone understood. If we could keep politics out of it, what a better place it would be.'

The 100 metres competition was, as always, the first major track event, and so Morrow missed the opening parade, and watched on TV from the village. Apart from the American team there were few top-class sprinters to worry about, although the 25-year-old Australian Hec Hogan, a refrigeration engineer and the darling of the crowd, had equalled the world record for 100 yards two years earlier on a grass track in Sydney, and could not be completely discounted.

Abilene Christian had sent Oliver Jackson to Melbourne to help out and to ensure that Morrow was in the right frame of mind, and they worked together on the relaxation exercises and went through his normal workouts, but in addition he and the three other American 100-metre contenders worked daily on baton passing for the relay, sometimes three times each day.

When the 100 metres competition finally opened, under blue skies and bright sunshine, Morrow and Murchison took complete control of the early rounds, both equalling the 10.3 Olympic record without looking unduly troubled. Disaster almost struck in the quarter-final when Morrow strained a groin muscle, but the team managers worked tirelessly to ensure that he would be fit for the next heat, using heat lamps, whirlpool baths and finally strapping it tightly to prevent the injury from worsening.

He did not suffer any after-effects, and although the press almost wrote him off because of the injury it didn't seem to worry him unduly. After the semi-finals, in which the 6ft 2in Morrow and 5ft 4½in Murchison both took first place, again equalling the Olympic record, the two Americans were made firm pre-final favourites.

The Australian starter came over to the US camp to join in the training, as he did with the other countries' teams, so that the sprinters would be accustomed to his technique, but Morrow did not pay much attention because he knew that he would be the last one out of the blocks and would then have to make up lost ground.

The six finalists included the three US stars, Morrow, Murchison and Baker, augmented by Hogan, the 21-year-old German Manfred Germar and British Empire Games champion Michael Agostini from Trinidad. As they settled into their blocks the wind gauge told them that there would be no world records, with a 9mph wind blowing straight into their faces. At the gun it was Hogan who leaped into an early lead but, by his modest standards, Morrow had not got a bad start and caught him at about the halfway mark, switching into overdrive and pulling away to win easily by five feet, in 10.5 seconds, with Thane Baker lunging past Hogan on the line to take the silver. The Australian took the bronze, while a disappointed Murchison finished fourth. 'I just couldn't believe it,' recalled Morrow, 'and I wondered to myself after I hit the tape, "What am I doing here?" It was a very big surprise to me, and all the sportswriters said, "Well, he's won the 100, but he can't win the 200."'

Standing at the top of the medal rostrum was one of the best moments of his life. 'It's the greatest experience an athlete will ever have. The American flag is raised on the centre pole and they play the anthem. There's dead silence in a crowd of 120,000 people and you could literally hear a pin drop. Chills ran up and down my spine as they gave me the medal and I'll never forget it as long as I live.'

The cynics among the American press corps predicted that Morrow would have tougher competition in the 200 metres, especially with reigning champion Stanfield, but they also thought that he would not last the pace of four rounds with his muscle problems. However, Morrow insisted: 'I felt confident, much happier than I did in the 100, because I liked to run the curve and I felt very comfortable.' Despite the bandaging wrapped around his left thigh he breezed through the heats and lined up with his old adversary Thane Baker, as well as Stanfield. Baker was given the unfortunate draw of the outside lane, while Morrow was in the middle. It was particularly galling for Baker because he had been allotted the same lane in the 1952 final. In Melbourne it made him so nervous that he put down his starting blocks pointing in the wrong direction and the race had to be delayed, the error pointed out and the blocks switched around.

But it was Morrow's race all the way. He powered past everyone on the curve, jaw muscles waggling in familiar style, and tore down the home straight to win by a yard and a half over Stanfield, with Baker overcoming his nerves to finish third. Morrow's victory made him the first double gold winner of the Games, and his time of 20.6 beat the old Olympic record set in Berlin by Jesse Owens, who was watching up in the stands and was among the first to congratulate the big Texan.

It was not the only record that Bobby would take from Owens. As everyone expected, the relay team, comprising arguably the four best sprinters in the world, had little trouble in winning the gold medal, with a particularly fast start from Murchison and efficient handovers to King, Baker and finally Morrow who galloped down the track. He broke the tape in 39.5, three-tenths of a second better than the world record set by the Owens quartet in 1936.

Murchison left the Army and went on to become a successful high school and college track coach in Chicago, before succumbing to bone cancer in 1994. Baker retired as a colonel from the US Air Force in 1983, worked research and development for Mobil oil and is closing in on his 90th birthday, while King returned to California where he became a school teacher. He died in 2001.

The saddest story was Australia's home-grown hero, bronze medallist Hec Hogan. Before the Games he had complained of unexplained tiredness and after a lacklustre showing at the 1958 British Empire and Commonwealth Games in Wales, he returned home to run a family-owned hotel in Queensland and was persuaded to go for a medical check-up. His health deteriorated rapidly and he was eventually diagnosed with leukaemia and died in September 1960 – just a day after the Olympic 100 metres final in Rome. As for Morrow, he became the first man to win three track and field gold medals at a single Olympics since Owens, and was instantly hailed as one of the star attractions of Melbourne and one of the main targets for the photo and autograph hunters.

He always shunned publicity, because he was a quiet and shy young man who felt distinctly uncomfortable in the role of the conquering hero. Throughout his life he insisted that he never read a newspaper or magazine article about himself, and although he was always helpful and responsive to most requests for interviews over the years, Morrow still tried to avoid publicity whenever he could. In Melbourne this took an unusual form when he and his close friend Glenn Davis, the hurdler, devised a foolproof scheme to escape the hordes of autograph hunters who stood guard outside the only entrance and exit to the village. 'There were so many people outside it was impossible to get anywhere, so when Glenn and I decided to go to a movie or ride downtown we came up with this scheme. We went to the training room and had the trainers wrap our hands with tape, so when we walked out of the gate our hands were all bandaged up and nobody bothered us.'

Morrow's reception in Australia was nothing compared to the one awaiting him when he returned home to Texas. In Abilene the entire college turned out at the airport as he flew in on a private plane from California, with a huge crowd of local banner-waving fans eager to catch a glimpse of their new star. His success in Melbourne saw his name written across banner headlines all over the United States and established Abilene Christian firmly on the map.

As Morrow was paraded through the streets, given the key to the city and attended banquets in his honour, little did he know of the traumas that would soon follow.

On the day he returned home, a local sports reporter wrote: 'If Abilene loved Bobby Morrow in October when it sent him around the world to compete against the best the world had to offer, it threw itself in admiration at his feet in December when he returned triumphant over all.' Morrow began to travel on the lecture circuit where his abilities as a public speaker kept him in high demand, talking to a variety of church, business and educational groups around the country. He was a good speaker, even an inspirational one, in the Jesse Owens tradition, but then he was a speech major at college and had preached to congregations in church and taught bible classes, so he had plenty of opportunity to improve his technique. His public speaking drew big crowds wherever he went, even winning a standing ovation at the state legislature, where he told the assembly: 'I sincerely believe that my greatest race, the Christian race, is the most important of them all and is yet to be won.'

In the months that followed his almost messianic return home he was in such demand that Abilene Christian assigned him a permanent public relations man, Bob Hunter, who toured with Morrow all over the United States, arranging his flights, booking hotels, paying bills and even writing the speeches. 'He did everything in the world for me,' explained Morrow. 'All I had to do was show up and be there. But it was real hard for an athlete that young to have all these things taken care of and even more difficult when you get out of that situation to then go out and do things on your own. It was very, very difficult for me.'

Morrow's epic tours were also placing a strain on his marriage to Jo-Ann and their young twins Ron Floyd and Vicki Jo. 'Because I was gone so long it put pressure on the family. I was away so much I couldn't keep up with my studies, so I laid out a semester because I was in South America, then in the Caribbean for the State Department and it was very hard to have a family life. It put a strain on everybody, not only on your wife, but the kids and yourself.'

Bobby Morrow had become the living embodiment of his country and all the things that made America great: God, clean living, family life and athletic success – he really was just too good to be true. His photo appeared on the covers of *Life*, *Sport* and *Sports Illustrated*, and politicians were eager to be photographed with him; he even appeared on the top-rated Ed Sullivan and Arthur Godfrey TV shows. A cascade of awards began to rain down on him, including the Sullivan Award, as the year's most outstanding amateur athlete. Similar awards came from *Sport* and *Sports Illustrated*, where he beat the top baseball and football players to be crowned America's number one sportsman. Early the following year, he was summoned to the White House for a conference with President Eisenhower, and the US Chamber of Commerce honoured him as one of the nine Great Living Americans.

Morrow was not allowed to remain as just the fastest man on earth, he was promoted as an example to everyone in the country, which put enormous pressure on him as he tried desperately to live up to his new reputation – a task that eventually proved as impossible as it sounded. Morrow continued to compete throughout 1957, tying the 9.3-second world 100 yards record at the NCAA championships, in Austin in June, and putting together a series of impressive relay times, including four world records with the fast quartet from Abilene Christian. Between races he continued his speaking engagements and even made a movie. 'I took acting lessons and I had a coach,' recalled Morrow, who personified the athletic, handsome, homeboy image that was admired in the mid-1950s. 'But I had to be up every morning at 6.30 for make-up, having already learned my lines the night before. It was an experience and I enjoyed it, but I didn't want to do it again.'

He played a high school coach trying to avoid the persistent attentions of a gorgeous student, but the movie was not a success at the box office and, much to his relief, Morrow's movie career stopped right there and then.

The following year, he graduated from Abilene and went to work as a vice-president at the Abilene Bank of Commerce, which allowed him time off to train and compete in major meets. His form was inconsistent and although he was beaten by his relay partner Bill Woodhouse and the improving Dave Sime, Morrow had already set his sights on defending his title in Rome in 1960. But he found training without the unequivocal support of the college very difficult, even though the bank was always sympathetic. 'I had a hard time when I got out of college,' he explained, 'because when I was in school I worked out with my team-mates and I had a coach who would tell me what to do. He'd tell me I had to run repeat 200s or 300s and of course I'd do it, because if I didn't I wouldn't be on the team and my scholarship would be cut. But when you're on your own it's hard to go out there and work out on your own.'

To counter this problem Morrow got permission to continue training with the college and with Jackson, although he still missed the motivation of running for the team. The 1959 season was similarly inconsistent and it was then, before Olympic year itself, that the curtain was finally, and painfully, brought down on his career, when he travelled to Houston for the Meet of Champions, and suffered a severe muscle spasm during the final of the 100 metres and crashed to the track.

A large knot appeared on his thigh muscle and as the trainers worked feverishly to try and push the injured muscle back into shape, photographers gathered around to take shots of the Olympic champion lying in agony on the track, his face contorted in pain. But the efforts of the trainers were to no avail and his leg was never the same again. For the rest of his life he would be unable to stretch it out properly. But it was not just the injury that put an end to his running career at the highest level. At that time, Morrow was on the verge of getting his pilot's licence, but he was still technically a learner and was accompanied by a qualified pilot when he flew down to Houston for the meeting. Naturally, he was not able to pilot the plane on the homeward-bound flight, so his 'minder' had to do the job for him. 'It was a very cloudy and overcast day,' remembered Morrow, 'and my wife and her brother were in the back of the plane as we took off and climbed up. I was on the radio trying to give Houston our flight plan when I looked over at the instrument panel and saw that the artificial horizon, which tells you how the plane is flying, was vertical. I told him and when he saw it he just went crazy, he grabbed the wheel to his chest and started screaming and hollering. I finally managed to pull the wheel away from him and pushed it down so we'd pick up our air speed and as we broke out of the clouds there was just enough time to see the ground and straighten out. We had flipped and stalled and if the clouds had been any lower we would have crashed straight into the ground. I had to fly on to Abilene and when we landed he got out of the plane, tore up his licence and vowed never to set foot in a plane again. It turned out he wasn't an instrument-rated pilot, we'd popped some rivets in the tail and he couldn't fly it. We were very close to being killed.'

The shock of escaping death so narrowly in the plane had a lasting effect on Morrow and after the incident he found it increasingly difficult to relax, which was the whole essence of his running. Willing to try anything, he accepted Jackson's offer of hypnosis in an effort to relax. 'I went to a doctor in Abilene and he did help me to relax and he told me that if he had enough time he could teach me to go into a hypnotic trance at the sound of the gun and come out of it when I hit the tape. We didn't have time to work on self-hypnosis, but he travelled with me to the big track meets, stayed in the same hotel and before each race he'd hypnotize me to relax.' Morrow was convinced that he had only touched the surface of his problem with the technique, which he likened to a form of deep concentration, and felt that today's athletes would do better trying to relax rather than dabbling in drugs.In the AAU championships, a route to the final Olympic trials, he strained a muscle during the warm-up and failed to qualify for the 100 metres, but he just managed to scrape a fourth place in the 200 metres, which meant he qualified to run at the Olympic trials. By that time the injury had healed, and although the break in his training was to prove critical, there were those who still felt that he would be good enough to make the team for the second time around.

Ultimately, he came in fourth in the 200 metres trials, just missing the team, but the US coaches and officials were keen for him to continue training with them and invited him out to the Olympic camp in California. So he gave up his job in Abilene to spend five weeks there in the hope that his performances would improve and he would be selected as a reserve. His form began to improve and in the pre-Olympic meets he started beating the athletes who had finished ahead of him in the trials. On the last day of the training programme, on the eve of the team's departure for Rome, Morrow asked the officials if he would be going. They told him that the decision would be made at a meeting that night. 'Finally they said I should meet them at the airport in the morning and they'd tell me then if I was going or not. I asked if that meant I had to pack for the Games or pack to go home, but they said they didn't know. So I packed for the Games and turned up at the airport all ready to get on the plane, and they said, "No, you're not going." So I turned around and came home.'

The decision and the manner in which it was executed devastated Morrow, and he admitted that it was a constant thorn in his side. He explained that there could have been two factors behind such shabby treatment of a reigning champion.

The first was, perhaps, an understandable fear on the part of some of the eastern coaches, who did not want Morrow to be vying for places with their own athletes, but the second was far more sinister. Shortly after the Melbourne Games, Morrow had spoken out about the misuse of money during the Games by the American officials and had met the attorney general in Washington to talk about the American Olympic Committee and a possible investigation of the AAU. A committee of inquiry held hearings on the AAU and Morrow testified with several other athletes, but nothing was ever followed up and the investigation fizzled out.

Morrow had been upset by the freeloaders who had flown in with the athletes to Melbourne and remembered clearly one official whose job it was to hand out the soap – and his wife went with him too. 'The Olympic team is supported through public donations,' he said. 'It's not government sponsored. But it's so political that all the AOC and AAU officials, their friends and relatives came along and jobs were found for them.' One of Morrow's biggest opponents during the investigation was a man whose name has appeared with unerring regularity throughout Olympic history, and that was AOC President and Olympic 'Godfather' Avery Brundage. Morrow and Brundage had crossed swords before over the issue of expenses for athletes, something that the AOC chief vehemently opposed, and Morrow felt there may have been an element of revenge in the way he was left out of the 1960 team at the eleventh hour. As it turned out, the Americans put up a poor showing, by their standards, in the sprints and relay and might well have benefited from Morrow's experience, but it was something the AOC would never have admitted.

After such a dramatic turn of events at the airport in 1960, Morrow decided to retire from the track and never ran competitively again. Despite failing to make the Olympic team he was still a popular figure in Texas, especially in Abilene, and it was at this time that he began to experience the attentions of commercial vultures, who were quick to descend on a man they perceived as an easy marketing ride because of his clean-cut image and good name.

Morrow and his family were still living in Abilene, but he decided to leave the bank for a short time and formed a company to market a pill called Stim-o-Stam, which he had used during his college days. It contained a mineral that helped relieve muscle soreness and fatigue, and was widely used in athletics at the time and even by hunters on long trips into the mountains. He employed a local man as sales manager and they set to work selling stock around the country to raise money to form the company. Many of the investors were friends from Abilene and the Texas area, some of whom were involved in the church and the college.

But it soon became clear that the business was not running properly and it transpired that his partner had been using Morrow's name to sell stock to his friends and pocketing the money. The partner was arrested, but all the money had been spent and Morrow's friends were not repaid when the marketing company collapsed.

'They were mad at me because everything had been done in my name,' said Morrow. 'But I really had no idea what he was doing. It hurt my image, especially in Abilene, and I had to have my phone disconnected because of all the strange phone calls I was getting. I was just one of many athletes who were being taken advantage of. People want to use your name and your notoriety for their own gain. Of course today athletes have agents and that's a good thing. That would have helped me a lot.'

The Stim-o-Stam affair was not the last occasion on which he got his fingers burned by an unscrupulous operator. A few years later he suffered another blow to his all-American image when he got involved with a man described by the locals as one of the state's most famous criminals, a man called Billy Sol Estes, who went to prison for fraud and conspiracy and wildly claimed to have aided and abetted President Lyndon Johnson in everything from fraud and conspiracy to the death of a US government official and even that of JFK.

Morrow had made a few speeches for Sol Estes before he fell foul of the law. He had been charged with selling mortgages for cotton allotments that did not exist, but was out of prison on a bond awaiting his trial when he telephoned Morrow one night in Abilene, persuading him to come out for supper. Morrow tried to refuse, but Sol Estes insisted, and during the meeting that followed he excused himself saying that he had to make a phone call. He returned a few minutes later and soon the place was crowded with reporters and cameras, wanting to know what was happening. It was an embarrassing scene, with Morrow trying to hide his face behind his hands and repeating 'No comment' over and over again. The whole sorry episode appeared on the front page of the *Abilene Reporter-News* the following morning.

'I think he did it primarily to get publicity for himself,' said Morrow, 'and to get public sympathy on his side. Of course that really hurt me being seen with him at a restaurant, and I had people calling me all hours of the night and eventually I had to have my phone disconnected again because of the animosity it caused. I definitely think Billy Sol did it on purpose to help himself.'

Sol Estes ended up in prison and the whole fiasco put additional strain on Bobby's marriage and Jo-Ann went on record as saying: 'Nobody can stay on a pedestal and he fell pretty fast. It was really hard on him and our marriage, too. Neither one of us was very communicative. He came through the Stim-o-Stam deal pretty well, but he was disappointed in people because they were disappointed in him. But the blow he couldn't take was when he tried to go to the '60 Olympics. They strung him along and used him to help other sprinters train. When they didn't take him after that, it was a hard blow. That was a kind of turning point. He felt used and got down on himself and then he got down on everyone else. He got more cynical and chose some friends that he would never have chosen before.'

The strain finally proved too much and Bobby and Jo-Ann were divorced in 1968, which estranged him from his twins for nearly 20 years.

Morrow worked for a couple of banks and, while in Houston, became involved in some promotion and coaching work with the Houston Striders athletic club, where he helped future Olympic champion and world record holder Jim Hines, especially on his starting, which seemed ironic as that was the weakest part of Morrow's racing make-up. He was delighted when Hines won in Mexico in 1968 but never felt like taking up coaching on a permanent basis.

On leaving Texas he got involved in a children's education programme in Ohio, where he met his second wife, Judy, who already had two children. Together they also had a daughter of their own. In the early 1970s, Bobby returned to his roots to run the family farm when his father underwent back surgery. When the economic realities of the farming business caught up with him, he switched from farmer to store owner, opening a clothes store in the city of Harlingen, followed by a pool and leisure centre, but he did not persevere with either and decided to move to Austin, the state capital, where he ran an insurance business from home.

Eventually the lure of the old family cotton and carrot farm proved too great and he moved back to San Benito, an area where he was always regarded as something of a legend. In 2006 they even named the new high school stadium after him.

One noticeable change in Morrow's life was the reduced influence of the church. He no longer attended church regularly and explained: 'I think because I was brought up in a strict, religious family, it's probably a rebellion on my part. I'm still a religious person, I just don't go to church and participate in church activities.'

He was always interested in speed – running fast, cars, planes and boats. He had a pilot's licence and a ski boat and admitted that speed was a lifelong passion. He last ran, just for fun, in an Olympians veteran relay race in 1976, alongside old rivals Thane Baker and Ira Murchison, but the next morning he could not get out of bed. He never aspired to the ranks of the morning joggers and promised himself that he would never run again. 'I don't keep that keen an interest in track,' he said, 'because there aren't many big meets in Texas, but I watch the ones on TV.'

Winning three gold medals affected Morrow's life in many ways, enabling him to travel around the world and meet people, but he also admitted that his Olympic success prompted a lot of people to try and take advantage of him, and some of them succeeded. Oliver Jackson, who died in 2007, often compared Bobby to Carl Lewis, saying: 'He had great strength and he was unbelievably disciplined. He never jumped a gun in the four years I had him and that was when you could jump and not be disqualified. We said he had ice water in his veins. I'm biased but I've never seen anyone I thought could beat Morrow. He ran on cinders in Melbourne, and the track had been laid the week before the Olympics and it was so mushy you could stick your fingers down into it. If he ran on the tracks we have today there's no telling what he could do.'

Many people in athletics mistook Morrow's laconic style and dismissive words about his career for a sign that he wished he had never competed in the Olympics, but that is far from the truth. A Texas magazine quoted him as saying that he regretted winning the gold medals, but they only got half of the story, because he always felt that those days were the greatest of his life. It was only the negative things that subsequently happened to him as a direct result of that success that he regretted.

In recent years his public appearances grew fewer and fewer, prompting one newspaper to describe him as 'the greatest sprinter you've never heard of'. But even in his seventies he could still chase and catch the jack rabbits on his farm.

As he grew older the years gave him a lot more peace and perspective. He figured he'd won the medals and enjoyed the experience immensely, but his days on the track and that period of his life were finished and forgotten. Morrow died in May 2020, in a hospice near his home in Texas, after he chose to discontinue treatment for a blood disorder. He was 84.

Forgotten by many perhaps, Bobby Morrow nevertheless remains arguably the greatest white sprinter of all time, by virtue of his competition success and world records, and certainly one of the most graceful runners ever to set foot on a track.

Not long after he returned from the 1956 Olympics, *Sports Illustrated* wrote: 'The amateur's only reward – and his gift to the world – is simply the knowledge of excellence. Bobby Morrow is one of the rare ones who achieved – and gave – a little more; a distillation of excellence, in his case as pure and heady an essence as the Olympic Games have ever known.'

More than sixty years on it is a perfect epitaph for one of the greatest 'Fastest Men on Earth'.

Rome 1960

Armin Hary

By the time of the 1960 Rome Olympics, the United States had dominated the sprints for nearly thirty years. Although the rise of the fast-starting young blonde European champion Armin Hary from West Germany had caused a few ripples of interest in the world track scene, little thought was being given to the possibility of an American defeat in the forthcoming Games.

As the Olympic year began, the world 100 metres record of 10.1 was held jointly by no fewer than four athletes – Willie Williams, Ira Murchison, Leamon King and, most recently, the 22-year-old Ray Norton. And they all had something else in common. They were all American. Norton was widely regarded as the world's premier sprinter and had taken his share in the world record at a San José meeting in 1959, a year in which he also swept the board in both sprints at the big USA–USSR meeting and the Pan American Games. Apart from Norton, the Americans also had the improving Frank Budd and big Dave Sime, now back to full fitness and ready to prove a point after the disappointment of missing out on Melbourne through injury.

Of the nine athletes who jointly held the 9.3 world mark for 100 yards, an astonishing eight were American, including Norton and Sime, while at 200 metres only Britain's Peter Radford could claim a share in the world record alongside the USA's Stone Johnson and the inevitable Norton. In fact, the 6ft 2 in Ray Norton held world record marks at 100 yards, 100 metres, 220 yards and 200 metres, as well as claiming the inaugural US Men's Athlete of the Year from *Track & Field News*. As one US columnist trumpeted in the run-up to the Games: 'They might as well mail him the medals now.' So it was hardly surprising that the American coaches were sceptical about the seriousness of the challenge from Germany and were supremely confident that one of their 'boys' would successfully retain the 'Fastest Man on Earth' title for the United States.

They ought to have paid more attention to what was happening across the Atlantic. After years of turning out top-class sprinters, such as Houben, Kornig, Jonath, Fütterer and Germar, only to see them beaten in the major international championships, in young Hary the Germans had at last unearthed a real world-beater.

Hary enjoyed a short but controversial career and was regarded by the German athletic establishment as an oddball character who seemed to delight in causing friction in the sport. His arrogant style and off-beat behaviour often upset other athletes and his incredible 'speed' out of the blocks earned him the title of 'The Thief of Starts' because of his persistent gun jumping. Off the track his antics continued to provide copy for the newspapers, though mostly for the wrong reasons, with stories about an abortive film career, a ban from the track for bringing the sport into disrepute, a fairy tale romance and marriage to a wealthy society heiress and finally the shame of arrest and prison.

Now in his eighties, Armin Hary's often difficult relationship with the German public finally appears to be softening, though he is still not widely regarded as a national hero despite setting up a foundation to help under-privileged German kids into sport and making more frequent and often high-profile media appearances.

But back in the 1950s all that was ahead of him as he practised hard to fulfil his childhood dream and become a football player in a small village near the industrial town of Saarbrucken, where he was born in March 1937, the son of a miner. His father was also a versatile sportsman and had a reputation as a wrestler, so it was no surprise when Hary Junior began to excel in sports, particularly soccer and gymnastics, before he switched his attention to athletics.

He first became a keen decathlete and sprang to prominence during 1956, when he established a new Saarland area record of 5,376 points and ranked among Germany's top 15 decathletes by the end of the year. However, while competing in the ten-event discipline it became clear that by far his best event was the 100 metres and he proved the point in Düsseldorf the following year by running 10.4 seconds, followed by a 10.5 second place in the German championships behind the favourite, Manfred Germar.

The year proved to be a crucial one for Hary, because he left his athletic club in Saarbrucken to join the big Bayer club in Leverkusen, which was backed by the giant Bayer chemical works, where he worked as a precision toolmaker. Once there he came under the influence of coach Bertl Sumser, who quickly spotted Hary's potential as a top-class sprinter. 'Hary has the temperament, unprecedented ability and enormous start speed,' he told pressmen. 'He is powerful and muscular, has a good supply of ambition and in addition a real charge of nervous energy – vital in a sprinter.'

During a series of tests conducted on German athletes at the Freiberg University Clinic, eminent professor Herbert Reindell also discovered that Hary's body had the capacity to endure a tough campaign of athletic training because his heart was that of an undeveloped non-athlete.

Sumser recalls the day he first saw the young Hary: 'I knew straight away he was going to be a world-class sprinter. He had everything, marvellous reactions and he was so well motivated. Although he had tremendous natural talent, he allied that to hard work in training – he was just a genius.'

So during the winter of 1957–58, Sumser worked tirelessly with him to improve his sprint times and hone his technique, with cross-country runs and hours of gruelling gym work, including weight-lifting, wall bar exercises and medicine ball training. The result was a new-look Armin Hary – stronger, quicker, more confident and with additional stamina allied to his natural speed and ability. When the 1958 indoor season opened and he was able to beat Germar over 60 yards, many knowledgeable people in European athletics began to take him seriously.

His electrifying start, referred to by the German press as the 'Blitz Start', was clearly his main weapon, and in most races, when he was not called back for jumping the gun, he would be two or three strides in front of the rest of the field within the first five metres. Naturally there were cynics who suggested that Hary was simply a master at anticipating the gun, so a series of tests were conducted using a high-speed camera which showed that his reaction time was genuinely superior to that of other athletes. The researchers suggested that the average human reaction time to a starting gun was 15 hundredths of a second, whereas the reaction time of top German sprinter Heinz Fütterer was eight hundredths. But when they studied the films of Hary's starts, his reaction time was an astonishing three hundredths of a second. Some scientists doubted that anyone could react to a gun at that speed, and it was suggested that the new boy must have a sixth sense to anticipate the gun.

His reaction time was only a part of Hary's phenomenal starting ability, because he himself admitted that a more important part was getting into full stride quicker than the other athletes. 'In the time it takes other runners to take their first step,' said coach Sumser, 'Hary has taken two or three.' Hary had learned, through hard training and relaxation, how to achieve full power soon after the gun and, together with his explosive reactions, this created the 'Blitz Start'. Hary himself believes: 'It was my speed of reaction to the gun. There was no real technique – just pure reaction speed.'

His ability was appreciated more widely during the 1958 European Championships in Stockholm, where he won gold medals in both the 100 metres and the sprint relay, although his start in the 100 seemed a little too good. His excellent form continued right through the year, and in September he actually recorded the first time of 10 seconds flat for 100 metres in Friedrichshafen, but when officials investigated the time they discovered that the track had an 11 centimetres downhill gradient – just one centimetre more than permitted – and the time was invalidated. His 1959 form was a disappointment compared to that of the previous year, but he was still persuaded to try his luck in America, with San Jose State College in California, where his big rival Ray Norton was based, and the prospect of a full sports scholarship was put on the table. However, he didn't settle and an agreement couldn't be reached, so in early 1960 Hary returned home. One of the big problems Hary had encountered in America was his inability to speak English. He earned some money by washing dishes and when an offer came to return to Germany he jumped at it. He joined the athletics section of the FSV Frankfurt Football Club, where he trained under the auspices of Coach Helmut Hafele, who had aided the one-time European champion Fütterer in the early 1950s. The club also helped find him a job as a salesman in the TV and radio department of the giant Kaufhof department stores.

His form, which had dipped during 1959 because of the lack of proper training and his trips to America, began to return early in 1960 and a few months later, on a summer night in Zurich, he wrote his name indelibly in the record books, reaching an athletic barrier that many felt would not be achieved for another ten years.

It was an extraordinary night, illuminated not only by Hary's blistering speed but also by his staggering arrogance and nonconformity. He appeared to enjoy bucking the system and was unconcerned about upsetting anyone who got in his way. It was reported in the German press that before he left Frankfurt to fly to Switzerland for the big race, he called the organizer of the meeting and told him that he needed to be motivated 'additionally' before he would set foot on the plane.

It had been customary for some years to pay a small amount of expenses to athletes, but under-the-counter payments were more unusual. Hary was well aware of his value to the meeting in terms of pulling people through the gates, and the organizers agreed to his demand for 1,000 Swiss Francs, but the episode caused West German track boss Dr Max Danz to describe him as 'a little urchin, a tough kid and a little loudmouth'.

But on June 21 he did not disappoint the promoters or the large crowd packed inside Zurich's Stadion Letzigrund, all hoping to see some fireworks from the new German sprint star. On that warm and sunny evening, Hary tore out of his customized starting blocks, clearly before the gun, and won easily from the rest of an international field to record another 10 seconds flat. One official timer clocked him at 9.9 seconds. There was no re-call from the starter – because, it was later discovered, the second shot would not go off – but the officials agreed that it had been a false start, and again his time of 10 seconds flat was struck off.

Hary protested vehemently, claiming that it was not his fault that the re-call had not gone off. The organizers eventually conceded to his demands for a re-run to take place some 50 minutes later. Only two of the original line-up were persuaded to race again with him, so just three of them took their places at the start. Now, however, there was no question of Hary jumping the gun – he just sprang out of the blocks incredibly fast and strode away from the two other athletes, hitting the tape in yet another 10 seconds flat. This time it was legal and his run became a sprinting landmark.

Three weeks later, on a balmy, 70-degree evening in Saskatoon, a city right in the middle of Canada, 19-year-old Harry Jerome became the second man to run a legal 10-flat during the national trials. However, despite these two world record shattering performances, both Hary and Jerome were still expected to play second fiddle to the Americans Norton and Sime when the Olympics began in Rome.

The Italian capital was bathed in summer sunshine for the opening of the seventeenth modern Olympics, a setting that contrasted the beauty of the ancient world with the ultra modern facilities of the 1960s.

As usual, the 100 metres competition was among the first to get underway and 61 competitors from around the world were in the Olympic stadium to contest the first round. The most notable absentees were the defending champion Morrow, the double NCAA sprint champion Charlie Tidwell, who had crashed out in the final of the trials, and the new Italian discovery Livio Berrutti, who wanted to save himself for the 200 metres, which he considered his best event.

While Hary and the other favourites cruised easily through the first round, one big casualty was fellow German Manfred Germar. An athlete who did impress was the young

Cuban Enrique Figuerola, who had set a national record of 10.2 before leaving for the Games. The packed stadium had not seen much of the real Armin Hary, but in the second round he unleashed one of his famous 'Blitz Starts' and sped to a new Olympic record of 10.2, beating his close rival Dave Sime in the process.

The following day, all the favourites had made it through to the last twelve for the two semi-finals, but tragedy befell the Canadian joint world record holder, Harry Jerome, when he pulled a muscle at 50 metres and crashed to the track. Bitterly disappointed, he threw himself on the infield turf and wept. At the finish of the race it was Britain's Peter Radford, a Walsall school teacher, who demonstrated his famous blazing finish to pip Figuerola on the line, with Budd just making third place to qualify for the final. In the second semi, Hary led from the gun to the tape, with Sime and Norton trailing in behind, so with the exception of Jerome, all the really big guns had qualified.

With the Canadian now out and Norton looking as though he had peaked a year too early, the final seemed to be a question of whether Sime could catch Hary, with Radford, Budd and Figuerola as outsiders.

The draw for the final, in blazing sunshine, put the two favourites, Hary and Sime, as far apart as they could be, with Sime in lane one and Hary on the outside. The field was under starter's orders for fully 20 minutes before the starter got them away. The delay and the heat would take their toll on some of the athletes, but Hary was among those who remained relaxed. At the first attempt to start, both he and Sime bolted before the gun fired, but it was declared a faulty start and neither was penalized. Then Figuerola decided to adjust his blocks, so there was a further delay, and when the starter tried a second time to get the race underway it was Hary who jumped early and was warned by the official. One more false start and he would be out of the final. However, the warning did not appear to worry the cool German – it had happened to him before on many occasions and it was what his racing was all about.

Finally, at the third attempt, the field got away cleanly and, as predicted, it was Hary who catapulted into an extraordinary early lead, taking a metre out of the field in the first five, a lead that seemed impossible to close. On the inside, after a terrible start, big Dave Sime was accelerating fast and as the tape loomed it looked as if he might get there first, but the German just managed to hang on and as he hit the line the big American lunged desperately forward and crashed in spectacular fashion on the red track. The two of them were clear of the rest of the field, in which Radford had suffered another poor start before his amazing finishing speed brought him past the field to pip Figuerola for the bronze, with Budd fifth and the pre-Games favourite Norton a disappointing last. Hary and Sime were given the same time – 10.2 seconds.

When the judges examined the photograph it was clear that Hary had won the gold by a foot from Sime, with the American appearing to lean a little too early, though it was widely felt that the result might have been different had the two men been drawn together instead of in opposite lanes.

Speaking recently to the Olympic Channel, Hary recalled: 'I know I may sound arrogant, but I had already beaten Dave Sime twice in Rome. Why should he beat me in the final race? It was not possible. I knew it was quite close and he was a little disappointed, but you have to be able to handle losing and Dave Sime was such a noble person and a great athlete. I would not have been against both of us winning the gold. That wouldn't have spoiled it for me.'

Sime, who had beaten Hary earlier in his career, remembered: 'The German had a tremendous start, but I didn't see him at any time during the race. I might have beaten him had I been in the lane next to him because then I would have known when to dip.'

The big American became a respected eye specialist in Miami for over 40 years and treated the likes of President Richard Nixon and boxing legend Sugar Ray Robinson. He also remembered Hary as an arrogant champion and said that he did not want anything to do with him. Sime had only just made the US team because his medical studies had not enabled him to train properly, but once he made the Olympic line-up he then spent some time getting back into shape, beating the seemingly invincible Ray Norton in three of their four pre-Olympic meetings, defeats that may have damaged Norton's confidence and contributed to his poor performances during the Games. As for that famous Hary start, he was never close enough to see exactly what the German was doing, but he said: 'Our initial reaction to the gun was about the same, but after the first step Hary would be two feet ahead. He had a second and third step that were out of this world.' Sime, who died in January 2016, could have chosen a career in football or baseball and was one of many fine sprinters who fell just short of Olympic greatness. Following his death, declassified papers revealed he had been signed up by the CIA to try and recruit Soviet athletes at the Rome Olympics, including bronze medal-winning long jumper Igor Ter-Ovanesyan. Sime was, as his son Scott so eloquently explained, 'a guy who has lived his life with the accelerator touching the floor.'

The bronze medallist Radford was clearly in the best place to understand how the Hary 'blitz start' had worked, and he has his own views on how the German won his gold medal. A respected academic and writer on physical education and sport, he recalls: 'There was a lot of debate about Armin Hary and his start. The German press had been carrying stories about how he had the fastest reaction time ever recorded, and there were stories going around about how he'd been in a laboratory and demonstrated that he reacted faster than anyone who ever lived. The stories were put around quite deliberately by his coach, so there was a lot of tension at the Olympics and the Americans were quite hostile to him.'

The final itself gave Radford the opportunity to experience the Hary starting phenomenon at close quarters, and he agrees with those who feel that the German could easily have been disqualified for false starting twice, holding him to blame for the first faulty start as well as the 'jump' for which he was officially warned. As for Radford, his concentration was wrecked by the long delay in getting the race underway, as well as by a well-meaning group of cheering British fans in the stands who were chanting his name – and by his realization of how Hary had been getting off the blocks ahead of everyone else. 'When we'd had our first run out of the blocks Hary was in lane six and I was in lane five, we were shoulder to shoulder, and I knew instantly how he'd set his world record and how he had a reputation for being a stride and a half faster than anyone else out of the blocks. I knew how he did it and I then had to make a decision whether to do the same, because it was a technique rather than an ability.'

Radford explains that under the international rules that applied at the time, the athletes moved into the 'set' position on the command 'Set'. Once they were all in the 'set' position, the starter then fired the gun and the race was underway. The starter alone decided when all the athletes were motionless in the 'set' position before he fired his pistol. 'In unison all the athletes moved into the 'set' position,' says Radford, 'but Hary didn't move. He came into the position later than everyone else. The starter couldn't start the race until everyone was still and Hary knew that, so the starter waited for Hary to get into position before he fired the gun. Hary knew as soon as he was still the gun would fire, so after waiting a moment he moved into the 'set' position, paused momentarily and then charged off. Most of the time his move would coincide with the gun.'

Shortly after the Games the rules were changed, making it illegal for an athlete to stay down after the 'Set' command, but in 1960 Hary had the flying start down to a fine art. 'My opinion of Hary is tainted by the knowledge that he tricked us all in the final,' admits Radford, and he has little feeling for the 1960 champion, something unusual in the close fraternity of the sprinting world. 'He wasn't an easy person to like. I think a lot of athletes have to be arrogant in a way, they have to believe in themselves and their own ability. There can't be any half measures or fraternizing with the 'enemy' too much, so you don't expect a warmth with your main rivals as you go around the world, but you do expect a certain sort of respect, almost like fellow professionals in the same trade. You never got that feeling with Hary. He was quite aloof and he had an uncomfortable arrogance about him that wasn't just based on his ability as a sprinter, but his feeling that somehow nobody else counted but himself. That was unusual with sprinters and he was very different in that respect.'

But respected or not, it was Armin Hary who climbed on to the rostrum to accept his gold, the first German to win a medal for the 100 metres since Arthur Jonath's bronze in 1932 and the first German to win an Olympic gold in a track event. Even in victory, standing in the gold medal position as his national anthem played and his flag was raised, he was causing a furore. As the cameras beamed pictures around the world, millions could see that to ensure he made some money from his Olympic enterprise he was wearing Adidas shoes on the podium, when he'd run the final in Puma shoes. In the eyes of the sporting world, particularly in Germany, his fame turned to silver on that medal rostrum.

On his return, the German press exacted revenge, with stories about his wealthy fiancée Christine, and even scandalous suggestions of causing a road accident in which he irreparably damaged his knee – an injury that would ultimately end his sprinting career just two months after the Games.

Germany wanted a winner but Armin Hary did not project the desirable clean-cut, gracious image they needed. His old coach Sumser said: 'I found Armin a nice, honest boy, not the bad boy the newspapers liked to paint him. He got a lot of success very quickly and he simply couldn't handle it.'

He had returned home with two gold medals in his pocket, one for the 100 metres and the other for the sprint relay alongside Bernd Cullman, Martin Lauer and Walter Mahlendorf. They had finished second behind the USA quartet of Budd, Norton, Johnson and Sime, but took the gold when the Americans were disqualified after the luckless Norton ran out of the passing zone trying desperately to compensate for the acute disappointment of coming last in both the 100 and 200 metres finals.

The 200 metres, which Hary did not enter, was won by the home crowd's favourite, Berruti, dark glasses and all, in a world record equalling 20.5, with the USA's Lester Carney second and Frenchman Abdoulaye Seye in third place. Peter Radford was eliminated in the semi-finals. With just a silver medal to show for their efforts, it had been a torrid time for the American sprint team and an Olympics they would want to forget in a hurry.

And what on earth happened to the out and out pre-Games favourite Ray Norton? Many years later legendary *Los Angeles Times* columnist Jim Murray spilled the beans. Norton had been suffering from amoebic dysentery and lost 20 pounds in the days before the Games began. 'He got so gaunt, his shoes didn't fit,' wrote Murray. 'His only chance to win would be if they shifted the event to the men's room. Nobody knew about it because Norton told nobody but the doctor. Ray kept hoping the stomach ache might go away in one of the heats. It got worse.'

Though still a young man, Norton quit the track after Rome and was drafted into the NFL by the San Francisco 49ers, though he played only one season. He later carved out a successful career as documentary and commercials producer and, now in his early eighties, is happily retired in Nevada.

Meanwhile, back in the Rome Olympic village, Hary had committed the ultimate sin, especially for a German sprinter, bearing in mind what had happened in 1936. He had snubbed Jesse Owens. The great man had asked him for an interview but the new champion had refused point blank, reportedly saying: 'I'm sorry, I haven't the time to fool with him.' Owens memorably remarked: 'I've been snubbed by bigger jerks before, but never faster ones.'

Three days later it seemed clear that efforts had been made to ensure the insult was rescinded, and Armin Hary was part of a large German retinue that descended on the US sector of the village and the traditional 'champions together' photos were taken. 'He is a strange boy sometimes,' admitted Gerhard Stöck, the chief of the German party. 'He can be difficult. When Owens asked to meet him Hary was busy and he said so. I don't think he intended to be so rude.'

But Hary's individualism was taking on monstrous proportions and on his return from the Olympics he decided to cash in on his new-found international fame and voiced his intentions of becoming a major movie star. It was not to be a smooth passage, and in a highly publicized row with a big German film distributor it became clear that he had demanded the lead roles in a western and a detective film for a fee of 100,000 marks each. The film company maintained that for a totally unproven, inexperienced 23-year-old, this was sheer arrogance, and Hary's claim that his name was as valuable as that of the major German film star Curt Jurgens was, they said, plainly ridiculous.

The affair earned him another nickname - the 'Callas of the Race Track', after the temperamental opera star Maria Callas, and he eventually rejected an offer from the company of 7,500 marks to appear in one of their films in a character part.

As one row finished, another began. After his car crash in November he fell foul of the German athletic establishment in another highly public row, this time over the alleged fiddling of his expenses and damage caused to the image of German sport. In January 1961, he was banned from competition for a year after being found guilty of having brought the sport into disrepute by painting a poor picture of athletics in a magazine article the previous summer, and of having injured team spirit prior to the Olympics. He admitted that he had claimed travel expenses to and from two sports festival meetings even though he had shared a car with a team member from Frankfurt.

The 'trial' at Frankfurt Sports College lasted eight hours and the normally cheerful and bouncy Hary could not hide his disappointment when he heard the result. 'I was so sure of myself and did not expect a single day's ban,' he told one newspaper. 'I had plans for the near future. I had been invited to Tokyo and the USA. The Japanese I could have beaten on one leg, but the American competition was a challenge and I would have loved to run. Now everything is over. What I did and admitted, others would also have done. With me they set an example of German thoroughness, but I shall fight this hard sentence. If I don't succeed I shall stop running. I will not be slapped in the face.'

Hary recalled later: 'I don't think I was the one who started demanding money for racing. There were sums of money floating around and all I did was the same as the others at the time – I took my share.'

Whether it was his threat to retire or mounting public pressure at the severity of the sentence that ultimately changed the mind of the athletic establishment is unclear, but a fortnight later the punishment was rescinded by the German Athletics Association. Instead it reprimanded Hary for his actions and substituted a ban which would effectively stop him competing for just the first week of the track season in May.

The GAA Committee stated that 'too much attention was paid to Hary from sport and other circles and he obviously lost the right sense of measure. Anyone who was pushed to the forefront in public life would require an enormous amount of maturity. This maturity is not possessed by someone young and still growing, such as this egotistic Olympic winner.'

However, there was no happy return to the track for Hary because the condition of his left knee, injured in his car crash, had not improved. In fact, doctors warned that the chronic inflammation would not clear up unless he took a year's break from sport. It was discovered that Hary could not stand or run for any length of time without considerable pain, and he decided that rather than wait a year in the hope of reviving his career he would bow out now at the top and try and make some money from his success while he was still a big name.

'If I am forced to take such a long break,' he told reporters, 'I will lose contact. It makes sense for me not to begin. My career as a sprinter is over.' He quit the track and went into business, including selling shirts, telephones, gambling machines, his own brand of sports shoes, insurance and finally property, becoming an estate agent.

In 1966 he married his fiancée Christine, the beautiful daughter of the wealthy Bagusat family, whose fortune was founded on the production of 'Rex' motorcycles and a brickworks, and whose family home was the magnificent Bavarian Castle Possenhofen. It seemed to be a fairytale ending to a troubled story, and although Hary and his family did not live in the castle itself, but in a smaller house in the grounds, he seemed content as a finance and property broker in what appeared to be an idyllic existence.

In 1980, however, the world caved in on the former Olympic champion, just as he was setting off on a skiing holiday in the Austrian Tyrol. He and Karl-Heinz Bald, a friend and business associate, were arrested by the police and charged with defrauding the German Catholic Church of more than a million marks and causing financial damage to the Archdiocese of Munich estimated at several million more. Although the older Bald, another property dealer, was clearly the prime mover in the sad affair, 43-year-old Hary worked as his right-hand man and together they had milked large sums of money from buying and selling property for the Church. The original trial lasted several months and at the end he was sentenced to two years in prison. The once proud track star spent a nightmare five months in a tiny cell at the Stadelheim Prison before he was released on bail pending an appeal, at which his punishment was commuted to an 18-month suspended sentence.

The sorry affair, which understandably made banner headlines in the German newspapers, ruined him, both as a businessman and in the eyes of the German public. After the trial, his licence to work as a property agent in West Germany was withdrawn and he made a living selling mobile steam baths. He did not win back his licence until 1986, but was then able to continue his business career. In a rare interview with the German newspaper *Der Tagesspiel*, he said: 'I don't think about the race every day like I used to fifty years ago. I'd rather think about the here and now.' But the resentment against officialdom clearly remains. 'I had all of Germany against me. The German athletic federation did not like me much, but I wanted to do things my way. I reached my goals. I wanted to be the fastest man on earth and Olympic champion. And that's what I achieved.'

In 2004 Hary launched a foundation to raise funds to help support under-privileged kids in Germany to play sports, and he spends much of his time today cajoling and persuading potential partners and sponsors to donate funds to the cause. 'All young talent between four and 12 years old that come from a socially poor or vulnerable environment will be supported,' he says. 'That's where we lose the most talent. It's social difficulties, family tensions, school problems and children that sit in front of the TV and push their families away. Every commercial partner we find creates hope for a young athlete.'

In 2010 he agreed to take part in a fiftieth anniversary celebration of his 10-second world record in Zurich, an event attended by the two greatest sprinters of the day, Usain Bolt and Tyson Gay. An old cinder track had been laid down for the exhibition, and timekeepers Omega built a special stand to test reaction times. American Tyson Gay registered a superfast 0.231.

Hary false started. 'That was on purpose,' he smiled.

Hary may be an unappreciated champion in Germany and probably misunderstood elsewhere, but in many ways he was a man ahead of his time during his track career. He maintained a professional attitude to both running and winning at a time when such professionalism was simply frowned upon. Had he been running today he would probably enjoy a reputation as a showman and would certainly be wealthy from his track earnings, but in his day such enthusiasm to make money only succeeded in alienating the German press and public, and consequently he did not enjoy the popularity a man with his achievements might have expected.

But the record books never lie, and his name will always be synonymous with the first ever 10-flat 100 metres and an Olympic gold medal. And all the sneering headlines in the world will never change that.

In 2020 he gave an interview to *World Athletics* journalist Olaf Brockmann and told him: 'I feel good. I regularly go cycling on my e-bike. I want to get to the age of 100 at least.'

Tokyo 1964

Bob Hayes

From an American perspective, the sprint events at the Rome Olympics had been a complete disaster. It was one of their worst showings in the history of the Games, an embarrassing failure that they did not want to repeat. A new sprinting hero was needed; someone who could dominate like an Owens or a Morrow – and the United States found one. A special one.

'Bullet' Bob Hayes was tailor-made for the role of the avenging American sprinter, a muscular, all-American boy who hauled himself out of the Florida ghettos to beat the world. His extraordinary talent spanned two of the world's most demanding sports – track and American football – and he dominated in both camps. But while his sporting career was a series of breathtaking highs, the life that followed was one of heartbreaking lows, humiliation, tragedy, personal redemption and a sad early death.

Back in 1942, when Hayes was born, track and field did not figure prominently on the list of sporting favourites in the east-side ghettos of Jacksonville. He grew up in a tough neighbourhood, the youngest of three children in a struggling and broken family, and much of his early life was spent playing truant from school and hustling on the street.

His father Joseph Hayes ran a shoe-shine parlour, which doubled as a front for a numbers gambling racket, and young Bob's job was to open the store at 7.30am and close it up at 8.30pm. As the youngest, Bob was able to dodge the strict, almost military family atmosphere. 'I was always the best athlete in my age group and being the youngest in the family I kinda got everything I wanted,' he remembered. 'I wasn't the best student because I didn't have to hustle to get the best grades.'

From an early age, it was quite clear that he was a natural sportsman, but his real love was football, so he hardly gave track a passing thought, and it was not until high school that he began to attract attention as a possible sprint star of the future. 'I was in junior high and the coach had a physical education class,' recalled Hayes, 'and he saw me running in the class with the other guys. He noticed that they were in tennis shoes or running barefoot, while I had on my every-day shoes, but I was outrunning them, so he convinced me to take up running.'

The coach was Earl Kitchings, who worked at the single block Matthew Gilbert High

School, and he gave Hayes the nickname 'Crow'. 'I said it was because he was black, he looked like a crow and he could fly like a crow.'

His first real meeting for the high school saw him entered in no fewer than seven events – the 100, 220, 440 and 880 yards, the sprint relay, the long jump and the high jump – and he won them all. His speed not only earned rave reviews from the school's coaches, but it also proved to be something of a money-spinner. Hayes explained: 'My friends used to organize races for me against senior guys in the school and then bet on me. Naturally the older guys always thought they could win, but they never did.'

However, despite his athletic success, he was still convinced that his future lay on the football field, and it was his ability as a speedy running back that earned him a scholarship to Florida A&M University, in the state capital of Tallahassee. In his first year at college, he hardly set foot on a track, preferring to use his speed to run rings around opposing defence men in the college football league. But it was not long before the track department persuaded him to try out for the track team and he came under the caring eye of coach Jake Gaither, who not only helped Hayes become the world's greatest sprinter and vastly improved his football technique, but also became something of a second father to him.

Hayes certainly needed guidance in those early days – he had been on campus only a short time when he fell foul of the law and received ten years' probation for armed robbery and assault, although in reality the offence was hanging around with a young man who held up another youngster with a toy gun and took his chewing gum and 11 cents.

It was a ridiculously harsh sentence for such a petty crime, but Hayes promised himself and Coach Gaither that he would not get into trouble again. He began to pay back Gaither's faith in him on his very first college track meet, in March 1961, when he went out and equalled Jesse Owens's long-standing freshman record for the 100 yards of 9.4 seconds. Two months later, he narrowly missed a record in the 220 yards, and people were beginning to take an interest in the new boy from Florida.

His improvement on the track continued, and in June of the same year he became the thirteenth man to tie Mel Patton's 100 yards world record of 9.3, although it was never officially ratified because just over a fortnight later Villanova's Frank Budd became the first man to duck under the record with a run of 9.2 at the AAU championships in New York.

But Hayes was not downhearted – after all, youth was on his side – and he disappeared into a football season with his college team and did not return to track competition for more than six months. When he eventually exchanged his football strip for running spikes, things began to happen almost immediately. In his first race at the college, he tied Budd's world record, only for it to be ruled out because the starter had used a non-regulation, small-calibre starting pistol. His form earned him a trip to Europe, where he ran a 10.1 for 100 metres. Then, back in the States, he suffered his first ever defeat, to the Canadian Harry Jerome, in Modesto, although some people still maintain that the judges awarded the race to the wrong man. Hayes started the following year in similar style, putting together a remarkable series of races, including two sparkling runs of 20.5 in the 200 metres and 220 yards, both unofficial world records.

Hayes was now being hailed as the rising star of the sprint world, and all the press stories indicated that it would not be long before he took an official record of his own. That day finally arrived in June 1963, at the AAU championships, on the fast rubber-asphalt track in St Louis, where he hurtled to victory in the semi-finals in a new 100-yard world record of 9.1, and repeated the feat, albeit with wind assistance, in the final. Now he was out on his own as the premier sprinter in the United States, and there were few men elsewhere in the world who could give him a serious race.

If confirmation was needed that Hayes would be the man everyone would fear at the Olympics in Tokyo, then it was provided in chilling fashion during a series of indoor meets early in Olympic year itself. He had already given warning of the kind of form he was in when he ran a 9.1 in the 100 yards and a 20.1 in the 220 yards in Miami on New Year's Day, but when he came indoors he equalled the world record for the 60-yards dash on no fewer than five occasions, clocking six seconds flat.

One man who remembers the indoor series clearly – and one 60-yard race in particular – was the up-and-coming American sprinter Charlie Greene, who would become one of the great stars of the 1960s, but was then just starting out as a freshman at the University of Nebraska. 'Bob was simply the best sprinter I ever saw,' he says. 'At that time I was a brash young college boy. I knew I was good but I had a lot of trouble convincing other people. I was running indoors at Madison Square Garden and I'd won my heat and semi-final and felt pretty good. There were some newspaper people around, so I went up to Bob and said, "You're gonna' have to run a new world record to win this race, because I'm gonna tie this one." Sure enough I tied the record, but Bob ran 5.9 and broke it.'

Greene's amazing confidence and fast-talking showmanship would make him a hit with the public in the years to come, but for now he had to take a back seat while Hayes moved to centre stage. Tokyo was fast approaching and while he had endeared himself to the American track fans with his scintillating running, the coaching purists were not so sure. His running style, or rather the lack of it, had them holding their heads in disbelief.

'He doesn't so much run a race as beat it to death,' suggested one American sportswriter, an off-the-cuff description that accurately summed up the essence of Bob's running. He was a heavily built athlete and very muscular – in fact, he looked more like a boxer than a sprinter, and when he ran he seemed to roll from side to side as he pawed his way down the track.

The New York Times athletics writer Frank Litsky remembers vividly the first time he saw Hayes in action. 'I looked across the starting line at all these sleek model sprinters and there's this guy with these huge shoulders, he looked like a weightlifter in the wrong event. The gun goes and the others go gliding off and he's rolling all over the place. I figure he must be 20 yards behind in the middle of the race, but then he's in front and he wins going away. I was astounded, and after the race I saw his coach and said, "I've never seen Bob before, but it seems to me that he's wasting an awful lot of motion sideways and if he went straight he could go much faster." The coach agreed and I asked him if he had plans to do anything about it. He just looked at me and said, "No, I've got the best sprinter in the world here. He's going to win an Olympic gold medal."'

Hayes was one of the heaviest sprinters around, scaling over 190 pounds, and he is the first to admit that he was not the most beautiful runner in the world, with his unorthodox style, broad shoulders, flat feet and pigeon toes. But he pointed out: 'I might not have had the correct arm pump, the right body lean or the proper stance, but I won my races. I'm built funny, different from other athletes, so what I did got the job done. As I told some of the critics at the time, they don't take pictures at the start, only at the finish.'

But the Hayes juggernaut almost came off the road completely at a dramatic AAU championship, in 90-degree fahrenheit sunshine at Rutgers University, in New Jersey, just a few weeks before the first Olympic trials. 'All I could think of was the pain,' recalled Hayes. 'And then a second thought flashed through my mind. There goes the Olympics.'

It may have been caused by the new cinder track that Rutgers had paid $75,000 to import from England a few weeks earlier. The soft, crumbling surface was clearly not packed down properly and in the 100 metres final Hayes felt his left hamstring go at about 60 metres and almost stumbled through the tape, still winning in 10.3 seconds, but then veering around the curve, hopping and skipping to a painful halt. Doctors at Miami University confirmed his worst fears – a torn hamstring. It would be touch-and-go for the Olympics.

It was his first serious injury, but mercifully it coincided with new rules for the US trials, in which two sets of races had been organized. The first was held in New York, just a fortnight after Hayes was injured, and would guarantee the winner a place on the team. Everyone else would fight it out for the two remaining places at a second trial in Los Angeles in September, just before the team left for Tokyo.

When Hayes arrived at the LA Coliseum he had not run in anger for almost three months and the pressure was building. 'The thousands of miles I had run in training, all the practice starts, all the other races over the years, the records I had set, and the fame I had achieved – none of them would mean a thing,' he said. 'Those trials were the most pressure I've ever had, more than any football game I ever played in, more than the Olympics themselves.'

Hayes decided to reduce his pick-up speed to avoid any chance of damaging his hamstring, but once he got going the old speed returned and he coasted through the tape to win comfortably in 10.1 seconds, with the rest of the field trailing some way behind.

The following day, with the sun still shining, he felt good enough for a crack at the 200 metres. He was beaten into third place behind Paul Drayton and Dick Stebbins, but finished ahead of a strangely lethargic Henry Carr, the world record holder, who had to battle to claim fourth. Hayes wasn't too concerned when the US officials bumped him off the 200 metres to allow the 6ft 3in Carr to make the Games and it turned out to be a smart decision.So, with his closest rival Frank Budd dropping out of track in 1962 to try his luck in football with the Philadelphia Eagles, the American hopes of getting back their prized 100 metres title rested squarely on Hayes's big shoulders. The team set off for the Games in October, flying 12 hours from California via Alaska to Tokyo, where they arrived completely exhausted in the early hours.

The Japanese organizers, meanwhile, had no intention of allowing them to sleep, and had rolled out the red carpet. 'All we wanted to do was sleep,' Hayes remembered, 'but when we got off the plane they had laid out chairs with our names on the back, just like you were a movie star, and everyone wanted interviews. I'll never forget it – here I was, a kid from Jacksonville, and everyone wanted to talk to me.'

The atmosphere and the setting in Tokyo suited Hayes perfectly and he immediately felt at home in the village, where the athletes rented bicycles to get around and all the competitors were allowed to mix freely. The Games were a triumph of organization from start to finish and are now regarded as probably the greatest advertisement for the Olympics in their long history. The Japanese seemed to create a spirit of enjoyment and goodwill that has never been surpassed. So many of the Games that followed Tokyo would be tarnished by political problems, financial issues or controversy of some kind. The cost was massive, estimated at £30 million, but the stadium was always full, even for the most obscure qualifying heats.

A record 94 countries took part, and for the first time the Olympics reached an international television audience with the aid of satellite technology, so Hayes knew that all American eyes would be on him when he stepped on to the track for the first major final. 'I didn't know if I was going to win or not, because there was Harry Jerome, who I knew, and the Cuban Enrique Figuerola, who I had never met before. But I knew I was in the best condition of my life and I was going to give 100 per cent to win that gold medal back. We had lost that tradition to Germany in 1960 and we wanted it back, we felt it was ours to own, so there was a little pressure on me to win.'

No fewer than 75 sprinters entered the competition and in round one, on the first day of Olympic competition, Hayes battled through appalling wind and rain to ease home in 10.4, while the best time was recorded, perhaps fittingly, by Japan's Hideo Iijima, in 10.3. He would make it to the semi-finals. In the afternoon, when the wind and rain cleared, Bob romped through the quarter-finals in 10.3 and was through to the semis, which were held the following day.

The semi-final draw favoured Hayes by keeping him clear of his two main rivals, Jerome and Figuerola, but while the weather had been improving slowly, the track was still a little wet. Nevertheless Hayes set the packed stadium alight by running his semi in 9.9 seconds, although the wind gauge reading indicated there was a strong wind blowing in his favour, so it would never be a record.

The final itself was held just an hour and a half later, and after the semi Hayes felt confident of success, despite a practical joke that almost cost him the race. During his stay in the village he had been going around with long-jumper Ralph Boston and boxer Joe Frazier, and on the eve of the final they had been playing around in their room when, unbeknown to Hayes, one of his running spikes had been kicked under the bed. 'I was so nervous I had everything packed hours ahead of time,' he said, 'so you can imagine how I felt when I got to the stadium and found I only had one shoe. Fortunately I only wear size eights, small for a guy of my build, and I managed to find another American athlete with the same size shoes and he let me borrow them for the final.'

Hayes found that for the biggest race of his life he had been randomly assigned the inside lane, where the cinders had been chewed up so badly by the recent finish of the 20-kilometre walk that the officials had to rake it. The Americans tried to protest, suggesting that their man had run the best time in the heats and deserved a better lane, but their appeals fell on deaf ears. Hayes and Mel Pender were the only Americans in the field, with injured third man Trenton Jackson failing to make it, but the real competition for Hayes would come from Jerome and Figuerola, while the other finalists, Poland's Wieslaw Maniak, the German Heinz Schumann, Tom Robinson of the Bahamas and the Ivory Coast's Gaousso Kone, were really unknown quantities.

From the gun, Hayes was quickly into his running and from about the 20-metre mark he unleashed a sustained burst of power that carried him hurtling down the inside lane and crashing through the tape an incredible seven feet in front of the next man, Figuerola, with Jerome third. His time of 10 seconds flat, which equalled Armin Hary's world record and established a new Olympic record – all achieved on the most atrocious track surface, and with a borrowed left shoe – remains one of the greatest sprints in track history. Jesse Owens, watching from the stands, said, 'When he comes out of the starting blocks he looks like a guy catching a ball behind the line of scrimmage and dodging people.' Owens described the victory as the greatest since 1928. He estimated Hayes's margin of superiority as three metres.

Hayes remembered the race vividly, and just one thought was flying through his mind as he took off out of his blocks. 'I was thinking, "Well, I got a bad lane, I've just got to run faster and harder, I've got to be more determined." As I hit about 40 yards, my acceleration started coming on and I stayed calm and relaxed, made sure I didn't run out of lane and there was the tape. It was an unexplainable feeling.'

Cuba's silver medallist Enrique Figuerola, who had finished fourth in Rome, told reporters: 'This is the best race I ran all year. Yet Hayes beat me at my best. He's the greatest.' Figuerola retired from the track in 1968 after winning another Olympic silver in the sprint relay and became a top coach in Cuba and a key figure in the development of the country's athletics. He was also a favourite of former leader Fidel Castro and in 2000 he was voted amongst the 100 greatest Cuban athletes and today is happily retired on the island.

Third-placed Harry Jerome remains something of a legend in his native Canada, with a nine-foot statue immortalizing his achievements standing in Vancouver's Stanley Park. After his disaster in Rome, Jerome suffered an horrific injury during the 1962 British Empire Games, completely severing his quadricep tendon, but he courageously fought back to fitness and made it to Japan.

After Tokyo he won gold at the British Empire and Commonwealth Games, in Jamaica, and matched the world 100 yards record of 9.1. He retired from the track after finishing 7th in the 100 metres final at the Mexico Olympics and began tirelessly campaigning for better education, training and facilities for young Canadians. He and his family had suffered rabid racism growing up in North Vancouver and he ultimately used his fame to evangelize on social justice and civil rights, which included a seat on the British Columbia Human Rights Commission. He was awarded the Order of Canada, but tragically died, aged just 42, when he suffered a brain aneurism in Vancouver in 1982. He had been suffering from mysterious seizures since his thirties and had left hospital to attend the funeral of his friend – the legendary Canadian sprinter Percy Williams – when a few days later he suffered the seizure that killed him. Aside from the statue, Jerome's memory is kept alive by his annual track meet and a black business and professionals' awards held each year in Toronto. In 2010, a powerful documentary movie was made about his life – it was entitled *Mighty Jerome*.

Back in Tokyo, Bob Hayes had become one of the heroes of the Games and the Japanese fans loved him, especially when he wore his distinctive cowboy hat around the stadium. Nor did he disappoint them at the medal ceremony, standing at the top of the rostrum looking as if he had stepped out of a John Wayne movie. He had to bend a long way for the tiny Emperor Hirohito to put the medal around his neck and as he walked back across the track studying his medal, he looked up into the stands and spotted his mother. Mary Hayes was a housemaid who had hardly set foot outside Florida, but thanks to the generosity of the people of Jacksonville she had been able to fly over to watch her son in the Games, and he ran straight up and gave her his gold medal.

Understandably, this was one of Hayes's greatest moments, but another one was just a few days away in the sprint relay, a run that some experts maintain was the fastest ever run by a human being. But first he had a little score to settle with a certain boxer about a shoe – having been told how it went missing. 'I got a bit cocky then,' said Hayes, 'and I went back to the village, found Joe and told him, "I know you're a world-class boxer, but if you ever kick one of my shoes again I'm going to knock you out." Then I smiled real quick and said, "Hi, Mr Frazier, how are you? I love you."'

Later that night he and his mother celebrated the gold medal with a special dinner for two in Tokyo's upmarket Ginza district – where they spotted a giant red, white and blue neon picture of Hayes lit up with the banner headline: 'Bob Hayes, USA, World's Fastest Human'. It was a day that neither of them would ever forget.

Then it was time to get back on the track as part of the American relay team. However, there was concern about the lack of proper preparation, poor baton-changing and the fact that Mel Pender had torn rib muscles in the 100 metres semi-final and was in hospital. So alarm bells were ringing. Would the USA see a repeat performance of their 1960 disaster? Just before the race the French anchorman, Jocelyn Delecour, approached Paul Drayton, the American lead-off man, and dismissed the US team, saying, 'You can't win – all you have is Bob Hayes.' His prediction looked like coming true when poor changeovers between Drayton, Gerry Ashworth and Dick Stebbins put Bob in a terrible position in fifth place for the anchor leg and about three yards behind the leaders.

What followed was astonishing. Hayes's pick-up was electric and he roared after the field, catching and then passing them in just 30 yards, as if they were all standing still, and running on to hit the tape a clear three yards ahead in a new world record of 39.0. Various times were given for his anchor leg, but the slowest was an amazing 8.9, while the fastest clocked him at 8.5. It is enough to say that his performance has never really been equalled and the run went down in history – just as his 100 metres final did – as one of the landmarks in sprinting. Hayes also felt that it was the fastest he had ever run. Fittingly, it was to be his last race.

The late British journalist Neil Allen, reporting for *The Times*, remembered the gasps of amazement in the stand as Hayes got the baton. 'I'd never seen any sprinting that impressed me as much as Bob Hayes's final leg. The man just exploded, he was absolutely fantastic, just like a clenched fist travelling along the track, and as he crossed the line up went the baton into the air and his team-mates were rejoicing.'

US Army private Paul Drayton enjoyed marching up to the Frenchman Delecour after the race, in which the French took the bronze medal – the American just smiled as he saw him and said, 'All anyone ever needs, pal!' Dick Stebbins, who handed off to Hayes, recalled: 'On my last steps I was really moving and Hayes was only in his twelfth or thirteenth stride, but I could feel the force of him about to explode and in one more step he'd have been out of my reach. In 10 yards he was going faster than I was at 110 and I think he ran the last leg in 8.5. It was unbelievable to make up all that ground and win going away. Just to have won in the circumstances would have been superb, but to annihilate them was out of the question. The good Lord gave Bob Hayes something most people don't have. Pure unadulterated speed.'

So Hayes returned home with two gold medals and to a hero's welcome. US President Lyndon Johnson invited all the golden athletes to a special dinner in Washington, where Hayes, at just 21, and the quadruple gold medal winning swimmer Don Schollander, who was only 18, were the stars of the show.

With the Olympics over, Hayes returned to college and the football season, but his track career was finished. He had decided to give up running and was drafted by both the Dallas Cowboys and the Denver Broncos, at a time when there were two different football leagues, and opted to play for Dallas in the National Football League in 1965.

It is likely that had he continued to run he would have broken more records, especially with more specialized training and synthetic tracks, because at just 21 he had many more years' running in front of him. Lindy Remigino, the 1952 sprint champion and a lifelong coach, thought that Hayes was simply the greatest. 'If he'd have run on the plastic tracks he'd have just taken off. I really feel he would have been running then the same sort of times as Usain Bolt.' Hayes only lost two 100-metre races, the first being the doubtful verdict against Harry Jerome, and the second at the NAIA meeting in 1962, when he was beaten by Roger Sayers after missing training for three weeks with a viral infection. No other sprinter can claim a record anything like his. 'A lot of folks asked me to stay in track because they felt I hadn't reached my potential, but there was no money in the sport and I didn't know all these all-weather tracks, better equipment and training methods were coming, so I decided to join Dallas and play football. I suppose I could have brought my 100 time down a couple of tenths.'

After the Tokyo Games a new sporting career beckoned for Hayes. Even though he had been an outstanding college football player, however, there were many people in the sport who poured scorn on the idea of transforming track stars into football players, simply because history had told them it had never worked. Glenn Davis, the 1956 and 1960 Olympic champion in the 400 metres hurdles, had one disappointing season with Detroit; sprinter Ray Norton only fared a little better with the San Francisco 49ers; and

Frank Budd was disappointing, too. Worse still was the tragedy of Stone Johnson, who finished fifth in the Rome 200 metres and joined Kansas City, where he died after breaking his neck during a pre-season game in 1963.

Undeterred, Hayes joined the Cowboys, while the Olympic 200 metres champion, Henry Carr, teamed up with the New York Giants. They actually faced each other in one of their first games, a 31–2 win for Dallas at the Cotton Bowl, in September 1965.

The Cowboys signed Hayes to a three-year contract worth around $100,000, but there were some anxious faces during his first practice games as a wide receiver when he kept dropping the ball. These problems were soon ironed out and he introduced himself to the Dallas fans by pulling in a wobbling pass from quarterback Don Meredith and sprinting 45 yards for his first touchdown.

Legendary former Dallas head coach Tom Landry, who died in 2000, recalled: 'It wasn't too difficult for Bobby to make the transition because he had played college football. He wasn't just a sprinter, he was a football player who could sprint.' The Cowboys's then President and General Manager Tex Schramm, who signed Bob, remembered: 'He had such speed and such unusual skill that instead of him learning the game, it was more a case of the game having to learn him, because he revolutionized our game in the early years.'

Schramm, who died in 2003, was absolutely right, because no one in the NFL had ever had to cope with world-class speed allied to a football brain, and Hayes was creating havoc in some of the best defences in the league. Finally the coaches around the country decided to abandon the tried and trusted man-to-man marking system and introduced a zonal defence scheme, which is still used today, and all because they could not cope with Bob Hayes.

He played for nine years at Dallas, an unusually long career in a game with an enormous casualty rate, and was rated as one of the greats. His high point came in New Orleans in 1972, when the Cowboys beat their arch-rivals the Miami Dolphins 24–3 in Super Bowl VI.

From his very first season in football, when he married his college sweetheart Altemease Martin and adopted baby girl Rori, the Cowboys fans took Hayes to their hearts.

The legendary Cowboys quarterback Roger Staubach, who joined Dallas midway through Hayes's career and remained a close friend, rated Hayes as one of the all-time great football players and the fastest wide receiver he had ever seen. 'He made me look a hero,' he said. 'We played in a lot of key games, including the Super Bowl, and not only did he have incredible speed, but he was also a great football player. It's very rare to have both attributes.'

Tom Landry added: 'I regard him greatly. A coach can't say anything but good things about a player as great as Bobby Hayes. He came to us when we became a championship team and in 1966 we won a division for the first time and went into the world championship game that year. It was mainly because of Bobby.'

The record books show that Hayes boasted an astonishing record with Dallas, with 365 receptions for 7,295 yards and 71 touchdowns and the best record in punt returns. He averaged 20 yards a catch and made three trips to the Pro Bowl, while in 1966 he chalked up 1,232 receiving yards and in November, against divisional rivals, Washington Redskins he managed 246 yards in receptions, a record which stood until 2009. 'I knew I was faster than anyone in the league,' said Hayes, 'and they had to prevent me from getting behind them. But I was in good condition and I could run around the big, aggressive linemen instead of getting hit head-on and I think that's the reason I stayed in the game so long.'

The Cowboys were one of the most successful sides during Hayes's career, and from 1966 through the seventies they won more games than any other team. There were plenty of good moments, such as his record 95-yard touchdown in 1966, but there were also some unhappy ones, especially the infamous 'Ice Bowl' game on New Year's Eve 1967, in Green Bay, when the Packers beat the Cowboys 21–17 for the NFL championship, with the temperature at 15 degrees below zero – and a wind chill which dropped that to a brutal minus 36. It was so cold that members of Green Bay's marching band were taken to hospital with hypothermia, an elderly fan in the stands died of exposure and the whistle stuck to the lips of the referee. Several players even suffered from frostbite. 'I never could get a drink of water on the sidelines,' said Hayes. 'Every time I'd squirt the stuff near my mouth it would freeze before it got there.' Former Arizona Cardinals head coach Dave McGinnis said: 'As a kid from West Texas, the Dallas Cowboys were everything. After you'd watch them play you'd go out in the front yard and all the receivers wanted to be Bullet Bob Hayes. That's just what you grew up with.'

While Gil Brandt, chief scout of the Cowboys for almost 30 years, explained: 'If he had been playing today he would be so rich he wouldn't have needed to do anything for extra money after his career.'

At the peak of his career, it was estimated that Bob was earning around $75,000 a year, but he was certainly not among the highest paid players in the league, and when persistent injuries and complacency dogged him in 1974, he was traded to the 49ers. However, things did not improve there, and after just six months with the San Francisco club he quit the game. This sudden departure from the sport marked the beginning of Hayes's dreadful decline. Despite taking deferred wage payments, he struggled with money and had made no plans for future financial security. He also had a tendency to trust people – to try and please them – and that translated into a raft of failed business deals. At just 31 years old, the worst period of his life was about to start. 'It was a kind of empty feeling,' he remembered. 'We all say we can adjust, but it's very difficult. All of a sudden you're down and no one recognizes you. Anyone who says they don't miss that is lying. I certainly did and everyone I've spoken to did as well.' The problem was that Hayes achieved his greatest sporting highs at a very young age, so the downward journey was a tough one. Many people tried to use him as a front, and being the simple, down to earth and kind-hearted man he was, he found it difficult to differentiate between the good ones and the bad. Hayes later admitted that he was just an immature boy in a grown-up body who tried to please everyone, and that landed him in trouble.

Roger Staubach explained: 'Bob could have gone on playing longer, though he had a good career, but he certainly wasn't as dedicated as he could have been. Athletes in his position are put on a pedestal. You are earning good money, but many don't have the vision to look ahead to when they stop playing. They are more interested in having a good time and living for today rather than tomorrow. So when they do stop playing they are just not prepared.'

However, finances were the least of his problems, because he still had money in the bank, and even when his football career finished he earned a little on the professional running circuit for a while. He became an alcoholic and got involved in the drug scene, both of which combined to pull the Cowboys's famous No. 22 all the way down. Hayes stressed his problems with alcohol were rooted in his family, because his grandfather and father were both alcoholics and died from the disease. 'I suffered just like they did because when I drank I just wanted more. I wasn't a social drinker, I was greedy and after a while my tolerance for alcohol increased and it started to destroy me.' At the same time, he got involved in drugs, mostly cocaine, and fell prey to the NFL hangers-on who liked to brag to their friends that they knew the big names and sold their merchandise to the starry-eyed.

It is possible that playing football for so long could have made Hayes susceptible to the drug scene, because drugs were, and still are, widely used in the NFL to ensure that players are back in action as soon as possible after injury. 'During that time your body gets accustomed to it,' said Hayes, 'and all of a sudden it's cut off, but you still want it. While you're playing it's legal, but when you're not it's illegal, so you get caught.'

The *Washington Post* sportswriter Ken Denlinger felt that Hayes's problems stemmed directly from his sudden departure from the NFL, because he was using the drugs and alcohol as a substitute high for the thrills of sport, but it is more complex than that. 'We have a wonderful flair for shooting our youth with large doses of fantasy, for getting them passionate about sports,' he wrote, 'but shockingly few bother to consider the trip back down, or that some sort of sporting phase-out, or at least an academic cushion, is necessary for someone whose career ends before middle age.' Hayes's former Cowboys team-mate Pat Toomay told the Dallas newspapers that it was 'like telling a carpenter at the age of 32 that he couldn't hammer a nail again – ever'.

It was an eerily similar tale for the Tokyo 200-metre champion Henry Carr. He quit the track after Tokyo and played three seasons as a defensive back with the New York Giants, but his life collapsed after injury ended his football career and he descended into a spiral of drugs, gambling and prostitutes. His eventual redemption came in the form of the Bible and Jehovah's Witnesses. He wrote: 'Even when one becomes the best, it's a deception. Why? because it's not lasting, nor really satisfying. Stars are soon replaced and generally forgotten. Then disappointment, depression and physical problems often follow. Rather than competing with others to be the best, helping and serving others is what brings true satisfaction.' Carr died in 2015 aged 73 in Griffin, Georgia, after a long battle with cancer.

Hayes was convinced that it was his alcoholism that drew him further into the downward spiral, and that was caused by his childhood. 'It doesn't affect just big sports stars, it's an across the board illness,' he said. 'It's not black or white, it has no religious boundaries, it's not people that have money and it's not just a problem – it's a disease. If there's someone who's an alcoholic or a drug addict in your family, then it can carry on to you. It started when I was young because my dad was an alcoholic, he gave me whisky when I was 12 and I had been drinking ever since.'

He recalled those dark days as the worst of his life, both physically and emotionally. In 1974 he was divorced from his wife Altemease, and shortly afterwards he married Janice and they had a son, Bob Junior.

Finally, his chaotic lifestyle caught up with him and in 1978, while he was working for a computer firm in Dallas, the police arrested him for acting as a middle-man in a drug deal and one of the would-be purchasers turned out to be an undercover narcotics agent. There were questions about entrapment and whether the authorities had pursued Hayes because he was a big name, but none of it really mattered, because for Hayes everything was now out in the open. He had to sink right to the bottom before he could start to climb back up again.

Within a year he was in court to face the charges, and as he sat quietly in the dock his world crumbled dramatically around him. Although he had not taken a cent in any drug deal, his lawyers advised him to plead guilty to the drug trafficking charges, hoping for a lighter sentence, and they paraded an array of character witnesses before the judge. Among them were Tex Schramm, Tom Landry and Roger Staubach, while Hayes told pressmen: 'I could see my wife out there with tears in her eyes. I could see Jake Gaither with tears in his eyes. On every row I could see someone I could say I was personally close to. It was a rock bottom feeling, the emptiest I ever felt in my life.' He took the stand admitting, 'I'm not the smartest guy in the world. If I was, I wouldn't be up here. I'm guilty, I was wrong, but I've paid the price in my image and my respect. People see me as Bob Hayes dope dealer, not Bob Hayes the citizen, and that hurts.'

Judge Richard Mays listened carefully as he heard how Hayes had a tendency to say 'yes' to the wrong sort of people and how he had lost untold commercial opportunities as a result of the offence. Staubach stated that Hayes was a good person who had fallen in with the wrong crowd, while a psychiatrist explained that he had found it difficult to sustain himself as a person of value since quitting football and would not gain anything from prison. But the prosecution lawyers argued just as persuasively that a special case should not be made for Hayes – after all, a similar incident had recently ended with a disgraced track star going to jail for 15 years on similar charges. Apart from that, they said, there was concern about the influence Hayes had on young people. The judge decided, after listening to both sides, that Hayes would go to prison for five years for selling cocaine and receive a seven-year probation on another charge of selling methaqualone.

He was taken to the Texas State Penitentiary in Hartsville to start his sentence, a completely broken man. 'You're standing on the rostrum winning a gold medal and all of a sudden you're in jail,' said Hayes. 'It's like going from the penthouse to the outhouse. It's very difficult to explain, but it's the lowest and worst I have ever felt. And the prison gates really do swing shut with a heavy metal clang. It's just like the movies.' As prisoner No. 290973, he certainly did not receive any star treatment inside, but he kept his head down, refused all but one interview, which was for the Cowboys newspaper, and did everything he was told. 'I didn't learn anything,' he said. 'There was no rehabilitation.

You were just locked up and developed anger and resentment. All I did was play some basketball and softball and lift some weights.' But his good behaviour earned him a parole, and in February 1980 he was back home in Dallas after serving just ten months of his sentence. By then his commercial value had vanished. Lucrative contracts to promote Hershey Foods and American Express were torn up and a Miller Lite commercial he'd filmed before his arrest was abandoned.

Back home, Hayes soon returned to his old way of life, sinking into drink and drugs, as he tried unsuccessfully to rehabilitate himself into society and build a better future. Fortunately, Hayes was the sort of person who attracted a lot of friends as well as hangers-on and it was his real friends who came to his rescue when he needed them most. 'I tried living my way, but it didn't work,' he said, 'so I decided to try it another way and that meant going to a rehabilitation centre. It was there I found out who Bob Hayes really is. Not the track star, not the football star, but the real person. I'm fortunate because now I do know who he is.'

The people responsible for pushing him into the centre were old friends like Staubach, Drew Pearson, Ron Horowitz and Jethro Pugh, and they paid for him to stay there for six months. 'It was there that I got my life back in order,' said Bob, 'and there that I found a greater power in my life that I choose to call God. I had been taking drugs for about three years – they were stimulating, they improved my reflexes, but they also made me miserable. Cocaine is very powerful, it's very fatal. It takes away your ability to think, it takes away your ability to live, it takes away your ability to remember, it takes away all of your goals and I know that if I ever did it again I would end up in a mental institution or I would die. So I made a willing decision to hand my life over to the care of God and He's still in my life.'

The centre made Hayes acutely aware of his problems and how to cope with them, and he believed that he was a much more balanced person for the experience, a bit older and a lot wiser. He owed his real friends a huge debt and said of Roger Staubach: 'He's the kindest man who has ever been in my life. He did more than just help, because if I had continued to drink and take drugs I would probably have died. He was probably the most important guy in my life; without him I wouldn't be here today.' But Hayes was also a realist and the centre taught him that there was no cure for his problem. 'I just take one day at a time and I can't promise that I won't do it again, but I'm not doing it today.'

Speaking in the late 1980s, Tex Schramm said: 'He did some things that were wrong, but he's paid the debt and now he's doing a very fine job and we're all extremely proud of him.' Shortly after coming out of rehabilitation, Hayes worked in the real estate business for Roger Staubach's company, and then spent some time working for Athletic Associates, a company that looked after professional athletes in all sports, handling their finances, their marketing and their problems. There was no man in the world better qualified to counsel on all those things than Bob Hayes.

He also kept in close touch with track and football, attending the annual Bob Hayes Invitational track meet, in his home town Jacksonville, and attending regular Cowboys games, where he was always instantly recognized as 'Speedo', the nickname he had throughout his career, and fans besieged him for autographs and demanded to see his Super Bowl ring. But the years were still not kind to Hayes and he continued his daily struggle with alcohol, spending time in rehabilitation as well as working with vulnerable kids' groups and charity events explaining the perils of addiction.

For many years it seemed that while the Dallas Cowboys fans had forgiven him for what happened, the club had not, stalling on adding his name on their famous 'Ring of Honor', which runs around the giant Texas Stadium celebrating their greatest stars. This was finally put right in 2001, when a greying Hayes was paraded around the stadium in an open-topped car to the rapturous applause of his once adoring fans.

Cowboys owner Jerry Jones had flown him in on his private plane to see his name and No.22 added to the ten other superstar names on the Ring, joining such Dallas legends as Landry, Staubach and Tony Dorsett.

'It feels great. I'm the eleventh, so it makes a full team,' smiled Hayes. 'It's the icing on the cake.'

Jones told a gathering of reporters: 'Bob Hayes was a once-in-a-lifetime talent who was a dominant performer in two sports. He enters the Ring of Honor on the basis of his contributions to this organization. He was a cornerstone to the success of this franchise, someone who helped turn an expansion team into "America's Team".'

In the same year he was able to jog slowly through the middle of the field at the Bob Hayes Invitational track meeting in his home town Jacksonville, brandishing a giant flaming torch, despite struggling more and more with his health. For years he suffered the consequences of his long sporting career. He walked very slowly, pronounced himself a middle-aged cripple and on some mornings he could not even get out of bed, such was the pain in his damaged knees and shoulders. As time went by his health continued to deteriorate and he became a more reclusive figure, living with his mother in Jacksonville and disappearing from public view. The reality was the diagnosis of prostate cancer and the draining rigours of the resulting radiation treatment.

He made a brief public appearance in 2002 to accept a Lifetime Achievement award at the Florida Sports Awards, albeit in a wheelchair. He received a standing ovation as he was wheeled on stage and then stunned the audience by pulling himself out of the chair and walking slowly to a standing microphone.

His short, halting, two-minute acceptance speech was hugely emotional and, true to Hayes's character, also typically mischievous and humorous. Gesturing toward Delores Barr Weaver, the wife of the owner of the local NFL franchise, the Jacksonville Jaguars, he suggested he was still in the market for work if she could put in a good word for him with her husband. The wave of applause seemed to go on forever.

In the mid-1970s Hayes had been inducted into the Track and Field Hall of Fame, but to his everlasting disappointment he had not been inducted into the Professional Football Hall of Fame. It was suggested that his earlier misdemeanours had conspired against him.

Hayes finally succumbed to his illness, which had been further complicated by kidney, liver and heart damage, in September 2002, in hospital in Jacksonville. He was only 59.

More than three thousand people attended his funeral, and his silver casket was draped with a white Olympic flag, flanked by a large black and white photograph of him in a Dallas Cowboys helmet.

The world of football and track turned out in force to pay tribute to him and the Reverend Jesse Jackson, who played football against him in college, told the gathering: 'He held up the nation when he was a second-class citizen living under legal segregation. He couldn't use a downtown toilet in Jacksonville. He couldn't use the public library. He couldn't stay at the Holiday Inn. But a first-class man lifted the nation to heights no exalted one could. If only Bob had observed this gathering when he was alive. He was not just a champion. He was a hero.'

On a more personal level, the former Cowboys running back Calvin Hill said Hayes should be remembered for his kindness and humour. 'Here was a guy who talked to emperors and kings, yet he could meet a janitor and make that janitor feel like he was the most important person in the world.'

The pressure to include Hayes in the Professional Football Hall of Fame continued after his death, and in 2004 he was denied inclusion on the last round of decision-making. One of the judges, the respected *Sports Illustrated* writer Paul Zimmerman, resigned from the selection committee in protest.

But early in 2009 he finally made it, and his son Bob Junior accepted the induction on his behalf. 'In his last days he used to talk about the Hall of Fame,' he said. 'It hurts because he should have been here to witness this special occasion. But unfortunately he didn't make it. I know wherever he is, he's smiling now. He's happy.'

Hayes will be remembered as a giant on the American sports scene and remains the only athlete to win an Olympic gold medal and a Super Bowl ring, but his sporting prowess shouldn't hide the real man. He was kind-hearted and funny; self-deprecating and generous; he made some poor choices and faced some tough challenges throughout his life, and while he couldn't beat them all, he smiled back at them just the same.

The last word should go to his long-time friend and Cowboys quarterback Roger Staubach, because at the Professional Football Hall of Fame induction ceremony he described Hayes, in every sense, the most succinctly.

'He was just a big guy.'

Mexico City 1968

Jim Hines

When Bob Hayes retired from the track after Tokyo and headed for football superstardom, it opened the door to a new wave of sprinters who were all keen to establish themselves as America's next number one. The obvious successor came in the pocket-sized shape of Charlie Greene, who was still beating himself up over the hamstring injury that torpedoed his run to the 1964 Olympics, when he had been the only man to push Hayes all season. 'Sometimes when I'm by myself at night I still think about it,' says Greene, a retired major in the US Army, 'and I really believe I'm two medals short, because I feel I could have got second or third to Bob in Tokyo and a place on the relay team.'

A lacklustre sixth place in the trials meant he missed the trip to Japan, but the disappointment galvanized Greene into action, and he dedicated himself to ensuring that he did not miss out when the Games opened in Mexico the next time around, quickly establishing himself as the world's top performer for the next two years. He even created a larger-than-life image for himself on the track – a fast-talking, super-cool, unsmiling façade aimed at frightening his rivals and entertaining the fans.

'I was so disappointed after the trials in '64 because I knew I had to wait four years, so I devised a kind of poison for myself, so that every time I raced I made it a deadly serious business. I developed this really tough exterior and I ran for one purpose only and that was to be the best sprinter in the world.'

His most famous prop was his dark sunglasses, and he delighted in telling reporters who questioned him about running in them, 'Hey, these aren't sunglasses, they're re-entry shades!' The reasoning behind the idea – which he'd picked up from Henry Carr – was that nobody could see his eyes, and this, coupled with the rest of his image, presented a psychologically intimidating figure on the track, especially for the other competitors.

It was not until midway through the 1967 season that his dominance was seriously challenged by a new hope, a 20-year-old from Oakland, California, called Jimmy Hines. They had met during the previous season when Greene, then at the University of Nebraska, had shown the younger man the way home on each occasion, but in 1967 Greene began to recognize that Hines was a genuine threat to his supremacy, and when he only narrowly beat both John Carlos and Hines in winning the Drake Relays, in April 1967, Greene realized that he had to be very careful indeed.

The next time they met was about a month later at the Modesto Relays, and Greene went into the 100-metre race knowing that he was unbeaten at the distance since September 1964, so when Hines not only beat him, but also equalled the world record in 10 seconds flat, it was a shocking experience for the Nebraska man – but one to which he would grow accustomed. Jim Hines had arrived and he was not going to go away.

Hines was actually born in Dumas, Arkansas, in 1946, but his parents moved with him and his nine brothers and sisters to California when he was only a five-year-old. It was at junior high that he discovered his ability to run fast, when a track coach spotted him darting around in a baseball match and asked him to try out for his team.

He remembers running the 100 yards in 10.6 at the start of the ninth grade and by the end of the same year he had reduced the time to 10.2, so when he started at McClymonds High School he already had something of a pedigree as a sprinter.

In his second year at high school he cut his 100 yards time to a very respectable 9.6 and then managed to drop it by a tenth of a second in the next two years until he matched Jesse Owens's high school record of 9.4. His talent ignited the usual mass interest from big colleges, but he chose Texas Southern, in Houston, not because it was a black college, but because it had the best track and field team in the country and a top coach in Stan Wright at the helm.

As an 18-year-old freshman, he won his first international vest in early 1965 with a team touring Europe, but back home he was still finding Charlie Greene a difficult hurdle to overcome. It was not until early in 1967 that he started to set the sprinting world alight, when indoors he reeled off three world record equalling 5.9s for 60 yards, made some impressive runs for Texas Southern and in May tied Bob Hayes's world 100 yards record in 9.1. The next big race was the confrontation at Modesto between Hines and Greene, where for the first time he managed to beat his old adversary and match the world 100 metres record.

The victory started a riveting rivalry between the two men, of a kind not seen in the sprinting world since the days of Owens and Metcalfe, and it created an immense amount of interest in the sport wherever they ran. Even now Greene and Hines argue about who won more races and who was the better man, although it is more good-humoured than it used to be on the track in the 1960s.

'When I lost that race in Modesto to Jimmy it was shocking for me,' says Greene, 'and it wasn't just because I lost or that I made a mistake, it was because on that day he was better than I was. But I found that hard to understand after being unbeaten for so long. How could he be better than me?'

Greene's confusion was further compounded when less than a month later Hines beat him again in the AAU championships, helped by a dubious start, with the evening temperature still in the nineties. Both men ran 9.4 for the 100 yards into a 5mph headwind and appeared to hit the tape together, but the judges gave the verdict to Hines. It was at about this time that Hines got some extra coaching from the 1956 sprint champion, Bobby Morrow, who was then working in Houston. He helped him to improve his starting, which had been causing him problems and even disqualification from races.

The coaching obviously helped in the run-up to the Games in Mexico City and may have proved a decisive factor in the races that led him to the Olympic title.

Hines and Greene were still running neck and neck, prompting one *Sports Illustrated* journalist to describe them as 'the fastest four-legged sprinter ever sent to the Olympics'. Greene had tied Hayes's 9.1 for 100 yards in the summer of 1967 and, despite losing a couple of races to Hines, he went into the Olympic year still confident of becoming the Olympic champion, but nevertheless aware that Hines was the man he would have to beat.

As the 1968 season began, it was Greene who still held the upper hand, with wins in the Drake Relays, Modesto and San Diego, but the biggest sprinting occasion would be the AAU championships in the heat of Sacramento, California, in June. The 80th running of the championships – which were instantly branded the 'Night of Speed' by the newspapers – are recorded quite correctly as the greatest evening of sprinting in track history, with a wholesale assault on the world record that had never been seen before and probably never will be again. The stars of the show? Who else but Jimmy Hines and Charlie Greene. But they were ably supported by one of the finest line-ups of sprinting talent in the world, most of whom would return to do battle in the Olympics in October.

The scene was set for a memorable evening in the heats, when Hines ran an astounding 9.8 in the 100 metres, which would have smashed the existing 10 seconds flat world record to pieces had it not been for a tailwind of about 6mph, but it sent a rush of excitement through the crowd of 23,000. In the next heat it was Greene's turn to get the fans on their feet, running a legal 10 seconds flat to equal the world record, but slowing down from about 15 metres out.

A couple of hours later, in the first semi-final, Jim Hines made history by becoming the first man to claim a legal run under 10 seconds, with a 9.9, beating, by a metre, Ronnie Ray Smith, who was given the same time. Not to be outgunned in his semi-final, Charlie Greene then went out and ran exactly the same time, becoming the next man to run a legal 9.9 and setting the scene for an epic confrontation in the final to decide who was America's number one.

On this occasion it was Greene, just pipping Hines at the tape, but despite a strong tailwind the time was 10 seconds flat for both men, with Jamaican Lennox Miller third, Smith fourth, the Frenchman Roger Bambuck fifth and Mel Pender sixth. It was one of the classiest sprint fields ever assembled and probably the greatest outside an Olympic Games. Five of the athletes there that night would be among the eight finalists in the 100 metres in Mexico.

'I felt confident after that race that I had a hold on Jimmy,' says Greene, 'because I'd beaten him the first five times we'd raced in '68, but I knew if I made the tiniest error, he'd beat me.' Hines remembers: 'In the final, Charlie jumped out on me, but I made a close race of it. But I had run an official 9.9 and become the first man in history to break the 10-second barrier, so for me that night was the greatest series of sprinting of all time.'

The American organizers decided to leave the Olympic trials to the very last minute, opening a training camp in the middle of a forest at Echo Summit, just to the south of

Lake Tahoe, in California, where the altitude of 7,350 feet would closely simulate the conditions in Mexico. They were not disappointed with the results, as world records fell in the 200, 400 and 400 metres hurdles. The stunning 19.7-second run of John Carlos would, however, never be ratified as a record because he had worn unauthorised 'brush' spiked shoes, a Puma invention that deployed 68 tiny, piranha-toothed spikes at the front of the shoe. They were banned, after Adidas allegedly strong-armed the IAAF to change the rules, on the dubious grounds that they damaged the tracks.

For the final trial of the 100 metres, arguably a stronger field than the Olympic final itself, the temperature had dropped to 63 degrees Fahrenheit. It was Hines' 22nd birthday and he celebrated by powering to victory in ten flat, with the slow-starting Greene second and the veteran Pender squeezing out Ronnie Ray Smith by just a few inches for third.

With the Games now in full view, the 'score' in terms of finals won and lost was Charlie Greene seven, Jimmy Hines four. They still argue about the other races and who won more, with Hines saying: 'We were battling for three years and I still say the record stands about 80/20 in my favour, but I know Charlie will say differently.' Not surprisingly, Charlie does: 'Jimmy was a great sprinter, not a mathematician, so if he read the record books he would see. But it's not important, because it's all there in black and white; in our head-to-head matches I won by far the greatest number of races.'

The US trials meant the 1-2-3 line-up for the 100 metres team was Jimmy, Charlie and Mel Pender, who had been given leave from the US Army in Vietnam to run in Mexico and would return there after the Games, while Ronnie Ray Smith would take his place on unarguably the strongest relay team in the world. Hines says that he would have liked to run in the 200 metres, despite the presence of Tommie Smith, John Carlos and Larry Questad, because he could have run a world record, but it was impossible to double up when the events were held back to back in the trials. Hines and Greene may not have been the closest of friends, but when they found themselves together in the American team, the Olympic cause became something of a common bond between them. As Greene says: 'Overnight we were transformed from a group of competitors into a close-knit outfit. Stan Wright told us it was absolutely vital that one of us win the 100 metres to be the world's fastest human – a title that traditionally the American sprinter holds. So for the good of the country individual ambitions and ideas were suppressed, so we developed a common appreciation for our talent. Going to Mexico we had one objective – that one of us should win.'

The political temperature in Mexico was red-hot, and for weeks beforehand it looked as though the Games might not take place at all because of student demonstrations at the university opposite the Olympic stadium. The students were objecting to alleged government corruption and the huge amount of money the government had spent on staging the Games, a luxury that contrasted sharply with the abject poverty experienced by the majority of the people in the country.

They threatened to disrupt the Games, and as the opening day drew nearer, so the demonstrations grew bigger. The government reacted by sending in the army, and tanks were a common sight outside the university, but few people expected the kind of solution to the problem that the Mexican military finally adopted. On October 2, in the Square of

Three Cultures, in the middle of Mexico City, the army surrounded the demonstrating students and coldly opened fire on them. Official government figures stated that 34 were killed and hundreds injured, but no-one believed them. Contemporary reports varied wildly, suggesting anything between 200 and 500 had been killed and thousands more injured. It was an unimaginable atrocity that would have abruptly ended any sporting event today. Thousands were arrested and somehow the Mexican government of the day managed to persuade the world they had put down a violent anarchist uprising and the Olympics went ahead.

When the Games finally opened, there was a lot of discussion about the effects of the heat and the altitude, the city being 7,000 feet above sea level. The thin air was expected to make life easier in some events and much more difficult in others. Tests showed that the altitude meant 27 per cent less atmospheric pressure and 23 per cent less air density, both of which made life better for the explosive events, particularly the sprints.

These would be the Games where millions of people around the world first saw the Fosbury flop used in the high jump, but they will be remembered most for the prodigious long jump of Bob Beamon, who almost jumped out of the pit with his 29ft 2½in (8.90m), and the other long-term world record from the Games, Lee Evans's incredible 43.8 seconds in the 400 metres.

But they could also have been remembered as the Games that had to go ahead without the talents of Jimmy Hines, who had been seriously considering giving up track before Mexico because of his precarious financial position. He was married and had a one-year-old son, but sprinting was not paying the bills, so when the Miami Dolphins football team stepped in and offered him a lucrative contract to sign and become the new Bob Hayes, he saw an immediate solution to his money problems. 'I almost signed that contract, I really did,' he says. 'But after talking it over with my wife and my parents I finally decided to go for the goal I had set myself in college. I wanted to be like Bob Hayes, who was my idol, so I decided to do it his way.'

Arriving in Mexico City, Hines could not believe the scenes that greeted him: 'There were soldiers everywhere, down all the streets, all around the Olympic village. We had to be guarded when our bus took us to the stadium, and my mind wasn't actually on training for the race, but more on would I be safe? Was I going to make it to the stadium to be able to compete?'

The 100 metres competition, the first to be held on a synthetic track, was a tough one, with 64 sprinters lining up for a first round that saw all the favourites come through unscathed, with Charlie Greene looking particularly good in a slightly windy 10-flat and repeating the feat in the quarter-finals held about six hours later. Meanwhile, Hines was unhappy because his races had been against the world's top men and he was having to run hard just to qualify, especially in the quarters when Lennox Miller pipped him on the line.

It was such a tough competition that in the very next heat Heinz Erbstösser, a sprinter from East Germany – which was running a separate team for the first time – had the distinction of being the first man ever to run a 10.2 and not even make the semi-finals. After the first day of racing in the 100 metres, fate was still pointing her finger in Greene's direction and Hines knew that he had to come up with something special for the semi and the final on the following day. He decided that the best thing he could do was to go and see his wife Joyce, who was staying some miles from the village on the other side of the city, so he went to the coaches and told them where he was going.

'They looked at me like I was crazy,' he said. 'The coach said, "You wanna do what, you wanna stay with your wife the night before the biggest race of your life?" They thought I was joking, so I went back to my room, packed my things and left. Meanwhile, the coaches had been on the phone to my wife and told her to stay away from me. So when I got to the hotel, with a couple of bottles of champagne, she would not let me in. Finally I persuaded her to open the door but she's acting like she doesn't know me, because I'm drinking the champagne and she won't have any. After a while I said, "It's time to go to bed," but she's still not sure, so I said, "We're married, aren't we, let's go." So I had sex with my wife and the next day I got up and went down to the stadium and the rest is history.'

The night's entertainment had relaxed him so much that he felt almost unbeatable when he stood on the track for the semi, running an easy 10-flat to beat Bambuck, Jerome and Pender. In the other semi it was Greene who now looked a little ragged, even though he managed to win in 10.1, holding off Miller, Cuba's Pablo Montes and the little man from Madagascar, Jean-Louis Ravelomanatsoa. As the final would prove, Charlie Greene had been 'up' on the first day of competition, but he was just under 100 per cent on day two, just enough to make him beatable as far as Hines was concerned.

At last the moment came for the final, which saw the first all-black field in Olympic history. After a false start by Ravelomanatsoa, the gun sounded and the sixty thousand crowd erupted as the veteran Pender, the captain of the US track and field team, burst out of his blocks and into an early lead, holding on until the 30-metre mark. Then Hines drew level and in a few strides had passed him smoothly, with Charlie Greene on the inside lane struggling to go with him. But Hines was not going to be caught and kept on accelerating to run through the tape unopposed in a new electronically-timed world record of 9.95, with Miller edging out the lunging Charlie Greene for the silver.

'I just hoped and prayed I could come out near Mel,' said Hines, 'because he was the fastest starter. I think I got the best start of my life and there was Mel out in front and Charlie and I were together. But I felt good because I knew I had another gear and when I switched it on I just went away. As soon as I hit the tape I knew it had to be the greatest race of my life, with a good start, good acceleration and a strong finish, so I felt it had to be a world record time.'

Both Miller and Greene recorded 10 seconds flat, but for Greene it was a disappointing end to his four years of hard work and dedication. 'From about 30 metres Jimmy and I started to make our move,' he said, 'but at 60 I felt a little pull on the outside of my left knee, just like somebody tapped me. So for a split second I had to decide whether to stop or keep going, but in that short space of time I decided I'd come this far and I was going to get one of those medals. But I couldn't increase my speed and I couldn't go with Jimmy the way I normally did and I ended up with third.'

Greene was sporting in defeat and one of the great pictures of the Games was of him and Jimmy hugging each other in the middle of the track. Even on the rostrum they were clowning around as Hines stepped up to receive his gold medal. 'It was – and still is – the greatest feeling of my life,' says Jimmy, 'because you are number one and nobody can take that away from you. There will never be anything to surpass it.'

Jimmy's time, which was an electronic timing, would remain the Olympic record for 20 years and, incredibly, the world record for nearly 15 years, so it remains one of the greatest track runs ever at any distance. But there are plenty of people who have poured cold water on it because it was set at altitude, where the thin air meant less resistance and helped the sprinters achieve better times.

Hines disagrees: 'Since that day people have been saying I ran so fast because of the thin air, but it was the hardest race I ever ran in my life. It was the only time in my life that I finished a race and felt absolutely dead. That thin air didn't help me one bit, in fact it hindered me, because at 80 metres my chest was burning and if that hadn't happened I probably would have broken 9.9. I know I could have run faster if I'd been in any other part of the world.'

So Jim Hines was indeed the fastest man on earth and there now seemed to be time to sit back and enjoy the feeling, because the relay was not scheduled to start until the end of the track competition. But a few days later a new political storm erupted right in the middle of the American team, and every athlete in Mexico was touched by it. It happened when the 200 metres gold and bronze medallists from the United States, Tommie Smith and John Carlos, conducted their infamous Black Power demonstration on the medal dais as the Star Spangled Banner echoed around the stadium. Both Smith and Carlos were members of the Olympic Project for Human Rights, a group of athletes organized to campaign for better treatment of blacks in the USA, and they caused an enormous storm by standing barefoot on the rostrum with their heads bowed and each with one black gloved hand in the air. It was a gesture to express the view that freedom applied only to whites in America.

Hines and Greene were present at the meetings that followed and both saw the demonstration first-hand. Hines says: 'I was a member of the US Olympic track team and although there had been talk of a possible black boycott we all stepped on that plane to Mexico as Americans. What happened was something that was done by those two individuals, while the 40 or so other black athletes, including myself, were just as surprised as everyone else when the gloves went up.'

He told a BBC radio documentary that the protest had a profound effect on him and the US team: 'It was certainly detrimental to my career in terms of finances. Prior to the Olympics, companies were saying to me that if I won a gold medal in the 100 metres there would be endorsements. When I came back they said sorry – we just can't fulfil them. I knew where it came from. It personally cost me a million and a half dollars because contracts were torn up, and a lot of black Americans lost jobs because of it – it really cost black America.'

Greene expresses a different view. He recently told the *Lincoln Star Journal*: 'The public display by Tommie and John was to bring attention that America was lying. Lying about how they treated their own citizens. Every generation of African–Americans have a part to play on the shoulders of the ancestors we stand on.'

The architect of the Olympic Project for Human Rights was sociology professor, Harry Edwards, who had hoped to organize a total black boycott of the Games, and he takes a rather different view of Hines's position after Mexico. 'I don't see why it would have cost him any money,' he said. 'He did not do anything, he wasn't about anything, he didn't understand what was going on then and probably doesn't understand what was going on today. The reality was that the average black Olympian came home to the same thing that every other black Olympian had come home to. It didn't make any difference.

'If he thought that by not being part of the movement and by not speaking out and supporting the effort he was going to make some money then he was dumber than I thought he was. The only reason there is money to be made for black athletes today is because of people like Smith, Carlos, Jim Brown, Muhammad Ali and Arthur Ashe who said things had to change. Jim Hines had no impact.'

But Hines feels that the whole Black Power issue diluted his achievement. 'The 100-metre dash is the No.1 event, but when I came home to America after the Games all anyone wanted to talk about was the gloved salute and the disrespect it showed. It completely overshadowed what I'd done.'

The storm had not really died down when the sprint relay team went out. Although the coaches knew that Greene was still not completely fit, they decided to persevere with him, but in the final it was more poor baton passing that left anchorman Hines about five feet behind Cuba in third place. But in a storming run, reminiscent of Hayes's performance in Tokyo, he tore past the field and hit the tape about a yard clear of the Cuban Figuerola, then jogged, smiling, to the side of the track and hurled his baton into the crowd with delight. The time was a new world record of 38.24 and one watch clocked Hines's final leg at a staggering 8.2 seconds.

He now had two gold medals and Greene had finally got his, but as they stood on the rostrum they knew their careers would now take completely different paths. Greene would carry on running until 1972, where he could only manage the quarter-finals of the Olympic trials, and continue his career as an officer in the US Army, as well as his his charitable work with the Special Olympics in Washington DC.

A few months after Mexico, he married Linda, a *Philadelphia Inquirer* reporter, and they had two daughters. He retired from an outstanding military career in 1989 and went on coaching, working as assistant manager on the US Olympic team at Atlanta 1996. He's since moved back to Nebraska, where sadly he has struggled with his health, first undergoing a heart triple-by-pass operation, then a serious neck problem that required radical surgery, and finally kidney failure, which needed hours of dialysis and then, in early 2010, a kidney transplant.Greene isn't talking or moving quite so fast these days, but his keen sense of humour has survived his brushes with near-death. 'It was St Valentine's night and I got a call from the hospital asking if I still wanted a kidney. They had found a match. I said yes and they said I had to get to Omaha inside six hours. There was a big snowstorm outside, but we made it.'

He has had to learn to walk all over again and today any distance requires a cane and a great deal of patience and endeavour. But asked about his future, he says it's 'to keep on mending'. He still loves the sport and follows track just as keenly as ever. 'I'm pretty sure I could beat all these guys today,' he laughs, 'but maybe not Usain Bolt. Man, he was fast.'

Silver medallist Lennox Miller went on to run a dental practice in Pasadena for thirty years and still holds a world record – albeit as part of a USC quartet that broke the record for the rarely run 4 x 110 yard relay at the 1967 NCAAs, where he took the baton from a certain O. J. Simpson. Miller's daughter Inger would win gold in the sprint relay at the Atlanta Games of 1996.

And it's worth a nod to Ronnie Ray Smith, the second man to record a legal 9.9 seconds and a gold medal winner in the relay. After retiring from the track and spending a largely uneventful career in the Los Angeles parks department, he died in a hospice in 2013, at the age of 64. But it was his funeral that caught national attention – an Olympic-themed send-off that aired on a US cable network show bizarrely entitled *Best Funerals Ever*. It featured Smith's casket being raced over the finish line of a track and then stood up on a makeshift podium surrounded by family and friends adopting a black glove-fisted salute.

Meanwhile, back in the post-Mexico limelight, Jim Hines was now confident of becoming the next Bob Hayes, and even as he stood on the rostrum the men from the Miami Dolphins were waiting in the wings with a contract and a pen, eager for him to sign.

Looking back, Hines genuinely believed that at just 22 he could have carried on running for a good many years and been a top contender for medal honours in the 1972 and 1976 Olympics; he was even quoted recently as saying that he should have stayed in track and earned a few thousand dollars under the table. At the time, however, the attraction of big money in the NFL was impossible to resist and he signed for the Dolphins almost as soon as he returned home, with both parties hoping to see a re-run of the success Bob Hayes was having with the Dallas Cowboys.

Sadly it was a false hope, and although his arrival and four-year $150,000 contract were fanfared in real American fashion, with Miami President Joe Robbie claiming it was 'the safest bet we ever made', Hines could not produce the goods on the field.

There was a major difference between Hayes and Hines in terms of their footballing careers. At college, Hayes was a football star who ran track, but Hines didn't actually touch a ball. He had gone to Texas Southern on a track scholarship and, while he had been a good football player in high school, the coaches at college were not keen to see their sprinting investment knocked around on the football field. 'I think I suffered a little bit because the Dolphins drafted me with the expectation of me being another Bob Hayes. But they didn't realize, or perhaps they didn't particularly care, that I had missed four very important years of college football. They were expecting me to come in and do what Bob had done with the Cowboys and that put me under pressure.'

Meanwhile, some of the other Miami players resented a newcomer arriving from nowhere with no college pedigree and picking up a big pay cheque. The Dolphins wanted to use his speed as a wide receiver, but Hines was having trouble catching the ball and the

Miami fans uncharitably christened him 'Oops', while others suggested he had 9.9 feet and 12.9 hands. So he spent most of his time on the bench, and although in three years at Miami he caught 11 of the 14 passes that were thrown his way in game competition, the press only seemed interested in the ones he dropped or fumbled.

He feels that, given more opportunity, he could have done better at Miami. After he was cut from their side he tried his luck briefly with the Kansas City Chiefs and finally joined the Oakland Raiders, but he never got on the field for the Californian club. In early 1973 he was laid off, and he decided to give up his dream of emulating his hero Hayes for good.

Throughout his football career he had been running occasional professional races, sometimes against other former Olympic stars and at other times against horses, but the one good thing about hardly setting foot on a football field was that he came out of the game without a scratch. So when a professional track circuit was set up in 1973, he was able to take advantage of it. For three years he plied his trade around the world, even setting a world record of 11.7 in Australia for the 130 yards on grass.

It was nearly ten years after his triumph in Mexico when the pro circuit folded and he had to start looking around for work, but ten years is a long time and he had little to show for his efforts during that time; the money had gone and so had his fame. Even though he was still the fastest man in the world, there were no commercial opportunities and he was not even recognized on the streets of his own home town.

He had to face the unpleasant fact that he was a former Olympic champion who was looking for a job, and those years since Mexico had effectively been nothing more than a waste of his time and talent. First he worked in recreation in Houston, then moved to Austin, where he became director of the city's Human Services Department, an important and responsible position, organizing welfare programmes, helping the underprivileged and doing counselling work. However, he gave that up and came home to Oakland where he got involved in more local government work, before he ran into an old friend, Dr Thomas Jones.

Dr Jones had known Jimmy for 25 years and was saddened by seeing him unable to fulfil his potential, especially when he watched him racing horses in 1984 and losing. He put Jimmy to work in his own company, a business that looked after men and women at all levels of sport, from high school through to top professional competition, and gave him a job as an agent and scout. Now retired, he pops up regularly on the hall of fame circuit and is always good for a sharp quote or a biting recollection. The waistline is a little wider and the hairline receding, but he still talks the talk. 'I am still the greatest sprinter,' he says. 'I am the original world's fastest. I won 99 per cent of my races in the 100. Nobody ever did that.'

'You know life is hills and valleys, ups and downs, and I've experienced that', he says. 'But I've always been a positive person. Of course, people always expected you to be rich, with a gigantic car, a million-dollar house and fine clothes, but when I meet people I just let them know I'm not like that. I've had ordinary eight-till-five jobs and I'm just an everyday person.'

His story has a lot of parallels with the life of Jesse Owens, in that Jesse spent a lot of years in limbo before he found his way, so perhaps the same thing will happen to Hines. 'I can relate to Jesse Owens' story step by step,' he says, 'and I consider him to be the greatest sprinter who ever lived.'

It is strange to think that, even though Hines was the first man to break the 10-second barrier, his name is rarely mentioned when track people start talking about the greatest, but perhaps that is because he was so quickly off the scene and forgotten. He admits that he will not be mentioned in the same breath as Owens or even Hayes, but he hopes that when knowledgeable people talk about sprinting his name will come out.

Perhaps the whole Black Power furore did disguise his achievements, and to this day he cuts a somehow disappointed figure, a man still described as the greatest athlete never known.

Unknown perhaps, but never lacking in confidence. 'I hear there are plans to make a computerized race of all the greatest sprinters of all time,' he says. 'That would be exciting and if they did I think I'd be pretty close.'

Munich 1972

Valeri Borzov

'The Fastest Human is a Commie'. Not a headline you see every day, and certainly not one that was particularly welcome in the United States. But that was the excitable view of *The New York Times* after both sprint events at the 1972 Munich Olympics were completely dominated by the powerful and fluent running of 22-year-old Soviet star Valeri Borzov.

The poker-faced hero of Eastern Bloc athletics, nicknamed 'The Ukraine Express' by the newspapers, destroyed two top-class fields in successive sprint finals, tearing from the grasp of the Americans the two gold medals that they considered virtually their own property. It almost started a second front in the Cold War.

What was even harder for the United States to stomach was the calamitous bureaucratic foul-up that saw their two best contenders, Eddie Hart and Rey Robinson, who had both equalled the 9.9-second world record before Munich, comfortably win their first round heats and then crash out of the competition without putting another foot on the track. When that controversy finally started to die down, the US press turned its venom on the inoffensive Borzov, describing him as an automaton and hinting that the reason for his emergence was the existence of a high-tech sprinting 'factory' somewhere in the Soviet hinterland which was busily churning out dubiously-fuelled athletes in production-line fashion. It read like the pages of poor science fiction, but it demonstrated the strength of feeling in the United States about losing their prized 'Fastest Man on Earth' title. Today, Valeri Borzov, a little wider and a little heavier than in his prime running days, just smiles when he's reminded of those newspaper stories, 'R-O-B-O-T,' he says with a big grin, giving an admirable impression of how a T-800 Terminator might have tackled an Olympic sprint final. He can afford to laugh about it now, but even today there are still people who write him off as a man-made sprinter, who was pushed into a pair of spikes just because he was the right height and weight and could pass a few biological laboratory tests. The reality is different, and the obvious reply to those who doubt Borzov's right to a place alongside history's great sprinters is to ask them to name all the other top Soviet sprinters.

Borzov was the only world-class sprinter to emerge from the old Soviet Union, in fact the only one to come out of the Eastern Bloc. Even their advanced training methods cannot create the ability to sprint – it requires an inborn quality and few have it. The old Soviet coaches quickly recognized Borzov's potential, trained it well, allowed it to develop and flourish naturally and then applied science to hone his technique to world-class standards. However, without the original talent all the work that followed would have been to no avail.

Borzov's speed first materialized as a child in the town of Sambir, about 75 kilometres southwest of the Ukrainian city of Lviv, close to the Polish border, where he was born in 1949. When the family moved to a town near the Black Sea, his new home was close to a long stretch of sand dunes, and the young Borzov spent many hours playing in them, unconscious of the fact that the soft ground was strengthening his legs. The sand gave way underfoot and anyone trying to walk over it would sink in ankle-deep, so each footstep needed two or three times more effort, which in turn strengthened the muscles and tendons and encouraged him to move fast so as not to sink.

'Only now I understand that spending a great deal of time playing all those energetic games on the sand contributed to the development of my leg muscles,' says Borzov, 'and as I got older I often used sand in my training, either on the beaches of Novaya Kachovka, where I used to live, or in Kiev. It was very effective.'

He was always running as a child, whether it was an errand for his parents or racing his friends at school, but he did not realize how fast he really was until the day he overtook a moving car. 'I used to try and catch the cars in the town as they went past,' he says, 'and on one particular day I succeeded in catching and passing one. It happened on several other occasions and it was then I realized I had an aptitude for sprinting.'

Before his twelfth birthday, he was spotted by coach Boris Voitas, who kindled in him a genuine love of athletics, and although he put him through a rigorous basic coaching regime to prepare him for what was to come, Voitas always stressed that sport should be enjoyed. His methods ensured that Borzov would not tire of athletics before he fulfilled his true potential. To that end he invented games for Borzov to play, which stood him in good stead for the years ahead and included one essential lesson for a great sprinter – relaxation.

'We made paper tubes and Voitas would order us to run 100 metres holding them in our teeth,' recalls Borzov. 'The one who did not bite or squeeze the tube was considered a sprinter, while the rest were considered to be simply runners.'

After Voitas laid the foundations he handed over his protégé to the scientific approach of Valentin Petrovsky, a senior lecturer at Kiev's Institute of Physical Culture, where Borzov was studying biomechanics. When he came under Petrovsky's guidance, he possessed natural speed, all the correct basic habits and the right mental approach to the sport; so all that was needed was to tap his vast potential.

Petrovsky's method of achieving this goal was to take a scientific view, breaking down the 100 metres race into small component parts and analysing the requirements for each section and how Borzov should reach them, even to the extent of studying in forensic detail his running patterns, from the push-off at the start, the pick-up and the middle of the race, right through to the finish. Modern coaches apply the same rules today.

His movements were calculated to within thousandths of a second and Petrovsky demanded that each individual movement was sped up in order to get a faster overall race. The calculations were made with slide rule accuracy and resembled the designing of an aircraft rather than the training of a sprinter, although Petrovsky liked to compare it to the detailed training of a top ballet dancer. In his quest to find the perfect sprinting model, he even made use of slow-motion films of some of the past sprint champions so that Borzov could watch and learn from them, both the things he should emulate and the bad habits he should avoid.

'After the basic preparation I had gone through there would not have been a better coach than Petrovsky,' says Borzov. 'We suited each other and I was good material for him. Voitas handed me over to him for a very specific purpose and it produced very positive results. I believe it is better to have a first coach, then a second to train you to the highest level of performance. I don't think that one coach can prepare an athlete from the beginning right up to Olympic standard, though there have been such cases.'

At the age of 17, Borzov ran 10.5 seconds for 100 metres in the Ukraine schools championships, and Petrovsky knew that he was ready to make the breakthrough from average sprinter to world class, although it was not to be a painless transition. For two years, he pushed himself to the limit only to be frustrated by repeated injuries and breakdowns, spending weeks hospitalized in plaster after a succession of tendon, ligament and muscle injuries – a depressing run that threatened to put an end to his track career before it even got off the ground. There were times when both athlete and coach feared that the breakthrough would never happen, but after two years their hard work and Borzov's suffering finally paid off.

In 1968, after winning the European junior sprints, he equalled the world indoor 60 metres best of 6.4 seconds – albeit hand-timed – and in 1969 he went into his first full season, clear of injury and with his body hardened to the stress he would now place upon it. He entered the Soviet championships in Kiev, where, on a rain-soaked, floodlit cinder track, he set the crowd alight by taking the 100 metres title in an electrifying 10 seconds flat, equalling the Soviet and European records – a star was born.

The Soviet sprint title was the first in a series of targets that Petrovsky had mapped out for his rising young star, but he never made the mistake of pushing him too far, too soon. 'We planned the targets according to the state of my preparations,' Borzov says. 'That is to say, we never planned any goal which I would not be able to achieve. This gave me great confidence in my potential and kept me mentally in balance. There were indeed stages. Winning the Soviet championships was the first, then trying to "look good", as Petrovsky would say, in the European Championships, then trying to compete with the Americans and, only when I had beaten the Americans several times, to try to get through to the final of the Olympic Games.'

In 1969, and now Soviet champion, Borzov had his athletics 'coming out' at the European Championships in Athens, where he ran for the first time on the new synthetic Tartan track, a surface which he liked immediately. He responded by surprising even his Soviet supporters and winning the 100-metre title. He followed this success with more victories around Europe, and then horrified the Americans by beating some of their best sprinters in a USA–USSR meeting in Leningrad, a result that the US experts put down to a temporary aberration on the part of their athletes.

But there could be no excuses when Borzov defeated them again – this time on

American soil. In another USA–USSR clash, this time in Berkeley, California, in the summer of 1971, Borzov beat Jim Green and Delano Meriwether – along with Jamaicans Lennox Miller and a young Don Quarrie – stunning the crowd of 17,000 and prompting an *Oakland Tribune* sports reporter to write: 'The race did prove that Valeri Borzov, the Russian champ, is for real. He just overpowered the field with a complete race.'

Borzov recalled: 'In Berkeley I won over all the American sprinters while the stadium was completely silent. The American fans sat with their mouths open and their athletes became afraid.'

He continued to beat the best the world had to offer, including the top US stars Ivory Crockett and Herb Washington, maintaining his unbeaten record over the 100-metre distance right through and, as it turned out, well beyond the Munich Olympics. He rounded out the 1971 season by taking both the 100- and 200-metre titles at the European Championships, in Helsinki. The workmanlike and unemotional way in which he went about his running led to his reputation as an automatic runner, almost programmed, which was something the Americans loved to claim, especially when their athletes were on the receiving end of another beating.

'There was a lengthy period when I lost to no one, but I never considered competitions in such a superficial way,' says Borzov. 'Not a single victory was automatic. It was always achieved in a sharp, competitive struggle, though it's true that at this stage I was much stronger. I simply had greater speed. For an outsider it looked as if I took part and won a competition automatically, but for me at that time it was not always important to win. In every competition I developed some kind of tactical variation that I would be able to use in a race of higher standard where there was greater competition.'

The more he won, the more attention and publicity he received, especially in the Western press, where he was berated as merely the latest in a long line of products from the Soviet sports system, a man-made sprinter, cold as ice, with all the personality of a robot. 'I'm used to certain titles given to sportsmen who achieved some outstanding or just good results,' says Borzov, 'and I was no exception. I was called the human rocket, a robot and many other names. My attitude towards it was a positive one. I thought journalists had the right to give sportsmen various titles, but I was never a machine, I've always been an active participant, not just a robot. The fact that I expressed no emotions was true, it was a tactic. I never jumped around after a race, and this contributed to the journalists' opinion that I was a robot. I was a normal human being just like now.'

The acid test of just how good he really was would be in the ultimate athletic competition, the Olympic Games, where his unbeaten record and consistency made him one of the favourites. His real competition, suggested the journalists, would come from the two Americans, 23-year old Eddie Hart and 20-year old Rey Robinson, who had both clocked 9.9 seconds in the US Olympic trials, as well as Jamaica's 1968 silver medallist Lennox Miller and the improving Hasely Crawford from Trinidad. After the heat, altitude and political chaos of Mexico, Munich was expected to be a much smoother and calmer affair – the friendly Games. The German authorities had spent £300 million on new state of the art facilities, including a vast canopied main stadium described by one British journalist as giving 'the impression that here was a circus that would never leave town'.

It would be the games in which Russian gymnast Olga Korbut captured the hearts of the watching world and where seven gold medals were won by American swimmer Mark Spitz. They saw the most controversial basketball game in history – when the Soviet Union controversially beat the USA after the officials ruled the last three seconds had to be replayed – and they witnessed the dominance of Finland's distance runner, Lasse Viren.

But the Games would be overshadowed by the spectre of a dreadful terrorist atrocity, when the Palestinian Black September group breached the low security surrounding the Olympic village, scaled an unguarded fence and broke into the quarters of the Israeli team. Two Israeli athletes died in the initial attack and nine more were held hostage. A list of demands was issued to the authorities, including a plane to fly them out of Germany, but after they were all driven by bus to an air base 15 miles outside Munich, a botched rescue attempt ended with the deaths of all the Israeli hostages as well as five of the terrorists. Three others were captured. It was the darkest day in Olympic history and though the Games continued, they were suspended for 24 hours as a tribute to the murdered athletes.

On Thursday, August 31 – a bright summer morning – the horror of this massacre was still five days away. The Games were just getting up and running, when 90 athletes from 58 countries arrived in the stadium for the first round of the 100 metres competition.

The first heat of the competition began just after 11am, with Borzov, Hart and Robinson all cruising easily through the first round and into the quarter-finals, which were due to start at 4.15pm, with the semis and the final on the following day. What subsequently happened is now part of athletics folklore and robbed the two American sprinters of the chance of continuing in the Games, because as their quarter-final heats were called neither athlete was in the stadium, both thinking they were not required on the track for several more hours.

The sad tale has never been explained properly and at the time US sprint coach Stan Wright took the blame for their non-appearance, but it was his out-of-date schedule, given to him by the US authorities, rather than suggestions that he could not read a 24-hour clock, that caused Hart and Robinson to be disqualified for turning up late. In an event so closely defined by the clock it was an unimaginable irony. The story goes that the three American 100 metres men, Hart, Robinson and Robert Taylor, were told that their races were at 7pm, so they were in the Olympic village, about to head to the stadium when, by chance, Robinson spotted a monitor at one of the gates which was showing athletes lining up for a 100-metre race. He asked one of the ABC-TV staff if it was a re-run of the first round. When he was told that it was a live transmission, he realized that he was watching the start of the very heat in which he was supposed to be running. The three athletes were driven at high speed to the stadium, in an ABC-TV studio van, but both Robinson and Hart were too late, while Taylor had just enough time to hastily get changed before running out on to the track for his heat.

The Americans tried vainly to get their sprinters back into the competition, but the IOC and the German organizers, sticklers for the rules, refused. Many people remember the resulting controversy over the debacle, especially in the United States, but few are aware that Valeri Borzov also came close to missing the same quarter-final.

According to the Ukrainian, he and Petrovsky were told by the German officials that their heat was to be put back by half an hour, which also suggests there may have been a little 'home' blame attached to the Americans's exit. Borzov wanted to go to the practice field but his coach told him to stay at the stadium, so he found himself a comfortable spot to sit and promptly dozed off. 'When I woke up I saw my race had come up on the board,' he said, 'and I could see the competitors going on to the track. I tried to get on to the track but I was not allowed to, a German official would not let me through. I told him who I was and that my race was about to start, but he still refused, so I lifted him out of the way and ran out on to the track. I had just about enough time to install the starting blocks and take off my tracksuit when the official commanded "Ready".'

To this day, he does not know what caused the confusion, but he thinks it was tragic that Hart and Robinson were deprived of the chance to take part in the event. 'These things just should not happen at the Olympic Games,' he says tersely.

As for America's number one sprinter, Eddie Hart, the pain of missing out on the biggest moment of his sporting life is something he has never forgotten. It became a defining experience for him.'I remember us driving to the stadium,' he recalls,' speeding the wrong way down one-way streets, swerving around police cordons. I had got halfway down the tunnel which connected the practice track and the stadium when my race went off – I was just seconds from making it.'

Hart is an intelligent and articulate man, but it is not easy answering the obvious question about what might have been had he made it through to the final. 'I was in the best shape of my life, with a 9.9 in the trials, and I felt very good. I really felt invincible and I was still on that plateau coming into the Olympics. At the very least I feel I would have given Borzov a real test, but I don't think I would have lost.'

One interesting facet of the sorry affair was that Borzov drew strength from the fact that his two main rivals were out of the competition, while Robert Taylor, the sole survivor of the US team in the event, was exposed to additional pressure. Hart was at least able to take a gold medal home in the relay, while Robinson left empty-handed, but for both men the feeling of disappointment and anti-climax was immense.

'I have managed to put it into perspective over the years,' says Hart, 'because I really had to come to grips with it. But it's still a big empty spot in my life. I could have accepted losing, but the idea of not even getting the opportunity to compete was really confusing for me.' As for Robinson, who was head track coach at Florida A&M, he described the incident as 'like being in a car accident that's your fault when you have no insurance and everyone on the freeway has stopped to look at you. It has stayed in the back of my mind forever because I really think I could have won it.'

Stan Wright was castigated on live television by ABC's legendary front man Howard Cosell, something Wright later described as 'unfair and inaccurate', explaining that he had been given outdated schedules by the US team, who in turn had been misled by the organizers. Wright, who was inducted into the Track and Field Hall of Fame in 1993 and died in 1998, was certainly made the scapegoat, but in a report prepared later for the US Olympic committee he was completely, but much more quietly, exonerated.

Despite the shock of almost missing the race, Valeri Borzov again proved his mettle by winning the quarter-final in 10.07, easily the best time of the competition, telling Soviet sports reporters after the race, 'You could say I produced my best time out of sheer fright.'

After winning his semi-final, he lined up in the final, the ultimate goal on the list of Coach Petrovsky's targets. Although Hart and Robinson were out, Robert Taylor was still a threat, along with Miller, Crawford and Borzov's fast-starting Soviet team-mate, Aleksandr Kornelyuk, so there was still plenty of excitement for the capacity eighty thousand crowd.

At the gun, the field seemed to get away together, but at the 30-metre mark Borzov, drawn in lane two and just coming upright after a copybook start, began to ease away and was never headed, crossing the line in 10.14, with his arms thrust high above his head in an uncharacteristic display of emotion, with Taylor a metre behind and Miller third.

'Straight after crossing the line I thought, "I can't believe the Olympic gold medal can be won so easily." I was absolutely elated,' he remembers, 'I even wanted to talk to journalists! But it's impossible to express in words the state one is in when you get an Olympic medal.'

Despite the convincing nature of his win, the mood of the post-race press conference was very uncharitable, especially from the American journalists. This was reflected in *The New York Times* article written by Red Smith, under the headline 'The Fastest Human is a Commie', which unkindly and inaccurately suggested that his race was 'mechanically perfect and in no respect remarkable'. Much of the questioning he faced at the conference centred on the absence of Hart and Robinson rather than the manner of his own victory, or the fact that he had become the first Soviet athlete to win a gold medal on the track in an event below 5,000 metres.

Some journalists even suggested that Borzov would not have been wearing the gold medal around his neck had the two Americans been in the final. It's a question that he has heard many times since and he always answers firmly. 'Both at the time and now I think that a victory in the Olympic Games gives one the right to be justifiably considered the best at the time. In this particular case I do not think that Hart and Robinson would have changed the situation, though I always considered them to be strong sprinters. I think at the time I was better than them and I achieved victory in an objective situation. After the 100 metres race I took part in the 200 metres race with American sprinters and I won.'

His 200 metres success was actually more convincing than his win in the shorter sprint, even though he had not intended to run in both events and had to be persuaded to take part by the Soviet team coaches. He was already committed to anchoring the sprint relay team and was worried that running in the 200 metres might affect his relay performance. But after his success in the 100 metres, he felt in excellent shape and ready to take on the world, especially the Americans who had tried to devalue his victory. He almost ambled through the 200 metres competition all the way to the final, and in one heat actually turned and spoke to US athlete Larry Burton as he cantered down the home straight, a sign of his relaxed mood and one of the factors that finally convinced him that he could win the final.

This time there could be no excuses from the Americans as the three US athletes – Burton, Larry Black and Charles Smith – had all qualified for the final and were beaten out of sight by a scintillating run from Borzov, who paced himself beautifully out of the turn, catching Black down the home straight, shifting gear and roaring home with two metres to spare. He had enough time to turn and give the rest of the field a derisory glance over each shoulder before flinging his arms into the air, with the clock stopping at 20 seconds flat, a new European record, with Black second and Italian Pietro Mennea third. Victory made Borzov the first man to take the sprint double since Bobby Morrow in 1956.

After the race he refused, with some justification, to attend the usual press conference, saying that he had been unfairly treated by the US journalists after the 100 metres final. One of the more interesting things he told the Soviet sports reporters was that he believed he had run only at 90 per cent power, although today he feels even that was probably an overestimate. 'I now think I used much less than 90 per cent, maybe 70 per cent,' he says, 'but if I'd used 100 per cent I would have just fallen apart.' His suggestion that he beat all the USA could offer without even turning on full power antagonized the American press still further, and from then on he always got a raw deal from them. He did get the last laugh, however, when a reporter from the respected *Track & Field News* asked him later about the percentage remark and he replied, with tongue firmly in cheek, that it was true and it had really taken it out of him throwing his arms in the air at the end of the race.

In the sprint relay final, the Soviet team was handicapped by injury and late replacement Juris Silovs got cramp on the third leg and only just managed to pass the baton to anchorman Borzov before he ran out of the end zone, which would have resulted in instant disqualification. Borzov was now way down the field in fifth place, with American Eddie Hart streets ahead, but another gutsy run brought him past everyone bar Hart and he crossed the line in silver medal position. He always insisted that had it been a 200-metre race he would have caught Hart. 'In Munich anything was possible for me,' he says.

For the first time since 1932, the winning 4 x 100 metres team did not include the 100 metres champion, but at least Hart got his gold medal, leading the US quartet alongside: Larry Black, who went on to be a personal trainer and died in 2006; Gerald Tinker, who played in the NFL for the Atlanta Falcons and Green Bay Packers; and silver medallist Robert Taylor, who became an elementary school teacher and died in Texas, in 2007.

Tinker ran a superb third leg to hand anchorman Hart a five-metre lead. He managed to hold that margin and smashed the world record in 38.19 seconds. 'Borzov wasn't going to run me down, any more than I would have run him down if he'd built the same lead,' said Hart in a 2017 book called *Disqualified*, in which he re-visited his career and his Munich experience, even returning to the stadium for the first time since 1972.

In the book, Hart completely absolved coach Stan Wright of any blame and instead pointed a finger at the US track and field team manager George Wilson. He was a US Olympic official who had failed to retrieve and distribute an updated race schedule from his mailbox because he'd been too busy dealing with a situation involving pole vaulter Bob Seagren being banned from using his own poles in the competition.

'Stan wrote things down. He had things in order. He was very organized,' wrote Hart. 'Stan and the sprinters became a family in Munich. The four of us were happy to win the gold medal, but we were just as happy to win it for Stan, because that gold medal was like a salve to the wound. It would have been devastating had we not won – both to Stan and us. But I truly believe Stan Wright didn't recover from that 100-metre mistake until the day he died.'

It's clear from the book that Hart believes the USOC threw Wright under the bus. When he returned home he never heard a word from anyone from the US Olympic family, though he did get a letter from President Richard Nixon expressing his sorrow for what had happened and commending Hart for how he handled the situation.

Hart retired from the track after Munich, enjoyed a successful coaching career and took part in Masters events, running a 10.8-second 100 metres aged 40. He now runs the non-profit Eddie Hart All In One Foundation for under-privileged kids in Pittsburgh, a blue-collar town 40 miles east of San Francisco. He found his recent trip back to Munich in 2015 emotionally overwhelming, but in his own words 'got a 43-year-old albatross off my neck' by pulling on his old USA vest, getting out on the old track and in front of just a handful of tourists actually re-running the 100 metres on his own. He was 64 years old.

'If Valeri Borzov wants to have a 100-metre showdown,' he concluded, 'I'll be ready. I've been ready since 1972'.

As the troubled Munich Olympics closed, it was Borzov, the Soviet Union's brightest star, who was given the honour of carrying the country's flag at the final ceremony, despite a threat that a bomb would be thrown at the team flag bearer, which came amid the international recriminations over the Palestinian terrorist atrocities. When Borzov eventually returned home he was treated like a superstar and had to deal with the hitherto Western problem of hero-worship, especially from the young fans. 'I had a great number of problems because people recognized me on the streets,' he says, 'and I was forced into spending a lot of time telling them how I became Olympic champion, which was very exhausting. But I felt that people respected me because I was representing the city of Kiev, our Ukrainian republic and the Soviet Union at the Olympics and was worthy of representing them.'

During the Games, the newspapers in the Soviet Union had devoted huge amounts of space to reports of his progress and medal-winning runs. In fact, in one edition of *Pravda* he got practically an entire page to himself, while on the same day one-time hero Boris Spassky was relegated to just three lines when he lost the world chess championship to American Bobby Fischer.

What Borzov could not have known was the effect that competing and winning in Munich would have on him, and for more than a year the world seemed to cave in on him. Almost a lifetime's work had been fulfilled by victory, during a few fleeting seconds, at the Olympics. Now that all his goals had been achieved, there was nothing left except a terrible feeling of emptiness. He could not sleep and even his work failed to interest him. His condition was diagnosed as nervous shock, and he was told that only time would bring a cure.

There was nothing that he could do to cure himself, so he surrendered to the depression and waited for it to pass. Gradually, as the months went by, it did diminish and his interest in both his work and the track slowly returned. However, to the outside world, especially the West, it appeared that he had gone into a sudden and premature retirement. Finally he forced himself back on to the track and began to train again, only then realizing just how important the feeling of running had become to him. He told a Soviet writer-friend at the time: 'I very often have the following urge. I suddenly feel on the street that I have to run. I absolutely have to run, dressed in a suit, wearing my hat and tie, not paying attention to the passers-by. I have to because I feel a certain rhythm inside me that completely dominates my body. It's like a melody that won't leave you alone. Then convention gets the upper hand and I restrain myself. It's painful but I feel happy inside.'

The remarks show the real drive inside Valeri Borzov and hardly represent the programmed thoughts of an automaton.

He finally made it back on to the track in the 1974 season and went on to reclaim his European 100-metre title in Rome, although he did not feel sufficiently strong to test himself over 200 metres. He returned home to begin preparations for the Montreal Olympics, with the Soviets convinced that he could hold on to the two gold medals he had won in Munich.

His rivals always respected his talent and knew that he would still represent a threat in Canada. In the Soviet Union, the younger athletes hero-worshipped him. Just prior to Montreal, Aleksandr Aksinin, then an up-and-coming sprinter from St Petersburg, described how he felt about Borzov to a sports reporter. 'He is unique in terms of talent, inner reserve and also will-power. Probably will-power is his strongest point. It's uncanny, when you line up alongside him for a competition you just know, you feel it in your bones that he'll win. You have no chance. Magnetism is just oozing out of him.'

Borzov clearly had a considerable psychological edge over his fellow Russian sprinters, but the rest of the world's top fast men, although holding him in high regard, genuinely felt that this time around he could be beaten. As it turned out, the improving Hasely Crawford took the gold, with Jamaica's smooth-running Don Quarrie second and Borzov third. He was disappointed, but the Soviets regarded his run as a success. After all, no previous Olympic champion at 100 metres had returned to an Olympics and won a medal in the same event.

After the 100 metres he pulled out of the 200 metres, blaming a niggling injury, but he still turned out in the relay, anchoring a well-drilled Soviet team to another silver.

During the Games, Borzov began making serious plans of a more personal nature. He and the four-time gold medal winning gymnast Lyudmila Turishcheva decided to marry, news that made major headlines, especially in the Soviet Union, where they were probably the two biggest sporting stars in the country. However, they were not brought together by their sporting success but by their political fervour.

'We first met at work,' says Turishcheva. 'Both of us were young Communists, active young Communists. We met at a Young Communist Central Committee Conference, and then at various meetings, though at that time we didn't know we were going to be husband and wife. But when we were in Montreal we were already good friends and started making plans.'

They were married in 1977, and just over a year later daughter Tania arrived on the scene, an event greeted with great enthusiasm in the Soviet Union, especially by the newspapers, which immediately christened her 'supergirl'. At this time, Borzov was still hoping to make the Soviet team for the 1980 Olympics, held on home soil in Moscow, but a series of injuries, culminating in complicated operations on both Achilles tendons, put an end to that dream and to his running career. However, he did take an active role in the Games behind the scenes and helped run the torch into the Olympic stadium.

Retiring from the sport was not the enormous wrench it might have been for Borzov, as he was frustrated by the constant stream of injuries he had suffered, and he was relieved to finally hang up his running shoes.

Through the 1980s, Borzov became a man of some influence, living and working in Kiev, in the Ukraine, where he became Deputy Director of the State Committee for Physical Culture and Sport, responsible for organizing and developing sport in the republic, encouraging youngsters to get involved and fighting for better facilities.

When Ukraine finally declared its independence in 1991, Borzov was appointed as the President of the Ukrainian Olympic Committee and quickly established the National Olympic Academy of the Ukraine. He has also worked tirelessly as a member of the International Olympic Committee since 1994. He remains one of the country's most famous sons, and after long spells in government and serving in opposition in the Ukraine parliament, he is regarded as one of the nation's elder statesmen of sport.

He still keeps fit and has lost none of the keen sense of humour or the razor-sharp intellect he displayed during his days on the track. The Olympics may have served as a platform on which Borzov based his career in sport, but it is likely that even without that triumph he would have still carved out a successful working life elsewhere.

'Of course, both winning the Olympic gold medal and the popularity that followed changed my life in every possible way,' he says. 'For example, when I studied at the university I was ashamed if I did not do well, because everyone knew me. If I work I'm ashamed if I do my work badly. If I'm amongst people I'm ashamed to say no to someone, not to tell them something, not to answer a question that someone asks me.

'That is to say, the Olympic medal put me in such a position that I have to behave as an Olympic champion, both at home and abroad, or wherever I am. I think it's a good saying that an Olympic medal has two sides – thorns and roses.'

Valeri and Lyudmila have been married for more than 40 years and although daughter Tania did not follow her famed parents into the sporting world, their three grandchildren – all boys – are huge sports fans and there are high hopes that at least one of them will have inherited those special Olympic genes.

Of all the Olympic 100 metres champions, there are probably five or six who stand out even among this elevated company, and many expert judges would place Valeri Borzov on this shortlist. Those who criticized him for being unspectacular forgot that his power, fluency and almost effortlessly efficient running style were really a spectacle in themselves. His consistency at the very highest levels of world sprinting, his record in major championships and the high regard in which he is held by other top sprinters are clear testimony to his undoubted class and superiority.

Montreal 1976

Hasely Crawford

At the precise moment that Valeri Borzov crossed the line to win the 100 metres final in Munich, more than 60 yards back down the track stood the cursing, fuming figure of Hasely Crawford. The big Trinidadian had pulled a hamstring in the semi-final and had only made the start of the final thanks to some intensive ice treatment and heavy strapping around his damaged thigh. But it took just four strides to undo all the team doctor's careful work and Crawford's Olympic dream had unravelled in the most heartbreaking fashion. As he stood on the track, watching the backs of the rest of the field disappearing towards the finish, he made himself a solemn promise to return next time and win.

From his earliest days, Hasely, who was born in 1950, the seventh of 11 children, had shown an intense, almost unnerving dedication to any task he set himself, whether it was on or off the track. It is possible that this characteristic stemmed from his humble background, growing up in the industrial capital of San Fernando, Trinidad's second city, within sight, sound and smell of the giant oil refineries that dominated the skyline. Life was tough for the Crawford family and made even worse when Crawford Senior, a rabies inspector with the Ministry of Agriculture, died of a heart attack when Hasely was just 14.

'We were very poor. I used to hate to see my Mom toiling to make ends meet. And I had only one good asset. I could run very fast and I was determined to use it to get ahead. My success came out of poverty, that was my driving force.'

By then Hasely had already been singled out by his school as a possible athlete after he was seen outrunning boys several years older in the playground. Just over a year after his father's death Hasely took part in his first major race, finishing third in the Texaco Southern Games 100 metres for the under-16s, but it was not until 1968 that he began to have serious designs on the Olympic Games. He was injured, and his close friend Carl Archer, who he had already beaten, was selected for the Trinidad team for Mexico. 'Since he'd made the team I thought, well why not me?' says Hasely, 'but when I told my friends that I'd be on the team at the next Olympics in Munich they all laughed at me.'

The Olympic year of 1968 was also his last at San Fernando Technical Institute. When he left, he took a job as an apprentice iron worker, spending much of his time in the docks working on the oil tankers. He might well have spent the rest of his life there had it not been for his running ability. He had only received a very basic education, starting school late at eight years old, so paying to go to an American college was completely out of the question.

But his luck began to turn after a promising track season in 1969, so much so that he was picked for the Trinidad team for the Central American and Caribbean (CAC) Games, which were to be held in Panama City in February of 1970.

Although Hasely had been running for the Texaco Sports Club, most of his training had been done on the tracks left by the sugar cane lorries at the giant Madeleine Sugar Factory, in the Philippines district of the island, so he was looking forward to his first ever trip abroad. It was one of his proudest moments when he walked out for the parade in the opening ceremony of the Games, wearing his maroon blazer and his welding goggles to shield his eyes from the sun. But the competition itself was strong, particularly from the Cubans, so he did well to make the final and finish a respectable fifth in the 100 metres, won by Pablo Montes, who had been fourth in the Olympic final of 1968.

Having enjoyed the competition so much, Hasely now set his sights on the Commonwealth Games, to be held later in the year in Edinburgh, Scotland, where he would come face to face with a man who would become his greatest rival throughout his career, Jamaica's Don Quarrie.

The Games were a key point in Crawford's life, even though he only managed a bronze medal in the 100 metres behind Jamaica's Lennox Miller and the winner Quarrie, because his performances in Scotland and also in Panama had been noticed by some of the major US colleges, who were always on the lookout for athletic talent around the world.

The University of Texas, in El Paso, had offered him a scholarship after the CAC Games, but following his bronze medal in the Commonwealth Games more offers began to arrive. To move forward, both on the track and in education, meant leaving his island home, as there were few educational opportunities, little financial help or sponsorship of sport to be had from his government, and very few local events in which Crawford could compete.

The college he selected, which was something of a tradition for Caribbean athletes, was Eastern Michigan University, where Trinidad's half-miler Eric Nesbitt was studying, along with a handful of other West Indian track and field stars. So after completing his Texaco apprenticeship in December 1970, Crawford left for what he hoped would be a better life and new opportunities in the United States.

Just before leaving, however, he was involved in a serious car accident and badly damaged his back, a condition that doctors diagnosed as a pinched sciatic nerve and which still causes him pain today. Thinking the injury would heal quickly, he headed to the States and kept quiet. 'But my right leg was almost completely numb,' he recalls. 'It would take me twenty minutes just to put on a pair of socks. I couldn't sneeze, I couldn't laugh, I couldn't even speak loud.'

So the college's new acquisition didn't put so much as a foot on the track for nearly 18 months, which put his scholarship under real threat, and it wasn't until the April of Olympic year itself when he began to show the sporting powers at East Michigan what he could really do. Crawford had beaten nearly every top sprinter in the world in the run-up to the 1972 Games, except for Borzov, Miller and the new American number one, Eddie Hart, so he felt that he had a chance of running well in Munich. The Russian star was a special motivation for him, particularly the way in which he was being held up by the press as the Great White Hope of international sprinting. 'I must admit that when I was at college I was influenced by the Black Power movement,' says Crawford, 'and going into the Games I felt he was eluding me, so I couldn't run against him, and when he was being billed as the Great White Hope, I didn't like it. So I built a kind of grudge against him, almost a rage inside me, and I was looking for him in Munich.'

This grudge was to prove Crawford's undoing at the Games, but before the team arrived in West Germany he embarked on a successful European tour, including a morale-boosting victory over the US star Hart, in Italy, so he was in good shape when the Olympic competition began.

Crawford finally got his wish to race against the Russian in the quarter-finals of the 100 metres, and he ran a national record of 10.18 in third place behind the American Robert Taylor and Borzov in what was to be the fastest race in the competition. It was enough to win him a place in the semis, where again he was drawn against Borzov, and he felt that he had something to prove. 'I got a very bad start but I caught him after about 20 metres,' recalls Crawford, 'and I looked across at him as if to say let's go, let's see what you can do. I tried to crush him and to show everyone that he wasn't so great after all, but I pushed so hard that I damaged my right thigh muscle.'

The injury meant he had to line up for the final heavily strapped and with virtually no chance of completing the race, but he decided to have a go and ignored offers of a pain-killing injection. 'I am not a doctor but I felt that in those days if you took an injection for an injury you may not feel the pain, but it does not cure the problem,' recalls Crawford, 'and I felt that if I do go and run in that state, I may win a gold medal but I may not walk for life. I was young and I had another chance and I could come back again, so I took the decision not to take the shot.'

Of course, it was a futile effort. The hamstring went completely after only a few metres and Borzov ran away with the final. But the defeat was an important factor in how Crawford fought his way back to compete in the next Olympics in Montreal, where he would become an even greater force. He became a much hungrier athlete, having to live with his defeat in Munich for four years before he could return to the Olympic arena and correct the mistakes he had made.

In 1972 he did not warrant a place in the world's top 10 sprinters, but in 1973 things had changed and he earned the number two spot, after an impressive victory in the AAU indoor championships in New York, where he beat the big US stars Herb Washington, Ivory Crockett and Steve Williams in the final of the 60-yard dash. His season continued in a similar vein, with a high point coming in the last race of the year, in Kingston, when he beat the local hero Quarrie and great rival Steve Williams in 10.1 seconds.

Now well established on the international scene, Crawford had earned himself a title in his native Trinidad, the nickname of Raj Paul, a local 'badjohn', a big, mean person that no one crossed. The language on the island reversed 'good' and 'bad', so Crawford's

TOP: Athens 1896. The first Olympic 100 metres final and much to the crowd's consternation and amusement, American winner Tom Burke (second left) adopts the 'novel' crouch start.

MIDDLE: The Boston Athletic Club contingent in the Athens stadium at the end of the 1896 Games. Tom Burke is seated at the front, on the far right.

BOTTOM: No pictures have ever been found of the 1900 Olympic 100 metres. The winner was Frank Jarvis, seated centrally at the top of this pre-Games Princeton group photograph.

TOP: Archie Hahn (right), the Paris 1904 gold medalist, arms raised in victory, canters through the finish of the 1906 'renegade' (Intercalated) Games 100 metres in Athens.

LEFT: Archie Hahn, aged 54, on the beach at a University of Virginia pre-season football camp in the summer of 1935.

ABOVE: London's White City crowd goes mad as the 'adopted' South African Reg Walker beats the Americans James Rector and Nat Cartmell and the Canadian Robert Kerr in the 1908 final.

TOP LEFT: Detroit's Ralph Craig – the double sprint winner at Stockholm 1912 – was a reluctant member of the US team and had to be cajoled into making the trip.

TOP RIGHT: Charley Paddock and silent movie superstar Bebe Daniels pose for a publicity shot for their 1926 movie *Campus Flirt*.

BOTTOM: Antwerp 1920. One of the most famous pictures in Olympic history. American Morris Kirksey's (far right) fateful look to the right costs him the 100 metres title as fellow countryman, the iconic Charley Paddock (second right), leaps past him at the tape.

TOP: Paris 1924 – the real Chariots of Fire final. Britain's Harold Abrahams drops through the tape to take the gold, with the American Jackson Scholz a close second.

ABOVE: Canada's double sprint champion Percy Williams is carried shoulder high around the Amsterdam stadium after his 1928 100 metres triumph.

LEFT: Percy Williams initially served as a civilian pilot during World War II and then became a flight instructor for the Royal Canadian Air Force. He said: 'I was too old to be a fighter pilot.'

TOP LEFT: The two greatest sprinters of the early thirties. The tall, elegant Ralph Metcalfe and the diminutive but powerful Eddie Tolan. Tolan would win both sprints at the 1932 Los Angeles Olympics – but not without huge controversy.

TOP RIGHT: 'Like watching water flowing downhill.' The wonderfully fluid Jesse Owens captured the hearts of the watching world with his seemingly effortless displays at the 1936 Berlin Olympics. But his later life would prove far less straightforward.

ABOVE: Nearly 30 years after his Olympic triumph, Jesse Owens takes a nostalgic tour of the stadium in Berlin where, in front of Adolf Hitler, he claimed four gold medals.

TOP: Cleveland's Harrison Dillard was the greatest high-hurdler of his era, but almost by accident won the Olympic 100 metres title on an unusually warm summer day in London, 1948.

ABOVE: A 91-year-old Harrison Dillard poses with the life-size statue of him hurdling in his racing prime at his alma mater Baldwin Wallace University in 2015.

TOP: Helsinki 1952. One of the closest finishes in Olympic 100 metres history. Four sprinters appeared to hit the tape together and American Lindy Remigino (lane 3) was eventually named the winner, ahead of Herb McKinley (lane 2) and McDonald Bailey (lane 5). The odd man out of the medals, 4th-placed Dean Smith (lane 4), was only 14 inches behind Remigino.

ABOVE: A 68-year-old Lindy Remigino at the athletic complex at Hartford Public in 1999. It was re-named the Lindy R Remigino Track at a special dedication ceremony.

LEFT: Regarded as one of the most relaxed sprinters in history, Texan Bobby Morrow rolls through the tape to clinch the 200 metres title and complete a sprint double at the 1956 Melbourne Olympics.

BELOW: The superfast-starting German Armin Hary (nearest camera) was the first sprinter to run 100 metres in ten seconds flat. At the 1960 Rome Olympics he took the gold but he was never far from controversy and scandal.

TOP: Bullet' Bob Hayes (702) destroyed the 100 metres field at the 1964 Tokyo Olympics, despite running on the inside lane of a cinder track that had been chewed up by an earlier distance race.

RIGHT: Bob Hayes enjoys the applause of a full house at the Texas Stadium, in September, 2001, less than a year before he died, after being inducted into the Dallas Cowboys' famed Ring of Honor, during half time at a Cowboys-San Diego Chargers game.

LEFT: Jim Hines (right) celebrates his sub ten second 100 metres success with great rival Charlie Greene in the thin air of Mexico City, in 1968.

TOP: 'The Fastest Human is a Commie.' So said a churlish *New York Times* as the 'Ukraine Express' Valeri Borzov (arms raised) won both sprints at the Munich Games of 1972.

ABOVE: The Borzov family on holiday in Sochi, on the Black Sea, in 1987, during filming for the TV series *The Fastest Men on Earth*, with wife Lyudmila Turishcheva, the former gymnastic champion, and daughter Tania.

TOP: Borzov couldn't repeat his success in Montreal, 1976. He was beaten into 3rd by the giant figure of Trinidadian Hasely Crawford (right) and runner-up Don Quarrie (yellow).

LEFT: Hasely Crawford, Trinidad 1999, showing off his Olympic gold medal and the bright yellow adidas spikes he wore in the 1976 final.

TOP: Britain's Allan Wells (near side) dips low to pip Cuban Silvio Leonard (lane 1) by the tiniest of margins on the line in Moscow, 1980. He would be the last white sprinter to make an Olympic 100 metres final.

LEFT: Arguably the greatest athlete of all time. Carl Lewis won nine Olympic gold medals – including two at 100 metres, in Los Angeles, in 1984, and Seoul, 1988, the latter following Ben Johnson's disqualification. His astonishing achievements remain a formidable target for today's track and field hopefuls.

RIGHT: Now assistant coach at his alma mater, the University of Houston, Carl Lewis may be about to hit 60 but he still looks in great shape.

TOP LEFT: Britain's most decorated sprinter, Linford Christie, enjoyed a stellar track career with the high points being his 100 metres triumphs at the 1992 Barcelona Olympics and the 1993 World Athletics Championships, in Stuttgart.

TOP RIGHT: The golden moment of realisation. An elated Donovan Bailey takes the 100 metres title in Atlanta, 1996, and sets a new world record of 9.84 seconds in the process.

LEFT: Donovan Bailey, flanked by a pair of Royal Canadian Mounted Police officers, recieves a place on Canada's Walk of Fame in 2017.

TOP LEFT: The 'Kansas City Cannonball' Maurice Greene celebrates his 100 metres gold at the 2000 Sydney Olympics.

TOP RIGHT: Dancer Cheryl Burke and Maurice Greene appear on stage during *Dancing with the Stars*, 2008.

ABOVE: A new world record of 9.76 seconds for American Justin Gatlin in 2006 – but it lasted only two days before the IAAF admitted a mistake in their calculations and rounded it up to 9.77, matching Asafa Powell's mark. Two years earlier Gatlin took the 100 metres gold in Athens, but was later banned for using performance-enhancing drugs.

TOP: The incomparable Usain Bolt – quite simply the greatest sprinter of all time – celebrates his 100 metres gold medal and new world record in Beijing, 2008, in his own unique style. He has since become the world's biggest sporting figure.

ABOVE: After injury and a supposed loss of form, Usain Bolt was actually written off by some sections of the track media in 2012, but he stepped up once again at a major event to reclaim the Olympic 100 metres title in London. Trailing in second was compatriot Yohan Blake (right), with American Gatlin (second right) in third.

ABOVE: Usain Bolt today – a 2021 picture of the current fastest man on Earth, snapped relaxing in the garden of his home in Jamaica.

running had been so good it became 'bad'. He is still known as Raj Paul even today. He had also been earning himself a reputation as the world's track tough guy, a man who would stop at nothing to win a race. At nearly 6ft 3in and over 190 pounds, Crawford was a big, intimidating man and he loved to frighten the life out of other athletes if he possibly could. 'I always believed that sprinting was relaxation, running and 25 per cent psychology,' he says, 'and I would do anything to win a race. I'd try to show you up, scare you, because I was always a bigger person than most other sprinters and I knew I could scare most people. I'd tease them, intimidate them and it often worked.'

After a dazzling season in 1973, he went off the boil the following year, partly because of a bone spur in his foot, but he returned in May 1975 with a bang, winning the NCAA and AAU indoor 60 yard titles and then clocking a wind-assisted 9.8 seconds in a 100 metres race in a blanket finish with Steve Williams, at the Hampton International Games at Arima, in Trinidad.

One problem that Crawford faced at this time was the end of his scholarship, so while he worked towards his masters degree in materials engineering he had to take a job and cut down on his training. Nevertheless, he won the outdoor NCAA 100 metres in June, before starting work in the summer at Nash Engineering, near Detroit, where he helped design gears for drag-racing cars, a job that lasted from six in the morning until four in the afternoon, so the only time he could train was in the evenings.

Despite these problems he still made Trinidad's team for the Pan American Games in Mexico City, in spite of pressure from his coach Wilton Jackson to rest and not attend. But the Trinidad Olympic Association were struggling to raise funds for the Games and without Crawford they would struggle even more. So he agreed to go. Ten pounds overweight and in poor shape, he passed out in the first training session in Mexico and performed wonders to finish second behind Cuba's Silvio Leonard in the 100 metres. When the 1976 season began, which would culminate in the Montreal Olympics, Crawford was still slogging towards his masters and working ten hours a day, and he had the additional problems of an eye inflammation that flared up occasionally following a stick-fighting accident as a boy.

Despite these problems, Crawford's hunger for Olympic success stayed as strong as ever and he kept his mind firmly on that 100 metres title. He qualified easily to run in the 100 metres, 200 metres and the relay in Montreal, and in the weeks leading up to the Games he chose his races carefully, ensuring that he did not overstretch himself and risk damaging any muscles. He chose well, because in a short pre-Olympic tour in Scandinavia he ran 20.2 for a national 200 metres record, virtually jogging the last 15 metres, and in Canada, on a cold, damp evening a few days before the Games began, he set a new national 100 metres record, running a 10-flat. 'It may sound cocky but I knew I was on a winner,' said Crawford, 'because I had corrected all my mistakes and I was running well, though I did have some respect for Quarrie and Borzov.' His coach thought the same. In his last training session before the Games began, Jackson had him practising starts and Crawford was literally flying out of the blocks. So the coach finished the session after only eight starts and said: 'Forget it. You ready. You going to win.'

His cause had also been boosted by injury to two of America's biggest hopes – the brash, lanky, 6ft 4in New Yorker Steve Williams and the fast-starting, enigmatic teenager Houston McTear.

Williams is often described as the greatest sprinter never to compete at an Olympics and there is good reason for it. Despite an unorthodox, shoulder-rolling running style, he'd clocked a world record-equalling 9.9 seconds on no fewer than four occasions, and looked to be coming into some consistent form in the summer of 1976. However, he suffered a muscle pull in the quarter-finals of the US trials in Oregon and didn't make the team.

It was even worse for McTear, who finished second to Harvey Glance in the final of the trials to book his place in Montreal, but in doing so suffered an Achilles injury that wouldn't heal in time. The smiling showman would have been a hugely entertaining addition to the Games. Born into abject rural poverty in the Florida panhandle, McTear was a naturally gifted sprinter who often put down a cigarette or a cheeseburger just before a race and strolled over to the start still in his street clothes, before decimating the field. He equalled the world 100 yards record of 9.0 seconds at a state high school meet in Orlando when he was only 18.

But even without these two flyers, the US team could still boast: 19-year-old double NCAA champion Glance, who had twice equalled the 100 metres world record in the summer; and Virginia-born powerhouse Steve Riddick and McTear's replacement, Johnny 'Lam' Jones, who would be a future NFL star.

They were all named among the pre-Games favourites, alongside Don Quarrie, who had equalled the world record in May; Cuban electronics student Silvio Leonard, the Pan American champion, and reigning Olympic champion Borzov. The one man who was hardly mentioned in despatches was Hasely Crawford.

The Montreal Games had been marred by an eleventh-hour boycott by 22 African nations and by the enormous cost of staging the Olympics, which had plunged the city and the state of Quebec into massive debt. The boycott was announced just 48 hours before the opening of the Games, and the nations involved justified their actions as part of the campaign against apartheid in South Africa and as a protest against the recent tour of the country by the New Zealand rugby team.

The Games themselves are remembered for the boycott and the race to finish the stadium for the official opening by Queen Elizabeth, but they were also the Games at which Finland's Lasse Viren retained both his 5,000 and 10,000 metres titles, Romanian gymnast Nadia Comaneci scored a perfect ten and the giant Cuban Alberto Juantorena strode his way to double gold in the 400 and 800 metres.

Crawford was looking confidently towards his own sprint double when the Games opened on July 17 and he was awarded the honour of carrying the Trinidadian flag. The 100-metre competition began a few days later and he breezed through the first and second rounds, beating Borzov comfortably in the latter, and then beating his other closest rival Quarrie in their semi-final. The final would take place with two notable absentees: Steve Riddick had been surprisingly edged out in the second semi-final; and Cuba's Leonard had gone out in the quarters. Leonard had been injured in winning the 1975 Pan American title after falling into the 10-foot moat that surrounded the Panama City track, but he had just regained some form and made the team. Just ten days before the Games were due to start, however, he stepped on a bottle, which broke and badly cut his foot, ruining all his training preparations.

The US men left in the final were the teenagers Jones and Glance, but Crawford knew how to deal with them, in his own inimitable style, in the room where the finalists gathered before they went on to the track. 'It was a room about 20 by 20 and I think I came in last,' he recalls. 'There were two attendants there. I came in singing a calypso to get their attention. Then I started swearing, cursing and shouting, pointing fingers at people, and I can remember Jones and Glance watching television like zombies. I shouted at them, "You two lose, you're in trouble, you're scared," and they started looking at me like I was a ghost and I knew I had them beaten.'

'Quarrie just kept saying, "Crawford's crazy," but I turned on him and shouted, "I'm crazy? You'll see how crazy I am when you go out there." The only person I couldn't move was Borzov. He just kept looking at me, making a kind of hissing noise, but he never once kept his eyes off me. So I went into the race knowing that he was the man to beat.'

Crawford had psyched himself up to an incredible pitch; he had hardly slept for nine days leading up to the final and the strain was beginning to show as he pumped himself up for the biggest race of his life. The night before the final he had been so restless that even his team-mates could not sleep. He had tried to read the Bible, he had got up and changed his outfit six or seven times, and was making such a noise that his colleagues apparently tried to quieten him by tying him to his bed and even cutting off chunks of his hair!

'I remember saying over and over again, "Something old, something new, something borrowed, something blue." A lot of things go through your mind and you want to make sure you have the right clothes on, so I decided to get something old, new, borrowed and blue. I think it was my jersey, a jockstrap, my pants and my socks. Then I got out of bed early, had lunch, warmed up and went into the room with the rest of the athletes.'

Both Crawford and Don Quarrie are convinced that had their great rival Steve Williams been in the field, then a world record could have been broken. 'I wish Steve had been there,' says Quarrie, still one of the most respected figures in world athletics. 'We were the best of friends but we had a great rivalry. Hasely and Steve also had a rivalry, because Steve hated Hasely to beat him and vice versa, and I think the tension would have been greater and the times a lot faster, maybe we would all have gone under 10 seconds.'

The eight finalists were Crawford, on the inside lane, the Bulgarian Peter Petrov, Borzov, Quarrie, Glance, Jones, East Germany's Klaus-Dieter Kurrat and Panama's Guy Abrahams. The gun went off but it was a false start, and Hasely jogged all the way to the finish line and then slowly back to the start, ever keen to pull some psychological advantage from any situation that arose. When they were all back in the blocks the seventy thousand crowd hushed again and this time the gun got the field away. Glance and Borzov were straight into the lead, but at halfway Quarrie was level with Borzov, while Glance was fading, and with 25 metres left the smooth-running Jamaican had eased clear of the Russian and was looking for the tape. Suddenly, out of the corner of his eye he could see for the first time what everyone else in the stadium had been watching. In lane one, running in his own race, Hasely had been hurtling along in the lead, and he hit the line just ahead of the fast-finishing Quarrie. Another five metres and Quarrie would probably have won.

Crawford's right arm was raised in triumph and the big man rolled right around the bend and kept going for nearly another 100 metres, after which the realization of what he had done must have suddenly hit him.

He hit the line in 10.06, with Quarrie second in 10.08 and Borzov snatching the bronze in 10.14, which was coincidentally exactly the same time in which he had won the gold in Munich. 'I went into the race figuring it was going to be between Hasely, Borzov and myself,' says Quarrie, 'and I didn't think the Americans would be a factor. I didn't get off that well and when I looked up I saw Borzov in front. Right away I said to myself, "Oh no, he's not going to win again." I took off after him, caught him and in going by him I thought I'd got it won. Then I saw Hasely. I made another effort but Hasely held on. But I wasn't too disappointed. I was hoping I would win, but that's what the Olympics are all about. I should have been concentrating more on just running rather than paying attention to any one particular athlete. But I had the 200 to come.'

Crawford's recollection of the race from the gun was similar to that of Quarrie. 'I saw Glance and Borzov out there, and Borzov made a kind of high-pitched hissing sound when he got off and I said to myself, "Jesus Christ, not again," because of '72. But in three strides I was past him and I opened a gap and I couldn't see anyone else. Then I saw Quarrie's yellow jersey and I picked it up again and went through the tape. The time was 10.06. If I'd had help I would have broken the world record that day, because I could have gone faster.'

Crawford's reaction as he cantered around the bend was a mixture of emotions – relief that he had finally achieved his long-time goal, and anger at the Trinidadian Government that he felt had not given him the kind of assistance he had needed in the build-up to the Games. But he had become a national hero overnight, Trinidad's first Olympic gold medallist, so it was a sweet moment when he stood on the victory rostrum to receive his medal and he admits that there were tears in his eyes.

For the first time since 1928, there were no Americans on the rostrum, and it was the second time in succession that an American had not claimed the Olympic gold and the title of 'Fastest Man on Earth'.

Crawford's next task was to take a second gold medal in the 200 metres, an event in which he had also run well in the build-up to the Games, but there was tough opposition in the field. After the traumas he had gone through before the 100 metres, he actually tried to get the Trinidad officials to pull him out of the competition, feeling that he could not face another four rounds of tension. But he was persuaded to join a field that included his great rival Quarrie, who was the clear favourite, plus the Italian Pietro Mennea, who had almost pulled out of the competition because of his poor performances in his national championships, and the Americans Millard Hampton and high school student Dwayne Evans.

One key man missing was the 1975 Pan American 200 metres champion, James Gilkes, but Guyana had decided to join the boycott of the African nations and, despite an appeal to the IOC by Gilkes to run under the Olympic flag, he was unable to take part. In the 200 metres heats, Crawford and Quarrie looked in good form, but in the final Crawford's injury jinx struck again and after about 50 metres he leaped high into the air and crashed on to the track with another muscle problem, this time a spasm in his left thigh. Again he had to watch as the rest of the field tore around the bend and Quarrie managed to hold off a late run by Hampton to take the gold, with 17-year-old Evans third.

Crawford is listed in the official report as not finishing the race, but an eagle-eyed track fan in the stadium noticed that he never actually left his lane as he pulled himself to his feet and jogged to the finish line to retrieve his belongings. His time is the slowest ever recorded in an Olympic 200 metres race and went down as one minute and 19.6 seconds.

For Quarrie it was the culmination of a long struggle to take his prized gold medal. He had been injured in training after selection for Mexico in 1968, then went to Munich as the Pan American champion, with the second fastest electronically timed 200 metres ever (19.86), only to pull a hamstring in the semi-final, and was carried off on a stretcher.

Few would begrudge him his moment of glory, and Quarrie – one of the nicest and most respected men in the sport – still works in the athletics world, after a hugely successful coaching career. Although he lost a battle in 2020 to become President of Jamaica's AAAs, he remains committed to helping develop the sport in his country and there is a statue honouring his achievements at the entrance of the national stadium in the Jamaican capital Kingston.

Back in Montreal, even without Crawford the Trinidad team made it to the semi-finals of the relay, but the final was dominated by the United States, who won comfortably in a time of 38.33. The winning quartet was Harvey Glance, Johnny Jones, Millard Hampton and Steve Riddick. Glance would go on to a stellar coaching career at Auburn and Alabama, with the US team at the Beijing Olympics and with 2012 Olympic 400 metres champion Kirani James.

In 1980 Jones signed the first million-dollar contract in the NFL and played for six years with the New York Jets. Post-football, he struggled with drink and drug problems and in 2019 he succumbed to bone marrow cancer after a long illness.

Hampton was a police officer in San Jose for 26 years before retiring and now runs his own website development business in Elk Grove, California. Steve Riddick started a coaching career, but was implicated in a fraud involving his athletes Marion Jones and Tim Montgomery. In 2008 he was sent to prison for five years for conspiracy, bank fraud and money laundering.

Houston McTear had a rollercoaster life. After the US boycotted the Moscow Olympics, he fell into drugs and lived on the streets in Santa Monica for more than three years. Then he met and married a former Swedish athlete, cleaned up and moved to Stockholm – where he actually won indoor races in his mid-thirties. He died there in 2015, from lung cancer, aged just 58.

Steve Williams fared much better. An idol of the young Carl Lewis, he retired in the early 1980s and worked as a coach in baseball, football and tennis. He also designed sports shoes and today continues a successful business career in Chicago.

In Trinidad, Hasely Crawford's triumphant homecoming on August 1, 1976, was a red-letter day – because it was also the same day that Trinidad and Tobago was officially declared a republic. The welcoming party at Piarco Airport was led by his proud mother, Phyllis, and the Prime Minister, Dr Eric Williams, who joined thousands of people to congratulate him as he stepped off the plane. After an overnight stay at the airport hotel, a motorcade took him and the rest of the team to a raft of civic receptions, where he glided past noisy, banner-waving fans in both the capital, Port of Spain, and Crawford's home town, San Fernando. The celebrations went on for weeks and the newspapers could print little else but eulogies to the island's new star.

One of the first honours to be bestowed on him was to have a British West Indian Airlines DC9-50 jet named after him, a plane that still runs regular services around the Caribbean, while Crawford was also appointed as a public relations officer for the company. At the end of August he received the nation's highest civic decoration, the Trinity Cross, for distinguished and outstanding service. There had been rumours that Crawford had received offers to play football in Canada for the Toronto Argonauts and that the New York Jets were keen to use his size, speed and power as a wide receiver in the NFL, but if the offers existed then Crawford was not really interested.

There were also reports in October 1976 that he was seriously considering giving up athletics because of persistent trouble with bursitis, a painful inflammation of the joints, but he was treated for the condition in the United States and resumed light training the following year.

However, there were still more honours to come, including a postage stamp minted by the Trinidad Post Office to commemorate his win. In 1977 he was handed the island's sportsman of the year award and appointed as a special adviser for sport and industrial education at the Ministry of Education and Culture. He was not even forgotten in the Carnival 1977, when no fewer than six calypsos were written about him, including one from Lord Kitchener called 'de people's man' and another from the Mighty Sparrow, which began:

Crawford like a bullet
Take off like a jet
Flash o' lightning
He keep moving
People bawling
Everybody glad
Is Craw-ford, Trinidad.

His achievement pushed him firmly into the public eye, which, being such a quiet and private person off the track, he did not always enjoy. 'Winning the gold medal gave me world recognition,' says Crawford, 'and it gave me the opportunity to travel the world. I must say I was a hasty person before I started competing, and it made me a disciplined person. I think I have a broader view of things now, though I must admit there are times that I do say to myself what was the purpose of winning this gold medal, because basically I'm a private person and there are times when people say nasty things to me and I feel resentful. I feel it's unnecessary, so sometimes I wonder what the purpose of it all was.'

Crawford did manage to squeeze in a few races in 1977, including the CAC Games in Jalapa, Mexico. There he won another medal, this time a bronze in the 100 metres, behind Cuba's Leonard, who won in the fastest time of the year, a 9.98, with Osvaldo Lara second.

At around the same time he poured cold water on suggestions that he was going to abandon the sport and sign up with a major international promoter in the Middle East to run professionally. Instead, he set himself a target of gold in the Commonwealth Games in Edmonton, in August 1978. It was to be his last genuine chance of medal success in a major international competition, and his old rival Quarrie was still on the scene, but now a newcomer was also challenging, Scotland's Allan Wells, for whom Hasely had enormous respect.

In the final in Edmonton, with a seven metres per second wind behind the finalists, Quarrie edged the gold as the three favourites hit the line together, with Wells second and Crawford taking the bronze. He won another bronze in the relay and went on to take some important scalps on a European tour, including Riddick, Gilkes and England's Mike McFarlane. In 1979, he ran alongside Wells and Quarrie in Australia in the hope of getting into shape for the Olympics in Moscow in 1980, so he could be fit enough to defend his 100 metres title.

He could not regain the form of 1976, however, and in Moscow he went out in the quarter-finals. That defeat looked like the end for Crawford and he disappeared from the track scene until March of 1982, when he started running in local meets to stay in shape. But he began to run some good times, including a 10.3 in Trinidad, so he went back into serious training in 1983 with one eye on the Los Angeles Olympics the following year.

At the age of 33, Crawford again carried the Trinidad flag into the famous LA Coliseum at the opening of the Games. He then won his way through to the quarter-finals of the 100 metres, having placed fourth in the first round behind winner Carl Lewis, and finally went out in a race won by Canada's Ben Johnson. It was his last major race – on returning from Los Angeles he decided to retire, after becoming the only Olympic 100 metres champion to race in four Olympics.

Since the Montreal Olympics, Crawford has worked for the government in the fields of youth, sport and recreation. 'I hope I'll be able to pass on a lot that I've learned,' he says, 'and right now my whole future is my job. I would like to see Trinidad & Tobago sport in the place it's supposed to be, and that's high on the charts.'

In 2000, he was named the Trinidad & Tobago Athlete of the Millennium and was inducted into the Caribbean Hall of Fame, one of only three track and field athletes to be included, alongside Ato Boldon and Arthur Wint.

In 2001 the local government renamed its national stadium in Port of Spain after Crawford. It's now the home of all the major sporting and cultural events on the islands. Although he is recognized everywhere he goes in Trinidad, Crawford lives a quiet life, though he suffers daily pain from his dodgy left knee and perennial back trouble and some mornings it can take him over an hour to get up. He turned 70 recently and is happily retired from the National Gas Company of Trinidad & Tobago, spending his time at his home in leafy Federation Park, just north of the capital, attending the occasional track meet and keeping up with his children, son Harlan and daughter Halli. But he is always prepared to offer an opinion or two on Caribbean athletics and athletes and is often the first person the local newspapers will turn to for a fiery quote or a biting comment.

A couple of years ago Crawford received arguably his most unusual honour. He was transformed into a comic-book superhero. It was an initiative run for schools by the island's gas company, which enshrined a number of its national heroes and their stories in cartoon form to inspire youngsters. Hasely's was called *A Runner's Life – Lessons From An Olympian*.

'They made me a hero and I hope it can be an inspiration for young people,' he explained. 'I learned to read from a comic book. I love to read comic books, I still do, and to make me into a comic-book hero is really quite an experience for me.'

He has come a long way since his struggling days by the oil refineries, but has not been spoilt by his achievements, even though he competed internationally for so long, racing and beating the best in the world. Perhaps his tendency to pull muscles and suffer other injuries conspired to rob him of a higher place in the rankings of the all-time great sprinters, but there are many top fast men who have suffered and never made it to the Olympics at all, let alone claim a gold medal.

Moscow 1980

Allan Wells

While Hasely Crawford was rocketing to success in Montreal, few would have believed that three thousand miles away, sitting quietly at home in rainy Scotland, his successor was watching the race unfold on television in complete anonymity.

Allan Wells, the man who would ultimately inherit Eric Liddell's famous title of 'The Flying Scotsman', had only just taken up serious sprinting at the grand old age of 24 – at which point many past champions had been retiring. He was not considered good enough for the British team in Montreal; in fact, the standard of sprinting in the country was so poor that the selectors decided to spare themselves the embarrassment of watching them lose and refused to send anyone to run in the 100 metres at the Games.

Wells had not long given up his dream of emulating his childhood hero Lynn Davies and becoming a great long jumper, but his lifetime best of 24ft ¼in (7.32m), which he'd achieved back in 1972, had been surpassed as a world record in 1898, and he eventually came to terms with the fact that he was never going to be an international threat at the event.

He had always been a fast runner, and during the long, tedious gaps at his club's long jump meetings he enjoyed watching the sprint races, particularly the 200 metres and the way in which the athletes ran the curve. The idea of running the curve himself really appealed, so after yet another mediocre performance in the long jump he decided to abandon the event and have a go at sprinting. Four years later he was the Olympic champion.

Scotland's capital and most beautiful city it may be, but most people agree that cold, wet, windy Edinburgh is hardly the ideal place to find a world-class sprinter. Yet that is where Wells grew up and developed as an athlete. He was born in May 1952, the son of a blacksmith and builder and one of five children, and his home was in Fernieside Crescent, a street that overlooked the famous Edinburgh Southern Harriers track. Later it could also boast two Olympic athletes living within 50 yards of each other, Wells and hammer thrower Chris Black.

Wells first raced at the tender age of six, finishing second in a primary school 60-yard competition, but his interest in sport did not really take off until he joined Liberton High School, where he played football, basketball and badminton and ran cross-country. But even before then he enjoyed winning races against the other children in the neighbourhood and he remembers: 'There was a friend of mine who used to leave his house in the morning and I could see him and he could see me. He would go around the bottom road and I would go around the top road and we would race each other to school. This would go on day in, day out and most of the time I'd win. I had further to go as well!'

Wells's greatest sporting success at school was winning the Scottish under-15 long jump title. At about the same time he also began to win trophies for his local Boys Brigade, the 9th Edinburgh Company, although his success came not in the sprints but in cross-country races, the type of character-building event into which the Brigade liked to push its youngsters. Wells joined the Brigade at a time when its code of strict moral and physical conduct, and its emphasis on clean living and manliness, contrasted dramatically with the creed of the swinging sixties, but he had always been something of a loner, so he fitted in well.

Of course, the Brigade boys were often the target of street jibes, aimed particularly at their uniforms, but after Wells enrolled in a Charles Atlas body-building course, few of the jokes tended to be directed at him.

His hero in those days also fitted the clean-cut, athletic ideal endorsed by the Brigade. It was long-jumper Lynn Davies, who had won the 1964 Olympic title and become one of Britain's top sportsmen.

There is a popular story about how Wells was spurred on to athletic success after raking the long jump pit for Davies during the 1970 Commonwealth Games in Edinburgh. There is no truth in it, but Wells did work as a steward at the Meadowbank Stadium and, on one occasion, did manage to meet his hero. 'He was training out at the back of the stadium,' he recalls, 'and I just went up and interrupted his session and started talking to him. It gave me a real feel for the guy, because he didn't swear at me or kick me out, but took the time to talk.' Fittingly, it was Davies who would be the British track and field team manager at the Moscow Olympics when Wells would make his own name in the athletics world.

Although Wells enjoyed the technical and practical classes at school, he was not a keen scholar and left at 15 to take up an engineering apprenticeship. Even then he didn't decide to devote his sporting efforts to athletics for another few years. When he did, it was the long jump and triple jump that he pursued, winning a Scottish junior triple jump title in 1971, but he dabbled a little in the sprints, which were dominated at the time by the young David Jenkins. He earned a couple of international vests for Scotland as a long-jumper, but his personal best in the event suggested that he would never excel in the way he wanted. Even though his relay times showed much promise as a sprinter, the best he could manage by the time of his twenty-fourth birthday was a 10.9 for the 100 metres. He realized that his long jump training – which involved lots of slow hill-work and weights – was holding him back, so he decided to switch events and devote his attention to improving his sprinting times. It was in 1976 that Wells joined a group of athletes trained by the coach Wilson Young, a man who had won at the Powderhall Sprints in the world of professional athletics but, more than forty years on, is a largely forgotten figure in Scottish athletics. He steered young Wells onto the road towards the Olympic Games and Wells considers the switch to be the watershed in his athletics career, a time when he began to pursue the sport seriously. 'I was at a crossroads in my athletic career, whether to carry on or take a completely new direction in training, and I was also looking for a new a motivation factor,' he says, 'and they both came together in one. I was still a long-jumper and he and the other athletes were happy for me to join the group and gain more speed for my long jump, but I think it took me about a fortnight to realize that I was going to be a sprinter. I think Wilson Young realized I was going to be a sprinter whether I was thinking of being one or not.'

The atmosphere of competition and motivation created by Young catapulted Wells into the national arena, and his performances began to reflect the new lease of life he was getting from working with the group. One of the first to see the change was athletics historian Tom McNab, who was then the British sprint coach. 'Allan came from the tradition of professional sprinting in Scotland, trained by a professional coach, and that's a very closed world. He carried a lot of professional attitudes with him into the amateur world, qualities like the ability to concentrate and work hard in training. He was very single-minded, and I give credit to him for being the catalyst in the revival of modern British sprinting.'

It might have been a closed world, but Wells's training included many of the old pro methods, such as the emphasis on speed, technique, strength and power, built up with special exercises, including the speedball, a device more familiar in a boxing gym than in the athletics world. But the new training and the highly charged atmosphere created by Young served to spark him into life, and he recognizes the debt he owes his old mentor, though sadly they fell out just as Wells was getting into high gear and they have rarely spoken since. Says Wells: 'I feel it was something that was always going to happen. He was motivating everybody in the group, not just me, there was no way that I was getting any more attention than anyone else, though maybe there are some people who would say otherwise. But I think that was the thing that spurred us on; he had one against the other, fighting each other physically and mentally. But the coach and I had our differences and me leaving the group was the best thing. I don't think the two of us came off any better, but at the time it was the only thing we could do. It was a sad day when we parted and I regret it now, and I'm sure he does too.'

Thanks to Young's influence, Wells began to attract attention as a sprinter and in 1976 he ran 10.55 for the 100 metres, the fastest time in Britain that year, earning a Great Britain call-up for the sprint relay team in an international against Canada. He continued to improve in the following year and managed second place in the British championships, but it was the winter training between 1977 and 1978 that really pushed him into the major league.

Wells allied some training ideas of his own to the tried and trusted ones he had been using, producing a regime of punishing exercises that would make a hardened SAS man wince. He was working under the auspices of coach Charlie Affleck, but also taking a more prominent role was his wife Margot, a guiding light in Wells's career and a formidable ally.

Wells put himself through hell during the winter, using a training system he maintained right up to and beyond the Olympics. He would leave work at Brown Brothers

Engineering and meet Margot and a training partner at a local park at about 5pm for a session of plyometrics, a series of dynamic bounding, hops, skips and other exercises which lasted for about 45 minutes. Having finished in the park, they would travel to the gym, a freezing converted single garage in Leith, where some nights they would have to shovel the snow away from the door to get inside. The one-bar fire made little difference to the temperature inside, especially with so many holes in the walls, but despite the conditions Wells pushed himself through an hour of constant exercising, including speedball sessions, press-ups, squat thrusts, chin-ups and all kinds of variations, using so much effort that by the end of the evening the sweat would rise like steam from his body and he could squeeze about half a pint of it from his vest.

The training went on six days a week throughout the winter, and when the 1978 season began, the new powerful Allan Wells bounded on to the scene, ready to take the sprint world by storm.

'It was complete concentration during the training,' says Wells, 'and I was a Jekyll and Hyde character. I would go to training and be somebody else, and when I stopped I became Allan Wells again. But when I was training I was Allan Wells, the athlete, though a lot of people could probably find other words. I was accused of being a right sod, but I didn't do it to make friends, it was an attitude of wanting to be the best.'

The early season of 1978 did not witness an immediate explosion, though he was buoyed by a sharp 6.68 seconds for the 60 metres, indoors at Cosford, but in July he announced himself by equalling Peter Radford's 20-year-old British 100 metres record of 10.29, in Gateshead, and doing so with his hands in the air five metres from the line. A week later, at the UK Championships and in untypically warm conditions, he broke the record and became the fastest-ever Briton, with a 10.15 on his home track in Meadowbank, and suddenly people were beginning to talk about the new 'find' from Scotland and how ironic it was that he should arrive in the same year that the last British gold medallist, Harold Abrahams, had died.

Wells's performances earned him selection for Scotland's team at the Commonwealth Games, in Edmonton, where he won two golds and a silver, firmly establishing himself on the international scene. In the 100 metres he ran a sensational, though wind-aided, 10.07 to finish second behind Don Quarrie but beat Hasely Crawford; he won the 200 metres in a windy 20.12, and took another first in the relay.

Running against some of the world's top fast men was tough enough, but meeting Crawford meant he had to undergo another test of character. 'Wells was running very well and I knew he was the one I had to beat,' recalls Crawford, 'so I went to the dressing-room before the final and his wife Margot was giving him a massage. I walked up and shouted at him, "I'm gonna beat your white ass," and said a lot of other things besides. I was really trying to upset him, to throw him off, but he just looked at me without a change on his face and I realized I couldn't move him. He was like a rock.'

Crawford has always had enormous respect for Wells and admits that throughout his own long career there were only two men he could not intimidate with his own bizarre brand of racing tactics – Wells and Borzov. Wells returned home triumphantly from

Edmonton, but he did not have the experience to cope with the European Championships four weeks later and finished a disappointing sixth.

Margot Wells, a member of the British teams at both Edmonton and Prague, was a good sprinter and an even better hurdler, but she decided to forgo her own athletic career and work full-time on her husband's. 'She decided to take a back seat in her athletic world and help me a bit more,' says Wells, 'but I felt I'd lost something, because when she ran it spurred me on. There was one occasion when we did train together, running 50s, and it brought the best out of both of us, but I couldn't have taken many sessions like that.' Margot's role in helping him drew a lot of publicity – there were not too many top-class athletes coached by their wives – but she still winces when she hears the description of her role as Allan's coach. She was much more than just a coach, because by this time Wells did not really need much coaching, he needed other help: motivation, organization and someone with sprinting knowledge to be his eyes during a race and point out anything that was going wrong.

'I always said to her after a race or a training session, "How did it look?" says Wells, 'and Margot would always be dependable in analyzing and discussing, with great accuracy, any technical or physical weaknesses. It tended to match with what I had experienced, but for me it was more the comfort of knowing that she was focused on what I was trying to achieve.'

From 1978 onwards, Mr and Mrs Wells were seen on tracks around the world, and it was Mrs Wells who earned the reputation as a tough character who would not take any nonsense from anyone. 'I just tried to let Allan run and think about his running, I did everything else,' explains Margot. 'I made sure his vests were there, he had two spikes, he got the right bus and all he had to worry about was preparing for the race. I wouldn't let anything get in the way and I wouldn't stand for officials hassling him or causing him problems. If anybody did get in the way it was always me that went to them and told them to stop. If I annoyed someone, but Allan won a race, then that was the price I had to pay. I always tried to be polite, but leading up to an Olympic final the last thing you're thinking about is being polite.'

During the 1979 season there were no major Games, but Wells managed to win the 200 metres in the Europa Cup final in Turin and finish third in the 100 metres, despite not using starting blocks and slipping at the start. He also placed second in the Golden Sprints in Zurich, behind the American James Sanford. The next major championships were the Olympic Games, in Moscow in 1980, but these Games were already being dogged by political rows over the Russian invasion of Afghanistan, and there were calls from all over the world to boycott them, led by the United States. Finally, the British team did go to the Games, whereas many Western countries did not, including the United States, but the athletes took heavy criticism from some conservative quarters about taking part and although the British team fared well, the furore served to illustrate the political nature of the boycott – and its futility.

The Olympic boycott may have had zero impact on the Afghan situation, but it saw the almost automatic retaliation of the Eastern Bloc countries in staying away from the next Olympics in Los Angeles; eight years of pointless political gesturing which served only to frustrate hundreds of athletes and satisfy the politicians who wanted to be seen to be doing something, without affecting their trading balances, stock and currency markets.

Wells was among the many British athletes who received piles of letters aimed at persuading him to pull out of the team. 'When the letters came through they had a little government stamp. I accidentally opened one,' recalls Wells, 'I suppose I was just curious, and there was a picture of a young girl in Afghanistan and it showed she was dead, her hand just a few inches from a doll. Obviously I felt sorry for the child and the parents, but also angry that I got this letter. It was quite difficult to deal with, but you had to look at these things sensibly. I just felt that, whether Allan Wells was at Moscow or not, it wouldn't have made any difference. It was left up to the individual athletes but we all felt that politics shouldn't have been at the Games at all.'

He had other things to worry about, apart from the problems caused by the pro-boycott lobby, and they included the IAAF's insistence that starting blocks would be compulsory at the Games. That was a problem for Wells because until three months before Moscow he had not used them in competition, preferring to start with his feet firmly on the track. In the winter prior to Moscow, he was told that he would be forced to use them, so he practised a little, but did not start using them competitively until just 12 weeks beforehand. Until then he had been happy to run without blocks, even at major championships like the European or the Commonwealth Games, because it felt more natural to him and he could start a fraction further forward than the other athletes. The only time it had worked against him was in Turin, for the Europa Cup, when his foot slipped on the track and he could only finish third.

Margot Wells suggests that there may have been another reason for Wells's reluctance to use them, and that was his laziness. Training at Meadowbank meant sharing the track with many other athletes, so each time Wells used blocks he would have to come back, pick them up and move them because other people wanted to use the track. So he began starting without blocks and soon realized that he could start just as fast that way. Wells himself thinks that other people worried more about him making the transition than he did, because he had used blocks before in training, and they were not totally alien to him, so it was just a case of getting used to them in competition. But it was certainly an added complication in the run-up to the Games, and it would have been interesting to see whether he could have been the first man to win the 100-metre title without blocks since Jesse Owens.

To ensure that Wells arrived in Moscow in first-class condition, his company kindly gave him six months' leave from work to prepare. He used the time wisely, running in the warm climate of Australia during the inhospitable British winter, then training with some of the Olympic team in the South of France before returning home to complete his preparations in the familiar surroundings of Edinburgh. The break from his job was crucial, because it would have been almost impossible to have reached the required level of fitness and race freshness while still working in a regular job five days a week.

For a while, however, it looked as if all this preparation might count for nothing after he injured his back during a starting practice just a fortnight before leaving for the Games. 'I felt something in my lower back but I just carried on,' Wells recalls. 'But when I woke up the next morning it had seized up completely and I couldn't move. I had to roll out of bed to phone one of the team doctors. I told him I didn't think I'd be making the plane, and he thought I was joking.' But intensive treatment at the Western General Hospital, in Edinburgh, three times a day for the first week and twice a day the week before he left for Moscow enabled him to make the trip – even though he hadn't done any sort of training.

Interestingly, Wells believes the injury may have been an advantage, because it helped him recover from the heavy pre-Olympic training sessions he had been putting himself through and acted as a buffer for the two weeks running up to the Games. When he started serious training in Moscow he began to look like a real champion, starting like a train on the practice track.

His dedication to the challenge of becoming Olympic champion prompted his team manager Lynn Davies to say: 'For want of a better word he really is a fanatic. Training, athletics and the build-up to Moscow are everything. I'm not saying other athletes are not dedicated or committed in their approach, but Allan is totally committed. In many ways I see some of my qualities in Allan that I used to have 10 or 15 years ago in approaching the Olympic Games. It's a life or death situation, whether you are going to do well or not. Unless you are totally committed these days you are not going to win an Olympic gold medal. He really does live for athletics, and to Allan a feeling of slightly less well-being than yesterday can affect his mood. For that day the quality of training is the most important thing.'

The intensity of Wells's preparations did, on occasions, alienate some officials and media people. The press, in particular, simply because they could get so little from him and often portrayed him as a dour moaner. Wells didn't really care what they wrote and his strong view was that, to be competitive and successful at the very top, he needed to completely alienate himself from the media. He was not the marketable kind of star, in press terms, that Sebastian Coe and Steve Ovett were, and as far as the British were concerned, it was the middle-distance races they were keen to see rather than the sprints, where Wells was given a chance of a medal, but not the gold.

Even though the three Americans, Stanley Floyd, Mel Lattany and Harvey Glance, were missing because of the boycott, and Floyd had the year's best time at 10.07, there was still a fine collection of sprinters in Moscow, including the talented Cuban Silvio Leonard, hoping to make up for his 1976 disappointment, and the Polish star Marian Woronin, who predicted he would win the title. East Germany's Eugen Ray and the home fans' favourite, Aleksandr Aksinin, were also tough competitors, so it was not going to be easy for Wells.

He breezed easily through round one, beating his old rival Don Quarrie into the bargain, looking relaxed and comfortable. It was at the next stage, the quarter-finals, that he really made everyone sit up and take notice, running a new British record of 10.11 to win a heavily loaded heat, which included defending champion Crawford, Italy's Pietro

Mennea, Cuban Osvaldo Lara and the Bulgarian Petar Petrov. He continued to improve through the semi-final. 'That was his best run,' says Margot even though the time was a tenth-and-a-half slower. 'The semi was phenomenal. He felt really good, he looked really good and he was supremely confident, but some people were saying he was too confident. Allan had gone back to the village after the race and I went down to the warm-up area to get the results, see the wind-reading and get all the details about who was trying and who was easing up. When I got there everybody was in a panic, they were saying he was too high and that I would have to get him down. Everyone was running around like their heads had been cut off.'

The hysteria was mostly on the part of the British team officials who, for the first time, saw the real possibility of a British victory in the 100 metres in a few hours' time, but when Margot returned to the village she found Wells lying quietly on his bed reading his book, *40 Years of Murder*. Perhaps he was also thinking about the dream he had had before the Games in which he saw himself winning the 100 metres but, intriguingly, the race was transformed into the 200 metres and the dream ended before the finish.

Allan and Margot then went back to the stadium, where she said simply, 'I'll see you when it's finished,' and they went their separate ways – she into the stands, he into the dressing-rooms. Strange things happen before Olympic finals, and this one was no exception: the first was the bizarre appearance of the Russian Aksinin, who Wells remembers walking into the dressing-room late and wearing just his underpants and making a point of moving around so that everyone present could see there was blood on them, possibly the result of an injection. Of course, it was unlikely that an injection could cause that amount of blood, or whatever he had smeared on them, but it was a psychological ploy that might have worked with someone else – not with Wells. 'I just thought, "You sod, you're going to have to run ten times harder for that."'

Once in the collecting area the Russian officials would not let anyone out, and Wells had to get special permission to pay a visit to the toilets, a disgusting wooden shack at the back of the stands, where the stench was so bad that the officials advised the athletes to wear masks. 'It reminded me of the old rugby clubs and their old changing rooms,' says Wells, 'and it brought back to me that here I was at an Olympic final. It really brought me back to earth. I was standing in there and thinking what the hell am I doing here, with this stench, and I was actually praying for help.'

When he lined up at the start, in front of a crowd of nearly 100,000 inside Moscow's magnificent Lenin Stadium, just after quarter past eight on a warm Friday evening, on July 25, he was drawn in the dreaded outside lane nearest to the stands, whereas his main rival, Leonard, was six athletes away, on the inside. In a short documentary film produced recently by the Olympic Channel, Leonard recalled: 'I never agreed with the lane allocation. The Soviets put me in lane one and the Englishman (*sic*) in lane eight. They always put us apart, putting the Soviets in the best lanes.' From the gun it was Leonard who appeared to have the lead, and as the halfway mark passed he began to push out in front and away from the rest of the field. What he could not have seen was that way out in lane eight Allan Wells was powering down the track, passing the rest of the athletes on his inside, and with five metres to go he began to dip. He seemed to hit the finishing line at almost the same instant as Leonard. There was confusion in the stadium and no one seemed to know who had won. It was a photo finish for the first and second, with Wells and Leonard well clear of the third-placed man, Petrov.

Wells recalls: 'It felt like I was in a tube, with that one lane stretching out in front of me and you are sort of outside yourself. You've done it all before, you've run it a hundred times before, you've slept it a hundred times before, but now it's real and you can feel the ground, but it's like you're looking through your own eyes at yourself.

'Lara was in the lane beside me and I used him as a gauge, because I'd seen him training with Leonard and I knew I had to pass him at 30 metres to be comparable, but I didn't get by him until 50 metres, so I just gave it all I had and I could see the line coming up in the distance. With about 40 yards left I allowed my eyes to glance across and I saw the Cuban Leonard. He was right up there and I thought to myself, "Well I'm going to get a medal anyway, I'll bloody well make a dive for the line and give it everything – that's why I'm here." But I wasn't sure and neither was Leonard.'

Margot, screaming memorably from the stands, remembers: 'I was just past the finishing line and from the angle I was in, I thought Leonard had won. The blood just seemed to drain from my body, I think it was all in my feet, I was so disappointed for Allan.'

Everyone in the stadium, including the athletes, stood on the track and waited for the action replay to come up on the stadium's giant electronic scoreboard. It was transmitted in slow motion and frozen on the line, showing clearly that Wells had dipped in front of the Cuban at the finish. Wells leapt into the air and began a victorious lap of honour, something he had promised himself if he won a gold medal, but when he returned to the finish a Russian official approached and told him that he had not won after all. Horrified that he had just embarrassed himself and his country by taking a lap of honour he had not earned, he watched in anguish for the scoreboard to put up the names of the winners. Finally it came up – in Russian – but he correctly assumed that even in Cyrillic his name was shorter than Leonard's and the shorter name had won, so it must be true. As he walked off the track and into the drugs testing room, Margot was receiving a bunch of flowers that he had organized before the race, but they did not see each other for several hours.

Wells and Leonard had been given the same time – 10.25 seconds – and the official photograph showed Wells's plunge for the line had beaten the big Cuban by just five one thousandths of an inch. It took the judges more than ten minutes to make their minds up.

Bronze medallist Petar Petrov, who still holds the Bulgarian 100 metres record he set in Moscow, recalled: 'For them it was difficult to see each other in their peripheral vision and to see who was ahead. And they were stunned somehow. I knew I was third, but the interesting thing was that the Cuban thought he was first and he started rejoicing, raising his hands, but from the replay on the screen it was clear that Allan Wells was first.'

Leonard, who is still coaching in his native Cuba, remembers not seeing Wells for the entire race. 'I was in the lead all the time, from when we took off. Then he lunged for the finish. I didn't lunge for the finish; if I had I might have won. When I passed the finish I thought I was the winner and then when the results came out there was a photo finish and I saw that, yes, Allan Wells's torso was in front of me. But anyway if you look at the photo finish, my full stride had gone over the finishing line. The thing is, when they decide on a photo finish victory they look at the torso.'

The medal ceremony was an anti-climax to Wells's success – a petty act on the part of the British Government ensured that the team would not see their flag rise nor hear the national anthem. Instead the Olympic flag and anthem were used, a sight that also greeted Britain's other major winners, Coe, Ovett and Daley Thompson.

'It hadn't really dawned on me that if I won I wasn't going to see the flag or hear the anthem,' says Wells, 'and it was really sad, a real disappointment, to see the Olympic flag and hear their anthem. I suppose it wasn't a really significant thing, but these are the moments you cherish and they weren't there.'

But standing on the rostrum with the gold medal around his neck was still a proud moment. He was the oldest man in Olympic history, at 28, to win the 100 metres. As Margot described it: 'Winning an Olympic gold medal has a kudos about it, a respect, because it's the one thing that you step on the track for, to race, to run, to train, whether you're five or fifty-five, it's the one thing you never dream about because you never think it can happen. When it does it takes a while to sink in.'

Wells was piped into the post-race press conference in Highland style, but the first question fired at him was about the late Harold Abrahams, the last Briton to win the title. One writer asked him if he had won it for Harold, and Wells quick-fired back, 'No, that one was for Eric Liddell.' It brought the house down for the Scottish journalists.

For a Scotsman, the last laugh was on him as, still elated from his win, he allowed himself to be persuaded by Margot to visit one of the Moscow tourist shops and buy her a new fur coat. 'She caught me at a vulnerable moment,' he recalls. 'She came out of the shop with a big smile and I came out with an empty wallet.'

Although there were many celebrations, Wells had to be careful because he had plenty of running still left to do and a double sprint victory was on the cards with his best event, the 200 metres, still to come. Again he made the final in some style, but standing in his way was the Italian 'Blue Arrow' Pietro Mennea, who was still smarting from his Europa Cup defeat over 200 metres on his home soil at the hands of Wells. Despite breaking the world record in 1979, with an incredible 19.72 – a record that would stand for nearly 17 years – Mennea still regarded Wells as his biggest threat. The Scot became known as 'The Beast' in the Italian's household, so the 1972 bronze medallist in the 200 metres was fired up to win this time. The race progressed as in Wells's dream, with him tearing into the lead, making up the stagger on Mennea, who was running just outside him in lane eight, and taking a perfect curve leaving Mennea some three yards in his wake. But the Italian did not give up and, as Wells began to tire, Mennea fought back and – just at the point where Wells's dream had ended – Mennea nipped by him in the last few metres to win, with Wells second and Don Quarrie third. The Italian retired after finishing 7th in the Los Angeles Olympic 200 metre final and became a respected lawyer, sports agent and member of the European parliament. He died from pancreatic cancer in 2013. He was 60.

In coming second in the Moscow 200, Wells had set a new British record of 20.21, so he was not too disappointed. Significantly, however, neither of the other two medallists in the 200 metres final had also run in the 100 metres final. A few days later, after taking fourth place in the sprint relay alongside Mike McFarlane, Cameron Sharp and Drew McMaster – in a race won by the Soviet Union – the British team set off for home. The typical reaction to Wells's victory was simply that he would not have won had the Americans been there. Even in Britain people were sceptical, while in the United States the little coverage that the Olympics received added to the general feeling of apathy about Wells. *The New York Times* track writer Frank Litsky explains: 'The American reaction was who? Scotland don't have sprinters. We knew an American sprinter hadn't won because we weren't there, but the record books don't have an asterisk by Allan Wells's name saying the Americans were not there. He was the right man at the right time and after those Olympics he raced against the Americans who were missing from the Olympics and he beat them. He won the Olympic title legitimately and won his number one ranking legitimately.'

Naturally the American sprinters felt that they could have given him a tougher challenge. The three sprinters who would have made the US 100 team were 19-year-old Stanley Floyd, Harvey Glance and the University of Georgia's Mel Lattany.

Floyd had collected a unique triple in the 1980 season, winning the NCAA, US Championships and the US Olympic trials – the first time this feat had been achieved in the 100 metres since Bobby Morrow back in the fifties. Floyd had run 10.07 seconds that year and had not been beaten indoors or outdoors for more than eighteen months. His opportunity to show the world what it had missed in Moscow came in the first major post-Olympic meeting in Cologne. A huge 35,000 crowd watched an incredibly close 100 metres, but it was Wells who dipped at the line to pip the American by just two hundredths of a second, in a time of 10.19. Lattany was third.

Floyd retired from the track in 1984 and, after an abortive attempt at an NFL career with the Atlanta Falcons, became a police officer with the Houston drug squad. On retiring from the force, he continued to coach and even helped his daughter, a first-class quarter miler, qualify for the 2008 Beijing Olympics.

Lattany was a popular figure on British tracks in the 1980s and after retiring he also tried a move into football; however, his career as wide receiver with the Dallas Cowboys lasted only a few months. He became a high school teacher, coach and business consultant.'I could never say that the Americans wouldn't have won the gold medal,' says Wells, 'and I have never said I would have won if the Americans were there, because it's total speculation. Politics came between us, but what I would say is a couple of weeks after Moscow I was given the opportunity to run against the Americans and if you look back they were second and I won.'

Although Floyd did manage to beat him in a couple of subsequent races, in Zurich and Brussels, by then it was academic as far as Wells was concerned, although he would make the point far more forcibly at the Golden Sprints the following year. At his triumphant homecoming, where thousands of fans turned out to see the fastest man on earth, the police had to control the Edinburgh crowds as Wells's open-topped bus moved slowly along the streets to a big reception at Meadowbank stadium.

As reigning Olympic champion Wells was invited to scores of meetings around the world, but if 1980 had been a good year then 1981 was probably his greatest, starting with victory in the European Cup 100 metres in Zagreb, and second place in the 200 metres. He followed this with his most decisive victory over the Americans, by winning the Golden Sprints in rainy Berlin, coming second behind the flying Frenchman Herman Panzo in the 100 metres, and winning the title on aggregate by storming to victory in the 200 metres by five metres from Mel Lattany – a win that he feels was probably his finest run. It was Lattany who told Wells it wouldn't have made a difference had the American sprinters been in Moscow. 'He came up to me and said, "Allan, it didn't matter we weren't there, you were the best man."' It meant a lot to Wells to hear it from one of the US team. Lattany managed to beat him in the IAAF World Cup 200 metres, in Rome, but in front of 54,000 fans at the Stadio Olimpico he claimed the 100 metres title with a tight win over the Ghanaian lawyer Ernie Obeng.

When the following season got underway, Wells was 30 years old and many people were writing him off, but he pushed himself hard through the winter and the run-up to the Commonwealth Games – so much so that Margot even admitted to reporters that their marriage had been under enormous strain, but the effort certainly paid off. He took three medals at the Commonwealth Games in Brisbane, Australia, winning the 100 metres from the emerging Canadian Ben Johnson, running a memorable tie for first in the 200 metres with England's Mike MacFarlane and adding a bronze from the relay.

His subsequent performances in major championships did not live up to his own expectations, but he continued to defy media prediction and athletics logic by making finals and winning international meetings around Europe.

At the 1983 World Championships he qualified for both finals and was placed fourth in the 100 and 200 metres, and the following year, despite a toe injury, he elected to defend his title in the Los Angeles Olympics. It ended disastrously, with him finishing an embarrassing last in his semi, and as he trotted forlornly back down the tunnel, he could see the future champion in front of him – Carl Lewis. It looked like a symbolic moment, but it convinced Wells that he was not finished, so he battled back again.

An operation on his toe caused him to miss the entire 1985 season, but he came back in style in 1986 to finish fifth in both sprints at the European Championships, at the grand old age of 34. Although he did not warrant selection for Scotland's team for the Commonwealth Games in Edinburgh, he answered the selectors in ideal fashion by beating both the 100 and 200 metres Commonwealth champions at a famous meeting at Gateshead, where he turned out in long, *Chariots of Fire*-style shorts and beat both Canadians Ben Johnson and Atlee Mahorn. Wells went on to run some impressive times during the early part of the 1987 season, which earned him selection for Britain's World Championship sprint team, but injury forced him to pull out. However, he set a different kind of world record, becoming the first man over 35 to run under 10.30 for 100 metres.

In November 1987, Allan underwent a hernia operation, in the hope that he could regain a level of fitness to get him on the plane for Seoul, but it was not to be and he would spend the 1988 Olympics as a studio guest for British television.

'It wasn't the money that made me carry on for so long,' he says. 'It was the sheer enjoyment the sport gave me and the pleasure I got from training and competing. I wasn't too sad to give up, because I had my share of injuries and I won't forget the good moments. The feeling of running fast is unforgettable; the exhilaration you experience running around a bend, it's like you're in charge, you're like a Ferrari.'

If he were the Olympic sprint champion today, Wells would be a multi-millionaire, but at the height of his track powers the 'big professional break' had not yet arrived and payments were a closely guarded and haphazard affair. 'I do regret there wasn't the financial rewards,' says Wells, 'but my event at the time wasn't as financially rewarding as the middle-distance events. Even though I was the first British gold medallist in the sprints for more than fifty years it still didn't seem to have much power behind it. But the way things have changed now I would certainly be getting top-notch money.'

While there may be some regrets, Margot values the gold medal more than wealth, and believes that athletics has suffered from loaded races and ridiculously high payments to mediocre athletes.

Allan Wells was always a racer rather than a record breaker, although he has had his fair share of national records. He never really received the credit he deserved as a sprinter, even in his own country, where he always ran in the shadow of the Coe and Ovett circus, and he played second fiddle to them on the European circuit, with the middle-distance men getting the money, the publicity and the kudos. Wells never courted popularity and maybe that is why he never attained real superstar status in Britain. In fact, even during his most successful years he was never voted athlete of the year. However, he was awarded an MBE in 1982.

After retiring from the track Wells did a little coaching, including working with the British bobsled team, the Lawn Tennis Association, the London Scottish rugby union side and long term with Scottish athletics. He continues to work at Surrey University, where he's spent a large part of his working life, as a much-respected technical engineer. At home he and Margot's two children, Zoe and Simon are grown up – Zoe providing two grandchildren – and Margot successfully runs her own business, Wellfast, a fitness and speed coaching enterprise that has specialized in training some of the country's top rugby players, as well as a raft of footballers, skiers, golfers and swimmers.

In March 2012 Wells returned to Moscow for the first time since 1980 as part of a British Embassy event to promote the London Olympics. He found it quite an emotional experience. 'They took us back to the stadium and all these years later it seemed so much more colourful and modern,' he said. 'Even the city seemed a happier place. On the pillars they showed us plaques showing the names of the 1980 gold medal winners, and Daley Thompson and I found our names on the same pillar. Muscovites are very proud of the Olympics they displayed in 1980. It was a really special trip and brought back a lot of memories.'

To many people Wells has always been an enigmatic, almost mysterious character – he was typecast by the press as a dour, difficult Scot and track fans around the country actually believed it. Wells admits that as an athlete he was interested only in winning races, but off the track he was a different person: a quiet, unassuming man who enjoyed family life, his children and his job. Years after his career ended he seems a much calmer and contented person.

'He's totally the opposite to the commentators' portrayal on TV,' says Margot. 'They say he's dull and he never smiles, but actually he smiles quite a lot and he's got a very dry sense of humour. The problem is that he's a perfectionist in everything. It doesn't matter what he does, everything has to be just so. In his job he's working to thousands of an inch, and if he does anything in the house it has to be exactly right. He does everything at a snail's pace and he's always late, in fact the only thing he does fast is run.'

Today, Wells now feels he better understands his place in Olympic history. 'I know I made huge sacrifices to achieve things in athletics. It was a really physical thing, almost a hypnotic state of mind. And during my career I never once let my guard down. It took me two or three years after my career ended before I actually did let my guard down. It was the most important thing I ever did. I dreamt about it and it came off. It was one of those unreal stories that actually happened.'

Margot's influence on her husband's career was fundamental, and without her it is difficult to imagine how he could have achieved half of the things he did. He was driven by an almost insatiable pursuit of excellence, and during his long career his intense dedication and hard work brought to the sport a sense of professionalism that encouraged a new generation of sprinters in Britain and perhaps elsewhere in the world. There may have been greater sprinters, but in fighting his way to the top with guts, determination and sweat, Allan Wells proved himself to be an outstanding role model.

He had earned the right to be included amongst Scotland's greatest ever sportsmen. Indeed, two Scottish newspapers recently named him alongside such luminaries as Andy Murray, Kenny Dalglish and Sir Chris Hoy. He was a bid ambassador for the London 2012 bid; he received an honorary doctorate from Edinburgh Napier University and when the Commonwealth Games came to Glasgow in 2014, it was Wells who was honoured as the first baton carrier in the Queen's Baton Relay, standing proudly standing next to Her Majesty The Queen at Buckingham Palace. Life as a retired and revered elder statesman of Scottish athletics was assured.

But Wells's peaceful existence was shattered in the summer of 2015 by revelations broadcast in a BBC television investigation about allegations of performance enhancing drug-taking in athletics, produced by the flagship current affairs series *Panorama*. It was ostensibly directed at American track coach Alberto Salazar, who worked with distance runners Mo Farah and Galen Rupp, but a thirteen-minute section of the one-hour programme focused on the whistle-blowing claim of a disgraced former team-mate of Wells, sprinter Drew McMaster.

Wells and McMaster had endured a spiky relationship in their running career, compounded by the fact that Wells routinely beat McMaster throughout the seventies and eighties. McMaster had confessed back in the nineties to taking performance-enhancing drugs and, in the programme, he claimed that Wells had also taken performance-enhancing steroids during his running career. He said that he had secretly tape-recorded conversations with a former British team doctor, the late Jimmy Ledingham, which confirmed these allegations. The programme did not play these tapes, but highlighted selected lines from the transcripts, before revealing they had corroborating evidence from two other athletics figures, albeit anonymous ones.

However, no new evidence was submitted and, as Wells's lawyer suggested, the programme seemed to be basing its allegation on the hearsay evidence of a disgraced former team-mate and the unheard and covertly-acquired recordings of a dead doctor. In truth it was an oddly assembled and unconvincing programme, with the historic Wells segment strangely shoehorned into a much more modern story.

Wells himself was aghast. He had never failed a drug test in all his 14 years as a sprinter and the allegations, which he categorically denied, had come out of the blue some 35 years after his Olympic triumph in Moscow. He refused to take part in the programme, which he described as a 'hatchet job' motivated by the malice of his former team-mate, who he described as 'a Walter Mitty character. The truth is that McMaster turned to steroids because I started beating him and I was not using drugs,' said Wells. 'These allegations go back years and have resurfaced at regular intervals. I've never enticed or advised people to get involved with illegal substances and I've never got involved with them. Having watched the show, I couldn't believe what was being said and the cynical manner in how it was put together. I won't lose any sleep over this as I know what the actual truth is. I hope that anybody in Scottish athletics will be able to split the difference between reality and fiction.'

Despite persistent enquiries, the BBC failed to respond to a list of questions posed in the preparation of this book. These included questions related to McMaster's credibility, the identity of the anonymous witnesses and why the tapes had not actually been broadcast. Whether viewers were convinced by the programme or not, it was certainly a damaging distraction from the enduring Wells legend, and this alone would seem to be a colossal injustice to a British sportsman who had achieved so much. It has to be hoped that the golden memories of Moscow will stay alive for far longer than the more recent attempts to destroy them.

It was ironic then, that in the summer of 2020 Wells – who was now approaching 70 – featured prominently in a month-long on-line series called *Sporting Nation*, which reflected on the 'greatest feats and personalities from Scottish sporting history'. No mention was made of any alleged impropriety on his part. The producers? The BBC.

But his unique place in Scottish athletics is assured. He is, after all, the nation's only Olympic track gold medallist since Eric Liddell – who was running nearly a hundred years ago.

Mark Munro, the CEO of Scottish Athletics, invited Wells to Glasgow recently to present the awards at a hall of fame ceremony. 'The response and warmth for him was overwhelming,' he explained. 'He spent most of the evening doing selfies for fans. He still has a massive impact in Scotland and is arguably our greatest-ever athlete. I know some of Eric Liddell's fans may disagree, but they were very different eras. Allan's achievements on the track make him the greatest of all time in Scotland.'

Los Angeles 1984 & Seoul 1988

Carl Lewis

In the summer of 1980, in a quiet, middle-class Philadelphia suburb, a skinny teenager sat with his family and watched transfixed as the Olympic Games opened in Moscow.

He had qualified for the USA team, but the American-led boycott of the Games, made in protest at the Soviet invasion of Afghanistan, meant he'd have to wait for his first big chance on the Olympic stage until Los Angeles four years later. Unlike some of the US athletes, he knew he had time on his side.

His name was Carl Lewis and in 2000 he would be named as the athlete of the century and lauded as the greatest Olympian ever to grace the Games.

Those twenty years would witness the most extraordinary athletic career – a rollercoaster of exhilarating performances, gold medals, world records, a colourful Hollywood lifestyle, million-dollar riches, lurid headlines, fights, feuds and a ringside seat at the biggest sporting scandal of the twentieth century.

His great rival, Ben Johnson, may have written a far darker chapter in the history of the 100 metres, but as his story faded from view, the legend of Carl Lewis continued to grow.

Off the track his tireless campaign to drag the sport into the professional era was genuinely ahead of its time and proved pivotal in paving the way for the next generation of athletes to earn their living in the sport. The track and field stars of today owe him an enormous debt and he was at the heart of a seismic shift that freed the sport from its amateur shackles.

On the track, his natural talent was boundless, his phenomenal speed effortless – but his showmanship polarized opinion. His manager once predicted that Lewis would be bigger than Michael Jackson, while his passion for fast cars, flashy clothes and a personal entourage that wouldn't have shamed a Hollywood A-lister meant the paparazzi were never far behind him. Wherever Lewis went, there was usually a story.

Happily, there were no media flash bulbs present when Carlton Frederick Lewis arrived into a close-knit, sports mad family in July 1961, in Birmingham, Alabama. Father Bill had been a good quarter-miler and mother Evelyn was one of the top high hurdlers in the 1950s. Young Carl spent his time playing catch-up with older brothers Mack, who was a decent sprinter, and Cleve, who would become a professional soccer player. Little sister Carol would be the first American woman to clear seven metres in the long jump.

When Lewis was just two years old the family left the south and moved to Willingboro in New Jersey, about 15 miles north east of Philadelphia, where his parents worked as high school teachers and coached at the local track club. With his sporting background, it seemed natural that young Carl should follow in the family tradition, but he was a slow developer and at one stage it seemed that he might be the only member of the Lewis family not to excel in sports. He was shy, quiet and, for a time, smaller than his sister Carol, who was two years his junior. Incredibly, for the graceful, 6ft 2in Olympic great he would become, his first nickname was 'Shorty'.

'I was kind of a slow learner, and a non-developer, or whatever you want to call it,' says Lewis, 'and it was interesting to see my brothers and even Carol far exceeding the things I could do. They were all very successful at a young age and I was just the opposite. I was reserved and shy, but as time went on I started to evolve, to mature and grow a little bit, then the talent just came to me.'

It was not until he attended high school that he began to develop physically and blossom as an athlete, but before that, at the age of 12 he was introduced to a man who would fire his athletic ambitions and whose achievements he would one day emulate – the great Jesse Owens. Lewis met him at a local track and field meet and was immediately impressed.

The ageing Owens joined sprinter Steve Williams and long-jumper Arnie Robinson as his childhood heroes. A year after meeting Owens he began to take a more serious interest in long-jumping, which he had first tried as a nine-year-old, jumping into some sand his father had put down as the foundations for a patio. He even marked off the distance of Bob Beamon's miraculous world record jump of 29ft 2½in (8.90m) during the 1968 Olympics in his front garden. The shy kid began dreaming of making a 30-foot jump long before the idea of competing in an Olympic Games even entered his head. It was not until 1979, the year before Moscow, that he realized he had a chance of making the US team. The metamorphosis had begun in 1976, when in one month he grew an amazing two-and-a-half inches in height and started to attract the attention of discerning people within the sport.

He made steady progress in the sprints, dropping his 100 yards time to a world-class 9.3 seconds and he began to jump regularly over 20 feet. It was in 1979 that his athletic career really took off. Still under the careful coaching guidance of his parents, he leaped an impressive 8.07 metres at a high school meeting, taking the US high school record and a world best for a 17-year-old. Soon after that triumph he came second in the US senior championships with an 8.09m, a jump that prompted *Track & Field News* to notice Lewis and describe him as 'a tall, lean high schooler with mind boggling potential'.

His performances earned him a place on the US team for the 1979 Pan American Games, in Puerto Rico, where he took a bronze medal with a jump of 8.13 metres just six days after his eighteenth birthday, a leap that ranked him fifth in the world. Carl Lewis had arrived.

In the autumn of 1979 he arrived at the University of Houston and came under the keen eye of coach Tom Tellez, who had been a key figure in the athletic careers of triple jumper Willie Banks and high jumper Dwight Stones. Tellez, who coached Lewis throughout his career, began working with Lewis to completely change his long jumping style and also helped improve his sprint skills, so much so that he was able to make a clean sweep of the sprints in the 1980 US junior championships.

For Tellez, Carl was something of a perennial experiment. He compared it to programming a computer; he fed in the information and he saw the results out on the track or in the long jump pit. Although the Americans had decided to boycott the Moscow Olympics, the trials were held as planned, with Lewis making the 'shadow' team in the long jump. Additionally, as fourth-placed man in the sprints, he was also selected for the relay team, alongside Stanley Floyd, Harvey Glance and Mel Lattany.

Missing the Olympics did not seem to faze him. 'It really wasn't that bad for me, because I was 18 when I made the team and 19 when we made the alternative tour in Europe. I was young and I felt the world was in front of me. I don't think I would have won anything anyway, but I think I would have got a medal in the long jump and I might have run in the relay, but I just looked to the future and I knew I'd be back and I'd have another opportunity.'

During the winter of 1980–81, Lewis toiled through a gruelling weight-training programme devised by Tellez to develop his physique and strength. The benefits were apparent when the indoor season opened in February 1981 and he ran a 6.06-second 60 yards, just outside the world record, and then jumped 8.49 to smash Larry Myricks's indoor long jump world mark.

1981 would be a special year. In May, running for Houston at the South West Conference Championships in Dallas, he performed the greatest double in history, leaping 8.25m and running a 10-flat 100 metres – the fastest sea-level run ever. He followed that with another double, this time taking the NCAA titles in the long jump and the 100 metres – the first man to accomplish it since Jesse Owens in 1936 – and if that wasn't enough, he followed it up with yet another double at the TAC Championships, despite the searing 100-degree heat in Sacramento.

At the end of the year, his performances ranked Lewis at number one in the 100 metres, ahead of reigning Olympic champion Allan Wells and his countrymen Floyd and Lattany. *Track & Field News* voted him the US Athlete of the Year and second only to middle-distance king Sebastian Coe in the world. To cap it all, he was presented with the prestigious Sullivan Award by the AAU, the first black athlete to win the title of the top sportsman or woman, since Wilma Rudolph back in the 1960s.

'It was a very gratifying end to a great season,' said Lewis. 'Being number one really motivated me and helped me to move on, because a year before everyone had said I couldn't be a world class jumper and sprinter.'

It was a ranking that Lewis would retain for the next four years in the 100 metres. The following year began with problems when the University of Houston declared him academically ineligible after he failed a history course. Lewis maintained that the reasoning behind the university's action was fear of a much-heralded NCAA investigation into college track programmes in the USA. He lost his athletics scholarship and that meant he had to pay his own fees to complete his degree in TV and radio communication. Given the money he was now earning on the track, it didn't turn out to be too much of a hardship, especially as one of the school's worries about the NCAA probe was how to explain away Lewis's new Porsche.

He only stayed on at Houston until the spring, before it became clear he would be financially far better off without having to tip-toe around the onerous NCAA rules. Consequently, he left college, signed up with manager Joe Douglas and ran under the banner of the Santa Monica Track Club, a high-performance centre for elite athletes set up in 1972 by Douglas.

His new manager had been a track coach but he was also a shrewd commercial operator and there were mutterings about a masterplan, drawn up as early as 1981, to commoditize and market Lewis as a lucrative brand.

It was clearly starting to work. The Dallas Cowboys wasted a twelfth-round draft pick on him, and even the NBA's Chicago Bulls tried to draft him, despite the fact that Lewis hadn't touched a basketball in almost ten years. In rejecting both approaches, Douglas was suitably dismissive: 'He couldn't afford the pay cut.'

Talking recently on the Houston sports show *Q'D UP*, Lewis recalled: 'Growing up, I didn't realize that track and field was amateur and basketball was not. It was glorified slavery and for so long many athletes just accepted it and you either fell in line or you try to change it. I wanted to change it because we were doing the same things as the other athletes, but we weren't being paid for it. I wanted to be a millionaire, I wanted to be rich like the other athletes.'

It was in the following year, 1983, when the fluent running and easy smile of Carl Lewis were launched on the international stage, at the inaugural World Athletics Championships in Helsinki. Until then, apart from the occasional foray into European grand prix meetings, his best performances had been reserved for the few home fans that turned up at the various track meets around the United States.

In Finland, it was decided that he would only compete in the 100 metres, long jump and relay, with Lewis figuring he was a little too inexperienced in the 200 metres. This was despite the fact that he had run the second-fastest time ever at the TAC Championships in Indianapolis, which doubled as the trials for the world championship – a jaw-dropping 19.75 seconds – just three hundredths of a second off Pietro Mennea's world record, which had been set at altitude. If he hadn't coasted the last ten metres, broken into a beaming smile and thrown his hands into the air he would almost certainly have shattered the world mark. In the same trials he leaped 8.79 metres, the second longest jump in history and half the competitors stopped their own preparation to watch him run the 100 metres. A sharp 2.37mph wind into the faces of the finalists meant there would be no world records, but Lewis charged to victory by two feet from Emmitt King and Calvin Smith, in a sedate 10.27.

In Helsinki, he was simply in a different class from the rest of the athletes on show and he comfortably won his two solo events, the 100 metres and the long jump. In the 100 he accelerated smoothly past everyone at about 75 metres, leaving fellow countryman Calvin Smith, the new world record holder, in his wake.

Smith had come to the Games confident of beating Lewis, especially after shaving two-hundredths of a second off Jim Hines's long-standing world record of 9.95 in the thin air of Colorado Springs a month before arriving in Finland. Considering that Lewis was behind both Smith and Emmitt King at 70 metres, his margin of victory – about a metre and a half – and his time of 10.07, was nothing short of remarkable and demonstrated perfectly what later became known as the Lewis 'gas jets', an almost turbo-charged extra gear into which he clicked with about three-quarters of the race gone – a spectacle that made the rest of the field look as if they were moving backwards. It showcased the very essence of Lewis's running, his ability to stay relaxed and maintain his speed to the finish, while other athletes began to tire and tighten.His form continued in the long jump: his first jump of the competition, an 8.55m, proved to be the winner and he only bothered to jump once more before withdrawing from the event, convinced that he would win. Finally, he anchored the USA's formidable relay quartet of King, Willie Gault and Smith to victory in a new world record of 37.86. By the end of 1983, Carl had recorded the fastest ever sea-level time in the 100 metres (9.97), the second longest jump in history (8.79m), the fastest sea-level 200 metres (19.75) and a share in the world 4 x 100m relay record. He had all the credentials with which to establish himself as the greatest athlete in the world, so when he emerged from Helsinki to tell an eager media that he would shoot for four golds and try to emulate Jesse Owens, no-one was the slightest bit surprised. Worryingly for Lewis, who had only turned 23 a month before the LA Games, in the minds of many track fans he had already won them.Lewis started Olympic year 1984 where he left off, with a series of stunning sprinting and jumping performances leading up to the US Olympic Trials, in Los Angeles, where he reeled off an incredible 10.06 into a 2.2 metres per second headwind, regarded by some track experts of the day as the greatest 100 ever. At 90 metres he was two metres clear of the field and hit the line with his arms in the air, with second-placed Sam Graddy clocked at 10.21 and third man Ron Brown at 10.23. World record-holder Calvin Smith just made the relay squad by a matter of inches in fourth place. Lewis then leaped 8.71m to win the long jump and clocked an impressive 19.86 seconds in the final of the 200 metres to ensure that he qualified for all four events as the undisputed number one.

The Los Angeles Olympics was boycotted by the Soviet Union and all the Eastern Bloc states, with the exception of Romania, in protest over the commercialization of the Games, but it was generally regarded as retaliation for the Moscow boycott four years before. The Games opened at the famous Coliseum on August 3 and the packed crowds and millions watching at home expected Lewis to take his place among the track immortals and comfortably walk away with four gold medals. But that was the problem. The American public not only expected him to win, they expected him to break the world records, too. The weight of expectation was overwhelming.

'Don't Step on Superman's Cape,' opined *Track & Field News* in the build-up to the Games. But the first fault lines were beginning to appear. 'Lewis has betrayed little of the pressure that surely must haunt him, if only in his dreams,' said the magazine. 'But the pressure leaks out in little ways. Some fellow athletes take umbrage at his "no sweat" attitude, but the public and even most of the press mostly look the other way when Lewis displays a studied nonchalance bordering on arrogance. They overlook the insularity, the flippant nature of many of his remarks. They smile at the gaudy fashion displays – the black and orange Spiderman warm-up suits, the solid gold belt buckles, the white framed sunglasses left on for just a moment as the cameras roll.'

Meanwhile the rest of the world's media was lying in wait, all wanting a piece of the new superstar. It was like a lamb to the slaughter. In the build-up to Los Angeles, Lewis and his associates had made some wild claims about the financial potential of winning four gold medals, and the commercial battle for his signature had begun.

Lewis had made commercials for Nike and the Japanese company Fuji, but in a report in the respected *Newsweek* magazine, his manager Joe Douglas described his search for a high-class corporate giant for which Lewis could be a blue-chip marketing front man. Even the Association of National Advertisers suggested that if he won four gold medals he would be 'very hot property'. It was nothing new for athletes to cash in on their Olympic fame – the new rules regarding payment to competing athletes now enabled them to earn money both on and off the track. Swimmer Mark Spitz and decathlete Bruce Jenner had both made handsome fortunes in the commercial world after their Olympic feats. What was different in Lewis's case was the advance planning for his marketing after the Games – before he'd won anything.

On top of his race earnings and countless endorsements, he was earning about $500,000 a year from Nike when the Games began, but Douglas was keen to broaden his commercial appeal. In *The New York Times* he said: 'We hope he'll be a multi-millionaire, but we'll wait and see. I don't think anyone knows how much he'll be worth.'

So while Lewis was busily preparing for the track, his backers were already doing battle in the boardrooms of potential employers, a tactic that actually dampened his appeal because at the start of an Olympics it appeared somehow unseemly and served to devalue his sporting contribution. Douglas even admitted to *The New York Times* that a marketing plan had been drawn up to cash in on Lewis's ability as far back as 1981, designed to turn him into a national hero whose commercial value would rocket after the Games.

The key principles of the plan were published in *Sports Illustrated*:

1. Prioritize appearance offers in Los Angeles or New York to maximum media attention.
2. Transcend track and field and gain access to all Americans via magazines such as *Esquire*, *Newsweek*, *GQ* and *Ebony*.
3. Limit participation in track meets to ensure that Lewis would be well-rested and prepared for each.
4. Limit endorsements and wait until after the Olympics to bag the big one. Douglas: 'We want Carl to be identified with one major company, the way O. J. Simpson is with Hertz or Bob Hope is with Texaco.'

5. Prepare for the post-Olympic stampede by continuing communications studies at Houston, taking acting lessons and, if possible, working part-time for a local network affiliate. Lewis: 'Mark Spitz and Bruce Jenner were not prepared. How can you train 15 years toward becoming the best athlete in your event and not one minute toward becoming an actor or singer and expect to do well?'

6. Emote openly to the public after major track achievements. Douglas: 'I never told him to show an emotion he didn't feel, but if he was going to gesture, to do it large enough so everyone could see.'

However, an avalanche of other stories were appearing too – though not the usual flattering tributes, like the two cover stories in *Time* during the three weeks running up to the Games. First, there was a particularly vitriolic piece about him in the special Olympic edition of *Sports Illustrated*, a brutal character assassination that portrayed him as a self-obsessed, preening diva. It quoted Lewis saying: 'I could set a world record in the decathlon if I trained for two years. I could be an All-Pro in the NFL within three years – but I never would, because in football, the athlete controls nothing. If I get sick of all this entertainment crap, I'll go into business, and if not that, maybe politics. I'm not ruling out anything. It's all there if I want it.'

The magazine pulled no punches and focused on Lewis's superstar behaviour. Entitled 'I Do What I Want To Do' it began thus: 'He stands at the top of the runway, his warm-up jacket collar flipped up over his neck in the style of someone who wants very much to be different, which he does, and his expression saying *Oh, it's up. Breeze must've caught it*.

'Around his neck is an orange headband – quite happy to be the only headband in the arena being worn around a neck – advertising the TV station he works for in Houston.

'On his feet are a pair of long-jump shoes moulded specially for him. That was his idea, too. On the back of his custom-tailored warm-up suit, in case you confused him with another jogger, is stitched his name. Oh, *that's* Carl Lewis.'

After that hit the newsstands, a Scandinavian scandal sheet then printed some unpleasant allegations about his sexual preferences, and yet another publication even suggested that he was taking drugs. Suddenly, instead of being hailed as the all-conquering American hero, he was being hounded by the popular press. He did not help his own cause, at the few press conferences he did give, by turning up late, dressed outrageously and often attended by an entourage more befitting a heavyweight boxer.

In the eyes of many seasoned Olympic observers, it was as if he had already won the four medals, taken his place on the champion's pedestal and been knocked off it, all before he had set foot on the track in Los Angeles. If he did not win all four golds he would be branded a failure. If he succeeded, no one would be surprised because he was expected to do so.

Stories about his opulent lifestyle began to appear in the press, detailing the splendours of his Victorian mansion in Houston and his penchant for collecting fine crystal. A *Newsweek* article described how its reporter was greeted by a uniformed servant and led into a luxurious living room for an interview with Lewis, who then appeared in a blue silk

Japanese bathrobe and complained that the athletic authorities were 'very strict' about billing furniture to his trust fund.

Even the other athletes on the US team joined in, including the respected hurdler Ed Moses, who accused Lewis of 'showboating'. Larry Myricks, for so long the bridesmaid to Lewis in the long jump, bleated: 'There's going to be some serious celebrating when Carl gets beat.' Lewis dealt with the adverse publicity the only way he knew: by denying the more unpleasant stories, especially about drugs and his private life; and by refusing to live in the Olympic village and shunning the accepted daily press conferences.

In the middle of the pre-Olympic storm was the respected track writer of *The New York Times*, Frank Litsky. 'Carl Lewis was a superb athlete, make no mistake about it. But he had a problem with a bad public image. He went into the Olympics with an opportunity to win four gold medals and become one of the great merchandising stars of our generation, of our century. He won four gold medals and actually went downhill as a merchandising attraction. I think it was just bad handling by his people, many things went wrong and any opportunity they had to present him in a good light they either forgot or did the opposite.

'At a press conference before the Games he arrived 45 minutes late, dressed outlandishly with his huge entourage. During the Games he didn't hold a daily press conference like most of the other athletes, saying he would only speak to the media after the gold medals events, that's four times in something like 11 days. Instead of spending 15 minutes a day answering questions and getting the media off his back, he stayed away and the media got angry, especially those members who were not track writers and had no knowledge or interest in track and just wanted to ask the guy a few questions. He just seemed to lose ground everywhere.'

With such a three-ring circus going on it was a miracle that Lewis managed to perform as he did on the track, but he is philosophical about the experience. 'The problem I had was that everybody had their idea of what they wanted me to be or how I had to act. In most cases I didn't fit the mould and people created things. Reporters sought out athletes to say negative things about me, and I never went out and said a lot of things about the money, it was just taken out of context. Joe made a statement once that if I won four gold medals it would put me at the same level in sport that Michael Jackson was in music. That turned around to read Carl should be as rich as Michael Jackson.'

Lewis brushed off some of the scurrilous things that were written about his private life and suggestions that he was involved in drug taking. 'It didn't hurt me as much as people think it did,' he says, 'because I knew where it was coming from. It was other athletes in my sport, and a lot of the press people wanted something like that to write about, but they couldn't say it until someone else did. Once they got a little bit they snatched it like a baton on an anchor leg. It didn't bother me that much because only a couple of these athletes made the team and they didn't do well.'

He managed to reduce the pressures by avoiding newspapers and living away from the village, which earned him strong criticism in the United States, even though other top athletes like Mary Decker, Ed Moses and sprinter Ron Brown also stayed clear of the mayhem. Lewis decided to treat his mammoth task in the simplest possible way, taking each race as it came and not putting pressure on himself by expecting to win every one. His philosophy was that winning the four gold medals was important, but going out and doing his best was even more so. Looking back today he recalls: 'I had no idea how big it was going to be. By the time we got there, there was tons of pressure. A lot of the branding things I learned from the entertainment business. It's normal now, but no-one was doing it then. In the 1980s sport and entertainment were separate. In 1984 there was Prince and *Purple Rain*, Michael Jackson and *Thriller* and me running around a track. We were the most famous people in the world. I made mistakes and look back and think I wish I had done this or that different, but we just focused on the competition and took it event by event.'

The first event at the LA Coliseum was the 100 metres, in which his toughest rivals all came from the USA, with British reigning champion Allan Wells injured and no surprises from the Eastern Bloc. It was a copybook run and Lewis totally outclassed a decent sprint field, turning on the 'gas jets' at about 60 metres and hurtling past everyone to win by the biggest margin ever in an Olympic final, an amazing two-and-a-half metres, from second-placed American Sam Graddy, in 9.99 seconds. The improving Canadian Ben Johnson took third, but he was nowhere near Lewis.

'I didn't react well at the gun,' recalls Lewis, 'and when I stood up at about 15 metres I saw Sam was ahead of me, in fact quite a few people were ahead of me, but I just stayed relaxed and the whole time I knew I was going to win. When I hit the finish line I really didn't know what to feel at the time because you're always so removed, it didn't really sink in until I saw my parents.'

Lewis's mother Evelyn could not bear to watch the race, and father Bill would not let her go down to the track to congratulate her son. He simply waved Carl away to do his lap of honour, something he did in some style, grabbing a huge American flag and trotting around the track waving it enthusiastically as the 92,600 sell-out crowd cheered wildly. Lewis eventually got to Coach Tellez, who proved to be just as outwardly emotional as Carl's father. 'He just stuck out his hand, shook mine and said, "You should have had a world record." So this is what I have to deal with. The man wants perfection.'

The medal ceremony was a highlight for Lewis, even though he would go through the routine another three times before the Games ended, but he remembers it particularly because Graddy was on the podium with him. 'It was nice to have another American there and the crowd was very vocal and very pro-American and every move you made they just cheered. It was really a great experience to think that the whole world was sharing the moment with you, it was more like a religious experience because it was really spiritual and really special. I remember feeling very tall, very strong, like I'd just conquered the world.'

It seemed as though all the bad publicity had been blown away in less than 10 seconds of explosive running, but a few days later events took another wrong turn, this time during the long jump competition. The final was held on the Monday afternoon, just a few hours after Lewis had run a couple of heats in the 200 metres, and he was feeling a little soreness in his leg. He opened up with a leap of 8.54, just a fraction over 28 feet, fouled the second and then decided to sit out the rest of the competition, just as he'd done in the 1983 World Championships, confident that no one would exceed his jump.

Again he was technically right, but when it became clear to the enormous crowd, who had paid top prices to see the competition, that Lewis was not going to jump again, they began to get frustrated and then angry. They even booed him during the medal ceremony that followed.

'People were very upset,' remembers Frank Litsky, 'because they'd spent sixty dollars a ticket. Carl was supposed to jump six times, that's ten dollars a jump. If he and his people had thought about this they could have got him to clutch his hamstring in agony after the second jump and he would have had all the sympathy in the world, but he didn't do it and he lost more ground with the American public.'

Lewis was philosophical about the incident at the time, commenting that it was flattering that they were booing because they wanted to see more of him, which seemed a rather self-serving interpretation. He explains: 'I remember having a problem with my leg and as the afternoon went on the temperature began to drop and I didn't want to take a risk on getting injured, because I had two more events still to go.

'I don't fault the crowd at all for booing, because I don't think most of them were very knowledgeable about track and field. I do fault the media for making a big deal out of nothing.'

In the 200 metres a couple of days later he produced another awesome piece of running, perhaps the best demonstration of curve running ever, to win his third gold medal, hitting the finish line well clear of his two American rivals, Kirk Baptiste and Thomas Jefferson, in a new Olympic record of 19.80, despite a strong headwind that was blowing down the home straight.

A few days later he trotted back on to the track to complete the formalities of his quadruple gold by anchoring the USA relay team to victory in another world record time of 37.83, alongside Sam Graddy, Ron Brown and Calvin Smith. His personal clocking from a flying start was an incredible 8.94, and he stormed away from the rest of the field to double the American winning margin to an astonishing eight metres. It was his thirteenth competition in just eight days. 'To duplicate one of track and field's greatest feats is an honour,' he told reporters. 'Everybody said it couldn't be done, even I said over a year ago that I didn't think I could do it. Jesse Owens is still the same man to me he was before – he is a legend.'

The relay record would last more than six years, though neither the 20-year-old Graddy, who won silver in the 100, nor the LA-born Brown, would see another Olympics. Brown, 23, had already been drafted into the NFL (he had turned down a multi-million-dollar contract to miss the Games and sign for the Cleveland Browns) and immediately joined the LA Rams as a wide receiver, where he became a major star for more than five years and made All Pro. After graduating in 1987, Graddy was drafted by the Denver Broncos, but played only a handful of games before joining the LA Raiders. He and Brown actually played there together for a season. Post-football,

Graddy worked for many years at his alma mater, the University of Tennessee, and at a non-profit housing group. In 1991, Brown retired from the NFL a wealthy man and today has interests in a variety of businesses and charities, as well as helping NFL and military veterans. Calvin Smith would return to the Olympics in 1988 for arguably the most high-profile 100 metres in history.

Back in Los Angeles in 1984, Lewis's job was complete: he had taken the four gold medals he was expected to win, emulated the achievement of the great Owens, and was now ready to accept the predicted avalanche of commercial offers and the cascades of dollars that would obviously be coming his way. But it did not happen that way at all.

The pre-Games publicity and some of the poisonous stories that had been appearing about him during the Olympics had hurt him more than he knew. Worse was still to come when Britain's decathlon gold medallist Daley Thompson took his lap of honour around the stadium wearing a T-shirt bearing the slogan: 'Is the world's 2nd greatest athlete gay?' It was a cheap shot from Thompson and compounded the more salacious stories circulating in the run-up to the Games.

Thompson tried to laugh it off at a press conference by pretending that the word gay in England meant happy, but understandably Lewis was far from happy about the whole affair, although to his credit he managed to keep cool and never let it show.

'I never developed the macho side as a lot of boys do,' he told one newspaper. 'Even my sister Carol shows more masculinity, but that doesn't make me a homosexual. They say I am, but I'm not. They say it because nobody knows what I'm doing. I don't even stay in the same hotels as the other athletes – I could be sleeping with a horse for all they know.

'Basically I'm a loner and that's why they say it. They said it about Michael Jackson for the same reason. If I was weak minded I could become paranoid about the accusations, instead I feel that as long as I know what I am it doesn't matter what people say.'

In his 1990 autobiography *Inside Track*, Lewis wrote: 'Sometimes when a reporter asked if I was gay, I would answer with a question. "Are you?"

'"No."

'"Well, if I called you that, what would you do?"

'"Nothing, I'm not gay, so nothing."

'"Thanks. You just answered your own question for me."

'Sometimes I would use a different approach. "I guess saying that someone is gay is the easiest, most effective way to attack a male, especially an athlete, who is supposed to be all macho. I should really be upset, right? Well, what am I going to do, raise my voice and kick your ass? Why do I have to do that? I don't have to prove anything to you. You don't seem to like me, so why am I going to waste my time with this?"'

So much mud had been thrown at Carl during the Games that some of it was obviously going to stick, true or not, and as a result the anticipated landslide of corporate work simply didn't materialize. Even the giant Coca-Cola Corporation, which had been keen to link up with Lewis and use him as a headline marketing weapon, backed off after the Olympics.

'Some of the offers before the Games were very, very good, but then came the negative publicity,' said manager Douglas, at the time. 'We are very disappointed. We lost Coca-Cola and we've not had the kind of deals we'd expected since then.'

Looking back at the Games and the way in which Lewis was treated, it is clear that he was the victim of a major smear campaign by the press. He had created some friction by failing to attend conferences or extend the normal pleasantries to reporters, and they reacted in the time-honoured way.

'I remember one reporter saying that I may have matched Jesse Owens,' said Lewis, 'but I would never be Jesse Owens, no matter what I did. I told him he was right, because thanks to people like Jesse I could use the front elevator and not the back elevator. Some people thought that was too calculating, but I was just well prepared. I think some of the media just wanted me to be to be a bit more "aw shucks".'

Lewis could certainly have been faulted had he not performed on the track in the way he did, but he came away with four gold medals. 'I don't think a lot of the media know how much it takes to compete in four events at an Olympics,' says sister Carol, who saw the campaign at first hand. 'He competed almost every day and they didn't realize that to run qualifiers at nine in the morning, you can't get up at 8.30, take a shower and leave, like you're going to work. You have to get up at five in the morning, then nap in the afternoon, between heats, then go home and eat dinner and be in bed about 8.30 so you can be back up the next day functioning correctly.'

The general public, however, did not care about the hard work and dedication that went on behind the scenes, with effortless grace and good-humoured humility. As it turned out, the real hero of the Games, at least as far as the USA was concerned, was the gymnast Mary Lou Retton, who thrived in the absence of the sport's 'heavyweights' from the Eastern Bloc and won the hearts of the nation in much the same way as Olga Korbut had done back in Munich in 1972.

Lewis admits that after the Games he felt very different, but for perhaps the wrong reasons because his profile was higher than ever before. As for the commercial disappointments, he can now afford to laugh at some of the things that were being said about him. 'After the Games some of the companies were saying, "Oh, he's so strange, his haircut is strange," and this and that. But a few months earlier I wanted to change my hair and one corporation said, "Don't change it, because it's unique." I don't think they really knew what they wanted.'

After the Olympics there were no further major titles for him to aim at until the next World Championships in 1987, so he focused on trying to beat Beamon's long jump record. However, despite remaining unbeaten and coming very close once or twice, it proved to be a frustrating time. When he suffered an injury during a long jump competition towards the end of the 1985 season, he decided to use the time it would take to get back to peak fitness to have a break from the track. He concentrated on his acting and singing careers, a decision that led to a couple of movies, some TV appearances and some records and live shows, including a TV special in Japan, where he was acclaimed as the new Michael Jackson.

It was a comparison that was often made, and once, when a reporter enquired whether he felt he might be as big as Jackson, Lewis famously answered: 'Physically definitely. I can't sing as well as he does, but he can't run as fast as I do.' But he always maintained serious intent on a post-athletics career in acting and music. He studied at New York's Warren Robertson Theater Workshop and began writing and producing his own songs. 'To me it almost feels like athletics,' says Lewis, 'because there's the preparation, the hard work, study, practice, dedication and the satisfaction of doing it, finishing and sitting back to enjoy it. I'd like to be recognized as a singer. If I sell fifty or fifty million records a year it doesn't matter, I just enjoy it. I'd like people to respect me as a singer, and as far as the acting goes I'd like to play in some action adventures. Of course the good thing about it is that after the financial success I've had in track and field I don't have the pressure of trying to be a millionaire out of entertainment.'

What Lewis and Michael Jackson did at least have in common was an appreciation of the bizarre and the pleasure they both took in being eccentric. 'He was his own person,' said Lewis of the singer, 'and he kept people dancing as to what he was like. In my world I do the same thing. People don't see me very often, but when I'm out I'm very flashy and outgoing.'

Actually, the real Carl Lewis is a much more reserved and quiet person than perhaps even he cares to admit, and it was rare to see pictures of him taken at clubs or big events appearing in the newspapers or magazines.

Within a few months of the LA Olympics he was no longer in the headlines, and after his injury in 1985 he even disappeared from the sports pages, choosing his competitions sparingly during 1986. He'd also moved from his much-publicized house in Houston, which had suffered two robberies and a constant stream of tourists, some of whom would camp on his front drive waiting to catch a glimpse of him.

On the track he still managed to merit a number one ranking in 1985 in the 100 metres, but his comfortable existence at the pinnacle of his sport was about to be challenged. The sport's biggest pantomime villain, Canada's fast-improving Ben Johnson, was about to enter the story as a leading player and the tale of the fastest men on earth was about to take an extraordinary and quite devastating new twist.

Johnson had built a reputation as a world-class short sprinter, but he tended to burn up in the closing stages of 100-metre races and had been largely discounted as a genuine contender for anything over 60 metres. The view was that Johnson had been around for a while – he was actually the same age as Lewis – and had done little to worry his domination. But all that was about to change.

Born in December 1961, Ben Johnson grew up in a small Jamaican town called Falmouth, a few miles east of Montego Bay, and as an infant survived a local outbreak of malaria. It was a traditional Jamaican family, loving, but strict and hardworking, and Johnson thoroughly enjoyed his childhood, especially the sun and the sea.

However, the family were finding it hard to make ends meet and in the mid-1970s they decided to try for a better life by moving to Canada, though Johnson's father Ben Senior remained with his job in Jamaica and would send money north. In April 1976 his mother Gloria brought Ben and his four brothers and sisters to Toronto, where she found work at Hilton Hotels and took a second job at night to enable young Ben to train and not be forced to take a job after school.

Initially, Johnson found it difficult to adjust to life in the big city. But his big sporting hero was sprinter Don Quarrie and he liked the idea of emulating him. After all, he loved to run and thought he was pretty quick too. He was just 15 when he first met the man who would turn him into a global superstar, when he went to the local track with his older brother Eddie in the early summer of 1977.

Coach Charlie Francis ran a sprint group called The Scarborough Optimists, the largest and most successful track club in Canada, and recalled first seeing Johnson at a Toronto high school workout.

'I can't say that Ben bowled me over,' he wrote in his 1990 book *Speed Trap*. 'At 15 he was the ideal age to start training, but he looked more like 12 – a skinny awkward kid of 93 pounds. He wore tattered, black, high-top sneakers that seemed too heavy for his long, pipe-stem legs.'

This unpromising first impression was compounded by an almost impenetrable Jamaican accent and a noticeable stutter. But Johnson found the track scene a happy diversion from his academic problems at school, and when he finished a creditable fourth, running against grown men, in a 50-metre race at an indoor meet in Montreal in 1978, Francis began to think he might have a new talent on his hands.

Johnson made steady, if unspectacular progress on the national track scene, but as the 1980s began Coach Francis realized that if his sprinting group was to move on to success at an international level, they would need more than just his creative coaching techniques. He learned with growing interest about performance-enhancing drug programmes in Eastern Europe and beyond, and it became crystal clear to him that many of the world's top performers at the time were taking these drugs. Eager for his own athletes to succeed, he arrived at a critical crossroads.

'An athlete could not expect to win in top international competition without using anabolic steroids,' he concluded.

Johnson has always maintained that taking steroids didn't make him run faster, which clearly begs the automatic question – then why take them? His slightly disingenuous remarks disguised the real reason for the widespread use of steroids in explosive sports, from the track to baseball, from cycling to the NFL. It was true that by themselves they were not a miracle 'speed injection', but they did stimulate the muscle fibres, resulting in faster muscle contractions, which is the foundation for greater speed and reactions. More importantly, they allowed athletes to train harder and longer, helping them grow bigger, stronger and more durable.

The physical difference between the Ben Johnson of the early eighties and the Ben Johnson of the 1988 Seoul Olympics wasn't purely about growing-up, but stemmed from a systematic use of steroids that turned him from the skinny high school kid into the heavily muscled monster who twice smashed the world 100 metres record.

'Steroids could not replace talent,' said Francis, 'or training, or a well-planned competitive programme. They could not transform a plodder into a champion. But they had become an essential ingredient within a complex recipe.'

So the die was cast. As soon as Johnson was ready, he would follow another of Francis's sprinters – Angela Issajenko – into a controlled steroid programme.

The race that persuaded Francis that Johnson was ready to challenge the best in the world came in August 1981, at the World Cup trials, in Venezuela, when at the age of 19 he ran 100 metres in 10.25 to finish second. It was a Canadian junior record, and he went on to make the finals in all three of Europe's biggest track meetings, in Zurich, Cologne and Berlin. Suddenly, Ben Johnson was looming large on the international track and field radar.

It was also time for him to confront what Francis described as the track and field facts of life. In September 1981 they sat down to discuss his training plan for the following year. At the elite level, Francis explained, steroids were worth about one per cent of performance – or a metre in the 100 metres. 'Though the decision to take the drugs was Ben's,' said Francis, 'he had little choice if he agreed with my conclusions. He could either set up his starting blocks on the same line as his international competition, or he could start a metre behind.'

Johnson agreed with the conclusions and within a few days of the meeting he began his first steroid programme that, with a little tinkering, would carry him all the way to Seoul. The plan began to bear fruit almost immediately and Johnson took his first major medal at the 1982 Commonwealth Games, in Australia, running a wind-aided 10.05 and finishing a close second to reigning Olympic champion Allan Wells.

In 1983 he won his first Grand Prix event, in Munich, where he started to get a name for himself for his extraordinary starts – he seemed to leap out of the blocks, almost losing control of his forward momentum, as if he'd been fired out of a cannon.

A scientific study conducted at the University of Ottawa suggested that his speed was unique among sprinters. The researchers' evidence had been gleaned from poring over slow-motion film of his technique during an indoor meeting in Canada. They found a number of stunning facts: first, that Johnson used 3,000 watts of energy in one stride, which is more than enough to light up an average mansion; and second, that he braked more efficiently than a car.

Johnson also intrigued the scientists by running in what they described as a completely different style from that of other sprinters. Leading the inquiry was Professor Gord Robertson, who explained: 'We have always felt that sprinters landed high on their toes and the heel would barely touch the ground. But this is not what happened in Ottawa. Everybody was landing on their heels, but Ben wasn't.' The professor explained that Ben ran high on his toes with the ankle fully extended upwards, just like an animal. 'Dogs run like that,' says Robertson. 'They run on their fingers with their heels inches off the ground.' The scientists concluded that this strange style was responsible for Ben's incredible spring.

By early 1984 Johnson was using a cocktail of performance-enhancing drugs, together with testosterone, vitamins and even human growth hormones. He proceeded to take bronze at the LA Olympics in both the 100 metres and the sprint relay, but still looked a long way from beating Carl Lewis.

Dr Jamie Astaphan, a sports injury expert hired by Francis a few years earlier, took control of Johnson's drug programme from 1985, administering the steroid injections himself at his Toronto office and planning a regimented, but scientific cycle of use.

The changes in Johnson were dramatic. By the end of the 1985 season Johnson was bench-pressing 365 pounds, more than double his body weight, and had famously picked up and thrown his Canadian team-mate Lennox Lewis, the future world heavyweight boxing champion, across a pool table during some horseplay at the LA Olympics. He was strong, and getting even stronger.

Through 1985 the rivalry with Lewis grew until Johnson managed his first win against the reigning Olympic champion in Zurich. Lewis had won their previous seven races and shrugged this off as a minor blip, but even though Johnson would be placed second behind Lewis in the year's official rankings, many track experts could see the writing on the wall.

By the beginning of 1986, Johnson had started using a new and then undetectable steroid called furazabol, which Astaphan had researched and introduced. It seemed to have immediate benefits, and in January Johnson set a new world indoor record of 6.50 for the 60 metres, in Japan.

By May he had beaten Lewis again, in San José, and in July they would face off at the Goodwill Games, in Moscow, in what the media were already labelling the big grudge match of the year. There Johnson showed why serious questions were being asked about the old order, blazing a fastest ever sea-level time of 9.95, with Lewis back in third.

The standard excuses were made by the Lewis camp. He was fatigued by the national championships, his training had been interrupted by his recording career – but it was all beginning to sound a little desperate. After dominating Johnson for so long, it appeared that the tables had genuinely turned. Another Johnson win over Lewis in Zurich meant a first ever number one ranking for the Canadian, and suddenly all the talk was of the World Championships, in Rome, the following year. In Rome, said both camps, everything would be settled once and for all.

Francis and Astaphan programmed Johnson's training and drug routine to peak in Rome at the end of August 1987. He started the year well, breaking his own indoor 60 metres record in 6.44 in January, and then lowering it again at the World Indoor Championships, in Indianapolis, with a 6.41. Incredibly, he was travelling so fast through the finish that he flipped over the waist-high safety wall some 20 metres beyond the finish line and landed flat on his back, though mercifully unhurt, on the concrete floor some six feet below.

Johnson was flying, and he started the outdoor season and the long run-up to Rome by beating Lewis again in Spain in an incredibly close finish. So close, in fact, that Lewis queried the result. 'Look, clown,' Johnson growled at him. 'Let's run another one right now, then you'll know who won.' They almost came to blows.

The media loved it, of course, and when they quizzed Johnson about the bust-up, he told them: 'Carl seemed to be confused over who won the race today. Next time I'll make sure he's not confused.'

The two would not meet again on the track before Rome, and track fans the world over waited with bated breath for the race of the year, with one Italian newspaper cartoon placing them in a boxing ring and superimposing their heads on the bodies of Muhammad Ali and Joe Frazier.

It was an extremely appropriate analogy. In the blue corner there was Lewis, bright, educated, articulate and natural; while in the red corner there was the brooding, uneducated, stammering and, it was whispered, man-made Johnson.

However, just a few months before Rome, Lewis forgot all thoughts of Ben Johnson and the World Championships when he learned that his father, a guiding light in his career, as well as devoted parent, had finally succumbed to cancer.

On the day of the funeral in New Jersey, Lewis pulled the Los Angeles 100 metres gold medal from his suit pocket to put in his father's hand. He later wrote: 'My mother asked me if I was sure I wanted to bury the medal, and I was. It would be my father's forever. "But I'm going to get another one," I told my mother. Turning to my father, I said: "Don't worry, I'm going to get another one." That was a promise – to myself and to Dad. He was lying there so peacefully, his hands resting on his chest. When I placed the medal in his hand, it fit perfectly.'

By August, it was back to business and although the final, as a genuine contest, turned out to be a huge disappointment, as an event it took over just about every newspaper, every radio station and every TV network.

Ben Johnson, all in red, won by half a metre and smashed the world record by the unheard-of margin of a tenth of a second – in 9.83 seconds. Carl Lewis, all in blue, was second in a new personal best of 9.93. 'I got out so quickly over the first 10 metres I thought I'd come out of my lane,' admitted Johnson. 'By 60 metres I knew that people would have to do something quite remarkable to pass me.' Lewis just could not catch him and it was his sixth straight defeat at the hands of the Canadian, bringing the match score to Lewis eight, Johnson six. Said a dismayed Lewis: 'I feel I've been KO'd.'

The seventy thousand spectators roared as they saw the time on the big screen, and then roared again at Johnson's reaction, with the cameras capturing a rare and enormous smile from the victor and new fastest man on earth. There was no confusion now, but there was a new king in town.

The Rome victory and new world record meant a new course could be plotted for Johnson, and in the year that followed his management pulled together some of the most lucrative endorsement deals in sport, including a four-year, $2.3 million sportswear agreement with Diadora.

But nagging at the back of many people's minds was something Carl Lewis had said in a British TV interview in the aftermath of Rome, in which the American gave voice to his own long-held suspicion. 'There are gold medallists in this meet who are definitely on drugs,' he said. 'That race [referring to the 100 metres] will be looked at for many years, for more reasons than one. I don't think it's fair to point fingers. I'm not bitter or anything at anyone. But there's a problem and I just want to take a stand. If I were to jump to drugs, I could do a 9.8 right away.'

Johnson reacted in his characteristically calm and non-committal way, but if the dam hadn't yet broken, there were already some visible cracks appearing in it.

Lewis later wrote: 'I had been hearing that he was on drugs. People on the track circuit had whispered here and there that Ben was using steroids, doing whatever he could to bulk up, speed up and beat me.' At the time it was just hushed rumours around the track circuit, but rather than prompt serious investigation, all Lewis's comments and accusations got him was a reputation as a finger-pointing bad loser. His time would come.

The Olympic year did not start well for Johnson, with a hamstring injury curtailing his indoor season. Then, in his first outdoor race, in Japan, another more serious muscle tear destroyed his summer preparations.

With the biggest race of his life a few months away, fault lines began to appear in his relationship with Francis over his treatment and training. Johnson appeared like a rabbit in the headlights, his nerves frayed by the injury, and he was feeling depressed at the thought of fulfilling all the commercial and business commitments demanded by his new deals in Europe and beyond. Without a word to Francis, he suddenly took off for the small Caribbean island of St Kitts, in order to escape.

As with a married couple who have had a tiff, it took a little while for the two of them to resolve their differences, but with Seoul now looming on the horizon they both reasoned they had come too far to throw everything away at the final hurdle.

In August, Johnson returned to action, winning the Canadian national 100 metres and then running a 9.98 at the high altitude of Sestriere, in Italy. With pre-Games hype now at fever pitch, the two rivals met at the Weltklasse, in Zurich, where Lewis beat Johnson for the first time in three years. But the Johnson camp knew he was still on the road to recovery and there was plenty more in the tank.

He returned to Toronto to complete his final drug programme – three injections of furazabol and three more of growth hormone – giving him, he thought, a more than ample 26 days for it all to clear his system before the 100-metre final in South Korea and the next test.

He was ready. Carl Lewis was ready. The world waited in anticipation of the greatest sprint race of all time.

Francis recalled the confidence he felt at the time: 'To deliver a sprinter's personal best, you must bring several components to bear: strength for the start and acceleration, speed for maximum velocity, and endurance to stay the last 30 or 40 metres. I was now certain that Ben could run into the low 9.80s, that he would win the gold medal and erase any doubts that he was the fastest sprinter of all time.'

When the two heavyweight contenders finally arrived in Seoul the scenes at the airport were more reminiscent of a rock star's arrival than the opening of an Olympic Games. A massive force of police and private security people battled unsuccessfully with the crowds of media and fans as both men were manhandled through the mayhem and stampeded into waiting cars.

The opening salvo in the psychological battle was fired by Lewis, who reopened his complaint about Johnson's starting technique at the World Championships. The suggestion was that Johnson had cheated the starter by lifting his hands and arms before the gun, and Lewis was now demanding that the IAAF make an official review. But the sport's governing body merely re-affirmed Johnson's win and his world record.

Neither Johnson nor Lewis could cope with the zoo atmosphere of the athletes' village, and both decamped to alternative accommodation. Johnson went to the Seoul Hilton, and Lewis to a quiet rented house, part of a Baptist ministry, with his family and friends.

The heats of the 100 metres began on Friday, September 23, and in heat eight Johnson almost jogged the last 30 metres to win in a sedate 10.37. Lewis won the final heat in 10.14.

A few hours later they both returned for the second round, with Johnson in a tough heat alongside fast-improving British sprinter Linford Christie and American Dennis Mitchell. Only the top two finishers were guaranteed passage to the semis.

Once again Johnson shut off the gas early, but this time it was too early and Christie won in 10.11, with Mitchell second and Johnson third in 10.17. The stadium was in shock. Had he made the most colossal mistake? Had he just destroyed the biggest moment of his life?

Johnson had to sweat until the end of the heats before finding out, to his obvious relief, that he would qualify as one of the fastest losers. Meanwhile, Lewis looked smooth and stylish in his heat, winning comfortably in 9.99. The temperature was rising, and as the competition went into its final stage on the following day the media now favoured Lewis.

In the semis, Lewis ran first and sprinted away from the field in 9.97. Now it was Johnson's turn, and he knew there could be no mistakes this time. At the first gun Brazil's Robson Da Silva false-started. At the second it was Johnson. Trackside, nerves began to fray among the Canadian team. But at the third time of asking he was away and powered into a strong headwind to win in 10.03.

They had 90 minutes to wait before the final. For both men it felt more like 90 years. It would become one of the most watched sporting events in history, the final showdown between two of the greatest track rivals for years. A true heavyweight battle.

At just before one o'clock in the afternoon, a global television audience estimated at more than a billion, the biggest ever for an Olympic event, leaned closer to their screens as the eight finalists emerged on to the track: Brazil's Da Silva, Jamaica's Ray Stewart, Carl Lewis in lane three, Linford Christie, Calvin Smith, Ben Johnson in lane six, fellow Canadian Desai Williams and Dennis Mitchell.

As Coach Francis wrote in his book: 'From gun to tape, a 10-second race is a study in compression; it is there and then it is gone. For most Olympic finalists, the great adventure of their athletic lives goes with it.'

For Lewis it was even more personal. This was the gold medal he vowed to win for himself to replace the 100-metre gold he had won in 1984 and had buried with his father, but when he set eyes on Johnson as they walked to their blocks just minutes before the start he knew he faced an uphill task.

He said: 'I just remember his little yellow eyes, a sure sign of drug use, and I just couldn't stop thinking about them. I said to myself, "That bastard, he did it again."'

As always, a deathly hush fell across the noisy stadium as the starter called 'Set', and then the bang of the gun heralded an overwhelming explosion of power as the eight fastest men in the world leaped out of their blocks – and a deafening roar from the seventy thousand spectators.

Johnson got out fastest, but only marginally in front of Lewis. But within 10 metres the Canadian was perceptibly ahead, and by 20 metres there was a couple of feet of daylight between him and the rest of the field.

By 60 metres it was a race for second place as Johnson continued to pull away from the field. By 80 metres he knew the job was done, even though Lewis had edged into a clear second. The Canadian looked back and left to check his rival's position and, seeing no threat, streaked over the line, his right arm up and forefinger pointed skyward.

His time was 9.79 – an incredible new world record. Heaven knows how fast he would have run had he not decided to celebrate 5 metres before the line.

Lewis was second in 9.92, a new personal best, with Christie edging Smith for the bronze. For the first time ever four runners had broken the 10-second barrier in the same race.

Lewis wrote: 'About 80 metres down the track – with the finish line flying toward us – I looked at Ben again, and he was not coming back any. He still had those five feet on me. Ben pretty much had the same lead all the way through, and I knew I couldn't get him. Damn, I thought, Ben did it again. The bastard got away with it again. It's over, Dad. God, I wanted to win it for Dad. But that was impossible now. It wouldn't happen.'

Lewis chased after Johnson as the Canadian went looking for a flag in the crowd and performed a very public, though clearly awkward congratulatory handshake.

The race of the century had delivered, and the Olympic and wider sports world rejoiced in the moment and the excitement of it all.

The medal ceremony was staged a little over half an hour after the race. Watching it today, in the knowledge of what was about to happen, gives it an almost surreal quality, with Johnson turning and shaking hands with the unsmiling Lewis, who by then was utterly convinced about what was going on behind the scenes in the Johnson camp. After the presentation of medals, Johnson was escorted into the stands by Royal Canadian Mounted Police to take a brief phone call from Prime Minister Brian Mulroney, who offered him the congratulations of the Canadian people.

'Here I was at age 26,' wrote Johnson, in his 2010 autobiography *Seoul to Soul*, 'a multi-millionaire just for being me, Ben Johnson. The hard work, discipline, sacrifice and commitment had paid off. But all seemed to be in vain. For when all was said and done, none of the awards and honours mattered. In the end, most would remember me not for my achievements as much as they would remember me for my downfall.'

The Mounties had one final duty to perform, to assist Johnson to his final engagement of the evening. The standard post-event drug test in the doping control room.

While Johnson spent two hours in the testing area trying to provide a urine sample, Lewis attended a post-race news conference and manfully responded to the media in the only way he knew how. 'My objective was to run a personal best and do the best I can,' he said. 'I did both those things, so that's why I'm happy with the way I ran.' He tried to duck making any comment on Johnson's race, but finally conceded: 'He ran a great race, obviously, because he had a great time.'

Tired and dehydrated, Johnson had struggled to pass water and needed ten beers to finally get the job done. In a precursor to a bizarre conspiracy theory that would follow, an unofficial figure was also in the testing area with Johnson, while he got a post-race rub-down. His name was Andre Jackson, a well-known face on the track scene and a friend of Carl Lewis who had been staying with him in Seoul. He handed Johnson several of his beers.

Johnson complained afterwards that Francis and Astaphan had been denied entry to the room, while so many other people seemed to have access. In his book, he wrote: 'According to the officials Charlie and Jamie did not have the security clearance to come in. Meanwhile, Andre, who did not seem to have any real purpose in being there, made himself at home in the doping room.'

Johnson was convinced Jackson must have spiked his beer, because he had not taken any drugs before the race and had tested negative at the last pre-Olympic meeting in Zurich.

When Johnson finally made it to the news conference, he told the assembled journalistic gathering: 'I'd like to say my name is Benjamin Sinclair Johnson Junior and this world record will last fifty years, maybe a hundred. The important thing was to beat Carl Lewis.'

The sporting world was at his feet, and estimates on the value of his new commercial deals, on top of the bonus payments for his gold medal and world record, ran into millions of dollars. Johnson felt he would be able to spend at least another four years in the sport and have a real run at the Games in Barcelona. He was not only the fastest man on earth, but he was about to become one of the richest.

Tragically, he would only enjoy these dreams, his seat at the summit of Olympic sport and his hard-won position as the world's fastest man for a little over three days.

In the early hours of the morning, on Monday, September 26, the head of Canada's Olympic team and its chief medical officer were woken in their hotel rooms with the worst possible news. One of their athletes had tested positive for a banned substance. The nightmare scenario was that this time it wasn't a minor weightlifter or obscure shot-putter, but their number one superstar and newly crowned national hero. Their world was about to cave in. It was Ben Johnson.

A global sporting scandal on a previously unparalleled scale was about to break, so after a sleepless night they called Johnson's coach Charlie Francis and together they drove downtown to the IOC's drug testing laboratory. The Canadian Olympic team bosses simply couldn't believe that Johnson could be a drug cheat, so they hoped there would be a rational explanation for the positive test.

Francis was also bemused by the test result – not, of course, because he knew Johnson was innocent but, as it would later emerge, because his planning of Johnson's drug regime had been meticulous. His credulity was stretched even further when he was told by the IOC testers that the substance they had discovered was the popular and easily detected steroid stanozolol. To his knowledge, Johnson had never taken the drug, because his sprinters had been using another steroid, furazabol, which the IOC testers, at that time, could not identify.

Francis wrote: 'After seven years of using steroids, Ben knew what he was doing. It was inconceivable to me that he might take stanozolol on his own and jeopardize the most important race of his life. My first instinct was that he had been set up.'

Johnson told the Canadian delegation and the IOC that he'd been shadowed by a then unidentified man while waiting in the testing area and the man had given him beer to drink. Could he have tampered with it?

Francis, who died in 2010, attended an appeal hearing later that night at which the second sample was confirmed as also testing positive for stanozolol. They argued convincingly that there had been a security breach, but within a few hours their worst fears were confirmed. The IOC commission had rejected the appeal, confirmed the positive test and recommended Johnson's immediate disqualification. Worse still, it was clear that word had got out and a media feeding frenzy of unprecedented proportions was about to kick off.

It is possible that, had the IOC only considered the traces of stanozolol in Johnson's sample, he might have been able to argue successfully against disqualification on the grounds of a clear breach of security and the element of doubt it created. But, unbeknown to Francis, the drug testers had dug a little deeper and pulled together an 'endocrine profile' – effectively a measure of Johnson's hormone levels – which demonstrated clearly that he was a long-term steroid user. It was game over.

Johnson was stripped of both his gold medal and his new world record. His career and multi-million dollar future collapsed overnight, and as the biggest sports story of the year broke worldwide, his character and reputation were torn to shreds. The news pictures as he was manhandled through the mayhem of Seoul airport were proof positive of the kind of treatment he was going to get as the biggest cheat in sporting history.

Johnson recalled in his book how Canadian officials Carol Anne Letheren and Dr William Stanish came to his room to retrieve the gold medal. 'It was a very emotional moment for everyone present. Unable to contain herself, Carol Anne began crying. I could tell they all felt sorry for me. I was tired. I had been through enough. Dr Stanish asked for the medal. It was in my carry-on bag. I opened my bag, removed my gold medal and handed it to him. He took it. Right after I won my medal, my intent was to offer it as a gift to my mother. More than anyone else, she deserved it. But this was not meant to be. Now I had to give it back. The next day, my gold medal would be awarded to Carl Lewis.'

Johnson managed to battle his way back to Toronto and went to ground, while Francis was effectively told to leave on the next flight.

Hero to zero in record time. Prime Minister Mulroney, who had feted Johnson only a few days earlier, told the Canadian media it was 'a personal tragedy for Ben and his family and equally a moment of great disappointment for all Canadians'.

The *Toronto Sun*'s front page simply asked: 'WHY, BEN?' The *Ottawa Citizen* was more personal: 'Thanks a Lot, You Bastard.' *Sports Illustrated*'s front cover was arguably the most apposite. Over a picture of the 100 metres finish, it simply said: 'BUSTED!'

In Seoul, everyone beat a path to the door of Carl Lewis, and his first instinct, albeit an emotional one, was to attack Johnson as a cheat who got caught – you live by the sword, you die by the sword. But instead, Lewis chose a more diplomatic course, saying publicly that he felt sorry for Ben and hoped he could straighten out his life and return to the track.

After the first shock waves subsided, the next question for the Canadians was how to deal with such a national disgrace. A major inquiry was quickly established with wide-ranging powers to get to the bottom of the whole sorry saga and restore some integrity to Canadian sport. It would be presided over by Ontario's associate chief justice, Charles Dubin.

A week after the Games, Johnson surfaced to tell Canada's now sceptical media: 'I have never knowingly taken illegal drugs, nor have had illegal drugs administered to me.'

Johnson's position was clear. He was trying to suggest his unwitting part in the whole affair and point the finger at the 'Svengali' coach Francis and his 'Frankenstein' doctor Jamie Astaphan. It was a sorry attempt at obfuscation and did him no credit, but the vultures were already circling. The whole truth was about to emerge and, once and for all, destroy the conspiracy of silence that had existed over drug taking at the very highest levels of athletics.

Johnson was banned for two years and not only lost his Olympic gold medal and world record, but also his 9.83 world mark, set in Rome, which was likewise wiped from the record books.

Francis would go to his grave baffled at how Johnson was caught doping in Seoul – in his view for using drugs he didn't actually take. It was an extraordinary, and for Johnson, Francis and his team, extremely unfunny irony that he had not been caught and punished for the systematic and wholesale cheating they had created with their sophisticated drug programme, but for a drug they claim not to have administered and one they knew would fail the most basic of athletic drug tests.

Francis revealed that, as far as he knew, the last steroid injection Johnson received was on August 28, in Toronto – a good 26 days before the 100-metre final. He also knew that the drug would not be discovered by the IOC because he'd been using it for years and it had returned negative results on the previous 29 tests.

Five months after the Seoul Games the Dubin Inquiry finally began in Toronto, and Charlie Francis, his career over and his character vilified in the media, decided his only course of action was to tell everything. His 29 hours of testimony laid bare the level of performance-enhancing drug taking in athletics and the detailed plan behind Ben Johnson's record-breaking run in Seoul.

Francis was handed a lifetime coaching ban in Canada, while Johnson himself waited until the end of the inquiry to take the stand, finally admitting to drug taking and warning young athletes not to do the same. The inquiry report was submitted in July 1990, nearly two years after Seoul, and summarized the testimony from 122 witnesses across 91 days.

At the end of his ban, in 1991, Johnson attempted a track comeback, running his first race in front of seventeen thousand fans in Hamilton, the biggest ever crowd at a Canadian indoor meeting, and finishing a decent second in a 50-metre race.

Despite this promising return, he didn't make the Canadian team for the 1991 World Championships, but he was selected for the Olympic team for Barcelona in the following year after finishing second to Bruny Surin in the trials. But it was something of a false dawn and Johnson looked a pale shadow of his old self, finishing last in his semi-final after appearing to stumble coming out of his blocks.

The comeback didn't last long and early in 1993, just after winning an indoor 50 metres only four-hundredths of a second outside the world record, he failed another drug test in Canada, this time for excess testosterone, and the IAAF banned him for life.

Thereafter Johnson continued to make high-profile news, first running against a stock car and, shades of Jesse Owens, even running against a racehorse in a charity event. He made more headlines when he took a job as fitness coach for Diego Maradona and then Al-Saadi Qadhafi, the son of the Libyan leader, who was keen on a professional football career.

It would be six years until he appeared on another track, after successfully challenging the life ban on a legal technicality, but in another bizarre twist the Canadian authorities ruled that anyone running against him would also risk a ban, so in late 1999 he turned out for a meeting in Ontario and ran solo in 11 seconds flat.

A few months later the final nail was hammered in his sporting coffin when he failed yet another drug test, this time for a banned diuretic that was often used as a masking agent for other drugs. For Johnson, at 37 years old, the game was well and truly up.

He retreated into the shadows, spending much of his time in the house he shared with his mother in the Toronto suburbs. As his money began to dwindle, he tried a couple of abortive commercial ventures, a 'Catch Me' clothing line and then as a spokesman for an energy drink called Cheetah Power Surge. In several jaw-droppingly awful TV commercials, Johnson looked straight to camera and told would-be consumers: 'I Cheetah all the time.' If that wasn't desperate enough, a few years later he was paid handsomely to star in a TV commercial for an Australian online gambling company and their 'juiced-up' phone betting app, in which he was mercilessly parodied. It included lines such as 'nobody knows performance enhancement like Ben Johnson' and 'putting the 'roid in android'.

The company, SportsBet, claimed it was clearly a spoof, but after a deluge of complaints, including one from the Australian sports anti-doping authority, it was banned by the advertising watchdog for making light of both cheating and drug use.

It was awful to see how far he had fallen, because while he was never regarded as the smartest man in the world, equally Ben Johnson was not a bad man either. While he obviously knew what he was doing, he was also easily led and made poor choices throughout his sporting life. Sadly for him, his legacy will never be as one of the fastest men on earth but as the most high-profile cheat in sporting history, and it's clear that without the major drug programme he adopted he would never have competed at those extraordinary heights.

Carl Lewis's manager Joe Douglas feels Johnson was more victim than villain. 'I think Ben was a pawn in a man's desire for success,' he said. 'And yes, he could have said no, but I'm not sure it's that easy, I don't think some kids are sophisticated enough. Ben wasn't a university graduate, he didn't have the intellectual equipment to deal with it. When a coach tells an athlete, "Everybody does it," that's an easy line but a convincing one too. And, by the way, everybody doesn't do it.'

In 2010 Johnson finally issued his extraordinarily odd autobiography, in which he not only replayed his conspiracy theory about Andre Jackson, who he claimed had confessed to spiking his drink for financial gain when they'd met six years earlier, but also revealed that he'd teamed up with a spiritual adviser named Bryan Farnum who would provide detailed explanations 'discerned' from God about the major issues in Johnson's life. Described by one Canadian newspaper in a masterpiece of understatement as 'unconventional', the book included the view that Johnson and Lewis had been rivals in a previous life, where Johnson was an Egyptian pharaoh and Lewis a scheming villain. Just when you thought Johnson's story could not get any stranger, it did.

Aside from its largely esoteric and often bizarre content, the book did provide one heartfelt remark. 'If I had a chance to do it again, based on my experiences, I would choose not to take steroids at all,' he wrote. 'Furthermore, I would encourage others not to succumb to the pressure and avoid steroid use or any other performance-enhancing applications completely.'

Whatever your view of the spiritual assistance Johnson receives, it is clear it has genuinely helped him find some lasting peace. 'I spent the past twenty years punishing myself for letting so many people down,' he wrote. 'By forgiving myself, I could stop beating myself up.' His father died in 1990 and his beloved mother in 2004, but his life is now built around his daughter and eleven-year-old granddaughter – far away, mercifully, from the glare of public scrutiny and opinion.

Returning to Seoul in 1988, Carl Lewis had been quietly presented with the gold medal in a hastily arranged and untelevised ceremony behind the main stand of the stadium. Christie was promoted to silver and Smith the bronze. There was something rather seedy about the event, with no podium, no flags and no media. A dirty little secret kept out of the public gaze and Lewis would complain bitterly about it. Bronze medallist Calvin Smith co-wrote a coruscating book on the whole affair, in 2016, unambiguously titled *It Should Have Been Gold*. Renowned for being the quiet, decent man of the track and priding himself on running clean, he was suddenly very vocal and hugely critical of just about everyone involved in the event and accused the three men who finished in front of him of drug taking.

'It would have been an honour, if I didn't already know the secrets hiding behind the Olympic curtain,' he wrote. 'I deserved the gold and they knew it. Yet nobody said anything. The cost would have been too great for all of us. If they talked, a worldwide audience would have known that drugs had fuelled so many of the athletes at these Games. The Olympics would have become a joke.'

But when the dust settled the cold facts were clear. Carl Lewis had become the first man in history to retain an Olympic 100-metre title and while Johnson's career would now disintegrate, Lewis would scale even greater athletic heights and ultimately become the greatest athlete of the twentieth century. Straight after the 100 final, Lewis went back out on to the track and cantered through two demanding 200 metres heats, before taking the gold medal in the long jump. He won a silver in the 200 metres final, losing to his Santa Monica team-mate Joe DeLoach, but missed out on a potential seventh gold medal when the sprint relay team was disqualified in its opening heat. The US team were so confident, they didn't bother including Lewis or De Loach in the heats of the competition, so they watched in horror as Smith and Lee McNeill, who was running an anchor leg for the first time, made a mess of the final handover. Three countries protested that the US team, running in bizarre, hooded race suits, had run out of their zone and video evidence confirmed it at the Jury of Appeal. It was only the third time in Olympic history that the USA would not appear in the sprint relay final. In the aftermath of Johnson's dramatic departure, Lewis was not only presented with the gold medal, but also the new world record. Johnson's 9.79 and his 9.83 were wiped off the books and Carl's Seoul run of 9.92 became the new global mark.It was beaten in June 1991 by his University of Houston team-mate Leroy Burrell, who ran a 9.90, but Lewis got his revenge later that year at the World Championships, in Tokyo, with a stunning 9.86. Lewis's delight was obvious and his reaction was unusually emotional. 'The best race of my life,' he beamed. 'The best technique, the fastest. And I did it at thirty.'

He also accomplished it fuelled by a completely new diet. Lewis had decided to switch to veganism before the championships, claiming it meant he could eat more and that it improved his performances. He's followed a similar diet ever since.

In Tokyo he also took part in arguably the greatest long jump final in history, which finally brought to an end his astounding run of 65 consecutive victories. In a titanic duel Lewis jumped a personal best of 8.91 metres, but his team-mate Mike Powell not only beat him for the first time but eclipsed the 1968 world record of Bob Beamon with a leap of 8.95 (29ft 4in).

Despite this defeat, *Track and Field News* suggested that it had become 'hard to argue that he is not the greatest athlete ever to set foot on track or field'.

Lewis spent much of the early nineties engaged in a running and often bitter battle, primarily over transparency around professionalism and money, with the US track and field authorities, most notably The Athletics Congress (TAC) which had taken over the organization of the sport from the AAU in 1979. When he published his autobiography, *Inside Track*, in 1990, he subtitled it 'My Professional Life in Amateur Track and Field', and he unashamedly used his status to lead the vanguard for lasting change in the sport. It now owes him a great deal, especially the athletes themselves, after it finally shook off its 'shamateur' cloak and became transparently professional.

Though he failed to qualify for the 1992 Barcelona Olympics in the sprints, his legend grew even greater when he won his third Olympic long jump title in a row and anchored the US sprint relay team to gold – alongside 200 metre champion Mike Marsh, Leroy Burrell and Dennis Mitchell – in a new world record of 37.40.

That made it eight Olympic gold medals in three Games, but he wanted one final Olympic encore – at his home Games in Atlanta in 1996.

There, he won his fourth Olympic long jump title and became one of only three Olympians to win the same individual event four times. A year later Carl Lewis retired from the sport as its undisputed king. His last competitive outing was due to be 1997 Texas Relays, but he was waiting at home for a floral delivery and told his teammates to leave for Austin without him. He'd catch up. 'I ended up waiting for my plants,' he recalls, 'and then I thought, it's time to retire if your plants are more important.'

In 1999 his place in the track pantheon was made official when the IOC voted him Sportsman of the Century; the IAAF elected him World Athlete of the Century and *Sports Illustrated*, a magazine that enjoyed a chequered history with Lewis, named him Olympian of the Century.

In 2003, in a bizarre echo back to Seoul, the US Olympic Committee's former director of drug control administration, Dr Wade Exum, inexplicably handed 30,000 pages of documents to *Sports Illustrated* containing the names of some 100 US athletes who had failed drug tests in the past and should have been banned from competing. One of the names on the list was Carl Lewis.

It was revealed that he had tested positive three times before Seoul for banned stimulants and had actually been banned from competing in the 1988 Games. However, Lewis and his lawyers had argued that the drugs had been used inadvertently in an over-the-counter Chinese herbal supplement, and also that they were below the level required to register as an offence. The USOC had accepted the explanation and overturned the decision, describing Exum's accusations as 'baseless'. While the story made headlines worldwide – and his exoneration just a few paragraphs – it actually did little to tarnish the Lewis legend. For nearly twenty years he performed heroics in athletic events around the world, filled stadiums, became a hero to many and remains one of the sport's most enduring superstars.Of course, he continued to court controversy off the track, famously appearing in a global Pirelli ad, posing in the 'set' position, wearing red stiletto heels. Photographer Annie Liebowitz took the shot and the tag line on the billboards, which ran everywhere except the United States, was 'Power Is Nothing without Control.' It rekindled questions about his sexuality, but typically unfazed, he brushed them aside, saying: 'People all around the world can bring out psychologists to read my mind all they want. But when it all comes down, I did it for two reasons. Number one it's a commercial and they paid me to do that. Secondly, I like working with Annie.'

He will admit to being mortified by some of the things he did as a young man, but life has certainly softened him. 'I'm a simple person now, he says. 'I tell people I used to be flash and cash, now I'm wash and wear!'

Lewis continues to travel around the globe in a whirlwind of media work, charity work, acting, speaking engagements – and simply being a professional Carl Lewis. While his films – such as *Alien Hunter*, *Atomic Twister* and *F*ck You, Pay Me* – have not yet threatened to break any box office records and his singing seemed only to excite the Japanese teenage market, Lewis seems content in his role as an articulate, often outspoken, track and field elder statesmen. Despite the grey hair, he still looks in excellent shape and his sharp wit and easy smile are always in demand with everyone from the United Nations to McDonalds' charities. He set up the Carl Lewis Foundation to promote health and fitness in young people, along with his FitForever on-line campaign, and he was even hired to help London 2012 market their ticket sales programme in the run-up to the Games.

Intriguingly, when he appeared at the opening of a Nike Town in London with some of the Premier League's top soccer stars, it was the likes of Cesc Fabregas, Didier Drogba, Ashley Cole and Theo Walcott who seemed star-struck. Age may be merciless, but as the cliché goes, class is certainly permanent.

So in April 2011, it came as no surprise when he announced his intention to enter politics and run as a Democratic candidate for the US Senate, representing South Jersey, with a strong emphasis on promoting education, especially physical education. 'We're getting into a culture of mediocrity where people think it's OK to be average,' Lewis told reporters. 'Well, it's our opportunity to inspire young people, to inspire families. I never forgot about my roots in South Jersey. It's where I grew up and learned what matters – that hard work, family values and commitment to others can make a difference.' Disappointingly for Lewis, his political career failed to get off the ground, but asked what he'd like his legacy to be, he answers simply: 'I hope I can inspire people to work hard, get educated and do something they never thought they could do.'

He will turn sixty a few weeks before the opening of the Tokyo Olympics and his passion for the track remains undiminished. He moved back to Houston in 2013 and recently returned to his alma mater, the University of Houston, to coach track alongside his old rival Leroy Burrell. Perhaps unsurprisingly, he became one of the breakout stars of an impressive documentary series, entitled *Speed City*, which followed the college's track team, the Cougars, as they claimed an impressive third spot in the 2019 NCAA season.

He says he never intended to get into coaching, but once he started volunteering at Houston his competitive instincts kicked in. Today he spends 90 per cent of his time coaching (though he's quick to point out it returns only five per cent of his income!) and now craves championships and the need to push his athletes to the Olympics.

Lewis's place in history is assured and his record will be a tough one to beat: nine Olympic golds, eight world championship golds and the first ever multi-millionaire to come from track and field. But perhaps his greatest achievement, after such a tumultuous career, is that he has grown into a much calmer, happier and contented soul. The veil was even lifted, just a little, on his closely guarded private life, when it was revealed that not only was he married, but that he has a 25-year-old son, who is in the US Army. He's even talked excitedly about trying to keep up with his four-year-old granddaughter.

Talking to a Houston TV show during the lockdown in 2020, Lewis said: 'Sports and athletics have given me the most amazing opportunity to do so many things – to get an education, to travel the world, to meet people and broaden my horizons.' Asked how he would like to be remembered by history, he explained: 'I hope that I am remembered by what I left – not what I did. That sports were changed financially for athletes, that I mentored kids and coached national champions and that I changed things for the better.'

None of that can be disputed and maybe he will get the chance to bring the story full circle. Perhaps we will see him back in Los Angeles, at the very track where his Olympic tale began in 1984 – though this time as the coach behind a new generation of athletes competing in the Games of 2028.

Barcelona 1992

Linford Christie

Linford Christie always looked like he had been chiselled from stone. He still does. Even in his sixties.

A muscular, powerful 6ft 3in, he used his physique to great effect in a record-breaking track career that saw him become arguably the most famous British athlete of his generation and certainly the most decorated in history. He used it to generate the extraordinary speed required to harvest the countless medals, titles and championships he won through the eighties and nineties, but he also used it to play mind games with his rivals.

The stone-like, unsmiling façade, the pre-race muscle flexing and the almost psychotically staring eyes were all a prescribed part of the Christie armoury; a ritual that always seemed to be more in tune with the boxing ring than the track. Critically, it all worked. Today, a far calmer and more contented Linford Christie looks back with a fond smile on the posing and posturing, but regrets none of it. 'I always tell people I was never the fastest, I just made everyone believe I was,' he laughs. 'Once you know you can get in people's heads, then you just go out and do it.'

Christie remains just as passionate about running as he did in his athletic heyday, but now it's coaching that stirs the emotions rather than competing. At the Sydney Olympics of 2000, he coached sprinter Darren Campbell to silver in the 200 metres and Katharine Merry to a bronze in the 400 metres.

The man still crackles with energy, passion and ambition. 'You get a real buzz from it, but it's not the same,' he says. 'I get more nervous now, which I never did before. When I ran, I knew exactly what I had to do. But now I'm teaching others and it's totally different. Even if you tell them what to do, you're never quite sure how they'll execute it.'

If there was one thing you could be sure of about Christie the athlete, then it was the certainty that when he walked on to the track he would give 100 per cent. 'I trained hard, but the real difference was I was such a competitor,' he recalls. 'There were times when my opponents didn't match that, even if they had the talent. I try and pass that experience on to my athletes.'

He's become a very successful businessman, accepted an OBE and an MBE from the Queen and runs a street athletics programme for kids. Christie has had his local stadium named after him, makes regular TV appearances, and lives comfortably in Buckinghamshire; he also owns the sports company Nuff Respect, which he helped to set up in 1992.All in all, life has been pretty good to Linford Christie, but it has not been an easy ride and some of the bumps along the way have been hard. A classic perfectionist, he had his run-ins with the athletics authorities; enjoyed a combative relationship with the British press; endured family tragedy; and on two occasions made unfortunate, lurid headlines for taking banned substances, neither of which seemed to make a great deal of sense.

A fierce patriot and a British team captain, he even fell out with several top British athletes, most notably quarter-miler Derek Redmond, who famously described Christie as the most balanced athlete in the world. 'He has a chip on both shoulders.'

This then is the extraordinary story of Linford Christie – a complex man, a driven man, a private man, a family man, a funny man – sometimes a difficult man. But always a fast man. It began in the calmer surroundings of St Andrew county, near Kingston in Jamaica, where he was born in April 1960. He clearly had a profound effect on his parents, because a few months later his father James left the island to seek a better life for his family in England, and his mother Mabel followed him over when her son was just two years old.

Linford, however, was considered too young to make the trip and remained in Jamaica with his beloved grandmother. His memories of those early carefree years are of fetching water for the house and picking mangoes and coconuts from the trees in his garden. All a far cry from the harsh reality of the tough west London estate to which he came as a seven-year-old, when the family finally decided it was time for him to join them in England.

He travelled over with his elder sister Lucia, and not only would be reunited with his mother, he would also be meeting two more sisters and a brother, all born in England. His father had first found work at a factory making cast-iron baths and later as a porter at the BBC, while his mother was a nurse, and Linford moved into their small house in Shepherd's Bush, near Queen's Park Rangers football ground. It was quite a culture shock. Money was very tight, the weather wasn't exactly Caribbean and despite the easy-going, swinging sixties image, London was a difficult place for a young black kid.

Christie was always a big football fan and his hero was Manchester United star George Best. Even in the big playground matches, where inevitably the sides ended up being blacks versus whites, he would pretend to be Best. It was in one of these games that his speed was first noticed by a teacher who was watching casually from a classroom window. 'He came up to me and said, "You look quick, would you like to try out for the school team?" To this day I can't quite understand how he could have just looked at that game and known that I was quick.'

He won his first race at primary school and even ran for his school at the famous old White City Stadium, just before it was torn down, wearing plimsolls bought for him by one of his teachers.

At secondary school in Fulham he continued to run, but without creating any real excitement, and left at 16 to take a job as an electronics apprentice at a TV rental company. But he hated it and quit after a month, joining the accounts department at a local Co-op department store. He also joined the London Irish Athletics Club, but Saturday work continued to interfere with his running and training, so he ended up working in a tax office at Elephant & Castle.

In reality, his training regime was virtually non-existent and Christie's attitude was that he could beat most of the guys he raced without bothering. The breakthrough came when he was selected to run at the English Schools Championship, in Nottingham, in 1979. At 19 he was still just eligible and he ran the 200 metres. A young Phil Brown, who was already an international, beat him comfortably, but offered young Linford some lasting post-race advice.

'I had finished second in the race and I was tall and gangly. They called me "Horse" because of the galloping way I ran. Phil came over and said that I was quick. He told me I could be really good if I trained hard.'

Within a year Christie had twice broken the British indoor 200-metre record, but he knew he needed more serious training and competition, so he left London Irish to join the famous Thames Valley Harriers, which brought him together with coach Ron Roddan, a man who would play a pivotal role in Christie's athletic career.

'I love that man, says Christie. 'I really have a lot of respect for him. He was my only coach, and even today we're best friends. He's one of those quiet, humble kind of people. I still use his training methods now.'

But it would be a few years before Roddan's influence would take effect, and while Christie continued to enjoy running and had some limited success, he concedes that his life lacked direction. He left the tax office and then decided to leave home. He was 23. He had no money and a one-bedroom rented flat, but he begged and borrowed an old cooker, fridge and furniture and moved in with his girlfriend.But his track career had run into a cul-de-sac. Despite some decent 100-metre times, he wasn't selected for the Los Angeles Olympics. 'I felt I should have been there,' recalls Christie. 'I realized if I wanted to be on the team, then I would have to do something about it.'

Two pieces of advice put Christie on the right path, the first from his grandmother and the second from Coach Roddan. 'She told me to do it because you want to do it, don't go through life thinking "if only". Ron wrote me a letter saying that I should come back to training and take things seriously. Or forget it. But don't waste my time any more.'

Christie finally realized it was now or never. At the age of 24 he began his first winter of serious training, and the effect was immediate. He started the 1985 season with a wind-assisted 10.2-second 100 metres in Finland, and despite some hamstring problems he was hopeful of selection for the British team in the European Cup. Much to his annoyance it was only from the newspapers that he discovered he'd been left out of the team, but he was still progressing and the way he'd been treated drove him on.

In his 1995 autobiography *To Be Honest with You*, Christie recalled: 'I suddenly realized what hard training was really about. I can't say I enjoyed it. In fact, I hated it. But the results were soon evident.'

Christie's career finally lifted off in early 1986 at the European Indoor Championships, in Madrid, where he won the 200 metres, his first major international title. Outdoors he started brightly, lowering his personal best in the 100 metres to 10.33 and in the 200 metres to 20.79.

But it was at an invitational meeting in Madrid that he suddenly made the world sit up and take notice, by beating a decent field that included Americans Thomas Jefferson and Emmitt King, in a new British record of 10.04. Frustratingly for Christie, the performance hardly registered on the British sports pages, which were dominated by England and Scotland's football performances in the Mexico World Cup.

'After that I started thinking that maybe I could do something at the Olympics,' recalls Christie. 'I thought I could beat everyone in the world. Your attitude just changes. You're not in primary school any more. I still didn't realize at that time how good I could be, but I wanted to be the best.'

The Commonwealth Games, held in Edinburgh about a month later, were something of a farce, with a mass boycott by Caribbean and African nations in protest over New Zealand's sporting links to South Africa's apartheid government, but Christie took a silver medal behind rising star Ben Johnson.

'Ben Johnson and I always got on well together,' recalled Christie. 'Maybe it was because we were both from Jamaica. Regardless of the controversy surrounding his athletics I always found him to be a very nice guy.'

A few weeks later, at the Neckarstadion in Stuttgart, Christie took his place on the starting line of the European Championships 100 metres, a race built up by the British press as a battle between new boy Christie and 1980 Olympic champion Allan Wells. In the event, Wells finished fifth and wasn't a factor, but Christie streaked past the field to win the gold in 10.15 seconds.

'This was the first time that Britain had won the 100 metres in the European Championships for 40 years,' recalled Christie. 'I felt a great sense of pride when I stood on the rostrum with a Union Jack, given to me by a British supporter on my lap of honour, draped around my shoulders. But even that would cause trouble.'

Not for the last time, Christie was reprimanded by the athletics authorities. On this occasion it was for wearing the flag on the podium, which was apparently banned. Then he even got criticism from members of the black community in Britain who didn't feel part of the country and objected to Christie wearing the flag.

'I was representing Great Britain,' said Christie. 'I couldn't somehow stand there and say I'm Jamaican. But I knew my roots and, as far as I was concerned, this was kudos for Jamaica too. Wearing the flag was an impromptu thing, but it said everything about how I felt. I have no regrets whatsoever.'

Christie rolled into the 1987 season ranked third in the world at 100 metres, behind Johnson and Nigeria's Chidi Imoh, so the obvious target was a medal at the World Championships, in Rome. The run-up went well, and despite missing the World Indoor Championships with a hamstring injury, he took a sprint double at the European Cup, in Prague, before lowering the British 100-metre record to 10.03 in Budapest.

However, another row with team boss Frank Dick, this time over the make-up of the relay team, then spilled into the press and threatened to undo all the preparations he'd made for Rome. Christie lost his temper in front of the cameras and the resulting headlines were not pretty.

'I may have been number one in Britain and Europe, but this also proved that I didn't know how to handle the media,' recalled Christie. 'I was inexperienced and I was learning my lessons the hard way. I felt I had gone out of my way to help the media in the past. Now they had turned on me. I felt very bitter about it. One day I was running for fun, the next thing I was forced into the public eye and not really given any kind of training to deal with it.'

Christie even went so far as to suggest that the hangover from the row damaged his run in the 100 final, which was won by Johnson in a new world record 9.83. Christie ran poorly but still finished fourth. It was an early illustration of the difficulties Christie would have with the track authorities and the media throughout his career.

Frank Dick, now a popular speaker on sport and motivation and president of the European Athletics Coaches Association, was Britain's director of coaching from 1979 to 1994 and found himself in the eye of the Christie storm. He explained: 'I have huge respect for Linford Christie. He was an incredible example of someone who developed through sport as well as from sport. I think that Ron and others who influenced him at that time really saved him from coming off the rails.

'He was so focused, so angry, but he channelled that anger into his running. It became a total expression of who he was. He was a competitor the minute he entered the warm-up area and that crystallized on the track when he would remove everyone in the world, everything except a channel that he ran through. It was almost as if the white lines became walls and all he saw was the end of the track.

'I could have a cup of tea and a chat with him outside of that environment, but two to three weeks out from a competition his attitude would change and his competitive behaviour would begin. In many ways he was similar to Daley Thompson, who was also a very difficult man if you were close to him on a professional level.'

As the Olympic year of 1988 rose into view, Christie tried to put these issues to one side and focus on his first tilt at the Games. He won both the 100 and 200 metres at the AAAs, effectively the British Olympic trials, but the press wouldn't let him relax.

At the big pre-Games meeting in Zurich, Christie ran a 10.07, his third fastest time ever, but finished fifth in a race won by Carl Lewis, with Johnson, Imoh and Calvin Smith all in front of him. One British newspaper superimposed Christie's face on an Olympic gold medal under the headline 'Fool's Gold' – suggesting that the sprinter had no chance in Seoul.

Christie's simmering distaste for most of the British press began to intensify further on the plane to South Korea. Rather curiously, the athletes and the journalists had been booked not only on the same flight, but into the same hotel as the British team.

'It was like stalking the royals. Everywhere we walked there was a lens following. We weren't happy with it; to be honest, I was totally pissed off.' His mood was darkened further when his coach Ron Roddan had to fly home because he couldn't get accreditation for Seoul.

In his autobiography, Christie recalls the morning of the 100-metre final and how he drank cups of black coffee to offset the early start needed to make a 10am race time. 'I felt completely knackered and I was knocking back the black coffees to keep me awake,' he wrote. 'A crazy thing to do because you can be found positive on too much coffee. It was naivety on my part because I had nothing to fear; I had made a big issue over the fact that I was not on drugs.'

Christie had been a vocal advocate of drug-free athletics, proclaiming himself 'clean as a whistle' and publicly wearing T-shirts with slogans like '100 per cent Natural' and 'Pure Talent. Body by me. Training by Ron.' But imbibing the bucket loads of coffee and the ginseng supplements he'd been buying in the South Korean shops near the team HQ at Nihon could never have prepared him for what was to come.

The final went according to script, with Ben Johnson destroying the field in a startling new world record of 9.79. 'Ben just went,' recalled Christie. 'I don't think I'll ever forget that. He just went. We had been preparing with Ben in mind because he was known to be a 60-metre man. He would go hard for 60 metres and then just hang on.'

Christie ran the race of his life to finish third in 9.97 – the first European athlete to duck under 10 seconds.

The whole spectacle then began to unravel with the news that Johnson had tested positive for steroids. 'I cried that day,' Christie wrote. 'I really cried because I have always felt that people who get caught for drugs should be banned for life. I had wanted the officials to catch these people. But I never expected it to happen to Ben. Believe me, I had been in Ben's company and I never thought he was on drugs – never, ever. He was such a nice guy. There are stories that people on drugs tear up rooms and go loopy-loo. But Ben was so cool, he was really funny.

'On the day he won the gold, we were on the rostrum and he was admiring the girls carrying the medals. He was a laugh. I felt so sorry because it was a sad day for athletics.' For Christie, it was about to get a whole lot worse.

Despite the Johnson scandal and rumours of further positive tests, Christie went out and finished fourth in the 200 metres, with a new British record of 20.09, and he was relaxing with some of his friends in the team back at the Olympic village when team manager Mike Turner approached him with some devastating news. Linford Christie had tested positive.

A distraught Christie emotionally protested his innocence, assuming the drugs the IOC testers had found were steroids. The British team management questioned him and he told them: 'If they want their medal, they can take their medal. I don't want it because I don't take steroids. Don't tell me that I'm on drugs because I'm not.'

It wasn't long before the news leaked to the media – notably the eager British press. The British team continued to quiz him, and Christie even had to resort to sleeping tablets to escape the nightmare. 'I just wanted to die,' he recalled. 'At one point I almost wanted to kill myself. Things like that went through my mind because they were really grilling me.'

But the substance in question was not a steroid, it was a stimulant called pseudoephedrine, something found commonly in over-the-counter medication such as cough medicines. It would need to be taken in vast quantities to be performance enhancing – and the amount found was tiny – but still the IOC decided to stage a full inquiry.

The post-Johnson media feeding frenzy was almost off the charts, and the British Olympic Association appointed a QC, Robert Watson, to handle Christie's defence. He explained that the ginseng Christie had been taking was to blame, and the inquiry finally accepted, by the narrow margin of 11 votes to 10, that Christie had done nothing wrong and he was exonerated. However, the language they used in the press conference that followed suggested they had given Christie 'the benefit of the doubt', which was hardly a ringing endorsement of his innocence.

In the official report of the Games, published by the BOA, its general secretary Dick Palmer criticized the need to employ expensive legal counsel to defend its athletes and called for an overhaul of the protocols used to tackle the issue of performance enhancement. 'I believe that the time has come for the BOA to insist that medical officers of the sports attending the Games give a full and detailed account of **all** products taken by competitors in the period prior to and during the Games,' he wrote. 'Furthermore, I believe that the BOA needs to embark on an urgent educational campaign aimed at appraising competitors, coaches and indeed doctors on matters of diet, supplements and drugs. We must never again be in the situation in which we found ourselves in Seoul.'

Christie was angry at how his name had been leaked – for which the IOC blamed the BOA, and vice versa. 'I felt like a little kid who had taken a penny bubble gum from a shop and ended up in the Old Bailey,' he said. Nevertheless he returned home to a positive welcome from Britain's sports fans, despite the media furore.

The following year he repaid the faith shown in him by Britain's athletics fans, by captaining the team to its first ever European Cup win, ending 25 years of dominance by the Soviet Union and East Germany. Memorably, it was achieved on home turf, in Gateshead, and Christie was selected to collect and lift the trophy. It remains one his career highlights.

Despite a foot injury, the season was also punctuated by another career highlight, Christie's first defeat of Carl Lewis, over 100 metres at a Grand Prix event in Monte Carlo. Jamaican Ray Stewart actually won the race, but it was a timely boost to Christie's confidence going into the 1990 Commonwealth Games, in New Zealand, early the following year.

In Auckland, he won the 100 metres in a wind-assisted 9.93 seconds and took another gold medal in the relay. He followed that in August, a few months after his thirtieth birthday, with gold in the European Championships 100 metres, in 10 seconds flat.

But the 1990 season would forever be remembered for Christie's more outrageous attire – most notably his leopardskin body suit and the rise of the 'lunchbox' legend.

He first wore one of his multi-coloured body suits at the tail end of the 1990 season, at an otherwise uneventful meeting in Sheffield. The media lapped it up, and Christie's outfits sometimes outplayed his performances. He had them personally designed, famously wearing a skeleton version at one meeting, which had been designed by a reader of the teen magazine *Look In*. While the suits were popular with the athletics crowds, they also played a practical role, keeping Christie's temperamental hamstrings warm.

A by-product of these suits, one that turned out to be quite unwelcome for Christie, was the tabloid newspapers' fascination with what they described as Linford's 'lunchbox', the rather obvious bulge in the groin area of the Lycra.

Christie hated the description, and while the *Sun* had fun baiting him with more and more lurid 'lunchbox' headlines and pictures, his sense of humour over the whole matter began to fail. 'They don't talk about Sally Gunnell's breasts; if they did, there would be an uproar – sexual harassment and everything else – and they know it. So why do I have to put up with this?'

The reality was that while the tabloid papers certainly did go overboard – when he finally retired the *Sun* headline was 'Linford's Hanging Up His Lunchbox' – Christie had brought a lot of the attention on himself by wearing the suits. But even today he struggles to see the funny side of it.

'I was a very serious person. I wasn't out there to make jokes and lark around. I was out there to do what I did. Some of the press couldn't cope with that. And, I guess, familiarity breeds contempt. I never had any problems with the press guys from abroad. But the British press couldn't deal with me and there were times when I wasn't used to dealing with what they needed from me. When they wrote something bad about me, I would want to know why. When I was growing up in Jamaica, my grandmother always told me if you haven't got anything good to say, then don't say anything.'

Back on the track, all eyes were on the 1991 World Championships, in Tokyo, and a new rival for Christie had appeared on the scene in the shape of American Andre Cason, who duly delivered his credentials in emphatic form at the World Indoor Championships, in Seville, beating Christie into second place.

But it was the old guard from the States who dominated in Tokyo, with Carl Lewis winning gold in 9.86 – a new world record, now that Ben Johnson's old figures had been stricken from the record books. Leroy Burrell took silver and Dennis Mitchell completed an American clean sweep, both recording personal bests in 9.88 and 9.91 respectively.

In fourth place, out of the medals, Linford Christie ran his fastest ever race, breaking the national and European record in 9.92. Six of the eight finalists ran under 10 seconds. It was one hell of a fast race, but he still left Tokyo empty-handed and began to wonder if he could run any faster. The press compounded his anxiety by suggesting that, at the age of 31, he was probably past his sell-by date.

'Never in my wildest dreams had I thought I would run 9.92 seconds, he recalled. 'It was a British, European and Commonwealth record. For the first time in my life I felt satisfied. I thought this is as good as it's going to get. It's time to get out and get away from all the crap the media were giving me.'

He announced his decision to retire to the media, but he hadn't bargained for the reaction he would get from his fans and the British sporting public at large. He received hundreds of letters from everywhere asking him to change his mind and have a go at the Olympics in Barcelona the following year.

After a long sit-down meeting with Coach Roddan, Christie decided not to quit the sport as a loser. In the end, he didn't want to be remembered for finishing fourth in the World Championships, no matter what the time was. So, having talked to Roddan, his partner Mandy and some of his closest friends, he decided to do one more year.

'Ron and I sat down and asked what went wrong in Tokyo,' recalls Christie. 'Because I honestly thought I was going to win. We looked at two things. First, there was my start and we worked hard on that. We didn't let anyone know we were doing it.

'I remember I got out well in the Tokyo final, but as soon as Carl came on my shoulder, I tightened up because I could see him. I thought there had to be a way of dealing with that, so after '91 that's when the scary-eyed stare down the track came in. It worked because it blurred my peripheral vision, so I couldn't see anybody coming up on my shoulders. We thought of trying so many things, even wearing "blinkers" like racehorses. But the stare worked, and it changed everything for me. It's quite likely that had I got a medal at the World Championships, I wouldn't have won the Olympics.

'But although I was in great shape in '91, by the time '92 came around I was definitely a better athlete. I'd had a few personal problems in '91 and I wasn't as mentally strong. But in '92 I was a changed person.'

Christie launched Olympic year by ducking the whole indoor season and electing to warm-weather train in Australia. It clearly worked and the outdoor season featured some very promising performances in Rome, Edinburgh, Oslo and Lausanne.

To reinforce Christie's new, upbeat view about Barcelona, his great rival Carl Lewis had unexpectedly finished sixth in the US Olympic trials and had not made the team for the 100 metres. Dennis Mitchell won and qualified alongside Leroy Burrell and Mark Witherspoon. Christie firmly believed he could beat all three.

He flew in to Barcelona a few days before the 100-metre competition was due to begin, and arriving at the Olympic village he discovered the poor standard of accommodation. 'Colin Jackson and I shared a box room which was so cramped we had to leave our suitcases in the corridor,' he recalled. 'There were eight or nine people sharing two bathrooms. We had a big metal shutter on our bedroom window, but it broke not long after we had arrived and we couldn't use it. It was an awful place, certainly nothing like the image people have of athletes travelling the world and visiting all these exotic locations.'

The beds were so small that Christie's feet stuck out of the end, but as team captain he knew he'd have to grin and bear it. There was no way he could swan out of the village and check into a five-star hotel.

Despite the discomfort in the village, Christie looked in complete control during the first day of heats, winning his first-round race at a canter and then squeezing out Burrell with a fast 10.07 in the second round.

'There were arguments over just who was the favourite,' recalls Christie. 'Dennis Mitchell was saying he was the best; Leroy Burrell claimed he was going to win. They asked me who was favourite and I said Dennis and Leroy both were. I wasn't getting into that kind of discussion because I didn't give a damn who the favourite was. Certainly, I didn't want it to be me; I wanted to sneak in around the back.'

The following day, Christie was drawn in the first semi-final, along with Mitchell and Burrell. The two runners who most concerned him, Namibian Frankie Fredericks and Nigeria's Oladape Adeniken, were in the second semi.

Burrell served notice of his intention with an impressive 9.97 into a 1.3-metre headwind, with Christie second in 10 flat, Mitchell third and Nigeria's Davidson Ezinwa fourth. They would all qualify for the final. Ben Johnson, returning from his ban, stumbled out of his blocks and finished last. 'I sat behind [Burrell] all the way,' Christie recalls, 'feeling that I could run past him at any time. I just left it at that and let everyone continue the debate over who was favourite.'

Fredericks took the second semi, with Surin, Adeniken and Ray Stewart. The third American, the 6ft 5in Mark Witherspoon, who finished second in the US trials, crashed to the track after 30 metres with a ruptured Achilles tendon.

A few hours later the eight men lined up for the final and Christie took on to the track some advice from an unlikely source. 'I had read an article on Carl Lewis in which he said he didn't go on to the track to race other athletes. He went out to run the best he possibly could and, if he did that, then it should be good enough to win. Barcelona was the first time I went to the blocks imagining my lane was a tunnel, with everything else on either side a blur.'

Canadian Surin was in lane one; Stewart, in his third Olympic final, in lane two; then Fredericks, Mitchell, Christie in lane five, Burrell, Ezinwa and Adeniken on the outside.

After a false start from Burrell, the race itself turned out perfectly for Christie. Out of the middle of the field, he got an excellent start and by halfway he took complete charge, edging ahead of the pack and cruising through the finish in 9.96 seconds to win the gold medal and, at 32, become the oldest man ever to win the Olympic 100 metres title. The Americans looked shell-shocked, especially pre-race favourite Burrell, who finished a disappointing fifth.

Christie was the only man on the day to run under 10 seconds. He powered over the line, with both hands raised in victory, and quickly found a British fan who handed him a Union Jack flag which he waved wildly on a well-deserved lap of honour.

'I can't tell you anything about the reaction of the crowd,' said Christie. 'You don't hear the noise when you're running. It's like being in a trance. If you hear anything, you are not concentrating. You can see through the side of your eyes when people are getting close. I didn't see anybody, and when I don't see anybody, I know I'm winning.'

Christie admits to having a large lump in his throat as he stood on the medal podium with the national anthem playing, but he fought the urge to cry. It was only then that he discovered that Ron Roddan wasn't actually in the stadium to witness his greatest triumph. He'd tripped and sprained his ankle getting on the bus to the stadium and was receiving treatment back in the village. He'd watched it all on TV.

The predictably churlish American press poured cold water on Christie's triumph, suggesting his victory had only been accomplished in the absence of Carl Lewis. The smouldering resentment in the *Washington Post* report summed up the sour American media view: 'Christie led all the way to defeat a lacklustre men's field in the relatively slow time of 9.96 seconds.'

Christie was emotionally drained and was knocked out of the 200 metres in the semi-finals. But he anchored the British sprint relay team of Marcus Adam, Tony Jarrett and John Regis to fourth place in a final won in a new world record time of 37.4 by the American quartet of 200-metre gold medallist Mike Marsh, Burrell, Mitchell and Carl Lewis.

He returned from Barcelona to a hero's welcome, but also to growing and irritating media speculation about the absence of Lewis. It was a bandwagon that the American seemed happy to jump aboard, despite Lewis's form being poor throughout 1992 and the fact that soon after the Games Christie defeated both Mitchell and Burrell again at the big Grand Prix meeting in Berlin.

Shortly after the Olympics, in partnership with friend and fellow athlete Colin Jackson, Christie set up his business Nuff Respect, an agency that represented athletes, and to run it day to day he hired the highly rated Sue Barrett from Alan Pascoe Associates. She's still there today, despite many saying the venture wouldn't last.After his Olympic triumph, all talk of retirement had been put on the back burner and after suffering a back injury in early 1993, he returned to the track and the goal of winning the World Championships, in Germany, an event now held every two years.

The clamour for a Christie–Lewis match race grew through the summer, and when it was finally agreed the global media interest and demand for tickets was stratospheric. The race would be held in the UK, at Gateshead, in July. Lewis arrived via Concorde, private jet and chauffeured Rolls-Royce; Christie via a DanAir scheduled flight and team bus. The running score offered Christie scant comfort – Lewis 12, Christie 1. A happier statistic was that each of them, it was reported, would receive £100,000 for the race.

A capacity crowd of nearly fifteen thousand, and tens of millions more watching live on television, piled the pressure on the two athletes. 'You would be forgiven for thinking that this was the Olympic Games,' recalled Christie. 'My heart was thumping more than ever, I was as nervous as hell. To me, this was more nerve-wracking than being in Barcelona, because Carl was one of the greatest athletes of our time.'

The race itself was another dream run for Christie. He got away well and chased down the fast-starting American Jon Drummond to win in 10.08, with Lewis third. The roof nearly came off the old stadium. 'If it had been a boxing match, Carl would have been on the canvas,' Christie recalled. 'It gave me so much pleasure.'

Hugely enjoyable, and profitable, though it was, Gateshead was not the World Championships, and Christie's next date with Carl Lewis would be on a far bigger stage. His preparation for Stuttgart was reasonable, though he lost to Burrell in Zurich, and he arrived in Germany in good shape.

The American team of Lewis, Mitchell and Andre Cason looked formidable on paper, and in the first day's heats they all looked in decent form, with Cason running a blistering 9.96 seconds in the second round.

The following day young British sprinter Darren Campbell, a protégé of Christie's, got a personal glimpse into his mindset in Stuttgart. 'I went to the track with Linford and watched him prepare. He looked calm as we walked into the stadium and he was looking to intimidate and scare. We went into a little waiting room with Ron, and when we sat down Linford was shaking. Even Linford, the Olympic champion, was nervous. But when he left the room he didn't show any of that. I learned that day what it was to be a champion, how to have total belief in yourself and how to portray yourself to the outside world. The key was how to manage your nerves.'

The times continued to drop in the semi-finals. Christie was walking through the tunnel for his when he heard the roar of the crowd as, in the first semi, Cason blitzed a 9.94, with Nigeria's Daniel Effiong second, Lewis third and Fredericks fourth. But Christie was no slouch either and he took the second semi in 9.97, comfortably ahead of Mitchell, Surin and Stewart. This was going to be some final.

As the preparations for the race began, so too did the mind games. Christie remembers: 'We all think size is strength, even though we know it's not really true. Warming up, I saw Carl Lewis and the other guys, so I took off my top and flexed my muscles. I saw Carl looking at me, and then he looked at his coach Tom Tellez and mouthed something that looked like "Fucking hell, look at that." Automatically, I knew I'd beaten him. As for Cason, I noticed as we were warming up that he was running up the same lane that I was running down. We both kept running and I thought to myself, I'm not going to move. And when I got close enough to him, he moved and went into the next lane. I knew he wasn't going to beat me.'

The race was another perfect one for Christie. He got a terrific start and seemed to be out in front almost from the gun. The reaction times would show he had the second fastest start after Dennis Mitchell, with the normally electric-starting Cason the slowest.

Christie just continued to pile on the pressure and was never headed, hitting the line in 9.87 seconds, a hundredth outside the world record, with Cason half a metre back in a battling second place in 9.92 and Mitchell third in 9.99. Lewis finished fourth and didn't break 10 seconds.

Christie, at 33, had recorded the second fastest time ever and had completed his full set of championships – national, Commonwealth, European, Olympic and now World titles in 100 metres.

'It was quite simply my greatest race ever,' Christie recalls. 'The level changed, the playing field changed. I had lost in 1991, I had won the Olympics in 1992, but Lewis and Cason hadn't made the US team. That didn't seem to matter. A lot of people still said I had only won because they weren't there. So I had to raise my game and do it all again. But like they say, the tougher the battle, the sweeter the victory.'

Christie ducked the 200 metres, but anchored the British relay team to a silver medal, with a new European record, behind the gold medal-winning Americans.

So that was that. Christie was reigning Olympic and world champion and had run his fastest ever race. Talk of retirement was put back on the table. But Christie was having too much fun to think about calling it a day.

He romped through the 1994 season, equalling the European indoor 60 metres record of 6.48, winning a seventh AAAs 100-metre title to equal McDonald Bailey's record, and taking a sprint double at the European Cup in Birmingham. In July, he was actually commentating for the BBC in Lausanne when Leroy Burrell broke the 100-metre world record, running a 9.85 seconds, and re-igniting the clamour for another match race. After all, Burrell wasn't in Stuttgart! Christie just couldn't win.

A hamstring injury slowed down his summer season, but he emerged in decent form for the European Championships, in Helsinki, which he duly won; then beat Burrell in a wet and windy Zurich Weltklasse before flying out to begin preparations for the Commonwealth Games, in Canada, where he took another gold medal with a dazzling 9.91 seconds. However, the post-Games tour proved a bridge too far at 34, and he suffered a string of losses, most notably to Dennis Mitchell, who would end the season rated as the number one sprinter by *Track & Field News*, which even for their strange ratings system seemed a little partisan.

Once again there was talk of retirement as the 1995 indoor season opened, but Christie belied the approaches of Father Time and within 90 minutes of a meeting in Liévin, in northern France, he broke the European indoor 60 metres record in 6.47 and then, to his own astonishment, smashed the world indoor 200 metres record, in 20.25 – becoming the first Briton to hold a world indoor record for 35 years.

But his outdoor season didn't follow the same pattern and, perhaps more out of frustration than desire, he tearfully told a British TV show that he'd had enough and would retire before the Atlanta Olympic Games. In June his mother passed away, but shortly after the funeral he still turned up to represent Britain at the European Cup final, where he won both the 100 and 200 metres.

A knee injury disrupted his preparations for the World Championships, in Gothenburg, where he was aiming to hold on to his 100-metre title. He was now 35, and the media also revelled in the story that he'd become a grandfather a week earlier, which was actually untrue. In Sweden he looked comfortable in the heats, but his troublesome hamstring problem reared its head in the semis and although he just managed to qualify, he knew the final wasn't going to go well.

'Deep down I knew I wasn't going to finish. I thought the hamstring would go halfway through the final. But if they wanted my title, I was not prepared to hand it over, just like that.'

Canada's Donovan Bailey won the title, but Christie managed to finish, almost trotting over the line in lane one with a respectable sixth place in 10.12 seconds. As soon as he crossed the line he dropped to the track in pain and medics rushed to apply ice to his torn hamstring. But he did manage to recover sufficiently to win the Zurich Weltklasse in 10.03, where he beat both Bailey and Drummond.

Christie then played several months of 'will he, won't he?' games with the media about his intentions for the 1996 Olympics. Perhaps with hindsight it might have been better had he not made the trip, but Christie was never one to duck a challenge.

Despite a '96 season of indifferent form and niggling injury, he won the British Olympic trials and an eighth AAA title and decided to make the trip. He listed public support as one of the key reasons for his decision, along with loyalty to his long-time coach Ron Roddan, who, he felt, would leave the sport if he didn't go, as well as a more stable relationship with the British Athletic Federation following a long-running dispute over appearance fees, in which he supported fellow internationals John Regis and Tony Jarrett. 'It's a risk that in the end I had to take,' he told the *Independent*. 'It would have been easy to have sat at home. But then if someone won the Olympics in 10 seconds flat it would be something I'd regret for the rest of my life.'

But the times would be a little quicker than that in Atlanta. Once there he managed to antagonize the organizers by turning up at a pre-race press conference wearing contact lenses embossed with a Puma logo. The event had been sponsored heavily by their rivals Reebok.

On the track he made his way through the heats in unspectacular fashion, finishing third in his semi-final, with a reasonable 10.03. But the infamous spectacle in the final saw him false-start twice, get disqualified and refuse to walk off the track. It was certainly not his finest hour, but it was also a traumatic and unparalleled moment. Before then no Olympic champion had ever been disqualified from defending his title on the start line of a final. It later transpired that the officials confirmed he hadn't false-started the second time, but in their opinion reacted too quickly to the gun.

Finalist Ato Boldon was among a chorus of athletes who railed at Christie's lack of professionalism and respect in not immediately accepting the decision and sparing the field the extra delay and pressure while he contested the call. But Britain's team spokesman Tony Ward said there was no disgrace in the way Christie had gone out. 'It was disappointing but he's been a fabulous champion,' he said. After elimination in the heats of the 200 metres, Christie returned home and embarked on the lucrative post-Games tour of Europe, finishing a creditable third in Zurich in a blanket finish with Bailey and Mitchell.

But he had already announced that this would be his swansong and that he would quit top-class racing at the end of the season. This was duly accomplished in Sheffield, where although he was beaten by a Briton for the first time in ten years, 21-year-old Ian Mackie in the 100 metres, he milked the rapturous applause of the crowd and then stripped off and threw them his running outfit.

But Christie didn't stay out of the news for long. While training in Australia in December, he received the devastating news that his younger brother Russell had been murdered in a street fight in a row over drugs in west London. A distraught Christie got on the first plane back to the UK. The police had arrested the culprit, a known drug dealer, who was later sentenced to five years, and it emerged that although the wayward Russell Christie had for many years been in and out of prison for GBH and theft, Linford was still very close to him.

It was a very difficult and emotional time and Christie didn't run much in 1997, but promised to make his farewell international appearance at the European Cup, in Munich, in June. At the age of 37, he duly won the 100 metres for the eighth consecutive time, in 10.04, the fastest time in Europe that year and equalling the meet record. For good measure he went out and dead-heated the 200 metres.

Christie's retirement created a huge hole in British athletics. He would continue to run some minor events in the coming years, but his attention would be entirely on coaching and his Nuff Respect company, even though he had split acrimoniously with his partner Colin Jackson some years earlier, when he left the business to focus more on his hurdling.

But early in 1999 two significant things happened to Christie. First, he became embroiled in a libel case in the High Court over an article in a defunct magazine called *Spiked*, which under the headline 'How Did Linford Get This Good?' suggested he used performance-enhancing drugs. The jury ultimately found 10–2 in favour of Christie.

Second, having run in a one-off minor indoor meeting in Dortmund in February, he was informed that he had tested positive for the steroid nandrolone, a charge he vehemently refuted. 'I have consistently opposed the use of banned substances and it is ridiculous to imagine that I would take them after my retirement,' he said. In fact, he was only supposed to be in Dortmund to oversee three of his athletes – Darren Campbell, Katherine Merry and Jamie Baulch – and it was they who had challenged him to run.

In September he was cleared by UK Athletics, who ruled they could not prove 'beyond reasonable doubt' that the substance in the sample had been derived from a prohibited source. Nandrolone, it was revealed, was produced naturally by the body, and medical studies indicated that the metabolites found in Christie's urine could have come from a combination of hard exercise and food supplements.

After nearly a year of delays, and in a masterpiece of bad timing, right on the eve of the opening ceremony at the Sydney Olympics the sport's ruling body, the IAAF, bizarrely rejected the UK Athletics' ruling and upheld the two-year ban originally imposed on Christie before he was cleared. Their opposing view was that Christie hadn't proved the substance had *not* come from a banned substance.

David Moorcroft, the CEO of UK Athletics at the time, was dumbfounded and condemned the IAAF's inept handling of the affair. 'If they wanted to bring greater negative attention to the sport they would be hard pressed to find a better way. The UK panel, which arrived at its conclusions using British law, said that in its view where there is reasonable doubt it must go in favour of the athlete. It seems to me that the IAAF's panel is saying that where there is reasonable doubt it should go in favour of the system.'

Despite the dubious nature of the IAAF conclusion, Christie continued to coach his athletes in Sydney, with Darren Campbell and Katharine Merry both winning medals on the track. But it was a desperately unhappy postscript to an extraordinary career, and even today no newspaper or magazine article on Christie is complete without reference to the stigma of being labelled a 'drug cheat' – which, given his position on drugs over the years and what he's done for the sport, seems wholly unfair.

The respected *Daily Mail* sports writer Neil Wilson, who followed Christie's career from its earliest days, found him a fascinating, but demanding subject. 'From the beginning of his career to the end, Christie was focused on ego. The name he chose for his management company said it all. "Nuff Respect". He expected it, demanded it and would not tolerate it when he did not receive it. I always assumed it came from his fractured upbringing. Leroy Burrell once said, "He runs on hate." But the French paper

L'Equipe caught him more perfectly when it headlined an article "Dr Linford and Mr Christie". There were two men inside him, one whom friends found funny, charming and even a little shy, and the other a man of aggression, hatred and vitriol who needed to wind himself up to compete. It was disrespect by officialdom – not picking him for the GB 4 x 100 metre Olympic squad – that wound him up enough to start training properly for the first time. The athletic press's attitude is "take as you find". They didn't like Ovett and Thompson because neither would give them the time of day; they did like Coe because he always had time for them. This applies to Christie. He was regarded as a difficult man to deal with, so he did not make friends among them.'

The name Nuff Respect had an unusual genesis. Sue Barrett recalled: 'It was the result of a shopping trip to Safeway, in Acton. Linford had just returned from racing on the circuit and it was the only time we could meet to discuss the forming of the company. Every aisle saw a different person approaching him and saying "respect" to him. It was all new to me, but when I knew he didn't want to name the company after himself, I went back to work and mentioned it to a colleague. Linford loved the idea and added the "Nuff" to it.'

It's no surprise to find a more positive view of Christie coming from his inner circle of friends and colleagues. Darren Campbell, sprint relay gold medallist in Athens, 200 metres silver medallist in Sydney and now head of short sprints and relays at British Athletics, was 14 years old when he first met Christie at a teenage sprint competition at Crystal Palace. 'The biggest thing I remember is how friendly he was. I was a nobody, but he spent time so much time with me and the other kids. I decided there and then that if I was going to be successful that's what I wanted to be like.'

Campbell's insight into Christie's on-track psychology is also interesting. 'Linford believes anything is possible and he instils that in his athletes. He always told me never to chase money, only medals. If I got the medals the money would follow. Winners have a different mentality. When something looks impossible you have to brainwash yourself that it can be done. You cannot stand in an Olympic 100 metres final and not believe you can win it. Potentially it can look like arrogance, but it is total confidence.'

As for the running battle with the British press, Campbell concedes that it was a shame that the lack of understanding on both sides has coloured the public's view of his achievements. Ironic too.

'The fact is he doesn't actually like confrontation,' he laughs. 'People say he is aggressive, but really he's just a big fun-loving softie. He doesn't wear his achievements on his sleeve. I've stayed at his house loads of times and there are no medals on display. I never saw his gold medal until I won mine in 2004.'

Campbell was one of Christie's greatest coaching achievements, and he continued his coaching career, with a good deal of success. But even in retirement controversy continued to dog him and when the Olympic Games returned to London in 2012 a simmering feud with 2012 boss Lord Coe meant there would be no official role for him at the Games. Even an invitation from the London Mayor's office to take part in the torch-carrying relay was embarrassingly rescinded.

On the brighter side, the old West London stadium was renamed the Linford Christie Stadium, and he remains committed to working with kids in the area. Looking back now, he explains: 'I really enjoyed my career. I retired when I stopped enjoying it. I love being part of athletics. I love trying to make my athletes better. It would be great to coach an athlete who was winning at the Olympics. I try and coach the way Ron coached. I'm not saying that I'm better than the other coaches, but I have a lot of experience. I'm certainly not a jacket and tie man and money is not my motivation.'

One of his biggest developments in recent years has been the Street Athletics campaign that he created with Darren Campbell. It runs programmes of sport, music and dance, designed to persuade kids in cities up and down the UK to use their local sports facilities. 'We try and replicate how we got started,' says Christie. 'Sport takes your mind off things you shouldn't be doing. It can do so much good.'

He has also featured on British television shows, fronting the BBC's *Linford's Record Breakers*, acting in the comedy-drama *Hustle* and even appearing in a movie called *Don't Go Breaking My Heart*. But his biggest TV role came when he entered the Australian jungle in 2010 to take part in the hugely popular ITV series *I'm a Celebrity Get Me Out of Here!*, where he was the sixth star to be eliminated, in show 15, and was generally well received.

'I really enjoyed the jungle experience,' said Christie with a smile. 'I'm not really a reality TV type of person, I'm really very private, so for me to do it was a big thing. They had been asking me for years. In the end my kids pushed me into it so they could have a laugh at Dad. My eldest daughter Briannah said the rules were I wasn't to drop out of anything and I wasn't to embarrass her. So with those rules behind me I went along.'

He was less fortunate with another British TV game show, the third series of Channel 4's winter games special *The Jump*, in which he became the fifth celebrity to get injured and was forced to pull out in early 2016. Undeterred, he then signed up for another reality TV show in 2019, Channel 4's *Sink Or Swim*, which aimed to raise funds for the Stand Up To Cancer campaign. Linford had been a poor swimmer as a child but bravely joined a relay team that included British Olympic gold medal winners Tessa Sanderson and Greg Rutherford, training to take on the hazardous swim across the English Channel. Unfortunately, bad weather halted their attempt just five miles from the French coast – with Christie saying he felt he'd gone a round in the ring with Mike Tyson – but the team still helped the campaign raise millions for cancer charities.

He continues to coach at Brunel University in north-west London and predicts his long-standing British 100 metres record of 9.87, set back in 1993 when he won the world title, will soon be broken by one of the new generation of British sprinting stars.

'We want to try and be up there with the Americans,' he says. 'That's what I'm looking for – I'm trying to look for the next guy who is going to come up and help keep British sprinting on the map.'Christie's legacy is more difficult to forecast. As Britain's most decorated athlete he clearly ought to have a more elevated position in the sport, but circumstances seem to have militated against that. Perhaps only time will bring his extraordinary achievements on the track back into sharper focus – when the personal feuds, rows and recriminations are long forgotten.

Until then Christie is happy to continue doing things his way and looks back on his career with enormous pride. 'There are so many sports and so many people. Ours was one of the few where you could say you were the best in the world. You can't say you're the best doctor or the best surgeon, but you can say you're the fastest man in the world.

'When I'm gone I would like people to remember me,' he laughs. 'I'd like them to think the only thing I couldn't beat was death. But I outran everything else!'

CHAPTER TWENTY

Atlanta 1996

Donovan Bailey

At just 23 years old Donovan Bailey seemed to have it all. A self-made man with an array of successful businesses in marketing, finance, property, import/export and clothing, he drove a Porsche convertible and owned an impressive house in a smart, lakeside Toronto suburb.

Bailey had graduated from college with an economics degree, and although he was always a big sports fan, playing basketball and running modestly in track at school, it had never entered his head to earn his living as a sportsman. But this was 1991. Canada was still reeling from the Ben Johnson scandal and the country needed a hero.

Much to the amusement of his disbelieving friends, Bailey the entrepreneur made a snap, but life-changing decision. Even with all his businesses booming, he would step back from his wheeler-dealing lifestyle, dust off his running shoes and get back out on the track.

'I had done very well, but I was stuck in the office all the time and I really needed to get out,' recalls Bailey. 'It was starting to get detrimental to my mental health. I needed to travel, I needed to be stimulated, and then one day when I was feeling a little burned out, I was watching TV and saw some of my old high school friends winning titles in the Canadian championships. I thought, I can beat those guys without even training, because I never trained in high school. People said I was an idiot, but I knew I could smash them.'

Self-confidence was seldom an issue for Bailey, and a strong ethic of hard work, personal discipline and thrusting ambition had been instilled in him from an early age. Born in Manchester, Jamaica, in December 1967, one of five boys sharing a single bedroom, he got up at dawn every day to feed the family's goats, chickens and pigs before heading off to school.

'I realized I was fast as an eight-year-old, competing in races in middle school, winning trophies, certificates and ribbons,' says Bailey. 'But because I was only beating my classmates, I didn't know just how gifted I was. I didn't know that until I eventually turned professional.'

He loved sport, but the overriding need for academic success was drilled into him every day by his parents. They also decided the family's future prosperity would benefit from a new location, so they upped sticks and emigrated to Toronto, in Canada, when young Donovan was just 13.

Bailey attended Queen Elizabeth Park High School and excelled on the track and the basketball court. He told *Sports Illustrated*: 'I could have left high school and run track right away, but that wasn't what I wanted. I wanted a nice house, money and fast cars. I was taught to work real hard and to work on my own.'

A smart and articulate young man, he was driven by these goals towards a business career, via economics studies, but he still found time at Toronto's Sheridan College to play forward for a season on the basketball team. After college his financial acumen went into overdrive and he seemed set on a life in the business fast lane, until that moment when the call of the track proved too much.

He started to train seriously in 1991, and in his first year he made the Canadian sprint team for the Pan American Games, in Cuba, winning a silver medal in the relay. But through that year and 1992 his personal best for the 100 stayed locked on a relatively sedate 10.42, and the Canadian athletics bosses overlooked him for the World Championships and the Barcelona Olympics.

An early success came in January 1992, at the Ottawa Winternational Indoor Games, where he took second place to the USA's Boris Goins in the 50 metres in a virtual dead heat at 5.78 seconds. It was the first and last time he lined up alongside the disgraced but returning Canadian sprinter Ben Johnson, who finished dead last.

Bailey continued to make slow progress into 1993, and although he made the Canadian team as a reserve for the World Athletics Championships, in Stuttgart, he was forced to sit on the sidelines, frustrated, while Canada won a bronze medal in the sprint relay, behind Great Britain and the USA. In the heat, semi and final, the Canadians used the same four sprinters and Bailey didn't get a look in.

Nevertheless, Stuttgart heralded a very important turning point for Bailey and his dreams of a stellar track career. It was there that he met the coach who would help turn his natural talent into tangible reward. American Dan Pfaff, who is now head coach at an elite track and field training centre in Phoenix, Arizona, had been enjoying huge success coaching athletics teams at Louisiana State University and saw something in Bailey's passion and drive. But he also told him: 'I never saw anyone run so fast who looked so bad.'

Pfaff recalls: 'He had run well enough to be selected for the relay pool, and I was coaching Glenroy Gilbert who was running second leg. We were having a relay workout and Donovan was whingeing about not being on the team. It was getting disruptive and I asked him to take his garbage elsewhere. He got a bit ruffled and after practice he laid out his anger and frustration. I said, if you think you've got what it takes you're welcome to come down to LSU and do a training stint and we'll see if you really have it.'

Three months after Pfaff invited Bailey down to train with him in Baton Rouge, he finally arrived to show what he could do. 'Every month he'd call and say he was coming,' said Pfaff, 'and I thought, here's a guy that's not serious. He was basically a basketball player – that was his love then and still is now – whose ego convinced him he could sprint.'

At just over six feet tall and around 180 pounds, Bailey was built like a light-heavyweight boxer and, as Pfaff recalls, the trial didn't start well. 'The first thing we concentrated on, biomechanically, was for him to learn how to walk correctly, then jog, in a straight line, with proper balance, with his joints working in the right order, and with the appropriate posture. It was a lot like setting up a Formula 1 race car.'

Pfaff was also coaching the powerful Bahamian javelin thrower Laverne Eve, and he asked her to show Bailey how to lift weights. He left them together and said he'd be back at the end of the session to check out how he'd got on.

'When I got back I found him sitting outside the gym and he told me he wasn't going to do that any more,' Pfaff explains. 'I asked why and he said that she had added so many weights – then lifted them – but he couldn't move them off the floor. I told him he either left right then or went straight back in and figured it out. He went back and figured it out.'

From early 1994 his scientific programme of sprinting, weights and diet began to bear fruit, with Bailey's 100-metre time dropping from an altitude-assisted 10.36 to a sea-level 10.03 seconds in just three months.

'Dan was just a blessing in disguise,' said Bailey. 'I remember the first day, he asked me, "Do you lift weights?" and I said no. Then he asked me, "Do you train?" and I said no. And then he asked, "Do you party all night?" and I said, well, yes.'

But the speed of his progress changed Bailey's attitude to training, and also caused him to revise his opinion on what he might be capable of achieving, something which had been soured by several years of disappointment, injury and stasis.

'He was a big over-strider and had suffered a lot of hamstring injuries because of that, so he tended to over-compensate,' explains Pfaff. 'In addition, as a young kid he had fallen out of a tree and fractured his sacrum [the large bone at the base of the spine], and that's why he always ran with a bit of a hitch and we could never quite clear that up. He was a walking injury when he came to us.'

But the improvement began quickly and in early 1994, after only a couple of months' training, Pfaff recalls watching him run at the Texas Relays and recording an impressive 10.12 into a rainy headwind. His new personal best of 10.03 seconds came in his first major track win, at a meeting in Duisburg, Germany, in June, where American 200-metre specialist Michael Johnson finished seventh. It would be the start of a lasting 'fastest man' rivalry.

But a genuinely defining moment in the Donovan Bailey story happened in Rome a week later in a race in which he finished fourth. 'It was the race where I first recognized that I belonged,' says Bailey. 'My first kick at the big show. All the big guys were there, Carl Lewis, Leroy Burrell, Linford Christie, Frankie Fredericks, and I was winning at 80 metres. But I had such respect for these guys, I had to look for them. In a split second they were past me. But I understood the mistake I'd made and vowed I'd never lose to them again.'

A month later, as if to prove the seemingly random nature of sprinting form, American Leroy Burrell produced a stunning run in Lausanne to break the 100 metres world record for a second time, nipping a hundredth off Carl Lewis's world championship winning time in Tokyo to lower the mark to 9.85.

But Bailey was determined not to get left behind. By the spring of 1995 he was running even better, and in the first outdoor meet of the season, an LSU invitational, he ducked under 10 seconds for the first time with a 9.99. 'After that race,' he recalled, 'I thought I could crush these guys, it was really awesome. I felt I had a loaded AK-47. After that I knew no one could touch me. There had been a lot of glimmers of great things in '94, but at that race in Baton Rouge, it just all came together.'

One of the key reasons for his improving form and surging confidence was that Pfaff had managed to completely rebuild his starting technique, something that had been a consistent problem.

The coach recalled: 'He had starts that were OK at times. But we wanted him to make a start that would set him up to run better later in the race and not rush the rate of acceleration. We wanted him to reach his maximum velocity at 50–70 metres, so we set up a start schematic to get us there.'

The result was a decent tour of the European summer circuit, with wins at Lausanne and Crystal Palace, but the best was to come on home soil, when he shattered the Canadian record at the national championships, in Montreal, with a 9.91 – the fastest time in the world that year. With Surin second in 9.97, it was the first time two non-US sprinters had run under 10 seconds in the same race.

The run made him one of the favourites for the World Championships in Gothenburg, Sweden, and the media immediately began to promote Bailey and Surin, not only as favourites, but also as the men who could restore Canada's damaged reputation after the national embarrassment of Ben Johnson. It would become a recurring theme.

Bailey told *The New York Times* that he'd been tested for drugs nearly 20 times during the year under the new no-notice programme instituted in Canada. 'I think we can change the public perception that anyone in the world who runs fast is on something,' he said. 'I don't go out of my way to say I'm clean, but it's important.'

Sometimes the testing got out of hand. On one occasion in Norway he was targeted, unusually, at Oslo airport as he was en route to the famous Bislett meeting. Perhaps unnerved by the incident and a false start, Bailey didn't even make the final. Coach Pfaff observed: 'I'm all for drug testing, but where does credibility and the right thing stop and harassment start?'

But all that was forgotten in Sweden, and after an impressive season he delivered in style, winning the final in 9.97, with his team-mate Bruny Surin second in 10.03. Gold and silver to Canada, but to Bailey's intense annoyance, the Canadian press still seemed intent on continuing the national hand-wringing over Ben Johnson rather than hailing the coming of a new hero.

The American press were a little more objective, with the *Chicago Sun-Times* summarizing the situation perfectly. 'Like Johnson, Bailey was born in Jamaica and is big, strong and muscular. But unlike Johnson, Bailey is personable and outgoing. And Bailey wants nothing to do with Johnson.'

'We don't answer questions about Ben Johnson,' Bailey told the post-event press conference. 'Bruny wasn't running when Ben Johnson was running and neither was I.' He gave it to them straight.

Bailey, Surin and the rest of the Canadian sprint team then added further lustre to the national fervour and deepening American gloom by winning gold in the relay, with the US team failing to make it out of the heats.

As usual, the athletes then took off on a whistle-stop European tour, where reigning Olympic champion Linford Christie, making a remarkable recovery from a hamstring injury sustained in the Gothenburg final, beat Bailey in Zurich, Brussels and Crystal Palace. Bailey's only revenge was a photo finish victory in Berlin that deprived Christie of a share in the lucrative prize pot for winning the Golden Four European track events.

A frustrated Coach Pfaff recalled: 'There were only about ten times in his career that he was motivated to run. Gothenburg was one and I can clearly count them. There were injuries and illnesses, but a lot of times he went down the track just to pick up the cheque. It was rare for him to be motivated. I remember he was running in Germany, I had to pull a rabbit out of the hat, so I told him that in all the years I'd been coaching I'd never had an athlete win in Germany. My ancestors are German and I said it would be great to say I coached an athlete that won a meet in Germany. He said, "You got it," then ran an amazing race of 10.02 into rain and wind. He just needed weird motivations to run.'

Despite little training, the Olympic year 1996 opened positively, with Bailey taking the Canadian 50-metre indoor record, in Hamilton, and then launching into the year's mind games with Christie, accusing him of faking his injury in Gothenburg.

Christie had finished sixth in the world final, crashing to the track and clutching his right hamstring. Bailey poured scorn on the injury, suggesting it took a couple of weeks to recover from such an injury and Christie had beaten him a few days later in Zurich.

Christie kept quiet, but his agent Sue Barrett said: 'There is no secret to what happened with Linford. He was injured in the final, and he went away the next day to get excellent treatment to which he responded very well.'

Bailey rounded off a successful indoor season by winning the Millrose Games 60 metres at Madison Square Garden and then breaking the 23-year-old world record at 50 metres, in 5.56, at the Reno Air Indoor Games. It was only February, but Bailey was already flying.

He comfortably won his first outdoor event in Brazil, and then paid an early visit to the new Olympic stadium in Atlanta, where he was soundly beaten by Dennis Mitchell in 9.93 and a 34-year-old Carl Lewis, who ran a 9.94, his best race for five years. Bailey came in third in what he called a 'pathetic' 9.97.

June saw some impressive 100-metre times from all over the world. First out of the blocks was Ato Boldon, winning the NCAA title, in Oregon in his last collegiate race for UCLA, with a stunning 9.92. Linford Christie, now 36 years old, confirmed his credentials by beating Bailey in Nuremburg, but the Canadian then ran a timely 9.98 a few days later in Germany. All of which warmed him up for the Canadian Olympic trials just over a week later, where he won the 100 metres in 9.98, beating Surin and training partner Glenroy Gilbert.

The US Olympic trials were also held in June, at the new stadium in Atlanta, with searing temperatures soaring into the nineties and cooling machines hired to sit on the infield. The heat and stifling humidity proved too much for some athletes, but Dennis Mitchell made light of the conditions and steamed to a comfortable win in 9.92, ahead of Mike Marsh and Jon Drummond. It was the end of the road for Carl Lewis, who had a terrible start and finished last, while his training partner and world record holder Leroy Burrell came home sixth. It would be Mitchell, Marsh and Drummond who would do battle with Bailey on the same track just a few months later.

But the muscle-flexing wasn't over just yet and Namibia's Frankie Fredericks, generally considered a better 200-metre runner, astounded the track world by running a 9.87 in Helsinki to claim the fastest 100 metres in the world for the year, with Bailey trailing in a disappointing third. Fredericks then cemented his decision to run both the 100 and 200 by lowering that time again, beating a top-class field in Lausanne with 9.86, with Bailey second in 9.93, and Boldon, Drummond and Christie behind him.

But Bailey arrived in Atlanta concealing a big secret. At the last major European meeting before the Games, in Nice, Bailey chased down Linford Christie to win an exciting race in a photo finish with both athletes clocking 10.17 seconds. 'Linford's Lost It!' screamed the unhelpful headline in the *Daily Mirror*, but the real story was that in desperately pushing to overhaul Christie on the line, Bailey had over-extended his stride and torn three adductor muscles.

Bailey recalls: 'Even when we were flying back from Europe on the plane I was getting treated, which was a strange sight for the rest of the passengers. And for four of five days after I got back from France I couldn't physically run down a track. Dan told me he really didn't know if I could compete, but I told him I was going out there even if they had to glue the muscles together. But I knew I had to be careful and if I was guilty of over-striding again then my Olympics would be over.'

Pfaff remembers: 'For the two weeks prior to the Olympics it was 24 hours a day therapy, acupuncture and bike riding. It was a mad house. The first time he really put his foot on a track was when we flew into Atlanta.

'In hindsight I think the injury might have allowed him to win, because we told him he had to control the injury. One bad step and he was out of the game. He had to run vigilantly and drive through the rounds with the parking brake on. Once he got to the final he could let go. Did it conserve vital energy and increase mechanical efficiency? Yes.'

So the scene was set for the Games of the XXVI Olympiad, in Atlanta, Georgia, where a record 197 countries would take part and sporting giant Muhammad Ali set the world's hearts racing by lighting the Olympic flame.

The first-day heats saw all the usual suspects through comfortably, with Trinidad & Tobago's 22-year-old Ato Boldon running an impressive 9.95 in the second round, only to see Frankie Fredericks drop that to 9.93. Bailey cantered in second to Linford Christie in his second-round heat and went back to the village to prepare for the biggest day of his life.

While all was calm in the Bailey world, outside in Centennial Park a man was planting a 40-pound nail bomb at the base of a sound tower at a music concert in what was the 'town square' of the Olympics. It detonated in the early hours, killing two people and injuring more than a hundred, prompting President Bill Clinton to declare it an 'evil act of terror'.

It turned out to be an overt but warped plan to force the cancellation of the Games by ex-US Army junior Eric Rudolph, who had been responsible for a spate of bombings across the southern states, apparently in protest at the availability of abortion on demand. The 'Olympic Park Bomber', as he became known, was finally captured by the FBI in 2003 and was sentenced to spend the rest of his life in a maximum-security prison.

Bailey remembers: 'I woke up really fresh on the morning of the semis and the final. I slept nine hours straight. I came down to breakfast and Dan told me there had been a bombing. At first I thought it was another one of his motivational tools, but I watched the TV and saw what had happened. I wondered what they were going to do. There was a lot of talk about cancelling the Games, but in the end the competition continued.'

So, with the world still reeling from the shock of the bombing, the sharp end of the track competition began. 'They escorted us all to the stadium,' says Bailey, 'and for me it was just another day of business. I focused hard on trying to relax, but at the same time maintain a race-day intensity.'

The semis went to the form of the competition so far, with Fredericks winning the first in 9.94, with Bailey second in 10 flat, America's Mike Marsh third and Jamaica's Michael Green fourth. In the second semi, Boldon pulled out a 9.93, ahead of America's Dennis Mitchell, Christie and Nigeria's Davidson Ezinwa.

These were the eight fast men who would contest the 1996 Olympic 100 metres final in a few hours' time, but for Bailey there was only one person he wanted to impress. His father George had come to Atlanta, having never previously seen his son run at any level.

'My parents were not that interested in sports,' Bailey recalls. 'They always wanted me to focus on my academic work and my business career. So the first time my father ever saw me run was the 100 metres final at the Olympic Games. He was so mad at me when I left business to go into track, so I had to prove that I did make the right decision. It was a real father-son bonding moment.'

The noisy 83,000 crowd began to hush as the eight men went to the blocks, but the deafening roar as the gun went off was short-lived. Christie had clearly false-started, and back they went to the blocks. At the second attempt it was Ato Boldon who jumped out a little early, but the third attempt looked clean.

Then the recall gun sounded again, prompting huge shouts of frustration from the athletes and the crowd. Sensationally, it was the defending Olympic champion again and, as Christie looked on in disbelief, the official held up a second yellow card to signify his infringement. He walked over to the judges' table and started to argue about the decision. He then went back to his lane and took his position as if to start the race again.

Meanwhile, the rest of the field paced nervously up and down the track, waiting for the panicked American officials to make a call. Eventually the track referee, John Chaplin, emerged from the tunnel, pulled a red card out of the pocket of his green jacket, and Christie stalked off, shaking his head in disgust, but insisting on watching the race from the sidelines.

'I asked him to leave,' Chaplin said. 'He said, "Fine," and left.' Christie then came through the tunnel, picked up the plastic crate that held his warm-ups and departed without comment. Later, he issued a brief remark: 'I smile now, but inside I am hurt.'

Later on he told the British press: 'I'm sorry for the people of Britain. I feel I have let them down. I went with the gun and I've been told the reaction was 0.089 seconds.

Others have got away with that. There were cameras flashing everywhere. It was mayhem. How can you expect people to concentrate in a situation like that?'

So, with an empty lane two, the athletes were called for the fourth time, and this time they got away cleanly – except that Bailey was left for dead, the last out of his blocks and trailing the whole field. But with an extraordinary burst of acceleration he'd caught up at 30 metres, and by 70 he had passed everyone, screaming through the line in an astonishing new world record of 9.84 seconds, with Fredericks narrowly squeezing out Boldon for the silver.

The now famous pictures of Bailey, his face angled right and eyes wide, yelling towards the stands as he eases down around the bend became one of the iconic moments of the Games. Donovan Bailey, at 28, had made history in the most exhilarating fashion, and he grabbed the customary Canadian flag from the crowd to complete a well-earned lap of honour.

'Despite all the kerfuffle with the false starts I still felt really relaxed,' remembers Bailey. 'I was just totally at ease with myself. I had a terrible first 30 metres, but by then I knew I'd won. The last 30 metres were poor too. I could have transitioned faster and I really believe I could have picked up another tenth of a second.'

In the post-event press conference, he told reporters: 'I wasn't thinking world records. Any time I've gone into a race thinking about times, I've always screwed up.'

The subject, naturally, moved to Ben Johnson. 'I'm not trying to undo what Ben did in Seoul,' he said. 'My name is Donovan Bailey. What happened is history. Because it was a huge story, it's always going to come up.'

Looking back today, Bailey recalls: 'I really didn't want to answer any questions about Johnson. We're both Canadian, we both came from Jamaica, so some people still connect him with me, but they are people with no knowledge of track and field. Because of what he did, Ben Johnson still financially disadvantages young sprinters today, just for being mentioned.'

As for the world record, Bailey didn't actually realize he'd broken it until the time came up on the scoreboard. Then, a few days later, there was another golden moment for him in Atlanta, with the sprint relay. Canadian sports fans couldn't quite believe their eyes as their quartet of Robert Esmie, Glenroy Gilbert, Surin and Bailey gave an exhibition of relay running to beat the US squad by nearly half a second in 37.69 seconds.

Gilbert is now head coach of Athletics Canada, while Esmie is known as 'Doctor Speed' and heads an elite speed training business in Sudbury, Ontario. Bruny Surin became a hugely successful entrepreneur, business coach and motivational speaker.

Bailey left Atlanta with two gold medals in his pocket, but within a few days his statutory position as the world's fastest man had been challenged by America's Michael Johnson, who destroyed the 200-metre world record in 19.32 after first winning the 400-metre title. It would further fuel the rivalry between the two and initiate plans to get them together on a track to settle the issue once and for all.

Bailey told journalists: 'The fastest man in the world has always been determined by the 100 and I don't think history is going to change in 1996.'

The track world licked its lips at the thought of a truly heavyweight confrontation – Bailey versus Johnson, both 29 years old, for the undisputed title of 'Fastest Man on Earth'. To ensure fairness, the battle would be conducted over a curved track of 150 metres, constructed to simulate lanes 3 and 4 from Atlanta, and the race organizers went to work building up the biggest grudge match in track history.

To add extra spice to the event, which would take place in Bailey's home town, in the Toronto Skydome, in June 1997, the promoters offered each athlete $500,000 just to take part and a $1 million bonus to the winner.

In a strange, but riveting live conference-call media interview with both athletes, Bailey re-ignited an old argument about the lack of respect accorded to non-American athletes in Atlanta.

In front of the rapt media, he told Johnson: 'If there was going to be a 'Fastest Man in the World' title then I would be participating with Ato, Frankie, Linford and those guys. You wouldn't be part of the race. You're not ranked in the top 10 in the US in the 100 metres. At 23 miles per hour (the fastest speed Johnson ever reached) you might go out in the quarter-finals of the Olympic 100 metres.'

Johnson replied: 'So now gold, silver and bronze Olympic medals are being given out based on how many miles an hour you run?'

'That's what speed is about, Michael. Fastest speed,' said Bailey.

Johnson ran down Bailey's Atlanta achievement. 'You didn't make any history. I'm sorry to disappoint you.'

'You'll have your chance', said Bailey.

The promoters rubbed their hands in glee. It wasn't exactly Ali-Frazier, but it got plenty of column inches across the world, and with American network CBS and Eurosport acquiring the rights for 'The Challenge of Champions' or, as the media translated it, 'The Dash for Cash', the whole project seemed to be heating up nicely.

On the day it turned into something of a non-event, with Johnson pulling up lame and grabbing his left thigh about halfway around the curve, coincidentally just as Bailey appeared to be pulling away from him. Bailey won, pocketed an extra million dollars and a priceless set of bragging rights. But the rivalry didn't end there.

'He didn't pull up. He's a coward,' Bailey told reporters. Johnson dismissed his claim, saying he felt his leg cramping: 'That shows you what kind of person he is and to show you what kind of person I am, I'm not going to comment.'

It was a genuinely oddball event, watched by a crowd of just over 25,000, which was significantly below expectations, and although the time hardly mattered they saw Bailey clock 14.99 seconds for the distance. Taking their lead from the booing and hissing of the partisan Toronto crowd, the Canadian press warmed to the theme of Michael Johnson as pantomime villain.

'BAILEY FOR PRIME MINISTER' screamed the banner headline of the *Toronto Sun*, but their jingoistic pride about sticking a thumb in Uncle Sam's eye was better revealed with the second headline: 'Oakville Sprinter Crushes Lame Yank.'

A few days after the race, Bailey was mortified at some of the things he'd said in TV interviews and offered an apology to Johnson. 'I think I just got caught up in the whole race thing,' he said at the time.

There's certainly a hint of regret as Bailey looks back now on the biggest match race in track history. 'There was a lot of talking, but it was nothing personal. I have a lot of respect for Michael. The American press whipped it up. I don't think they liked the idea of me running away with the top sprint prizes in Atlanta and taking them back to Canada.

'For me it was simply a significant economic opportunity, and the fans got to see the two biggest stars in track and field go head to head. I really trained hard for that race; I don't think I ever prepared for a race as well as that. I was so focused on winning I really think I let the World Championships go that year.'

'I understood the finances, but it was a stupid race,' said Coach Pfaff. 'If Donovan was healthy there was no way MJ could run with him. Donovan ran repeat 150s in training, it was a big part of his programme and he could run those very well. He had run a 9.84 100 compared to a guy whose PB was 10.12 or something, so it was never going to be much of a race.'

As the dust settled on the Toronto shoot-out, minds began to focus on August and those World Championships in Athens. Michael Johnson's injury turned out to be serious enough to rule him out of the national championships, and it also caused him to lose his first 400-metre race in eight years and to have to sweat on a wild card invitation from the IAAF for defending champions to take part in Greece.

Meanwhile, Bailey churned through the gears around the European circuits, winning in Germany and France, and even took part in another 'winner take all' event, this time in England, beating Linford Christie over 150 metres, in Sheffield, and walking off with £50,000.

So Bailey went into the sixth World Athletics Championships in the summer heat of Athens as favourite to retain his 100-metre crown, despite the emergence of a new sprinting talent, the fast-talking Kansas cannonball Maurice Greene, who had won the US trials with a superb 9.90 and beaten Bailey in Lausanne a month earlier. The American's stunning form continued, and it was Greene who prevailed, equalling the championship record with an impressive 9.86, with Bailey second in 9.91 and American Tim Montgomery third in 9.94.

Bailey salvaged some national pride with another relay gold, after the heavily tipped American quartet of Brian Lewis, Montgomery, Mitchell and Greene crashed out in the very first heat of the first round after another all-too-common fumbled baton change.

Bailey hit the European circuit straight after Athens and helped mark the final track appearance of Carl Lewis in front of sixty thousand fans in Berlin, where he was lead-off man for a winning 'dream team' relay squad, alongside Leroy Burrell, Frankie Fredericks and anchor man Lewis himself. His final race of the season was a September defeat to Fredericks in Tokyo.

'In '97 he was tired, said Pfaff. 'He'd had the build-up in '94, the world champs in '95, a world record and the Olympics in '96, then the pressure from sponsors, and the stupid match race with MJ, and all that drained him. He was really ill in '97 in Athens. It's not an excuse, but he was. He made everyone around him miserable. I left Athens straight after the 100 and told him he had to find another coach.'

So, with the 1997 season over, Bailey returned to Toronto to consider his plans for the next campaign. But it was a season that nearly didn't happen at all after a terrifying brush with death.

In the early hours of a freezing late October morning, driving home from a friend's house in his powerful Mercedes, he hit a patch of black ice. His car skidded out of control, hit a power pole, flipped into the air, rolled three times, landed on its roof and burst into flames. Bailey managed to crawl out and was picked up by a passing motorist. Miraculously, he suffered only a separated shoulder and a police charge of careless driving.

Bailey believes his sprint training saved him from more serious injury. He recalled: 'I saw the pole coming and what I did was, I tried to stay relaxed as much as possible. You always hear about people when they tense, they brace themselves in these accidents and it leaves a lot of trauma to their bodies. So what I did was basically become fluid and rolled with it. I just ended up with a busted left shoulder.'

Bailey embarked on a lengthy and money-spinning global sprint tour through 1998, which started in Melbourne, Australia, in February, where he was beaten by Maurice Greene, and stopped off in Rio de Janeiro, Qatar, Montreal, New York and ended abruptly in Zurich. The highlights were trademark Bailey wins in Doha, Barcelona and Paris, but his best time of the year – a 9.93 – came running second to Bruny Surin in the Canadian nationals in Montreal.

After a disastrous appearance at New York's Goodwill Games, where he virtually trotted over the line in seventh, he looked back to form in Monte Carlo, where he almost ran down Ato Boldon in 9.96. But his next race would be his last for the year, when he pulled up halfway through the Zurich Weltklasse meeting with yet another hamstring problem. Back home in Toronto, he was well on the road to recovery when bad luck struck again.

The beginning of the end for Bailey's fabulous track career came in unusual circumstances, when he ruptured his left Achilles tendon running backwards in a friendly game of pick-up basketball. The injury was a bad one. The Achilles had rolled up like a ball at the bottom of his calf muscle and the rupture had been both up and across the tendon. To make matters worse there was collateral nerve damage too. The surgery was complicated and the rehabilitation long and painful.

Coach Pfaff, who had returned to coach the Canadian star, explained: 'It was like being a paralysis patient from a car wreck. He had to learn to stand again, walk again, move every muscle again, a total neuro-muscular re-education project.'

The obvious decision was to call time on his sprinting career, but Bailey said it took him only the five-minute journey from the basketball court to the hospital to rule that out as an option. 'It's not about fame or money. It's because it's never been done and people say it can't be done,' he told one journalist.

So Bailey began the long climb back to fitness, describing it as driving a fast car with one foot on the accelerator and the other on the brake. He struggled through 1999 and at the end of the year was ranked outside the world's top 50 sprinters. To make matters worse, that summer Maurice Greene had smashed his world record with a 9.79 run in Athens, and team-mate Bruny Surin had equalled his Canadian record of 9.84.

Although he finished third in the Canadian trials in June, he didn't line up in the 100 metres at the 1999 World Championships in Spain. He did take the lead-off spot on the Canadian relay team, the defending champions, but they failed to emerge from the first heat after being disqualified.

The rest of the season was a disappointing plod around the European circuits – finishing behind athletes he'd beaten routinely just a few years earlier – but, at 32, Bailey still hankered after another crack at the Olympics and the chance to defend his title. In the spring of 2000 he started running some low-key events in the Caribbean, even running a decent 10.03 in Martinique, but he never looked consistent or entirely comfortable.

The real highlight was a stunning return to form at the big Lucerne meeting, in Switzerland, on a balmy June evening, when he won with a storming 9.98. It remains one of the high points of his career. 'There would be three great races I'll always remember,' he recalls. 'The 100 in Rome, where I first knew I had what it takes; obviously the Olympic final in Atlanta; and that race in Switzerland. It came after the Achilles injury and I was just so worried that it would snap.'

Bailey's erratic form, hampered by a partial hamstring tear, continued in the run-up to Sydney, in the course of which he rolled in last in Brussels and Gateshead, sixth in Berlin and finally won, albeit in a modest 10.26, in a pre-Olympic meet in Runaway Bay, Australia, a few weeks before the Games began.

All this made it very difficult to predict how Bailey would fare at the Sydney Olympics. Unhappily he slid quietly out of contention on the first day of competition, just making it through the first round with a third-placed 10.39 and then, in his second-round heat, trotting forlornly over the line in last place with a time of 11.36. It was a sad way for the Olympic champion to bow out.

Coach Pfaff recalled: 'The medical people did an amazing job just to get him back to running sub-10 seconds. But once you'd been at the pinnacle, we were now going through hours of prep just to run a single meet. The wheels were coming off. There was one last huge push for Sydney, but then he got a huge viral infection on his first week on the ground in Australia and that was that.'

In early 2001 the sport's respected *Track & Field News* voted him the sprinter of the decade, and in May he announced he would retire at the end of the season after a lucrative and valedictory tour of Europe and, hopefully, a last hurrah at the World Athletics Championships, which would be held in Edmonton, Canada, in August.

He opened his final outdoor season with a promising 10.13 win at the Texas Invitational meeting, in Austin, before heading to Europe. But his times continued to spin backwards as he struggled with fitness and form. It was something of a surprise that he won the Canadian trials, in June, albeit in a slow 10.24, so little was expected of him at the World Championships a few months later.

In Edmonton, the road finally ended for Bailey, and after struggling through the first round and posting his best time of the year, 10.11, in the quarter-finals, he went out in a semi, won by Maurice Greene, with a disappointing 10.33. He had desperately wanted to reach the final and bow out at the highest level in front of his home fans, but it was not to be.

Cheered and applauded loudly all around the stadium, he grabbed a Canadian flag for a final lap of honour as the fans gave him a lengthy standing ovation.

'I didn't really want it to end up with me not winning or not even advancing to the finals, he told reporters. 'I ran a pretty bad race today, but at the end of the day, I gave it all I had, and definitely it was my last race.

'The Canadian public has always given me respect and always given me support. I've done all I can. In all my years of hard work, that is really what I was working for. I did it every day. I ran proudly, cleanly and with the dignity of our country.'

It was fitting epitaph. At nearly 34 years old, Bailey retired from the track and returned to the financial and corporate world from where he'd originally emerged.

Coach Pfaff rates him among the ten best sprinters, despite the relatively short career he enjoyed. 'We were very close and still are relatively close. It was like a big brother relationship because the age differential wasn't that huge. There were times when I didn't enjoy it. He could be a moody cuss. There are about five Donovans that showed up. Two of them were tolerable and three of them you wanted to go and hide under a rock. All the great ones in sprinting are a bit of a diva.'

Today Bailey spends much of his time living between Jamaica and Toronto. Since his retirement, his businesses have continued to grow and Bailey Inc remains heavily involved in real estate, finance and media. He also set up the Donovan Bailey Fund to provide financial help for young amateur athletes in Canada, where he remains in huge demand as a powerful and persuasive public speaker.

He married his long-term girlfriend, British-born Michelle Mullin, in April 2004 and has two children, daughter Adrienna and son Alexander. The marriage ended in 2006, but Bailey claims to be 'happily divorced'.

In 2004 he was inducted in the Canada Sports Hall of Fame, and four years later he lined up with the Atlanta relay team to be inducted again, before leaving to work for the Canadian national broadcaster CBC at the Beijing Olympics. He continues to work as a commentator on major track events and in 2016 he was given membership of the Order of Ontario, the province's highest honour. A year later he was presented with a star on Canada's prestigious Walk of Fame. 'This is a gathering of the embodiment of success in Canada,' he said, 'I'm quite humbled.'

A couple of years ago Bailey's name was in the Canadian newspaper headlines again. This time the news was not so positive. It was reported that he had been investigated by the Canada Revenue Authority who accused him, and other prominent Canadians, of using offshore tax havens to dodge the tax man. Some $3.75m – his entire athlete's trust payments – had been invested by specialist tax lawyers.

In 2018, the *Toronto Star* and *The Vancouver Sun* reported that Bailey owed nearly $2.3m in unpaid taxes; however, the case was finally settled out of court, with a $750,000 settlement paid to the CRA by the company who constructed the original tax plan.

In a statement from his lawyers, which he issued on his twitter account, Bailey explained that, like a lot of high net worth individuals, he had invested in a tax plan in good faith and this had resulted in a significant tax liability. However, he was 'neither bankrupt nor destitute' and wanted to assure everyone that it was 'business as usual' and that he was writing his book and preparing a film about his life story.

However, his nation's highest honour, the Order of Canada, still eludes him and the omission has become something of a cause celebre. In the summer of 2020, a leader column in the *Toronto National Post* made a clarion call for his inclusion in its ranks, where he would join sports stars such as ice hockey's Mario Lemeieux and Wayne Gretsky; the NBA's Steve Nash and Olympic winners Catriona LeMay Doan, Marnie McBean and Curt Harnett. 'He has been forgotten or passed over year after year,' railed commentator Steve Robinson, who also pointed out that all the sporting recipients had, thus far, been white. 'Bailey happens to be black. You do the math.'

Looking back on his career, Bailey said: 'When I retired I felt I didn't want track and field to define me, I really wanted to get away from it all, so I went back into business. Perhaps I should have gone straight into the media, but now at least the business allows me the time to get involved again.

'I've not really been involved in the sport. We've been through a time when so many people were drug infested, with people turning up with no personality or a bad attitude. I was different because I could talk and I had no attitude.

'I had some great moments, some great partnerships and made some great friends.'

When his book finally arrives, it should be some read.

CHAPTER TWENTY-ONE

Sydney 2000

Maurice Greene

Will the real Maurice Greene please stand up? Is he the trash-talking motormouth who famously painted himself gold for a commercial, drove an unfeasibly flash sports car with the plates MO GOLD and had the tattoo G.O.A.T. – Greatest Of All Time – emblazoned on his right arm?

Or is he the sensitive soul who cried in the stands at the Atlanta Olympics because he failed to make the US track team, and then four years later, when he finally did make the team and fought his way all the way to the podium, was in floods of tears even before he heard a note of the Star-spangled Banner?

The reality, of course, is that the swaggering, self-styled Kansas City Cannonball is all of these things. And a good deal more besides.

'There are certainly two sides to me,' he says. 'On the track, I'm serious. But once I cross the line, OK, let's go have a party. You have to entertain the fans, give them what they want, and I wanted them to get a real sense of who I am.'

Greene arrived on the track scene in the mid-1990s with all the calm, tact and diplomacy of a cartoon Tasmanian Devil. He would go on to break world records, win Olympic gold and take multiple world titles. He would almost end his career in a bizarre motorcycle accident, become unwittingly embroiled in a major drug investigation and dance in front of tens of millions on network television. Dull, he wasn't. Dull, he isn't.

As a young athlete he strutted straight on to centre stage and told the world he was going to put American sprinting back on the map. Then he went out and did just that.

'Every morning in Africa a gazelle wakes up. It knows it must move faster than the lion or it will not survive. Every morning a lion wakes up and it knows it must move faster than the slowest gazelle or it will starve. It doesn't matter if you are the lion or the gazelle, when the sun comes up, you better be moving.' That was just one of the many lines from the Maurice Greene book of wit and wisdom that entertained fans and even enthralled a largely cynical media.

Welcome to the super-fast world of one of sport's great performers and one of the fastest men of all time. It began far away from the glare of Olympic glory and multi-million-dollar sporting superstardom, in the more tranquil waters of a Kansas City suburb, where he was born, the youngest of four children, in July 1974.

Even as a kid he could talk the talk. By the age of eight he followed his sister and three brothers on to the track. 'Being the baby, Maurice always said he was going to do it better,' recalled his mother Jackie. 'We encouraged all the kids in whatever they decided to do, to give it their all. We didn't let them quit. Whatever they chose, they had to finish it.'

By then he had already hooked up with local coach Al Hobson, a former US marine and General Motors car parts buyer. He became almost a second father to Maurice, who by the age of 10 would tell anyone who cared to listen that some day he would be the fastest man in the world. His father Ernest recalls: 'He was always confident and energetic. I told him to be careful his talking didn't overshadow his performance.'

Greene remembers: 'As a kid I had a lot of success growing up, and I would go to practices with my brother. My coach would make me run and tell my brother and the older guys to catch me and they never could. I was eight or nine and I thought, yeah, I'm pretty fast.'

While he was never going to win any academic awards at high school, Greene excelled in sports, playing football and winning the Kansas state track titles at 100, 200 and 400 metres for three straight years.

He saw his brother Ernest Junior make the semi-finals of the 1992 US Olympic trials, but Maurice's rapid progress on the track and less than stellar grades at school convinced his parents and coach to forgo college and begin training professionally and privately at Hobson's Kansas City Chargers track club. A poor ACT (American College Testing) score had deterred the usual college recruiters, but the educational foundation set up by the late owner of the Kansas City Royals baseball team, Ewing Kaufmann, handed him a scholarship to community college for two years while he trained.

Hobson later explained to *USA Today*: 'I'm a guy who stresses education. But colleges can't always provide personal attention on the track. We could work every day on mechanics and technique. We weren't pushed to run relays or score points for the team.'

Greene knows how much he owes to Hobson. 'If it wasn't for him I wouldn't have done any of the things I've done,' he recalls. 'He was the one that taught me about hard work and technique. Without him there would be no me. '

Greene odd-jobbed around Kansas City to earn money, working at everything from sweeping up at fast food restaurants to clipping cinema tickets and walking greyhounds at the local track. 'My parents were not wealthy, so they told me if I wanted something I had to go to work to get it myself. So I had a lot of jobs because I always wanted something!'

All the while he trained, grew stronger and waited impatiently for the big breakthrough.

There were signs of the things to come when he took a creditable fourth spot in the 1995 World Indoor Championships 60 metres in Barcelona, but the real explosion happened at the Texas Relays in Austin a few months before his twenty-first birthday, when Greene not only beat his idol, the legendary Carl Lewis, over 100 metres, but posted an astonishing, albeit wind-assisted, time of 9.88 seconds.

'Unknown Shocks Lewis in Sprint at Texas Relays,' screamed the headline in the *Washington Post*, while Greene explained: 'I tried to treat this race like it was any other. But any time you run against Carl Lewis, it is a pleasure. I think everybody thought Carl would win the race, but I knew I was just as capable.'

Soon after that he took second place in the US Track and Field Championships in Sacramento, California, in an extraordinary blanket finish with Mike Marsh and Dennis Mitchell, where only careful study of the photo finish picture could separate them and all three were given the same time of 10.23 seconds. Maurice Greene had arrived.

His first major international event would be representing the USA at the 1995 World Athletics Championships, in Sweden, but in a second-round heat he was caught napping in the blocks and eliminated, finishing a disappointing sixth in 10.35. Further disappointment came in the relay heats, where Greene ran a storming lead leg but then watched in horror as the injury-hit squad mishandled the next baton change and were disqualified.

Back home in the USA, Greene continued to progress, and he was among the favourites to qualify for the US team at the home Olympics in Atlanta the following year. However, a hamstring injury in the spring of 1996 came at precisely the wrong time and he laboured through the competition, finally crashing out in the second round of the Olympic trials.

'I was devastated,' Greene recalled. 'I ran a personal record in the first round at 10.08 seconds, but I couldn't duplicate it. It was the worst moment of my life. I remember sitting up in the stand and crying. I couldn't come to terms with it. I was handicapped by a pre-season injury, but this wasn't the standard I had set myself. I thought about quitting the sport, in fact I thought about it very seriously. But deep down I didn't want to quit. I'd come a long way and I enjoyed being a fighter.'

He watched the Atlanta Olympics from the stands and admitted to tears during the 100-metre competition, vowing that the event would not happen again without him being involved. But the experience forced Greene into a difficult but life-changing decision. He would leave the safety and familiarity of Kansas City and his long-time coach and 'father figure' Al Hobson, and move to Los Angeles to hook up with the globally renowned UCLA sprint coach John Smith.

'I felt for me I needed a change. I was good, but I wanted to be better. I wanted to be the best, so I felt I had to go somewhere else. Al was like a second father to me, I even stayed at his house for a while. But you have to do what is best for yourself. He was hurt, he didn't want me to leave, but he's always had my back, no matter what.

'I didn't only want to be the best, I wanted the Olympic gold medal, I wanted to be a world record holder and there was no coach out there who had coached more world record holders or gold medallists than John, so why would I go anywhere else?'

Former *Kansas City Star* journalist Mechelle Voepel, now an ESPN writer, recalls: 'That transition was very hard, especially for Al. He was a guardian angel figure in the city, a father figure too, to so many kids in track. He was worried about who would look after Maurice, and he certainly feared that he might become enmeshed in a win- at-all-costs culture.'

Greene and his father drove to LA in September 1996, and on their first day in the city they went out to the track at UCLA to wait for Smith to arrive. 'So you want to run fast?' Smith asked him. 'Yes, I do,' Greene said simply.

The Smith regime was a tough one, where relentless sprint repetitions and punishing workouts often left Greene vomiting on the trackside, but he would never give in. 'It was a school of hard knocks,' Greene recalls. 'It was very tough mentally and physically. I was doing new things and the people I was training with never gave me a break at all – not once. They were hard on me, but I kept asking for more. They had to tell me to stop working. John had to tell me to go home some days.'

Training partner Ato Boldon told *Sports Illustrated*: 'There were times when Maurice just stood all by himself out on the infield because he didn't want anybody to see him crying.' In the evening he would take Greene back to his house to watch videotapes of the day's practice and try and de-code some of Smith's directions. They also watched tapes of some of the world's great sprinters and analysed their techniques.

Life was no easier away from the track. Although was able to live rent-free for a while with an old friend of Coach Hobson's, he was forced to borrow money and work in low-paid jobs to supplement the modest $20,000 a year he received from a Nike shoe contract.

Smith's coaching was unique. By devising a low, measured drive out of the blocks, he delayed Greene's top-end speed so it could be achieved at 70 or 75 metres, leaving less distance for deceleration and less time for him to be caught.

He broke down each race to 45 steps, each stride allotted 0.083 of a second on the ground, the feet striking below the hips for maximum efficiency and the spikes raking the track instead of braking. He wanted his sprinters to think of their arms and legs as circular levers and themselves as human wheels.

'John taught me the structure of a race and he made my technique better,' Greene recalls. 'I learned a lot of things before John, but I only knew how to run. John gave you a game plan, structure and a reason why we did certain things. I got in deep about breaking down a 100 or 200 race into its component parts.'

It was nine months of hell before Smith's training began to pay dividends, but in the summer of 1997 a far quicker, more durable Maurice Greene emerged back on to the track scene. At 5ft 9in tall he was a comparatively small sprinter for the modern era, but at 180 pounds he had the muscle and power to challenge the best the world could throw at him.

His starting technique had also improved, with Greene now not lifting his head until at least 20 metres into a race, and Smith had also re-balanced his racing strategy, slowing his acceleration at the start to ensure he didn't burn out too quickly and had enough left in the tank for the finish.

Boldon was in no doubt that Greene had something special: 'Maurice is the most competitive human being I've ever known. Off the track, he's fun-loving, with all that Midwestern 'Yes ma'am, no sir' stuff. But on it, it's a hell of a contrast. He's tough.'

This bulletproof confidence, his raw speed and Smith's coaching sent him into the 1997 US Track and Field Championships ready to write a new page in American track history. 'People are saying that American sprinting is down, that we're not any good, that we're lost,' he told *The New York Times*. 'But I don't feel that way. It's just time for someone to step up and say, "I'm going to carry American sprinting on my back. I'm here to take responsibility for American sprinting. I'm going to carry it as far as I can."'

At the US championships, in Indianapolis, in June, Greene did exactly that, winning the title in a hugely impressive 9.90, the second fastest time in the world that year, and becoming the third fastest American in history after Leroy Burrell and Carl Lewis.

He repeated the feat at the Lausanne Grand Prix meeting, in Switzerland, a month later, beating a world-class sprint field that included Olympic champion Donovan Bailey, Frankie Fredericks and team-mate Ato Boldon.

Next stop: the World Championships, in Athens. A few weeks after his twenty-third birthday, Greene had already written the script. 'I'm going to run where it makes an imprint in someone's mind,' he said. 'When you get old you're going to say, "That boy ran fast." It's going to take sprinting to a whole other level.'

He wasn't far off the mark. In the final he ran a storming race, leading from start to finish and holding off Bailey in the next lane to flash through the line in a new personal best time of 9.86 seconds – the third fastest time ever, equalling the championship record set by his hero Carl Lewis – with Bailey second and Tim Montgomery third.

'It's not that the US has died down,' an emotional Greene told the post-race press conference. 'We have tremendous sprinters in the US and someone has to take charge. I'm an American and this is what I was here for – to get the gold medal for the United States and bring it back home.'

Predictably, the sprint relay squad fouled up once again, dropping the baton and failing to make the semi-finals, but Greene returned home to a hero's welcome.

The Maurice Greene era had begun, and when the 1998 season opened, Greene told the sports press his goal now was to attack and destroy Donovan Bailey's 9.84 world record for 100 metres and, just for good measure, nail Andre Cason's 60-metre world record of 6.41, which had stood since 1992.

It started well, with Greene first equalling the 6.41 mark in Germany, then two days later dropping the time with a new world record of 6.39 at an indoor meeting in Madrid. But breaking the outdoor record would not be so straightforward.

The season was warming up nicely, punctuated by the occasional VIP experience, including the honour of throwing out the first 'ceremonial' pitch of the season for his native Kansas City Royals, in April. But the first real hint of a serious challenge to Bailey's world mark came in Oregon, at the May Prefontaine Classic, when Greene ran a staggering 9.79 seconds. Sadly, the wind measurement was 0.9 metres per second over the legal limit, so the time would not stand. But just to show the kind of form he was in, Greene then went out and beat Michael Johnson in the 200 metres in a barely wind-assisted 19.88 seconds. 'It shows that American sprinters are not playing any more,' he told reporters. 'We're out for business.'

It looked like he meant it too. A few weeks later, at the US Track and Field Championships, in New Orleans, Greene equalled Bailey's mark in the heats with a 9.84, albeit wind-assisted again and not valid, and looked odds-on to beat the time in the more intense atmosphere of the final. But the 90-degree heat played havoc with Greene's preparations, and cramp and dehydration made him so ill overnight that he was forced to withdraw from the event.

After twice losing to Frankie Fredericks on the European circuit, Greene called time on talk of breaking world records. 'We've decided that we've put too much emphasis on the world record,' said Greene. 'Now, I just want to run the best I can, and if the world record comes, it comes. Maybe we've been getting too caught up in running against the clock.'

Though irked at his inability to break his great rival's world record, the frustration didn't stop him rounding off a hugely impressive year with a stunning series of performances around the European Grand Prix tour, with sub-10-second wins in Stockholm, Lausanne, Brussels and Berlin – the pick of the bunch being a 9.90 in Sweden. The world record would have to wait another year.

In February 1999, Greene matched Donovan Bailey's world indoor 50-metre mark of 5.56 in Los Angeles and followed it a month later with a 60-metre gold at the World Indoor Championships, in Japan.

He told the media that he'd abandoned all thoughts of records and was planning a low-key summer build-up to ensure he was in peak fitness for the US championships and the World Championships in Spain, in August. Then, in typically contrary Maurice Greene fashion, he went to a second-tier invitational meet in Athens to run a 200-metre race – and smashed the 100-metre world record by the biggest margin since the introduction of electronic timing.

On an almost windless night in the Greek capital, he made a last-minute decision to run both sprint races after he saw the 40,000 crowd and the strength of the 100-metre field, a race that included team-mate Ato Boldon, Dennis Mitchell, Frankie Fredericks, Tim Montgomery and the in-form Canadian Bruny Surin.

From the gun he tore out of the blocks and he and Boldon, in lanes four and five, pulled away from the field and fought each other all the way to the line, with Greene finishing just a metre ahead in an amazing 9.79 – five-hundredths of a second better than Bailey's Atlanta mark. Boldon's 9.86 in second was the fastest 100 metres runner-up time ever and matched his national record.

With his arm in the air, Greene began hopping and bouncing around the bottom bend, turning to hug Boldon and celebrate with the other athletes. He looked around for an American flag to wave but couldn't find one. He tried to call his mother with the news that he was now the world's fastest human, but she wasn't home. He had to settle for leaving a message.

He told a stunned press corps: 'They can't have a party without me. I knew something was going to happen with this race and I wanted to be part of it. I expected it. It was the best ever race for me. It felt very slow, all the way. I was very patient. Every move I made was the correct one for that race. I won't say that time slowed down, but I could see vividly every movement I was making. I have proved with this what I am, and I hope to improve the world record next time. This is a special place for me.'

Less than 90 minutes after breaking the record, Greene went back out on the track and finished second to Boldon in the 200 metres.

The cover of *Track & Field News* was unequivocal – 'He's the Fastest' – while his home town *Kansas City Star* covered the front page with a picture of his record-breaking run with the headline 'KCK Native Fastest Man Ever'.

Looking back on that night now, Greene recalls: 'The year before we were always saying we were going to break the world record. I was ready to do it, I was capable and it would just never happen. But I was getting into races and running for it, rather than just running the best race I could. But it never came, so I said forget it, I'm just going to run, I'm not going to chase it. It took the pressure off and I focused more on the technique of the race. Then the time came to me. I tell my kids today, don't run after it, let it come to you.'

His coach John Smith was not surprised by the record. 'Maurice knows how to compete. His biggest asset is that he isn't cowed by competition. On game day, he loves to match up against the best. He can be around another 10 years.'

Greene was still only 24 and his teammates were similarly positive about what he could achieve. Training partner Jon Drummond explained: 'He has blind faith. This boy believes. If we played a game and Maurice lost, we would have to play until Maurice won one time. And if he wins that one time, it's like he won all the others. It's almost to the point of being psycho.

'He goes to that edge. If he's got to run out of his legs, where his body is left at the starting line and his legs are at the finish line, then that's what he will do if that's what it takes to win.'

As for Greene himself, he told journalists: 'It's just the beginning. I believe there is a better time way out in the water. You all might not believe it, but I believe it within myself. And once I do that, I'm going to say that I can do it again, and it is going to be even faster.'

With his status as No.1 fast man now beyond dispute, all eyes were on the World Championships, in Seville. As defending champion he was able to skip qualification via the US championships, selecting to run only the 200 metres, where he was billed to meet reigning Olympic champion and world record holder Michael Johnson. But a few days before the event Johnson withdrew citing a leg injury, and Greene was able to stroll to the title.

In Seville, Greene was in supreme form, winning the 100 metres and retaining his world title with a championship record 9.80, a fraction outside his world record, despite almost losing his footing as he blasted out of the blocks, with Surin second and Britain's Dwain Chambers third.

Greene later said: 'I believe if I didn't stumble, my time would have been faster. The beginning was very shaky, but I didn't panic. I ran under control. I finished strong. In the 100, everything you do takes off hundredths of a second. I wasn't trying for the world record. I don't try any more. If it comes, it comes.'

After the finish, Greene kneeled on the track, holding his head in his hands for several seconds. Then he looked up at his injured training partner Ato Boldon in the stands and shouted, 'That's for you, Ato,' before setting out on the customary victory lap armed with the American flag.

US team coach George Williams was quick to praise Greene's effort. 'I thought he ran a great race except for the first step. He stuttered. And that cost him a world record.'

'In Seville I thought I was invincible,' says Greene. 'I was so in tune with my body. I was going through the rounds not wanting to run too fast. I was pushing my blocks back from the starting line so I could take my time and ease out. I felt on top of the world. But when the final came and I put the blocks back in place, I didn't execute the start like I could, so I didn't break the word record.'

A few days later he went out and took the 200-metre title with a season best 19.90, with Brazil's Claudinei Da Silva second and Nigeria's Francis Obikwelu third.

And for once the American relay team didn't make a mess of the final act. Despite some jittery baton handling, the quartet of Drummond, Montgomery, Lewis and Greene took the gold, although the double world champion had to do all the work on the anchor leg, receiving the baton behind Great Britain and overhauling Chambers in the last 50 metres. Greene returned home to the States with three gold medals in his bag. Job done.

The year 1999 would remain a high point in Greene's career, with a new world record and three gold medals at the World Championships, but after the disappointment of Atlanta in 1996, it was the Olympic Games of 2000 that would become the defining moment and mark him as one of the greatest sprinters of the modern era.

'The 1999 track season was just great,' he said at the time. 'I am happy I had a very good year. My main focus now is to win the Olympic gold. That comes first, not a record. Right now, I have a goal of 9.76 and the coach said I am capable of running faster, but I take small steps at a time. The most important thing is to win the Olympic gold. That's something I haven't done and I want to do.

'I think to be number one you have to train like you're number two. If you train like you're number one you have no place to go,' he continued. 'That's what it is like. I'm training like I'm trying to get the person ahead of me. I have goals in this sport that I want to accomplish and I can't stop now.' He added: 'I work too hard to lose. I don't go to practise and work as hard as I do every day to lose. The pain I go through in training, is compensated for by the joy I get out of crossing the finish line first. My coach believes I can run 9.60 seconds for 100 metres, but at this time I've set a goal for myself of 9.76. I'm not putting a time limit on when I want to do it, as long as I achieve it. The Olympics would be the perfect stage, but if it happens before that I would love it.'

As the Olympic year began, Greene's view was the only person who could beat him to gold in Sydney was himself. As usual, however, it would be a tough race and, with the 'Down Under' Games starting later than usual in September, the trick would be to pace himself through the year. It began well, with victory in the 60 metres at the Millrose Games at Madison Square Garden. 'I'm stronger than '96, my technique is a lot better than '96 and mentally I believe I am unstoppable,' he told an enthusiastic New York press.

In reality his preparation for the US trials was chequered. He ran the fastest 100 metres of the year, a 9.91 in Japan, but suffered three losses, including a woeful and tired-looking fifth place in a Great Britain v USA meeting, in Glasgow.

Questions were being asked of the world champion as zero hour approached, but Greene didn't blink. He told *The New York Times* that he practised his stride in the mirror, like a ballet dancer, and that sometimes he wrote down a time faster than he has ever run on a piece of paper and stuffed it in his racing spikes.

At the US trials he was the man everyone was gunning for. The man with the reputation, the world record and the seven-figure income. The European circuits were paying him $100,000 a race, but in Sacramento, in July, there would be no pay day, only the hazardous path of finishing in the top three in both the 100 and 200 metres to ensure a crack at three gold medals in Australia. The sell-out crowd in California was eager to see how the story would play out, especially the much-awaited showdown between Greene and world record holder Michael Johnson over 200 metres.

In the end Greene delivered with some ease. In the 100 metres, he stumbled coming out of the blocks, but didn't panic and caught training partner Jon Drummond at about 80 metres to win in a modest 10.01, albeit into a 4mph headwind. 'I made the Olympic team, I am an Olympian,' he sang to waiting reporters.

On Greene's twenty-sixth birthday, the big duel with Johnson dawned and even NBC, normally the most track and field ambivalent of the TV network heavyweights, promoted the race nationwide. For Greene and Johnson, however, the rigours of their wins in the 100 and the 400 metres respectively had taken their toll. In incinerating heat, both sprinters failed to make it out of the turn in the 200 metres final, dramatically clutching limbs and limping out of the action. 'I will go to Sydney and I will bring home two gold medals, said Greene. 'I wanted to win the 200 today. But I'm still alive. That's the most important thing.'

Greene needed some intensive treatment, but although he was forced to skip a few races, he still managed to embark on a lucrative pre-Olympic European tour, where 100-metre wins in Zurich, Monaco, Brussels and, with a fitting flourish, a season's best of 9.86 in Berlin made him the out-and-out favourite for the gold medal in Sydney.

The 2000 Olympics were an outstanding accomplishment by the Australian organizers, taking place in early spring, costing close to seven billion Australian dollars and boasting a record 199 nations and over two thousand athletes. Of the Olympic nations only Afghanistan failed to attend, owing to the ruling Taliban's prohibition on sports. Even North and South Korea entered a unified team.

The flame was lit by Australian track star Cathy Freeman, who would go on to win the 400 metres gold and become the only competitor in Olympic history to accomplish both feats.

Greene arrived in Sydney 12 days before the start of the 100-metre competition and the Australian media took to him straight away. 'A year before we had gone to Australia and ran some races and I was the first guy to run under 10 seconds down there,' he explained. 'When I crossed the line I thought I'd broken the world record because they started fireworks and everything. Then I looked and it was only 9.99 – I thought all of this for that! But that got me a lot of support there.'

He also played the entertainment game and seemed to be on every news bulletin, whether it was posing with the bikini babes on Bondi Beach, mugging to the cameras outside the Opera House or flashing around Darling Harbour in a rented red Ferrari. They didn't seem to mind that he opted to stay out of the Olympic village and stay with his sprinting group, which included rivals Jon Drummond and Ato Boldon, at a multi-million-dollar house on Coogee Beach, about five miles east of Sydney.

They loved the fact that his father was there with him too. Ernest Greene was certainly enjoying the ride. He smiled as Maurice told another media gathering that he was there for only one thing. 'A gold medal wrapped around my neck.'

'I like to see him like this,' said Ernest. 'It tells me he's relaxed. There's only one time you ever need to worry about Maurice and that's when he's being modest.'

Greene recalls: 'I remember talking to my manager Emanuel Hudson and telling him that after everything I'd done, these Olympics were mine to lose. If I didn't do the things I needed to do I could lose and I wouldn't get the thing I really wanted. I went into Sydney thinking nothing and nobody will take this away from me.'

The 100-metre competition got underway on the morning of Friday, September 22, and Maurice Greene cantered through his first heat in a sedate 10.31 just after midday. It wasn't until nearly nine in the evening that he was back in the stadium to stroll through the second round and into the following day's finale with a modest time of 10.10 seconds, and then watched as the reigning, but injured, champion Donovan Bailey exited the competition on the first day.

Greene laughs as he recalls the day of the final. 'Me, Ato and JD trained together and stayed in the house together. We did everything together. On final day, even though we did everything together, it all got separated. I woke up and the house was so quiet, you could hear a pin drop. I would hear a door open and close, hear people walking around, and then go back to their rooms. Everyone was in their own little space. As time got closer, I had my music on in my room, they had theirs, and we were all doing our own thing. Then JD came to me to say that Ato had told him we couldn't ride with him to the track. I said I didn't want to ride with him anyway and closed the door. After being so close, we all went to the stadium separately.'

Early on Saturday evening, Greene watched Briton Dwain Chambers win the first semi-final in 10.14 and American team-mate Curtis Johnson crash out a disappointing sixth. At just before seven o'clock, he blasted out of the blocks to beat both training partners Drummond and Boldon with a swift 10.06.

The final would take place less than an hour and a half later and the eight men contesting the greatest track prize on earth would be Britain's Darren Campbell in lane one, Ghana's Aziz Zakari, Chambers, Barbadian Obadele Thompson, Greene in lane five, Drummond, Kim Collins, from St Kitts & Nevis, and Boldon out in lane eight.

As the stadium announcer went into the introductions for the capacity 110,000 crowd, Greene prowled up and down the starting area like a cat, staring intently down the track, bobbing, weaving and sticking his tongue out at the cameras. His nervous energy could have powered the stadium lights. 'It might've looked like I was loose,' said Greene, 'but I was trying to play everything up like there wasn't a lot of pressure. When I get nervous, my tongue comes out of my mouth. I start biting my lips.'

At the gun he got out well, but the recall sounded immediately and Zakari was penalized for a false start. But the second start was clean and in typical Greene style he kept his head down for the first 20 metres, rising slowly to see that he was just in front of the pack. As he slowly pulled away, only Boldon in the outside lane seemed to be close, but he was never close enough, and Greene stormed over the line, right hand in the air, to win the gold in 9.87 seconds, with Boldon second in 9.99 and Thompson third in 10.04.

The two training partners embraced before Greene sank to his knees in silent prayer. He then got up and started a victory lap, hurling one of his running spikes into the crowd and handing another to a kid sitting in the first row. 'We owe a lot to the fans here in Sydney,' said Greene later. 'They've packed the stadium. I gave them the best that I could. And I gave them a little souvenir – my shoes.'

An emotional Greene told the eager media conference: 'You work four years for something that's only going to last nine seconds. It's hard to do. I'm overjoyed and overwhelmed and everything and just filled with joy.'

The podium was an emotional high point, and to millions watching around the world it appeared as if Greene was desperately trying not to laugh as the American flag rose and the anthem played. 'Actually, I was trying not to cry,' he said. 'I was just overwhelmed by the excitement of it all. In Atlanta, they were tears of sadness. Here they were tears of joy and of thanking God.'

He reserved a special mention for his coach John Smith, who had missed out on Olympic success at the Munich Games of 1972 because of injury. 'I hope I've filled a bit of that hole,' said Greene. 'I'm not in this sport for the fame and fortune. I'm in this sport because I love it. You have to love it to go through what we go through. I was thinking about being on the UCLA track with John Smith and my training partners. You don't have to go to practice, you know. No one makes you go to practice. You can go as often as you want and be as good as you want to be. That's what I like about this sport.'

As for the other medallists, Ato Boldon retired after the 2004 Olympics and held political office for a short time in his native Trinidad & Tobago. He's since made a name for himself as an outstanding TV pundit on CBS, ESPN and, most notably, NBC. His work on the network at the London Olympics won him a nomination at the Emmys – the TV Oscars – the first track and field broadcaster to receive one in US history.

Bronze medallist and fellow Caribbean islander Obadele Thompson became the first athlete to win an Olympic medal for Barbados. After a stellar college and professional running career he published an autobiographical book called *Secrets of a Champion Student–Athlete: A Reality Check* and took part in leadership, development and motivational programmes on sports management, performance and anti-doping. A former academic All-American, he qualified from the University of Texas Law School and practises in international arbitration and litigation. In 2007 he married the former Olympic sprinter Marion Jones. They have three children.

It was relay time back in Sydney and, perhaps surprisingly, the American squad didn't let anyone down on the track and the quartet of Jon Drummond, Bernard Williams, Brian Lewis and anchor man Maurice Greene took the gold in a tidy 37.61 seconds. Off the track, their theatrical celebrations, in true WWE style, generated a barrage of criticism from around the world, so much so that Greene was moved to apologize, explaining that it was a reaction of the moment. Fittingly, it was Henry Kissinger who presented the team with their medals.

Drummond became a successful coach, but was banned from the sport for eight years in 2014 when he was implicated in the use of banned products for his athletes. Williams would win silver in the 2004 Olympic 200 metres and become a successful sports performance coach, while Lewis continued running until 2002 and currently lives in Virginia.

In Sydney, Maurice Greene had now become the only man to hold, simultaneously, world records at 50, 60 and 100 metres, world titles at 100 and 200 and the Olympic title at 100. So he returned home a hero, and proceeded to enjoy the spoils of Olympic success, with a raft of commercial endorsements, promoting everything from super-fast broadband services to running shoes, and a once in a lifetime trip to the White House to receive the personal congratulations of President Bill Clinton.

But if Greene's rivals thought he would take his foot off the gas, then they were horribly wrong, as he opened the 2001 indoor season by equalling his 60-metre world record of 6.39, in Atlanta.

The goals for this year, aside from racking up a pile of cash from strutting his gold medal stuff around the European circuits, were an improbable third world title in Canada in the summer, matching the achievement of Carl Lewis, and a lowering of his own world 100-metre record. 'I want to be known as the greatest ever 100-metre sprinter,' said Greene. 'Jesse Owens took the event to one level. Carl Lewis took it to another. And I want to take it to the next.'

Greene ran into some decent form in the build-up to the World Championships, running a 9.91 in Athens and a world's fastest 9.90 at the US championships, in Oregon, but an increasingly painful problem with tendinitis in his left knee was hampering his training and he decided not to double up in the sprints in Canada.

It turned out to be a wise decision. The injury was clearly affecting him, but as the World Championships began in Edmonton, he still managed to blaze a 9.88 in the second-round heats to serve notice of what was to come. In the final, despite three false starts, he managed to run the fastest time of the year – and the third fastest ever – of 9.82, to win the gold and a third world title, leading a clean sweep for the United States, with Tim Montgomery second and Bernard Williams third.

He looked on course for something even better after a superb first 60 metres, but seemed to almost hop and bounce over the line, before limping painfully off the track. It would be his last action of the event. Having already reluctantly withdrawn from defending his 200-metre title, on the advice of John Smith he now decided against anchoring the relay.

'I was never able to finish my greatest race, explains Greene. 'I got hurt at 60 metres. If you look at the race closely, you can see I grimaced and felt it, then just hobbled along to finish and ran 9.82. I was just getting ready to do my thing in the race. That was my 9.6-something race. I always compare it to the scene in the movie *The Fast and the Furious* where the guys hit the nitro button and the bolts start popping on the car – that was me in Edmonton. I was moving so fast my body couldn't take it.'

It was a disappointing end to an impressive season, and after five years of dominance at 100 metres, questions were now being asked about how long the 27-year-old could keep going at such a rarified level.

Greene hardly set foot on a track in 2002, the result, as it appeared, of recovering from his Edmonton injury, missing a swathe of winter training, losing two close family members – his grandmother and a close uncle – and getting embroiled in a battle between Nike and Adidas.

He had been with Nike for some years, but when the contract came up for renewal in the wake of the World Championships, Greene felt they had reneged on an agreement to name a line of shoes after him. So after a protracted dispute, he signed for their bitter rivals Adidas, who immediately announced they would launch a 'Mo Greene' line of clothing and footwear.

But he kept very quiet about the real reason for his lengthy inactivity – a broken leg sustained in a motorcycle accident. While cruising outside Los Angeles on the 405 Freeway on his Suzuki 600, he was side-swiped by a car changing lanes and fell heavily off his bike. 'It was bad enough,' recalls Greene. 'It put me out for a few months. I didn't tell anyone because I didn't want to make excuses. If I step on the track, then I'm strong enough to win.' But the broken leg triggered a catalogue of injuries that destroyed his training and all his preparations for the season. Surely things could only get better?

The year didn't improve, however, and he continued to run poorly, even in the big European meetings. 'This year has been very trying for me,' he said. 'I have gone through a lot. That's why my season has been so up and down. Now I want to keep running fast and then I can start gearing up for next year and the World Championships.'

But the injuries kept coming and effectively ended his 2003 ambitions too. Although he qualified for the World Championships in Paris, as a wild card defending champion, he limped out of the event with another quadriceps injury after finishing a distraught seventh in his semi-final. He disappeared home to Los Angeles to rest and recover, putting all thoughts of track and field out of his mind.

For many, it was the end of the line for Greene, but he never doubted there was a dramatic comeback on the cards. 'You have to show them,' he said. 'Once you start running the times that you used to run, then what are they going to say? "Oh, well, we thought his best days were over. We thought he was finished, but he's showing us something different?" I am my biggest critic. I put more pressure on myself than anyone puts on me. They can say what they want to say.'

Greene emerged into another Olympic year in markedly better health and a far better frame of mind, and with the Games to be held in Athens – always a favourite city for him – his motivation to succeed returned too.

But the sprinting world was in turmoil. Fellow American Tim Montgomery, who had claimed a new world record of 9.78 seconds in Paris in September 2002, was now embroiled in a federal drug investigation, and Britain's Dwain Chambers had tested positive for steroid use and was facing a suspension. The track needed its hero back.

As if to signal the shape of things to come, Greene took part in a massive, year-long Adidas advertising campaign where through the wizardry of special effects he was seen jogging with Muhammad Ali, his daughter Laila, David Beckham, Ian Thorpe and basketball star Tracy McGrady. It was called 'Impossible is Nothing.' Maurice Greene was about to discover if that was true.

The world was sceptical, and when, in February 2004, he pulled out of the 60 metres in the US indoor championships, citing a 'touchy hamstring', the *Boston Globe* headlined its story 'Greene Not on Last Legs' and quoted the athlete's explanation: 'I haven't been this healthy in a couple of years. Now I have to get back to the technical aspect of running. I got into some bad habits because I was trying to compensate for my injuries.'

But the outdoor season went well, with early wins in the States and Japan, then a strong 9.86 in a televised race in Carson, where he took off his running shoes at the finishing line, dropped them on the track and a friend ran on and turned a fire extinguisher on them. The crowd loved it. A few weeks later he posted a stunning but wind-assisted 9.78 at the Peyton Jordan US Open, in California, where he beat the up-and-coming Justin Gatlin. A pumped-up Greene told reporters. 'I say everyone will be fighting for second.'

The only hiccup in this renaissance was the rumbling BALCO drug scandal, where it seemed every day a different athlete was caught up in the controversy. Greene's position was resolute. 'There is no room for drug cheaters in our sport,' he said. 'They should get lifetime bans.'

Greene moved into the crucial US Olympic trials in fine form, as well as boasting a brand-new tattoo to show off to his fans: a lion engraved on his right shoulder, with the letters G-O-A-T written across its mane – Greatest Of All Time. He explained: 'The lion is the king of the jungle, and the track is my jungle. And that's what I'm basically going to prove this year. That I'm the greatest of all time.' Nobody in the track media world doubted it after he stormed a meet-record 9.91 to win a closely run trial, with Gatlin second and Shawn Crawford third.

But the return to his spiritual sprinting home, the site of his world record run in 1999, didn't go entirely to plan. In the run-up to the Games, Greene turned 30 and suddenly looked vulnerable, losing his three warm-up races, twice outgunned by the young Jamaican Asafa Powell. But when the US team arrived in Athens most pundits still had him down as favourite for the gold.

In a tremendously close final, Greene could only manage a bronze medal, with team-mate Gatlin winning the gold in 9.85 and Francis Obikwelu, now running for Portugal, the silver in 9.86. Greene was a further hundredth back, while Shawn Crawford ran a 9.89 and didn't even get a medal.

A subdued but sanguine Greene told the press conference: 'I expected a very close race between seven people, as I knew the ability of the others. I came a long way to come back and compete at this level. The final is everybody's race, so I'm pleased I secured a medal.'

He added silver in the sprint relay, but returned home disappointed that he couldn't repeat his golden achievements in Sydney. When the dust had settled, he explained his feelings about it: 'I have a bronze medal from the Olympics and it really hurts to look at it. I lost it because of things that I did. That's how I feel. Of course it hurts. It never feels good to lose.

'In my semi-final race I should have won the race but I was conserving energy. That's when Obikwelu came up and I took third because I didn't know he was there. I believe that's what put me in lane seven and, while I was in lane seven, I couldn't feel anything in the race. I just felt like I was running all alone. I believe if I was in the middle of the race I would have been able to react to people that came ahead of me. It was a dumb mistake and I've had to live with it. If I'd been in lane three or six, I would have won. I was very mad. I was very upset because I always say I lost that race. I don't feel they beat me.'

Greene started 2005 with the target of a fourth world title in Helsinki and a sixtieth sub-10-second 100 metres. Neither would happen. After a mediocre outdoor season, he made the final of the US championships, only to crash spectacularly to the track after 70 metres with yet another injury. A month shy of his thirty-first birthday, Greene was always in contention in the race but pulled up with an obvious left hamstring injury. He hopped on his right leg, and then fell to the track. 'I'm not going to Helsinki,' said Greene, in tears after the race. 'I wanted to get my world championship title back. That hurts the most.'

The disappointment was compounded by Jamaican Asafa Powell lowering the 100-metre world record to 9.77 in a blistering run in Athens in June.

He eventually went to Helsinki with the relay squad, but lack of practice caught out the US team once again, and anchor man Greene watched in dismay as the team's very first handover in the heats of the competition was bungled and they were disqualified. He didn't run another step in anger at a major race. Father Time had finally caught up with the Cannonball, and a string of foot and leg injuries restricted his 2006 and 2007 seasons to rare cameo appearances. So it came as no surprise when Greene finally announced his retirement in May 2008, while on a tour of Olympic facilities in Beijing. 'It's a little sad for me,' he said, 'but it's happy at the same time because I've had a great career. I've done a lot of great things. For the last couple of years, I've had nagging injuries that have stopped my training. So I think it's better to just call it quits.'

It wasn't the difficult call for Greene that everyone imagined. 'It wasn't really that tough because mentally I wasn't into it any more. I had injuries and I thought do I want to come back? Mentally I wasn't strong enough to put my body through it again. I knew I was done. It wasn't anything but my mind. There were a lot of times when I wasn't prepared to run, but mentally I'd do it. But mentally I didn't have it any more.'

He had already made some US television appearances on shows such as *Blind Date* and *Identity*, so when the offer came to take part in the seventh season of the hugely popular ABC show *Dancing with the Stars*, he leaped at it. Competitive as ever, he put in a decent effort, partnered by professional dancer Cheryl Burke, and survived until week eight of the contest, finishing a creditable fifth. He even went on the theatrical tour with some of the stars of the show. 'I had a lot of fun,' he said. 'I made a lot of friends out here. I learned how to dance in front of millions of people every night. I had a great time.'

Bizarrely, one of the world's greatest sprinters is now recognized more in the States for taking part in the dancing show than for all his achievements on the track.

More worrying for Greene, though, was the sudden explosion of headlines surrounding a whistle-blower in a federal trial in the United States relating to the supply of performance-enhancing drugs. A Mexican former athlete called Angel Heredia, a prosecution witness in the trial, had named Greene in a list of athletes who had paid him $14,000 for a variety of drugs in 2003 and 2004.

Greene, an outspoken advocate of lifetime bans for drug cheats, vehemently denied the allegations, suggesting that he was part of a smear campaign, though he conceded that he did pay for 'stuff' for athletes in his training group. His manager Emanuel Hudson described the charges as 'ludicrous'.

The trial ultimately named a number of athletes, including Sydney 4 x 400 metre gold medal winner Antonio Pettigrew, who admitted using drugs and was stripped of his Olympic medal. He was found dead in August 2010, aged 42. Greene was never brought into the trial and, tellingly, despite Heredia's claims, Greene was also never charged by the US Anti Doping Agency or the IAAF, who have stood by him, and he remains a major advocate of a drug-free sport.

Since then, Greene has run a music business, worked as an ambassador for the IAAF, fronted his own TV show on Eurosport and, for a while, coached the sprint relay squad in Nigeria. He married wife Latoya in 2014 and settled in Gilbert, Arizona. Besides spending time with his three children, he trains, coaches and teaches physical education and multiple sports at a charter school, the American Leadership Academy.

A wealthy man from his years of track exploits and endorsements, Greene continues to be a popular addition to an eclectic mix of TV shows and events, from regular track and field to the more bizarre, such as hosting the American Pole Fitness Championships, in New York, in late 2010.

He remains the premier sprinter of his era and an entertaining, larger-than-life character who instilled a sense of fun and theatricality into the sport when it dearly needed it, as well as creating a wonderful legacy on the track – a world record, an Olympic gold medal and three world titles.

Greene wants to be remembered as a great competitor and there's no doubt that he will be. But he was a lot more than that. He has few regrets, and aside from that Olympic semi-final in Athens, there's only one thing he'd like to go back and change.

'I wish I could have spent more time appreciating what I achieved. I never really sat down after I achieved things and let it sink it. I always did it and moved on. I never took time out to enjoy what I achieved, and now that I've finished, I look back and think I should have appreciated it a little bit more than I did, but I was always looking ahead. I know I missed that. I look back and I think, yeah I did it, but I don't remember how it felt.'

In terms of legacy, the self-styled 'Greatest Of All Time' is clear about his place in sprinting history. 'I think of it as eras,' he says. 'Jesse Owens was the greatest of his era, Carl Lewis the greatest of his era, and in my era I was the G-O-A-T! – no one did it better than me.

'I was the first to run under 9.8, I had the world record, I had world titles and I had an Olympic gold medal. I surpassed what they did before me and more. In my time I'm the G-O-A-T.'

'The sport continues to move on; I'm no longer competing, so someone has to do it better. It's not for me to say where I am with the other champions, that's a debate for everyone else. So I am very comfortable with what I did.'

CHAPTER TWENTY-TWO

Athens 2004

Justin Gatlin

At the very moment Maurice Greene flashed through the finishing line in Sydney, a teenager in Florida jumped from his seat in front of the TV and punched the air in delight at another American gold medal.

Despite a growing reputation as a high school sprinter, the 18-year-old Justin Gatlin was barely known in his own state, let alone the wider track and field world. Within a month he would head off to college and begin a stellar but rollercoaster athletic career that would see him soar to the heights of Olympic superstardom and then crash to the depths of drug-abusing shame and a long-term ban.

Enmeshed in a nationwide performance-enhancing drug scandal, he became a key player in a sad and sordid tale involving some of the biggest names in sport. A scandal that reverberates to this day. Gatlin still vehemently denies ever knowingly taking drugs and fought tooth and nail to overturn the ban and win back his career. He then staged an extraordinary comeback, the success of which was matched only by the fierce vilification of it by the media. He is now approaching 40 and, improbably, shows no signs of slowing down. Despite taking gold, silver and bronze in three Olympic 100-metre finals his greatest dream remains – a golden and romantic farewell at the Games in Tokyo, followed a year later by an emotional goodbye at the world championships, on his favourite track in Oregon.Such storylines seemed a million miles away from Gatlin's modest upbringing in the Sheepshead Bay district of Brooklyn, New York, where he was born in February 1982, the real baby of the family, with a much older brother and two older sisters. His earliest memories involve running through the neighbourhood to get to school and jumping over fences and fire hydrants along the way.

Even then, Justin knew he was different. 'I was faster than all the other kids by far, and one day I told one kid to jump on his bike and race me while I was still on foot, and I still beat him. That really made me think, hey, I'm faster than normal.'

In the fourth grade his teachers called his parents when he handed in a spelling test with only a picture of a bird drawn on it. He had spotted it outside the classroom window. His mother had noticed his lack of concentration at home and took him for tests. He was diagnosed with ADD – Attention Deficit Disorder – and began taking medication to counter the problem.

Shortly afterwards, his hardworking parents, Willie, a retired US Army sergeant, and Jeanette, a jewellery shop owner, decided to uproot the family when Gatlin was just nine and move to Pensacola, on the north-west Florida coast.

There, at Woodham High School, Gatlin excelled in sports and got a reputation as a decent football player and an exceptional hurdler. By the time he was about to leave for college, he was rated in the top three high school sprinters and the major colleges began to call.

He puts his success down to his coach, Jay Cormier. 'He believed in me before I believed in myself. He kept pushing me to be the best and made sure I kept my discipline and got my grades for college. He was like a sensei to me, the first coach who really cared about me.

'I didn't know anything about being professional. My hero was Maurice Greene, but I didn't know how to get to that level. I used to have pictures of him all over my wall at home. Me and my best friend at High School, Paul Miller, used to call ourselves Justin Greene and Paul Drummond (he loved Jon Drummond). We used to watch those guys run and say that's what we want to be, just like them.'

Gatlin had seriously considered pursuing his love of art and drawing, but in the end his sporting prowess won the day and it was his potential as an out-and-out fast man that was spotted by coaches Vince Anderson and Bill Webb, who recruited him to the University of Tennessee, in Knoxville, where his impact was instantaneous.

In his freshman year he won both the 100 and 200 metres at the 2001 NCAA championships, in Oregon, despite them being run only an hour apart, helping Tennessee to their first title for 20 years. His final times of 10.08 and 20.11 made the US track and field fraternity sit up and start taking notice – he was only 19.

On his twentieth birthday, in February 2002, he took another sprint double at the NCAA indoor championships, in Arkansas, to clinch another title for Tennessee. He told the waiting reporters: 'I think I can still do good in the hurdles, but if you split your talent you take away from your ability. I like sprinting better.'

Already a powerfully built 6ft 1in, 175-pound athlete, he was criticized for his slow starts, but gained a reputation as a seemingly effortless and astonishing finisher. The modest Gatlin tried to deflect the praise on to his coach. 'I owe it all to Vince Anderson, our sprint coach. My arms used to come halfway up instead of being higher. My knees didn't come high enough. He changed my stride habits. He's helped my mechanics, my form and my technique.'

With the outdoor season beckoning, the future looked incredibly bright for young Gatlin, and the US track and field fans began to wonder just how far he could go.

The answer came in May 2002, but it was not the one they were expecting. It was from the US Anti-Doping Agency (USADA) and they announced they were banning Gatlin for two years for testing positive for a banned amphetamine discovered at a routine test at the US junior championships almost a year earlier.

It transpired that the stimulant in question was contained in the prescription medication called Adderall, something he took for his ADD problem, and although an arbitration panel conceded that Gatlin was clearly not trying to cheat and that his mistake was, at worst, a technical violation, the ban would have to stand.

Gatlin explained: 'My ADD was a case that I was too calm and nonchalant. If I got a D on a test – some kids were like "Oh my lord, my mom's going to kill me" – but I was like "Oh well, I'll do better next time." I was the total opposite of the hyperactive.'

He stopped taking the medicine after the positive test, adding: 'The drug was a de-enhancer instead of an enhancer. The thing was, when I'd get out there the drug would make me concentrate so much that I'd get tired.'

The ban applied to all track meets except the collegiate circuit, so at least he was able to continue running for Tennessee, which he did in some style, winning a second sprint double at the summer's NCAA meeting in Baton Rouge, Louisiana, and becoming the first man in 45 years to repeat the feat.

Just a month later there was more to celebrate, when he was reinstated to the track after serving just half of his two-year ban, with the governing body the IAAF accepting that he had a genuine medical explanation for his positive test. With this reprieve, however, came the warning that they still felt he had committed a doping offence and that any repetition would result in a lifetime ban.

With the way now clear to start a professional track career, Gatlin decided to terminate his college life at the end of his sophomore year, and in September he signed a substantial sponsorship contract with Nike. 'It's been a very good two years,' he said. 'I know I wouldn't be where I am today if I had attended another university. I feel that I'm not saying goodbye, but just stepping to the next level of track and field.'

A few days later his sprinting targets were redrawn when fellow American Tim Montgomery lowered Maurice Greene's 9.79 world record by just one-hundredth of a second to 9.78 in a blazing run in Paris. Gatlin, the new kid on the block, now had Montgomery to contend with as well as the reigning Olympic champion. And that was just at his own national trials.

He had hoped Montgomery was going to become a training partner, when he and his parents decided to hook up with Jamaican coach Trevor Graham and his Sprint Capitol group, which was based in Raleigh, North Carolina, but they never got to work together. After a bust-up with Graham, both Montgomery and partner Marion Jones, the fastest woman on earth, had already left to work with Ben Johnson's controversial old coach Charlie Francis.

'I was very young and Graham pursued me,' recalls Gatlin. 'I was just coming out of college and I didn't know anything about him other than he coached Marion and Tim, who had just broken the world record, so it seemed like a great idea. Looking back now I wish I could change that. I've learned to be careful about the people you keep close around you that are not your friends.'

Graham immediately went to work on Gatlin's notoriously poor starts and began to hone his pick-up technique. It all soon began to pay dividends on the track.

His pro career started solidly in February 2003 at the 96th Millrose Games, at New

York's Madison Square Garden, where he took second place to Terrence Trammell in the 60 metres but significantly did manage to beat Maurice Greene into third.

It stood him in good stead at the US Indoor Championships in Boston about a month later, when he took the 60-metre title and qualified to run for the USA at the World Indoor Games, in England, where he disarmed the cynical British athletic press with an unexpected American charm offensive.

The *Daily Mail's* athletics correspondent Neil Wilson wrote: 'For anyone expecting the traditional boastful, butt-kicking US sprinter, Gatlin is a disappointment. Quietly spoken and charming, he boasts not of what he will do to the Brits but instead suggests that he and Mark Lewis-Francis are the next generation.'

In his very first meeting outside the US, Gatlin then went out on the Birmingham track and let his running do the talking, taking advantage of an injury to team-mate Trammell in the heats to win the 60 metres gold medal in 6.46 seconds, in front of Kim Collins, from St Kitts, and Britain's Jason Gardener.

'I have status now on the world level,' he told the *Washington Post*. 'This is a message for everybody, not just Maurice and Tim. I'm trying to show them that I'm out there and able to compete on the world stage now. Everybody should be listening.'

And so they were. Listening and watching, especially when the US Track and Field Championships opened in California, and especially when Coach Graham suggested to the media that Gatlin's 2003 goals were to become number one in both the 100 and 200 metres.

But at his first senior national event, one that would decide the US team for the summer's World Championships, in Paris, Gatlin struggled with both the pressure of expectation and a hamstring strain and failed to make the semi-finals in the 100 metres, finishing a disappointing 17th out of 31 finishers. Intriguingly, support came from an unlikely quarter – world record holder Tim Montgomery. The South Carolina star said: 'I didn't have as much pressure. They weren't calling me the future.' Gatlin himself was sanguine. 'I'm not too disappointed. I'm a rookie and of course everyone makes mistakes. I just have to come back and do better.'

The pressure clearly got to Montgomery too, because he could only finish second to Bernard Williams in the final, with Jon Drummond third. Defending world champion Maurice Greene had an automatic spot, so he didn't have to compete.

Gatlin tried to put the disappointment behind him and set off for Europe and a tour of some of the top tracks, winning in Italy and Sweden, and dead-heating at the Zurich Weltklasse with compatriot John Capel.

At the World Championships, the US team unravelled spectacularly, with Greene, aiming for an unprecedented fourth world title, injured and eliminated in the semis and Montgomery, a pale shadow of his world record form, finishing a disappointing fifth in a final won, in an extraordinary blanket finish, by Kim Collins in a modest 10.07 seconds. The widespread media view was that the now in-form Justin Gatlin might well have won the race at a canter had he been there.

As if to confirm their suspicions, Gatlin went out and won the next big event – a $1 million 100-metre challenge held in Moscow, where he held off Britain's Dwain

Chambers, with Montgomery third and world champion Collins a distant sixth. The prize pot was $500,000 to the winner and the remaining half split amongst the other finalists. But it took months of haggling to get the cash out of Russia.

When the Olympic year opened, the 100-metre favourites were still Greene and Montgomery, but Gatlin was growing in confidence. 'I just try to be normal Justin Gatlin and not let all the hype get to me,' he told journalists. 'I know what I'm capable of doing. There's a lot of talented sprinters out there. And yes, I consider myself to be one of them.'

Under Coach Graham, he'd brought his personal bests down to 9.97 for the 100 and 19.90 for the 200, and with Athens looming he hired a new agent, the former hurdling golden boy Renaldo Nehemiah.

But Maurice Greene wasn't quite done yet and beat Gatlin in a wind-assisted 9.78 at a meeting in California in May. The 100-metre race at the US Olympic trials looked like being a titanic battle between Greene, Montgomery, rising star Shawn Crawford, Williams and Gatlin. Only three would make the cut.

Then yet another scandal began to unfold, one that would finally pull the rug from under an organized drug ring that provided performance-enhancing drugs to elite athletes across a variety of sports, from baseball superstar Barry Bonds to world 100-metre record holder Tim Montgomery. It centred on a federal investigation into a nutrition company based near San Francisco called the Bay Area Laboratory Co-Operative (BALCO). Within days the name BALCO would become shorthand for illicit drug supply in sport, and the ripples would spread far and wide.

Immediately, Gatlin's coach Trevor Graham met with federal investigators and accepted immunity from prosecution in exchange for co-operation. Details of the investigation had been broken by journalists working for the *San José Mercury News*, who claimed to have documents revealing that BALCO owner Victor Conte had provided banned drugs, notably the anabolic steroid THG and testosterone, to nearly 30 athletes, including 12 track and field competitors. The witch-hunt had begun and would form a dramatic backdrop to an almost surreal Olympic trials, in Sacramento, in July.

The anticipated titanic battle looked more likely to be played out in a courtroom than a track, with Montgomery and his partner Marion Jones under federal investigation and Greene fighting a recurring injury. The stage was set for a shift in the balance of American sprinting power.

In the event, the 100 metres final at the Olympic trials actually did live up to expectation, with a meet record and the closest of finishes. It was won by Maurice Greene in 9.91, with Gatlin second in 9.92 and Crawford third in 9.93. USA Track and Field CEO Craig Masback said: 'It was one of the classic 100-metre fields in history. There was great anticipation and the race matched the anticipation.'

A miserable-looking Montgomery finished way back in seventh. Escorted off the track by security and pushing his hand in front of TV cameras, he railed: 'This is the reason I couldn't win. I got y'all on my back every day.'

At the press conference Graham told the assembled reporters: 'No BALCO questions.' But it was an improbable demand. BALCO was the big story. Six athletes coached by

Graham had tested positive for banned drugs, and in addition he'd coached Montgomery and Jones. It was unavoidable, he said, given the current atmosphere of suspicion in the sport, that the performances of his athletes Justin Gatlin and Shawn Crawford would be questioned. But he maintained he'd never given banned drugs to any of his athletes.

Gatlin backed him up. Talking about coach Graham's sprint base in Raleigh, he said: 'I've been in the camp and I can honestly say that he only coaches us.'

All Gatlin and Crawford could do was get on with the job at hand. In the 200 metres they did just that, with Crawford taking first and Gatlin second. Now, with a spot on the relay team assured, there were three gold medals up for grabs. Next stop Europe.

But the pre-Olympic tour didn't start well for Gatlin. He could only manage a disappointing sixth place at a sweltering London Grand Prix, won impressively by the unbeaten Jamaican Asafa Powell in 9.91, with Greene second. Powell continued to set the pace in Zurich, again beating Greene into second, with Gatlin third.

So when the US team packed up its training base on the Greek island of Crete and headed for the heat of Athens, it had to consider the unthinkable. The 100 metres gold medal might not be returning to the States. Purely on form, the clear favourite was now Asafa Powell, closely followed by Portugal's Francis Obikwelu, world champion Kim Collins and the American trio of Maurice Greene, Shawn Crawford and Justin Gatlin. But it was going to be a tough one to call and the gold medal would go to whoever pulled out the big performance on the day.

Gatlin remembers: 'I felt everyone was a threat and I gave them all equal respect. There really wasn't an out-and-out favourite. Maurice was the reigning champion, but he was getting beat all over the place by Asafa. At the same time my team-mate Shawn Crawford was doing crazy things. He was like Superman. He'd go out and cruise a 9.88 like it was nothing.' Twenty-five-year-old Crawford was a hugely entertaining sprinter and actually described himself as 'Cheetah Man' – a name that stuck after he appeared in a Fox TV show *Man vs Beast* and raced a giraffe and zebra over 100 metres on a dirt track. The zebra won and Crawford accused it of false-starting.

The 'Welcome Home' Games of Athens 2004 opened in the stifling heat of mid-August amid unprecedented security in the wake of the 9/11 atrocity, which had happened a few years earlier, but more than ten thousand athletes from over two hundred countries would take part.

The sprints were immediately in the news when Greek stars Konstantinos Kenteris and training partner Ekaterini Thanou, who both won medals at the Olympic sprints in Sydney, withdrew from their events after apparently staging a motorcycle accident to avoid a drug test. It was an inauspicious start to the Games, but when the 100-metre competition began all the media focus returned to the action on the track rather than the troubles off it.

The first day was a predictable affair, with all the big names moving easily through the first round, but the speeds increased in round two, where Obikwelu threw down the gauntlet with a new national record of 9.93 in the first heat. But the Americans were not to be out-shone, and Shawn Crawford ran a sharp 9.89 in the next heat, with Gatlin following him in heat three with a 9.96. Greene and Powell both ran sub 10-second heats to keep the packed Athens crowd on their feet. The scene was set for a hell of a second day. The semi-finals saw all the big names go through, with Crawford edging Gatlin in the first and Powell beating both Obikwelu and Greene in the second, so with the final a few hours away, the eight finalists all found ways of controlling their nerves and avoiding the clock. All of them except Justin Gatlin.

His calm, pre-planned routine was destroyed by the bizarre intervention of an official. While Gatlin was in the call room putting on his spikes, the man came into the room and demanded to take photographs of his tattoos. Gatlin had a variety of these – the Virgin Mary on his right bicep, God's Speed on his left shoulder, Honor Thy Mother, Honor Thy Father in Japanese on his forearms, Live To Fight, Fight To Live, even an NYC sign on his chest. He's since added more. The over-zealous official, choosing precisely the wrong moment to confront Gatlin, wanted to ensure that his tattoos were not covert advertising transfers that might breach the regulations. The demand infuriated Gatlin.

'I was angry, I am not going to lie,' he explained later. 'This was the biggest race of my life and I don't want anybody that I don't even know taking photos of me. He wanted pictures of tattoos that I have had since I was 15.' He went on to suggest that the incident so fired him up that it gave him extra speed in the final. 'Maybe I should thank him,' he told reporters.

Barbadian Obadele Thompson recalled: 'He was pretty worked up. I think we got on the wrong end of his stick. It was nothing to do with any of the athletes. I just think the whole thing really got him keyed up for the race.'

Just before the start Gatlin simply paced up and down like a caged animal, staring down the track toward the finish. He didn't even react when the stadium announcer called his name.

'I was kind of confused because I didn't know how to approach the race. I had been in a lot of championships – but this was the Olympics. The stadium was really high and it felt like there were so many people. Even though I have a humble side, I also have a side that wants to show off. So every time I put my foot down in the stadium, this electrifying feeling comes over me. As I went into the "set" position I told myself to leave everything on the track. If I lose I'll go back to the drawing board. But just stay relaxed and run as fast as you can.'

In the neighbouring lane his team-mate and training partner Shawn Crawford was all winks and playing to the cameras. He looked supremely calm and relaxed. The eight finalists were Collins in lane one, Ghanaian Aziz Zakari, Gatlin in lane three, Crawford in four, Obikwelu, Powell, Greene and Thompson out in lane eight.

At the gun the 65,000 crowd erupted from near silence as the field got away first time. It was a dream run for Gatlin. He and Kim Collins appeared to get out the blocks quickest and the man from St Kitts held the slimmest of leads at the halfway mark, with Obikwelu and Greene just behind them. But Collins then started to fade and Gatlin powered on to win it, with the fast-finishing Obikwelu holding off Greene for the silver. Pre-race favourites Shawn Crawford and Asafa Powell trailed in a disappointing fourth and fifth. But it was extraordinarily close. Gatlin was timed at 9.85, with Obikwelu at 9.86 and Greene at 9.87. Fractions of centimetres separated first and fourth.

At the finish no one was immediately sure who had won – even the TV commentators weren't convinced. The cameras first went to fourth-placed Crawford and then, after the first slow-motion replays, it was clear that Gatlin had got it. For the first time he broke into a smile and hugged Crawford, then set off on a well-earned victory lap with the American flag.

'I only knew I'd won when I looked up at the scoreboard,' Gatlin recalls. 'It was so close. I felt that I'd won but sometimes it's a little confusing crossing the line. So I didn't want to skip about as if I'd won and then find out I hadn't. That would have been embarrassing. Then I looked up and saw I'd won. The whole thing was like an out-of-body experience, it was really quite surreal. Without question it was my greatest race, a real dogfight all the way to the line.'

He told the waiting reporters: 'I am still trying to feel how fast I ran. Shockingly fast. I am glad I have the gold medal. I knew I could take a 9.85, I just didn't know when it was going to happen. That is what I work so hard for on the track, to show everybody here and around the world that track and field can be positive and all sports can still be positive.'

With appalling timing, just over an hour after the race, his coach Trevor Graham triggered the next track and field scandal by admitting to sending a syringe of the designer steroid Tetrahydrogestrinone – helpfully abridged to THG – to the US Anti-Doping Agency (USADA). His purpose, he later told the *New York Times*, was 'just a coach doing the right thing' and to reveal that the hitherto undetectable drug – nicknamed 'The Clear' – was being created and sold by the BALCO comany. In truth it smacked more of self-protection, revenge or sabotaging a rival, possibly a combination of all three, rather than his claimed altruism.

Federal prosecutors simply saw it as a piece of theatrical sleight of hand by Graham and the resulting frenzy implicated eight of his athletes and would later lead to his own indictment for lying to investigators, a 12-month house arrest and a lifetime ban from coaching.

Despite this substantial distraction, Gatlin beamed happily from the top of the medal podium. 'I didn't know what to do, sing the anthem or not,' he laughs. 'I wasn't 100 per cent sure I knew all the words, but I knew the camera would be on me, so I thought I'd just keep quiet and smile.' After the ceremony he dedicated the medal to his high school coach Jay Cormier.

He then went back out on the track and took a bronze in the 200 metres final in a clean medal sweep by the Americans, with Crawford taking gold in 19.79, and Bernard Williams the silver.

That left the sprint relay, in which the Americans, with Gatlin, Crawford and Greene, alongside 27-year-old Mississippi farm boy Coby Miller, looked certain to take the gold and maybe even a new world record into the bargain. But lack of relay practice came back to haunt them and in the final pure speed simply wasn't good enough.

Poor handovers, first from lead-off man Crawford to Gatlin, then from Gatlin to Miller, where the 100-metre champion appeared to step on the back of his team-mate's foot on the changeover, left anchor man Greene about a metre down on Britain's Mark

Lewis-Francis. Greene closed the gap, but the Briton just managed to hold him off to win an exhilarating race by just one-hundredth of a second – the closest relay finish in Olympic history.

So Gatlin left Athens with a complete set of medals – gold, silver and bronze – and received a hero's welcome when he returned to Florida. He also made it on to the famous Wheaties breakfast cereal box, along with swimmer Michael Phelps and gymnast Carly Patterson – a post-Olympic tradition with the cereal makers General Mills that went back to the 1930s and Johnny Weissmuller and Jesse Owens.

It wasn't long before he was back on the track, running a sharp 9.97 at a big international meeting in Yokohama, Japan, to beat fellow American Leonard Scott, with Maurice Greene a tired-looking fifth.

The end of Olympic year saw a raft of awards and honours for Gatlin, none more prestigious than the Jesse Owens award for best male athlete, which was presented by USA Track and Field in Portland, Oregon.

The following year was another golden one for Gatlin, with a sprint double at the US championships in Carson, California, and a double gold medal-winning performance at the World Athletics Championships in Helsinki. His world championship 100 metres victory was utterly convincing, the widest winning margin in the history of the event, in a comfortable 9.88. But the fastest man of the year wasn't there.

Jamaican Asafa Powell had broken Tim Montgomery's world record in June, with a stunning 9.77-second run in Athens, and then succumbed to a groin injury. But even with a shortened season he still claimed the three fastest times of the year. Gatlin wasn't complaining and added the 200 metres title on a rain-sodden evening, powering across the line several metres ahead of the field in 20.04 to lead an unprecedented American 1-2-3-4.

He seemed to have the world at his feet and, despite 2006 being a year with no championships, Gatlin finally landed the big prize on May 12, when he broke the world 100 metres record – or so he thought. It was at an IAAF meeting, in Doha, in Qatar, and with a brisk but legal wind of 1.7 metres per second behind him he stopped the clock at 9.76.

Gatlin celebrated wildly, running into the stands to see his American team-mates and telling reporters: 'I felt in my heart that I could do it anywhere I went. My agent kept telling me to tone it down because I kept saying I could break the world record. I think I proved it.'

But Gatlin's celebrations lasted only four days before an acutely embarrassed IAAF realized they had made a mistake and had wrongly rounded down his official time of 9.766. After all the headlines, Gatlin had only equalled the world record of 9.77, not beaten it. This, however, was to be the least of his problems.

The IAAF record debacle was to presage a wholesale unravelling of Justin Gatlin's world. In July, he was informed by USADA that he had tested positive at the April Kansas Relays meeting for 'testosterone or its precursors'. The news was a hammer blow, and he loudly protested his innocence to a largely disbelieving media, saying: 'I cannot account for these results, because I have never knowingly used any banned substance or authorized anyone to administer such a substance to me.'

Whether he did or he didn't, Gatlin knew the positive test would be linked back to his earlier ban, albeit for what was acknowledged to have been a prescribed medication. But the automatic punishment for two infringements was clear. Justin Gatlin, the fastest man on earth, would be banned from the track for life.

The Olympic champion had become something of a poster boy for running clean. He had even told a *Sports Illustrated* reporter that if he were ever to test positive it might KO the sport. 'I know how important it is that I'm clean,' he said. He told another writer: 'I think that people who feel that they have to use drugs and manipulate their fans are criminals. You're cheating yourself.'

The explanation for the positive test, first proffered by Coach Graham and taken up by Gatlin himself, was sabotage. This was a bizarre tale involving the alleged actions of a vengeful masseur, Chris Whetstine, who had, they maintained, rubbed steroid cream into Gatlin without his knowledge.

Exactly what Whetstine's motives were for these strange actions never really became clear, the accusation that he did it in revenge against Graham and Gatlin being largely unsubstantiated. It was hard for the naturally suspicious track and field media and the disgruntled fans to feel anything but crushing disappointment at yet another re-run of the drug-abusing athlete story.

The masseur himself had enjoyed a chequered career. He was disciplined by the Oregon Board of Massage Therapists for 'unprofessional conduct' in 2003 and had been contracted to work exclusively with Gatlin by sports company Nike. He dismissed the allegations of sabotage out of hand.

Gatlin explains: 'Me and my family have put these dots together. He worked for me in 2004 and 2005 and towards the end of that year he told me he deserved a $50,000 bonus. I had some pull with Nike back then and I had got him a full-time job and a regular pay cheque, but when we said no to the bonus I think he felt slighted.

'Going into 2006 he started coming to meets and then disappearing. He wasn't around to do the work and he was really slacking, so we fired him. But for the European season we had to hire three guys to cover for him. The irony was that he was really good at his job, so we brought him back. That was my biggest mistake, firing and then re-hiring someone who was disgruntled.'

The sport's governing body, the IAAF, called for the statutory lifetime ban, but when Gatlin co-operated with USADA and accepted the provenance of the tests, the American authorities imposed a slightly less harsh punishment – an eight-year ban. For an athlete of 24, it was still effectively a life ban, and it looked like Gatlin's career was over. In addition, his world record was wiped from the record books.

As a sign of goodwill and thanks for Gatlin's co-operation with the federal investigation into the activities of his coach Trevor Graham, the ban was eventually halved to four years after arbitration. Even then, it wasn't short enough to allow him to defend his Olympic title. Gatlin's legal team continued to fight to get him back on the track sooner, and with the 2008 Beijing Olympics beckoning they made one last attempt to overturn the ban, suggesting he should be allowed to run in the summer's US Olympic trials because the earlier positive test for an amphetamine in his prescription medication violated his rights under the Americans with Disabilities Act.

The lawyers argued that if this earlier ban had been expunged, his ban for the later positive test would only have been two years, thereby allowing him to resume his career. But the 11th US Circuit Court of Appeals was unpersuaded and in June it turned down Gatlin's request for an injunction allowing him to run. The only course open to him was the Supreme Court, but Gatlin decided that enough was enough and he would see out the rest of his ban.

A month earlier Coach Graham had been convicted of lying to federal investigators about his relationship with a known steroids dealer. Gatlin had helped the authorities gather incriminating evidence on Graham, allowing phone calls between them to be taped.

In July Graham was banned for life by USADA. Bill Roe, the president of USA Track & Field, said: 'Through his involvement in fostering the use of performance-enhancing drugs, Mr Graham jeopardized the health of his athletes, to say nothing of their integrity and their future ability to compete in the sport.'

In October Graham was sentenced to a year of house arrest. His lawyers told the court he had been driving a school bus to make ends meet.

The BALCO scandal that engulfed American sport led to prison terms for the company's founder Victor Conte and one-time golden girl Marion Jones. Her former partner Tim Montgomery fell the furthest. In a San Francisco court he confessed to a systematic use of performance-enhancing drugs and was banned from the sport. Next he was arrested and convicted of a multi-million dollar cheque fraud and then heroin dealing. Montgomery, once the world's fastest man, spent six years in prison in Alabama, earning 12 cents an hour on the landscaping crew. His nine-year sentence was cut for good behaviour and he was released in May 2012, first to a halfway house, then to confinement at home with an electronic tag. It wasn't until October that year that he was finally released on probation.

He was married in 2009 while in prison and, although he lost custody of his son Monty to then-girlfriend Marion Jones, he managed to find happiness with wife Jamalee and daughter Tymiah, who is a member of the track team at the University of Florida.

Today he lives quietly in Gainesville, Florida, and has created a small business training youngsters for speed and fitness. It's called NUMA – Never Under-Estimate My Ability. His biography on the company's website reads: 'Tim Montgomery knows exactly what it takes to be the fastest man in the world. He also knows the price one pays when achieving such goals illegally.' His is a redemptive story, of sorts, and today he's calmer and philosophic about past misdemeanours. 'I didn't lose at the first part of my life. I just made a bad choice. I won't lose the second part of my life.'

Though Gatlin has steadfastly maintained his innocence, it must be said that the circumstantial evidence was very persuasive and, outside the tight circle of his family and friends, there seemed to be only a few people who felt willing to publicly support his position. His four years in the track and field wilderness were tough, but he managed to fill them. 'I learned to be a man,' he told a Florida newspaper. 'As a professional athlete, everything was handed to me. Things I needed to do, I had people do for me. No more.' He spent his time coaching kids, opened a gym, worked on a TV show, even tried out for a handful of NFL teams. But the real highlight was the birth of his son, Jace, in May 2010.

However, the lure of the track was strong, and Gatlin stuck to his guns, served his time and on August 3, 2010, he returned to the track in the rather modest surroundings of Rakvere, a tiny town tucked away in a remote part of northern Estonia, in Eastern Europe. He ran a solid, if unspectacular, 10.24 to win his first comeback 100-metre race, then improved a few days later to win his second in 10.17 at the ERGO Games, in the Estonian capital Tallinn. A few weeks later in Rovereto, Italy, he brought his time down to 10.06, running a close second to Jamaica's Yohan Blake, a training partner of Usain Bolt, and he finished his season running consistently in the ten zeros.

'Step by step it's a case of getting back out there,' says Gatlin. 'It's just like learning to ride a bike again. It's a little sketchy at first, but once the wheels start turning, it's OK. Maybe I'll start a new trend. I've always been one to be a little different. Maybe everyone will want to take a rejuvenating time out!'

The first few races were, perhaps predictably, a far cry from the world class-successes of Athens and Helsinki, but at least they were a start. For Gatlin the immediate goal was to make the 2011 World Championships in South Korea, the London Olympics of 2012 and prepare professionally for a genuine shot at redemption, both personal and professional.

Gatlin was uncertain about how his return to the track world would be received. His anxiety was not misplaced. The media were largely dismissive and the big European track bosses ran an informal agreement to exclude many previously banned athletes, even if they had served their time. Gatlin was clearly on the list.

As Patrick Magyar, the man behind the Zurich *Weltklasse*, told journalists: 'Mr Gatlin has massively damaged our sport. It is very clear that we will not be in a position to invite him in this or upcoming years.' So Gatlin simply had to find other races to run, which he certainly did. He travelled around obscure track outposts in the Caribbean, Scandinavia, the US and even a bizarre appearance on a Japanese game show to 'break' the world record with the aid of wind turbines. Steadily the old Justin Gatlin was put back together again, piece by piece.

Naturally, the past continued to haunt him and at one press conference the *New York Times* journalist Jere Longman, who believes Gatlin is in complete denial over the whole affair, asked him pointedly: 'Why don't you just admit it? Then people would probably embrace you more.' Gatlin calmly replied: 'For the whole five years since it happened, I've stuck by my story. It hasn't swayed. That's the way I was raised and if I did it, I would have said so.'

Despite friction with the media, the comeback continued. In June 2011 he ducked under the ten second barrier for the first time since his return, with a 9.97 at the Prefontaine Classic 100 metres, in Oregon. Less positively, he only finished sixth, but progress was being made and the next stop was a big one: the national championships, effectively the trials for the World Championships, to be held later that year in South Korea.

It was here that the beginnings of a truly remarkable comeback story really took shape, when Gatlin claimed his spot on the American team by finishing second to Walter Dix in the 100 metres with a time of 9.95. As the TV cameras closed in on him at the finish, he lifted his head to the heavens and screamed, before dropping to his knees in floods of tears. 'I had a lot of pent-up frustration, sadness and anger at the end of the race today, I just let out a roar. I just let it all out. I cried at the end, I was so happy,' Gatlin told the US press. 'I have lots of support from my fans. They gave me so many well-wishes on the Internet and there wasn't a lot of hatred.'

Preparations began immediately for Daegu, with a training camp in Florida run by veteran coach Brooks Johnson, a man who publicly predicted Gatlin would run world class times again if he could regain premium fitness.

The motivation clearly worked for Gatlin, though he remained typically sanguine. 'Maybe it's something about my ADD. I just don't over-analyse things. I'm able to channel all the hard work into the big days. They don't bother me.' His laconic style even lent a hint of comedy to his arrival in South Korea, where he matter-of-factly announced to an incredulous media that he was suffering from the after-effects of frostbite to his feet. He'd been using a cryogenic chamber to speed recovery from training and ventured in one day wearing damp socks. The result was that after just two minutes he suffered burns and blisters to his feet. Playing it down, he said:' I definitely don't want to sit in the stands eating popcorn and watch other guys run. I am hungry. I have a sensational appetite to go out there and run my heart out. Just to know that I am here, I feel blessed.'

However, the World Championships came a little early for him and he went out, albeit narrowly, in the semi-finals. Despite that frustration, he was philosophic. Asked immediately after his race if he still envisioned beating Usain Bolt next year, he smiled: 'I envision beating everybody next year.'

And that remained his real target: London 2012. 'My dream is to stand on the podium in 2012 and run around the track holding my son,' he explained. 'Now I have him I want him to grow up smiling and look at me and say "Wow, that's what you did Dad, that's great." I want him to have the best.'

His performances continued to improve and he was even welcomed back into elite competition, when in May 2012 he ran a 9.87 to win the Diamond League opener in Doha, out-dipping the in-form Jamaican Asafa Powell on the line. Six weeks later he went to the US Olympic Trials in Eugene, Oregon, and won the 100 metres in a post-ban personal best time of 9.80. With reigning champion Usain Bolt's form in apparent flux, it was Gatlin who was now installed among the favourites to depose him in London.

But Bolt found his form at the right time, striding imperiously to the second fastest time ever – 9.63 – with team-mate Yohan Blake second in 9.75. Gatlin was a long way back and had to settle for a bronze medal, albeit with a new personal record of 9.79. He did, at least, fulfil his dream of a podium. 'I want to beat Bolt,' he said. 'He's a stellar athlete, he's a showman. People pay a lot of money to see that. He's the incentive to train even more and I think I can step up to the plate. It's not about times, but running to the line, being the first across it. Running for me is an out-of-body experience. I will compete until I can compete no more.'

And compete he has. From the end of the London Olympics a recurring pattern was set – the big American chasing the tall Jamaican, a high-speed soap opera played out on the tracks around the world. And the song remained the same, with Gatlin playing second fiddle to Bolt in major championships, though edging inexorably closer with every race. He did manage to beat his old foe at the IAAF Rome Golden Gala in the summer of 2013 and took a Diamond League 100 on home soil at Oregon's Prefontaine Classic in an impressive 9.88, joking that he was ageing 'like fine wine'.

His next big target was the 14th World Championships, in Moscow, and he looked ominously strong in qualifying. On a wild and rainy night he fell short once again, though, splashing in behind the Jamaican to take the silver in 9.85 – half a metre and almost a tenth of a second away. 'I went out there to compete in the last half of the race instead of running a technical race and that's why I got silver and not gold,' he told reporters. 'I thought I had it for a while but then I saw those long legs coming on my right.'

Gatlin continued to wreak sprinting havoc around the big global meets through the end of 2013 and 2014, especially as Bolt rarely made an appearance. But while his bank account grew appreciably, he knew that only a win in a major championship against the Jamaican would cement his place in history and perhaps erase, in some small measure, the darker elements of his running past. In September 2014 he lowered his 100 metres personal best to 9.77 while winning the Diamond League final in Brussels, and completed the sprint double with a 19.71 in the 200 metres. Usain Bolt, as the media duly noted, was not competing.

Still the barbs continued to fly, and it wasn't just the press. When Gatlin was nominated for IAAF Athlete of the Year, German discus thrower Robert Harting asked for his name to be taken off the list of nominees in protest.

Eyebrows had already been raised when Gatlin appointed another former US Olympic sprinter, Dennis Mitchell, as his coach. During his running career, Mitchell served a two-year ban after testing positive for testosterone. As journalist Doug Gillon suggested in the *Glasgow Herald*: 'This is the incestuous world of doping and coaching which Lord Coe (the new President of the IAAF) must unravel.' All Gatlin could do was to keep working, keep training and keep winning. Back on the track, in May 2015 he improved his 100 metres personal best to 9.74 at the Qatar Super Prix, but what he really wanted was to beat Usain Bolt in a major championship final. The 2015 World Championships in Beijing, he felt, would be the place.

Incredibly, in a sport brought low by relentless revelations about drug-enhanced performances, entire nations conspiring to cheat the system and even the sport's own governing body mired in corruption, it was Gatlin who was still routinely singled out for character assassination, even a full five years after he returned from his ban. Somehow he had become a poster boy for everything that was wrong with the sport – the personification of all track and field evil. It seemed incredibly unfair and one-eyed.

Guilty or not, Gatlin had served his time. He had expressed remorse and sought to be a better role model for the sport, following the rules and – which nobody had foreseen – returning bigger, better and faster. But perhaps that was where the real problem lay. The media was content for him to return after serving his ban, but they seemed to view it as somehow impolite that he had also returned better than he was before.

So why single out Justin Gatlin? Why was he guiltier than everyone else? What about the Russians, the Chinese, the Kenyans, even the other Americans? Were they not famous enough? More likely was they were not running against Usain Bolt.

Could it be that the media simply needed to create an 'Anti-Bolt' as the 'baddie' in their storylines? As Gatlin was now the man regarded as the biggest threat to the sport's true hero and flag bearer, he was perfect for the role – a convicted 'heavy' straight out of Hollywood central casting.

British journalist Oliver Brown wrote in the *Daily Telegraph*: 'Athletics quite simply deserves a better ambassador than Gatlin. He might well be a "good guy" to his friends, but equally he is a bothersome impediment to the sport's rehabilitation in the eyes of a jaded public. Yes, his continued demonization is a reductive exercise. But when you carry an indelible taint like his, in an event meant to be the purest athletic test that exists, then that is the soup you swim in.'

It was a strange, hugely over-simplified and astonishingly myopic summary. Had Gatlin ever portrayed himself as an ambassador? Does this book suggest the 100 metres was ever the purest athletic test that exists? And more pointedly, was Gatlin the only athlete who had ever fallen from the path? It seemed that Gatlin's broad shoulders would need to carry all the ills of decades of drug abuse, appalling governance, poor oversight and old-fashioned corruption. As the perceptive writer Richard Moore asked in *The Scotsman*: 'Where was the outrage before Daegu 2011, London 2012 or Moscow 2013?' The answer now lay in Gatlin's competitiveness.

Ultimately, whatever the reasons, whatever anyone believed, this 100 metres was not going to be simply a titanic battle between two great sprinters, but more a moral play about the future wellbeing of athletics. Bolt v Gatlin – The Sequel. It was like when Muhammad Ali fought Joe Frazier for the second time in 1974. The media and the fans chose sides. Battle lines were drawn, and not just on the track.

Leaving all the hype and intrigue behind, it was actually a terrific race. Gatlin had a picture book start and was flying by halfway. This time the big Jamaican couldn't get away from the field, and with 20 metres to go it looked good for the American. But in the end Gatlin lost again. The gap to Bolt, though, had closed still further. An almost imperceptible 0.01 seconds separated them on the line. Bolt took gold in 9.79, with Gatlin a hair's breadth behind in 9.80. It seemed as if the American had just dipped too early and his chance had gone.

His long-time agent and former hurdling legend Renaldo Nehemiah summarized it perfectly. 'I just think he wanted to get to the line before the line was there. I told him, when you look back on this, you'll realize you handed him that race.'

Afterwards, at least for the public and the media, Gatlin was all smiles and good grace, but Nehemiah revealed the disappointment had hit him hard and that there were tears when they finally saw each other outside the stadium. Bolt's victory in the 200 metres was more decisive, but Gatlin still claimed another silver and the right to be the sole challenger to the Bolt crown in Rio. On paper, at least, it was going to be mighty close in the Estadio Olimpico. The media opprobrium showed no sign of abating. During the Championships the BBC's respected commentators Steve Cram and Michael Johnson both ventured the view that Gatlin had showed no contrition and had done nothing to endear himself to the public. After Beijing, an exasperated Nehemiah released letters revealing the extent to which Gatlin cooperated with US anti-doping investigators and apologised for his own wrongdoing. Even US Track & Field wrote to the IAAF explaining that Gatlin had gone into colleges to talk about the consequences of doping and the importance of competing clean. 'When people say he never apologized,' said Nehemiah, 'I say: you haven't done your homework. What is he supposed to do, go to every country and say sorry?'

Gatlin, for his part, says simply: 'Obviously I am the most criticized athlete in track and field but at the end of the day I am a runner and that's all I can be. I just keep my head down and keep running.'

During 2015, Gatlin estimated he was tested more than 70 times, the majority of them when the testers turned up unannounced at his home in Florida at all times of the day and night. 'It's fine with me, I have nothing to hide, nothing to run from,' he said. 'So I'm happy with how many times I'm tested.'

As Olympic year dawned there were dark mutterings around the sport that injuries were catching up with Usain Bolt. While the Jamaican champion hardly set the track alight in 2016, even missing his own national trials with a hamstring problem, Gatlin was racking up more and more impressive times. He'd lost just a single 100 metres race in the previous two seasons – the 2015 World Championships final – and he was simply irresistible on the Diamond League circuit. At the US Olympic Trials, in front of a vocal 22,000 crowd in Eugene, Oregon, Gatlin posted a world leading 9.80 in a smoothly run 100 metres victory, with youngster Trayvon Bromell second and Marvin Bracey third. He followed that with a 19.75 win in the 200 metres. It was game on.

'If you look at it, me and Usain are the only guys who've run 9.7 in the last couple of years,' he told the American press pack. 'He's going to do just enough to get on the podium. We both have run very fast so it's not like we need to make any kind of statements by running superfast, super early. It's about both of us running fast at the right moment.

'Sprinting and the 100 metres is a science, but when it comes to true competition there's no science to it. You got to go out there and you got to execute your race and when you do that you got to have some guts, you've got to be able to get to the finish line and stay focused.'

As Rio approached more and more pundits began to switch sides and back the American to take the gold. They had all forgotten what genuinely motivated Usain Bolt – competition at the very highest level. And so it proved.

The Jamaican recorded the fastest time in the semi-finals – a swift 9.86 – and just over an hour and a half later the eight finalists walked out into the cauldron of a near sold-out stadium to a roar of chanting – 'Bolt, Bolt, Bolt.'

This time it wasn't even close, and Bolt emerged from the pack at 40 metres and bounded across the line well clear of the field in 9.81 seconds, with Gatlin second in 9.89 and Canada's Andre de Grasse third. Bolt had won three in a row, but Gatlin was the oldest man, at 34, to win an Olympic 100 metres medal and although his time was slower than his 2004 and 2012 finals, he now had an unprecedented set of Olympic 100 medals – gold, silver and bronze.

'I'm just happy to be on the podium,' he told a packed press conference. 'I'm the oldest guy in the field, so for me to be able to get on the podium is an honour.'

He then took a rather unwanted record in the 200 metres, running a 20.13 and becoming the fastest man not to qualify for a final, and was part of yet another American relay disaster. The 4 x 100 was won by the Jamaican team, with Japan pipping the USA for the silver, but the American team had almost completed their bronze medal celebration lap when the scoreboard told them they had been disqualified for a changeover zone infraction.

It was possibly the Rio disappointment as much as the injury niggles that dogged him through most of a disappointing 2017 season, but the relentless Gatlin competitive spirit would return at the World Championships in London, in August.

He went into the US trials, in California, with a best time of just 10.14 to his name. No fewer than 17 entrants in the competition had run faster that year. But the 35-year-old had timed his peak to perfection and took the win in 9.95 seconds, ahead of rising star and NCAA champion Christian Coleman and Christopher Belcher.

A final showdown beckoned with the soon-to-be-retiring Usain Bolt. One last chance to defeat his old foe in a major championship. Gatlin described the opportunity as 'surreal' and explained: 'As your career goes on, the more success you have, that window of hunger becomes smaller and smaller. The quest for me is to find that hunger again. This is something I want to fight for.'

And so he did. All the way to the finish line in a raucous, packed London Stadium, late on a clear-skied August Saturday night.

Running from lanes two to nine – the finalists were China's Bingtian Su, Jimmy Vicaut of France, Usain Bolt, in his last-ever individual race, Christian Coleman, who had the year's best time of 9.82, then South Africa's Akani Simbine, Yohan Blake, Justin Gatlin in lane eight and Britain's Reece Prescod on the outside.

As the smiling and relaxed-looking Bolt strolled onto the track the roar of the crowd almost took the roof off, in complete contrast to the barrage of booing that greeted the announcement of Gatlin. Pantomime season had started early.

A loud but electrifying 'sssssh' echoed around the stadium as the eight men went to their blocks. The crowd roared as they got away first time and the diminutive Coleman shot into an early lead, pursued by a very slow-starting Bolt. All the focus seemed to be on those two in centre field, but out in lane eight, away from their peripheral vision, Gatlin was catching, catching, catching. He dipped hard on the line and the three athletes spun to a halt and the whole field, indeed the whole crowd, stopped to look at the big screen replay and the scoreboard to confirm who had won. It was that close.

The scoreboard lit up. Gatlin, a 25 to 1 outsider, had won it and more boos rang out from the crowd. The American roared at the sky, put his fingers to his lips and spotted Bolt. He immediately dropped to his knees in mock adulation and subservience. Bolt gave him a big hug and told him: 'Man, I didn't see you.'

With tears in his eyes, Gatlin sank to his knees again just as his time – a season's best 9.92 – flashed up on the big screens, with teammate Coleman second in 9.94 and Bolt taking the bronze in 9.95. Bolt's fairytale finale had not materialized; the sport's bogeyman had finally won his big day. Justin Gatlin was the world 100 metres champion.

Bolt was typically magnanimous: 'Over the years I've always said he's done his time and if he's here it's ok. I've always respected him as a competitor. Over the years he's worked hard and I've always said that he's one of the best competitors I've ever competed with. I know that if I don't show up he's always going to win and tonight he showed up. He was a better man tonight and he came out and killed us.'

Gatlin explained: 'I wasn't really focused on the boos or thinking that my win tonight was a disaster. I really did it for my fans, my support staff, my country, my people who really believed in me when I didn't believe in myself. I stepped on the starting line and it was the first time I've ever run a race where I really wasn't thinking about myself. I was thinking about them and it took the pressure away from me.'

The press reaction was predictably hostile. *The Observer* journalist Sean Ingle opened his report of the race thus: 'As a full moon rose over the London Stadium, athletics' greatest pantomime villain, Justin Gatlin sank his teeth into the carefully laid plans for Usain Bolt's retirement party.'

'Bolt was no longer stunning. He was just stunned,' cried the *Los Angeles Times*; 'Spoiler Alert: Bolt Upset', headlined the *Chicago Tribune*, and 'Justin Gatlin Steals Gold' shouted the *Daily Mail*.

IAAF President Lord Coe seemed even less impressed, telling the BBC it was certainly 'not the perfect script'. He added: 'I'm not eulogistic that someone who has served two bans walked off with one of our glittering prizes.'

That prompted a spiky response from Gatlin's manager Renaldo Nehemiah. 'I don't condone doping but Justin Gatlin is not the poster child for it. He's done his time, he plays by the rules, the IAAF reinstated him. They said if you come back we should accept that. So to put a narrative out that it's just Justin Gatlin and he's the bad guy, it's not really fair. It's inhumane, it's unsportsmanlike.'

Looking back on the victory and the reaction to it, some months later, Gatlin explained: 'I kind of predicted that was going to happen, so I guess it didn't really affect me that much. I looked at the variables going into it. It's Usain's last season, it's Usain's last world championships, it's Usain's last race. I looked at it and said "if any time I've been the black hat to his white hat, it's going to be the most right now. He is the adopted child of London, of England. They love him there just as much as they do in Jamaica. For me, it was like I knew I was going to be the bad guy. Did I know to that magnitude?

No, I didn't. But I did know I was more of a threat than I had ever been in the past.'

Before leaving London, Gatlin took silver as part of the American relay team beaten by Great Britain, but if he expected life to calm down as the sport moved into its winter hibernation, he was sadly mistaken.

In December 2017, the British newspaper, *The Daily Telegraph*, splashed its front page with the banner headline 'Gatlin embroiled in new athletics doping scandal'. The story detailed a lengthy undercover investigation by the paper in which they revealed members of Gatlin's team offered to supply them with illicit performance-enhancing drugs. It was alleged that Gatlin's coach Dennis Mitchell and an agent named Robert Wagner had offered to supply and administer testosterone and THG, via a doctor in Austria, for an actor requiring bulking up for a movie role.

The newspaper conceded that: 'There is no evidence Gatlin is currently using any banned substances' but questioned his judgement over the make-up of his entourage.

Gatlin reacted by immediately firing Mitchell and strenuously denying any involvement in the allegations levelled by the *Telegraph*. The Athletics Integrity Unit found Wagner guilty of serious violations under their code and banned him from the sport for two years. Ominously, they say their investigation is still on-going.

The emotional upheaval pushed Gatlin back to his old mentor, the veteran coach Brooks Johnson, then in his mid-eighties, to get himself back on an even keel. The following year would be a usefully quiet one for Gatlin, with no major championships, so he used the time to rest his ageing body, spend time with his family and re-organize his coaching plans. He first connected with the Florida-based Gary Evans, who looked after Bahamian quarter-miler Steven Gardiner and Jamaican hurdler Omar McLeod, but by the summer of 2019 he was back with Mitchell.

It wasn't until June that Gatlin troubled any of the scoreboards on the Diamond League circuit, when he came home second to Christian Coleman in Eugene, Oregon, with a 9.87 – his fastest 100 since 2016. Wins followed in perfect conditions at both Lausanne and Monaco and they helped re-build form and confidence – and as reigning world 100 metres champion, his wild card meant he didn't have to go through the perilous US trials.

So Gatlin arrived in Doha for the 2019 World Championships well rested but also running into decent form. With Usain Bolt happily retired, the trials winner Christian Coleman would be the man to beat, an athlete Gatlin described competing with as 'like running against a 23-year-old version of me'.

But the 37-year-old version couldn't quite get the job done, once again following Coleman over the line to take a silver medal in 9.89. Coleman peaked perfectly and ran a personal best 9.76 to take the title. 'I had an up and down season,' Gatlin conceded. 'I had some injuries, I had a question mark over my head whether I was even going to come to the championships and I still made the finals and the podium. I'm just thankful.'

Unlike many athletes, when the Covid-19 pandemic shut down the sport in early 2020, it didn't trouble Gatlin too much. After all, another year's rest and rehabilitation might further protect his ageing muscles, extend his speed and allow him a final shot at Olympic glory in Japan.

There may be some grey flecks in that close-cropped black hair these days, but his competitive streak still burns deep. He'll be an almost unbelievable 39 years old when the re-arranged Olympics gets underway, but he continues to post impressive times (including a 9.98 at the Miramar Invitational, in Florida, in April 2021) and a lifetime dream for him is for his son Jace, who will be eleven by then, to watch him run in Tokyo.

'We said maybe we'd go and watch from the stands, but then I thought that maybe there's an opportunity to get on the podium,' he says.

Justin Gatlin has certainly seen both sides of being the fastest man on earth and admits: 'With great privilege, comes great responsibility. Everyone expected me to win every race and break every record. Everywhere you go, you're the man, even outside of sport. It was a golden ticket to get in anywhere, the key to the city. It felt good.'

There is talk of a forthright documentary about his life – working title *Gatlin Untold* – and an opportunity to set the record straight. 'I'm not trying to get anyone to believe me, or be on my side,' he says. 'I just want to get my viewpoint across. Usually the first thing that people ask me once they get to know me is "what really happened?". That's one of the questions I want to answer. Just lay it all out there.'While he admits to making mistakes during his career and sometimes trusting the wrong people, the likeable, quietly-spoken Gatlin still wants to leave behind a lasting and positive sporting legacy. 'I let people down, my parents have been through all the joy and all the pain with me. I let the world down for not being careful and I am sorry for the actions that I caused. But I'd like people to remember me as a survivor – an Olympic champion, a world champion, a world record holder too – but through all those things I've been through, positive and negative, that I fought all the way.'

It's going to be a long, hard road, but maybe, just maybe, the rollercoaster story of Justin Gatlin is not quite done yet.

CHAPTER TWENTY-THREE

Beijing 2008, London 2012 & Rio de Janeiro 2016

Usain Bolt

It's hard to imagine today, but Usain Bolt's extraordinary Olympic adventure began with defeat and disappointment.

Just three days after his eighteenth birthday, back in 2004, Bolt ran his first Olympic race in the 200 metres competition in the stifling summer heat of Athens. It went badly.

Great things had been expected of him, especially in his native Jamaica, where two years earlier, as a spindly 15-year-old, he'd won the 200 metres title in the world junior championships.

Then, in April of Olympic year, he broke the world junior record at the CARIFTA Games, in Bermuda, running a sensational 19.93 seconds. Everyone agreed it was time for him to mix it with the big boys. Everyone, that is, except Bolt himself.

He didn't feel ready for the Olympics and, instead, wanted to focus on defending his world junior title in Italy.

Two weeks after breaking the junior record he badly damaged his hamstring in training and missed the trip to Italy. After several months of rehabilitation and treatment he began running again, but he wasn't right and he knew it. He didn't want to go to the Olympics because he knew he wouldn't be able to run at his best – but everyone ignored him, including his coach back then, Fitz Coleman, and the rest of the Jamaican athletic authorities. They thought it would be a positive experience for him and they wanted their new *wunderkind* on show to the world.

In the first round of the competition it would be the first four to qualify, but Bolt finished a poor fifth and clocked a dreadful 21.05, a time he would normally beat in his sleep. As he loped forlornly off the track in the half-empty stadium, the skinny Jamaican teenager felt only a huge sense of relief that the whole thing was over.

He recalled: 'My legs were heavy and every step felt lousy. I had no energy and my strength had gone to God knows where.'

Outside Jamaica, little was written about this fleeting cameo appearance and the early exit of Usain St Leo Bolt, and this rather unpromising Olympic debut offered absolutely no hint of the explosion of talent and success that was to come.

When he returned home to Jamaica, the widespread negative reaction to his performance from the media and general public bordered on the vitriolic. The prevailing view was that their big new sprint hope had let them down and should have done better. It genuinely shook Bolt and provided a valuable lesson for the future.

It also provided the catalyst for a seminal change of direction that would help propel Bolt into the stratosphere of the sport. With their relationship effectively broken down, he decided to drop Coleman and select a new coach, the sprint expert Glen Mills. A new partnership was born and it would prove to be a golden one.

Mills had already enjoyed a great deal of success with sprinters at Jamaica's High Performance Centre and Bolt had heard good things about him. He'd also coached Kim Collins, the St Kitts sprinter, to the 2003 world championship 100-metre title. His more collaborative, less dictatorial, approach to coaching suited the laid-back Bolt far better.

The first job at hand for Mills was to get to the bottom of why Bolt suffered so many injuries, especially to his hamstrings. The diagnosis was a total bombshell. After a detailed medical examination, the doctor told Bolt he had an innate condition called scoliosis, which caused his spine to curve to the right. 'I always had a sore back and the doctor told me that was the reason,' said Bolt. 'It also made my right leg half an inch shorter than the left and affected my pelvis. It wasn't the news I wanted to hear.'

It was about to get worse. The doctor's view was that the condition was so bad that he ought to seriously consider giving up athletics altogether. But a referral to an expert in Germany persuaded Bolt that all was not lost.

The man who effectively saved his career before it even really began was the pioneering Hans Müller-Wohlfahrt, a Munich doctor famed for his unorthodox, homeopathic treatment of some of the biggest sports stars in the world, from footballers Michael Owen, Ronaldo and Jurgen Klinsmann to top track and field stars such as Maurice Greene and British distance runner Paula Radcliffe. He was also the club doctor at the Bayern Munich football club for nearly 40 years, having been personally recruited by former club president Franz Beckenbauer.

Bolt received regular treatment at Wohlfahrt's German clinic throughout his career and his enormous success on the track is a ringing endorsement of the good doctor's work.

With the back problem now under control, Coach Mills set about preparing a more bespoke training regime for his new charge. Mills immediately understood the delicate balance of handling an athlete of Bolt's obvious talent along with his more casual relationship with training.

'It was difficult to keep yourself motivated all the time,' said Bolt. 'It's easy to get a little bit lazy. But I had a lot of great people around me and my coach was always on me, ensuring I kept focused and training. And my parents and friends were always around too, so I got plenty of support.' Bolt's background is fundamental to his success, and while his upbeat personality and humour are pure Jamaican, so too is the discipline he got from his parents, who brought him up in a quiet little town called Coxeath, near Sherwood Content, in the Trelawny district in the north of the island.

Bolt was born there in August 1986 and grew up in a small two-bedroomed, rented house with his parents, younger brother Sadiki and older sister Christine. His father Wellesley worked for a local coffee company and was an old-school disciplinarian, while mother Jennifer was the more relaxed. She was also a devout churchgoer and together they instilled solid values in their children. While Bolt's playful, easy-going exterior is what the public sees today, his quiet, almost humble presence, good manners and genuine politeness were instilled way back in sleepy Trelawny.

Today you can't miss it. As you arrive at Sherwood Content a big sign with a picture of Bolt in his famous pose is there to greet you, beneath which it says simply: 'Welcome to Sherwood Content, Home of the World's Fastest Man, Usain Bolt'.

Back in the town's more anonymous days, his first school, Waldensia Primary, had a grass running track in front of it, with a two-foot dip at the end of the straight, and it was here that the future Olympic star took his first racing steps. Strangely, his first experience was defeat to a classmate, but the sports master clearly saw something special in the young Bolt and bet him a free lunch that he could beat his friend if they raced again.

Bolt got the free lunch and never lost on that grassy track again. But track and field wasn't his biggest thrill. Like most Jamaicans, football and cricket were the main attractions, and Bolt excelled at both. He fancied himself as a goalkeeper and was a fast bowler and number three batsman for his school. 'They were carefree days and I would often get in trouble because I was a bit of a prankster,' says Bolt. 'But Mum and Dad and the teachers kept me in line. They were pretty strict.'

While Bolt might have been the fastest kid in Trelawny, when he started competing against other schools on the island he quickly realized that he still had a long way to go. But he was still quick enough to get a sports scholarship to William Knibb School, one of the best establishments in the area. It was here that Bolt discovered that, no matter how impressive it was, raw talent without hard work simply wasn't going to fly, and that while skipping training to play video games and hang out with his friends was certainly much more fun, it wasn't going to make him quicker. And he wanted to be quick.

'I got a lot of lectures about the importance of training and they said that my athletic ability was the reason the school accepted me,' recalled Bolt. 'They said if I didn't do the training they would take the scholarship away. I also knew that Dad would kill me if that happened, so from then on I made training a priority and it's been like that ever since.' For the tall, gangly fourteen-year-old, it was a watershed moment, and with this new-found commitment to training came genuine and eye-catching advances on the track.

'It was certainly at high school that I first realised I could be really fast,' says Bolt. 'Before then I never trained too hard and I kept running and breaking records. It suddenly dawned on me that I was pretty good at this. That's why I really enjoyed the last two years of high school.'

With a proper training regimen helping Bolt become stronger and fitter, he took silver in the 200 metres at the Jamaican high school championships and in March 2002, at the CARIFTA Games, a Caribbean athletic celebration, held that year in the Bahamas, he won golds in the 200 and 400 metres, setting championship records in both.

A few months later he entered the World Junior Athletics Championships, held in his own backyard, in Kingston, Jamaica. He was still only fifteen, more than a month off his 16th birthday, but now a slim 6ft 5in tall he didn't look as out of place as he might. He ran only the 200 metres and to this day describes his performance in the final of the event as his greatest race ever, better than his record-breaking Olympic and World Championship performances.

'You have to understand how nervous I was running in Kingston,' says Bolt. 'As I was coming out of the tunnel in the stadium for the final I heard this loud roar. At first I thought it was for a girl sprinter Anneisha McLaughlin, who was with me, but as I got to the end of the tunnel I could hear they were chanting "Bolt, Bolt, Bolt".

'Oh my God, it really messed me up. I was just so nervous I couldn't even put my spikes on the right feet. I was shaking, I couldn't warm up properly, I couldn't stride out, I couldn't do anything. But I ran and I won. After that it was easy. After that I told myself if I could win here I could do anything. If I can win in Jamaica in front of people I know, I can certainly win in front of strangers.'

Bolt shook off his nervy start and blasted through the field to win by four metres in an impressive 20.61. The stadium went wild and the Jamaican newspapers plastered his pictures on the front, back and centre pages. He followed his 200 metres triumph with silver in the sprint relay, in a new Jamaican junior record. Jamaica could truly boast a new home-grown star and the whole world of track and field was now on notice. There was a new kid on the block.

After the championships Bolt returned to William Knibb, where the school and his parents organized a mentor to help him with the often difficult balancing act of schoolwork, training, competing – and to help keep him out of trouble. This rather unusual role was taken by Norman Peart, a tax officer from Montego Bay, and he would help smooth Bolt's path from promising young athlete to global superstar, eventually becoming his full-time manager.

Bolt passed his exams, with Peart's help, and when he broke the records for both the 200 and 400 metres at the 2003 Jamaican High School Championships, it was decided that a career as a professional athlete was clearly beckoning. He moved, along with Peart, to the Jamaican capital Kingston and signed his first professional contract with the sports company Puma, which had been a long-term sponsor of the Jamaican team.

The head of Puma's sports marketing for track and field, Pascal Rolling, first saw Bolt at the 2002 CARIFTA Games and then again at the World Junior Championships, where he was convinced he'd seen someone very special. 'Everyone could see that he was fast on the track, but even back then he was an entertainer too, playing with the fans and having fun,' said Rolling. 'He fitted perfectly with Puma's attitude and mentality – great performances, but not taking himself too seriously. He was the ideal ambassador.'

He wasn't the only one to see the staggering potential. American magazine *Track & Field News* put him on the front cover of their September 2003 edition, with the headline 'Teen Sensation Usain Bolt – The Next Great Long Sprinter?' In what seemed like just a heartbeat, Bolt had leaped straight from the schoolyard to the competitive world of professional track and field; but the first few years would not be as easy as he thought.

His agent Ricky Simms, at PACE Sports Management, recalls: 'Usain joined us in 2003 and came to Europe at the start of the 2004 summer to prepare to defend his world junior 200 metres title and compete in the 2004 Olympic Games. I had heard a lot about this amazing talent since he won the world juniors in 2002, and everyone was very excited about his future potential. Unfortunately he came to Europe with an injury, and more time was spent arranging appointments with different doctors and physios than organizing competitions that year.'

One highlight was the new world junior record for the 200 metres, but cracks were already appearing in his relationship with coach Fitz Coleman.Coleman demanded Bolt seriously step up a training regime that had largely consisted of short sprint runs and the young athlete struggled to keep up. Coleman demanded longer runs, more repetition and regular gym visits for strenuous weight sessions. His view was that he needed to help Bolt develop physically from schoolboy to professional athlete, but the transition was becoming too painful for Bolt to bear.

The disaster of the 2004 Olympic Games in Athens was the last straw. It broke their relationship, but it prompted the arrival of Glen Mills, who helped deliver a definitive diagnosis and treatment of his long-term back problem. The foundations for Bolt's career were now firmly laid. 'I trusted Coach Mills completely and I had total confidence in him,' says Bolt. 'If I had a problem with anything I knew I could talk to him and we could sort things out. He knew I could get a bit lazy, but if I missed training for more than a day he'd be on top of me. I respected that.'In 2005 Bolt began a new phase of his career with success in the less demanding Caribbean Championships, and the goal of making the 200-metre final at the World Athletic Championships, in Helsinki, in August. That too was achieved, but held on a cold, damp night, Bolt made the headlines for all the wrong reasons. He cramped 60 metres from the line and limped home in a distant last place, watching America's Olympic hero Justin Gatlin celebrate the win. But Bolt was not downhearted. He had achieved his goal of reaching the final and he genuinely believed that without the injury he could have made the top five of a world-class 200-metre field.

After more treatment in Germany he returned to Jamaica and prepared for a low-key 2006 season, ducking the Commonwealth Games, in Melbourne. Despite rumblings of discontent on his home island about lack of progress in big championships, Bolt and Mills felt they were heading in the right direction.

This was proved accurate as he powered to a new personal best of 19.88 in the 200 metres in Lausanne, despite finishing third behind Americans Xavier Carter and Tyson Gay. Two months later he claimed his first senior world medal with a bronze at the IAAF World Athletics final, in Stuttgart and then silver at the World Cup, in Athens, behind Wallace Spearmon. Bolt had just turned 20 years old.

Coach Mills was keen for him to try the longer 400 metres, but the level of training the event required wasn't a great attraction to Bolt, even though he could comfortably run 45 seconds without any real training of any kind. What he really craved was a chance at the shorter, but far more glamorous 100 metres, an event he had never run competitively. Mills told Bolt that he would let him try the 100 metres, but only once he'd broken the Jamaican 200 metre record. It proved an inspirational piece of motivation. In early 2007 he stormed to an impressive 19.75 to break the legendary Don Quarrie's 36-year-old record and, perhaps more importantly for Bolt, earn a crack at the blue riband 100 metres.

His debut run at the event, in a small meeting in Crete, saw him win in 10.03, and he had proven, to himself at least, that he could be a genuine contender at the shorter distance. Coach Mills's hopes of building a formidable 400-metre champion were starting to recede.Still only 20, Bolt rolled into the meat of the 2007 season with genuine expectation of success at the World Athletics Championships, in Japan. He didn't take part in the 100 metres and emerged from Osaka with two silver medals and another learning experience at the hands of Tyson Gay, America's man of the moment. Gay had taken the 100-metre title in 9.85, beating Bolt's Jamaican team-mate and world record holder Asafa Powell into third place. He then lined up for the 200 metres, confident of claiming a remarkable sprint double.

Despite Bolt running one of the best corners of his career, Gay blitzed the 200, winning in a championship record 19.76, with Bolt second on 19.91 and Spearmon third. Bolt told the waiting press that the best man on the day had won, but added ominously that he would be back.

He left Japan after claiming another silver and a new Jamaican record in the sprint relay, sure in the knowledge that another winter of really intensive training would bring him a seismic move forward, one that would take him beyond the seasoned pros who were beating him to the top of the podium. 'It really hit me in Japan that I could be a really great athlete, if I put the work in,' recalled Bolt. 'Coach Mills told me I had to get stronger and more focused and he just convinced me that if I put my heart into it I could be the best in the world at both the 100 and 200.'

And so it transpired. Bolt emerged from a winter of rigorous training with Coach Mills – with a lot less partying – fully energised and with a real point to prove. Incredibly, early in the May of the Olympic year, on his home track in Kingston, Usain Bolt ran only the third competitive 100-metre race of his life in an astonishing 9.76 – just two hundredths of a second outside Powell's world record. Any debate in the Bolt camp about which events he would run at the Beijing Olympics that summer was over – he would double up in the sprints and be part of the relay.

At the end of May he travelled to New York to run the 100 metres at the Reebok Grand Prix, at Randall's Island. It was his first opportunity to tackle the seemingly unbeatable Tyson Gay over the shorter distance.

The meeting was held up for over an hour by fierce rain storms and, rather poetically and perhaps portentously, lightning bolts. Then, on a sodden track, dotted with pools of water, and with a healthy but legal tail wind, the normally slower-starting Bolt got out ahead of Gay and blasted down the track to win in a blaze of flash bulbs. He'd finally laid the ghost of

Tyson Gay to rest and he didn't even realize what he'd really done until he was halfway round the back straight, where he slowed to a jog and then sank to his knees in apparent disbelief.

The clock had stopped at a new world record of 9.72 – two hundredths of a second faster than Asafa Powell's record set in Italy less than a year earlier. In the psychological battle with Gay, a decisive blow had been struck.

In typically understated fashion he told the US press corps that he was 'pretty happy' with the run. But he underlined his real focus by saying: 'This world record means nothing unless I get the Olympic gold medal. Tomorrow if someone comes and runs faster than me I'm no longer the fastest man in the world. If you're the Olympic champion then they have to wait four more years to get you again.'

'The unique thing about Usain is that 15 minutes before that race in New York he was still making jokes and showing no signs of nerves,' recalls Simms, his agent. 'I think my heart was beating faster than his in anticipation of the clash with Tyson. Usain has a great ability to stay calm under pressure.'

New York newspaper headlines screamed 'Bolt From The Blue' but knowledgeable track fans knew he hadn't simply sprung from nowhere. Analysts were quick to compare the stride patterns of Gay, at 5ft 11 in tall, with Bolt, at 6ft 5in. Bolt had run the distance in 41.5 strides to Gay's 45. The American sprinter who chased Bolt home simply lamented: 'He was covering a lot more ground than me.'

More worryingly for Gay would have been Coach Mills's suggestion that there was still a lot more to come from his young charge. 'He's not as strong as he should be,' he said. 'If he gets stronger, his stride frequency will improve and when we achieve that in perhaps the next two years, he is going to run even faster.'

Soon after New York, Bolt and his team moved over to London for the rest of the season as the build-up to Beijing began to intensify. In Europe the big man continued his serene progress to the Games, lowering the Jamaican 200-metre record in Athens to 19.67, the fifth fastest run of all time. Only a Grand Prix defeat to Powell, in Stockholm, marred his 100 per cent record in 2008. Bolt put it down to a 'daydreaming' start and it clearly did little to dent his bullet-proof confidence.

Across the Atlantic Tyson Gay had endured a rollercoaster US Olympic Trials, in Oregon. In the 100 metres he ran a national record 9.77 in the heats and then a wind-assisted 9.68 in the final to claim his spot on the Olympic team. The track and field world was already licking its lips with anticipation at one of the greatest Olympic 100 metres of all time. But a few days later, in the 200 metre final, he crashed to the track after only 40 metres clutching his left hamstring and was stretchered out of the stadium. It was an injury that, despite his best efforts, would sadly make him an irrelevance in Beijing and rob the world of what could have been a truly earth-shattering showdown.

The Olympic pendulum had swung decisively in Bolt's favour. On the plane to China Bolt's confidence had risen so high he recorded a prediction on his mobile phone saying he would win three gold medals.

Unlike some of his more aloof predecessors, Bolt loved life in the Olympic village, hanging out and playing video games and dominoes with his friends on the Jamaican team and meeting athletes – especially the girls – from all over the world. 'I could never understand why anyone would stay anywhere else,' he said. 'It's what the Olympics are all about. The people, the buzz, the fun. I just loved it all.'

In China it was Bolt's eating habits rather than his performances on the track that first hit the headlines. On his first full day in Beijing he'd tried a local Chinese meal and it hadn't gone down well, so he decided to find the local McDonalds and then lived on chicken nuggets – 15 at a time, for breakfast, lunch and dinner – for the duration of the Games.

For the 29th Olympic Games more than eleven thousand athletes from 204 countries converged on Beijing, where the most breathtaking structure was the main stadium, a $423 million piece of modern architecture, with criss-crossing metal bands, that was immediately dubbed 'the Bird's Nest'. It was here, at 10am on August 15, that Usain Bolt began the hunt for the three gold medals that would finally put behind him the Olympic catastrophe of four years earlier.

Despite the bright sunshine, the heats were pretty routine and Bolt cantered to first place in the opener in a sedate 10.20, with rivals Gay and Powell also winning. In the second round, some ten hours later that day, Bolt upped the ante with a run of 9.92, while Gay and Powell also eased through to the semis. It all looked effortless, and Bolt called home that night to say he was feeling good and looking forward to the next day's competition. He was rooming with his friend, Jamaican decathlete Maurice Smith.

'We were like kids on a camp,' Bolt recalled. 'We stayed up late talking and messing about. He filmed everything and we were always laughing. One night Coach Mills, who was next door, came in at two in the morning and told us to go to sleep like we were naughty schoolboys!'

Bolt was supremely relaxed and confident on the day of the 100-metre semis and final, and a packed stadium saw him power to a comfortable 9.85 in the first semi-final with clearly plenty left in the tank. It was an ominous sign for his rivals, but the Chinese fans just loved him. The second semi saw the end of the struggling Tyson Gay's Olympic dream for 2008 as he laboured to fifth place in a race won convincingly by Bolt's team-mate Asafa Powell in 9.91. The final was in less than three hours and Bolt decided there wasn't enough time to go back to the village, so he hung around at the stadium with Coach Mills and the other athletes.

'Prior to the Games, Coach Mills and I had discussed what he would do between the semi and the final,' said Simms. 'We wondered if the occasion, the crowd or the Olympic atmosphere would get to him, but when he came back to the warm-up area he was full of his usual jokes and banter. I remember looking around with about thirty minutes to go to until the final call, and all the other athletes were stone cold serious and Usain was lying on the ground laughing at one of his own jokes. Coach Mills looked at his watch and said, "OK, Usain, it's time – let's go."'

There would be three Jamaicans in the final, with Michael Frater joining Bolt and Powell. The other five starters would be Trinidad's Marc Burns and Richard Thompson, with Americans Walter Dix and Darvis Patton, plus Churandy Martina from the Dutch Antilles.

'As I walked on to the track I felt happy and relaxed,' said Bolt. 'I was disappointed

Tyson didn't make it because I wanted all my rivals out there, but I felt very calm. I was actually thinking about computer games, but as we were called forward I focussed on my start, looked up at the finish line and settled into the blocks.'

The gun went and the noise from the crowd was deafening as the stadium lit up with tens of thousands of flash bulbs exploding on all sides. Powell and Thompson got away the fastest and the reaction time statistics show that Bolt, in lane three, was only the seventh fastest starter, but once he was up and running he simply blew the field away.

At 60 metres it was all over. At 80 metres he glanced right, saw no one and spread his arms wide, cruising over the line and slapping his chest with his right hand.

Men against boys. A new world record of 9.69 and he made it look easy. Simply unbelievable. The crowd in the stadium erupted at the performance – and then again at the time on the scoreboard. They had just witnessed an astonishing piece of history.

'At 55 metres I was starting to go away from the pack and at 85 I knew I'd won it', he recalled. 'Nobody was going to pass me.'

In the stands the TV cameras found his family going crazy and then Bolt found them. Draped in a Jamaican flag he set off on a victory lap. And that's when it happened.

'I just pointed both arms skywards and mimicked the action of a bolt being fired. It wasn't pre-planned, it just came and I did it.' It would become Bolt's signature and the crowd loved it. A few curmudgeonly purists poured scorn on Bolt for showboating in the greatest race on earth, even IOC President Jacques Rogge jumped on the grey bandwagon, stubbornly ignoring the exhilaration and joy it gave to hundreds of millions watching around the world.

Bolt was rightly non-plussed. 'Not for a moment did I mean any disrespect to my fellow athletes, but the excitement of the moment had taken over. To be honest even I was surprised how far out I'd eased up.'

The rest of the awestruck watching world simply wondered what kind of time he could have run had he not slowed up 20 metres from home. Some experts suggested a 9.5 – we were heading into the realm of track and field fantasy.

By the time he'd politely navigated dozens of media interviews and attended the now routine drug test it was nearly midnight and the stadium was closed and silent. Even the shuttle buses back to the village had stopped, so he and agent Ricky Simms had to order a car to drive them back. At one in the morning he dropped into McDonald's for more nuggets, then more excited conversations with his coach and team-mates before falling into a contented sleep around 2:30.

The following evening was the medal ceremony and half of Jamaica cried as he stood, smiling, on the top step of the podium while 'Land We Love' rang across the stadium and the Jamaican flag rose into the Beijing night sky. 'Catch Me If You Can' was the front page headline on the *China Daily*, while Britain's *Sunday Times* emblazoned their sports pages with '9.69 – And He Didn't Even Try'.

The American papers mourned the loss of Tyson Gay and majored on swimmer Michael Phelps claiming an astonishing eighth gold medal, but the *New York Daily News* ran a huge headline across two pages that declared: 'It's Bolt With No One Close', marvelling at the fact – along with a close-up photograph – that he had crossed the line with his right shoelace untied.

Then it was back to the business of the Games – and the 200-metre heats, which started less than 24 hours later. Bolt cruised easily through the heats and expectations grew of a spectacular double. 'To be honest I felt I had more chance of winning the 200 than the 100,' he said. 'But I was starting to feel the effects of the week. All the reporters wanted to know if I would break another record and I played it all down.'

But when he arrived for the 200 final the next day he felt fresh and ready to go. The world record was held by one of his heroes, Michael Johnson, who had run a stunning 19.32 at the Atlanta Olympics in 1996. Since then no one had got near it.

This time there would be no showboating, he would run hard for the whole 200 and see where it took him. As fastest qualifier from the semis, Bolt had Lane 5 for the final, which meant a nice, open and sweeping corner. He was calm and relaxed, mugging to the cameras at the start and performing his now celebrated bolt-firing action to the delight of the stadium crowd.

While the 100 metres generated all the glamour and excitement in track and field, for Bolt the 200 metres was his day job and he meant business. 'I just love the feeling of coming off a corner. That's the great thing. You get that slingshot feeling, like someone grabs your hand and is pulling you round. Whoosh – it slings you out of the corner.'

Michael Johnson was working as an analyst for the BBC and watched in astonishment as Bolt took away his world record in 19.30 seconds. Into a headwind. Bolt started well, swept round the corner like a tornado and just kept going all the way through the line. He finished more than 4 metres ahead of second-placed Churandy Martina and third-placed American Wallace Spearmon. This time he didn't make it too far beyond the bottom bend before collapsing onto the track and theatrically lying flat on his back. Two gold medals down. One to go.

Then, just minutes after the race, the event was plunged into controversy as Wallace Spearmon was disqualified for stepping out of his lane. The Americans appealed and accused second-placed placed Martina of doing the same. The result was both were disqualified and Americans Shaun Crawford and Walter Dix, who had finished fourth and fifth, were elevated to the medal positions. It was an unhappy end to a glorious night.

Bolt summed up how he felt about the race: 'Winning the 200 metres and breaking the world record was better than winning the 100. Michael's record seemed to be a barrier no one could get beyond. But on that day it all clicked. I was in the best shape of my life and I left everything on the track. After that I was finished.'

Fittingly, the medal ceremony for the 200 took place the following day, which was Bolt's twenty-second birthday. As the Jamaican flag rose the ninety-thousand strong crowd serenaded their new hero with 'Happy Birthday' in English.

He was grateful to sit out the sprint relay heats as his team-mates roared to the final, and he was still sceptical about whether he could put in another gold medal performance. Despite an almost complete lack of relay preparation, the Jamaican squad of lead-off man Nesta Carter, Michael Frater, Usain Bolt and anchorman Asafa Powell got it all right on the night and took the gold medal, smashing the world record by an amazing three tenths of a second in 37.10.

It was an exhausted Usain Bolt who left the stadium after hours of interviews and drug tests, but that didn't stop him hitting China Doll, a famed champagne bar in the city, to celebrate what had been an extraordinary Olympics.

As usual the Olympics were followed by a whistle-stop, but lucrative, tour of European circuits, with 100-metre wins in Zurich and Brussels and a 200-metre win in Lausanne – Bolt's favourite track.

Then it was time to head to Jamaica and the biggest welcome home party the island had ever seen. Despite the September rainstorms, thousands crowded Norman Manley Airport, in Kingston, to see the new king of Jamaica, and even Prime Minister Bruce Golding turned out. It was a wholly new and frankly scary scenario for Bolt, who had been used to being able to cruise around Jamaica without any hassle.

Finally he was able to elude the hordes of well-wishers, autograph hunters and back slappers and escape back to the tranquillity of Trelawny. Even there, motorcades and celebrations were planned and it was several days before things began to calm down.

'As Usain went back home to enjoy his success, our work was just beginning,' explained Simms. 'His Beijing heroics had projected him to become one of the most famous sportsmen in the world and he was now generating daily interest from the media, TV chat shows, commercial sponsors and so on – everyone wanted a piece of Usain Bolt. Our office was inundated with calls and emails to see if Usain could be an ambassador or make an appearance for them. The interesting thing was that the requests were coming from all corners of the world. His life was never going to be the same again.'

Bolt's success and Jamaica's reaction to it even prompted the normally tough Coach Mills to give Bolt an extra three weeks off training. He was simply worn out. Before the year ended there was one final award to receive and it was the prestigious World Athlete of the Year, which included a big trophy and a $100,000 cheque, presented by Prince Albert of Monaco.

It was a suitably starry finale to the most stellar of years, but now the hard work of winter training loomed and 2009 would bring with it the World Athletics Championships in Berlin. The world would be waiting. But how on earth would he be able to follow that?

He nearly didn't make the 2009 season at all after crashing his BMW M3, a present from Puma, when it rolled off Highway 2000, the new motorway linking Kingston and Montego Bay. Driving barefoot, he skidded in the rain and the car plunged backwards off the road, rolling three times and landing in a ditch on its roof. Miraculously, he escaped serious injury.

A stunned Bolt crawled out and then went back for the two girls in the back of the car. They hadn't been quite so lucky, but with only a broken knee and strained back between them, they could also count themselves fortunate. Ironically, the only injury Bolt suffered was from walking over the large thorn bushes where the car had rolled as he tried to pull the girls out.

The crash and the injury to his foot made worldwide headlines and kept him out of training for a fortnight, but he managed to recover in time to take part in a special city-centre event in England, in May. A 150-metre straight track was laid in the middle of Manchester, where predictably it rained throughout the day. The sun finally broke through in time for Bolt to storm to a new world record of 14.35, eclipsing by almost half a second the 1983 record of Italian sprint legend Pietro Mennea.

Soon after he got home it was the Jamaican national championships, which were effectively trials for the World Championships a few months later. Despite lacking full fitness, he took the 100- and 200-metre titles with solid, if not spectacular times of 9.86 and 20.25.

He returned to England and his base at Brunel University, where a strength-building programme of 400-metre runs was constructed with the help of quarter-miler and friend Jermaine Gonzales. He also embarked on a tortuous repetition programme of 150-metre runs, each completed in less than 17 seconds with only a minute's rest in between. Bolt could put eight of these together in one session.

Meanwhile, Tyson Gay was back to fitness and recorded the fastest 100 metres of the 2009 season so far in Rome, with an impressive 9.77. Bolt had run an equally promising 19.59 for the 200 metres in Lausanne a few nights earlier, albeit on a windy, rainy night and had suggested he wasn't pushing too hard. The two great rivals were ready to rumble again.

Bolt arrived in Berlin with the Jamaica team in mid-August in fantastic shape and already dialled into a winning mentality, but the press was intent on building the head-to-head rivalry with Tyson Gay.

The heats were a procession for both men, and it wasn't until the semi-finals the following day that the excitement really started to grow. Before the first semi-final Bolt was fooling around with training partner Daniel Bailey, and they laid a bet on who would start the quickest. Bolt went a fraction too early and was false started, then Brit Tyrone Edgar did the same. At the third time of asking they got away and Bolt cantered to an easy 9.89, after which Gay took the second semi in 9.93.

Two hours later, on a warm summer evening, the biggest race of the year was ready to go, a heavyweight battle between the laid-back Bolt and the high-tension Gay, with hundreds of millions watching around the world.

As the track camera moved along the start line, Bailey sparred into the lens, Bolt played to the crowd, Powell pretended to eat his vest number and only Gay seemed to stay focused with a perfunctory wave to the crowd when his name was announced.

The crowd hushed for a moment and then the gun sounded. The field was up and running and, despite registering the third slowest reaction time, Bolt was up and out quickly and was ahead of Gay after just 10 metres. To his credit Gay never gave up, and it must have been his presence on Bolt's shoulder that drove the Jamaican hard over the line to yet another jaw-dropping world record – 9.58.

Astonishingly, Bolt had lopped more than a tenth of a second off his Beijing world record in an event that was used to having records shaved by hundredths. He didn't smash the world mark – he decimated it. The time was the biggest jump in the 100 metres world record since the advent of electronic timing back in the mid-1970s.

Tyson came in a bewildered second, having run the race of his life and claiming a new American record of 9.71, while Asafa Powell took the bronze with a season's best 9.84.

Gay was gracious in defeat, admitting he'd run his greatest race but that it simply wasn't enough, expressing happiness for Bolt, but complaining of a groin problem that would ultimately see him withdraw from the 200 metres.

But the night belonged to Bolt and he swept around the bottom bend, arms spread wide, pursued by TV cameras and photographers, stopping only to show off his 'Bolt action' pose to the roar of the 50,000-plus crowd.

Once again Bolt had delivered when it mattered and the race had lived up to all the pre-event hype. Surely nothing could compare.

And then he did it again in the 200.

Breezing through the heats and the semi-final, he admitted to reporters that he was feeling tired, that he wasn't in the greatest shape and that more world records were beyond him. But as Britain's *Daily Telegraph* declared: 'We should have known not to believe him. Usain Bolt does not do anti-climaxes.'

Bolt had the start of his life and came out of the blocks as if fired from a cannon, making up the stagger on everyone outside him within the first 50 metres and running the fastest bend ever seen. He had eight metres on the field in the closing stages, but instead of shutting down the engines he drove through the line and smashed yet another world record.

The clock stopped at 19.20, but that was then rounded down to a scarcely believable 19.19, which meant he'd taken another 11 hundredths of a second off the old record, the same as he'd done in the 100.

It left former world 200-metre champion Michael Johnson, again working as a BBC pundit, almost speechless and clutching at superlatives. 'It was unbelievable, just ridiculous,' he stammered. 'No one has run a bend like that and no one ever will.'

Bolt seemed typically unbothered, fooling around with the Berlino, the mascot bear, shooting bolts and milking the thunderous applause.

Interviewed after the race he declared that his next aim was to defend his titles, then admitted to another ambition. 'If Queen Elizabeth knighthooded me and I would get the title Sir Usain Bolt,' he said. 'That sounds very nice.'

'I never expected a world record tonight,' he added. 'I was really tired, but I told myself I just had to do my best. Now I am tired.' Astonishingly, he even managed to find fault with his performance. 'I was too upright,' he said. 'It wasn't a good race, but it was a fast one.'

Panama's Alonso Edward took the silver in a distant 19.81, with Spearmon snatching the bronze in 19.85, while even the fifth-placed man finished in under 20 seconds.

Then once again Bolt completed a major championship tour de force with a third gold medal in the sprint relay, holding it together on the third leg to hand the baton to anchorman Asafa Powell, who beat off the Trinidadians.

With prize money and win bonuses, Bolt celebrated his twenty-third birthday, the day after the 200 metres, around $320,000 richer. To add lustre to the medals and the money, world athletics chief Lamine Diack publicly hailed Bolt as the greatest star of the sport. 'He is now one of the best-known people on the planet,' he said. 'We need stars and he brings so much prestige to the sport.'

Before Bolt left Berlin, there was still time for the city's delighted mayor to present him with a most unusual gift. It was a 12-foot-high section of the Berlin Wall, bearing a mural of Bolt winning the 100 metres. Although the painting bore little resemblance to Bolt, and weighed nearly two tons, it was shipped back to Jamaica, where it has pride of place on an army-training base. The press reaction all over the world was ecstatic, but one of the more interesting contributions to the sports pages was the view ventured by long jump world record holder Mike Powell that Bolt could be the man to break his 20-year-old mark and become the first man to jump nine metres.

The idea always intrigued Bolt and it certainly presented a more appealing prospect than moving to 400 metres. 'I'm really going to try and stay away from the 400,' he said in Berlin, 'It's just so tough. But me and my coach definitely want to try the long jump. I'd really love to give it a go. Maybe I'll aim for the Brazil Olympics in 2016.'

Frank Dick, the president of the European Athletic Coaches Association, always believed Bolt could have been the first man to hold world records at 100, 200 and 400 metres, with him training simply for occasional one-lap races. But as Bolt grew older and the physical demands of the sprints took their toll, the idea of tackling new events disappeared. The excitement of Berlin was followed by the traditional tour of the European sprint circuit, with success in Zurich and Brussels, before he finally boarded the plane back to the Caribbean, where a much quieter welcome home was planned. Bolt also moved into his new house in Kingston, where he promptly lost his world championship medals.

The 2010 season was to be low key and largely uneventful on the track, without any major championships to motivate Bolt to stellar heights. 'I talked to my coach and he says you just can't train hard every year,' he said. 'If you do you start damaging your body. So in 2010 we took it easy and tried not to do too much and then we picked it up again in 2011 and got back into serious training.'

But in Kingston he still managed to turn in the fourth fastest 200 metres of all time, a 19.56, early on in the 2010 season before heading for Asia in May and strolling to comfortable wins in the 100 in South Korea and the 200 at the opening Diamond League event in Shanghai.

He even found time to tackle the rarely run 300 metres at the 49th running of the famous Golden Spike track meet in Ostrava, in the Czech Republic. Michael Johnson had set the world record ten years earlier, albeit at altitude in Pretoria, with a stunning 30.85.

On a rain-soaked track Bolt won by a huge margin in a time of 30.97, not quite good enough to beat Johnson's time, but better than the 31.30 of American LaShawn Merritt's sea-level world record. 'I'm not in the shape I was in the last two years,' Bolt told reporters. 'If I was I'm sure I could take this record.'

Though he wouldn't want to hear it, the performance also suggested a fully fit Bolt would seriously threaten Johnson's then long-standing 400-metre world record of 43.18, set in Seville back in 1999. That would be eclipsed by South African Wayde van Niekerk, at the 2016 Olympics, when he ran a 43.03. But Frank Dick insists that Bolt was capable of running below 43 seconds.

The 300-metre run left him nursing a sore Achilles tendon and he ducked out of competition for a month before returning to action with a win over 100 in Lausanne, before suffering his only 100-metre defeat to Tyson Gay in Stockholm, in August. The 27-year-old Kentuckian looked fitter and fresher than the clearly labouring Bolt and took the Grand Prix event in 9.84, with Bolt second in 9.97.

The American, though pleased to win, was again honest and gracious enough to concede Bolt wasn't in tip top shape. 'It feels great to beat Usain, but deep down inside I know he's not 100 per cent. I look forward to beating him when he is 100 per cent.'

The quiet, humble and respectful Gay would certainly be a dominant force in the sprint world were it not for the man from Jamaica. Growing up in a sporting family in Lexington, Gay realized he was exceptionally quick when he was able to steal more bases than other kids in the little league baseball games he played.

He rose through the ranks at high school and the University of Arkansas, under the tutelage of coach Lance Bauman. A mark of Gay's integrity was that when Bauman was imprisoned for ten months for falsifying students' entitlements to funds, Gay looked after the coach's wife and daughter – as well as his own daughter – until he was released. Tragically, his daughter Trinity – an outstanding high school sprinter – was killed, aged just fifteen, in a shooting in Lexington in 2016. She was an innocent bystander in the incident, which involved four men outside a restaurant. All four were eventually convicted.

Tyson Gay is now retired from the track and his story is one of extraordinary highs and terrible lows. He began to make real headway in the pro-sprint world with a personal best 9.84 at Zurich in 2006, he then swept the board in the 100, 200 and sprint relay at the 2007 World Championships in Japan before his injury in the US trials ruined his chances in Beijing. After claiming the US record of 9.71 running second to Bolt in Berlin, he then lowered that further in Shanghai, in September 2009, with a fabulous run of 9.69 seconds, which made him the fastest American sprinter in history. Fit and healthy, he still looked like the only athlete that could seriously challenge Bolt.After his 2010 Stockholm defeat by Gay, Bolt admitted that the lack of championships and minor injuries to his Achilles and hamstring had meant he'd slacked off in training, but he was still clearly disappointed to lose. 'You can get beat any day,' he said. 'You have good days and bad days. I still need to work on my strength. The first 10 metres was rubbish. I had no power, no nothing. I have tried to work on it but it didn't work out. But Tyson was in better shape than me and was better prepared.'

With that Bolt departed the 2010 track season and headed back to Jamaica to recuperate and plan his winter training and an assault on the 2011 World Championships, in Daegu, South Korea, and the 2012 London Olympic Games.

For Bolt, track is all about the big championships and bringing big performances to them. Such is his popularity now that his agents PACE Management can ask for $200,000 a race on the European circuit and that certainly helps pay the bills, but it's not his driving force and he insists that the money hasn't changed him.

'The money hasn't made any difference to how I am as a sportsman or as a person,' he says. 'I'm still the same as I've always been. I was brought up a certain way, I was a simple kid and humble, so nothing changes. Of course it helps me get a lot of stuff and it allows me to do what I want, to chill, see my friends, play video games and so on, but I'm not the sort to travel for no reason. I love cars and speed, but otherwise it's just the normal stuff at home.'

Back in 2010, Bolt lived in Jamaica with his brother Sadiki and best friend NJ (old school pal Nugent Walker Junior) and clearly enjoyed being king of the hill. But even then he was finding it difficult to simply disappear on the island as he used to. He still appeared at a club now and again, but his hard partying and big-time dancehall days were over.

'It's still hectic in Jamaica, but it's not too bad,' he says. 'When I go back home people still want to talk about a race, but people stop me to talk about all kinds of things. But to be honest when I'm in Jamaica I'm inside at home most of the time so it's not so bad.'

Bolt's smooth Jamaican lilt has also softened, but if he's back in Jamaica for any length of time he'll relax back into patois, the local language. Bolt revealed that when he first moved to Kingston to start running professionally, he actually took English lessons to make media interviews easier. Today he can duck in and out of both skills without a problem.

But the island remains home and it's clearly important to him. He is regarded as a genuine role model for kids across Jamaica and it is a responsibility he takes very seriously. He's helped schools with tracks, shoes and clothing and continues to work closely with health education, community development and sports on the island. His priority is to leverage his fame to raise funds to provide piped water in Sherwood Content, where in some places rain water is still collected in tanks.

To add to his growing list of honours the island awarded him the prestigious Order of Jamaica, making him the Honourable Usain St Leo Bolt, though it's not a title he tends to use. But he clearly loves the title of 'Fastest Man on Earth'.

'It is surprising sometimes to sit and think that you are the fastest man on the planet,' he says. 'There is only one. At first it was all about championships, but after breaking the world record for the first time everybody started saying you're the fastest man in the world and then you start thinking about it.

'It's good to know that you could be in a room with thousands of people and understand that if something goes wrong, you're going to be the first one out of there! No-one has been able to explain why I'm so fast. Maybe I'm a freak of nature, maybe the back problem helps. Whatever it is, it works.'

Bolt was always acutely aware that he helped re-build the credibility not only of his own event, but the sport as a whole. Such was the damage done to track and field by a procession of drug scandals, that Bolt's smiling success became a beacon for athletics and even the Olympic movement. Bolt was probably the most tested athlete in the world and had to provide the authorities with details on his whereabouts on a daily basis. Just like today, they could arrive on his doorstep at six in the morning and demand a test or at the most inconvenient moments in training.It didn't stop a handful of cynical newsmen, ambulance-chasing sports commentators and the occasional former athlete taking cheap shots at Bolt, but he always waved it off with the simple line: 'I have never taken drugs and I never will.' He won't even take a cold remedy for fear of its contents showing up on a banned list and his only small slip was once trying a cigarette as a 13-year-old. He hated it.

Bolt was always profoundly aware that he carried the future prosperity and health of the sport on his broad shoulders. It was for that reason that his sponsors Puma agreed a stratospheric deal with Bolt in 2010, making him the richest track athlete there's ever been. Reported as worth more than $30 million over the first three years, Bolt turned down rival company attempts to derail a relationship he's enjoyed since he was 15. In 2013 they renewed and improved the deal for another three years. 'There were others interested,' said Bolt. 'But for me Puma is the number one in my book. We've been together for years now, they are my family so I don't want to start with a new family. You want money, but it's also got to be about the comradeship between you and your company.'

Puma's Pascal Rolling, the head of running sports marketing, explained the rationale behind their huge investment, saying that Bolt had 'broken out of world athletics and become a truly global superstar. You cannot compare him with any other track and field star because he is one of the biggest stars of any sport today, you have to compare the contract to people like Cristiano Ronaldo and Lionel Messi. That's where he stands in world sport.

'But the really great thing is that he's still just the same guy. Of course, he's certainly a lot more professional than he was at sixteen, but apart from that he hasn't changed. He still has that sense of humour and sense of fun and that's a very important part of the relationship for us.'

The Puma deal saw the marketing of his famous 'shooting Bolt' logo, which they freshly christened 'To Di World' and comparisons have been made between that and NBA legend Michael Jordan's 'Jumpman' logo adopted by Nike and now worth more than a billion dollars a year in sales.

For Bolt his split-second stance is already worth a fortune, but it still causes him problems. 'It just came to me and I did it, but sometimes it can get pretty annoying. After a race when I'm still on the track it's fine, but when every autograph hunter wants their picture with me doing it, it gets pretty hard. So now I just say I can't do it.'

As the 2011 season unfolded Bolt clicked unspectacularly through the gears, hindered by a series of niggling injuries, but seemingly unbothered by running just a handful of races that barely troubled the headline writers, preferring to focus on gold at the World Championships in South Korea, in August.

He looked casual in qualifying for the 100-metres final, but the 60,000 crowd inside the Daegu Stadium and the millions watching on TV around the world wanted only one winner. They were ready for fireworks. The line-up was Frenchman Jimmy Vicaut in lane one, then Daniel Bailey from Antigua, Kim Collins from St Kitts and Nevis, American Walter Dix, Bolt in lane five next to teammates Yohan Blake in lane six and Nesta Carter in seven, with Frenchman Christophe Lemaitre completing the field in the outside lane. The four fastest men of the year were not even in the stadium. Mike Rodgers and Steve Mullings had been banned for doping offences and Tyson Gay and Asafa Powell, who had the fastest time in the world for the year at 9.78, were both injured.

As the crowd grew silent and the field came under starter's orders, Bolt's training partner Blake seemed to make the tiniest of movements, but it was the champion who broke first and flew out of his blocks. He knew instantly what he'd done, tore off his yellow Jamaica vest and howled in fury and frustration. To the audible horror of the stadium, and the incredulity of the watching world, Usain Bolt had false started in the final of the World Championships. Under the IAAF's new 'one strike and you're out' rules he was done. The man was human after all.

While he stomped around in the background, unable to find a hole big enough to swallow him and barely able to watch the replay on the big screen, the rest of the field got back to business. It was Blake who took the race by the scruff of the neck, surging past the fast-starting Kim Collins to win in 9.92. American Walter Dix edged past Collins for the silver, but at 35 years and 145 days the Saint Kitts and Nevis man took bronze and the title of oldest-ever-medallist for the 100 metres at a World Championships.

Bolt was left to rue what appeared to be a pretty straightforward opportunity to add to his medal tally, and his anger with himself was clearly evident in a documentary film made by a French TV crew at the time. Sprawled on a sofa in the apartment he shared with Blake, he looks beyond the camera and says: 'I pretty much squandered it, I would say. I don't know what happened. Can't believe it happened. I kept saying to myself, "Why did you false start, why did you false start, why did you false start?" It's never happened. Major championships. That's what I live for. All I could hear was something said "Go" in my head and I just went.'

Although his dark mood began to subside in the days that followed, helped in part by watching his beloved Manchester United, playing video games with his team-mates as well as spending an evening with his parents, he still couldn't figure out what had caused such an aberration.

That nagging fear was still with him as he entered the stadium for the final of the 200 metres six nights later, but it was a bunch of kids in the South Korean crowd that pulled him back into the zone. In his autobiography, *Faster Than Lightning*, he described what happened next. 'I went over to say hello and, as we goofed around, the reality of my situation dropped with me. You know what? To hell with this stressing! I thought. I'm supposed to be having fun.' The moment seemed to lift a weight off his shoulders and although he registered the slowest reaction time to the starting gun, he romped home to the gold in 19.40 seconds, his third fastest time ever, with Dix and Lemaitre trailing way behind him for silver and bronze. The Bolt Bandwagon was back on the rails and the next day, as if to confirm that very fact to himself, he anchored the Jamaican relay team to gold and a new world record of 37.04.

Crisis averted, it was time for Bolt to concentrate on his real goal. London and history. 'Beijing was fantastic and London has a lot to live up to,' he said. 'But if you want to make your name in history London is going to be the place. It's one of the greatest cities in the world and everyone will be watching, not just the sports fans. So you will be huge. When I win in London I'm thinking about jumping into the stands with the Jamaican fans! I'm working on being a living legend. I want to be remembered as one of the most fun-loving people, a joy to watch and one of the greatest athletes there's ever been. Anyone can win one Olympics, but I want three.

'Me and my coach know the importance of being an Olympic champion. Some people think it's easy, but I came in really young and I've learned a lot. I pick up quickly on things, I work very hard when it matters and I've got a lot of good people around me.'

Training had gone well through the winter, but for the first time the track world began expressing real doubts about his ability to repeat his Beijing performances in London. It was as if the false start had pierced his apparent bulletproof invincibility.

Chatter in the sport began to focus more on his injuries, his mental state, his partying and, of course, the quality of the competition, not least his young team-mate and friend Yohan Blake, who sent further shock waves through the sport post-Daegu when he ran the second fastest 200 metres of all time – 19.26 – at a Diamond League meeting in Brussels.

But early season form in 2012 looked promising for Bolt, with wins in Rome and Oslo in 9.76 and 9.79 respectively suggesting he'd beaten his injury niggles and was back to his best.

All the old anxieties returned at the Jamaican national championships in June, however, when Blake completely out-raced him to win the 100 metres title in 9.75 – his best ever time – with Bolt more than a tenth of a second behind him. A light year in terms of the 100 metres. To make matters worse Blake won again in Bolt's favoured 200 metres, and suddenly Bolt was no longer the London favourite. But as he would concede after the Games it turned out to be an extremely valuable wake-up call. The alarm bells were ringing and an Olympic year was not the time to be sleepwalking. He needed to get his act together.

Yohan Blake was now regarded as the genuine threat to the Bolt era. He was also someone who knew the big man inside out, having trained with him almost daily since the autumn of 2008. If anyone knew his Achilles heel, so the story went, then it must be Blake.

Born on Boxing Day 1989, Blake grew up one of 11 kids in grinding poverty in Montego Bay. The family moved south to Clarendon when he was 12, and it was the local school principal who spotted his track potential while playing cricket as a very fast bowler. He moved to St Jago High School, in Spanish Town, where progress was swift under the watchful eye of coach Danny Hawthorne. He was a finalist in the world youth championships at 15 and a Caribbean junior title winner at 16, but it was in 2007 that he grabbed the attention of the track world outside Jamaica when he ran 10.18 to beat Ray Stewart's 28-year-old national junior 100 metres record by just one hundredth of a second. A year later he joined the Glen Mills camp and in May 2009, in Paris, he became the youngest sprinter, at just 19, to duck under ten seconds when he ran a scintillating 9.94.

However, the wheels came off spectacularly a month later when it was discovered that he had tested positive for a stimulant at the national trials. He was initially cleared because the stimulant wasn't actually on the banned list, just close to one that was. But after much debate he was suspended for three months, and that meant missing the World Championships in Berlin.

In 2012, though, after his World Championship win and triumph over Bolt in the Olympic trials, everything appeared to be turning Blake's way. To pile further pressure on Bolt, the American Justin Gatlin was also running into form, recording his fastest ever time of 9.80 to win the US Olympic trials.

London had promised a stellar Olympic Games and it did not disappoint. The city and its people put on a party that nobody would forget. In his autobiography *Faster Than Lightning*, Bolt prefaced his memories of the Games with one line: 'London 2012. Talk about crazy.'

The city was buzzing, a sea of colour and chatter. Yes, Londoners were even talking to each other – on buses, trains, in shops, on the street. It was unheard of. It was said that the last time the city pulled together like that was the wartime Blitz. Bolt's face peered down from billboards, store fronts, even a giant mural on the side of a building near the Olympic Park. Unfortunately for him, he could only view this on a laptop from the quiet safety of his room. 'There was no way I could walk around the streets to catch the sights,' he explained. 'Unlike Beijing there wasn't a moment of calm before the storm, and from the minute I landed the Olympic Village became my home, where I had to stay out of view, away from autograph hunters and fans. That was tough. There was a shopping mall by the Olympic park and my friends were always calling up to say how jam-packed it had been with pretty girls.'

But Bolt didn't need distractions. This was almost zero hour and legends do not create themselves.

The 100 metres competition lived up to every expectation. Bolt marvelled at the fact that, unlike previous Games, capacity crowds filled the stadium for every round, and the electricity they generated seemed to help energise the early performances. The preliminaries were unbelievably quick, with American Ryan Bailey recording the fastest ever Olympic heat in 9.88. The three semis went to form, Justin Gatlin taking the first in 9.82 (the fastest ever Olympic semi-final); Usain Bolt cruised the second in 9.87 and Yohan Blake the third in 9.85. How on earth would they be separated in the final?

A couple of hours later, on a warm August night, just before 10pm, the eight finalists stepped up for their introductions. Trinidad's Richard Thompson bounced and shadow-boxed; Jamaica's Asafa Powell narrowed his eyes at the camera; a tense looking Tyson Gay seemed to be talking himself into the race; Yohan Blake went into full 'Beast' mode and clawed at the camera with a big smile; but it was Justin Gatlin who looked more like a caged animal as he paced up and down and saluted to the crowd. The noise of the crowd rose as Bolt was introduced and he went straight into his repertoire of antics; spinning imaginary discs, pointing down the track to the line and looking up to the stars. Outside him Ryan Bailey smiled and waved and the Netherlands' Churandy Martina gave the camera a little wink.

At Olympic level, a sprint final is like a superfast game of poker. Everyone looks for a sign or a tell. Who's stressed? Who's nerves will crack? Bolt surveyed the field and saw only glimmers of anxiety in teammates Powell and Blake. Coach Mills had warned him about Gatlin – 'You are the two people who step up for the big occasion' – but Bolt dismissed the idea. Then those words flashed into his head. DON'T FALSE START.

Before he had time to process the thought a loud 'Ssssssh,' came like a wave from the crowd. Usain Bolt took up the hint and pressed his finger to his lips. Then it was down to business.

The gun sounded and a line of the fastest men on earth took off.

Bolt explained: 'I realized Gatlin had made one of the best starts I'd ever seen in my life. It was powerful and sleek and I could not work out for the life of me how he had moved away so quickly.' But experience told him to keep calm, maintain his technique and in seconds they were level. His head told him the race was over. It was his giant 41 strides against everybody else's 45.

At halfway it was close and then Bolt began to push ahead of the pack and pull clear, stopping the clock at an incredible 9.63 – the second fastest time ever. Yohan Blake was a metre behind in second, equalling his personal best of 9.75, with Gatlin just pipping Gay for the bronze in another personal best of 9.79.

'The champion becomes a legend,' shouted BBC commentator and former Olympian Steve Cram to 20 million people watching on British television as the 80,000 crowd roared its approval. The whole electrifying field finished under ten seconds except for the injured Powell who limped over the line more than two seconds behind everyone else clutching his hamstring. But Bolt knew he had switched off too early. A new world record was there for the taking and in his rush simply to win and grab the gold he'd forgotten a basic principle. Run through the line.

Bolt stopped halfway around the bottom curve and slowly sank to his knees and kissed the track. Then he rose and went into his famous pose. Blake caught him and they hugged before heading for a bunch of Jamaican fans in the crowd to grab a flag and celebrate.

As he made his way off the track he spotted a familiar face. 'Amateur', said Coach Mills, shaking his head in disappointment. 'Bolt, you're an amateur.' Mills believed that a rare opportunity for an extraordinary time had been within reach, but Bolt had ignored it. How fast? Maybe under 9.5, he thought.

'My start wasn't the best,' Bolt explained later, 'but my coach already explained to me, "Forget about the start. You're never a good starter, stop worrying about this." I just came out there and won gold, got out with a good start and then just executed, because the last 50 metres is where I shine.'

The world's media began to thumb through every thesaurus and dictionary to find a superlative that somehow did justice to what had just happened. And that hadn't already been used. In the end *The Guardian*'s columnist Marina Hyde trumped them all. 'When his career comes to an end, they will retire the adjective "effortless".'

Bolt didn't finish with the media until well after midnight, when he told them he needed to go back to the Village and get some sleep. So it was with a certain degree of bemusement that Olympic journalists greeted the pictures of him on Twitter at 3am posing in his bedroom with some of the Swedish women's handball team. 'It was all innocent fun,' Bolt explained. 'If anything had happened do you think I would have put in on Twitter?'

Four days later he was back for the 200 metres final and another appointment with history. Nobody had ever retained an Olympic 200-metre title and the opposition in the final was genuinely first class, so he would need to bring his best game to add another line to the Bolt legend. At the start he betrayed no nerves and waved to the crowd, in classic Queen Elizabeth II style, as his name was announced. Lying in wait were seven athletes with their own designs on the title – Frenchman Christophe Lemaitre, Alex Quinonez from Ecuador, Blake, Churandy Martina, American Wallace Spearmon, compatriot Warren Weir and young South African Anaso Jobodwana.

Again Bolt put a finger to his lips and enjoined silence. Quiet swept instantly across the stadium. The athletes seemed to be in their blocks for an eternity before the order to set, followed by the bang and a deafening roar.

Bolt flew off the line like a Formula One car and the roar grew even louder as he blasted into a clear lead and came off the bend in front. It looked all over, but Blake wasn't giving in and pushed his team-mate the whole way to the line. Bolt had become the first man to retain an Olympic 200-metre title and equalled the time set by Michael Johnson back in Atlanta in 1996 – 19.32, the fastest time of the year. Blake registered 19.44 and Warren Weir took third in a personal best 19.84 for a Jamaica 1-2-3.

Before the lap of honour began he dived into the crowd and then dropped to the track and did five push ups – one for every gold medal he'd won. 'For me that was for all the doubters,' he said in the post-race media room. 'That was for all the people that were saying I wasn't going to win and I wasn't going to make myself a legend.'

'Bolt seals place in pantheon with another stunning run', announced *The Guardian*. Exceptional, Remarkable, LEGEND,' screamed Jamaica's *Daily Gleaner*, whose reporter struggled to find a suitable description of what he had just witnessed. 'No superlative adequately captures the performances of Jamaican sprinting sensation Usain Bolt.' While the *New York Times* simply stated 'Usain Bolt is an all-but-impossible track and field act to follow.'

Impossible for everyone, that is, with the exception of Usain Bolt himself. There was still time for another display of sprinting that was simply out of this world. The Americans had been revving up for the relay showdown for some time and believed they could beat the Jamaican quartet. In the first semi the Jamaicans, without Bolt, ran the fastest preliminary in history in 37.39. Not to be outdone, the American four then beat that mark, as well as the US record, with a 37.38. This was a final worthy of its prime-time billing.

NBC commentator and analyst Ato Boldon predicted something spectacular was about to happen to the Jamaican world record of 37.04. 'You may see one, if not two, teams go under 37 seconds.'

Jamaica lined up in lane 6, just inside the US team, with Nesta Carter, Michael Frater, Yohan Blake and Usain Bolt. The Americans switched Trell Kimmons and Gatlin to the first two legs and added Tyson Gay and Ryan Bailey to finish.

From the gun it was incredibly close and for once the baton changes on both sides were slick and professional, but Bolt had a tiny edge over Bailey on the final changeover. After that it was vintage Bolt as he turned on the gas and swallowed the home straight in an astonishing 8.8 seconds, beating the Americans by a clear metre and smashing the world record to pieces in an astonishing 36.84. The USA claimed the silver and a new national record of 37.04, though the run would be chalked off after the team was controversially disqualified by the IOC, nearly three years later, after Tyson Gay was suspended for a doping offence. The Jamaican team held court with the media in typically eclectic style. Carter dedicated the win to the country and its fiftieth birthday; Blake told reporters that they were not human and, in fact, came from Mars. 'What I mean is we are not normal,' he explained. '36.84 is not normal. We are flying.' A laughing Bolt clarified the whole situation. 'I said to Yohan "You need to stop talking like that. Somebody's going to put you in a straitjacket one day."'

The fun, laughter and smiles of the Jamaican team, especially of Usain Bolt, not to mention the exhilarating performances, would remain an indelible and uplifting memory of a wonderful Olympic Games. But while the world continued to savour one of the greatest ever exhibitions of sprinting, thought was already turning quickly to the future. 'In a perfect race I really don't know what I'm capable of,' said Bolt. 'After every race where I've broken a record I've said to my coach that's a perfect race and he always says no. He keeps finding fault in everything I do.'

Like most post-Olympic years, 2013 started slowly with Bolt struggling to garner the motivation to perform at his superfast levels. At a June event in Rome he was even beaten by Justin Gatlin.

Then the roof truly fell in on the Jamaican sprinting fraternity, when only a month after seven-time Olympic medal-winning Veronica Campbell-Brown was reported to have tested positive for a banned diuretic, no fewer than five failed drug tests were revealed from the Jamaican national championships, including former world-record holder Asafa Powell. Campbell-Brown would be cleared of any wrongdoing, but Powell voluntarily withdrew from the World Championships in Moscow as a result of the test. It would be nearly a year before he received an 18-month suspension from competing, a ban that was only lifted in the summer of 2014.

Then a few days after recording a sharp 9.79 in a Diamond League 100 in Lausanne, Tyson Gay admitted he had failed a doping test on an out-of-competition sample he had submitted in May. It was an anabolic steroid. 'I don't have a sabotage story. I don't have any lies. I don't have anything to say to make this seem like it was a mistake or it was on USADA's hands, someone playing games. I don't have any of those stories. I basically put my trust in someone and I was let down.'

The popular Gay would eventually get a reduced one-year ban for assisting the US authorities (his coach Jon Drummond subsequently got an eight-year ban) and while his admission was certainly a bombshell, the Jamaican infractions, although seemingly minor in scale, were all fuel to the growing fiery argument about the integrity of athletics on the island, and moreover the quality of the drug testing and control. And of course at the apex of this was Usain Bolt.

At a press conference in London in July, he decided to speak out. 'I was made to inspire people and to run. I was given a gift and that's what I do. I'm confident in myself, my team, the people I work with. I know I'm clean, so I'm just going to continue running and using my talent and trying to improve the sport and help the sport.'

In Richard Moore's fascinating book *The Bolt Supremacy*, which presents a hugely interesting insight into the mindset of the people in and around the Jamaican track world, he offered a thought-provoking comparison to disgraced cyclist Lance Armstrong.

Despite endless suspicion over the years, Armstrong had consistently denied any involvement in performance enhancing drugs, but just a few months earlier he'd made a spectacular confession on *The Oprah Winfrey Show*. Moore had written extensively on cycling and saw a distinct difference in the tone and mood of Bolt's press dealings to Armstrong's. Bolt was all relaxation and bonhomie, whereas Armstrong exuded confrontation and hostility. And there was one critical line that is worth repeating. 'There is at least one difference between Bolt and Armstrong, however,' he wrote. 'Bolt says: "I am clean." Armstrong used to say: "I have never tested positive."'

The implication was clear, and while Moore concedes there are no quick and easy conclusions to explaining Jamaica's domination of sprinting in recent years (genetics, poverty, training, diet and the elevated position that track maintains in Jamaican society are but five), he thinks it's unlikely that it's down to a pervasive doping programme across the island. Back at the London press conference, a reporter asked Bolt if he knew that only one of the five fastest men in the world now hadn't failed a drug test. 'Can they trust you?' she asked.

Bolt was keen to answer. 'If you've been following me since 2002 you would know I've been doing phenomenal things since I was fifteen. I was the youngest person to win the world juniors, at fifteen. I ran the world junior record, 19.93, at eighteen. World youth record at seventeen. I've broken every record there is to break in every event that I've ever done. For me, I've proven myself since I was fifteen. I'm just living out my dream now.'

It is interesting to note that in 2012 Bolt was tested no fewer than 25 times and never failed one. If that statistic had ever changed, given the pivotal role he performed, there would have been calls to roll up the tracks, tear down the stadiums and pack up the five rings. But it never did.Back on the track, Bolt seemed to be running into some long overdue form, just in time for the World Championships in Moscow. He ran a hugely impressive and world-leading 19.73 in the 200 metres in Paris, and back at a packed Olympic Stadium, in London, he cantered easily to a 9.85 win in the Anniversary Games. He was ready for Russia.

The fourteenth World Athletics Championship was a crowd-pleasing show, despite the weather, which even delivered a Hollywood-style electrical storm right on cue for the 100 metres final. 'I thought they were going to postpone the race, to be honest,' said Justin Gatlin. 'But they wanted to see a great race in the rain and I think we delivered that.'

For the 100 metres it was as if time had stood still between London and Russia. Three Jamaicans made the final and the big man seemed calmness personified as he stood for the introductions in the lashing rain at the Luzhniki Stadium, entertaining the 87,000 spectators by opening up an imaginary umbrella. The lightning that lit up the Moscow skyline was clearly a good omen. Bolt reacted well to the gun but it was Gatlin who broke out in front and led after 45 metres. At 50 Bolt drew level and the American began to tread water, as if he was trying to match the Jamaican's giant stride. By then the race was over and Bolt powered over the line in a world-leading 9.77, Gatlin second in a season's best 9.85 and, in another race entirely, Nesta Carter took bronze in 9.95.

'The 100 is always just for the fans, for the people, for the show, because it's the event everyone always wants to see,' Bolt explained. 'Who's the fastest man in the world, who's the best? But for me it means a lot more to come out here and defend my 200-metre title.'

He reclaimed that crown in equally emphatic fashion six days later, with another world-leading performance, catapulting off the curve to canter home in 19.66, with fast-finishing team-mate Warren Weir claiming a personal best 19.79 in second and American Curtis Mitchell unable to break 20 seconds back in third. To restore 'normal service', he then anchored the Jamaican relay squad and took his third gold, starting more or less level with Gatlin and the Americans on the last leg, but easing away to yet another world-leading win in 37.36.

The big smile and the old swagger was back. In the post-relay press conference he was asked how much of a lead the Americans would need to beat him on the final leg: 'About ten metres'. And he wasn't joking.

A hamstring injury in April 2014 meant surgery and nearly three months of missed training, so he didn't compete again until August and the Commonwealth Games in Glasgow, where he anchored the Jamaican relay team to gold in a games record of 37.58.

A few weeks later he won an exhibition 100 metres in Brazil, and then took yet another world record, albeit an unusual one, when he ran an 'indoor' 100 metres in Poland under the closed roof of the National Stadium in Warsaw, and won it in 9.98. But with no major championships to chase the Bolt spark was missing, and he decided to curtail his season, with coach Glen Mills saying: 'It is now time to shut it down while he is healthy and injury free with a view on his preparations for the 2015 season.'

The season started slowly and was heavily punctuated by injury and disappointment as he pulled out of three big meets in June and July, citing leg pain that was diagnosed as a blocked sacroiliac joint. The litmus test would be the Diamond League event at London's Olympic Stadium in late July, but which Bolt would turn up? Maybe it was the memories of those summer nights and the 2012 London roar, but that night there was no doubt the real Usain Bolt was alive and well, as 40,000 fans watched spellbound while he strode magnificently through the cold wind and rain to win the final in 9.87 seconds. His start may have been lethargic, but he seemed happy enough. 'I've been running fast in training,' he told the waiting press corps. 'But it's easier in training because you're under no pressure and you can execute well. It's all about getting race ready now.'

'Bolt is back,' screamed the stadium announcer. Or as *Track & Field News* succinctly summarized – 'The Stage Is Set For A Monster World Championship 100'.

The 2015 World Athletics Championships, at the Bird's Nest stadium, in Beijing, was another homecoming of sorts, the scene of his first Olympic triumph back in 2008 and still a bastion of Bolt Mania. The media drew clear battle lines. This was Good versus Evil, pure and simple. Usain Bolt had to win for the good of the sport and Justin Gatlin had to lose for, er, the good of the sport. This rather binary précis of a complex and personal event was quite at odds with the views of both athletes. It was almost bullying.

Bolt had no issues with Gatlin and had never seen himself as any kind of saviour. For the likeable Gatlin, his quiet demeanour and shy humility were the very antithesis of the moustache-twirling pantomime villain contrived by the media, especially the British press.

The Times fretted that Gatlin, the odds-on favourite with the bookies, looked ready to claim Bolt's world title, reporting that the new IAAF President Lord Coe felt 'queasy' about the possibility of crowning the American as champion. Bolt refused to be drawn into the Gatlin witch-hunt, wisely reminding anyone who asked that it was just a running race.

He may have been the only one who was taking it that calmly. 'High Noon' beckoned, but the early rounds were not encouraging for the followers of the world record holder. He was controlled but unimpressive in 9.96 in his heat and stumbled out of his blocks to win his semi in the same time. By comparison Gatlin stormed both his races with a wind-assisted 9.83 and a stunning 9.77 in the semi. But would his blistering early pace cost him in the final?

The line-up from lane one was Jimmy Vicaut; local hero Su Bingtian, the first Asian-born sprinter to break ten seconds; American world junior record holder and fastest ever teenager, Trayvon Bromell; Mike Rodgers; Bolt; Tyson Gay; Gatlin; Asafa Powell and young Canadian Andre de Grasse.

As he went to the blocks Bolt still had coach Glen Mills's final words ringing in his ears. 'Look, you will have to run the 100 metres if you are going to win this race.' Bolt knew he had to get a decent start and run all the way through the line. It was going to be tight.

On the gun the field got away pretty evenly, but by 20 metres Gatlin was flying and by 50 he'd pushed in front. By 70 metres Bolt drew level, but this time Gatlin didn't fold and Bolt couldn't pull away. Perhaps the only difference was Gatlin seemed to dip a little early and as they flashed through the line it was Bolt who had won it by the slimmest of margins. The timers gave him 9.79 and Gatlin 9.80. And the photo finish picture showed how close it really was.

BBC commentator Steve Cram went into overdrive: 'Bolt has saved his title, he's saved his reputation. He may have even saved his sport! It was the result that everyone wanted, apart from Justin Gatlin. How could we ever doubt him?' Outstanding commentator Michael Johnson, also working for BBC television, summarized the event perfectly. 'Usain Bolt was challenged here more than he has been at any time during his career. Put on top of that the burden of "saving the sport" which was placed on his shoulders, it means that the pressure was there. I have to give him so much credit for that performance.'

Bolt's confidence duly rocketed and four days later he returned to the track with a stampeding performance in the 200 metres final – powering off the curve to beat Gatlin by a clear two metres in an impressive 19.55 – the tenth fastest of all time.

Then came the strangest thing of all. Halfway round his victory lap, an over-excited Chinese cameraman, perched on a Segway, bounced off an advertising hoarding and crashed into the back of the champion, sending them both crashing to the ground. Mercifully no harm was done – though heaven knows what the insurance company would have made of it had Bolt been genuinely injured – and it soon became a viral hit on the Internet. 'The rumour I'm trying to start right now is that Justin Gatlin paid him off,' laughed Bolt in the post-race press conference. 'That's what I'm going with, but I'm all right.'

Gatlin responded immediately. 'I want my money back. I want my Yuans back please.'

Bolt's golden hat trick was duly claimed in the relay, where he anchored a strong quartet of Nesta Carter, Asafa Powell and Nickel Ashmeade to victory in a world-leading 37.36. Bolt flashed past a stricken Mike Rodgers on the final leg as he almost stopped to grab the baton from Tyson Gay. The Americans would later be disqualified for passing the baton outside the correct zone.

Bolt was happy, but philosophic about his victories and the road ahead. 'The key thing is not to get injured. It's hard because the older you get, the rougher things are. But if I can get one season with no problems, I know I'm going to be in the best shape that I can be when I get to Rio. And I know Justin and the other athletes are going to be coming up and pushing me to run fast.'

So with his gold medals collected, Bolt called time on his season, pulled out of a scheduled appearance in Brussels and headed home for a well-earned break and to plot the long build-up to Rio. Olympic year opened to the spectacle of much hand-wringing amongst the sport's leaders and writers. Their greatest star was halfway out of the door and no-one was prepared for it. While visiting London to help promote the 2017 World Championships – where kids' tickets would go on sale for the Bolt-type price of £9.58 in honour of his world record – he told the press that after the event he would probably retire.

'It'll definitely be my last Olympics. It's going to be hard to go four more years for me, to keep the motivation that I want, especially if I accomplish what I want in Rio.'

What he wanted was three more gold medals – a dizzying triple-triple. 'Somebody said I can be immortal,' he smiled. 'Three more medals to go and I can sign off. Immortal.'

IAAF President Lord Coe could not ignore the six feet five-inch elephant in the room. 'When Usain Bolt leaves it is a high-class problem. Will the sport survive? Yes. But we will need to work even harder.'

His old Olympic teammate Daley Thompson was less diplomatic. 'He's really important because he's probably the only reason we're not ranked with tractor pulling and mud wrestling, because he is an incredible athlete.'

The fabled triple-triple would not be easy. As well as his great nemesis Justin Gatlin there were some fast new kids emerging on the block, including Canada's Andre de Grasse, American Trayvon Bromell and South Africa's Akani Simbine.

As usual Bolt seemed unconcerned and his 'Road to Rio' began sedately enough in the Cayman Islands, followed by his annual pilgrimage to the Golden Spike meet in the Czech Republic, where he dipped under ten seconds.

But injury worries continued to dog his progress and a hamstring tear forced him to pull out of the Jamaican trials, which were dominated by his old rival Yohan Blake, who was looking healthy and quick following a return from long-term injury.

The pro-Bolt sports press worried that Gatlin had been too close for comfort at the previous year's World Championship and that Bolt had hardly raced a 100 in anger. The heavy money was once again being wagered on the American breaking Jamaican hearts and ending the fairytale Olympic finish. But, as ever, Bolt saved his best for the biggest stage.

Rio would not be quite the sporting showstopper that London created, but the stunning Estadio Olimpico was almost filled to bursting for the 100 metres competition. All the key names whirred comfortably through the gears in the heats, but the times began to tumble in the three semi-finals, where the first two in each and the two overall fastest losers would qualify for the final.

Frenchman Jimmy Vicaut took the first semi in 9.95, with the Ivory Coast's Ben Youssef Meite a close second in 9.97 and Akani Simbine third in 9.98. In the next semi-final Usain Bolt upped the ante with a languid 9.86, with clear air to second-placed Andre de Grasse in 9.92 and Bromell in 10.02. But the clearest winning margin was reserved for the third semi, where Justin Gatlin bowled over the line in 9.94, a bus ride ahead of Yohan Blake in 10.01 and Christophe Lemaitre of France in 10.07.

An hour and 25 minutes later the eight men were back out for the final and the old football stadium rocked with noisy delight as Bolt emerged onto the track, the crowd endlessly chanting his name and happily booing Justin Gatlin. Bromell was drawn in lane two, then Simbine, Gatlin, Vicaut, Bolt in lane six, De Grasse, Meite and Blake on the outside in lane nine.

The relaxed, smiling champion, wearing the striking new yellow- and black-halved Jamaican team vest, went through his standard TV routine – shushing the crowd, mugging to the camera and pointing at the sky as if to call down assistance from the sprinting Gods. He didn't need them.

'Usain Bolt, Usain Bolt, Usain Bolt' chanted the crowd as he waved and nodded his approval.

He got a reasonable start by his standards and by 40 metres he'd emerged from the pack and simply sailed across the line, with a quick sideways glance as he effortlessly passed Gatlin about 20 metres from home. Not even close. No contest. The crowd went wild.

Bolt was timed at 9.81, his fastest time of the year, with the 34-year-old Gatlin taking silver in 9.89 and young Canadian De Grasse – who was 21 on the day of the final – breaking his own personal record to take the bronze in 9.91.

'Going into the race I felt confident,' he said later. 'My legs felt a little tired from the fact that the semi and final were so close, pretty much back to back races. But I was thinking about execution, that as long as I execute right and I don't panic and just run through the line, then I'll be fine. When I saw that I had won I felt good because personally I think it's my weakest event.'

'Bolt's Final Push', yelled the *New York Daily News*; 'Usain-ly Unique', sniggered the *Los Angeles Times*; and in an interview with the BBC, Jamaican Prime minister Andrew Holness suggested he'd already reserved Bolt a seat in the Cabinet. 'He could be minister of sport, but Usain could be minister of anything he wants,' the PM declared.

A few days later it was time for the 200 metres, an event Bolt regarded as his strongest and in which he still harboured serious record-breaking intent. But lowering his jaw-dropping 19.19 seconds was never on the cards and despite winning the gold medal by a huge margin he could only muster a 19.78 – though he was still light years ahead of the fast-finishing Andre de Grasse, who took the silver in 20.02, with Lemaitre taking the bronze by the width of a vest from Britain's Adam Gemili.

Still complaining of fatigue, Bolt found the energy to anchor the Jamaican quartet – alongside Powell, Ashmeade and Blake – to another gold in a world leading 37.27, with Japan second, Canada third and the USA once again disqualified for poor baton changing. Their anchor man, Trayvon Bromell, had to be stretchered away by the medical crew after his ankle gave way and he crashed to the track at the finish.

And there it was – the triple-triple. History made. Immortality confirmed. How long would it be, mused the world's sports commentators, before we saw anything like him again?

Bolt returned to Jamaica and didn't re-emerge until well into 2017 to start his valedictory parade to the final event of the Usain Bolt era – the World Championships in London.

'I've done everything I wanted to do in the sport,' he told a Reuters reporter. 'I asked Michael Johnson the same question. Why did you retire when you were on top? He said the same. He had done everything he wanted to do in athletics so there was no reason to stay in the sport. Now I understand what he means.'

After his annual visit to Ostrava, Bolt's back problems flared up once again and that meant another visit to his doctor in Germany and weeks of missed training. He managed an emotional last race in Jamaica, at Kingston's National Stadium, a five-hour 'love-in' in front of 35,000 fans called Salute To A Legend. The race itself was as forgettable as the time – a slow 10.03 – and although he was mobbed at the finish and fireworks lit up the capital's skyline, he still found time to describe it as 'one of my worst races'. In fairness to Bolt, he'd missed the previous two weeks of training after the death of his close friend, the Olympic high jumper Germaine Mason, in a road accident. However, he still smiled his way around a long lap of honour, threw some moves with dancehall legend Beanie Man and listened with embarrassment as the island's top politicians lauded him as the greatest Jamaican of all time. It was a heck of a night.

A little over six weeks later Bolt hit Europe to start his preparations for the World Championships, winning a non-competitive 100 metres at a Diamond League event in Monaco in 9.95 seconds, before heading to London.

En route he decided not to run the 200 metres, simply because he figured he wasn't in good enough shape to double-up, but he still managed to serve up enough drama to light up the old Olympic stadium.

A noisy crowd of 56,000 arrived to witness the last hurrah of a living sports legend, while tens of millions more watched on TV around the world. But this time there would be no fairytale ending, and the carefully laid plans for Bolt's retirement party were gate-crashed by the man the media loved to hate, American Justin Gatlin.

In full pantomime fashion the London crowd booed Gatlin at every turn, but the 35-year-old had the last laugh and dashed away from Bolt and the pre-race favourite, American Christian Coleman, to take his first 100 metres world title since 2005.

Bolt had no answer: his start was awful, he looked fatigued and frankly just happy that it was finally all over. He told the crestfallen, but still cheering crowd: 'London, I really appreciate the support you gave me. I'm just so sorry I couldn't deliver as I wanted. It's one of those things.'

Gatlin also wanted to deflect the glory onto the retiring superstar and explained that his win had done nothing to diminish Bolt's legacy. 'Usain is the man. I have the utmost respect for him and I thank him so much for pushing me to be the athlete I am today. You can't ask for a better champion. Mind-blowing times, gold medals after gold medals, being able to carry the whole sport on his back. He's a character, he's always been respectful to other athletes and to the fans.'

But the drama kept coming right to the very end. In the final of the sprint relay the Jamaican quartet of Omar McLeod, Julian Forte, Yohan Blake and anchorman Bolt were still hot favourites to take the gold. With the crowd roaring, Bolt grabbed the baton in third place, behind the Brits and the Americans, and the stage was set for a grandstand finish. But within a few strides he leaped in the air and stuttered to a dramatic halt, clutching his left hamstring and dropping to the track. A few days later he tweeted the diagnosis – with an accompanying photograph – a tear of the proximal myotendinous junction of the biceps femoris of the left hamstring with partial retraction. In old money – a plain old hamstring tear. Not perhaps the way for an immortal to take his leave of his sport, but certainly not short on drama.

Bolt genuinely had no regrets about the disappointing nature of his swan song. 'After losing the 100 metres someone said to me, Usain don't worry, Muhammad Ali lost his last fight also, so don't be stressed about it. I don't think that one championship or one race, or the fact that I didn't end my last race is going to change the facts of what I've done in the sport.'

So that was that. The reign of the world's greatest ever sprinter was over and he would retire quietly back to Jamaica and enjoy the rest of his life in comfortable tranquillity. Or not. Not even close.

As his agent Ricky Simms is happy to point out, Bolt is busier now than when he was at the peak of his athletic powers. 'To be honest it hasn't really changed at all. Prior to Covid his schedule was probably busier than when he was an active athlete. Ninety per cent of his business in recent years was off track and now that he doesn't have training restrictions he is able to take on a lot more opportunities than when he was an active athlete.'

And it looks like Bolt's enduring charm and box office magic will remain a powerful weapon for a long time to come. As the world edged into the re-arranged Olympic year of 2021, he was still the highest-earning track star in the world, even though he hadn't put a foot on a track for more than three years. The wealth-watching website Celebrity Net Worth estimated his fortune at more than $90 million.

Usain Bolt has more than a dozen high-end commercial partnerships, ranging from Puma and Gatorade, to Swiss luxury watch company Hublot, German financial services giant Allianz and Virgin Media. Gone are the days when appearing on a Wheaties cereal packet was the zenith of any 100-metre Olympic champion's commercial achievements and it was proof positive that Bolt's global appeal and the hard work of Simms and PACE Management had fashioned an enduring and hugely valuable brand from his God-given speed.

Since retirement he's been jetting all over the world in a blur of big PR stunts, business launches, TV ad shoots and media events, but it's not all been plain commercial sailing.

In May of 2018 the lustre of his triple-triple was dented by the disqualification of teammate Nesta Carter from the 4x100 metres relay at the Beijing Olympics. It was a hugely dispiriting tale that dated back to earlier the previous year when the IOC announced that as part of a series of more than 450 re-tests they had ordered on samples taken from athletes at the 2008 Games, they discovered the drug methylhexanamine (MHA) – a stimulant on their banned list – in a sample from Carter.

MHA had been part of a set of stimulants on WADA's prohibited list since 2004, though it was not specifically named, and it was then reclassified on the 2011 list as a 'specified substance'. This meant it was a substance that was more susceptible to a 'credible, non-doping explanation'. It had been sold as a nasal decongestant in the US, but more recently it was used as an ingredient in dietary supplements.

The IOC immediately disqualified him – and thus the whole gold medal-winning Jamaican squad – with Dwight Thomas, Michael Frater, Carter, Powell and Bolt all ordered to return their gold medals and diplomas. Carter appealed, arguing that he was prejudiced by the long delay – nearly eight years – between the original sample collection and the re-test, which happened just months before the expiry of the period of limitation. It made it almost impossible, he contended, to recall any products that he had taken, albeit inadvertently, that may have contained MHA.

His legal team also argued that there would be a 'fundamental unfairness' were Carter to be sanctioned for the presence of a substance that he did not know and could not have reasonably known was a prohibited substance at the time.

But the following spring, after a hearing in Switzerland, the Court of Arbitration For Sport said there was 'no merit' in Carter's argument and ruled in favour of the IOC.

With the programme of re-analysis of samples from past Games continuing, it must be worrying for Bolt that his 2012 4 x 100 relay gold medal may also be under threat, given that Nesta Carter was part of the Jamaica team in London.

However, Usain Bolt now has 'only' eight Olympic gold medals, rather than nine. He put a brave face on the whole affair, but it was clearly a serious disappointment to him.

Interviewed by CNN, Bolt said: 'I haven't spoken to him. But I have no hard feelings. It's just one of those things that happens in life. I haven't gotten to talk to him to find out exactly what happened or what went down. So, until I see him, I can't really say he did it on purpose or it was a mistake or I should be angry.'

When asked if he feared he would lose more of his Olympic relay medals, Bolt replied: 'I'm not worried about that. If I lose all of my relay gold medals, for me I did what I had to do with my personal goals and that's what counts.'

Better news came on the football field, where Bolt's well-publicised ambition to be a professional football player began to take more solid form. He had trials with Borussia Dortmund, one of Germany's top sides; Stromsgodset in Norway; and South African Premier League team Mamelodi Sundowns. Contract offers appeared from every corner of the globe. In the end it looked like he'd made the breakthrough he craved at Australian A-League side Central Coast Mariners, and after seven weeks of training and trials he made his first start, in October 2018, scoring twice in a 4-0 friendly win over Macarthur South West United, in Sydney.

But he never got to play in an A-League game and a few months later a disappointed Bolt announced he was calling time on his football ambitions. 'It's just one of those things you miss out on and just have to move on,' he said. 'I do think about it sometimes that it didn't work out the way I wanted it to, because football is something that I love. But it was fun while it lasted.'

However, Bolt did captain the World XI in two huge televised Soccer Aid matches against England, a big pro-celebrity fund-raising campaign for UNICEF, winning the man of the match award in the first, which was played at Old Trafford, home to his beloved Manchester United. It would be a golden memory he would never forget.

Back on the commercial trail he opened a Jamaican restaurant called Usain Bolt's Tracks & Records, in London's trendy Spitalfields – he already has three in Jamaica – and then began an electric scooter and car business, in New York and Paris, called Bolt Mobility.

However, when Covid-19 struck, his commercial enterprises slowed and he returned to Jamaica to wait it out – although he got in trouble for hosting a party for his 34th birthday that broke the nation's social distancing rules. He then tested positive for the virus and had to self-isolate, but exhibited few symptoms and was quickly back to full health.

Far better news was the arrival, in May 2020, of his daughter Olympia Lightning, with partner Kasi Bennett. Even the Jamaican Prime Minister tweeted about it. Usain is hoping to take her to Tokyo for the Olympics. 'One of my moments is to have my first-born just to walk on the track with me,' he said. 'That's something that I always thought about.'

The new arrival also prompted him to donate medical equipment, including twelve blood pressure monitoring machines, to Kingston's Nuttall Memorial Hospital's maternity ward.

He remains passionate about his charity work and the Usain Bolt Foundation, which was set up in 2013, continues to work hard for disadvantaged kids in Jamaica. In early 2020 it funded the donation of computer equipment to seven schools in his home parish of Trelawny – part of a campaign to ensure kids in rural Jamaica get access to the same education as others on the island.

Understandably, Jamaica reveres its greatest sporting star and they are not slow in showing it. The government plans to erect a statue to him in the city of Falmouth, in his home parish of Trelawny. It will follow the eight-foot bronze statue of him that was unveiled a few years earlier at the National Stadium, in Kingston.

At that event, World Athletics President Lord Coe sent a video message that neatly summarized the impact Bolt has had on athletics. 'Usain has changed the face of our sport,' said Coe. 'His has had an extraordinary career which has exemplified competitive excellence, extraordinary character, good sportsmanship and professionalism, all of which has made him a global superstar.

'Usain may have left the track but I know he will never leave the sport and we look forward to working closely with him on the next part of his journey in the greatest sport on the planet. On behalf of the world of athletics, thank you to a giant of world sport who has made an immense contribution to athletics worldwide.'

Does Bolt miss the track? 'I miss competing,' he says. 'I miss the thrill of the big stadiums, the atmosphere, the crowd and, of course, the race. But I really don't miss the training.'

That his place in athletics history is secure is in no doubt. He set out to be a legend and landed sporting immortality instead. His achievements are unlikely to be matched. His is the name on every school kid's lips when they race across a playground, a school field or a back yard. He transcended his sport and became something far, far bigger.

'I'd like history to remember me as a legend of the sport,' he says. 'I won many Olympic and world championship medals and set world records. But I also tried to put a smile on people's faces and elevate the sport of track and field.

'One of the biggest things I wanted to do was win three Olympics back to back and I did it. I wanted to set the bar so high for the next person who comes along that they have to work really hard – harder than I worked – to get to the level they need to get to.'

Asked if he thinks someone will one day beat his world records he remains a little gnomic. 'You never know. The possibility is there. I don't want it to happen, but then it would be great to see somebody new in track and field, because track and field needs great athletes; so if somebody comes along in twenty years from now and surpasses me, I'll be OK.'

CHAPTER TWENTY-FOUR

Chasing Usain Bolt

The king is dead, long live the king. Well, not actually dead, but certainly in happy exile. And definitely not planning to return. Asked for this book whether he fancied a surprise, one-off comeback for Tokyo Usain Bolt simply laughed: 'No chance!'

So as the 2018 season opened, the first without the presence of the three-time Olympic champion for almost 16 years, the media painted a gloomy picture of an apocalyptic post-Bolt world. Some pronounced the sport already dead, while even the more optimistic suggested survival would be an uphill struggle.

What they all seemed to agree on was that there was no obvious heir apparent to the great man's throne as the fastest man on earth. However, contrary to the pervading media wisdom, a bright new generation of sprinting superheroes was already assembling.

While Usain Bolt's retirement clearly created genuine anxiety amongst the sport's leaders – its promoters, sponsors and television rights holders – far from spiralling into an era of grey, identikit athletes, empty stadiums and blank TV screens, there was a clear and growing optimism about the track and field stars of the future.

Outside the sprint world there was a charismatic young Swede, the pole vaulter Mondo du Plantis, who was breaking world records at will; the extraordinary talent of South African quarter-miler Wade van Niekerk, who broke Michael Johnson's longstanding 400 metres world record in 43.03 seconds in Rio; and there was the stunning Bahamian sprinter Shaunae Miller-Uibo, the Olympic 400-metre champion who seemed to charm every track around the world with her brilliant running and striking new hair colours.

All were capable of selling tickets.

It was left to Olympic decathlon champion and the world's greatest all-round athlete, Ashton Eaton, to best articulate the prevailing climate from inside the sport. 'Usain won't create a vacuum. He's made a platform. We're not seeing the fruits of his labour yet, but we will see youngsters inspired by him in years to come. I was inspired by Michael Johnson at the age of eight and I didn't start to make an impact until I was eighteen. So give it a decade and we will see the effect he's made.'

Actually, the dividends of Bolt's enormous global popularity would be seen much earlier than that, especially in the sprint world. And it would take a hideous pandemic, rather than the departure of the sport's biggest box office attraction, to halt, albeit temporarily, the momentum of this exciting new wave.

So who were the members of this bright new generation?

Alongside the old guard of the 2017 world champion Justin Gatlin and Jamaica's evergreen Asafa Powell – both of whom steadfastly refused to slide quietly into the night – were two familiar names, albeit younger guns, who had given Usain Bolt a run for his money in London: American Christian Coleman and Canada's Andre de Grasse. And right behind them was another seam of real talent that included no fewer than five more extraordinary fast men from the unending American production line. There was the injured Rio finalist and world's fastest teenager Trayvon Bromell; the sublimely talented and wonderfully theatrical Noah Lyles; superfast Ronnie Baker; and youngsters Michael Norman and Matthew Boling. Chasing Uncle Sam's boys were Nigerian Divine Oduduru, who had been ripping up the US college circuit, and South Africa's Akani Simbine, who had finished fifth in the Rio final.

It was an exceptionally talented line-up. So, within just a few years of the Rio Games, a previously unthinkable question was already being given serious consideration. How long could Usain Bolt's seemingly unsurpassable world records survive?

The path to the next Olympic Games – originally to be held in Tokyo, in the summer of 2020 – began with the first of these new stars making an early bid as heir apparent with a series of record-breaking indoor runs in early 2018. Bolt himself had tipped the short, stocky, Atlanta-born Christian Coleman as a potential successor, but correctly observed at the time: 'The field for the next Olympics is wide open.'

In January 2018, at a minor collegiate event in South Carolina, Coleman ran the fastest 60 metres in history – a staggering new world record of 6.37 seconds. This cut two hundredths of a second off Maurice Greene's mark – a time widely considered to be unbeatable when it was set some 20 years earlier. Post-race, Coleman ducked suggestions that he was the natural heir to the Jamaican superstar and stuck rigidly to the script. 'A lot of people might consider me the next Bolt, but I just want to leave my own legacy, continue to work hard, be ready to compete and when the time comes, run for a gold medal.' However, when *Track & Field News* prodded Coleman a little more, he conceded that beating Bolt's world record times would be a dream come true. 'To be the fastest ever, that's anybody's dream.'

A month later, at the US Indoor championships in New Mexico, Coleman burnished his credentials still further when he lowered his indoor 60 mark to a previously unimaginable time of 6.34 seconds – albeit at altitude – but still grumbled about his start, describing it as a 'B effort' and promising more improvement to come.

Although improvements in times did not materialize at the World Indoor Championships – held in March, at the Birmingham Arena in England – Coleman still captured another major sprint title in 6.37 seconds. Afterwards, he neatly summarized the sprinting eco-system, explaining: 'I have a good chance to lead the sport in the post-Bolt era, but like I've told so many others, loads of guys have the talent.'

With his closest rival Andre de Grasse struggling to handle persistent hamstring injuries and Trayvon Bromell not setting a foot on the track since Rio, Coleman's title credentials were hard to ignore. Armed with a silver medal from the previous year's World Championships and following an electric indoor season, surely Coleman was the man who would be king? He was the reigning NCAA champion at both 100 and 200 metres and, during his time at the University of Tennessee, he had lowered the six-year-old college 100 record to 9.82 seconds – smashing Ngoni Makusha's time of 9.89 by seven hundredths. It remained the fastest time of the year. Was there a quicker sprinter running anywhere in the world?

In fact, there was another viable contender just 600 miles south of Coleman's Knoxville base – an eight-hour drive down the I-75 freeway to Clermont, in Florida. A hamstring injury had robbed Noah Lyles of most of his rookie pro season, but the Virginian sprinter still managed to win the 200 metres title at the Diamond League finals meeting of 2017. On a chilly, rain-sodden evening in Brussels, his 20-flat time signalled a mightily impressive return to the track and now, happy, healthy and fit, Lyles planned a wholesale assault on all the major events in 2018. No lesser expert than NBC television analyst Ato Boldon hailed him as 'the new Michael Johnson'.

Alongside Lyles was the smiling, muscular figure of Ronnie Baker, who has a unique claim to fame as a sprinter. He started his athletic career as a cross country runner – in Alaska. Although he was born in Kentucky, in October 1993, his family moved to Anchorage when he was just five years old. 'My Mom lived in Alaska when she was growing up and I think she just wanted to go back. We were there for seven years and I started running cross country at elementary school. It was freezing cold, we wore hats and gloves, and there were tons of kids running a course through the woods!'

Ronnie did not even see a running track until the family moved back to Louisville when he was thirteen, but very quickly his natural speed was spotted and he won his first 100 metre race in the sixth grade. At Ballard High School he claimed the state titles at 100 and 400 metres in 2011 and 2012 and his continued success on the track brought him a scholarship to Texas Christian University, in Fort Worth. There, Ronnie made steady progress under coach Daryl Anderson, winning two national titles, breaking college records and running a 9.89 before graduating with a degree in kinesiology and turning professional.

In 2017 – Baker's first year as a pro – he demonstrated his extraordinary acceleration to win the national indoor 60 metre title and claimed his first victory in the Diamond League, when he took a wind-assisted 9.86 seconds win in Eugene, Oregon.

So Coleman, Lyles and Baker all looked fast. Bromell would be back and De Grasse had run a stupendous 9.69 – the fastest 100 metres of 2017 – albeit with a strong wind behind him, at the old Olympic stadium in Stockholm, Sweden. Sadly, a hamstring injury would then take De Grasse out of the picture for the rest of the year.

Who else would challenge them? Jamaica's Yohan Blake was still on the scene and had posted the second fastest time of 2017 – a 9.90 in Kingston – but a return to the days of his fastest-ever time of 9.69, set back in 2012, now seemed beyond him. His younger teammate Julian Forte could certainly be a contender and there was Texan Cameron Burrell – son of the former world record holder Leroy – and his fellow American Chris Belcher, as well as the two Africans, Oduduru and Simbine.

Born in a poor Johannesburg suburb in September 1993, the young Simbine had dreamed of being a football star with the city's premier club, the Kaizer Chiefs, but his high school principal spotted his speed and re-directed him to the track. As an Information Science student at the University of Pretoria, Simbine equalled the South African 100 metres record in 2015 and the following year smashed it with a run of 9.89 in Hungary. A few months later he finished just outside the medals in the Rio Olympics. At the 2018 Commonwealth Games, in Australia, he would take gold in the 100 metres.

Back in the States, two even younger talents were beginning to emerge from the shadows: Californian phenomenon Michael Norman had torn up the record books at everything from 100 to 400 metres; while Texan Matt Boling became the first high school athlete to run a 9.98 in the 100 metres. The US tabloid press immediately, and lazily, dubbed him 'White Lightning'.

The race for Tokyo was already heating up.

First blood of the 2018 outdoor season went to 20-year-old Lyles, who ran the season's first Diamond League 200 metres in a showy personal best of 19.83 and followed it up at Oregon's annual Prefontaine Classic, in May, where he went faster still, streaking away from a world-class field, which included the Turkish world champion Ramil Guliyev and Trinidad's bronze medallist Jereem Richards, to win in 19.69.

'I'm in love with the time,' he told journalists, 'but I'm a little scared because I didn't expect to run this fast this soon. So it just means the rest of the season is going to be even faster.'

At the same meeting, Baker ran a windy 9.78 seconds to take the 100 metres, ahead of Coleman, and throw his hat into the ring for a ticket to the post-Bolt shakedown.

However, Lyles vividly demonstrated his own 100 metres pedigree at the US Championships, held at Drake University, beneath cloudy skies in Des Moines, Iowa, in June. The 36-year-old Justin Gatlin elected to miss the event, while Coleman was forced to pull out with a hamstring problem, so the scene was set for the fast-starting Baker to make an early claim for the title of America's number one. But young Lyles hadn't read the script. Just before the race his coach, Tyson Gay's old mentor Lance Brauman, told him: 'I'm giving you the all-clear to go all-out.' And he did just that, starting slowly, but not panicking and inching back on Baker to burst ahead in the final couple of metres to win the title in a personal best of 9.88. Baker was timed at 9.90 – also a personal best.

Perhaps more intriguingly, Lyles broke into a spontaneous dance routine after the race, which went viral and got the attention of sports fans all over the world. Could Lyles be the man to inherit the mantle of Bolt the entertainer, as well as Bolt the racer?

As he headed back to the Diamond League caravan for the rest of the summer, Lyles would major on the 200 metres, while Baker and Coleman would battle each other in the 100 metres. Baker opened with a time of 9.78, albeit with an illegal tailwind, to beat Coleman in the Prefontaine Classic, in Oregon that May. The rest of the season was an epic ding-dong, head-to-head battle between them, with Baker winning four – including a 9.88 in Paris – and Coleman three. Baker then ran a world-leading 9.87 at a small meet in Poland, but Coleman would have the last laugh. It came, fittingly, at the Diamond League 100 metres final in Brussels, where he saved the best until last: a season-leading and personal best of 9.79 seconds, with Baker just behind in 9.93. It was a neat book end – starting and ending the season on a high. 'I put myself back in the conversation,' said Coleman. 'It was the first time this year I was able to come into a race fully confident in my health and fitness and I think it showed.'

In the 200 metres Noah Lyles was a class apart, winning almost at will and lowering his own personal best at Monaco's Diamond League event in July to 19.65 seconds, which lifted him to equal No. 8 in the all-time list. He retained his 200 metres title in text-book style at the Zurich Weltklasse, gliding almost effortlessly to victory in 19.67 seconds.

With Gatlin cutting down his track activity to manage his ageing body and De Grasse struggling with more hamstring issues, the scene was set for another big World Championship showdown in Qatar in 2019. Would there be any real challengers for the three young Americans – Coleman, Lyles and Baker?

After a stellar 2018, the sprinting world waited with bated breath for a Baker–Coleman sequel in 2019 and a battle royale at the US trials and the world championships. But disappointingly, long-term hamstring and adductor injuries virtually wrote off Baker's entire season.

'While I was injured in 2019 I watched him destroy everyone and win the world championships,' says Baker of Coleman. 'But if I'm healthy there's not a doubt in my mind that I can beat him. I've done it before and we're very close.'

With Baker spending the bulk of the 2019 season in rehab, it was left to Coleman and Lyles to begin the battle for supremacy.

Coleman told *Track & Field News*: 'My mentality is just so totally different from a lot of guys. Growing up and especially being from Atlanta, it's just so competitive, it's dog eat dog, so I'm coming in every single day just trying to outwork the next person. I'm not just going against my training partner, I'm trying to beat the guys on the other side of the world that are training, the guys that are my competitors that are trying to make the USA team and take my spot.'

It would be fair to say that Christian Coleman has had his eyes fixed firmly on the prize from a very early age. Born in Atlanta, Georgia, in March 1996, Coleman's parents Seth and Daphne recall him running for student president as a ten-year-old – and recruiting a campaign staff to ensure that he won. He always dreamed of being an American football player and his father spent hours on the road driving him to camps all over the country. But the same reaction kept coming back: good player, too small.

Coleman's first high school coach Robert Wilson said: 'In the ninth grade he was a hell of a long jumper. I saw that power and explosion in him, it was just a matter of his body catching up. Back then he looked like a kid who played violin.'

'I know that Christian has always been kind of the underdog,' said mother Daphne. 'When he played football he was small and people doubted him. I think he's always had this chip on his shoulder.'

Another high school coach, Mark Tolcher, recalled: 'He would win races before they started based on how he carried himself. Athletes in his heats were intimidated just being in a race with him, they were psyched out.'

That combination of natural speed, laser focus and brooding intensity served Coleman well. During his senior year at Atlanta's Our Lady of Mercy high school he won four state titles – three of them in one day – and as an all-state wide receiver he was about to sign up to play football with a minor school in Indiana when he was spotted running at a track meet by the University of Tennessee. They immediately offered him an 80 per cent track scholarship and he never looked back. In his freshman year the college upped the ante to a 100 per cent scholarship when Coleman was named South Eastern Championship (SEC) freshman of the year, after becoming the first collegiate athlete to run a sub-ten second 100 metres and a sub-20 second 200 metres on the same day.

At college, now a muscular 5ft 9in and 150 pounds, Coleman made rapid progress through 2016, winning the NCAA indoor 200 metres and placing second in the outdoor NCAA 100 and 200 metres, before qualifying for the Rio Olympics on the relay squad. The following year he won the sprint double at the NCAA championships and a week or so later announced he was leaving college and turning professional.

The record books show that Christian Coleman was the fastest man over 100 metres in 2017 and 2018, and no lesser voice than Usain Bolt surmised that he had the race in Tokyo 'sewn up'. Only a few were keen to doubt his wisdom.

One of them was Noah Lyles, an athlete with a very clear vision of his own future. 'I'm trying to be great, not good. There are tons of people who are good, there are tons of people who have gotten to where I am now. But to be great I've got to do what most people haven't. You have to win the gold medal, you have to do it more than once, you have to do it three times in a row; break a world record, do it again. These are the things that make you great.'

The word 'prodigy' is bandied about a lot in track and field; but for Lyles, it is the only one that fits. On the track his personality, charm and showmanship light up the dullest of meetings, while his electric performances have already given us a glimpse of an exhilarating future. He'll sing, he'll dance, he'll change his hair colour, he'll throw himself into the crowd and he'll play to the cameras. He'll also run exceptionally fast. He won't admit to idolizing Usain Bolt because he doesn't want to put him on a pedestal. 'I admire and respect him, but I'm coming after his records,' he says.

Born in Gainesville, Florida in July 1997, young Noah had a tough start in life, suffering so badly with asthma that he was constantly in and out of hospital. He missed so much school that his mother held him back a year and he ended up repeating the first grade, alongside his younger brother Josephus. His parents – father Kevin and mother Keisha – met while running track at Seton Hall University, in New Jersey, and Kevin won a gold medal as part of the 4 x 400 relay squad at the 1995 world championships. However, they split up when the boys were still young and Noah recalls a hand-to-mouth existence living in a one-bedroomed apartment in Alexandria, Virginia, close to Washington DC, where it was a constant struggle for single mom Keisha to pay the bills.

Noah struggled academically at school, suffering with ADD and dyslexia, but he always loved sports and began competing as a gymnast and then a high jumper. He didn't start seriously running track until he and his brother were inspired by watching the opening ceremony of the 2012 Olympics in London. They decided there and then that one day they would go to the Olympic Games.

Two years later, at just 17, Lyles strode to a gold medal by a huge margin in the 200 metres at the 2014 Youth Olympics in China. On the start line, wearing shades and playing to the crowd, Noah gave the world its first glimpse of the superstar to come.

Keisha drove her sons to meets all over the country and Noah knows that without her sacrifices and hard work he and his brother would never have made it as far as they have. In 2015 and 2016 he was named high school athlete of the year, and after winning 100 metre golds in both the US junior championships and world junior championships, he then made it to the final of the senior 200 metre US trials for the Rio Olympics. At 18 years old he finished 4th – breaking a 31-year-old high school record in the process – but didn't make the team and vowed to return and win it all next time around.

It was in 2016 when Noah had a dream in which he ran the 100 metres in 9.41 seconds. He told *Athletics Weekly*: 'I ran up to my Mom and said "Mom, I just ran 9.41". And she was like, "That's nice, Noah". And then she turned around and said: "What did you just say?" I said 9.41. She said: "That's a world record!" I said: "I know. I didn't even feel like I was pushing in the race.'

'It's funny how you can take things from reality and put them into dreams. I do think I can run 9.41. I don't know when it's going to happen but I'm going to try my best, do everything in my power, to make it happen.'

When Lyles left TC Williams High School in Alexandria, the original plan was for him to head to the University of Florida. Instead, he broke with convention and shortly after the trials turned professional, signing an eight-year deal with Adidas, along with his brother Josephus, who is a 400-metre specialist.

The start of Lyles' first pro season in 2017 augured well. In New Mexico he broke the world record for the rarely run indoor 300 metres in 31.87 and followed that up in May with victory in the 200 metres in his first Diamond League event in Shanghai, China – recording a time of 19.90, his first sub-20 second run.

Hamstring problems kept Lyles out of the US trials and the world championships in London and he did not run in another major event until the Diamond League final in Brussels in September, when he once again won the 200 metres.

After his exceptional 2018 season, when he was named US men's athlete of the year, he conceded that the 100 metres was still very much a work in progress. 'The 200 metres is my bread and butter,' he explained. 'It's my thing I know that I can do it almost to a science and that it's getting faster each time I run. In the 100 I feel there is so much that I have to learn that it's still a little early for me to get excited about it.'

As the 2019 season opened, it took until only the second Diamond League race of the year for that to change and the balance of power to shift.

On a warm May night in Shanghai, as the 100-metre athletes were being introduced to the crowd, Christian Coleman looked subdued and nervy. On the contrary, when the camera moved in front of Lyles, he drew an imaginary pistol from an imaginary holster and fired it, blew the smoke away like a Western gunfighter and spun it back in the holster. Unlike Coleman, he was calmness personified.

At the starting gun, Coleman catapulted out of his blocks as we had seen so many times before and simply tore away from the field. Game over, apparently. Except Lyles didn't get the message. At 50 metres he wasn't in the race, but out of nowhere he came flying past the rest of the field and astonishingly dipped to beat Coleman on the line by just six thousandths of a second. His time was a new personal best and world-leading 9.86 seconds. 'The 100 has never been my dominant thing,' he said, clearly elated after the race, 'so I wanted to make everybody aware that this year I am a 100 runner, not just a 200 runner kind of running the 100'.

Back in the United States, a few weeks later, Divine Oduduru posted another twist in the tale when he won the NCAA 100 metres in 9.86 seconds – equalling Lyles's time. His coach at Texas Tech, Calvin Robinson, had clearly succeeded in transforming his sluggish starts, though the Nigerian had a far simpler explanation. With his wide trademark grin, he said: 'Sometimes you wake up on the right side of the bed, sometimes you wake up on the wrong side.' Astonishingly, a little over 30 minutes later he took the 200-metre title for the second year running, in a jaw-dropping 19.73 seconds – the second-fastest college time ever.

Oduduru's story is an interesting one. Born the youngest of ten children, in Ughelli in southern Nigeria, in September 1996, Divine and his family worked a hand-to-mouth existence on their tiny farm, where they sometimes went for days without eating. Despite the grinding poverty, Divine's mother Christiana pushed him to attend school and it was there that his natural speed was first discovered. He used it to good effect at the D. K. Olukoya Championships – a regional event staged to promote young sporting talent – and from there he went on to win multiple titles at the African youth level before landing a silver medal in the 200 metres at the World Junior Championships, in Oregon, in 2014. The following year Oduduru won both sprints in the African under-20 event and in 2016, aged just 19, he won the Nigerian 200 metre trials and a place on the national team for the Rio Olympics. His performance in Brazil, where he made the semi-finals of the 200 metres, prompted the offer of a scholarship and new life at Texas Tech.

At around the same time as Oduduru was performing his 2019 NCAA heroics in Texas, nearly six thousand miles away in the suitably historic setting of Rome, 21-year-old Michael Norman chose his moment to crash the party, winning an incredibly close 200 metres in a world leading 19.70, with favourite Noah Lyles just a fraction behind him.

Not to be outdone, Coleman then won the 100 metres at a packed Bislett stadium in Oslo. His time of 9.85 seconds was the world lead time that year, only for him to lower it again a few weeks later in Oregon to 9.81 seconds, as the perilous US trials in Des Moines beckoned. But Lyles wasn't finished. In perfect conditions at the Lausanne Diamond league event, he lowered his 200 metres time to an eye-widening 19.50 – the fourth-fastest run of all time – with only Usain Bolt, Yohan Blake and Michael Johnson having run faster.

Before then there was still time to see the returning Andre de Grasse back to something like vintage form, with a confidence-building 200 metres win at the Diamond League in Morocco. He had switched coaches after two years ravaged by injury and was now with sprint specialist Rana Reider in Florida. The strength training and stamina building were clearly paying off. The Canadian made good use of the time he was injured, first becoming a father to daughter Yuri alongside his partner, the American Olympic silver medallist high-hurdler Nia Ali, and joining the team campaigning to bring the 2026 Commonwealth Games to Hamilton, Ontario.

De Grasse grew up in Scarborough and Markham, tough neighbourhoods in the eastern suburbs of Toronto, and is happy to admit that a career on the track probably saved him.

When his basketball team folded in 2012, he began staying out late, hanging with the wrong crowd and forgetting his school work. By complete chance he found himself on a local track and betting with an old friend about who was the fastest.

'I was at the bus stop going home from school and I got on the bus and bumped into my friend,' he explains. 'He was wearing track attire and I asked him where he was going. He said he was going to the university for track practice, so I asked him what events he was running and he said the 100 and 200 metres. I said "no way, you're not that fast" and he said that I should come out and train. I turned up and I was shocked because everyone was wearing spikes, compression shorts and uniforms and I was in basketball shorts, basketball shoes and didn't know how to use the starting blocks. But I ran anyway and recorded 10.90 seconds. People told me that was really fast – but more importantly I beat my friend.'

Incredibly, four years later.De Grasse lined up in the Olympic 100 metres final in Rio.

His local track run had been spotted by coach Tony Sharpe, who had won an Olympic sprint relay medal in 1984. He handed Andre his business card and suggested he join his track club. 'I wouldn't be here today if it wasn't for my friend and Tony recruiting me that day,' he recalls. His mother Beverley could also take some credit. She was a sprinter in her native Trinidad, and one of his early coaches wryly observed: 'He did a great job in selecting the right parents.'

In 2013 Andre shipped out to a community college in Kansas, then on to the University of Southern California, where in 2015 he won the sprint double at the Pan American Games in front of his family in Toronto, as well as another double at the NCAA, and a bronze medal in the world championships.

By the end of the year Andre de Grasse was one of the biggest stars on the sprint scene, prompting Puma to pay him over $11 million for a long-term commercial deal. He immediately went out and bought … a Honda Accord! But he also fulfilled a promise he made to his mum and graduated from USC with a degree in sociology. 'I had good values instilled in me by my mother,' he smiles. 'She taught me so much. Everyone seemed to have a Honda in my neighbourhood when I was growing up and there was a dealership near where I lived. Of course, I've got a few different cars now!'

At Puma, Andre became friends with Usain Bolt – the wonderful image of them chatting over the finish line in the Rio 200 metres semi-final became one of the most iconic during the Games. 'I remember being nervous when I first raced him,' Andre recalls. 'I was only nineteen and I'd watched him in the Olympics in 2008 and 2012 and – wow. So when the best in the world is telling you that you can be one of the best, that brings a lot of confidence for me.'

The Canadian 100 metres record of 9.84, held by Donovan Bailey and Bruny Surin, is a major goal – 'I really want to be the fastest Canadian' – and a fit and healthy De Grasse, one of the nice guys of the track world, will certainly be one of the major contenders in Tokyo after benefiting enormously from the extended lay-off in 2020.

De Grasse was just an interested observer when the 2019 US trials rolled around in July. As always, it would be the first three men over the line that would make the USA team for the World Championships in Qatar. No excuses, no appeals. As world champion, only the veteran Justin Gatlin could afford not to bother qualifying. He was going anyway, happily holding a free-entry golden wild card. Coleman decided to run both sprints, but Lyles elected not to run the 100 metres and save himself for the longer sprint.

On the day, Coleman won the 100 final easily, with a time of 9.99 seconds into a headwind, with veteran Mike Rodgers second and 25-year-old Chris Belcher third. Two days later, on a wet and rainy track, he was looking good in the 200 metres until Lyles casually overhauled him at the end of the curve and strolled away down the home straight to win in 19.78 seconds.

With the team and events for Doha settled, Lyles then headed back to Europe and in quick succession won the Paris 200 in 19.65, then the 100 in Zurich in 9.98, before completing a remarkable double by taking the 200 in Brussels in 19.74. In doing so, he became the first man to win both 100 and 200 trophies in the ten-year history of the Diamond League. He was also $100,000 richer just from the prize money.

But it wasn't just Lyles' performances on the track that won rave reviews. In front of a packed house at the Zurich Weltklasse he teamed up with Swiss band Baba Shrimps, and US pole vaulter Sandi Morris, to perform one of his own songs, written and performed under the name Nojo19, on a makeshift stage in centre field. Lyles the rapper was beginning to make Usain Bolt and even Carl Lewis seem like shrinking violets. He has now released seven singles and an album.

If Christian Coleman was downhearted by playing second fiddle to his great rival, he did not have too much time to dwell on it. A far more unpleasant turn of events was just around the corner. In August it was widely publicized that USADA (the US Anti Doping Agency) discovered that Coleman had broken their 'whereabouts rule' for a third time. This rule ensured that all athletes were always available for drug testing and had to let testers know where they would be for one hour each day, along with where they were training and where they were spending the night. The rule was simple – breaking it three times meant a suspension. With the World Championships in Qatar a matter of four weeks away, this was desperate news for the 23-year-old from southside Atlanta.

In the end, the case was dropped due to a filing error. For the charge to stick, the three breaches of the rule had to take place within a twelve-month period; although Coleman's breaches had been logged in June 2018, January 2019 and April 2019, the first missed test was now technically out of date. Coleman dodged the bullet and the internet raged with indignation. He posted a 22-minute video online defending himself, explaining that he had changed his training schedule. On his Instagram page he said: 'I have never failed a drug test and never will. I'm the biggest advocate for clean sport because I know the sacrifice and what it takes to make it to this level. There have been a lot of inaccurate things said in the media over the last few weeks.'

So he ran. And on a late September night after a spectacular light show in the Khalifa stadium in Doha, he managed to channel all the emotion, pressure and pent-up anger into his best ever 100-metre run – a gold medal-winning 9.76 – to completely destroy a first-class field. As Coleman flashed across the line he screamed into the sky and wheeled around the bottom curve before sinking to the track as the enormity of what he had just achieved finally hit him.

Justin Gatlin trailed in a distant second in 9.89 and a rejuvenated Andre de Grasse took the bronze medal in 9.90. Simbine, Blake, Britain's Zarnell Hughes, Italy's Filippo Tortu and Canadian Aaron Brown filled out the rest of the places, with the first five all running under ten seconds.

'This is just something I'll never forget,' Coleman said in the post-race interviews, grading his performance as an A-minus. 'I'll never take for granted that opportunity to come out here and compete and then be crowned world champion. People don't see behind the scenes, the amount of blood, sweat and tears that goes into it, just to step on that line and be able to make it to a world championship final. So hats off to all the competitors out there.'

The media seemed immediately disappointed that they didn't have the usual post-race pyrotechnics of Usain Bolt, but Coleman's manager Emanuel Hudson was quick to point to the upside. 'Are you going to see Usain Bolt-dancing and stuff? You're not going to see that. But at the same time what he gives you is going to be genuine, it's not going to be made up. And he's a purist. He's like the old school guys.'

Asked if his post-race reaction meant he had something to prove, Coleman replied: 'That's just my lifestyle. I feel like I always walk around with a chip on my shoulder. Just being from where I'm from, not many people are expected to make it out or expected to do something of this magnitude.'

Some of the media still wouldn't let him forget his 'whereabouts' transgressions and even Michael Johnson, working for the BBC, poured cold water on his success, suggesting that the missed tests meant he could never be the face of the sport. Coleman reacted tetchily. 'Michael Johnson doesn't pay my bills or write my cheques, so I don't necessarily care what he says.'

For his part, Justin Gatlin was simply delighted to make the podium after a season of injuries, while de Grasse seemed almost stunned that he had managed to land a medal. 'To go through these injuries and battle back for the past couple of years, all I can say is I'm grateful for it. It's an amazing feeling to get back here and be on the podium.' His gratitude grew still further when he took an unexpected silver medal in the 200 metres a few days later, with Noah Lyles catching and passing him down the home straight to win comfortably in 19.83 seconds. The Canadian's medal haul, collected so soon after a lengthy period of injury, augured well for Olympic year.

Lyles, his hair tinted silver, exuded an air of relief in landing his first major championship gold medal. 'So many times this year I've thought of being world champion you wouldn't believe it. I have it on my phone. I said it to myself in the car, I think it all the time, and finally to have done it feels unbelievable. I don't know how many people come to their first world championships and get the gold, but I've done it. I just knew that no matter what position I found myself in I can always find a way to come through. And when I crossed the line I just felt relief. Don't call me the new Bolt. I'm me. If you like me, I'll happily entertain you. It's my time.'

Buoyed by his 200-metre success, he then went out and anchored the US relay team, alongside Coleman, Rodgers and Gatlin. The American quartet won a superb gold in the sprint relay, with an unusually slick display of changeovers and great speed, in a new national record of 37.10.

No sooner had the lights gone out at an electrifying World Championships in Qatar, than the build-up to the 2020 Tokyo Olympics began in earnest.

For the sprinting world it would be the first opportunity to witness the new generation of fastest men up close and personal, butting heads before a colossal global audience. It was a truly exciting proposition.

And then the world stopped. The catastrophic Covid-19 pandemic would cost more than three million lives, crush national economies and put untold millions out of work. Somehow, the postponement of the world's major sporting events – even the Olympic Games themselves – hardly seemed relevant or important. So when the official announcement was made in March 2020, the reaction was not simmering outrage, but one of resigned comprehension and muted disappointment.

Ominously, while announcing the new dates for the Games, from July 23 to August 8 2021, Japan's then Olympic boss Yoshiro Mori confirmed that there would be no further postponement. If the Games could not be staged on those dates, for whatever reason, then they would be scrapped and the next Olympics would not take place until 2024 in Paris.

Inevitably it was slim pickings for track fans, as the sport's biggest stars were forced to train in public parks, soccer pitches, golf courses – even on the streets. They posted videos of their endeavours on social media and pontificated on the pros and cons of a competitive gap year before track returned in 2021. Or so they hoped.

Everyone was in the same boat. It was impossible to make any new evaluations on the potential candidates for 100 metres glory in Japan, because hardly anyone had set foot on a track in a competitive race since the World Championships.

But there were still headlines to be written. Some good, some less so.

The funniest story was probably that of Noah Lyles believing, at least for the briefest of moments, that he had broken Usain Bolt's 200 metre world record in a jaw-dropping solo run timed at 18.90 seconds at the newly created Inspiration Games, in July.

The event had been dreamed up to work in a global lockdown so that around 30 athletes could run solo, but simultaneously, at different tracks around the world. In the 200 metre race, Lyles was racing in Florida, Frenchman Christophe Lemaitre in Zurich and Dutchman Churandy Martina in Arnhem. The race would be televised worldwide on split screens.

Embarrassingly, the organizers somehow contrived to start Lyles from the wrong line and he actually only ran a distance of 185 metres. The race (and $10,000 prize money) went to Lemaitre, who posted a sedate time of 20.65 seconds. Lyles tweeted afterwards: 'You can't be playing with my emotions like this – smh.' [shaking my head]. At the same games Andre de Grasse won a 100 yards race into a strong headwind in 9.68 seconds.

The most disappointing story concerned Christian Coleman, arguably the favourite for the Olympic title, who having narrowly avoided a ban from the authorities over the 'whereabouts' rule in 2019, contrived to get on the wrong side of the rule again. Once was careless – twice meant a suspension.

In mid-June, the World Athletics Integrity Unit (AIU) announced they had provisionally suspended Coleman for missing another drug test – this time on December 9, 2019.

Coleman was apoplectic, claiming on social media that he had been Christmas shopping at a mall five minutes away from his home in Lexington, Kentucky and there had been no attempt by the testers to contact him by phone. Exactly why he had chosen to go shopping in the hour he'd set aside for drug testers is unknown.

The testers, who are not obliged to alert athletes by phone, had reported they had made 'multiple, loud knocks every ten minutes for the entire hour' without a reply.

'I've been contacted by phone literally every other time I've been tested,' railed Coleman, who appealed the decision, but could not compete until the hearing on the case. If the suspension was upheld, he faced a two-year ban from competition and would miss the Tokyo Olympics.

In a lengthy, rambling and emotional tweet to his fans and fellow athletes, Coleman pointed an admonitory finger at the authorities and issued a *cri de coeur* for reform to the system. 'Last year I publicly addressed my stance on clean sport when I was dealing with USADA, when they wrongly charged with missing three tests,' he wrote. 'And today nothing has changed. I have never and will never use performance-enhancing supplements or drugs. I am willing to take a drug test EVERY single day for the rest of my career for all I care to prove my innocence. I have nothing to hide but it's not possible to show that if I'm not even given a chance to. I am committed to the fight for clean sport. I support USADA, WADA and the AIU to keep athletes and competition clean and fair. But the system must change. I thought the point of the organization was to keep the sport clean by testing everyone and catching cheaters – not attempt to catch people when they're not home and make no attempt to actually test them and mess with the livelihoods of people who are clearly not doping. This isn't justice for anybody. Not me, not them, not the sport, who wins here? And the consequences are huge – they are messing with my opportunity to build generational wealth. Unlike other sport leagues, there is no face card who makes these decisions and has to stand on this nonsense. Only my reputation takes a hit and I don't even know who has the final say. The organization just looks as if they're doing a job, but they're not.'

Though clearly passionately stated, Coleman's position was not widely defended in the athletics community. Michael Johnson wrote: 'After a close call last year for three whereabouts failures or missed tests, for Coleman to allow this to happen again will lead people to believe either you're doping or you don't take seriously the anti-doping efforts of the sport.'

Former world 400-metre hurdles champion, Welshman Dai Greene, posted a lengthy rebuttal to Coleman's protest. 'Last year you got off for the same sanction. To let it happen to you again is astounding. Being at your hour slot each day is a small price to pay for the life this sport has given to you and to help fight for an equal playing field for all athletes. Regardless of whether you are doping or not, the rules are there for the greater good of the sport. Being the best in the world means that you should be leading the way by example. Try treating the sport, your full-time profession, and fellow athletes with the respect they deserve.'

Greene was one of many athletes who criticized Coleman's stance, including his own American teammate and recently appointed President of the newly formed Athletics Association, triple jumper Christian Taylor, who suggested his actions showed a 'lack of respect'.

As the furore subsided, Coleman told one website he was prepared to work out a deal so long as he could run in Tokyo. But the boss of World Athletics, Lord Coe, suggested that he would be surprised if any special cases were made – without specifically naming names.

'I don't think it is that complicated, I really don't,' Coe explained. 'The athletes are asked to give their whereabouts for one hour a day, and there is plenty of scope if that one hour suddenly becomes a problem. It's not arcane maritime law. You don't need a degree in logistics from Cambridge to figure that out, it's what you are expected to do. If you are hanging by a thread on one or even two of those, then my instinct would be to be sitting by my front door for that hour. You wouldn't risk not being there and if they fall foul of this regularly they will be banned. I can't put it in any blunter way and that is what the AIU is there to do.'

Once the first wave of Covid had passed, some events began to appear – albeit behind closed doors – in various countries around the world. These enabled athletes to stretch their legs, check their fitness and tick off some of the unfulfilled appearance clauses in their shoe contracts. Decent times were recorded by Akani Simbine, Noah Lyles, Andre de Grasse and Ronnie Baker.

Top prize for the fastest 100 metres in this rather unusual and challenging mini-season went to Michael Norman, who took a break from his 400 metres training to smash his own personal best with a hugely impressive 9.86 seconds, at a meeting in July, in Fort Worth, Texas. This was a time that would have ranked him second in the world in 2019.

Starved of meaningful action for so long, the track media went into overdrive. Norman, at just 22, had become only the second man in history – after 400 world record holder Wayde van Niekerk – to run a sub-ten second 100, a sub-20 second 200 and a sub-44 second 400. And Norman hadn't run a 100 metres race since high school in 2016. The internet went into meltdown and pictures of the powerful 6ft 1in track star with the model looks began to appear everywhere. It was all a new experience for him.

Norman had been pleading with his coaches, USC's Caryl Smith Gilbert and Quincy Watts, to allow him to run a 100, but they routinely turned him down. However, with the pressure of real competition forgotten under Covid-19 restrictions, they finally relented. Both coaches can see his potential at 100, as well as the commercial value, but still suspect he will attack only the 400 metres in Tokyo. There's been talk of doubling-up – even a bizarre 100/400 metre permutation – but it will all depend on the schedule at the 2021 US trials as much as at the Olympics themselves.

Norman himself appears sanguine about it all, exhibiting a rare humility and maturity for such a young athlete. Taking a lead from his hero Usain Bolt, he explains: 'Saying that you're world champion is cool, saying that you're Olympic champion is amazing, but leaving a legacy is what's most important.'

Norman was born in San Diego, California, to a Japanese mother and American father, in December 1997. At Vista Murrieta high school, about an hour north of San Diego, he tore up the record books at everything from 100 to 400 metres, leading his school to its first ever state title in any sport – virtually single handed. In the summer of 2015, he ran his first competitive 100 metres in an astonishing 10.23 seconds and then headed off on a track scholarship to the University of Southern California.

Norman's parents Michael and Nobue had been athletes at school – his mother a middle school 100 metre record-holder in Japan. But he was ten years old when his Olympic dreams were fired by a familiar name at the 2008 Olympics. 'I remember exactly when I was like, 'I want to do that,' he says. 'I was watching Usain Bolt, with that side camera panning across the track as he ran the 100. And that moment really fuelled my motivation and continued to inspire me to keep working over the years.'

A state champion at high school and national champion at USC, Norman turned pro after his sophomore year and ran the two fastest 400-metre times in both 2018 and 2019. But injury and fatigue caught him out at the world championships in Qatar and he failed to make the 400 metres final.

Make no mistake, however, Michael Norman is a special athlete. Coach Quincy Watts, himself a 400 metres Olympic winner in 1992, is convinced he is destined for greatness – maybe the first man to run under 43 seconds in the 400. Gold in Tokyo, then switch to the 100. Maybe both. 'I've seen Butch Reynolds, Steve Lewis, Michael Johnson and Wayde van Niekerk. I have never seen anything like him,' he says. 'He has the potential speed-wise to be faster than them all.'

A few days after Norman's stellar 100, it was time for the long-lost Trayvon Bromell to emerge back onto the scene. He had hardly been seen since he was wheelchaired out of the Estadio Olimpico after the 4 x 100 metres relay final at the Rio Olympics almost four years earlier. So it was with some satisfaction that he threw down a promising 9.90 seconds in Florida and then, a couple of weeks later, followed it with a faster-still 9.87, albeit with a slight tailwind. Was it possible, after all his injury problems and setbacks, that the first junior to break ten seconds at 100 metres was back? The humble, quietly spoken Bromell certainly deserved a break.

Bromell came from a poor, crime-ridden neighbourhood on the south side of St Petersburg in Florida, a city that ranks as one of the most dangerous in the United States. 'It ain't no Disneyland, it ain't no theme park. We called it "The Trenches"', he explains. 'It's the very bottom of the barrel. Growing up there was hard, no other word for it. My Mom didn't have a lot, so we had to work with what we had. I did what everyone had to do, find a way to survive. That's what it's like growing up in poverty, you have to find a way to survive. There's a right way and a wrong way.'

Thanks to his mother's influence and hard work, Trayvon grew up the right way, along with his two brothers and a sister, but his real potential as a sprinter wasn't really noticed until he reached Gibbs high school. Bromell always wanted to play football and had inadvertently tried hard to ruin his future athletic career, first injuring his left knee in the eighth grade trying to do backflips; then the following year injuring his right knee and forearm while playing basketball.

All through elementary and high school Bromell was coached by Garlynn Boyd, a former state shot put champion, and she began to teach him the basics of sprinting. 'Mom worked all the time to make sure I was good, to make sure we had somewhere to live. When I went to practice, coach G was like another Mom. She and my Mom were the only people who believed I was special, even in times when I didn't believe it myself.'

Coach G knew what she was doing. Aged 17 Bromell won the Florida state 100 metres title in 10.45 and the US Junior Championship 100 metres in 10.47. A year later, after landing a track scholarship and heading to Baylor University in Texas, he won the NCAA in a world junior record of 9.97 seconds – the first American teenager to duck under ten seconds. The following year he ran a windy 9.84 at the US national championships, aged just 19, and qualified for the World Championships in Beijing, where he took an incredible bronze medal.

It was a whirlwind start to his professional career and he signed with shoe company New Balance.

In early 2016 Bromell won the world indoor 60 metres title, but that spring, at a Diamond League meeting in Rome, while leading a 200 metre race he felt pain in his left heel and slowed to finish a distant seventh. A few days later, warming up for a meet in England the same thing happened, so he flew back to the States. An x-ray revealed a bone spur growing near his Achilles tendon; but instead of attending to it immediately, his training was modified and he managed to qualify for the US sprint team for the Rio Olympics. Unwilling to give up on an Olympic opportunity, he trained for Rio in a pool and on an anti-gravity treadmill and it was against all odds that he made the final, where he trailed in a disappointing last. 'I wasn't going to run,' he recalls, 'I was telling myself that I was in too much pain. I just couldn't perform how I wanted.'

But five nights later he went back out on the track to anchor the US relay team in the final of the 4 x 100. Desperately trying to chase down the flying Usain Bolt, Bromell threw himself over the line to grab third spot and crashed to the track. The heel pain returned, the team was disqualified for an earlier changeover violation and he was ferried off the track in a wheelchair.

He underwent surgery straight after the Games and was in a protective boot for two months and unable to do any proper rehabilitation for six. It would be ten months before he raced again, where he was eliminated in the heats of the 2017 US Championships, with a time of 10.22 seconds. To make matters worse, the pain had returned in his heel.

Another doctor was consulted and expressed surprise that Bromell was even capable of running the time he did. 'Your tendon should have torn off the bone,' the doctor told him. Another operation was organized, this time to lift the scar tissue off the bone and he started the rehab all over again. This time it would be two years before he raced again, at a meeting in Florida in July 2019, but after an easy win in the heat he blew an adductor muscle in the final and was back to square one.

'I was on the road to great prosperity in the sport.' he says. 'It was looking good and this stumble happened and I had to be tough. I can't fold, I had a lot of people who kept me mentally strong. It was definitely hard, but what helped me from breaking was my humble beginnings. I remember times when I was hoping my Mom could pay the bills so we didn't get kicked out into the street. It's been way harder than me getting injuries in sports.'

This time he decided a change of coach might help and left his old mentor Mike Ford behind and joined the team led by sprint specialist Rana Reider, who had a reputation for helping injured athletes, including Andre de Grasse, return to action. Reider went back to basics, focusing on strength and conditioning, before upgrading to actual sprinting. In July 2020 – on Independence Day – in a small meet near Orlando, Florida, Trayvon Bromell ran his first 100 metres without pain for four years, posting a decent time of 10.04.

Trayvon's mother prayed over him after the victory. His beloved coach G had planned to be trackside as well, but tragically she had died ten days before his comeback race. After years of struggle with diabetes – she had her right leg amputated in 2013 – it was reported that she had contracted Covid-19. She was 54. Bromell's tweet read: 'Lord knows this one hurts. Not being able to hear your voice. No matter the circumstance, you knew how to bring the best out in me. Even though you're gone, you live on forever in me. I promise to keep running.'

And so he did. Later that month he ran a 9.90 and in early August a 9.87, with just too much wind behind him to make it legal. But the signs were encouraging. One of the world's greatest sprinting talents was back in the house. 'It gave me a lot of confidence that I'm getting healthier,' he says. 'I'm very spiritual and it showed me that God hasn't finished with me and I'm not done in this sport.'

Bromell knows that it has been a long, gruelling journey, but it's not over yet. In the midst of all this rehab, he still graduated from Baylor with a BA in kinesiology and a Masters in business and sports marketing. 'Who knows, it could be Dr Bromell,' he smiles. 'My plan is to take it day by day. That's how I operate. I know that's a bit of a cliché but I really live by that. I can't jump to Tokyo. It's like a book, you don't read the first pages and then jump to the end, you read each page and each chapter.'

The new generation of sprinting talent suggests it could be an especially memorable new chapter come Olympic year. And if the list of pretenders for Usain Bolt's crown was not already impressive enough, just as we thought all the avengers had assembled, then another arrived in the unlikely form of Houston-born Matt Boling.

Known for its high-quality journalism and adherence to factual veracity, even *Sports Illustrated* disappeared into wordy hyperbole when, in the April of 2019, the 18-year-old high school senior ran a 9.98-second 100 metres at a regional Texas boys meet. Admittedly, it was wind-assisted, but it was an historic high school record in all conditions, and when he continued to run a series of extraordinary times through the rest of the season his exploits would hit every newspaper in America.

Unusual? In a nation that widely acknowledges track and field in only four-year cycles, it was frankly amazing. But Matt Boling was different. He was white. He even had red hair!

'He is the vessel into which the track and field community has poured its endless hope for youthful potential that might grow into breakout relevance,' gushed America's number one sports magazine.

Boling, born in Houston in 2000, was immediately and stereotypically dubbed 'White Lightning' by the headline writers of the US tabloid press, and his run became a YouTube smash with over three million views. Before his 100 metre pyrotechnics he had 1500 Instagram followers. By the end of 2020 he had nearly 200,000.

Boling's performances at Houston Strake Jesuit high school – which culminated in a legal 10.13 – not only broke the 29-year-old state high school record, but was the second-fastest high school 100 metres ever run. It was all the more remarkable for the fact that he had only taken up the event less than a year earlier. Previously, he'd specialized in the 400 metres and long jump. His precocious talent persuaded the University of Georgia to sign him up on a scholarship, but in early 2020 when Covid shut down the sport in the States, Boling's extraordinary momentum went with it.

His high school coach Chad Collier says he has heard people compare Boling to the iconic golfer Tiger Woods, suggesting he could inspire more white kids to take up sprinting: 'The one thing about Matthew is the bigger the stage, the bigger the performance, and that is just the type of young man he is.' And Boling's dreams are straightforward – to line up alongside the likes of Coleman and Lyles at the Olympic Games.

One thing is for certain. The odds are dropping on the Texan phenomenon throwing a major curve ball into the accepted global order of the 100 metres.

So maybe it is a little surprising to know that Matt Boling is not alone in the teenage phenomenon stakes. Alongside him sits fellow American Erriyon Knighton, who crushed an AAU junior Olympic 200 metres field in the summer of 2020, setting the second-fastest time for an under-18-year-old of 20.33. Only Usain Bolt ran faster. The long-striding, 6ft 3in Knighton also did it at only sixteen years of age and, quite impressively, after six months of Covid-driven inactivity. He then elected to turn pro, signed with Adidas and opted out of competing at high school – and, of course, any aspirations of college. He runs with the My Brother's Keeper Track Club, a stone's throw from his home in Florida, in the Tampa suburbs. His agent is former British 200 metres ace John Regis and he firmly believes Knighton, who only turned 17 in January 2021, has the right stuff to follow in Bolt's footsteps. It might sound a little premature, but Knighton's target is the Tokyo Olympics. 'I believe if I train hard enough, I can make it,' he told *Track & Field News*. A record-breaking victory in his professional debut at the PURE Athletics Invitational, in Clermont, Florida in April 2021 only strengthened that belief.

Of course, every Olympic year tends to throw up a wild card, but we won't get much more of a feel for how the Tokyo 100 metres will shape up until the world of athletics returns to a more regular shape with the hoped-for restart of the calendar in 2021. Much of the indoor season was cancelled, but in the few events that did take place there were encouraging performances in the States for Trayvon Bromell and a gold medal at the European Indoor Championships, in Poland, for the American-born Italian sprinter Marcell Jacobs, with a world-leading 6.47-second 60 metres. At the NCAA Indoor championships, in Arkansas, freshman Micah Williams powered his way to the 60 metres title in a personal best-equalling 6.49, but the real fireworks happened in the 200. Favourite Matt Boling powered off the start but was almost caught on the line by LSU's fast-finishing Terence Laird – they were separated by just one hundredth of a second – with Boling setting a new personal best of 20.19 and Laird another in 20.20. Boling's run put him sixth on the all-time world list for the indoor 200. Asked afterwards to name his best event he said: 'My best event and my favourite event is probably the 200. I feel like I can use my 100 speed and my 400 strength and combine it in the 200.'

As for the outdoor season, by then there will barely be enough time to qualify in the national trials and win a few early mind games on the Diamond League circuit, which is due to start at the end of May, before all eyes switch to Japan. In mid-April, however, Justin Gatlin announced that he should not be discounted in the chase for Tokyo gold, winning the 100 metres at the Tom Jones Memorial Invitational, in Gainesville, Florida, in a time of 9.98, against some pretty tough opposition. Andre de Grasse (9.99) finished second and, in his first outdoor race of the '21 season, Noah Lyles placed fourth in 10.08.

The new generation of sprinters are obviously hoping the Games will happen and that crowds are welcomed back. And they all agree that without Usain Bolt the field has been appreciably levelled.

'Usain was so dominant and people were used to seeing him win all the time,' says Andre de Grasse. 'Now it makes it more fun and more exciting. We don't know who is going to win, everyone is close. When I watch football I want to see Ronaldo and Messi going at it, or LeBron James and Kevin Durant in basketball – you want to see the big match-ups. Everyone is so good, we're really going to see a show.'

'Usain Bolt was a level above,' says Ronnie Baker. 'No-one is clocking 9.6s on the same basis and he makes the 9.8 guys look really slow. The guy you gotta watch out for is Noah Lyles. He's a great 200 runner, but he can run a really good 100 too and he's going to double at some point.'

Baker would like history to remember him for winning two Olympic 100-metre gold medals – in Tokyo and Paris. 'I'd like to break the world record too, but maybe I'll bow out after Paris and use the influence and impact I'll have built to encourage kids trying to get into college. It's not just about making a load of money.' A world-leading 9.94 at the Texas Relays in Austin, in March 2021, brought those goals into sharper focus.

Similar sentiments are expressed by Trayvon Bromell. 'Obviously winning a medal or running a fast time is cool, but that doesn't last long. I want to leave a mark on people. I don't care about the medals or the times, but I'm in a position to be able to speak to people and change their lives. If I can stand on that podium in first place what I'm going to be thinking about is completely different from what the world is thinking about when they see it. They'll think that guy won gold, but I'll think this guy just changed the life of a little kid who was watching and was maybe thinking of giving up on this sport. That's my prize.'

In 2020 Noah Lyles revealed that he needed therapy and medication for depression and was greeted with widespread support for his candour. He was equally clear about the next Olympics. 'Going into Tokyo, the gun is going to go off and I'm going to break the world record.' But he also appreciates what winning gold will do for him in terms of history. 'You definitely need to know your sport because the more you know about it, the more you see what people have done in the past that hasn't worked, the more you learn from it. Your sport is history and history repeats, so if you don't know it you're just going to repeat the same faults that other people made.'

Perhaps a history lesson on the darker aspects of the 100 metres may have been instructional for Christian Coleman. In early October 2020 the AIU's disciplinary tribunal was held into his 'whereabouts' issues, via video conference, and a few weeks later it announced its decision to ban him for two years, until May 2022. He would miss the Tokyo Olympics.

The decision made banner headlines worldwide and would not only spell a tragic end to Coleman's Olympic dreams but completely shredded what was left of his standing in the sport.

The tribunal's findings were damning and while it stressed that there was 'no suggestion that the athlete had ever taken any prohibited substance' it summarized that 'the consequences for athletes who are subject to three missed tests are draconian. But, rather than learn from his experience with USADA, the athlete's attitude to his obligations can fairly be described as entirely careless, perhaps even reckless.' It criticized Coleman for attacking the authorities for their conduct rather than admitting fault and did not accept his confusing explanation for a third missed test – that he had been Christmas shopping in a nearby mall, bought some food and then driven back to his house towards the end of the pre-arranged one-hour testing window, watched the start of a football game and then left again to return to his shopping. They were clear he had not been at home at any point in the window.

The tribunal summary explained: 'Despite the narrow escape from a potential ban and despite the fact that the athlete knew that he still had two Whereabouts Failures on his record, and – as he accepted in the hearing – was on high alert, by December 9, the athlete went shopping throughout his 60-minute slot. As he himself stated, he was simply assuming that the DCO (Doping Control Officer) would call him and that he would then be able to drive back to his residence within a few minutes to provide a sample.'

It concluded by saying: 'We understand that it is very difficult for a young man, blessed with prodigious talents which the athlete obviously has, to find himself suddenly at the centre of public gaze. But success of this nature, and the financial rewards that follow, also give rise to responsibilities that must be taken seriously and observed, day after day, just as all other athletes in the Registered Testing Pool must do.'

In pure racing terms it was obviously an immense disappointment that the reigning world 100 metres champion and fastest man in 2017, 2018 and 2019 – and the only man to have broken 9.80 in the last five years – would not be lining up for what still promises to be an epic competition in Japan. That said, it was clear that the integrity of the sport, as well as the competency and virtue of its anti-doping machinery, were just as much on trial as Coleman himself.

Pulling no punches, the *Daily Telegraph* lambasted Coleman's 'feeble excuses' and described the 22-page tribunal verdict as 'an enduring monument to his stupidity'.

It concluded: 'Remarkably, he still has his apologists in the US, who play the folksy card that beneath all the bravado, he is a wonderful son and a true Christian. Perhaps he is, but all that matters for athletics is that nobody can believe another word he says. The Olympics will be better off without him.' Even his home newspaper, the *Lexington Herald-Leader*, conceded that Coleman had run out of chances. 'To believe that the evidence supporting Christian Coleman's two-year ban from track is flawed is to believe that the 24-year-old sprinter really has redefined the title "World's Fastest Man."' 'It is to believe that in the span of 29 minutes last December 9, Coleman bought dinner from a Chipotle near his house, hurried back home and ate it, watched the kickoff of "Monday Night Football", then headed back out to a nearby Wal-Mart, where he purchased 16 items and checked out.'

"It would have been simply impossible," a panel of arbitrators wrote Tuesday in delivering a two-year sanction that, if upheld, will keep the 100-metre world champion out of next year's Olympics.' Coleman kept unusually quiet after the decision, but his manager Emanuel Hudson immediately announced: 'The decision of the Disciplinary Tribunal established under World Athletics Rules is unfortunate and will be immediately appealed to the Court of Arbitration for Sport. Mr Coleman has nothing further to say until such time as the matter can be heard in the Court of Jurisdiction.' The appeal was lodged with CAS toward the end of November 2020, with Coleman requesting the decision be expunged or reduced. However, unless Coleman introduces new evidence, recent history suggests there's more chance of the panel increasing the punishment, based on the existing facts, than reducing it. Currently there is no date set for the appeal hearing. So first no Usain Bolt and now no Christian Coleman. However, there is no doubt that a brilliantly executed Tokyo Olympic Games would be a marvellous antidote to the global hardships of Covid-19. And the remaining array of stars from the new generation of the sprinting world will certainly be keen to play their part.

Usain Bolt hopes to be there. But just watching. Like the rest of us.

However, unlike previous years, the next chapter of *The Fastest Men on Earth* is going to be much more difficult to predict.

Index

The Men's Olympic 100 Metres

Final Results

(All results given in seconds)

ATHENS 1896

1 Tom BURKE, USA, 12.0
2 Fritz HOFFMAN, Germany, 12.2
3 Frank LANE, USA, 12.6
4 Alajos SZOKOLI, Hungary, 12.6
5 Alexandros CHALKONIDIS, Greece, 12.6
DNS Tom CURTIS, USA

PARIS 1900

1 Frank JARVIS, USA, 11.0
2 J Walter TEWKSBURY, USA, 11.1
3 Stan Rowley, Australia, 11.2
DNF Arthur DUFFEY, USA

ST LOUIS 1904

1 Archie HAHN, USA, 11.0
2 Nat CARTMELL, USA, 11.2
3 Bill HOGENSEON USA 11.2
4 Fay MOULTON, USA 11.4
5 Fred HECKWOLF, USA
6 Lawson ROBERTSON, USA

ATHENS 1906

1 Archie HAHN, USA, 11.2
2 Fay MOULTON, USA, 11.3
3 Nigel BARKER, Australia, 11.3
4 Bill EATON, USA
5 Lawson ROBERTSON, USA
6 Knut LINDBERG, Sweden

LONDON 1908

1 Reg WALKER, South Africa, 10.8
2 James RECTOR, USA, 11.0
3 Bobby KERR, Canada, 11.0
4 Nat CARTMELL, USA, 11.2

STOCKHOLM 1912

1 Ralph CRAIG, USA, 10.8
2 Alvah MEYER, USA, 10.9
3 Don LIPPINCOTT, USA, 10.9
4 George PATCHING, South Africa, 11.0
5 Frank BELOTE, USA, 11.0
DNS Howard Drew, USA

ANTWERP 1920

1 Charley PADDOCK, USA, 10.8
2 Morris KIRKSEY, USA, 10.9
3 Harry EDWARD, Great Britain, 10.9
4 Jackson SCHOLZ, USA, 10.9
5 Emile ALI-KHAN, France, 11.0
6 Loren MURCHISON, USA, 11.1

PARIS 1924

1 Harold ABRAHAMS, Great Britain, 10.6
2 Jackson SCHOLZ, USA, 10.8
3 Arthur PORRITT, New Zealand, 10.9
4 Chester BOWMAN, USA, 10.9
5 Charley PADDOCK, USA, 10.9
6 Loren MURCHISON, USA, 11.0

AMSTERDAM 1928

1 Percy WILLIAMS, Canada, 10.8
2 Jack LONDON, Great Britain, 10.9
3 Georg LAMMERS, Germany, 10.9
4 Frank WYKOFF, USA, 11.0
5 Wilf LEGG, South Africa, 11.0
6 Bob McALLISTER, USA, 11.0

LOS ANGELES 1932

1 Eddie TOLAN, USA, 10.3
2 Ralph METCALFE, USA, 10.3
3 Arthur JONATH, Germany, 10.4
4 George SIMPSON, USA, 10.5
5 Daniel JOUBERT, South Africa, 10.6
6 Taka YOSHIOKA, Japan, 10.7

BERLIN 1936

1 Jesse OWENS, USA, 10.3
2 Ralph METCALFE, USA, 10.4
3 Martinus OSENDARP, Holland, 10.5
4 Frank WYKOFF, USA, 10.6
5 Erich BORCHMEYER, Germany, 10.7
6 Lennart STRANBERG, Sweden, 10.9

LONDON 1948

1 Harrison DILLARD, USA, 10.3
2 Barney EWELL, USA, 10.4
3 Lloyd LABEACH, Panama, 10.4
4 Alastair McCORQUODALE, Great Britain, 10.4
5 Mel PATTON, USA, 10.5
6 MacDonald BAILEY, Great Britain, 10.6

HELSINKI 1952

1 Lindy REMIGINO, USA, 10.4
2 Herb McKENLEY, Jamaica, 10.4
3 McDonald BAILEY, Great Britain, 10.4
4 Dean SMITH, USA, 10.4
5 Vladimir SUKHARYEV, USSR, 10.5
6 John TRELOAR, Australia, 10.5

1956 MELBOURNE

1 Bobby MORROW, USA, 10.5
2 Thane BAKER, USA, 10.5
3 Hec HOGAN, Australia, 10.6
4 Ira MURCHISON, USA, 10.6
5 Manfred GERMAR, Germany, 10.7
6 Mike AGOSTINI, Trinidad & Tobago, 10.7

1960 ROME

1 Armin HARY, Germany, 10.2
2 Dave SIME, USA, 10.2
3 Peter RADFORD, Great Britain, 10.3
4 Enrique FUGUEROLA, Cuba, 10.3
5 Frank BUDD, USA, 10.3
6 Ray NORTON, USA, 10.4

TOKYO 1964

1 Bob HAYES, USA, 10.0
2 Enrique FUGEUROLA, Cuba, 10.2
3 Harry JEROME, Canada, 10.2
4 Wielsaw MANIAK, Poland, 10.4
5 Heinz SCHUMANN, West Germany, 10.4
= 6 Gaoussou KONE, Ivory Coast, 10.4
= 6 Mel PENDER, USA, 10.4
8 Tom ROBINSON, Bahamas, 10.5

MEXICO CITY

1 Jim HINES, USA, 9.95
2 Lennox MILLER, Jamaica, 10.04
3 Charlie GREENE, USA, 10.07
4 Pablo MONTES, Cuba, 10.14
5 Roger BAMBUCK, France, 10.16
6 Mel PENDER, USA, 10.17
7 Harry JEROME, Canada, 10.20
8 Jean Louis RAVELOMANATSOA, Madagascar, 10.28

MUNICH 1972

1 Valeri BORZOV, USSR, 10.14

2 Robert TAYLOR, USA, 10.24

3 Lennox MILLER, Jamaica, 10.33

4 Aleksandr KORNELYUK, USSR, 10.36

5 Michael FRAY, Jamaica, 10.40

6 Jobst HIRSCHT, West Germany, 10.40

7 Zenon NOWOSZ, Poland, 10.46

DNF Hasely CRAWFORD, Trinidad & Tobago

MONTREAL 1976

1 Hasely CRAWFORD, Trinidad & Tobago, 10.06

2 Don QUARRIE, Jamaica, 10.07

3 Valeri BORZOV, USSR, 10.14

4 Harvey GLANCE, USA, 10.19

5 Guy ABRAHAMS, Panama, 10.25

6 John JONES, USA, 10.27

7 Klaus Dieter KURRAT, East Germany, 10.31

8 Petar PETROV, Bulgaria, 10.35

MOSCOW 1980

1 Allan WELLS, Great Britain, 10.25

2 Silvio LEONARD, Cuba, 10.25

3 Petar PETROV, Bulgaria, 10.39

4 Aleksandr AKSININ, USSR, 10.42

5 Osvaldo LARA, Cuba, 10.43

6 Vladimir MURAVYOV, USSR, 10.44

7 Marian WORONIN, Poland, 10.46

8 Hermann PANZO, France, 10.49

LOS ANGELES 1984

1 Carl LEWIS, USA, 9.99

2 Sam GRADDY, USA, 10.19

3 Ben JOHNSON, Canada, 10.22

4 Ron BROWN, USA, 10.26

5 Mike McFARLANE, Great Britain, 10.27

6 Ray STEWART, Jamaica, 10.29

7 Donovan REID, Great Britain, 10.33

8 Tony SHARPE, Canada, 10.35

SEOUL 1988

1 Carl LEWIS, USA, 9.92

2 Linford CHRISTIE, Great Britain, 9.97

3 Calvin SMITH, USA, 9.99

4 Dennis MITCHELL, USA, 10.04

5 Robson DA SILVA, Brazil, 10.11

6 Desai WILLIAMS, Canada, 10.11

7 Ray STEWART, Jamaica, 12.26

DISQ Ben JOHNSON, Canada, 9.79

BARCELONA 1992

1 Linford CHRISTIE, Great Britain, 9.96

2 Frankie FREDERICKS, Namibia, 10.02

3 Dennis MITCHELL, USA, 10.04

4 Bruny SURIN, Canada, 10.09

5 Leroy BURRELL, USA, 10.10

6 Olapade ADENIKEN, Nigeria, 10.12

7 Ray STEWART, Jamaica, 10.22

8 Davidson EZINWA, Nigeria, 10.26

1996 ATLANTA

1 Donovan BAILEY, Canada, 9.84

2 Frankie FREDERICKS, Namibia, 9.89

3 Ato BOLDON, Trinidad & Tobago, 9.90

4 Dennis MITCHELL, USA, 9.99

5 Mike MARSH, USA, 10.00

6 Davidson EZINWA, Nigeria, 10.14

7 Mike GREEN, Jamaica, 10.16

DISQ Linford CHRISTIE, Great Britain

2000 SYDNEY

1 Maurice GREENE, USA, 9.87

2 Ato BOLDON, Trinidad & Tobago, 9.99

3 Obadele THOMPSON, Barbados, 10.04

4 Dwain CHAMBERS, Great Britain, 10.08

5 Jon DRUMMOND, USA, 10.09

6 Darren CAMPBELL, Great Britain, 10.13

7 Kim COLLINS, St Kitts & Nevis, 10.17

DNF Aziz ZAKARI, Ghana

2004 ATHENS

1 Justin GATLIN, USA, 9.85
2 Francis OBIKWELU, Portugal, 9.86
3 Maurice GREENE, USA, 9.87
4 Shawn CRAWFORD, USA, 9.89
5 Asafa POWELL, Jamaica, 9.94
6 Kim COLLINS, St Kitts & Nevis, 10.00
7 Obadele THOMPSON, Barbados, 10.10
DNF Aziz ZAKARI, Ghana

2008 BEIJING

1 Usain BOLT, Jamaica, 9.69
2 Richard THOMPSON, Trinidad & Tobago, 9.89
3 Walter DIX, USA, 9.91
4 Churandy MARTINA, Dutch Antilles, 9.93
5 Asafa POWELL, Jamaica, 9.95
6 Michael FRATER, Jamaica, 9.97
7 Marc BURNS, Trinidad & Tobago, 10.01
8 Darvis PATTON, USA, 10.03

LONDON 2012

1 Usain BOLT, Jamaica, 9.63
2 Yohan BLAKE, Jamaica, 9.75
3 Justin GATLIN, USA, 9.79
4 Ryan BAILEY, USA, 9.88
5 Churandy MARTINA, Holland, 9.94
6 Richard THOMPSON, Trinidad & Tobago, 9.98
7 Asafa POWELL, Jamaica, 11.99
DISQ Tyson GAY USA 9.80

RIO DE JANEIRO 2016

1 Usain BOLT, Jamaica, 9.81
2 Justin GATLIN, USA, 9.89
3 Andre DE GRASSE, Canada, 9.91
4 Yohan BLAKE, Jamaica, 9.93
5 Akani SIMBINE, South Africa, 9.94
6 Ben Youseff MEITE, Ivory Coast, 9.96
7 Jimmy VICAUT, France, 10.04
8 Trayvon BROMELL, USA, 10.06

The Men's 100 Metres

World Record

Seconds

10.6 Don Lippincott, July 1912, Sweden
10.4 Charley Paddock, April 1921, USA
10.3 Percy Williams, August 1930, Canada
10.2 Jesse Owens, June 1936, USA
10.1 Willie Williams, August 1956, Germany
10.0 Armin Hary, June 1960, Switzerland
9.99 Jim Hines, June 1968, USA
9.95 Jim Hines, October 1968, Mexico
9.93 Calvin Smith, July 1983, USA
9.92 Carl Lewis, September 1988, South Korea
9.90 Leroy Burrell, June 1991, USA
9.86 Carl Lewis, August 1991, Japan
9.85 Leroy Burrell, July 1994, Switzerland
9.84 Donovan Bailey, July 1996, USA
9.79 Maurice Greene, June 1999, Greece
9.77 Asafa Powell, June 2005, Greece
9.74 Asafa Powell, June 2007, Italy
9.72 Usain Bolt, May 2008, USA
9.69 Usain Bolt, August 2009, China
9.58 Usain Bolt, August 2009, Germany

N.B.: The world records of Ben Johnson of 9.83 seconds in Italy in 1987 and 9.79 seconds in South Korea in 1988, as well as Tim Montgomery of 9.78 seconds in France in 2002, were erased from the record books after they were banned for taking performance-enhancing drugs.

Acknowledgements

Adidas, Amateur Athletics Association, Amistad Research Center, Ancestry.com, Athletics Integrity Unit, *Athletics News*, *Athletics Weekly*, *Austin American-Statesmen*, Baldwin Wallace College, Boston Athletic Club, Boston Public Libraries, *Boston Globe*, *Boston Journal*, *Boston Post*, British Athletics, British Columbia Sports Hall of Fame, British Museum Library, British Newspaper Library, British Olympic Association, British Veterans Athletics Federation, Cleveland Board of Education, *Cleveland Plain Dealer*, Court of Arbitration for Sport, *Daily Mail*, *Daily Mirror*, *Daily Telegraph*, Dallas Cowboys, *Dallas Morning News*, *Detroit News*, Detroit Public Libraries, Duke University, Envision Sports & Entertainment, *The Field*, *Florida Times-Union*, Gateshead Public Libraries, German Press Association, Global Athletics & Marketing, *The Guardian*, Hammersmith & Fulham Libraries, Harlingen Public Libraries, Hartford Courant, International Olympic Committee, International Society of Olympic Historians, Jamaican AAA, *Los Angeles Times*, Peter Lovesey, Michigan University, *Milwaukee Journal*, National Centre for Athletics Literature (Birmingham University), National Olympic Committee of Ukraine, National Union of Track Statisticians, New Balance, *New York Times*, Northwestern University, Ohio State University, Olympic Channel, PACE Sports Management, *Pasadena Post*, Patent Office, *Philadelphia Inquirer*, Powderhall Stadium, Princeton University, Puma, Ricky Simms, South African Press Agency, Soviet Sports Committee, *Sports Illustrated*, Temple University, *Texas Monthly*, *Times Newspapers*, *Track & Field News*, *Trinidad Express Newspapers*, Trident Sports Management, US Olympic Committee, Ukraine Olympic Association, USA Track & Field, *Vancouver Sun*, *Washington Post*, Mel Watman, Neil Wilson, World Athletics.

And special thanks to my editor Ross Hamilton and proofreader Guy Croton, without whom this entire story would have made far less sense.

Picture credits

The publishers would like to thank the following sources for their kind permission to reproduce the pictures in this book.